Windows 2000 SYSTEMS PROGRAMMING Black Book

Al Williams

CORIOLIS™

President, CEO
Keith Weiskamp

Publisher
Steve Sayre

Acquisitions Editor
Stephanie Wall

Marketing Specialist
Tracy Schofield

Project Editors
Dan Young
Meredith Brittain

Technical Reviewer
Emmett Dulaney

Production Coordinators
Laura Wellander
Jon Gabriel

Cover Designer
Jody Winkler

Layout Designer
April Nielsen

CD-ROM Developer
Robert Clarfield

Windows 2000 Systems Programming Black Book

The Coriolis Group, LLC
14455 N. Hayden Road, Suite 220
Scottsdale, Arizona 85260

480/483-0192
FAX 480/483-0193
http://www.coriolis.com

Library of Congress Cataloging-in-Publication Data
Williams, Al , 1963-
Windows 2000 systems programming black book / by Al Williams.
p. cm.
Includes index.
ISBN 1-57610-280-7
1. Systems programming (Computer science) 2. Microsoft Windows NT. I. Title.

QA76.66.W55 2000
005.4'4769--dc21 99-42701
CIP

Printed in the United States of America
10 9 8 7 6 5 4 3 2 1

CORIOLIS

14455 North Hayden Road • Suite 220 • Scottsdale, Arizona 85260

Dear Reader:

Coriolis Technology Press was founded to create a very elite group of books: the ones you keep closest to your machine. Sure, everyone would like to have the Library of Congress at arm's reach, but in the real world, you have to choose the books you rely on every day *very* carefully.

To win a place for our books on that coveted shelf beside your PC, we guarantee several important qualities in every book we publish. These qualities are:

- *Technical accuracy*—It's no good if it doesn't work. Every Coriolis Technology Press book is reviewed by technical experts in the topic field, and is sent through several editing and proofreading passes in order to create the piece of work you now hold in your hands.
- *Innovative editorial design*—We've put years of research and refinement into the ways we present information in our books. Our books' editorial approach is uniquely designed to reflect the way people learn new technologies and search for solutions to technology problems.
- *Practical focus*—We put only pertinent information into our books and avoid any fluff. Every fact included between these two covers must serve the mission of the book as a whole.
- *Accessibility*—The information in a book is worthless unless you can find it quickly when you need it. We put a lot of effort into our indexes, and heavily cross-reference our chapters, to make it easy for you to move right to the information you need.

Here at The Coriolis Group we have been publishing and packaging books, technical journals, and training materials since 1989. We're programmers and authors ourselves, and we take an ongoing active role in defining what we publish and how we publish it. We have put a lot of thought into our books; please write to us at **ctp@coriolis.com** and let us know what you think. We hope that you're happy with the book in your hands, and that in the future, when you reach for software development and networking information, you'll turn to one of our books first.

Keith Weiskamp
President and CEO

Jeff Duntemann
VP and Editorial Director

For Jerid, who had the courage to start over, and always for Pat.

❧

About The Author

Al Williams has programmed numerous computers ranging from tiny embedded systems to giant mainframes. Al's columns appear in each issue of *Visual Developer* and *Web Techniques*. He is the author of many programming books including the very popular *MFC Black Book*.

When Al is not writing, he does software and hardware development as a consultant. He also conducts training seminars all around the U.S.

An avid amateur radio operator, Al lives near Houston, Texas, with his wife Pat, a varying number of kids, and two spoiled dogs. You can find Al on the Web at **www.al-williams.com**.

Acknowledgments

Producing a book is a team effort, and this book had an unusually large team. My thanks to the Coriolis editorial and production staff including Meredith Brittain, Jon Gabriel, Stephanie Wall, and Dan Young and Laura Wellander who saw it through. Robert Clarfield did his usual fine job on the CD-ROM. Of course, I can't forget my technical editor, Emmett Dulaney, and my copyeditor, Tiffany Taylor, who have helped so much.

On the home front, I can't even begin to thank my family for putting up with the maddening schedule books demand. Finally, I can't forget Oscar the tow truck driver and his son Scott the mechanic. Without them I'd still be stranded in Blytheville, Arkansas with a blown head gasket.

Contents At A Glance

Chapter 1 Windows 2000: The View From Above 1

Chapter 2 ActiveX Survival Kit 21

Chapter 3 Processes, Threads, And Fibers 121

Chapter 4 Synchronization 161

Chapter 5 File I/O 199

Chapter 6 Interprocess Communications 233

Chapter 7 Memory Management 331

Chapter 8 Windows Security 353

Chapter 9 Registry And Logging 381

Chapter 10 Shell Tricks With ATL 419

Chapter 11 Internet And Network Programming 475

Chapter 12 Console Applications And Services 537

Appendix A Beyond The Frontier 591

Appendix B Windows 2000: A Programing Odyssey 597

Table Of Contents

Introduction .... **xxi**

Chapter 1
Windows 2000: The View From Above **1**

In Depth

A New Language? 3
A Brief History Of Windows 3
Windows Versions 7
Windows Architecture 7
Windows Quirks, Oddities, And Differences 10
Development Tools 15

Immediate Solutions

Development Tool Choices 17
The Architecture Of Windows 17
Understanding Processes 18
Calling The API From C++ 18
Calling The API From VB 19
Calling The API From Visual J++ 19
Internet Resources 20

Chapter 2
ActiveX Survival Kit **21**

In Depth

ActiveX Vs. Java 23
Definitions 24
The Structure Of An ActiveX Object 25
That's An Object? 26
Code Reuse 27
Polymorphism 29
A Few Miscellaneous ActiveX Oddities 30
About **IUnknown** 32
Creating Objects And Finding Interfaces 33
More About Reference Counts 34

About Aggregation 35
More Oddities 37
The ActiveX/C++ Connection 40
Why Not Use C++ Directly? 41
The System Registry 41
The Registry: Up Close And Personal 42
Registry Oddities 44
That's It? 46
Registering Objects 46
Class Installation 50
Using REGEDIT 50
Self-Registration 51
Impersonating Objects 53
Type Libraries 54
Macro Mania 60
Learning Client Basics 60
A Simple Server Design 64
A Simple Client 66
An EXE Server 68
A DLL Server 78
Supporting Multiple Interfaces 82
MFC Techniques 83
MFC Aggregation 95
IDispatch 97
New Frontiers: COM+ 113

Immediate Solutions

ActiveX In A Nutshell 115
Understanding The Registry 117
Guide To Common Interfaces 118
Using MFC For **IDispatch** 118
Using MFC For Ordinary Interfaces 119
About ATL 119

Chapter 3
Processes, Threads, And Fibers 121

In Depth

Other Operating Systems 122
Processes 124
CreateProcess 126
Jobs And Working Sets 131
Threads 132

MFC And Threads 135
Thread Local Storage 136
Fibers 139
APCs 141

Immediate Solutions

Running A New Program—The Easiest Way 144
Running A New Program—A Little Harder 144
Running A New Program—The Macho Way 144
Waiting For A Program To Complete, Setting (Or Reading) The Exit Code 145
Creating A New Thread With The Windows API 146
Creating A New Thread With The C++ Library 146
Using Threads And MFC 146
Creating An MFC Worker Thread 147
Creating An MFC UI Thread 148
Making Windows And Message Boxes Appear On Top 148
Obtaining Process And Thread Handles 149
Waiting For A Thread To Complete, Setting (Or Reading) The Thread Exit Code 149
Manipulating MFC Threads 150
Learning The Return Value With MFC 151
A Complete MFC Example 152
Using Thread Local Storage 158
Using Fibers 159
Using Alternatives To Threading 159

Chapter 4
Synchronization 161

In Depth

Defining The Problem 163
More About Synchronization 165
Synchronization Details 165
The Interlocked Calls 167
Events In Detail 168
Mutexes In Detail 170
Semaphores In Detail 171
Secure Synchronization 172
Using **WaitForMultipleObjects** 173
Alertable Waits 174
Waitable Timers 174
Critical Sections 174
A Major Example 176
Other Waitable Handles 184

Immediate Solutions
Selecting A Synchronization Method 187
Avoiding Deadlock 189
Using Events 189
Using Mutexes 190
Using Critical Sections 190
Using Semaphores 191
Waiting For Multiple Objects 191
Using Interlocked Variables 191
Understanding MFC And Synchronization 192

Chapter 5
File I/O 199

In Depth
Why Asynchronous I/O? 201
File I/O Review 201
Using Threads 206
Overlapped I/O 207
I/O Completion Ports 210
An Example Application 211
A Completion Port Example 215
Another Way To Access Files 219
An Example 220

Immediate Solutions
Opening A File 225
Reading Or Writing A File Synchronously 226
Detecting EOF (Synchronous) 226
Duplicating File Handles 226
Closing A File 227
Using Methods For Asynchronous I/O 227
Using Asynchronous I/O With Threads 228
Starting Overlapped I/O 230
Completing Asynchronous I/O 230
Detecting EOF (Asynchronous) 231
Using **ReadFileEx** And **WriteFileEx** 231
Using Completion Ports 232
Memory Mapping Files 232

Chapter 6
Interprocess Communications 233

In Depth

Why The Big Deal? 235
Overview of Windows 2000 IPC Mechanisms 238
Simple IPC 240
Using DLLs For Shared Memory 247
Another Shared Memory Technique 251
Anonymous Pipes 252
Named Pipes 256
Mailslots 257
About Sockets 267
MFC Sockets 290
About RPCs 310
Microsoft Message Queue (MSMQ) 319

Immediate Solutions

Summary Of IPC Methods 322
Using **WM_COPYDATA** 323
Using DLLs For Shared Memory 324
File Mapping Shared Memory 325
Using Anonymous Pipes 325
Using Named Pipes 326
Replacing A Standard Handle With A Pipe 327
Using Mailslots 327
Using Sockets 328
Using RPCs 329
Understanding When To Use Obsolete Or Little-Used IPC Methods 330

Chapter 7
Memory Management 331

In Depth

Why Bother With Memory Management? 332
Memory Paging 333
Using **VirtualAlloc** 334
VirtualAlloc In Practice 335
Working With Page Attributes 337
Using Heaps 343

Immediate Solutions

When To Use **VirtualAlloc** 345

Using **VirtualAlloc** And **VirtualFree** 345

Setting Page Protection 346

Reading Page Protection 347

Responding To Exceptions 347

Creating A New Heap 348

Finding The Default Heap 349

Allocating And Freeing Heap Data 349

Compacting A Heap 350

Debugging A Heap 350

Heap Performance Considerations 351

Chapter 8

Windows Security 353

In Depth

Goals Of Security 354

Privileges And Rights 355

Filling In The **NULL** 357

Inside SIDs 358

ACEs And ACLs 359

Types Of Security Objects 360

Using The Default 360

Building SDs 361

Tokens And Impersonations 362

Building Arbitrary ACLs 363

Using **AccessCheck** 367

Private Security 368

Privileges 372

Kerberos 372

Immediate Solutions

Learning An Object's Owner 374

Converting A SID To A Name 375

Converting A Name To A SID 376

Creating A Descriptor 376

Converting Between Absolute And Self-Relative Descriptors 377

Using The Default Security Descriptor 377

Using A Universal Security Descriptor 378

Using A Specific Security Descriptor 378

Using Private Security 379

Chapter 9
Registry And Logging 381

In Depth

Give Up INI Files? 383
The Registry: Up Close And Personal 384
Registry Oddities 386
That's It? 399
What's In There? 400
Building REG Files 400
Inside A File Type 402
Logging 404
Event Sources 405
Creating Message Files 405
System Messages 407
Operating On A Log 408

Immediate Solutions

Opening A Registry Key 412
Finding Subkeys 412
Finding Values 412
Using The Registry Instead Of INI Files 413
Creating REG Files 414
Creating INF Files 415
Creating A Message DLL 416
Registering A Message DLL 416
Logging Events 417
Converting Errors To Messages 418

Chapter 10
Shell Tricks With ATL 419

In Depth

Shell Extensions 421
Essential ATL 423
Using MFC Instead Of ATL 428
ATL Vs. MFC 436
Icon Tray Programs 436
About Smart Pointers 440
Shortcuts 441
MMC 446

Immediate Solutions

About Shell Extensions 470
Resolving Shortcuts 470
Creating A Shortcut 471
Writing Icon Tray Programs 472
Miscellaneous Shell Calls 473
About MMC 473
Writing MMC Snap-ins 473

Chapter 11
Internet And Network Programming 475

In Depth

Internet Shortcuts 477
Using Internet Explorer 486
The Web Post API 502
MFC Internet Support 517
Active Directory Services Overview 529

Immediate Solutions

Working With Internet Shortcuts 532
Methods Of Internet Communications 532
Using Resource URLs 533
Inside Internet Explorer 534
Using The Scripting Object Model 534
Using HTML Dialog Boxes 535
Using MFC's Internet Support 535

Chapter 12
Console Applications And Services 537

In Depth

Creating A Simple Console Application 538
Services 568
An Object-Oriented Service 577

Immediate Solutions

Starting A Console Program 585
Using MFC From Console Programs 585
Methods For Accessing Consoles 585
Creating A Main Console For A GUI Program 586
Creating And Using Auxiliary Consoles 587
Handling Console Events 587
Finding A Console's Window Handle 588
Inside Services 588

Accessing A Service 589
The C++ Service Base Class 589
Debugging Services 590

Appendix A
Beyond The Frontier 591

Appendix B
Windows 2000: A Programming Odyssey 597

Index 601

Introduction

To quote the Grateful Dead: “What a long, strange trip it’s been.” If you’ve been programming for any length of time, you know that things have changed. In my lifetime we’ve gone from punched cards and paper tape to CD-ROMs and megabytes of RAM; from computers the size of refrigerators to computers that run your refrigerator; from Snoopy calendars to online printers to calendars running on palm-top PCs.

The rapid pace in this business often results in programmers getting stuck in one of two kinds of rut. The first trap is sticking with what you’re comfortable with. It’s fine to a point, but eventually the world (or at least your company) moves on to new things. For example, when a company I used to work for switched from Unix to Windows, many of the old Unix guys complained loudly and more than one left. I like Unix—but I’m always willing to learn something new.

The second trap is more insidious. As operating systems (like Windows) grow and change, it’s easy to stay stuck in time and ignore new techniques and features. This situation is especially bad if you started early with a particular system. Programmers who began with Windows 3.1 should unlearn old habits, but sometimes they don’t. It’s easy to write code in an old-fashioned way because, for the most part, new versions of Windows still support the old ways of doing things.

Old-fashioned programming may be comfortable, but it’s often detrimental to your programming efforts. Using older programming techniques may cause your programs to consume additional memory, impact multitasking performance, and make it harder for you to take advantage of new operating system features.

With Windows 2000 here, there has never been a better time to learn about Windows or unlearn some of your old habits. If you’re familiar with Unix or other operating systems, you’ll find that Windows 2000 is a fully capable environment. It will do pretty much the same things any modern operating system will—although you may have to learn a new way to do an old trick. If you’re an old hand at Windows programming, you’ll find new features and subtle differences in Windows 2000. Either way, this is a great time to examine Windows.

What's In This Book?

This book talks about how to use Windows 2000 to your best advantage. The topics, ranging from memory management to networking, include illustrative programs that you can examine—you might even be able to "borrow" some of the code.

Many of the example programs use a bare-bones console interface so you can drill down directly to the pertinent details. Although these programs don't require much knowledge of standard Windows programming, others use MFC and require at least some understanding of basic Windows application programming.

Using modern tools, you can easily create Windows programs. But without making use of special Windows features, you aren't really getting the most bang for your buck. After all, if you're just using standard C or C++, you might as well write your programs for Unix or DOS. Why use Windows if you won't take advantage of it?

As an example, consider this scenario: Suppose you're writing a program to analyze video signals. Any modern operating system will let you allocate large blocks of memory (say, with **malloc**) to store the signals. But with Windows, you can use special operating system features to allocate memory on demand, for greater efficiency.

That's what this book is about: How to take advantage of the fact that you're running Windows 2000. What special features are available that can make your programmer faster, smaller, or better in some way?

Is This Book For Me?

To get the most from this book, you should first know something about Windows programming. This book primarily focuses on the services provided by the operating system. Although it contains some traditional GUI programs, most of the programs emphasize functions like memory management, multitasking, and networking.

If you're a C++ programmer looking to make better use of the tools provided by Windows, this book is for you. Even if you're using a different language, you'll still benefit from the information about the services Windows provides.

By the time you finish this book, you'll be able to work with Windows multitasking, memory management, and interprocess communications. You'll also learn about services, the management console, and overlapped I/O. In addition, you'll find out about security, the Registry, logging, and shell programming.

If that sounds like a lot to cover, it is. Windows has a lot to offer. Armed with the details in the chapters and the practical advice in the immediate solutions at each chapter's end, you'll be in a better position to exploit Windows quickly.

What Do I Need?

Any version of Windows 2000 will run most of the example programs in this book, although I used the Windows 2000 server. In some cases, you can try the programs on Windows NT 4. You can run a few of the programs on Window 98 (perhaps with reduced functionality).

All the programs in this book use Microsoft's Visual C++ (particularly the version included with Visual Studio 98). If you're using a different language, you'll find some guidance in Chapter 1. However, you'll have to make your own connection between the material in the book and the language of your choice.

Get Started!

The longest journey begins with a single step. Your next step depends on your exact needs. If you want the full effect, you can read each chapter in sequence. If you don't have that luxury, you can review the table of contents and select the chapters that meet your immediate needs.

Like all *Black Books*, this book features detailed chapters including immediate solutions to give you a quick summary of the topics. If you're in a big hurry, you might consider starting with the immediate solutions and referring to the main part of the chapter only as necessary.

Each chapter contains code listings to illustrate its topics. The complete listings are included on the accompanying CD-ROM. In some cases, the code has highlights to point out especially important portions. You should be able to find enough context in the listings to help you see the relationship between wizard-generated code and code you must add.

Regardless of your path through this book, you won't learn much reading the introduction! Pick a topic and start your own strange trip through the insides of Windows 2000.

Chapter 1

Windows 2000: The View From Above

If you need an immediate solution to:	*See page:*
Development Tool Choices	17
The Architecture Of Windows	17
Understanding Processes	18
Calling The API From C++	18
Calling The API From VB	19
Calling The API From Visual J++	19
Internet Resources	20

In Depth

It isn't a great secret that I'm a big science fiction fan. However, even I will admit that practically all of it is ridiculous. Oh, I can accept alien ecologies and stellar empires. I can even swallow a faster-than-light star drive. What I can't accept is that it will be so easy to communicate with aliens. Of course, on *Star Trek*, all the aliens speak English. But really, very few science fiction stories consider what it would be like to make first contact with an alien culture. Most of the time, the aliens learn English from radio and TV. Other times they have a magic translation machine. Either way they do the work out of sight so as not to obstruct the story.

Consider human communications. No matter who you are talking to, no matter what subject you want to discuss, most of the communications between two people are implied, not expressed. Want an example? Consider this odd, but correct, sentence:

"I saw the Grand Canyon while flying to New York."

You know and I know that the speaker was flying to New York, and saw the Grand Canyon. But you could also parse this sentence to mean that the Grand Canyon was flying to New York, and I saw it! Rubbish, of course, because we all know that the Grand Canyon doesn't fly. But aliens (or computers, for that matter) don't know what the Grand Canyon is. You understand the sentence because you have a certain baseline knowledge that everyone takes for granted.

The problem is worse when you cross cultural boundaries on Earth. Here's an actual headline from a British newspaper a number of years ago:

"British Left Waffles on Falklands"

Typically, Americans wonder why it is newsworthy that the English forgot their breakfast. However, if you follow events in the UK, you know that the British Left is a political party. The headline is saying that they can't make up their minds about the Falkland Island situation.

Was the British newspaperman crazy? Not at all. He simply assumed (correctly) that his readers had a certain base level of knowledge that most Americans do not have.

This same idea holds true of programming at any level of complexity. When you discuss programming with others, you have to make assumptions about what they know. Try stopping the average person on the street and asking them why **printf** fails to link in your code. Chances are they won't have a clue about what you are saying unless they happen to be a C or C++ programmer.

A New Language?

Suppose for a minute that you are a C++ programmer. You share a certain base of knowledge with other C++ programmers. If your boss decides you have to fix Year 2000 problems in Cobol (shudder), no one would expect you to just walk in and start with no problems. Cobol programmers have a different base of knowledge. Communications between a Cobol programmer and a C++ programmer are usually difficult, at best. Everyone expects that.

However, operating systems, for some reason, don't share this luxury. Dilbert-style, pointy-haired bosses seem to expect you to switch from Unix, VMS, MVS, MS-DOS, and Windows with ease and no learning curve. This is especially true if you are experienced in one variant of Windows. But the truth is, these tasks are all quite different. If you learned to program under Windows 3.0, you can limp along with Windows NT or Windows 2000, but it is a struggle.

If you are moving from another operating system, things are particularly painful. As an old Unix guy, I've watched a lot of my friends make the transition from Unix to Windows. Most complain often and loudly about how things are so terrible in Windows.

The truth is, 32-bit versions of Windows are really not that different from Unix. But it is different. It is very hard to lose that base of knowledge and have to start over. If someone says, "create a new process," and you are a Unix guru, you think **fork** not **CreateProcess**. Sure, you can look it up in the help, but that's like traveling to another country and trying to use one of those silly phrase books. It can work, sort of, but it isn't comfortable or convenient. You need that base level of knowledge.

The purpose of this chapter is to make sure everyone is starting from the same point. I'll show you some things about Windows that you ought to know (and might even know already). Along the way, you'll build the base level of information that you'll need to understand the rest of the book.

A Brief History Of Windows

If you and I had formed a company way back when and tried to market the Windows operating system, we would have been looking for jobs soon afterward.

When Windows first appeared it was frightful. Only a company like Microsoft could prop up Windows until it developed into something actually useful.

Not that Windows' problems were all Microsoft's fault. Don't forget that the computers of the day had sluggish processors, narrow busses, and pitiful amounts of memory. That Windows worked at all was a triumph. But it just wasn't ready for prime time.

The Intel 386 was the first PC-compatible processor that could really handle a system like Windows. Microsoft quietly introduced a product named Windows/386 to take advantage of it. This was the first version of Windows that performed well enough for most people to take seriously.

Not long after Windows/386, Microsoft rolled out Windows 3.0. This was the first commercially viable version of Windows. Not that it didn't have its share of problems. But it didn't have enough problems to keep people from buying it *en masse*. With enough potential buyers, software companies rushed to build Windows programs (commonly known as applications).

Soon thereafter, Microsoft introduced Windows 3.1. Not only did this release fix many bugs in Windows 3.0, but it also introduced many important new features. Many programmers first learned Windows programming under Windows 3.0 or 3.1.

Although users really liked these versions of Windows, most programmers hated them. These versions of Windows had a lot of baggage left over from the earlier versions. Memory management was pernicious at best. Segmented memory models were a constant pain. Multitasking was crude and required cooperation from all the programs involved. If any one program didn't cooperate, then the whole system crashed. The 16-bit roots of the system made it tough to port code from Unix or other 32-bit operating systems.

Still, market forces demanded Windows applications, and that's what programmers delivered. For better or worse, this is where most programmers started out.

Microsoft did release several variants of Windows 3.1, including Windows for Workgroups 3.1 and 3.11 as well as Windows 3.11. From a development standpoint, these were not very important.

Enter NT

However, the real action was when Microsoft decided to develop Windows NT. Microsoft knew that Windows could be better if it were not for the limitations it suffered for the sake of older processors. It also knew that Windows was not able to compete with operating systems like Unix when it came to networking and distributed processing.

Another thing that worried Microsoft in those days was that another operating system or microprocessor architecture would rise to crush Windows or the Intel platform. Microsoft decided to make sure this would not affect it by making NT agile so that it could emulate other operating systems and run on different platforms.

NT's release was lackluster to say the least. It required hardware far in excess of what most people had at the time. You got minimal performance with 16MB of memory (at a time when few people had more than 8MB). You needed a CD-ROM to install it. Very few people had CD drives then (in fact, I bought my first drive just so I could install NT).

Even if you had the hardware, there were two major problems with NT: lack of device support and lack of applications. Only a fraction of the PCs in the world were running NT; most ran Windows 3.1. Hardware and software vendors had very little incentive to support NT. Sure, NT could still run most Windows 3.1 programs, but not all of them. And why buy NT just to run Windows 3.1 programs? Especially when NT costs more and probably would require an expensive hardware upgrade, too.

However, Microsoft kept NT propped up (just as they had the original Windows product) and quietly improved NT over several releases. Still, Microsoft knew it had to entice third-party developers into writing NT applications.

The 95 Connection

The answer turned out to be Windows 95. Instead of releasing Windows 4.0, Microsoft rolled out a new product—Windows 95. Microsoft wanted you to think of Windows 95 as Windows NT Lite (tastes great—less filling). However, the truth is that it was more like Windows 3.1 pumped up on illegal steroids.

The key to Windows 95 is that it nominally supports the same programming interface as Windows NT. So why not write code that runs on Windows 95 and NT? This would boost the amount of NT software available, right? To make this work, Microsoft needed to make sure that everyone running Windows 3.1 would rush right out and buy Windows 95 That led to some design choices that are otherwise hard to justify.

Not only did the strategy work—it worked very well. The number of 32-bit applications grew at a frantic pace. So how about the vendors that already had NT products? Wasn't that a boon for them to open up the Windows 3.1 market? Not really. The Windows 95 Applications Programming Interface (API) is a subset of the Windows NT API. If you were very careful, you could make code run on both, but unless you planned on that from the start, it was unlikely that your code would work right away. Technically, the Windows 3.1 API is known as the Win16 API and the other releases use the Win32 API. However, Win32 under Windows 95 and Win32 under Windows NT are not exactly the same thing.

However, porting Windows 3.1 code to the new Windows 95/NT API was a snap. Many programmers jumped right on the bandwagon. As a salve for those still running Windows 3.1, Microsoft released a product for developers known as Win32S. If you used the Win32S libraries in your program, you could make an even smaller subset of the Windows NT calls. The Win32S library would then convert your calls to Windows 3.1-style calls automatically. So, in theory, you could have one piece of code that worked on Windows 3.1, Windows 95, and Windows NT.

In truth, Win32S flopped. Part of the reason was that it didn't work very well. Another reason was that the subset of calls you could actually make was quite small and restricted developers too much. Eventually, Microsoft dropped Win32S, although you'll still find a few developers struggling to make it work.

However, overall, Microsoft's strategy was overwhelmingly successful. Windows 95 applications that would also run under NT sprang up everywhere. Suddenly, you could run real 32-bit programs on Windows NT.

Meanwhile

Meanwhile, on the hardware front, things were changing rapidly. Pentium-class processors were the norm, and memory prices dropped daily. High-end video cards and printers had 8MB of RAM, and many people had PCs with 64MB of RAM or more. These PCs could easily handle NT and many people switched to NT 3.5 or NT 3.51. The dropping prices of multiple processor motherboards also spurred people to make the switch to NT. (Running Windows 95 on a multiprocessor is a waste because Win95 only uses one processor anyway.)

The explosive growth of the Internet also fueled interest in NT. NT is a good networking server, and best of all, Microsoft gives away the Internet tools with NT server software.

The only major problem was that Windows NT 3.51 still looked and acted a lot like Windows 3.1 from the user's point of view. Many users wanted the Windows 95-style shell, plug and play, and other features available only in Windows 95. The release of Windows NT 4.0 brought most of that (and some new things) to the NT user.

With Windows 2000, Microsoft brought more features to Windows that users wanted (like support for multiple monitors) and also added a few new things for programmers. So that brings us to today. Right now, most (but not all) home users are running Windows 95 or Windows 98. Most corporate users, developers, and power users (but not all) are running Windows NT and will likely migrate to Windows 2000.

Windows Versions

Each version of Windows comes in several flavors. For the most part, programmers don't care which they use. The main differences between the flavors are what extra software Microsoft puts on the disk and a few licensing issues (like the number of concurrent users allowed).

The Professional edition is usually a good choice for a single desktop user. It has everything you need to use Windows as a personal operating system. You can even run a small network with the Professional edition.

If you really want to run a network or Web server, you should opt for the Server edition. There are several variations on the server product depending on what you want (for example, Site Server comes with the Microsoft Personalization System and other tools for high-volume Web sites).

Finally, there is the Windows Advanced Server and Datacenter Server, which enables programs to potentially address more virtual address space. These special versions of Windows also provide advanced networking features and additional multiprocessing support.

As a programmer, however, there isn't really any difference between these flavors of Windows. You make the same calls, in the same ways, using the same tools. If you depend on extra components (or the 3GB virtual memory limit), you might need a particular version, but in general, you won't care which type of Win32 platform your programs have to use.

Windows Architecture

From a programmer's standpoint, Windows 2000 presents a fairly simple environment. Each program has a flat (that is, nonsegmented) memory space that ranges from address 0 to 2GB. Of course, most programs don't use all of this space, and indeed, not all systems today have that much free disk space and physical memory. That's not a problem because Windows only allocates real memory as the program uses it.

Addresses are simple 32-bit integers from 0 to 4GB (although only 0 to 2GB are legal). You don't have to worry about segmentation or locking memory or any of the other odd things you used to in older versions of Windows.

The Pentium processor, by the way, allows up to 4GB of space. However, the operating system reserves the top 2GB. Does the system really use that much space? No. However, one of the processors that can run some versions of Windows has 2GB of user program space and 2GB of supervisor (operating system) space. So this model matches that processor very well.

The Windows API is the normal interface to the system. You make calls to the operating system that actually reside in system dynamic link libraries (DLLs). If you are used to other operating systems, the calls won't be familiar, but the functions will be. There are functions to allocate memory, open files, and so on. Many of these features are used mainly by people writing languages (like C++). You'll most often use constructs in your language to do many of these functions. For example, you probably won't call **CreateFile** in the Windows API. You'll call **fopen** in the C++ library instead. On the other hand, there are some things **CreateFile** can do that **fopen** can't handle.

If you have prior Windows programming experience, you'll find the function calls familiar—sort of. Many functions are the same as in Windows 3.1 and even earlier. Others are similar with subtle differences. Sometimes, Microsoft changes the call's name slightly to indicate that the parameters or return values are different. One common change to the name is to add **Ex** to the end. So in Windows 3.1, you use **GetCurrentPosition** but in Windows 2000 (or NT), you'll use **GetCurrentPositionEx**. The difference? **GetCurrentPosition** returns the current drawing position as two 16-bit words packed into a 32-bit return value. **GetCurrentPositionEx** returns two 32-bit words in a point structure you pass as an argument. The functions have the same purpose, but the Win32 variant works with 32-bit quantities.

Another change occurs to any function that accepts strings. NT and Win2000 don't use ANSI strings internally. Instead, they use 16-bit characters known as UNICODE (more on that later). However, most programs use ANSI (or what you may think of as ASCII—8-bit characters). So every function that accepts a string has two versions: one that takes ANSI strings (and converts them to UNICODE), and another that accepts UNICODE strings directly.

For example, consider the Windows 3.1 function **MessageBox**. As you probably know, this function pops up a dialog box with a text string. In Win32 there is no such function. Instead, there is **MessageBoxA**, which takes ANSI arguments, and **MessageBoxW**, which handles UNICODE. However, the documentation still refers to **MessageBox**. This is because C++ compilers and many other tools select the correct one depending on your preference regarding UNICODE. In a C++ program, when you refer to **MessageBox**, you are really using a macro that expands to **MessageBoxA** or **MessageBoxW** depending on your instructions to the compiler. Of course, that means that compiler error messages still refer to, for example, **MessageBoxA**, which can be confusing.

That's It?

If that were all there were to the Windows architecture, this would be a short section. But in reality, this view that your program has of Windows is a sham. Windows 2000 (and Windows NT) actually does not do its work using the Win32 API. Instead, it uses a special set of APIs that comprise the Executive. Microsoft does not publicly document the executive, but it is a set of primitives that Microsoft and its licensees can use to build operating system APIs. The executive does all the work.

However, user programs never directly call the executive. Instead, they call into a subsystem. A subsystem presents the program with a personality. The Win32 subsystem, for example, implements functions like **GetCurrentPositionEx** and **MessageBoxA** and calls the executive to make them work. There are other subsystems (for example, an anemic POSIX subsystem is present).

Prior to NT 4, the Win32 subsystem was a separate module just like other subsystems. However, by the time NT 4 and Windows 2000 appeared, Microsoft realized that nearly all programs actually use the Win32 subsystems. Therefore, in current versions of NT, the Win32 subsystem is actually part of the executive. This makes no difference to application programmers, but it does speed things up a bit.

Below the executive is the Hardware Abstraction Layer (HAL). This piece of software is even further removed from normal programmers. It is a piece of code that knows how to perform all the machine-specific tasks that Windows requires. So if you want to port Windows to another type of computer, you need only compile the Windows code and write a custom HAL. Of course, to get all the code and documentation, you would need some sort of agreement with Microsoft because they don't publicly support the HAL (or the Windows source code). There are different HALs for single- and multiprocessor machines. You'll also find HALs for different machine architectures like the Power PC.

What About 95 and 98?

How do Windows 95 and Windows 98 (collectively, Windows 9x) fit into this picture? As I mentioned earlier, Windows 9x isn't as much Windows NT Lite as it is Windows 3.1 on steroids. Although most of the Win32 API calls are present in Windows 95, most of them do not do anything more (functionality-wise) than their Win16 counterparts. There are a few exceptions to this, but in general, if you can't do it in Win16, you can't in Windows 95 or 98.

At first, this seems strange. Why would Microsoft release a new product based on old technology when it already had new technology (in the form of Windows NT) available? The answer lies in marketing. One key goal for Windows 95 was to spur the development of 32-bit programs. For this to work, almost all Windows 3.1 users had to switch. Otherwise, Windows 95 would become another 32-bit albatross like Windows NT was at the time—a great system with no software.

Microsoft wrote the Windows-On-Windows (WOW) module that allows Windows NT to execute Windows 3.1 programs and got a surprise. Many important programs took advantage of bugs or undocumented features present in the Win16 API. These programs failed when run with WOW, which behaved according to the documentation.

Making WOW work exactly like the real Win16 API would be troublesome, so Microsoft's answer was to leave WOW so that it worked as it should. If your program didn't run, that was your fault. That means that some Windows 3.1 programs won't work properly under Windows NT.

With Windows 95, no one wanted to take that approach. Home users are very unlikely to upgrade their machines if they even suspect that some of their programs won't operate afterward. So Microsoft needed a way to duplicate the Win16 subsystem for Windows 95.

Microsoft took the obvious solution: It just took the existing Win16 subsystem. This ensures that practically all existing Windows 3.1 software runs under Windows 95. It also enables old Windows 3.1 drivers to work. Yes, Microsoft did rewrite some parts to use 32-bit code completely, but only a few parts (notably the font rendering and memory management).

So how is Windows 9x a 32-bit system? Because it contains a Win32 API that converts Win32 calls into Win16 calls (much like the ill-fated Win32S product). Because of this approach, many NT features are absent from Windows 9x. Other features work differently between Windows 95 and NT. The memory layout is different to accommodate Win16 programs.

This book isn't really about Windows 95 (and by extension, Windows 98). However, it is good to understand how it fits in with Windows 2000. Don't worry too much about Windows 95/98, but do be aware that it has significant differences from its cousin with NT heritage.

Windows Quirks, Oddities, And Differences

If you are used to a previous version of Windows, or a different operating system, there are a few things you might find odd about Windows 2000. These aren't necessarily showstoppers, but just things you have to get used to. Of course, if you have no predispositions, these are just comments on how Win2000 works.

Multitasking And Threading

If you are coming from a Unix background, multitasking with Win2000 can be frustrating. The reason is that Unix (and many other operating systems) has a different method for handling multitasking, but many of the terms are the same.

When you run a program under Win2000, you create a process. That's not surprising. What is surprising is that the operating system never schedules a process to run. A process owns open files, memory, and other resources. It also owns a thread.

What's a thread? A *thread* is just a set of processor registers. The thread knows where in the code it is executing and where its local variables reside. Windows schedules the thread. This seems like double talk. What's the difference between scheduling the thread and scheduling its process? When there is one thread per process, not much.

However, consider what happens if your main thread creates another thread. That thread might make several more. Now it is very important that Windows schedules threads, not processes. Each thread runs in turn, along with threads from other processes.

So what's the difference between a thread and a process? Easy. All the threads that belong to one process can easily communicate because they share memory and other resources. Threads that belong to different processes can't easily share data or communicate. Sure, they can communicate, but that requires interprocess communication methods.

Forking

Another frustration for former Unix programmers is the lack of a **fork** construct. In Unix, the **fork** call clones the current process. The two processes are just the same, each with a private copy of the program's data. Many times, right after a **fork**, you call **exec**. This loads a new file into the new process, wiping out the copy of the original process. A **fork** and an **exec** are about the same as a single call to the Win32 **CreateProcess** function.

But what about the times when you want to clone the process and maintain the two clones? Windows can't easily do this. Why is this important? Suppose you have a program that tries to optimize a production schedule of plastic pellets. This is a real-world example, because it is cheaper to make some plastics in a particular sequence. In other words, suppose you have to make plastic A, plastic B, and plastic C to fill your orders. If you make A, followed by B, followed by C, you might waste two tons of plastic. Why? Because every time you change the plastic you make, there is some waste while the chemicals mix with the residue already in the process. But what if type B is more similar to type A, and there isn't much chemical difference between type A and C? Then if you make type B, then A, then C, you might only waste 500 pounds.

The first step for this imaginary program is to read all the orders and current inventory and match them up. What's left is what you have to manufacture. Now, your program wants to try several strategies for optimization. Instead of trying the strategies one at a time, a Unix program might **fork** several times, creating new processes for each optimization method. Each new process gets a private copy of the data the first process gathered. At the end, the main process would examine the results and decide which method did best.

This would be more difficult to do in Windows 2000. You could start a new process using **CreateProcess**, but by default it will have no data in common with the old program. Sure, it could use a shared memory area, or even just a file, but it isn't as simple.

How about using threads? That's a possibility, too. However, if the optimization methods modify the data, this won't be viable because all the threads share the same variables. In the **fork** example, each process automatically had a private copy of the data. Each one could change variables without affecting the related processes.

Interestingly, the executive has the capability to perform **forks**, because it does so for the POSIX subsystem. However, there is no way to access this from Win32. Another note: Lucent Technology's David Korn has a POSIX library for Win32 (U/Win; see **www.research.att.com/sw/tools/uwin/** that, among other things, implements **fork**. As I understand it, the library uses **CreateProcess** in conjunction with special startup code that copies all data using interprocess communication methods. This may sound like a lot of work, but in practice it seems to work quite well.

NT And 2000 Vs. 3.1

If you are familiar with Windows 3.1, you'll also have to rethink multitasking. In Windows 3.1, of course, there are no threads. Each program you run is a process. Because processes all share memory and other resources under Windows 3.1, they really are more like Windows threads.

Another issue is how programs relinquish control of the processor. In Windows 3.1, programs execute until they call one of a handful of system functions (**GetMessage**, **PeekMessage**, or **Yield**). At that time, Windows could elect to suspend the program and resume another one. This technique, *cooperative* *multitasking*, is simple to implement and frees programmers from worrying about deadlocks and resource contention. As long as you didn't call any of the special functions, you didn't have to worry about another program trying to use resources you were using.

The downside to this scheme is that if a program doesn't call these special functions, the system locks up. This is why there is no **Sleep** call in Windows 3.1. If your program pauses without processing messages, the rest of the system appears to hang.

Windows uses preemptive multitasking. It is still possible to put yourself to sleep by making certain calls. However, if you don't make those calls, Windows will eventually put you to sleep anyway.

That's a good thing, right? Mostly. It prevents the system from locking up due to errant programs. It also makes the system appear more responsive to the user. But it does put an extra burden on the programmer. Suppose you have several programs that share an error log file. In Windows 3.1, you can open the file, write to it, and then close it. As long as you don't make any of the special system calls, you know no other program will open the file (because no other program can run).

With Windows 2000, it isn't this simple. You might open the file and then relinquish control (involuntarily) to another thread. If that thread tries to open the same file, what happens? Either the thread can't open the file, or it opens it for sharing (which isn't what you expect). Even if Windows does not preempt you, it is still possible for another thread to execute on another processor and cause the same problem.

This is an old problem for many operating systems (like Unix) and the solutions are not too complicated. Windows provides synchronization objects (see Chapter 4) that can help you work out these problems. But you do need to be aware that this sort of thing can happen.

UNICODE

Windows 2000 doesn't use ANSI characters by default. Instead, all internal strings are UNICODE. UNICODE is a 16-bit character set (unlike ANSI, which uses 8 bits). With the extra space, UNICODE can hold many different symbols and non-English characters.

Of course, most programmers (at least in the United States) still use ANSI. Windows does allow you to use ANSI, if you like (at least, in most cases). The trick is that every API function that accepts or returns a string is really two functions: one that works with UNICODE and one that works with ANSI. When you set up your project, your development tool (like Visual C++, for example) usually allows you to choose which you want to use.

Suppose you have a call to **MessageBox** in a C++ program. The compiler defines a symbol depending on if you are in UNICODE mode. The header files define a macro for **MessageBox** that expands to **MessageBoxA** for ANSI builds and **MessageBoxW** for UNICODE builds. This can cause confusion when error messages and debugging output refers to **MessageBoxA**.

If you ever need to convert strings from ANSI to UNICODE, you can use the **WideCharToMultiByte** and **MultiByteToWideChar** functions. Of course, a UNICODE string might not exactly convert to an ANSI string and Windows might have to substitute some characters that have no ANSI representation.

File System Issues

Windows 2000 utilizes installable file system technology. That means that you may have to deal with different file systems on the same machine. It is possible for one hard drive to use VFAT (the Windows 95-compatible system), and another to use NTFS (the preferred Windows file system) at the same time.

Most of the time, these problems won't bother you as long as you don't make assumptions about the file names. For example, if you assume that a file name has one to eight characters, a dot, then one to three characters, you will probably be wrong. If you treat file names as mysterious, unknowable strings, you won't have any problems.

Prior to NT 4, you could install an HPFS (OS/2-style) file system. NT 4 dropped official support for HPFS, although reports on the Internet indicate you can still install it from your NT 3.51 disk, if you really need it.

It is worth noting that NTFS doesn't work on floppy disks. With NT 3 that meant you couldn't have long file names on a floppy disk. NT 4 and Win2000 support VFAT (the Windows 95 file system), which does support long file names, and therefore you can use VFAT with floppies. However, you still don't get the other extra features that NTFS provides.

What are those features? NTFS is essential for security. You can't secure a file on a FAT or VFAT disk. Why have FAT and VFAT at all? Well, floppy disks are important and you can't format an NTFS floppy (well, not officially; see **www.ntsecrets.com** if you really want to do it). Also, many users boot Windows 95, Windows NT, and Windows 2000 from the same machine. Without FAT and VFAT, you'd be unable to share disks between the two installations (again, not officially; **www.ntsecrets.com** has a read-only NTFS driver for Windows 95).

All things being equal, you want to run Windows with NTFS. However, you can't count on it. Some users are using VFAT or even HPFS. Even without odd local disks, you can't depend on what you might find across the network. The key is to assume you don't know much about what a file name looks like.

DLLs

DLLs (dynamic link libraries) are the backbone of Windows. Every time you make a system call, you are calling into a DLL provided by Microsoft. This enables you to use libraries of code without actually including them in your program at link time.

This has three advantages: Your code is smaller, different programs can share the same library, and library updates don't require you to relink your program. Of course, you can create your own DLLs and use them, too.

Windows 3.1 DLLs had many quirks that Win2000 DLLs do not share. Unlike Windows 3.1, Win2000 calls a function in your DLL to notify you when a process loads your DLL and when it releases the DLL. This makes it simple to allocate resources for each process using your DLL.

When more than one process uses a DLL, the DLL can make certain variables private for each process or it can share common variables between processes. This allows for a rude form of shared memory and can be fairly useful if you need to communicate between processes.

When Windows attempts to load a DLL into a program's process space, it first checks to see if it has the same DLL loaded for another process. If it does, Windows will try to simply map the same memory that the DLL resides in into both processes (except, of course, for private data memory). This works well, but only if the second process has free memory at the same address that the first process uses for the DLL.

What happens if the second process is using some of the memory required? Then Windows has to reload the DLL fresh (except for shared memory pages). That means that two processes that use the same DLL might not agree on the addresses of that DLL. This isn't normally a problem, but it can be if you are using the DLL for shared memory. The bottom line: Don't put pointers in shared memory. Instead, consider using offsets from the beginning of shared memory. You'll learn more about this topic in Chapter 6.

Development Tools

Windows certainly has no shortage of development tools. Certainly most of the developer's materials for Windows have the C++ programmer in mind, and this book is no exception. Even if you don't plan on using C++, nearly all of the Microsoft documentation is in C++ (or at least is in C++ months before any other language), so you might as well get used to reading it.

However, it is true that there are many other viable development platforms for Windows. Java is now quite popular, for example. Borland has Delphi, a visual Pascal (and C++ Builder, which works the same way but uses C++). Another language often overlooked is Visual Basic (VB). With version 5, VB sports true compilation, great ActiveX support, and it can call the API without much trouble.

Whereas there are dozens of other development tools out there, C++, Java, and VB certainly cover the majority of development tools that you would likely use to work with Windows at the low level. Nearly all of the examples in this book will focus on C++, but the Immediate Solutions section of this chapter will show you how to call the API from these three languages.

Summary

This chapter should give you a good idea of what's inside Windows and how it is different from other operating systems you are familiar with. As you try to build up that base level of knowledge, keep in mind that Windows is different from what you are used to, but that's okay. Don't fight it.

In the following chapters, you'll read a lot more about Windows, including more information about some of the topics covered in this chapter. Over time, you'll start thinking of the Win2000 way as natural—believe it or not!

Immediate Solutions

Development Tool Choices

When working with Windows at the detailed level that this book covers, you will probably encounter more C++ than anything else. On the other hand, many programmers are turning to Java, which is also an acceptable choice for most projects. However, most of the examples in this book will focus on C++ with MFC, because most C++ programmers now seem to use MFC anyway. You should be able to follow the examples (the listings and accompanying text) with little difficulty. Where graphical user interfaces are not important, you'll see many examples written as console applications. A console application allows you to write normal C or C++ code with a **main** function, and standard I/O functions.

Another interesting language choice is Borland's Delphi (or the related C++ Builder). This environment is highly graphical, but perfectly capable of writing low-level code and calling the API in Pascal (Delphi) or C++ (C++ Builder).

Although Visual Basic has long been the scorn of system-level programmers, VB6 is not a bad choice. This is especially true if you need ActiveX—VB6 does a great job of making ActiveX painless. VB6 also offers native code compilation, which erases most of the performance problems VB had in the past. You can easily call most of the API. One major objection here is that VB programs require a sizable runtime library. Well, so do MFC programs, but that hasn't stopped people from using MFC.

Whatever language you choose, you need to understand the principles of what makes Windows tick. That's really what this book is about, even though most examples are in C++.

The Architecture Of Windows

To the application programmer, Windows provides a flat 2GB virtual address space for each program (3GB in the some editions). You use ordinary 32-bit pointers that are simply numbers between 0 and 2GB.

Calls that you make to the operating system reside in system dynamic link libraries (DLLs). These calls pass your requests to the Win32 subsystem, which in turn passes control to the Windows Executive, which does all the actual work. As a passing point of interest, the executive may further call on the Hardware Abstraction Layer (HAL) to handle the machine-specific portions of the operation.

Understanding Processes

It is very important not to confuse Windows processes with processes from other operating systems. In Win2000, a process is nothing more than a container. What does it contain? Memory, open files, resources, and *threads*. A thread is the actual unit of execution. Win2000 schedules threads, not processes.

A process starts with one thread, but the thread can create more (and those threads might create more threads, too). Threads within a process share all the things in the process. The only uniqueness they have is their execution point in the program and the location of their local variables in the process address space.

Threads that reside in different processes share nothing unless they choose to do so by using special interprocess communication techniques.

Calling The API From C++

Calling the API from most C++ environments (including Visual C++) is quite simple. Just make sure you are including the proper header file (usually WINDOWS.H), and that you have the correct library (you can find out which libraries you need in the online help). Then make the call. The API is designed to work best with C/C++.

You usually won't even need to do that much work because the environment will usually set things up for you so that you can just merrily call the API. If you are using a library like MFC, you'll include the library headers such as WINDOWS.H (and other files) for you.

One thing to keep in mind is that the compiler will change many of the API names behind your back; how they will change depends on if you are using ANSI or UNICODE. The **MessageBox** call, for example, becomes **MessageBoxA** for ANSI builds or **MessageBoxW** for UNICODE. You may see these names when you look at map files, debugging information, or compiler error messages.

It is just as easy, by the way, to call the API from Delphi. You have to include the correct unit and link with the appropriate library. Again, this is usually set up for you anyway.

Calling The API From VB

Although VB doesn't naturally call the API, you can make it do so with just a little work. The trick is that VB can call nearly any function in a DLL. Because the Windows API is nothing more than a collection of DLLs, VB can make API calls.

Because the API is so large, it would slow VB down to know about every API call each time you ran any program. Most programs just use a handful of calls anyway. Instead, Microsoft provides the API Text Viewer. Using the viewer, you can select calls you are interested in and the viewer exports them as **Declare** statements to a file of your choice. These **Declare** statements make it possible for you to call the API.

This is handy, but there are a few problems. The viewer doesn't understand dependencies. Depending on how you create the output file, you may have errors when you try to run your program. For example, you might get an error on the following line:

```
Public Const KEY_EXECUTE  = (KEY_READ)
```

Examining the file, you'll find that **KEY_READ** is defined later in the file. You'll have to manually move the **KEY_READ** definition so that it precedes **KEY_EXECUTE**.

The other problem is a related one. You may export a function or identifier, only to find that it depends on something else that you need to export (like **KEY_READ** in the preceding example). Once you fix it, you are likely to discover you need to add yet other items. This goes on for a while until you unearth all the dependencies.

Calling The API From Visual J++

Calling the API from Visual J−+ can be very challenging because you have to use Java's native method interface—very tricky. However, Microsoft's J/Direct makes it quite painless.

J/Direct consists of two parts. The first part enables you to call arbitrary functions in DLLs without much trouble. The second part is a simplified way to call the normal Win32 API.

Using the first part, you could define the ANSI **MessageBox** function using this special comment and line of Java code:

```
/** @dll.import("USER32") */
private static native int MessageBox(int w, String msg,
  String title, int flags);
```

You could call the UNICODE version like this:

```
/** @dll.import("USER32",unicode) */
private static native int MessageBox(int w, String msg,
  String title, int flags);
```

Of course, you don't want to do this for the entire API, so Microsoft supplies several classes that wrap the entire API. You might as well call **MessageBox** like this:

```
com.ms.win32.User32.MessageBox(0,"Hi","Java Message Box",0);
```

This isn't as much trouble, and the **User32** class takes care of all the data type conversion and DLL importing.

Internet Resources

Here are some interesting URLs to check out:

www.al-williams.com—My Web site, which has a variety of MFC tips each month, and any updates for this book.

www.sysinternals.com—A great place to find system utilities for NT and Windows 2000.

www.zdnet.com/pccomp/features/fea0797/nt/welcome.html—An interesting article titled "NT Lies" from *PC Computing* magazine.

Chapter 2

ActiveX Survival Kit

If you need an immediate solution to:	*See page:*
ActiveX In A Nutshell	115
Understanding The Registry	117
Guide To Common Interfaces	118
Using MFC For IDispatch	118
Using MFC For Ordinary Interfaces	119
About ATL	119

In Depth

When I was a kid, I did a lot of walking. I grew up in a small town—a really, really, small town. We lived about a block from a grocery store, so it was nothing to just walk down to the store for something. I would walk to the beach or to school. Bobbie Anne's bakery was a nice walk, because you could walk back home eating hot doughnuts (or cream horns, or these little custard pies).

Later, I started riding a bike. With a bike, you could go quite a bit further. The library was a favorite stop. I even rode my bike to work some days. I wasn't the only one, either. There were several old men in town that everyone knew who rode their bikes or walked everywhere. Mr. Pete, who was a retired butcher, rode around town on a red bicycle. So did Eddie, an ex-lawyer that everyone said had a nervous breakdown. Then there was Melvin on his big three-wheeler. After Melvin had a wreck, he drove wearing a helmet and had flashing lights on his trike. "Bad news." Jeff always had some bad news to tell as he walked around town. Of course, there were plenty of kids like me, too.

When I moved to Austin, Texas, I noticed something odd. No one walked or rode a bike anywhere. Sure, plenty of people walked and rode bikes, but they didn't go anywhere. They would drive to some park, unload their bike, and ride around in a circle for awhile. Then they would load the bike back up and drive away, waving at the runners as they drove off, too.

Some of this has to do with the specific town, I think. In New York, people walk blocks for a Hebrew National hot dog. But in Los Angeles, everyone drives everywhere. Houston (my current hometown) is the same way—we have no public transportation to speak of, so everyone drives.

So I've joined the crowd. It has been a long time since I've walked anywhere. My son and I occasionally ride our bikes to the convenience store at the entrance to our subdivision, but that's about it. If the weather is cold or bad, I've even been known to drive to the mailbox.

Programming is a lot like this. In the old days, everyone punched cards (or had a keypuncher punch them). Of course, minicomputers required you to toggle in some bootstrap code using the front panel switches. That bootstrap code was enough to load the real loader from paper tape. Then the real loader read whatever you wanted from paper tape.

Today, who's using paper tape? Who remembers what a paper tape *chad* is? Not many people. Not that many people mourn the loss of punch cards or paper tape, but back then who would foresee the eventual demise of these ubiquitous technologies?

Windows programming is not immune from this effect. There was a time when practically all Windows programmers used the C language and the API (also known as the SDK). Then, most migrated away from C. Many moved to C++ with the Microsoft Foundation Classes (MFC). Others moved to higher-level tools like Visual Basic, and still others migrated to Java.

Another migration is still occurring at the API level. In the past, when Microsoft introduced a new feature in Windows, it would also document the API—a set of system-level calls that you use to manipulate that feature. Today, most new technologies from Microsoft (and some other vendors) don't support a traditional API. Instead, they use ActiveX. ActiveX is a catchall word used for the latest versions of what used to be OLE and COM. Windows 2000 adds some extra pieces into the mix and names the whole thing COM+. Confused? Get used to it. It seems like every year, Microsoft changes the names associated with this technology. In general, I'll use the terms ActiveX and COM to refer to the traditional technology, and reserve the term COM+ for Win2000-specific additions.

Do you want to manipulate shell links? You need ActiveX. Want to work with advanced MAPI? ActiveX again. How about the Microsoft Transaction Server? You need ActiveX.

In this chapter, you'll learn enough about ActiveX to get through the rest of the book. However, ActiveX is a big, big topic and could fill a book by itself (in fact, I've written several different books on ActiveX). Because ActiveX is the core of so much new technology, you would do well to learn about it anyway, so you might as well start now.

If you already understand basic ActiveX concepts, you might want to just skim this chapter. If you've actually written ActiveX programs before, you'll probably want to skip this chapter and jump right into the rest of the book. However, if you aren't comfortable with ActiveX, I would encourage you to carefully read this chapter before moving on to other chapters that use ActiveX. It will be time well spent.

ActiveX Vs. Java

Many programmers don't want to commit to ActiveX because they feel Java may replace it. This is a media-driven argument that amounts to nonsense. The ActiveX versus Java battlefield is the Web browser (and other software that needs applet-style code). Even if Java completely supplants ActiveX in Web browsers and similar software, that is only a small part of what ActiveX does.

Microsoft is clearly committed to ActiveX, and at the API-level, whatever it wants to use is what you will use. So even if Web browsers universally embrace Java, it is very likely that Microsoft will still use ActiveX for new APIs. As you read this chapter, you'll notice that ActiveX is a technology with many applications, and it only competes with Java in a few cases. These cases just happen to be very high-profile cases and receive all of the attention.

So ActiveX is the Next Big Thing. How do you get started? Do you have to write OLE programs? These are big questions. Before you can write ActiveX servers and clients, you need to know about a few other things (like the system registry). In most cases, you don't have to write what most people think of as an OLE program. Traditional OLE programming enables you to embed or link one document inside another. This is a complex process involving many different ActiveX objects. However, writing ordinary ActiveX components isn't hard at all.

Definitions

One of the frustrating things about ActiveX is that there are a lot of unfamiliar words that seem to change from week to week. Let's define a few of these terms now:

- *ActiveX Component*—An ActiveX object that other programs can use.
- *ActiveX Control*—A special component that works like a control window.
- *ActiveX Client*—Any program that uses any ActiveX component.
- *ActiveX Container*—A program that can accept ActiveX document objects or controls.
- *ActiveX Server*—A DLL or executable program that provides one or more ActiveX objects.
- *ActiveX Document Object*—A document that you can embed or link into a container (this is the traditional OLE functionality).

Currently, Microsoft calls any ActiveX object a control. I don't think that's a good idea. I prefer to call any ActiveX object a component. Some components know how to act like traditional windows and those are controls. For example, an ActiveX object that converts names to Internet addresses is just a component. You can't drag it onto a Visual Basic form, for instance. On the other hand, a control that makes a spinning logo on the screen is both a component and a control. Controls are similar to the older style OCX (OLE Control Extensions) or VBX (Visual Basic Extension) controls.

The Structure Of An ActiveX Object

Here is the most startling and important sentence in this chapter: To a client program, an ActiveX object is nothing more than a table of function pointers. That's it. Read it again. When a client accesses an object, it simply calls functions using the pointers in the table (see Figure 2.1). Objects can supply any number of tables for different purposes, but the client works with one at a time. These tables are called *interfaces*. Of course, the client and server must completely agree on the order and form of these functions. The calling convention, parameters, and return value must match both sides' expectations.

Consider this example: you are writing a system that enables users to retrieve stock market data. You create an ActiveX object with functions to validate the user's ID, make an entry in the user's account (so you can charge him for the transaction), and get the data. The object then has three functions, **LogIn**, **AccountLog**, and **GetStockData**. You might use two interface tables; one for the logging and accounting (the **ILog** interface); another for the data retrieval (**IGetStockInfo**; see Figure 2.2). Could you use one single table? Yes, you could. However, consider another example.

Your stock market data program is so successful that you branch into providing data for mutual funds, too. You might then create the object in Figure 2.3. Notice that two of the functions are the same and they appear in the same interface as those in Figure 2.2. Only the **GetStockData** function changes. Keep this example

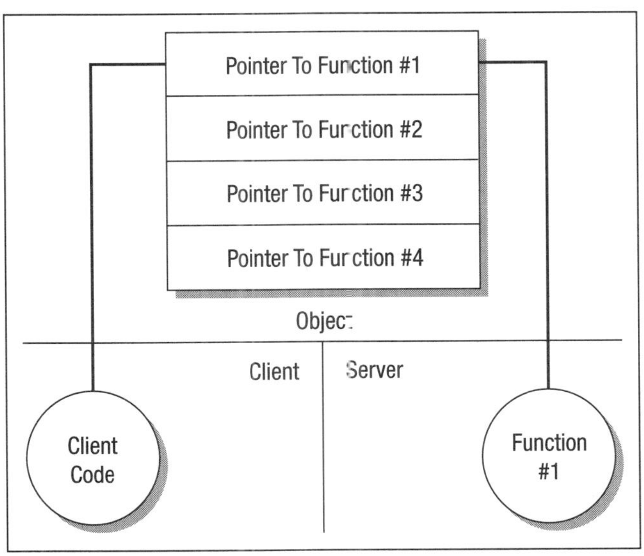

Figure 2.1 An interface table.

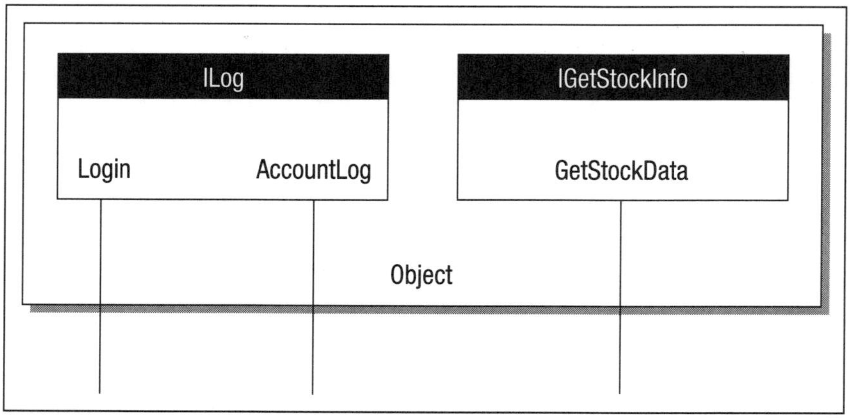

Figure 2.2 The stock market object.

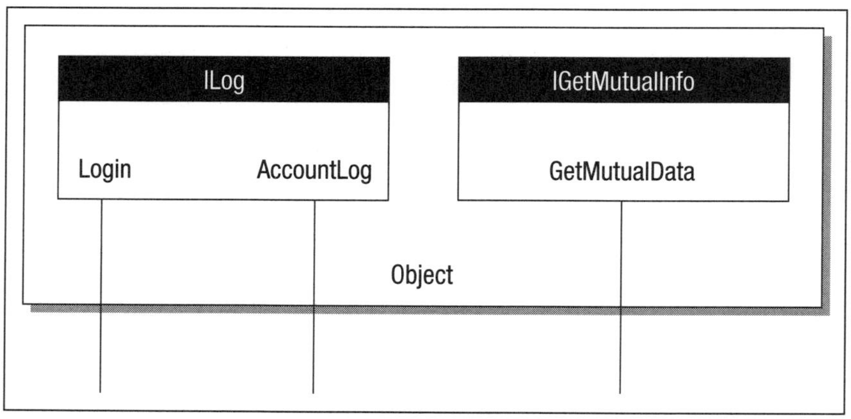

Figure 2.3 The mutual fund object.

in mind. We'll look at it more closely later in the chapter. By the way, it is customary (although not mandatory) to begin names of interfaces with the letter **I**, like **IGetStockInfo** and **ILog**.

It doesn't matter what language you use to create your object. Use C, C++, Delphi, or Visual Basic. The only thing that is important is that your language can create the magic table of function pointers. ActiveX servers can reside in DLLs or EXE files and supply objects to other programs. It doesn't matter what language you use to write the client or the server, so use the one you like best, as long as it supports ActiveX.

That's An Object?

That seems too simple, doesn't it? (In truth, there is a bit more to it than this, but not much more.) If you are familiar with objects from C++, this doesn't seem like the same thing. Well, it isn't exactly the same thing, but if you look closely, ActiveX objects allow the same fundamental operations as C++ objects.

Objects are important for several reasons:

- Objects hide their implementation of functions. You ask the object to perform, and it does, but you shouldn't know how. This is encapsulation and enables you to make major changes in the way an object operates without affecting any other code.
- Objects enable you to reuse their code to build other objects. In C++ you do this via derivation. When you derive one class from another, the derived class inherits all of the base class's code.
- Objects are polymorphic. If you have a base object for vehicles, for example, you can create more specific classes for cars, trucks, and vans. Polymorphism enables you to treat cars, trucks, and vans as vehicles. In other words, you can define a list of vehicles that may contain cars, trucks, and vans without knowing which is which. C++ handles this via derivation, also. If all three classes derive from the vehicle class, you can store pointers to them in a vehicle pointer.

How does ActiveX accomplish these goals? Encapsulation is easy. Because each ActiveX object exposes interfaces (and nothing else), client programs must call using the pointers in those interfaces. You are free to change the object in any way as long as the interface table contains pointers that work the way they originally did. If you agree that slot 4 in the interface table prints its three integer arguments, then that's what it has to do. However, exactly how you do that is up to you. You could write the object in C++ or Visual Basic, or you could connect over the Internet to a mainframe and print it there using FORTRAN. The client doesn't know or care.

That still leaves the question of derivation, right? Not exactly. C++ uses derivation to support code reuse and polymorphism. Derivation is not especially important to object orientation—it is simply one way to meet the goals of code reuse and polymorphism. ActiveX uses different mechanisms to provide these features.

Code Reuse

There are two ways ActiveX components can reuse other ActiveX components: containment and aggregation. Aggregation requires a good deal of work and design—we'll talk about it later. Containment, on the other hand, is quite simple. There is no reason that an ActiveX object can't use another ActiveX object in its implementation. Because of encapsulation, the object's user doesn't know or care what does the actual work. This is containment. The new object can provide the same interfaces as the base object as well as additional interfaces. When the object receives a call to one of the contained interfaces, it can do any of the following:

- Handle the call itself (this is similar to a C++ override).
- Call the contained object (this is similar to doing nothing in C++).
- Execute some code, call the contained object, and, perhaps, execute some more code (this is similar to C++ overrides that call their base class).

This enables you to reuse any number of other ActiveX components the same way a C++-derived class reuses its base classes. Look at the advantages to this method:

- You don't need the source code for the base class.
- The base class doesn't even have to use the same language.
- If the base class changes, the containing class will automatically use the new version without recompiling.
- You don't have to expose all the interfaces an object supplies—this allows you to selectively expose interfaces from a base class.

Because ActiveX components only expose interface functions (and never variables), you don't have the problems you see in C++ where the derived class depends on some internal state of the base class. The only communication permitted is via the interfaces.

Figure 2.4 shows an example of a contained object. Notice that the outside client has no idea what the contained class is. If the object later decides to use a different object to provide an interface, or provide the entire interface internally, it is free to do so. If the object needs to inherit from multiple base classes, it can simply contain multiple objects.

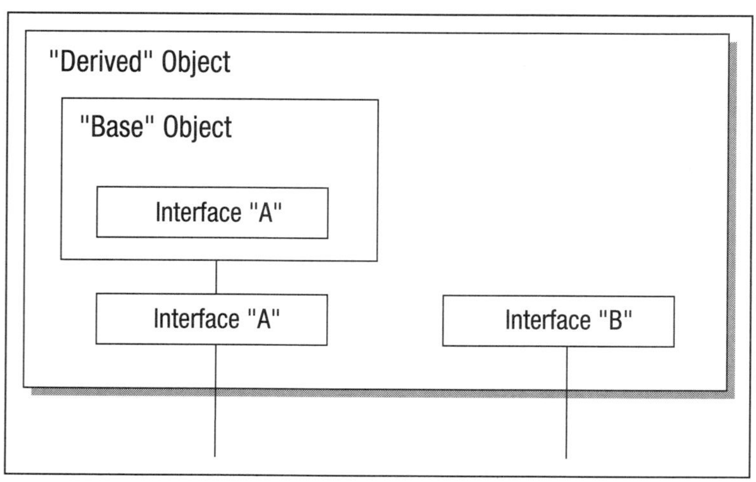

Figure 2.4 Object containment.

Polymorphism

Because objects can support multiple interfaces, they can be polymorphic. Returning to the vehicle/car/truck/van example, look at Figure 2.5. These three objects are polymorphic because they all support the **IVehicle** interface. A client can treat all of these objects the same by requesting their **IVehicle** interface table. If the client requires more detail, it can get the more specific interface table, too. Notice that if there is an object for vehicles, the other objects could reuse it through containment.

The only problem here is when you want the vehicle class to be abstract. In C++, an abstract base class is one that you can't create—you can only derive from it.

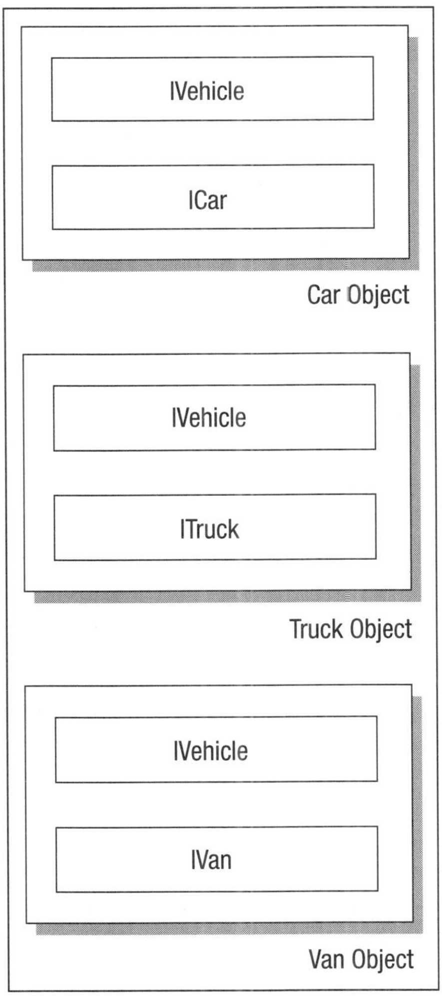

Figure 2.5 Polymorphic objects.

If you plan to reuse an ActiveX object via containment, then the "derived" classes must create it. Therefore, any other program can create the object, too.

There are some ad hoc solutions to this problem. For example, if you don't tell clients about the vehicle class, they can't create it. That isn't a very good answer, however. Usually, the idea of an abstract base class in ActiveX is just that: an idea.

This method of polymorphism has many advantages (some of which are similar to the advantages of containment):

- You can create unrelated objects that are polymorphic with respect to each other.
- The objects don't need to be in the same language, nor do you require the other object's source code.
- Any program can work with your polymorphic objects regardless of the language or origin of the program.

Another example of polymorphism occurs in the stock market/mutual fund example (refer back to Figures 2.2 and 2.3). Here the parts of your code that deal with logging in the user and computing his charges need not change. Regardless of the object in use, the interface remains the same. Only the data interface is special. If you later want another object that has a more complicated data interface, so what? The login interface remains constant.

A Few Miscellaneous ActiveX Oddities

There are a few other oddities that you ought to know about before you start exploring ActiveX. These aren't fundamentally important, but they are peculiar to ActiveX.

HRESULT And SCODE

By convention, many ActiveX functions return a type known as an **HRESULT**. This is simply a 32-bit value that indicates success or failure along with an explanation in either case (see Figure 2.6). The top bit indicates the error status. The next 15 bits identify what system causes the success or failure (the facility code defined by Microsoft). Finally, a 16-bit code tells you more information. On 32-bit platforms an **HRESULT** and an **SCODE** are the same thing.

An **HRESULT** is almost never zero, even when it succeeds, so you can't just test it for being zero or non-zero. While you can break the fields apart manually and test them, it is usually easiest to use the **SUCCEEDED** and **FAILED** macros to test for success or failure.

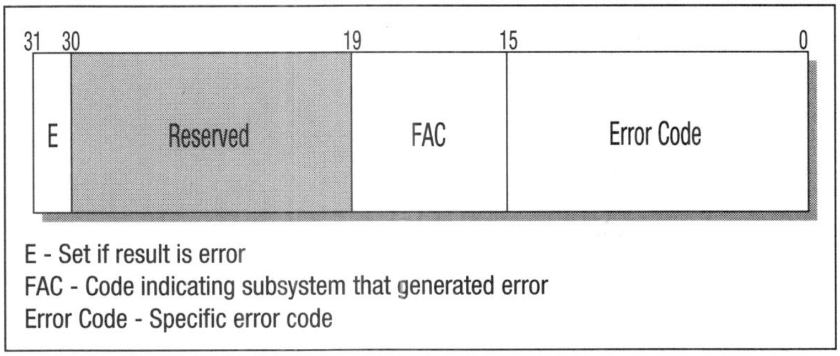

Figure 2.6 An **HRESULT**.

The ActiveX headers define many codes that you can return as **HRESULT**s. For example, you might return **S_OK** to indicate success or **E_FAIL** to indicate a failure. Other codes are more specific. For example, **E_OUTOFMEMORY**, **E_NOTIMPL** or **S_FALSE** indicate specific failures. This last code means that the function succeeded, but the answer is **FALSE** (whatever that means for a particular function).

Notice that not all ActiveX functions return **HRESULT**—they can return any type you want. However, if your functions will work across process boundaries (or over a network) they must return **HRESULT**s. When an **HRESULT** indicates failure, you can't assume anything about the state of any output parameters. A function that wants to succeed partially must return some sort of successful **HRESULT**.

GUID/UUID/IID

One of the daunting problems with ActiveX is identifying particular components uniquely—even across the Internet. This problem crops up whenever you have networking considerations. The Open Software Foundation's Distributed Computing Environment defines a Universally Unique Identifier (UUID) that addresses this problem. Microsoft calls UUIDs *GUIDs* (for Globally Unique Identifier), and often calls them *CLSIDs* (Class IDs) or *IIDs* (Interface IDs) depending on their use. All of these terms refer to the same thing. The name you use depends on how you are using the UUID.

What's a UUID look like? It is a 128-bit number formed in such a way as to be unique (or at least reasonably so). When you create a UUID, the system builds it using the current date and time and unique information about your machine (for example, a network card's hardware address).

So how do you create a magic UUID? You can call **CoCreateGuid** if you need one at runtime. More often, you'll run a program named UUIDGEN (this comes with most development tools). UUIDGEN will create as many IDs as you need at random, or in a sequence. For example:

```
C:\>UUIDGEN
f6d0f800-992a-11cf-a7b2-444553540000

C:\>UUIDGEN -n3
0c10ba20-992b-11cf-a7b2-444553540000
0c10ba21-992b-11cf-a7b2-444553540000
0c10ba22-992b-11cf-a7b2-444553540000
```


By the way, I ran those two invocations of UUIDGEN about 10 seconds apart. You can also ask UUIDGEN to create C structures (-S) and structures in a few other formats. Enter UUIDGEN -H to see a list.

Another way to create a UUID is with the Component Gallery (available in Microsoft's Visual C++ 4.0 and later). One of the components there enables you to create a UUID in one of several formats. It then places the UUID on the clipboard so you can paste it into your code (or anywhere else for that matter). Many other development tools (like VB5, for example) will also generate UUIDs for you automatically.

UUIDs usually go in your code, the System Registry, and type information files. You'll learn more about the Registry and type information later in this chapter. When you see text representations of a UUID in places like the Registry, they will look like this:

```
{f6d0f800-992a-11cf-a7b2-444553540000}
```

The braces and the dashes are not optional, although they are for cosmetic purposes. You also have to be careful not to get extra spaces anywhere in the UUID. This is especially bothersome at the beginning and end of the string where the blank isn't apparent.

Not all objects require a UUID—only objects you need to identify uniquely to the system. It turns out that most interesting objects will have a UUID, but you could have private objects that don't have a UUID.

About IUnknown

Does all this sound too easy? How does this simple protocol work so much magic? Well, there is one little thing I forgot to mention. There is one pseudo-interface called **IUnknown**. It isn't a true interface because it is really a part of every interface.

Remember earlier, when I said that an interface is a table of function pointers? That's true, but ActiveX reserves the first three slots in the table for the **IUnknown** interface functions. This enables you to treat any interface as an **IUnknown** interface. You never know or care exactly how many functions are in any interface—as long as there are at least as many as you plan on calling. If you think an interface is **IUnknown**, then it is because every interface has the same three functions appearing first in its table.

In C++ jargon, **IUnknown** is the base interface from which all other interfaces derive. What could be so important about three functions that every interface needs them? The **IUnknown** functions (see Table 2.1) are vital. Two of them manage the object's reference count. When you create an object, it has a reference count of 1. Each time you acquire a different interface for the same object, or copy an existing interface pointer, the count should go up by one. That's what **AddRef** does. When you no longer need an interface, you call **Release**. That decreases the count. If the count falls to zero, the object can destroy itself. Notice that the reference count is usually per object, not per interface. Interfaces may implement their own **AddRef** and **Release** logic, or they may call a common routine to do the work. Either way, they usually manage a single reference count per object.

Creating Objects And Finding Interfaces

The third function that **IUnknown** specifies is **QueryInterface**. You call **QueryInterface** with an IID (remember, that's a UUID that identifies an interface). If the object supports that interface, **QueryInterface** returns a pointer to the appropriate interface table. Let's go back to the stock market and mutual fund data objects in Figures 2.2 and 2.3. Suppose you are in some part of your code that doesn't know which of the two objects it is working with. It only knows it has an **IUnknown** interface. (Note: Figures 2.2 and 2.3 don't explicitly show **IUnknown**, but assume it is there.)

The first thing your code will do is call **QueryInterface** on the pointer it has, specifying the IID for **ILog**. Of course, the pointer might have been an **ILog** interface already. That's okay. **QueryInterface** will just return the same pointer. The difference is that now your code knows it is an **ILog** interface. In any case, **QueryInterface** will search the object looking for an interface that matches the IID.

Table 2.1 The IUnknown functions.

Function	Purpose
AddRef	Adds one to the object's reference count (not the interface's)
Release	Decreases the object's reference count; frees the object when count is zero
QueryInterface	Asks any interface if its underlying object supports another interface and returns the interface

If it finds it, it returns a pointer to the interface. Otherwise it returns **E_ NOINTERFACE** (a standard **HRESULT**).

All this assumes you know how to create an object. There are many ways you might get an initial interface pointer to an object. Here are the four most common ways:

- Call some function that specifically returns a particular interface pointer to you. This function might be part of ActiveX, or it might be code in a private library.
- You might call an interface function that belongs to one object to create another object.
- Someone else might pass you an interface pointer via a function or interface function in your code.
- Call a function that can create any ActiveX component. Usually, this is **CoCreateInstance**. You can think of this as the C++ **new** operator. You supply an object ID (a CLSID) and an interface ID (IID). The function creates the object and returns a pointer to the interface you requested (or returns an error if, for any reason, it didn't work).

More About Reference Counts

It seems like a lot of trouble to call **AddRef** each time you make a copy of an interface pointer, doesn't it? Luckily, you don't have to do it in every case. A little common-sense reasoning will show you that it doesn't always make sense. Consider this pseudo-code:

```
AnInterface *p,*p1;
p=GetTheObject();  // ref count == 1
p1=p;              // make "copy" of pointer to send to function
p1->AddRef();      // ref count == 2
DoSomething(p);
p1->Release();     // ref count == 1
p->Release();      // ref count == 0; object destroyed
```

Assuming that **DoSomething** is an ordinary C++ function, it is pointless to call **AddRef** and **Release** a second time. (It might make sense if you expected **DoSomething** to start a new thread of execution, however.) The original **AddRef** won't **Release** until the function returns. We really don't care what the value of the reference counter is as long as it won't go to zero until the object is not in use. The preceding code would work, but it is wasteful.

Consider what could happen if **DoSomething** started a new thread to work with the interface pointer passed into it. Then you wouldn't code the first **Release** statement in the preceding code. Instead, the **DoSomething** code would call **Release** at the end of the thread (or when it finished with the interface). You would need the first **AddRef** because the final release in the code might occur while the second thread is still using the object. It is very impolite to destroy an object while some other part of your code is using it.

Here are two common rules about when you must call **AddRef**:

- Any function that returns an interface pointer (like **QueryInterface** or **CoCreateInstance**) must call **AddRef** so the object has an initial count of one.
- Anytime you pass an interface pointer to another thread, you'll need to call **AddRef** first (see the previous example).

Usually if you think about it, it is plain where you'll need to call **AddRef**. Just make sure the reference count stays above zero until the object is no longer in use.

About Aggregation

Earlier, I told you about two methods you can use to support code reuse: containment and aggregation. Containment was very simple, but aggregation requires you to know about **IUnknown** and reference counting. Armed with that information, we are ready to tackle the idea of aggregation.

The only thing wrong with containment is that you usually have to write little stub functions for the entry points that you want to pass directly to the contained object. This is an advantage for the functions you want to override or alter, but it seems stupid if you just want to directly expose the contained object's interface (compare Figure 2.7 to Figure 2.4).

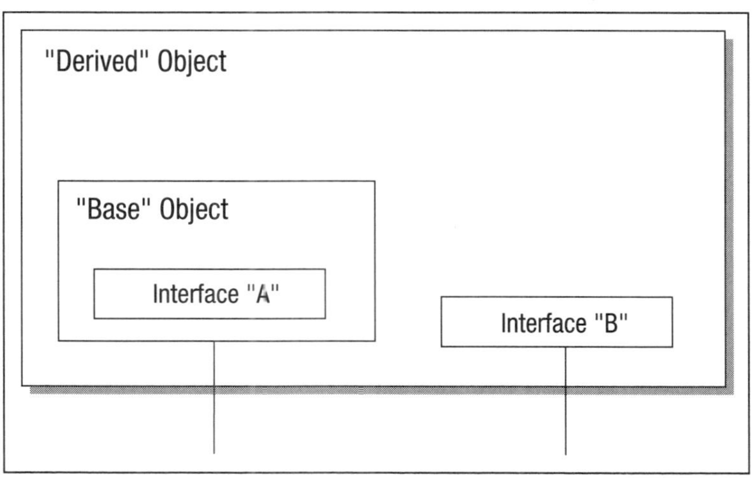

Figure 2.7 First attempt at aggregation.

If you think about it, you might try a simple solution. What if the main object creates another copy of the subordinate object? Using **QueryInterface**, the main object learns the address of the exposed interface. Then, when the main object receives the correct **QueryInterface** call from a client, it simply returns that address. That sounds good, but there is a slight problem.

What happens if a client obtains the exposed interface and calls **QueryInterface** on it to learn another interface that belongs to the main object? It won't work. The subordinate object doesn't know about the main object. The **AddRef** and **Release** calls won't work correctly either because the main object's reference count won't reflect calls made against the subordinate.

The answer is to use special features that ActiveX supplies to support aggregation. Both the main object and the subordinate object must do special things, so you may not be able to aggregate just any object. When the main class creates the subordinate one, it passes an address to an **IUnknown** interface (the controlling **IUnknown**). If the subordinate object supports aggregation, it will pass any calls directed at its **IUnknown** to the controlling interface (see Figure 2.8).

The subordinate object still has a private set of **IUnknown** functions; the main object requests a pointer to them when it creates the object. This enables the main object to call **IUnknown** in cases where that is necessary. If this seems a bit complicated, don't worry. You'll usually use containment to reuse any ActiveX component.

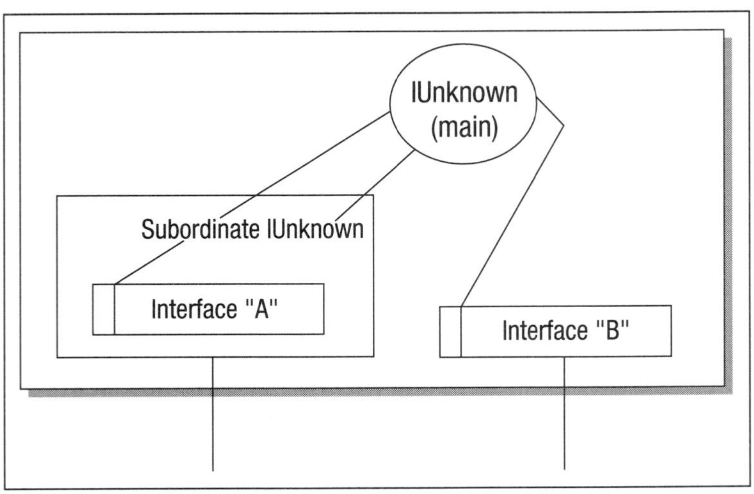

Figure 2.8 Correct aggregation.

More Oddities

There are a few other things you should be aware of regarding ActiveX. These are details that you may run across as you read ActiveX documentation or try to write your own programs.

Predefined Interfaces

ActiveX includes the definitions of many standard interfaces. You'll use some of these (like **IMalloc** to allocate memory), and you'll create others (**IDispatch**). In certain cases, you'll have to supply certain interfaces to work with some other part of Windows (for example, the browser).

However, there is nothing to stop you from adding your own interfaces. If you are writing an object that requires three interfaces, there is no reason you can't supply other custom interfaces, too. That's polymorphism again. If certain clients never ask for particular interfaces, who's the wiser?

Of course, you can also design your own objects with whatever interfaces you desire (predefined, custom, or both). The only thing you must support is **IUnknown**, and you need that in every interface. Other than that, you are free to do what you want. The only restrictions come when you want to interact with other ActiveX programs that you don't control (like the browser or Microsoft Word). Then you have to follow their specific protocols.

Here's a specific example: Suppose you want clients to create your component by calling **CoCreateInstance**. Then you must provide a specific object (a class factory) that has an **IClassFactory** interface. This component knows how to create your component, and **CoCreateInstance** uses it. However, if you have another method for creating your component and don't care about **CoCreateInstance**, you don't need a class factory object or the **IClassFactory** interface. Don't worry about the specifics of **IClassFactory** yet. Just realize that to work with certain parts of ActiveX you need to provide certain interfaces.

Type Libraries

Since you are free to design your own objects and interfaces, how can any program know what to expect? That's where *type information* comes into play. In brief, a type library contains information about objects and their interfaces in machine-readable format. You can use special function calls to read this information from a database that each component contains. You can also use functions to create the type library (often a TLB file or resource). However, you usually create a text file that describes the type information and pass it through a special compiler (MKTYPLIB) to generate the TLB file.

Proxies, Stubs, And Marshalling

One key aspect of the ActiveX object structure is that clients don't know or care where the interface table's function pointers go. If an ActiveX server is in a DLL, then the pointers probably go directly to the proper functions. The DLL loads into the client's address space and the functions run fast and efficiently.

What if the server is in an EXE file? You can't pass pointers across process boundaries. ActiveX creates a proxy in this case. The proxy is just a simple function that resides in the client's address space and forwards calls to a stub function in the server's address space. Then the stub calls the actual server function. Of course, the functions have to move any data back and forth between the address spaces (see Figure 2.9). ActiveX calls the process of translating data across process boundaries *marshalling*.

Here's an interesting twist on proxies: Why not have a proxy that forwards calls across network boundaries, not just process boundaries? Why not? Figure 2.10 shows a typical situation. The proxy receives a call, marshalls the data, and passes the call to a stub on the remote machine. The stub receives the data and makes the call to the server. Neither the server nor the client need ever know they are

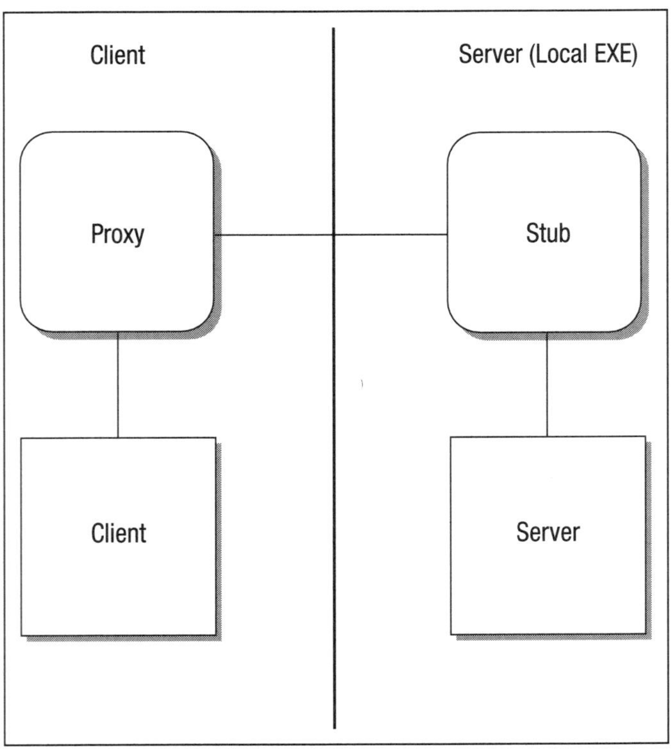

Figure 2.9 Proxy to an EXE.

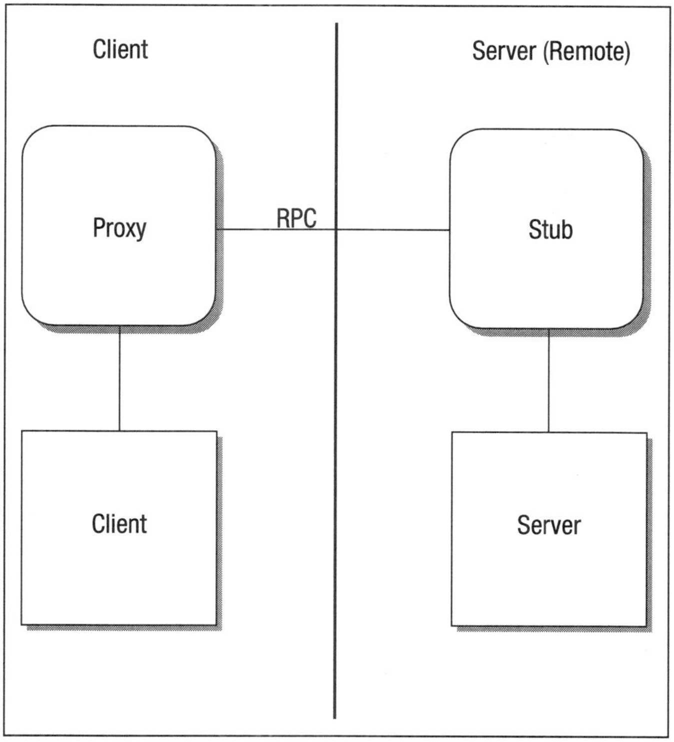

Figure 2.10 A network proxy.

not on the same machine. The exact mechanisms used to pass the data (named pipes, remote procedure calls, etc.) are unimportant and subject to change. ActiveX hides these details from both the client and the server.

The nice part about proxies and marshalling is that it usually happens automatically—at least for predefined interfaces. There are a few exceptions, but mostly it all happens with no effort on your part. The only problem is when a certain data type can't pass between process boundaries. For example, consider a device context (an HDC). What good would it do to send an HDC to another machine? You can't draw on it or even find out much about it. In cases like this, you'll often have a two-part server. One part (either a DLL or an EXE) can run on the remote machine. The other part (always a DLL) handles functions that must occur on the local machine and passes the other requests to the main server. If the main server is an EXE, this technique also can improve local performance because code in the DLL runs in the client's address space. An EXE server always runs in a different process space and requires marshalling.

If you want your custom interfaces to have marshalling support over networks, that is possible, too. The easiest way to do this is to describe your interface using Microsoft Interface Description Language (MIDL). (If you've ever done Remote Procedure Calls—RPC—this will look familiar.) You pass a MIDL script through the MIDL compiler and it generates all the marshalling code you need. You'll use that code to build a DLL. Then you'll need to inform ActiveX that it needs to use the DLL for your interface. You'll see how simple this is later. There is no reason you can't support network marshalling with your own private interfaces.

About Multiple Threads

All this seems simple, and it is. There is one small complication, however. An ActiveX server can contain multiple threads of execution. Clients also can call servers from multiple threads. This can lead to problems. ActiveX supports a threading model known as the Apartment Model. This is just an odd way to say that ActiveX treats each thread in a process as a separate process (or apartment, if you prefer).

This has several ramifications. First, each thread that will make ActiveX calls must initialize the ActiveX library separately. Also, each object belongs to a particular thread. Other threads that access the object must use a form of marshalling—just as if they were in separate processes. This special marshalling isn't to share data—it is to ensure that only one thread modifies the object at any time. If the object uses any shared data (like a reference count), it must take steps to protect that data using a critical section, a semaphore, or some other synchronization method. Supporting multiple threads using the apartment model is fairly complex. However, when you use MFC to create servers—and you will in later chapters—MFC will handle these details automatically.

ActiveX can also support a different threading standard called the Free Threading model. This model uses a pool of worker threads that handle each call to an object. This requires more synchronization on the part of the object. You can also write servers that are not thread-safe. ActiveX will attempt to load these servers into the main apartment. However, most multithreading clients (for example the new-style Windows shell) will fail if a server is not thread-safe.

The ActiveX/C++ Connection

If you've worked with C++ in detail, you might notice that an interface table looks suspiciously like a C++ VTBL (the table that stores virtual function pointers). Conveniently, most C++ compilers do generate VTBLs in the exact format required by an interface table.

This is a tremendous aid to C++ programmers, because you can express objects easily using C++ (you'll see how soon). However, this in no way ties ActiveX to C++. You can write objects in any language. You may have to create the interface table "manually," but you can do it.

The ActiveX SDK is usually C++ biased, although sometimes it has a slight C flavor to it. For example, the online help often uses the :: notation to indicate an interface function, as in:

```
IUnknown::Addref();
```

On the other hand, some versions of the help show function calls with an extra first parameter that you don't need with C++. The parameter, of course, is the C++ **this** pointer that points to the object. In C, you would need to specify that parameter directly. This makes the help a little difficult to read because you have to switch gears depending on what you are doing. If you are writing in C, you have to remember to insert the **this** pointer manually (regardless of what the help says to do). If you are writing in C++, you have to ignore any **this** pointer argument that the help specifies

Why Not Use C++ Directly?

For all this trouble, you might wonder why Microsoft didn't elect to use C++ directly. The key is that Microsoft wanted ActiveX to be a binary standard. You should be able to work with objects without having their source and without recompiling. You should be able to distribute objects without having to give away your source code.

ActiveX meets these goals. Although it may be easier to create ActiveX objects in C++, you can create them in practically any language. You can reuse code at the binary level via containment and aggregation regardless of the language you use. You can design objects that are polymorphic with other objects even if you don't have access to the source code for all the objects.

The System Registry

What do you think of when someone says database? Oracle, Sybase, DB2, and dBase? Sure, those are the traditional database products, but you usually don't use these in ordinary programs. In Windows 3.1, the most common database you might use in a regular application is an INI file. INI files are easy to use—just a few easy-to-learn API calls.

However, another system-level database exists: the System Registry. In times past, only a few types of programs used the Registry. With the advent of Windows 2000,

Windows NT, and Windows 95, Microsoft recommends using the Registry instead of INI files. So, what's that got to do with ActiveX?

ActiveX servers can reside in DLLs or EXE files. Objects a server can create often have CLSIDs (those long 128-bit numbers) that identify them. How does the system know that a particular CLSID goes with a given server? The Registry. There are many other ActiveX-related items found in the Registry—not just CLSIDs. To program ActiveX, you'll need to know all about the Registry. Luckily, the Registry isn't very difficult to understand (although it isn't as easy as INI files). The Registry database resembles a file system with directories (keys) and files (values). You use special APIs to create, manipulate, and destroy these items. If you can navigate the hard disk on your computer, you can learn to use the Registry.

Another source of information concerning ActiveX objects is type libraries. These ActiveX objects can provide information about the objects a server provides and their interfaces. After you find out more about the Registry, you can tackle type libraries.

The Registry: Up Close And Personal

Figure 2.11 shows REGEDIT, the standard registry editor (REGEDT32 is a similar NT- and Win2000-only program that presents the data a bit differently). You can see that the Registry resembles a file system with folders and files. The root of this pseudo file system contains six items: **HKEY_CLASSES_ROOT**, **HKEY_CURRENT_USER**, **HKEY_LOCAL_MACHINE**, **HKEY_USERS**, **HKEY_CURRENT_CONFIG**, and **HKEY_DYN_DATA**. These loosely segregate the various entries in broad categories.

Suppose you want to work with a value called **PATH** in the **HKEY_ CURRENT_USER\SOFTWARE\AWC\REALFAST\1.0** key. You have several choices. The

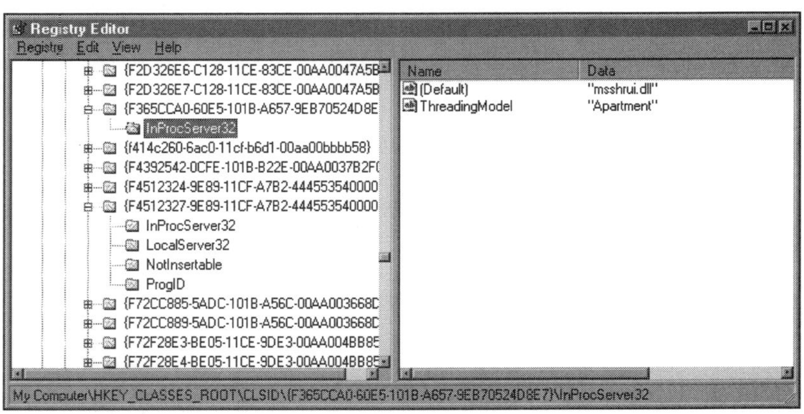

Figure 2.11 The Windows REGEDIT program.

best plan is to open the **HKEY_CURRENT_USER\SOFTWARE\AWC\REALFAST\1.0** key and then modify the **PATH** subkey. However, you could simply open **HKEY_CURRENT_USER** key and work with the **SOFTWARE\AWC\REALFAST\1.0** subkey. On Windows 2000, you may have security issues with the last method, so it is best to open the most specific key possible.

You'll use an **HKEY** variable (key handle) to refer to an open Registry key. You can obtain an HKEY with **RegOpenKeyEx()** or **RegCreateKeyEx()** (see Table 2.2 for a list of Registry-related calls). These calls present a chicken and egg problem: the first argument required is an **HKEY**. However, you can use a constant to refer to any of the root entries (listed previously). For example, you might write:

```
HKEY key;
RegCreateKeyEx(HKEY_CURRENT_USER,
  "SOFTWARE\AWC\REALFAST\1.0",0,
  NULL,REG_OPTION_NON_VOLATILE,
  KEY_ALL_ACCESS,NULL,&key,NULL);
```

Table 2.2 Selected Registry calls.

Function	Description
RegCloseKey	Close an open Registry key
RegConnectRegistry	Connect to a remote Registry
RegCreateKeyEx	Create a new subkey
RegDeleteKey	Delete a key
RegDeleteValue	Delete a value
RegEnumKeyEx	Enumerate subkeys (returns a different key on each call)
RegEnumValue	Enumerate values (returns a different value on each call)
RegFlushKey	Flush (write) key values (only required if you demand immediate update)
RegLoadKey	Load a key from a special file (see RegSaveKey)
RegOpenKeyEx	Open a key
RegQueryInfoKey	Query key information
RegQueryValueEx	Read value
RegReplaceKey	Replace a key after system restart
RegSaveKey	Save a key to a file
RegSetKeySecurity	Set key security
RegSetValueEx	Set a value
RegUnloadKey	Unload a set of entries

Once you have an open key, you can read a value (**RegQueryValueEx()**), change the value (**RegSetValueEx()**), delete the key (**RegDeleteKey()**), or enumerate the subkeys (**RegEnumKeyEx()**). You can also enumerate all of the named values for a given key (**RegQueryValue()**). After you are done, you need to close the open **HKEY** using **RegCloseKey()**. Table 2.2 shows the details of Registry-related calls.

The Registry has additional features I will mention briefly here but won't discuss in depth. For example, Windows 2000 includes advanced security features to protect portions of the Registry. A particular program may not have access rights to work with every Registry key on the system. Also, you can connect to a remote Registry and manipulate it over the network. These features don't have anything to do with ActiveX, however. Besides, once you understand the concepts, the remaining features are not difficult.

Registry Oddities

There are a few things about the Registry that don't work the way you would expect. Here, in no particular order, are the unusual things I've noticed.

RegEnumValue

RegEnumValue() has a peculiar property. The documentation says that this function walks through the values for a particular key. If the key has only a default value, the function returns it. However, if the key has nondefault values, this function will return them, but not the default value. That means if you want to be sure to get all the values, you'll need to get the default value explicitly (**RegQueryValue()**) and then enumerate. If you retrieve the default value during enumeration (it will have an empty string as its name), just discard it.

RegDeleteKey

If you attempt to delete a key that has subkeys under Windows 2000, the **RegDeleteKey()** call will fail. Under Windows 95 (and Windows 98) the call succeeds, wiping out the key and all subkeys. This can be very dangerous. In particular, you can get into lots of trouble under Windows 98 with code like this:

```
char subkey[100];
GetSubKeyName(subkey); // this fails--subkey is NULL
RegDeleteKey(HKEY_CLASSES_ROOT,subkey);
// if subkey is NULL, the entire HKEY_CLASSES_ROOT
// branch is now gone!
```

Error Returns

Don't depend on **GetLastError()** to check for error values from the Registry functions. These functions all return the error code directly. Calling **GetLastError()** will simply return whatever error some other API call generated earlier in your program.

Typed Data

If you browse the help files, you'll see that the Registry can contain many exotic data types (see Table 2.3). The system doesn't pay attention to these types in any real way. For example, the **REG_EXPAND_SZ** type is for strings that should have environment variables expanded inline. Don't think that the Registry will do this expansion for you. The flag implies that you should do the expansion yourself (use the Win32 function **ExpandEnvironmentStrings()**).

There are a few exceptions. For example, Windows 95 and Windows 98 will add a terminating zero to a **REG_SZ** string if you forget to do it. Some versions of Windows NT and 2000, however, will not add the zero. None of these systems adds the extra NULL to **REG_MULTI_SZ** or **REG_EXPAND_SZ** types.

Examining Registry Code

A picture is worth a thousand words, and so is a code listing. You can find a simple program that manipulates the registry in Chapter 9 (see Listing 9.1). The program has a simplified user interface and displays data from the registry. The program displays the keys and values.

Values have a type flag associated with them. This program checks for **REG_SZ** (strings), **REG_DWORD** (32-bit binary), and **REG_BINARY** (series of bytes). There are other types (see Table 2.3), but the system doesn't actually deal with them. They are for your program to interpret. Default values, by the way, are always **REG_SZ**. This dates back to when there was no support for multiple values or multiple data types in the Registry.

If you need to get a specific value from the Registry, you can use **RegQueryValueEx()**. Pass a NULL value name for the default. You can create new values with **RegSetValueEx()** or delete them with **RegDeleteValue()**.

Are you wondering why some of these functions have an "Ex" in their names while others don't? That's because Microsoft has changed the Registry in many ways since its first release. All the older calls are there, but you should use the "Ex" call when you program under Win32. This enables you to control issues like security, multiple values, value data types, etc. In some cases, the calls haven't changed. In these cases, you still use the original call. This is always very confusing when coding late at night.

That's It?

Is that all there is to manipulating the Registry? Yes and no. Physically working with the Registry is just this easy. However, you also need to know what goes where so that other programs (and Windows) can work with the information you provide. The API is like an alphabet. Even if you know all the letters, you can't communicate without words.

There are many standard places in the Registry that you should use to store data. For example, you can register a file type so that the shell can display custom icons, context menus, and so forth for your files. Another example is profile information (what you used to store in INI files). You should put your profile information in **HKEY_CURRENT_USER\SOFTWARE*company_name\product_name\version_number*** if it applies to the current user, or under the **HKEY_LOCAL_MACHINE\SOFTWARE*company_name\product_name\version_number*** key if it applies to the machine.

This book doesn't cover all the myriad places you can put Registry information—only a few that apply to the material in each chapter. If you want to find more information about the Registry's format, you'll find it scattered throughout the Microsoft documentation.

Registering Objects

For the ActiveX programmer, the burning question is: Where do I enter servers (or classes, if you prefer) in the Registry? There are several answers to that question depending on what you need to do.

Nearly all of the ActiveX Registry entries appear under the **HKEY_CLASSES_ROOT** root key. The first thing you'll need is something to identify the server. You place a key equal to the CLSID (with all the curly braces and dashes) under the

\HKEY_CLASSES_ROOT\CLSID key. The value of this key is a human readable name that identifies the server. The name can contain any characters you like—it is just for display. Further subkeys identify the location of the server. Consider this example:

```
HKEY_CLASSES_ROOT
   CLSID
      {73FDDC80-AEA9-101A-98A7-00AA00374959} = Word Pad Document
         LocalServer32=C:\PROGRA~1\ACCESS~1\WORDPAD.EXE
         InprocHandler32=OLE32.DLL
         PROGID=WordPad.Document.1
         Insertable=""
```

This entry—which is part of the one Windows 95 and Windows 98 use for WordPad—identifies WORDPAD.EXE as the server for this object. It is an EXE server because it uses the **LocalServer32** keyword. If the server were in a DLL (an inproc server), the key would read **InprocServer32** instead. Don't confuse this with the **InprocHandler32** key. This key specifies a DLL that stands in for the local server. The client communicates with the handler and the handler communicates with the local server. This enables the client to avoid making calls across process boundaries. It also enables the local server to perform operations in the client's address space. You almost always use the default system-supplied handler, OLE32.DLL.

It is permissible to have both types of servers for a single CLSID. Clients can request a particular type of server when they create an object. Inproc DLLs are very efficient because all operations occur in the client's address space. However, users can't start a DLL. What if you were writing a word processor program? You certainly need an EXE file that users can run. However, for better ActiveX performance, you might make a DLL that also serves the word processor objects.

Naturally, if you were dealing with old-style 16-bit OLE objects, you would omit the "32" suffix from all of the above Registry keys. You still may run into some older 16-bit OLE objects if you deal with Win32S or Windows 95 and Windows 98.

The **ProgID** key serves as a short (and hopefully unique) ID for the object. Some languages that don't support GUIDs will use the ProgID when creating objects. You can put most characters in a ProgID, but not spaces. In theory, it doesn't matter what you use for a ProgID because end users should never see it. However, in practice, the ProgID needs to be unique. The convention is to use your company name and a component name together. For example:

```
Coriolis.AutoMail
```

You can also support multiple versions of a component by tacking the version number on at the end:

```
Coriolis.AutoMail.2
```

The ProgID has its own entry under **HKEY_CLASSES_ROOT**. Here's an example:

```
HKEY_CLASSES_ROOT
   Coriolis.AutoMail.2=Coriolis Group Auto Mailer Version 2.0
      CLSID = {c353e4a0-9ce6-11cf-a7b2-444553540000}

   Coriolis.AutoMail=Coriolis Group Auto Mailer
      CurVer = Coriolis.AutoMail.2
   CLSID
      {c353e4a0-9ce6-11cf-a7b2-444553540000} = Coriolis Auto Mailer
         ProgID=Coriolis.AutoMail.2
         VersionIndependentProgID=Coriolis.AutoMail
            .
            .
            .
```

The version independent ID is for clients who want the current version, regardless of what that is. You can use **ProgIDFromCLSID()** and **CLSIDFrom ProgID()** to convert back and forth between CLSIDs and ProgIDs. In C++ programs, you won't often use the ProgID, but it is important for many other types of clients.

Notice the single **Insertable** key in the preceding WordPad example. This indicates that the client can display this class in a list of objects to insert. For example, many programs have an Insert Object... menu item. When you select this item, a dialog appears that enables you to create a new object (see Figure 2.12). The items on this list all have an **Insertable** key. If you have objects that are not for users to see, simply omit the **Insertable** key.

Many of the other keys you'll notice in Registry entries pertain to specific types of objects. For example, embedded documents may support a **DefaultIcon** key and a **Verb** key. However, for simple ActiveX components, these entries are all you need. Remember, you don't always need a CLSID and registration for simple objects. Components that require registration include:

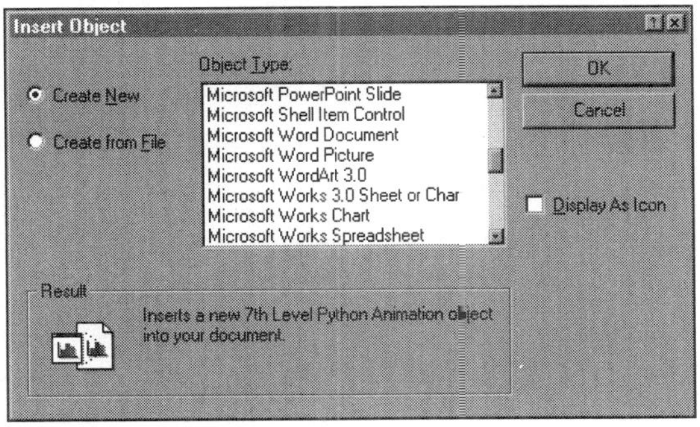

Figure 2.12 The Insert Object dialog.

- Any object that clients will create with **CoCreateInstance** (including most objects that other parts of ActiveX will create)
- Objects that want to expose information about themselves to clients before they are created
- Objects that marshal their interfaces

One of the best ways to learn about the Registry is to open yours up and browse through it. Many of the entries make sense right away. Others you'll read about later (or, if you can't wait, look them up in your compiler's help). You'll also find a brief summary for many entries in Table 2.3.

Table 2.3 Registry entries.

Key	Description
LocalServer32	Name of EXE file that contains the server
InprocServer32	Name of DLL file that contains the server
InprocHandler32	In-process handler DLL (usually OLE2.DLL)
Insertable	Indicates that server is an insertable object
ProgID	Short name for class (may include version information)
VersionIndependentProgId	Short name for class (independent of version)
TreatAs	Replacement class for this class (see the "Impersonating Objects" section of this chapter)
AutoTreatAs	Replacement class for this class (see the "Impersonating Objects" section of this chapter)
Interfaces	List of all IIDs that this object may support (optional)

Class Installation

Now that you know where to register classes, do you have to write a lot of code to do it? Not necessarily. There are three ways you can inform a machine about your Registry entries:

- Write code to manipulate the Registry in an installation program.
- Write a REG file and call REGEDIT to insert it for you.
- Make your servers self-registering by adding code to them.

Each of these methods has advantages and disadvantages. The first case is tedious, but not difficult to figure out. Just use the calls outlined in Table 2.2 to put whatever you like in the Registry.

Using REGEDIT is the easiest way to add entries to the Registry. You simply construct an ASCII file (see "Using REGEDIT," next) and use **WinExec** (or any other method) to launch the REGEDIT program. You pass the file name as a command line argument to the editor, and it provides a dialog box that reports its success or failure. If you don't want the user to see anything, pass a **/S** argument to REGEDIT and it will remain silent. Of course, you can also run REGEDIT manually to examine or manipulate the Registry by hand.

Self-registration is a convenience feature that enables servers to automatically register themselves. Of course, servers can reside in DLLs or EXE files. As you might expect, the mechanism you use to self-register is different for these two types of servers. Self-registration isn't really a specific technique. It is just a protocol for the system to ask your server to register itself. When you respond to the request, you'll use one of the other two methods (direct API calls or REGEDIT) to complete the task.

Using REGEDIT

By far the easiest way to make entries in the Registry is by using REGEDIT. You simply create an ASCII text file that you can install in several different ways:

- You can import the file using the commands on REGEDIT's menu.
- You can run REGEDIT with the file name to import the file and receive feedback.
- You can run REGEDIT /S with the file name to import the file silently.
- If your system associates REG files with REGEDIT (the default association), you can simply use the shell (or **ShellExec()**) to register the file if it has an REG extension.

Listing 2.1 shows a simple REG file. Notice that it has three main sections. The top line denotes that this is a REG file and what version of REGEDIT it supports. Older versions of REGEDIT didn't allow multiple values, for example.

The next part of the file is a key name surrounded by square brackets. REGEDIT will create as many keys as necessary to generate the full key. For example, if you specify **[HKEY_CLASSES_ROOT\X\Y\Z]** when there is no X subkey, REGEDIT will create all three subkeys. However, if any (or all) of the keys already exist, REGEDIT will not complain.

After the key name, you specify any values for the key. The default value's name is "@". Other values may have any name you like and may appear up to the next key name. Then the whole process repeats until you have specified all the keys you want.

Listing 2.1 An example REG file.

```
REGEDIT4
[HKEY_CLASSES_ROOT\CLSID\{F4512327-9E89-11CF-A7B2-444553540000}]

[HKEY_CLASSES_ROOT\CLSID\{F4512327-9E89-11CF-A7B2-
444553540000}\LocalServer32]
@="c:\\activex\\aawsound\\debug\\aawsound.exe"
"ExampleValue"="Some string value"

[HKEY_CLASSES_ROOT\CLSID\{F4512327-9E89-11CF-A7B2-444553540000}\ProgID]
@="AAW.Sound"
```

The easiest way to see how to generate a particular REG file is to find a similar entry in the Registry and export it using REGEDIT. Then you can modify the file to suit your needs instead of building it from scratch. Programming tools, like MFC's AppWizard, often generate REG files for you with no effort on your part.

There are a few tips about constructing REG files that you should know. First, the file should end with a new line. If it doesn't, REGEDIT will fail to process the last line in the file without warning you. Another annoyance is that you must backslash quotes in strings. If you use a single backslash, REGEDIT doesn't complain, but it ignores the entire string.

Self-Registration

To simplify registration, ActiveX supports an optional means for component servers to register themselves. This self-registration protocol also enables the system to ask a server to remove itself. In most cases, self-registration is optional, but it is handy and not difficult to implement.

There are three basic strategies you can use to implement self registration:

- Use the API calls to directly modify the Registry.
- Spawn a copy of REGEDIT to load a REG file.
- Create a temporary file (perhaps from a resource) and run REGEDIT.

Of course, to remove entries, you'll always need to use the API calls. The second method, loading an existing REG file, isn't as useful as the other two methods. The reason is because it requires a separate REG file. If a user forgets to copy the REG file with the component, the registration will fail. The other two methods allow a naive user to copy your server to another machine and still operate it.

It is optional, but you can indicate your server's ability to self-register by including a special version information string in your resources. Here's an example:

```
VS_VERSION_INFO VERSIONINFO
    .
    .
    .
BEGIN
BLOCK "StringFileInfo"
   BEGIN
   BLOCK "040904B0" // Unicode US English
      BEGIN
         .
         .
         .
      VALUE "OLESelfRegister","\0"
      END
    .
    .
    .
```

When your server self-registers, you'll need to make entries for every single object your server supports. You also need to register type libraries, if you have any. Unregistration should remove all the entries that registration makes.

Self-Registering EXEs

If your server resides in an EXE, you need to look for command line arguments to decide when self-registration should occur. For registration, the command line will contain **/RegServer**. Don't assume anything about the case of the string. Also, the option character may be a dash instead of a forward slash.

Not surprisingly, **/UnregServer** signals that you should remove everything. The same rules apply: The string may be in any case and may use a "-" character instead of the "/".

Self-Registering DLLs

DLLs don't typically process command line arguments. Instead, the system looks for two functions exported by name: **DllRegisterServer()** and **DllUnregister-Server()**. These functions take no arguments, and must return an **HRESULT**.

If the routines succeed, they return **S_OK**. If they fail, you can return **SELFREG_E_CLASS** indicating that class information failed to load, or **SELFREG_E_TYPELIB** if the type information failed.

Impersonating Objects

There is a different way you can register a class in the Registry that enables it to masquerade as a different class. This is handy, for example, if you upgrade to a new server with a different CLSID, but you don't want to break existing code. Another possibility is replacing a competitor's server with your own (which, of course, will be better in every way).

When you replace one server with another, you have to be sure you provide all the same interfaces with identical semantics that the existing server provided. You are free to implement them any way you want to, but the semantics must remain the same. You can also add additional objects and interfaces, so long as the server doesn't require clients to use them. Newer programs will use your "new" CLSID and can request the new objects or new interfaces. The old programs will use the "old" CLSID and will only request objects and interfaces they know about.

The entries required for this emulation seem odd at first. Suppose you want to replace component **ALPHA** (in ALPHA.DLL) with the **BETA** component (in surprise BETA.DLL). The Registry might look like this:

```
HKEY_CLASSES_ROOT
   {..Alpha CLSID here..}=The Alpha Component
      TreatAs={..Beta CLSID here}
      AutoTreatAs={Beta CLSID here}
      InprocServer32=ALPHA.DLL
         .
         .
         .
   {..BETA CLSID here..}=The Beta Component
      InprocServer32=BETA.DLL
         .
         .
         .
```

So what's the difference between **TreatAs** and **AutoTreatAs**? When a new server completely replaces an old server, you make entries in both keys. This indicates a permanent replacement. If you are not replacing the existing server, you only make an entry in the **TreatAs** key. That way, when your server unregisters, the old server (either from **InprocServer32** or from **AutoTreatAs**) gains control.

To put it another way, you might use both keys if you were upgrading your existing server with a new version. However, if you install a software package and want to emulate your competitor's server, you only make an entry in **TreatAs**. After all, the user might remove your software and resume using your competitor's (surely not).

ActiveX will automatically manage this process if you call **CoTreatAsClass()** in your registration routines. This function requires two CLSIDs. If the IDs are different, the function creates a **TreatAs** entry in the Registry. If the IDs are the same, that indicates that the replacement server is unregistering. Then, the function looks for **AutoTreatAs**. If it finds an entry there, it replaces any existing **TreatAs** key with the value from **AutoTreatAs**. If there is no **AutoTreatAs** key when both arguments are the same, then the **CoTreatAsClass()** function removes the **TreatAs** key.

Type Libraries

ActiveX is very extensible. You can add your own objects and your own interfaces. Your objects can mix predefined interfaces and custom ones. How can you communicate information about your objects to clients you didn't write?

The answer is type libraries. A *type library* is a database associated with a server. The library contains type entries. There are six types of elements (see Table 2.4). The library and each of its elements can have attributes (see Table 2.5).

Table 2.4 Type library elements.

Element	Description
importlib	Imports another type library
typedef	Defines a new elementary type
interface	Defines an interface
dispinterface	Defines an IDispatch interface
coclass	Description of a component class
module	Describes exported items from a DLL

Table 2.5 Selected type attributes.

Attribute	Description
odl	Required on all interface elements
in	Marks argument as an in-parameter
out	Marks argument as an out-parameter
vararg	Indicates that the function takes a variable number of arguments
optional	Marks argument as optional
lcid	Identifies a language for the element
public	Allows external visibility of typedef elements
uuid	Specifies the UUID associated with the element
version	Marks element's version number
appobject	Used with coclass to mark the class as an EXE application
control	Used with coclass to mark the class as an ActiveX control
dllname	Identifies the name of a DLL
entry	Specifies an exported item in a module
helpcontext	Context ID for help
helpfile	Specifies name of help file (no path; see text)
helpstring	Brief help
hidden	Indicates that the object should never appear to the user

At runtime, the library appears as a set of ActiveX objects you work with using interfaces. You can query for elements or enumerate them. You can set up type libraries to work with different languages. You can supply different libraries for particular languages.

Where Is The Type Library?

You can distribute a TLB file that contains the type information directly, or you can store it in the DLL or EXE server as a resource. If your application uses ActiveX compound files (a file format for storing ActiveX objects), you can place the type information in a special part of the file.

To identify the type library for an object, you need more entries in the Registry. First, you need a **TypeLib** key under the **CLSID** entry. Each type library has a GUID (you create it like any other). For example:

```
HKEY_CLASSES_ROOT
   {..object CLSID..} = Some Class With TypeInfo
   TypeLib={..TypeLib UUID}
```

Then you also need to define the type library:

```
HKEY_CLASSES_ROOT
   TypeLib
      {..TypeLib UUID..}=TypeInfo for Some Class
         DIR=c:\some_class\bin
         HELPDIR=c:\some_class\help
         1.0
            9
               Win32=English.TLB
            0
               Win32=Any.TLB
```

Some of these entries deserve explanation. The **DIR** and **HELPDIR** entries specify the directories that contain the library and the help files, respectively. These are important, because they vary depending on the installation. Help files named in the library must not have an absolute path. Instead, their paths are relative to the directory named in **HELPDIR**.

The next entry is the library version number (1.0 in this case). You can have multiple versions registered, if you like. The numbers below the version are language IDs (a locale). This identifies the library's language. The 9 is generic English, and the 0 is for any language. It is always a good idea to specify at least an entry for language 0. You'll use locales anytime you write programs that support multiple languages. If you want to learn more about locales see the sidebar "About Locales."

The **Win32** key, of course, specifies the file that contains the library. This can be a TLB file, an EXE or DLL server, or a compound file.

About Locales

A locale is a 32-bit number that identifies a specific language. Although locales (or LCIDs) are 32 bits wide, only the bottom 16 bits are significant. Windows reserves the top 16 bits—they are always zero.

Of the significant 16 bits, Bits 0 to 9 specify the major language. For example, 9 is English and 0x13 is Dutch. The top 6 bits specify divisions of the major language. Consider English. What people speak in London has many differences from what Americans speak. Spelling is different (honour versus honor). Sometimes meanings are different, as in "hood." In the United States this is the part of a car that covers the engine. In the United Kingdom it is a convertible's top (the engine cover is a bonnet). Also, time and money formats are different. So whereas 0x0009 is simply English, 0x0409 is U.S. English and 0x0609 is U.K. English.

You can find all the various language bits in WINNT.H. There are language IDs ranging from Afrikaans to Ukrainian defined symbolically there. You'll also find macros you can use in your code like MAKELANGID, PRIMARYLANGID, and SUBLANGID. The first macro builds an LCID from the two IDs. The other two macros extract the parts from an LCID. You can also find definitions for the *neutral* language—that is, the language to use when you just don't care.

Creating Type Libraries

This all begs the question: How do I create a type library? The easiest way to create one is to write an Object Description Language (ODL) script that describes your objects. You compile this file with MKTYPLIB to generate a TLB file. You can then use that file or include it in your server as a resource. Visual C++ will show ODL interfaces in your class view and allow you to jump to them by clicking them just like you normally jump to member functions and variables.

There are three things you can describe in an ODL script:

- A module
- Custom data types
- An interface

You can also describe scripting (or automation) classes and interfaces, but that is a special case of an interface.

Listing 2.2 shows a typical ODL file. There is a single line at the top that describes the library as a whole. This line contains the library's GUID, its help file, and any attributes (refer back to Table 2.5). It also names the library. Then after the first curly brace, you can use several special keywords:

- ***importlib***—The **importlib** statement is similar to a C++ **#include** statement. It reads in another type library. You often use this to read standard types from a common library (such as STDOLE.TLB, which contains the predefined types).
- ***typedef***—Use **typedef** to define structures, enumerated types, and unions.
- ***coclass***—To define an ActiveX component, use the **coclass** keyword. You'll precede this with a **uuid** line to identify the object, its help file, and its attributes. This is the same modifier used in the first line of the script to identify the library as a whole.

  Inside the **coclass** braces you can name interfaces that the object supports. These interface lines consist of an optional attribute (refer back to Table 2.5), the word **interface**, and the name of the interface. To describe the individual functions in the interface, see the **interface** keyword, below.

- ***interface***—Not surprisingly, the **interface** keyword describes an interface. You'll precede this with a **uuid** line to identify the interface, its help file, and its attributes. This is the same modifier used in the first line of the script to identify the library as a whole.
- ***module***—The **module** keyword describes any exported functions or constants from a DLL. You may precede it with any appropriate attributes (refer back to Table 2.5).

Listing 2.2 An example ODL file.

```
/*
*EXAMPLE.ODL
* Neutral Language Type Library
*
* "Neutral" language is usually English.
*
*/


[
uuid(5889EE60-AE68-11CF-A7B2-444553540000)
     , helpstring("AAWSound Type Library")
     , lcid(0x0000)
     , version(1.0)
]
   library AAWSoundLibrary
     {
     #ifdef WIN32
     importlib("STDOLE32.TLB");
     #else
     importlib("STDOLE.TLB");
     #endif

/*
 * IID_IAAWSound
 * 'interface' entries must have 'odl' attribute
 */
[
uuid(F4512324-9E89-11CF-A7B2-444553540000)
  , helpstring("Definition of interface IAAWSound")
  , odl
]
interface IAAWSound : IUnknown
  {
  //Methods
  [helpstring("Play the specified sound")]
```

```
  HRESULT Play([in] char *file);
  HRESULT GetOptions([out] long *val);
  HRESULT SetOptions([in] long val);
  }


//CLSID
  [
  uuid(F4512327-9E89-11CF-A7B2-444553540000)
  , helpstring("Type information for AAWSound")
  ]
coclass AAWSound
  {
  interface       IAAWSound;
  }
};
```


Type Library Wrap-Up

Some specifics of type libraries will have to wait until we look at other ActiveX details. For now, recognizing that they exist, and knowing their basic form, is enough. Soon, you'll see how MFC will create starter type libraries for you. You'll only need to maintain those libraries, not create them from scratch.

About The MFC Examples

Although the examples in this chapter use MFC, they don't use the traditional document-view architecture. To keep things simple, they just bring us a simple dialog box and do the processing there.

If you are at all familiar with MFC, you'll understand this type of program with no difficulty. If you haven't used MFC before, don't worry. So far, the programs don't use any special MFC features. Here are a few tips to help you follow the code:

- Each program has an application object derived from CWinApp. This object's InitInstance member is the closest thing you'll find to a WinMain in an MFC program. All of the startup code will be in InitInstance.
- There is a specific class that represents the dialog box. Functions with names like OnInitDialog or OnPaint handle the corresponding Windows message (WM_INITDIALOG or WM_PAINT). Other functions like OnPlay or OnOK occur when the user presses a button. In these cases, the corresponding message is WM_COMMAND with a particular control ID. Open up Class Wizard to view the mappings between functions and messages.
- Don't worry about the code that paints icons, handles data exchange, etc. The MFC AppWizard writes all of this code, anyway. The important parts are the portions that appear in the listings.

Macro Mania

Microsoft provides a plethora of macros to—ahem—simplify ActiveX programming. Some of these are part of the basic API. Others are specific to MFC. If you see macros in this chapter like **STDMETHOD** and **STDMETHODIMP_**, just check out the sidebar "ActiveX Support Macros."

ActiveX Support Macros

You'll encounter many odd macros when dealing with ActiveX programming. Here are the most common ones you'll see in both API and MFC programs:

STDMETHOD — Declares a COM interface function that returns an HRESULT. Notice that this has an odd syntax. The function name appears as an argument to the macro, as in:

```
STDMETHOD(function)(int argument);
```

STDMETHODIMP — Used to implement a COM function that returns an HRESULT. This macro has a more ordinary syntax:

```
STDMETHODIMP function(int argument);
```

STDMETHOD_ — Declares a COM interface function that returns something other than an HRESULT. The syntax, of course, is identical to STDMETHOD except that this macro takes a second argument to specify the return type.

STDMETHODIMP_ — Implements a COM function that doesn't return an HRESULT. (See the AddRef code above for an example of STDMETHOD_ and STDMETHODIMP_).

Why use these macros? Usually, they are a convenience. However, they can also assist you in porting code back and forth between different hardware and operating systems. For example, STDMETHOD expands differently if you are compiling for Windows 3.1, Windows 2000, or the Macintosh.

If you want a greater understanding of what these macros do, look up their definitions in the standard header files. None of them are very complex.

Learning Client Basics

The problem with learning about clients and servers is that you can't have one without the other. Instead of trying to plow through both, we will borrow an object from the new-style shell and write a client program that uses it.

The shell exposes an **IShellFolder** interface for each folder (including the desktop). You can obtain the desktop folder's interface by calling **SHGetDesktop-**

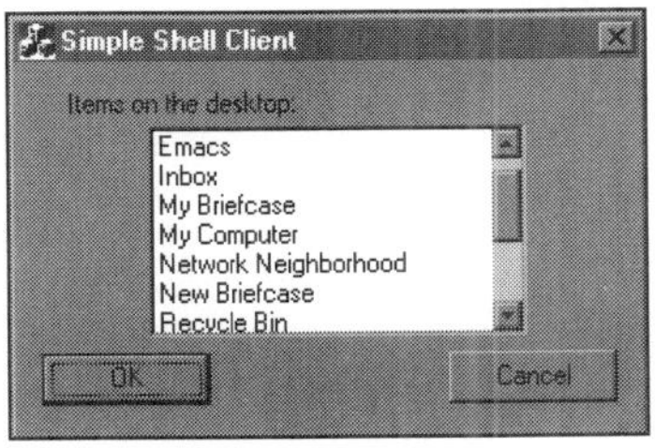

Figure 2.13 The shell client in action.

Folder. Armed with this interface, you can manipulate the folder in various ways. This example client will ask the desktop to name each item on it and place the names in a list box (see Figure 2.13).

One thing each ActiveX program (client or server) must do is call **CoInitialize** before making other calls. There are cases where you will make a different initialization call that itself calls **CoInitialize**, but either way your program must call this at least once. If the call succeeds, you must also call **CoUninitialize** before your program terminates. These calls are very simple. **CoInitialize** takes a single **NULL** argument for historical reasons. **CoUninitialize** takes no arguments. You should always check the return value from **CoInitialize**—don't call **CoUninitialize** unless the initialization succeeds. You may initialize more than once, but you must uninitialize once for each time you called **CoInitialize**.

Listing 2.3 shows the relevant portion of the simple shell client. Don't get too bogged down in the shell programming portions—focus on the ActiveX components. This program is an MFC dialog-based program. If you are not familiar with this sort of program, see the sidebar "About The MFC Examples." The program uses three separate interfaces. First, it uses the **IShellFolder** interface to manipulate the desktop. It also requests an enumerator to provide the items the folder contains. Finally, because the enumerator returns a string that the shell wants us to free, the program requires an **IMalloc** interface to free the memory.

Listing 2.3 Excerpts from the shell client.

```
BOOL CShellClientDlg::OnInitDialog()
   {
   .
   .
   .
   // First initialize ActiveX
   CoInitialize(NULL);
   IMalloc *shmalloc;  // IMalloc interface
   STRRET name;    // A union for returning strings
   HRESULT err;    // ActiveX result
```

```
ITEMIDLIST *list; // List of shell items
IEnumIDList *idlists;   // Enumerator for shell items
IShellFolder *desktop;  // desktop folder
// We need the shell's allocator so we can free
// things it gives us
SHGetMalloc(&shmalloc); // Get IMalloc
// Get desktop folder
SHGetDesktopFolder(&desktop);
// Ask for ActiveX enumerator object
desktop->EnumObjects(m_hWnd,SHCONTF_FOLDERS|SHCONTF_NONFOLDERS
  ,&idlists);
// Enumerate until done (S_FALSE) or error
while ((err=idlists->Next(1,&list,NULL))!=S_FALSE&&SUCCEEDED(err))
  {
  // Ask desktop to translate IDLIST to name
  desktop->GetDisplayNameOf(list,SHGDN_NORMAL,&name);
  // Put it in the box
  if (name.uType==STRRET_CSTR)
    listbox.AddString(name.cStr);
  // Free memory with shell's IMalloc
  shmalloc->Free(list);
  }
// Release all ActiveX interfaces
idlists->Release();
desktop->Release();
shmalloc->Release();
// Done with ActiveX library
CoUninitialize();
return TRUE;  // return TRUE  unless you set the focus to a control
}
```

Often the hard part about ActiveX is not writing custom interfaces—it's puzzling out interfaces that you want to use, but didn't create. **IMalloc**, for example, is a standard interface that enables you to allocate and free memory in a thread-safe way (see Table 2.6). You can get the standard ActiveX allocator by calling **CoGetMalloc**. In this case, we need the shell's allocator (which may or may not be the same as the standard allocator), so the program calls **ShGetMalloc**. Obtaining the **IShellFolder** interface is equally easy. A simple call to **ShGetDesktopFolder** does the trick. Table 2.7 shows the interface functions for **IShellFolder**.

Table 2.6 The IMalloc interface.

Function	Description
Alloc	Allocates a block of memory (compare to malloc)
Realloc	Changes the size of an allocated block of memory (compare to realloc)
Free	Frees memory (compare to free)
GetSize	Returns the size (in bytes) of a block of memory
DidAlloc	Determines if this instance of IMalloc was used to allocate the specified block of memory
HeapMinimize	Release unused memory to the operating system

Table 2.7 The IShellFolder interface.

Function	Description
ParseDisplayName	Translates a display name into an item identifier list
EnumObjects	Enumerates the objects in the folder
BindToObject	Retrieves the IShellFolder interface for the specified subfolder
BindToStorage	Reserved do not use
CompareIDs	Compares two item identifier lists
CreateViewObject	Reserved for use by the shell; do not use
GetAttributesOf	Retrieves the attributes of the specified file object or subfolder
GetUIObjectOf	Creates an interface that can be used to carry out operations on a file object or subfolder
GetDisplayNameOf	Retrieves the display name of a file object or subfolder
SetNameOf	Sets the display name of the specified file object or subfolder and changes its identifier accordingly

The heart of the program requests an enumerator interface (**IEnumIDList**) from the shell. ActiveX often uses enumerators. Enumerators enable you to walk a list of some type. In this case, the list is a list of IDs that the shell uses. Don't worry about what these are—you will pass them back to the desktop folder and it will convert them into regular names.

Because enumerators have to deal with different types, you use a different enumerator depending on the situation. In other words, there is no generic **IEnum** interface. However, by convention, enumerator names start with **IEnum** and have the same functions (see Table 2.8). The **Next** function returns **S_FALSE** if no more items remain, **S_OK** if it returns an item, or an error code if something bad happens.

Table 2.8 The IEnum pseudo interface.

Function	Description
Next	Retrieves a specified number of items
Skip	Skips over a specified number of items
Reset	Resets the enumeration sequence to the beginning
Clone	Creates another enumerator that is at the same point in the sequence

Once the client gets an ID from the enumerator, it passes it to **desktop->Get-DisplayNameOf** to convert the ID to a string. Don't worry about the **STRRET** type—it is a shell peculiarity that enables the shell to return different types of strings. It is just an ordinary union.

The documentation for **IEnumIDList** clearly states that you have to free the memory returned by the enumerator. That's why the program needs the shell's **IMalloc** interface. A simple call to **Free** does the trick.

When the enumeration is complete, the program calls **Release** on each interface. Why are there no corresponding calls to **AddRef**? The **AddRef** is implied in each call that returns an interface pointer. Any call that creates a pointer (**CoCreateInstance**, **QueryInterface**, or **ShGetDesktopFolder**, for example) must call **AddRef** for you.

This client uses API calls to retrieve different interfaces that it needs. This isn't always possible, or desirable, however. The more general way to create an object is via **CoCreateInstance**. Table 2.9 shows the arguments to **CoCreateInstance**. For this call to succeed, the server must make special entries in the Registry and make certain function calls. You'll see more about that as you write a server later in this chapter.

A Simple Server Design

Before you implement a server, you need to know what it does. Table 2.10 shows the **IAAWSound** interface. This is the single interface to a simple object that

Table 2.9 Arguments to CoCreateInstance.

Argument	Type	Description
rclsid	REFCLSID	CLSID of object to create
pUnkOuter	LPUNKNOWN	Controlling unknown for an aggregate; NULL for normal case
dwClsContext	DWORD	Request for EXE or DLL server
riid	REFIID	Requested IID
ppv	LPVOID *	Returned interface pointer

plays WAV files. The client doesn't need to know about multimedia or include any multimedia headers or libraries. It can create an object with an **IAAWSound** interface, call the **Play** member function, and the sound will play. Of course, a practical object will probably have more functions, but all objects will have the same structure.

General Server Issues

Servers can reside in EXE files or DLL files. Usually EXE servers are programs that can do something unrelated to ActiveX. Microsoft Word, for example, can create documents without ever using ActiveX (either as a client or a server). However, when called on, Word will act as an ActiveX server.

Most servers you want to host on the Internet will reside in DLLs (an in-process or inproc server). This is efficient, especially if the DLL and the client are on the same machine. However, users can't run DLLs to do other work.

For the AAWSound object, it could reside in either a DLL or an EXE, so you'll see both implementations in this chapter. If you run the server as an EXE, you can manually enter a WAV file name and play it directly.

Server Usage

There is one other consideration about servers. How many clients can use a single server? In the case of an AAWSound server, probably only one client can use the server. What does it mean to play two sounds at once (at least, on most hardware)? Other servers (Word, for instance) might serve multiple objects at once to a variety of clients.

Servers that are for a single use utilize the **REGCLS_SINGLEUSE** argument to **CoRegisterClassObject**. If multiple clients request the server, ActiveX must spawn a new copy for each client. **REGCLS_MULTIPLEUSE** servers, on the other hand, can service any number of clients simultaneously.

Table 2.10 The IAAWSound interface.

Name	Description
Play	Plays specified WAV file (pass file name as argument)
GetOptions	Returns options via single DWORD * argument
SetOptions	Sets options (single DWORD argument)

NOTE: *All functions return an HRESULT.*

Class Factories

If you want clients to create your objects without calling a special function, you must provide another object. This object is a class factory, and it exposes the **IClassFactory** interface (see Table 2.11). (There is also an **IClassFactory2** interface that enables you to control who can create the component based on any security scheme you like.) You have to tell ActiveX about the class factory (exactly how depends on where the server resides). Then the system (or a client) calls your class factory when it wants to create objects that your server provides.

The class factory isn't very difficult to write, and later we will trick MFC into writing it for us. If you provide API-style calls that create objects, you don't need a class factory. You only need a class factory if you want clients to create the server using generic calls.

A Simple Client

Before writing the server, you'll need a simple client for testing. Listing 2.4 shows excerpts from a client that requests a file name, creates an AAWSound object, and calls **Play**.

Table 2.11 The IClassFactory interface.

Function	Description
CreateInstance	Creates a new object
LockServer	Locks server in memory

Listing 2.4 Portions of the test client.

```
// We need to "know" about IAAWSound
#include "iaawsound.h"

void CClientDlg::OnOK()
   {
   DWORD err;
   IAAWSound *play;
   UpdateData(TRUE); // read edit control
   if (FAILED(CoInitialize(NULL)))
      {
      MessageBox("Can't initialize ActiveX!");
      return;
      }
   CLSID clsid;
#if 0 // Use ProgID instead of CLSID
   if (FAILED(CLSIDFromProgID(L"AAW.Sound",&clsid)))
```

```
      {
      MessageBox("Can't find AAW.Sound server");
      return;
      }
#else
   clsid=CLSID_AAWSOUND;
#endif
   CLSCTX servertype;

   // Use this line for EXE server
   // servertype=CLSCTX_LOCAL_SERVER;
   // Use this line for DLL server
   // servertype=CLSCTX_INPROC_SERVER;
   // Use this line if you don't care
   servertype=(CLSCTX)CLSCTX_ALL;

#if 0 // Use CoCreateInstance
   err=CoCreateInstance(clsid,NULL,servertype,
     IID_IAAWSOUND,(void **)&play);
#else  // "manual" create instance
   IClassFactory *fac;
   err=CoGetClassObject(clsid,servertype,NULL,
     IID_IClassFactory,(void **)&fac);
   if (SUCCEEDED(err))
      {
      err=fac->CreateInstance(NULL,IID_IAAWSOUND,
        (void **)&play);
      fac->Release();
      }
#endif
   if (SUCCEEDED(err))
      {
      if (FAILED(play->Play(fileName)))
         MessageBox("Server reports failure");
      play->Release();
      }
   else
      {
      CString s;
      s.Format("Create failed: 0x%08lx",err);
      MessageBox(s);
      }
   CoUninitialize();
   }
```

Notice that this is similar to the first client program, with a few exceptions. This client is simpler because the object it manipulates is also simpler. Another difference is that it uses **CoCreateInstance** to make the object from a CLSID. You'll also see some inactive code that can create the object from its ProgID or by obtaining its class factory (with **CoGetClassObject**) and using it directly. Remember, the ProgID is a short string that should be unique, but isn't as unique as a UUID. The Registry maps the ProgID to the corresponding CLSID. All **CoCreateInstance** does is obtains a class factory and calls it. Therefore, you might find it more efficient to use the class factory directly if you plan to create multiple instances of a class.

One thing you must specify in a client is what type of server you want. If you don't care, you can use **CLSCTX_ALL**. Alternatively, you can use **CLSCTX_LOCALSERVER** to get an EXE server or **CLSCTX_INPROC_SERVER** for a DLL.

Of course, you can't test the client until you build a server. For a first attempt, let's build the server in an EXE file.

An EXE Server

Listing 2.5 shows SERVER.CPP, which contains the code required to provide the server functions. It could hardly be simpler. However, this isn't all you'll need; you'll need a class factory (see Listing 2.6). An EXE server needs some user interface, too. If you run the server by itself, it will allow the user to enter a WAV file name, press the play button, and hear the sound over the computer's speakers.

Listing 2.5 SERVER.CPP.

```
// Server class

#include "stdafx.h"
#include "Server.h"
#include "resource.h"
#include <mmsystem.h>


CServer::CServer()
   {
// Initial Conditions
   ref_ct=0;
   options=SND_SYNC|SND_NODEFAULT;
   }

STDMETHODIMP CServer::QueryInterface(REFIID iid, void ** obj)
```

```
   {
   *obj=NULL;
   if (IsEqualIID(IID_IUnknown,iid))
      *obj=this;
   else if (IsEqualIID(IID_IAAWSOUND,iid))
      *obj=this;
   else
      return E_NOINTERFACE;
   ((IUnknown *)*obj)->AddRef();
   return S_OK;
   }

STDMETHODIMP_(ULONG) CServer::AddRef(void)
   {
   return ++ref_ct;
   }

STDMETHODIMP_(ULONG) CServer::Release(void)
   {
   if (--ref_ct==0)
      {
      AfxGetMainWnd()->PostMessage(WM_CLOSE);
      delete this;
      }
   return ref_ct;
   }

STDMETHODIMP CServer::Play(char const *file)
   {
   AfxGetMainWnd()->SetDlgItemText(IDC_FILENAME,file);
   AfxGetMainWnd()->UpdateWindow();
   return sndPlaySound(file,options)?S_OK:E_FAIL;
   }
```

Listing 2.6 CLASSFAC.CPP.

```
// Server class factory object

#include "stdafx.h"
#include "classfac.h"
#include "Server.h"


ClassFac::ClassFac()
   {
```

```
   ref_ct=0;
   }

STDMETHODIMP ClassFac::QueryInterface(REFIID iid, void ** obj)
   {
   *obj=NULL;
   if (IsEqualIID(IID_IUnknown,iid)||
       IsEqualIID(IID_IClassFactory,iid))
      *obj=this;
   if (*obj) ((IUnknown *)*obj)->AddRef();
   return *obj?S_OK:E_NOINTERFACE;
   }

STDMETHODIMP_(ULONG) ClassFac::AddRef(void)
   {
   return ++ref_ct;
   }

STDMETHODIMP_(ULONG) ClassFac::Release(void)
   {
   // No need to delete anything since class factory
   // is always static in this example
   return --ref_ct;
   }

STDMETHODIMP ClassFac::CreateInstance(IUnknown * control,
  REFIID id,void **obj)
   {
   CServer *newobj;
   if (control)
      return CLASS_E_NOAGGREGATION;
   if (!IsEqualIID(id,IID_IAAWSOUND)&&
       !IsEqualIID(id,IID_IUnknown))
      return CLASS_E_CLASSNOTAVAILABLE;
   newobj=new CServer;
   if (!newobj)
      return E_OUTOFMEMORY;
   // QueryInterface calls AddRef!
   return newobj->QueryInterface(id,obj);
   }

STDMETHODIMP ClassFac::LockServer(BOOL lock)
   {
   return E_NOTIMPL;
   }
```

```
// Local private function -- not accessible to clients
void ClassFac::GetObjID(CLSID *clsid)
   {
   *clsid=CLSID_AAWSOUND;
   }
```

An EXE server can run in one of two modes: as a standalone program or as an ActiveX server. ActiveX passes **/Embedding** (or **-Embedding**) on the server's command line if it is a server. The command line is always ANSI characters, so be sure to take that into account if you are programming with UNICODE. The main program's **InitInstance** checks for this switch (see Listing 2.7). If it finds the switch, it sets the **embed** variable to **TRUE**.

Listing 2.7 InitInstance for EXE server.

```
BOOL CAawsoundApp::InitInstance()
   {
   // Standard initialization
#ifdef _AFXDLL
   Enable3dControls();
#else
   Enable3dControlsStatic();
#endif

   CString cmd=m_lpCmdLine;
   cmd.MakeUpper();
   if (cmd.Find("/EMBEDDING")!=-1||cmd.Find("-EMBEDDING")!=-1)
      embed=TRUE;
   else
      embed=FALSE;
   if (cmd.Find("/REGSERVER")!=-1||cmd.Find("-REGSERVER")!=-1)
      {
      char fn[1024];
      GetModuleFileName(NULL,fn,sizeof(fn));
      if (SUCCEEDED(RegisterServer(fn)))
         AfxMessageBox("Registration successful");
      else
         AfxMessageBox("Registration failed");
      return FALSE;
      }
   if (cmd.Find("/UNREGSERVER")!=-1||
     cmd.Find("-UNREGSERVER")!=-1)
      {
      if (SUCCEEDED(UnregisterServer()))
         AfxMessageBox("Unregister successful");
```

```
      else
         AfxMessageBox("Unregister failed");
      return FALSE;
      }
   CsoundDlg dlg;
   m_pMainWnd = &dlg;
   int nResponse = dlg.DoModal();
   if (nResponse == IDOK)
      {
      // TODO: Place code here to handle when the dialog is
      //  dismissed with OK
      }
   else if (nResponse == IDCANCEL)
      {
      // TODO: Place code here to handle when the dialog is
      //  dismissed with Cancel
      }
   return FALSE;
   }
```

The real action occurs in the main dialog's **InitDialog** function (see Listing 2.8). Here, the code checks for the **embed** flag. If it is **TRUE**, the program does the following:

1. Calls **CoInitialize** because all ActiveX programs must call this function.
2. Calls the class factory's **GetObjID** member to learn the main CLSID. Notice that this is a private member function, not part of **IClassFactory**.
3. Calls **CoRegisterClassObject** to inform ActiveX that it can create the object.
4. Disables the play button and forces the dialog box edit control to read-only. The client, not the user, controls the program in server mode.

Listing 2.8 The OnInitDialog code.

```
BOOL CsoundDlg::OnInitDialog()
   {
   .
   .
   .
   // Register ActiveX Server here
   if (((CAawsoundApp *)AfxGetApp())->embed)
      {
      CLSID id;
      if (FAILED(CoInitialize(NULL)))
         {
```

```
        MessageBox("Can't start ActiveX");
        AfxAbort();
        }
      factory.GetObjID(&id);
      if (FAILED(CoRegisterClassObject(id,&factory,
        CLSCTX_LOCAL_SERVER,REGCLS_SINGLEUSE,&reg_key)))
      MessageBox("Can't register class");
      GetDlgItem(IDC_FILENAME)->SendMessage(EM_SETREADONLY,1);
      GetDlgItem(ID_PLAY)->EnableWindow(FALSE);
      }
   else
      localserver=new CServer;
   return TRUE;
   }
```


If the program isn't in server mode, it creates a private copy of the server and places a pointer to it in the **localserver** variable. This shows an important idea. If you want to use your own server, you don't need to register it with ActiveX or do anything but create the server and use it. In non-server mode, the play button uses the **localserver** object to do the work.

When the dialog box exits (see the implementation of **Release** in SERVER.CPP), the code in the **OnOK** routine revokes the class object. This is a fancy way to say it is telling ActiveX that the server isn't willing to create any more objects. Then it calls **CoUnInitialize** to end its ActiveX operations.

Will That Work?

What else do you need to get the server to work? Some Registry entries, right? You can find them in Listing 2.9. Notice that the path to the EXE must be correct and that you should double any backslashes in the REG file.

Listing 2.9 REG file.

```
REGEDIT4

[HKEY_CLASSES_ROOT\CLSID\{F4512327-9E89-11CF-A7B2-444553540000}]

[HKEY_CLASSES_ROOT\CLSID\{F4512327-9E89-11CF-A7B2-
444553540000}\LocalServer32]
@="c:\\activex\\aawsound\\debug\\aawsound.exe"

[HKEY_CLASSES_ROOT\CLSID\{F4512327-9E89-11CF-A7B2-444553540000}\ProgID]
@="AAW.Sound"
```

If you build this example and run it in standalone mode it will work fine. Running it with the client program causes an ActiveX error—error 0x80040150, to be exact. What does that mean?

To find out, look in the system header, WINERROR.H. The digit 8 simply means that the high bit is set. When the high bit is set in an **HRESULT**, it indicates an error. The important part of the code is the 40150. Searching WINERROR.H with a grep utility or an editor with a search feature will show you that 0x80040150 is **REGDB_E_READREGDB**. It can't read the Registry! This is as misleading an error as you are likely to see.

There are two places you'll want to look to find out what is wrong. First—the obvious suspect—is the Registry. The other candidate is the code itself. Try debugging the server to see what is happening (see the sidebar "Server Debugging Tips" to find out how to get started). Verify that the class factory is working. If you get calls into the server code, you can assume the class factory is at least doing something right. In particular, look at the server's **QueryInterface** (in SERVER.CPP, not CLASSFAC.CPP). Notice how many interfaces ActiveX requests. What can this mean?

Think about what else might be missing. Do you think it really relates to the Registry? When you think you know, go ahead and read the section "No Peeking," next.

Server Debugging Tips

Debugging a client is simple—just run the program with your debugger. Servers pose more of a problem because you don't execute them directly. There are several possible solutions.

If your server resides in an EXE file, you have two options. The first is to run the server under the debugger. If the server is a single-use server, you'll need to include **/Embedding** in the command line. Place any breakpoints you want to examine. Then start the client and create an object. The debugger should trigger a breakpoint at the appropriate place.

Another option is to modify the server's Registry entry so that the LocalProc32 entry is the debugger EXE combined with the command line arguments required to start the server. ActiveX will then start the debugger. If you use this method, you must make sure the server registers its class factory before the timeout expires.

Debugging DLLs is even easier. Just start with the DLL visible in the compiler's IDE. Select Build Settings from the menu and click on the Debug tab. Fill in the name of the client you want to run in the field labeled Executable for debug session. When you attempt to run, you may see a warning that the client doesn't have debugging information. That's no problem.

One common **HRESULT** you'll see when working with DLLs is 0x800401F9. This result usually means ActiveX couldn't find your **DLLGetClassObject** or **DLLCanUnloadNow** functions. Perhaps you forgot to export them, or the names don't match exactly.

No Peeking

Okay, so what's wrong with this server? The key is that the server resides in an EXE file. That means it is running in a separate process from the client. ActiveX knows this, and asks the object for *marshalling* interfaces. Remember marshalling? That's the procedure that moves data between process boundaries. Of course, our object doesn't supply marshalling interfaces.

When ActiveX discovers that our object doesn't know how to marshall its data, it looks in the Registry under **\HKEY_CLASSES_ROOT\INTERFACES** for the IID the client wants (**IID_IAAWSound** in this case). Guess what? There is no entry in the Registry for this. You didn't make one. This is the cause of the Registry-related error message.

If you want to verify this, change the client code to ask for **IUnknown** instead of **IAAWSound**. Then manually cast the pointer to an **IID_IAAWSound** interface. The object creation will then succeed, but the client will crash when you call any members in the object. That's because methods like **Play** will not cross the process boundary.

Of course, if the server were in a DLL, this wouldn't be a problem. It is worth mentioning that the client can ask for a particular type of server when it calls **CoCreateInstance**. This client passes **CLSCTX_ALL** to indicate that it doesn't care what type of server it obtains. This is usually the case, because the client interacts with the server in exactly the same way in any case. Of course, DLLs are more efficient because they do not marshall data.

Marshalling

So, you need Registry entries for marshalling. The **INTERFACES** key requires a subkey with the IID. The IID key will have two subkeys. The first indicates how many functions the interface provides (**NumMethods**), whereas the other names a DLL that will marshall the interface (ProxyStubCLSID32). Usually, this CLSID is the same as the IID. Then you need to register that CLSID under **\HKEY_CLASSES_ROOT\CLSID** and add an InProcServer32 subkey.

That's not hard, but where do you get the marshalling code? You could write it, but that is moderately difficult. The easy way is to write an interface description language (IDL) script and compile it with a program named MIDL. MIDL writes three C-language source files that you can compile into a DLL.

Besides the files that MIDL creates, you'll need RPCPROXY.H and RPCRT4.LIB. You'll usually include UNKWN.IDL in your IDL script (it defines **IUnknown** and it includes **WTYPES.IDL**). To compile, you still need to supply a DEF file and a MAKE file. You also need to register the DLL, which you can do with a REG file.

Writing The Script

You still need to know how to write the IDL. IDL isn't unique to ActiveX. It is actually part of the Open Software Foundation's (OSF) Distributed Computing Environment (DCE) specification for Remote Procedure Calls (RPC). Luckily, for ActiveX purposes, you need only a small subset of the entire thing.

Look at Listing 2.10. This is the IDL file required for the sound server. The first line encodes the IID and states that it is part of an object. The next line names the interface and indicates that it derives from **IUnknown**.

Listing 2.10 The IDL file.

```
[uuid(F4512324-9E89-11CF-A7B2-444553540000),object]
interface IAAWSound : IUnknown
  {
  import "unknwn.idl";
  HRESULT Play([in,string]char const *file);
  HRESULT GetOptions([out]DWORD *dw);
  HRESULT SetOptions([in] DWORD dw);
  }
```

The lines inside the curly braces are very similar to a C++ structure definition. The script imports UNKNWN.IDL instead of manually defining the functions for **IUnknown**. Following this are three almost ordinary-looking function declarations. The difference is that each parameter has a qualifier in square brackets preceding it. These qualifiers indicate if the parameter is an input, an output, or both. Also, in the case of some ambiguous pointer types, the qualifier tells what the pointer points to. For example, the string qualifier in the line that defines the **Play** function tells the IDL compiler to generate code to pass a NULL-terminated string.

After you get the DLL working, try removing the string attribute, rebuilding the DLL, and see what happens. You won't always use the string attribute with character pointers. Other IDL scripts you write might have different uses for a character pointer. It might point to a fixed-size buffer or even a single character. In this case, however, the string attribute is necessary. Notice that the **DWORD** * argument needs no qualification because it is usually unambiguous. Of course, if it pointed to an array of **DWORD**s, you would need to indicate that. For example:

```
HRESULT Proc(
    [in] short Length,
    [in, length_is(Length)] DWORD array[10]);
```

You can find out about all of the IDL modifiers by looking up IDL in the help. When you read the help, remember that the original intent of IDL was for RPC.

You'll often read about stubs and proxies. A *stub* is a piece of code that a client thinks is a server. It calls the stub to do some work. The stub then passes data transparently to the proxy (in a different address space or machine). The *proxy* reconstitutes the data and calls the actual server. When the server returns, the proxy packages any output data and passes it back to the stub. The stub reassembles the data and returns it to the client. The net effect is that the client thinks it directly calls the server and the server thinks the client directly calls it. The proxy and the stub are invisible to both processes.

Now It Works!

Once you use IDLIDE to process the IDL script, you can build the DLL using the make file. You'll also need to use REGEDIT to import the REG file. Then the client can call the server with no trouble.

The EXE server is much more complex than a DLL server. First, you need an independent user interface. Second, you need marshalling code to break process boundaries. Also, marshalling is never as efficient as directly passing data to a DLL.

More About The Server

Here are a few nonobvious points about the server. First, notice that this server can only handle one client at a time. That's why the call to **CoRegisterClassObject** uses the **REGCLS_SINGLEUSE** flag. This tells ActiveX to run a copy of the server for each client that requires it. Also, this server creates only one type of object. More sophisticated EXE servers will register all of their class objects at once.

Some servers can cope with multiple clients (for example, if the sound program had an MDI interface). Then, you would use **REGCLS_MULTIPLEUSE** instead. However, you would also need to prevent the server from exiting if the user interacts with it. Suppose a client opens a multiple use server (like Microsoft Word). The user switches to Word and opens a new document to edit. When the client destroys its object, you don't want to close Word—that would be rude. If a user interacts with the server it should never shut down unless the user explicitly closes it.

The EXE should also not close down unless its reference count is zero. However, the class factory's reference count isn't important. The EXE is free to close even if the class factory has outstanding references. That's why the class factory interface has the **LockServer** method—it prevents the EXE from closing even if the object reference count is zero. In the case of this server, we never care about locking it while it is supplying no objects, so the call returns **E_NOTIMPL**.

Because this server handles only a single client per instance, any ActiveX invocation disables the primary user interface. However, more sophisticated servers might need some of or its entire user interface active. Notice that a server might detect it is running in an ActiveX context and never even show a window.

One final touch is self-registration. This server finds its location and manually enters or removes the entries required.

A DLL Server

The next logical step is to transform the server into a DLL. It turns out that you can almost completely reuse the code in SERVER.CPP and CLASSFAC.CPP. However, the DLL version of the AAWSound server doesn't have a user interface, so the new versions delete the lines of code that manipulated the server's window. The only new code is in DLLMAIN.CPP (see Listing 2.11). Because this server has no user interface, it doesn't use MFC—it is just a simple C++ DLL.

Listing 2.11 DLLMAIN.CPP.

```
#include <windows.h>
#include "classfac.h"
#include "server.h"
#include <olectl.h>  // Required for SELFREG_E definitions


int in_use=0;
HANDLE inst;


BOOL WINAPI DllMain(HANDLE hInst,
   ULONG reason,
   LPVOID lpReserved)
   {
   if (DLL_PROCESS_DETACH==reason)
      // Could do detach processing here, if desired
      return TRUE;

   if (DLL_PROCESS_ATTACH==reason)
      {
      inst=hInst;
      return TRUE;
      }


   return TRUE;
   }
```

```
// You can't use __declspec(dllexport) here!
// Why? STDAPI is the same as EXTERN_C HRESULT STDAPICALLTYPE
// and these functions are prototyped in OBJBASE.H as STDAPI.
// STDAPI expands to EXTERN_C HRESULT STDAPICALLTYPE
// However, to use __declspec(dllexport) you would need to use:
// EXTERN_C __declspec(dllexport) HRESULT STDAPICALLTYPE
// if you try to write that and not use STDAPI it doesn't match!
// Therefore you must have a DEF file to export these functions.

STDAPI DllGetClassObject(REFCLSID rclsid,REFIID riid,void **ppv)
   {
   HRESULT hr;
   ClassFac *obj;

   if (CLSID_AAWSOUND!=rclsid)
      return E_FAIL;

   obj=new ClassFac();

   if (NULL==obj)
      return E_OUTOFMEMORY;

   hr=obj->QueryInterface(riid, ppv);

   if (FAILED(hr))
      delete obj;

   return hr;
   }


STDAPI DllCanUnloadNow(void)
   {
   return in_use?S_FALSE:S_OK;
   }


static char *ourCLSID="{F4512327-9E89-11CF-A7B2-444553540000}";
static char *prog="AAW.Sound";

HRESULT RegisterServer(void)
   {
   HKEY key,newkey,progkey,svrkey;
   char fn[1024];
   HRESULT err=SELFREG_E_CLASS;
```

```
    GetModuleFileName(inst,fn,sizeof(fn));
    if (RegOpenKeyEx(HKEY_CLASSES_ROOT,"CLSID",0,
       KEY_ALL_ACCESS,&key)!=ERROR_SUCCESS)
    return err;
    if (RegCreateKeyEx(key,ourCLSID,0,NULL,0,
       KEY_ALL_ACCESS, NULL, &newkey,NULL)!=ERROR_SUCCESS)
    return err;
    if (RegSetValue(newkey,NULL,REG_SZ,
       "AAWSound Server",16)!=ERROR_SUCCESS)
    return err;
    if (RegCreateKeyEx(newkey,"InProcServer32",0,NULL,0,
       KEY_ALL_ACCESS,NULL,&svrkey,NULL)!=ERROR_SUCCESS)
    return err;
    // don't forget to add 1 for terminating NULL
    if (RegSetValue(svrkey,NULL,REG_SZ,fn,strlen(fn)+1)
      !=ERROR_SUCCESS)
       return err;
    if (RegCreateKeyEx(newkey,"ProgID",0,NULL,0,
       KEY_ALL_ACCESS,NULL,&progkey,NULL)!=ERROR_SUCCESS)
    return err;
    // don't forget to add 1 for terminating NULL
    if (RegSetValue(progkey,NULL,REG_SZ,prog,strlen(prog)+1)
      !=ERROR_SUCCESS)
       return err;

    RegCloseKey(progkey);
    RegCloseKey(svrkey);
    RegCloseKey(newkey);
    RegCloseKey(key);
    return S_OK;
    }

HRESULT UnregisterServer(void)
    {
    char t[512];
    HRESULT err=S_OK;
    HKEY key;
    if (RegOpenKeyEx(HKEY_CLASSES_ROOT,"CLSID",0,KEY_ALL_ACCESS,
       &key)!=ERROR_SUCCESS) return SELFREG_E_CLASS;
    strcpy(t,ourCLSID);
    strcat(t,"\\InProcServer32");
    if (RegDeleteKey(key,t)!=ERROR_SUCCESS)
       err=SELFREG_E_CLASS;
    strcpy(t,ourCLSID);
    strcat(t,"\\ProgID");
```

```
  if (RegDeleteKey(key,t)!=ERROR_SUCCESS)
     err=SELFREG_E_CLASS;
  // don't overwrite worse error!
  if (RegDeleteKey(key,ourC_SID)!=ERROR_SUCCESS)
     if (err==S_OK) err=S_FALSE;
  RegCloseKey(key);
  return err;
  }

STDAPI DllRegisterServer(void)
  {
  return RegisterServer();
  }


STDAPI DllUnregisterServer(void)
  {
  return UnregisterServer();
  }
```


The code in DLLMAIN.CPP is very simple. The **DllMain** function is the customary code that executes when the DLL loads or unloads. The other two functions in this module are **DllGetClassObject** and **DllCanUnloadNow**. You must export these functions in a DEF file. Because of their definitions in the system headers, you can't use **__declspec (dllexport)** to export them as you might do for your own functions.

The **DllGetClassObject** function must create a class factory for the requested CLSID. ActiveX will call the function for each class it wants. Unlike an EXE server, DLLs simply respond to this request. If you support multiple class factories, you only respond with the correct one. Contrast this with an EXE server that registers all of its factories when it starts.

The code verifies that the CLSID is the one expected, creates the class factory with the **new** operator, and uses **QueryInterface** to return the interface and set the initial reference count.

The **DllCanUnloadNow** function checks a flag to see if the DLL is in use. When a client creates (or destroys) an object, the server increments (or decrements) this flag. Notice that creating a class factory is not sufficient to hold the DLL. If the client needs to lock the DLL without creating an object, it calls the class factory's **LockServer** function. This function also manipulates the flag that **DllCanUnloadNow** uses. When clients want to free memory, they can call **CoFreeUnusedLibraries**. This causes ActiveX to call **DllCanUnloadNow** and release any DLLs that reply affirmatively.

Of course, the self-registration portion of the code is different, too. You may wonder how you can execute the self-registration code in a DLL. Microsoft does ship a program called REGSVR32.EXE with several products (for example, look in your \MSDEV\BIN directory). You can use this program to register ActiveX DLLs. You'll also find code that performs the registration steps on the companion CD-ROM.

Other than these simple changes, the server code is essentially unchanged. Of course, the build process is for a DLL, not an EXE file. Since you can't execute a DLL directly, you'll need to use special techniques to debug it (see the sidebar "Server Debugging Tips," page 74).

The most important difference between an EXE server and a DLL server is the address space. A DLL server runs in the client process's address space (that's why it is an inproc server). This means it is much, much faster than an EXE server and easier to write. You don't need any marshalling to make the DLL server work.

Supporting Multiple Interfaces

This example server is simple and only requires a single interface. What if you have an object that contains multiple interfaces? There are several ways you can supply multiple interfaces. The most straightforward (but not the easiest) way is to supply each interface in a separate C++ object. Then you have to coordinate the ActiveX object behavior (for example, maintaining a common reference count). If you do this, you are responsible for maintaining the cohesion between the ActiveX object and the many C++ objects that implement it.

Another way to support multiple interfaces is via C++ multiple inheritance. Just as the example server object derives from an interface, you can create an object that inherits from all its interfaces. However, this leads to some messy issues because common elements (like **IUnknown**) become ambiguous. This method doesn't lend itself well to aggregation, either.

Perhaps the best method for creating objects with multiple interfaces is to use nested classes. Consider this piece of pseudo code:

```
class AnObject
   {
   int class_wide_data_item;
   int ref_count;
   .
   .
   .
   class Interface1 : public IInterface1
```

```
    {
    // Interface 1 data and members
    .
    .
    .
    }
  class Interface2 : public IInterface2
    {
    // Interface 2 data and members
    .
    .
    .
    }
};
```

This method is relatively simple and compact. There are a few issues you need to consider. For example, how does code in the **Interface1** object obtain a pointer to the outer **AnObject** pointer so it can access class-wide data objects? One answer is to pass the outer **this** pointer to the nested classes' constructors. In practice, this doesn't matter because MFC will handle this automatically. You'll see how in the next section.

MFC Techniques

MFC can greatly simplify many Windows programs, including ActiveX servers. However, the current version of MFC doesn't directly support building ActiveX servers. It does, however, enable you to build automation servers. An *automation server* is a special server that implements the **IDispatch** interface (something we have not discussed yet). By starting with an **IDispatch** server, you can easily modify the program to serve any interfaces, if you know how.

MFC can create DLL or EXE servers. It also generates REG files and ODL files, and handles issues such as multithreading and other thorny problems. If you support multiple interfaces per object, MFC will help you nest classes to support the interfaces. I suppose you could use another method to implement multiple interfaces, but then MFC wouldn't help you.

In MFC, ActiveX objects derive from **CCmdTarget**. **CCmdTarget** contains several useful functions that you can call. There are three calls (**ExternalAddRef**, **ExternalRelease**, and **ExternalQueryInterface**) that implement **IUnknown**, for example.

An MFC EXE Server

When you ask AppWizard to create an EXE Automation Server, it creates an ActiveX program that implements an **IDispatch** interface. AppWizard uses special MFC macros to create nested classes and maps those nested classes to particular interfaces. You can find out more about these macros in the sidebar "MFC ActiveX Macros," page 92.

If looking at these macros seems intimidating, don't worry. AppWizard uses nearly all of these macros and puts them in the right place. You'll only need to change some arguments in most cases. The process is a simple matter of applying a few steps. You can find an example server in Listings 2.12 through 2.14 with the steps marked. Here is a summary of the steps (the order isn't particularly important after you pass Step 2.

Step 1: Create An EXE With AppWizard

Use AppWizard to create an EXE-based project using any options you like—just be sure to select Automation on the AppWizard's third screen (see Figure 2.14).

Step 2: Create An Object

Use Class Wizard to create an object to represent your ActiveX object. It must derive from **CCmdTarget** and you must select Automation (see Figure 2.15).

Step 3: Remove Automation-specific Code

In the CPP file for the class you created in Step 2, locate and remove the line that calls **EnableAutomation**.

Step 4: Remove Dispatch Map

Only an **IDispatch** interface requires a dispatch map. Remove it from the CPP file and the H file. In the CPP file, you'll need to remove all lines from **BEGIN_DISPATCH_MAP** to **END_DISPATCH_MAP**. In the header file, remove the line that reads **DECLARE_DISPATCH_MAP**.

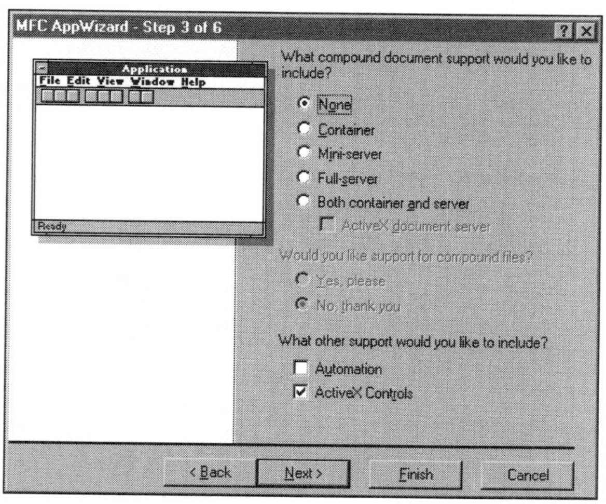

Figure 2.14 Creating an EXE server with AppWizard.

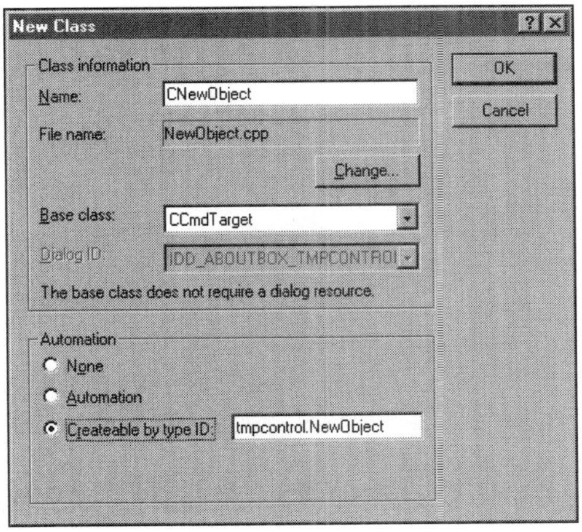

Figure 2.15 Adding a class with Class Wizard.

Step 5: Set Correct UUID

Class Wizard automatically generates a UUID for the **IDispatch** interface to use. If you need an ID for an object or an interface, you can use this one. If you already have an ID you are trying to implement, you can change the generated one to suit you. Look for a definition of a **CLSID** in the CPP file.

Step 6: Correct The Interface Map

The interface map informs MFC that a certain nested class implements a particular interface. The map will have one line for **IDispatch**. You can change this line or delete it and add new lines. The line contains an **INTERFACE_PART** macro that takes three arguments: the main class name, the interface ID, and the nested class name (without the preceding X). Be sure to use the interface ID and not the class ID in this macro.

Step 7: Set Up Class Factory

MFC uses a data-driven class factory. That means that the default class factory automatically knows how to create your classes. To enable this feature, you need to place an **IMPLEMENT_OLECREATE** macro.

You need to inform MFC's class factory that your object exists. You'll need to add the **DECLARE_OLECREATE** macro to the header and the **IMPLEMENT_OLECREATE** macro to the CPP file. The **IMPLEMENT_OLECREATE** macro takes three arguments: the main class name, a string that isn't important in this case, and the class ID. Don't use an interface ID here.

Step 8: Add Nested Classes

To add a nested class, you place a **BEGIN_INTERFACE_PART** line in the header file, define each member you want in the class after this line, and finally, you insert an **END_INTERFACE_PART** line. You don't need to declare the **IUnknown** functions (**AddRef**, **Release**, and **QueryInterface**). MFC uses internal code for the original **IDispatch** interface, so there isn't any code to delete. You can add as many nested classes as you like. The first argument to **BEGIN_INTERFACE_PART** names the nested class (remember, MFC will prepend an X to the name). The second argument is the interface this class implements.

Step 9: Remove Application Setup

In the application's main file (not the object's file), you'll find the definition of the application object. The **InitInstance** member of this class is the closest thing to a **WinMain** you'll find in an MFC program. One line in this code connects the MFC document template to the automation class. We aren't using automation, so you need to comment out this line. The call is **ConnectTemplate**, and you can remove the entire line.

Step 10: Write Member Functions For Nested Classes

Here's the real meat of the process. You must write functions for all the nested members you defined in Step 8. Remember, you have to put the X in front of each class name (except in the MFC macros). Although MFC declares the **IUnknown** functions automatically, it doesn't write them for you. You must write the functions explicitly.

However, MFC does provide a default implementation for the **IUnknown** functions in **CCmdTarget** (the base class of the outer class). How do you access it? You need the **METHOD_PROLOGUE** macro. This macro takes the outer class name and the nested class name (without the X) and fills in a pointer—**pThis**—with a pointer to the outer class. You don't need to declare the **pThis** variable because the macro declares it for you.

Once you have the **pThis** pointer, you can call **ExternalAddRef**, **ExternalRelease**, and **ExternalQueryInterface** calls to do all the work required to implement **IUnknown** in a thread-safe fashion. If you browse the MFC source, you may notice there are also functions for **InternalAddRef**, **InternalRelease**, and **InternalQueryInterface**. You shouldn't need to call these functions directly. The external calls work when your object stands alone or when it is part of an aggregate. You'll see more about aggregating MFC objects shortly.

You can also use **pThis** to access data or member functions in the outer class. This is a good way to store data and code that apply to the object as a whole from inside each interface class.

Listing 2.12 AAWSOUND.H.

```
// AAWSound.h : header file
//
```

```
/////////////////////////////////////////
// CAAWSound command target

class CAAWSound : public CCmdTarget
   {
   DECLARE_DYNCREATE(CAAWSound)
   // Step 7b: Add DECLARE_OLECREATE
   DECLARE_OLECREATE(CAAWSound)

   CAAWSound();

   // Attributes
   public:
      DWORD options;

   // Operations
   public:

      // Overrides
      // ClassWizard generated virtual function overrides
         //{{AFX_VIRTUAL(CAAWSound)
         public:
            virtual void OnFinalRelease();
         //}}AFX_VIRTUAL

      // Implementation
      protected:
         virtual ~CAAWSound();

      // Generated message map functions
         //{{AFX_MSG(CAAWSound)
         // NOTE - the ClassWizard will add and
         // remove member functions here.
         //}}AFX_MSG

      DECLARE_MESSAGE_MAP()
      // Generated OLE dispatch map functions
      //{{AFX_DISPATCH(CAAWSound)
      // NOTE - the ClassWizard will add and remove member functions here.
      //}}AFX_DISPATCH
    // Step 4b:Remove Dispatch Map
    //       DECLARE_DISPATCH_MAP()
      DECLARE_INTERFACE_MAP()
    // Step 8: Add Interface parts
     BEGIN_INTERFACE_PART(Aaw,IAAWSound)
```

```
    // IUnknown added automatically
      STDMETHOD(Play)(char const *file);
      STDMETHOD(GetOptions)(DWORD *opt);
      STDMETHOD(SetOptions)(DWORD opt);
      END_INTERFACE_PART(Aaw)
    };
```

Listing 2.13 AAWSound.CPP.

```
// AAWSound.cpp : implementation file
//

#include "stdafx.h"
#include "mfcexe.h"
#include "IAAWSound.h"
#include "AAWSound.h"
#include "mmsystem.h"
#include "MfcExeDoc.h"
#include "MfcExeView.h"
#include "Mainfrm.h"

#ifdef _DEBUG
#define new DEBUG_NEW
#undef THIS_FILE
static char THIS_FILE[] = __FILE__;
#endif

////////////////////////////////////////
// CAAWSound

IMPLEMENT_DYNCREATE(CAAWSound, CCmdTarget)
// Step 7a: Add IMPLEMENT_OLECREATE
IMPLEMENT_OLECREATE(CAAWSound,"AAW.Sound",
   0xf4512327, 0x9e89, 0x11cf,
   0xa7, 0xb2, 0x44, 0x45,
   0x53, 0x54, 0x0, 0x0);



CAAWSound::CAAWSound()
   {
   // Step 3: Delete this line: EnableAutomation();
   options=SND_NODEFAULT|SND_SYNC;
   CMainFrame *w=(CMainFrame *)AfxGetApp()->m_pMainWnd;
   w->playui=FALSE;
```

```
   ((CEdit *)(w->GetActiveView()->GetDlgItem(IDC_FILENAME)))->
     SetReadOnly(TRUE);
   }

CAAWSound::~CAAWSound()
   {
   }


void CAAWSound::OnFinalRelease()
   {
// When the last reference for an automation object is released
// OnFinalRelease is called.  The base class will automatically
// delete the object.  Add additional cleanup required for your
// object before calling the base class.
   CCmdTarget::OnFinalRelease();
   // Here we will close app but if this were a
   // MDI app, you'd need to make sure there were
   // no more open sessions -- especially user
   // initiated windows

   // We are running in a RPC context now, so don't
   // call DestroyWindow, OnFileClose, etc.
   AfxGetApp()->m_pMainWnd->PostMessage(WM_CLOSE);
   }


BEGIN_MESSAGE_MAP(CAAWSound, CCmdTarget)
   //{{AFX_MSG_MAP(CAAWSound)
   // NOTE - the ClassWizard will add and
   // remove mapping macros here.
   //}}AFX_MSG_MAP
END_MESSAGE_MAP()

// Step 4a: Remove dispatch map
//BEGIN_DISPATCH_MAP(CAAWSound, CCmdTarget)
//      //{{AFX_DISPATCH_MAP(CAAWSound)
//
//      //}}AFX_DISPATCH_MAP
//END_DISPATCH_MAP()

// Step 5: Change or remove this ID if you need to
//static const CLSID ID_AAWSound =
//{ 0xf4512327, 0x9e89, 0x11cf, { 0xa7, 0xb2,
// 0x44, 0x45, 0x53, 0x54, 0x0, 0x0 } };
```

2. ActiveX Survival Kit

```
// Step 6: fix up Interface map
BEGIN_INTERFACE_MAP(CAAWSound, CCmdTarget)
  INTERFACE_PART(CAAWSound, IID_IAAWSOUND, Aaw)
END_INTERFACE_MAP()

//////////////////////////////////////
// CAAWSound message handlers
// Step 10: Write methods
ULONG FAR EXPORT CAAWSound::XAaw::AddRef()
   {
   METHOD_PROLOGUE(CAAWSound, Aaw)
   return pThis->ExternalAddRef();
   }

ULONG FAR EXPORT CAAWSound::XAaw::Release()
   {
   METHOD_PROLOGUE(CAAWSound, Aaw)
   return pThis->ExternalRelease();
   }

HRESULT FAR EXPORT CAAWSound::XAaw::QueryInterface(
   REFIID iid, void FAR* FAR* ppvObj)
   {
   METHOD_PROLOGUE(CAAWSound, Aaw)
   return (HRESULT)pThis->ExternalQueryInterface(&iid, ppvObj);
   }

HRESULT FAR EXPORT CAAWSound::XAaw::Play(char const *file)
   {
   METHOD_PROLOGUE(CAAWSound, Aaw)
   CFrameWnd *w=(CFrameWnd *)AfxGetApp()->m_pMainWnd;
   CMfcexeView *v=(CMfcexeView *)w->GetActiveView();
   v->m_file=file;
   v->UpdateData(FALSE);
   v->UpdateWindow();
   return sndPlaySound(file,pThis->options)?
      S_OK:E_FAIL;
   }

HRESULT FAR EXPORT CAAWSound::XAaw::GetOptions(DWORD *w)
   {
   METHOD_PROLOGUE(CAAWSound, Aaw)
   if (w) *w=pThis->options;
   return w?S_OK:E_FAIL;
   }
```

```
HRESULT FAR EXPORT CAAWSound::XAaw::SetOptions(DWORD w)
   {
   METHOD_PROLOGUE(CAAWSound, Aaw)
   pThis->options=w;
   return S_OK;
   }
```

Listing 2.14 InitInstance for MFCEXE.

```
BOOL CMfcexeApp::InitInstance()
    {
    // Initialize OLE libraries
    if (!AfxOleInit())
       {
       AfxMessageBox(IDP_OLE_INIT_FAILED);
       return FALSE;
       }

// Standard initialization

#ifdef _AFXDLL
    Enable3dControls();
#else
    Enable3dControlsStatic();
#endif

    LoadStdProfileSettings();
    CSingleDocTemplate* pDocTemplate;
    pDocTemplate = new CSingleDocTemplate(
         IDR_MAINFRAME,
         RUNTIME_CLASS(CMfcexeDoc),
         RUNTIME_CLASS(CMainFrame),
         RUNTIME_CLASS(CMfcexeView));
      AddDocTemplate(pDocTemplate);

// Connect the COleTemplateServer to the document template.
// The COleTemplateServer creates new documents on behalf
// of requesting OLE containers by using information
// specified in the document template.
// STEP 9: No document template
// m_server.ConnectTemplate(CLSID_AAWSOUND, pDocTemplate, TRUE);
// Note: SDI applications register server objects only if
// /Embedding or /Automation is present on the command line.

// Parse command line for standard shell commands
      CCommandLineInfo cmdInfo;
```

```
ParseCommandLine(cmdInfo);

 // Check to see if launched as OLE server
if (cmdInfo.m_bRunEmbedded || cmdInfo.m_bRunAutomated)
    {
    // Register all OLE server (factories) as running.
    // This enables the OLE libraries to create objects
    // from other applications.
    COleTemplateServer::RegisterAll();

    // Application was run with /Embedding or /Automation.
    // Don't show the main window in this case.

    // Disregard the last AppWiz comment
    // In this case, open window
    OnFileNew();
    // should disable UI here!
    return TRUE;
    }

// When a server application is launched stand-alone,
// it is a good idea to update the System Registry
// in case it has been damaged.
m_server.UpdateRegistry(OAT_DISPATCH_OBJECT);
COleObjectFactory::UpdateRegistryAll();

// Dispatch commands specified on the command line
if (!ProcessShellCommand(cmdInfo))
   return FALSE;

return TRUE;
}
```

MFC ActiveX Macros

MFC supplies its own set of ActiveX macros. You can still use the others, too. MFC automatically creates a class factory and an IUnknown::QueryInterface for you. These macros tell MFC how to implement these things for you.

DECLARE_INTERFACE_MAP — This macro appears in your class's header file. It creates an interface map. This map designates which nested class corresponds to a particular COM interface. The built-in QueryInterface uses this to return pointers to the correct objects.

BEGIN_INTERFACE_MAP — This macro creates the interface map in the class's CPP file.

BEGIN_INTERFACE_PART — You place this macro inside the object's header file to automatically create a nested class that represents an interface. It automatically writes declarations for the IUnknown functions, but you must add declarations for any other functions after this macro. This macro does have an annoying way of handling things. You specify a class name, and the macro automatically prepends an X to the name. If you name the class, Cl1, for example, the class name becomes XCl1. You don't need to use the X in other macros (like INTERFACE_PART, below), but you do need to use it other places.

END_INTERFACE_PART — This macro ends the definition of a nested class. Your member function declarations appear between the BEGIN_INTERFACE_PART macro and this macro.

INTERFACE_PART — Use this macro after the INTERFACE_MAP macro to define the particular map entries. The macro takes three arguments: the main class name, the interface IID, and the nested class name (without the leading X).

END_INTERFACE_MAP — This macro ends the interface map.

DECLARE_OLE_CREATE — Use this macro in your H file to declare a class factory.

IMPLEMENT_OLE_CREATE — This corresponds to DECLARE_OLE_CREATE but appears in the CPP file. It takes the class name, an external name, and the object's CLSID.

METHOD_PROLOGUE — This macro appears in member functions of the nested classes that implement each interface. It creates a variable, pThis, that points to the main class.

INTERFACE_AGGREGATE — Specifies a variable that contains an interface to aggregate with the object.

Other Considerations

Once you know how to manipulate MFC, it is simple to write an EXE server. Of course, you still have to write your program, too. You also need to write any proxy DLLs and register them. Speaking of the Registry, MFC creates a REG file for your server, but you may need to modify it to reflect your choice of CLSID and your proxy DLL. You'll also need to change the ODL file if you want to create a type library. However, if you don't need a type library, you can just delete the file from the project and ignore it.

In the example's case, you don't need a type library. You also can reuse the proxy library built earlier in this chapter. The proxy library isn't in MFC, but since the MIDL compiler builds it automatically, who cares?

Another issue with EXE servers is what to do when a client starts your program. The example program notes that /Embedded appears in the command line while processing **InitInstance**. The automatically generated comments indicate that you should avoid showing the main window in this case. That's true for an automation server, but may or may not be true for your server. It depends on what you want to happen. The example code calls **OnFileNew** to show its user interface, ignoring the automatically generated comments.

The actual user interface implementation is trivial. Notice that the user interface changes when the EXE file is acting as a server. This is similar to the logic in the original EXE server, just redone for MFC.

Not every ActiveX object requires a CLSID. If yours doesn't, you can omit Step 7. You can also delete the ID in Step 5 if you don't need it. You'll see some objects that don't require CLSIDs in the next chapter. Of course, you can't use **CoCreateInstance** to generate objects without a CLSID.

Even using this roundabout method, MFC makes server construction more manageable. The library simplifies things by providing an **IUnknown** implementation, registering classes, automatically creating a class factory, and setting the basic structure of the server.

An MFC DLL Server

Writing a DLL server using MFC could hardly be simpler. Just ask AppWizard to create a DLL and make sure the Automation checkbox is checked. MFC will create all the required global functions and the same type of skeletal automation object that it did for the EXE file.

Again, it is a matter of a few simple steps to convert the specialized automation server into a general-purpose ActiveX server. The steps are very similar to the ones required for an EXE server. You'll find the code on the CD. Here are the steps:

1. Use AppWizard to create an automation DLL (see Figure 2.16).
2. Use Class Wizard to derive a class from CCmdTarget that uses OLE automation (refer back to Figure 2.15).
3. Delete the call to EnableAutomation in the constructor.
4. Delete the lines that relate to the dispatch map from the new class.
5. Change the automatically generated CLSID, if you want.
6. Fix the interface map, changing the **INTERFACE_PART** macro and adding any others that you require.
7. Remove the **BEGIN_INTERFACE_PART** macro that defines the **IDispatch** interface. Replace it with as many **BEGIN_INTERFACE_PART** macros as you need to define all the interfaces you want to create.
8. Add **DECLARE_OLECREATE** and **IMPLEMENT_OLECREATE** macros to the H and CPP files (unless your class doesn't require a class factory).

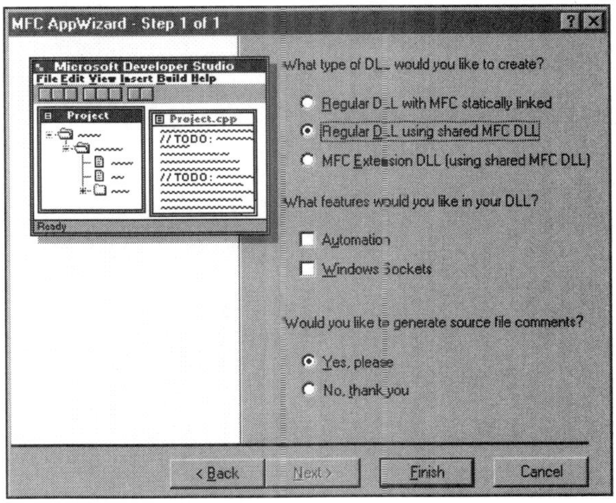

Figure 2.16 Creating a DLL server with AppWizard.

9. Write the interface functions you need (including the **IUnknown** functions).

This is, of course, very similar to the steps you need for the EXE server. Better still, the example code uses the same ActiveX object as the EXE server, except for the code that manipulates the user interface. You will need to manually write the REG file for a DLL server.

MFC Aggregation

Remember aggregation? *Aggregation* is the process that enables an object to expose interfaces from a contained object. MFC objects can easily aggregate another object or allow other objects to aggregate its interfaces.

Allowing aggregation is simple if you are using MFC. The first step is to call **EnableAutomation** during the object's construction. The only other thing to remember is to call **ExternalQueryInterface**, **ExternalAddRef**, and **ExternalRelease** instead of the internal versions. You can always call the external versions and you should rarely, if ever, call the internal versions.

Aggregating another interface isn't very difficult either. In your interface map, add an **INTERFACE_AGGREGATE** line. This macro takes two arguments: the main class name and the name of a variable in the main class that points to the aggregated interface. Obviously, this variable has to point to an **IUnknown** or something derived from an **IUnknown**. You initialize the variable during your override of the **OnCreateAggregates** function. When you create the aggregated object, you'll need to pass **CoCreateInstance** a pointer to the controlling **IUnknown**. You can get this pointer by calling **GetControllingUnknown**.

A partial example of aggregating an interface from a different object is shown in Listing 2.15.

Listing 2.15 Aggregating an interface from a different object.

```
class CMain : public CCmdTarget
{
public:
    CMain();

protected:
    LPUNKNOWN m_aggregated;
    virtual BOOL OnCreateAggregates();

    DECLARE_INTERFACE_MAP()
.
.
.
};

CMain::CMain()
{
    m_aggregated = NULL;
}

BOOL CMain::OnCreateAggregates()
{
    // Create new object with our controlling ID
    m_lpAggrInner = CoCreateInstance(CLSID_aggobject,
        GetControllingUnknown(), CLSCTX_INPROC_SERVER,
        IID_IUnknown, (LPVOID*)&m_aggregated);
    if (!m_aggregated)
        return FALSE;
    .
    .
    .
return TRUE;
}

BEGIN_INTERFACE_MAP(CMain, CCmdTarget)
.
.
.
    INTERFACE_AGGREGATE(CAggrExample, m_aggregated)
END_INTERFACE_MAP()
```

IDispatch

The **IDispatch** interface is arguably one of the most powerful ActiveX interfaces around. Yet it only contains four unique functions (see Table 2.12). These functions allow objects to expose variables and functions to other objects—even those from different programs.

Like all other ActiveX technologies, the **IDispatch** interface has to have obscure names. Instead of exposing variables, **IDispatch**-aware objects expose properties. This may be actual variables, or the object may execute code to store and retrieve the property value. Either way, the object's user accesses properties as if they were simple variables.

IDispatch-aware objects also don't have functions—they have methods. These are simple function calls.

You may recall that earlier in this chapter you asked MFC to create an automation server and then stripped out all the automation code to create ActiveX objects. An object that provides an **IDispatch** interface is an automation server (you can also say that the object supports ActiveX scripting).

If you allow MFC to create your **IDispatch**-aware objects, you'll find it quite easy. You can use Class Wizard to add members and properties with little difficulty. MFC also manages your **IDispatch** functions with no effort on your part. Class Wizard also allows you to add events, but these are only for ActiveX controls.

The key to the **IDispatch** interface is the **Invoke** function. This function allows ActiveX objects to select, at runtime, what variable (property) you want to access or what function (method) you want to call. Each property and method has a unique ID (a **DISPID**). This ID is just an integer that serves to distinguish the various methods and properties from each other. Microsoft predefines **DISPIDs** of zero or less (see Table 2.13). You won't always use any of these predefined **DISPIDs**.

Table 2.12 The IDispatch interface.

Function	Description
Invoke	Provides access to properties and methods exposed by the object
GetIDsOfNames	Converts a single member name and an optional set of argument names to a set of integer DISPIDs
GetTypeInfo	Retrieves the type information for an object
GetTypeInfoCount	Returns 0 if GetTypeInfo is not supported; 1 if the object can provide type information

Table 2.13 Predefined DISPIDs.

DISPID	Value	Description
DISPID_VALUE	0	The default member
DISPID_NEWENUM	-4	Returns an enumerator object that supports IEnumVariant and should have the restricted attribute specified in the ODL script
DISPID_EVALUATE	-5	The **Evaluate** method
DISPID_PROPERTYPUT	-3	The parameter that receives the value of an assignment in a property put
DISPID_CONSTRUCTOR	-6	The C++ constructor function for the object
DISPID_DESTRUCTOR	-7	The C++ destructor function for the object
DISPID_UNKNOWN	-1	Value returned by IDispatch::GetIDsOfNames to indicate that it could not resolve a name

When you want to call a method or access a property, you call **IDispatch::Invoke**, passing it a **DISPID**, some control flags, an array of arguments, a locale ID, a place to store any return result, and places to store error information. Before you look at these arguments in detail, you need to learn about some special types ActiveX defines.

BSTR, SAFEARRAY, And VARIANT

ActiveX defines three unique data types that you can use in a variety of situations. The simplest of these is the **BSTR**. As the name suggests, this data type is for character strings. A **BSTR** pointer is just like a C string pointer because it points to an array of characters that end with a **NULL** byte. The only difference is that the four bytes preceding the **BSTR** pointer contain the count of characters in the string (not counting the **NULL** byte). ActiveX provides several functions to manipulate **BSTR**s (see Table 2.14). If you are an MFC programmer, you can convert a **CString** into a **BSTR** by calling **CString::AllocSysString**. Newer versions of Visual C++ also support the **_bstr_t** type that you can use to represent **BSTR**s.

A **SAFEARRAY** is a simple structure that contains information about the size and shape of an array, along with a memory handle (and possibly a pointer) that contains the data in the array. ActiveX provides several API functions to manipulate **SAFEARRAY**s (see Table 2.15). A **SAFEARRAY** can contain **BSTR**s, **IDispatch** pointers, **IUnknown** pointers, or **VARIANT**s.

Table 2.14 BSTR functions.

Function	Description
SysAllocString	Converts an ordinary string into a BSTR
SysAllocStringByteLen	Converts a byte buffer (which may contain NULL bytes) into a BSTR
SysAllocStringLen	Converts a character buffer (which may contain NULL bytes) into a BSTR
SysFreeString	Deallocates a BSTR
SysReAllocString	Similar to SysAllocString except it uses an existing BSTR
SysReAllocStringByteLen	Similar to SysAllocStringByteLen except it uses an existing BSTR
SysReAllocStringLen	Similar to SysAllocStringLen except it uses an existing BSTR
SysStringLen	Determines the length of the BSTR by reading the embedded length (this may be different from **strlen** if the BSTR contains NULL bytes)

Table 2.15 SAFEARRAY functions.

Function	Description
SafeArrayAccessData	Locks the array and returns the array's pointer
SafeArrayLock	Locks the array and sets the array's internal pointer
SafeArrayUnaccessData	Unlocks the array and invalidates the pointer **SafeArray/AccessData**
SafeArrayUnlock	Unlocks the array and invalidates the internal pointer
SafeArrayCreate	Creates an array of a given type and size
SafeArrayAllocDescriptor	Builds a descriptor of a SAFEARRAY that may be of any type
SafeArrayAllocData	Creates a SAFEARRAY based on a descriptor (see SafeArrayAllocDescriptor)
SafeArrayGetElement	Returns a single element from the array
SafeArrayPutElement	Assigns a single element in the array
SafeArrayPtrOfIndex	Returns a pointer to an element in the array
SafeArrayRedim	Resizes an array
SafeArrayCopy	Creates a copy of the array
SafeArrayDestroy	Destroys the array and its data
SafeArrayDestroyData	Destroys data in the array
SafeArrayDestroyDescriptor	Destroys the array descriptor (no data)
SafeArrayGetDim	Returns the number of dimensions in the array
SafeArrayGetElemsize	Returns the size of the array's elements in bytes
SafeArrayGetLBound	Returns the lower bound for a particular dimension in the array
SafeArrayGetUBound	Returns the upper bound for a particular dimension in the array

The **VARIANT** (or **VARIANTARG**) union can hold almost anything. In essence, it is just a union and a variable that indicates what kind of data is in the union at any given time (see Tables 2.16 and 2.17). When a client passes a **VARIANT** to a server, you might expect it is a simple matter to just read the value from the proper field in the union. But, what if the client didn't pass the type of data you expected? ActiveX has two functions that can convert (or coerce) a **VARIANT** that contains one data type into a **VARIANT** that contains a different type (if the conversion is possible). The functions are **VariantChangeType** and **VariantChangeTypeEx**. These functions are very similar in form, but the **Ex**-flavor function understands language concerns (important for date and currency formats). Don't attempt to convert a **VARIANT** in place with these functions—provide a separate output **VARIANT** union.

Table 2.16 The VARIANT data structure.

Field	Type	Comments
vt	VARENUM	Type of data in VARIANT (see Table 2.17)
iVal	short	Short integer
lVal	long	Long integer
fltVal	float	Four byte real
dblVal	double	Eight byte real
bool	VARIANT_BOOL	Boolean
scode	SCODE	Error code
cyVal	CY	Currency
date	DATE	Date
bstrVal	BSTR	A BSTR
punkVal	IUnknown *	Note that this means IUnknown pointer, not an unknown data type
pdispVal	IDispatch *	Pointer to a dispatch interface
parray	SAFEARRAY *	An array
piVal	short *	Pointer to short
plVal	long *	Pointer to long
pfltVal	float *	Pointer to float
pdblVal	double *	Pointer to double
pbool	VARIANT_BOOL *	Pointer to Boolean
pscode	SCODE *	Pointer to error code
pcyVal	CY *	Pointer to currency

(continued)

***Table 2.16 The VARIANT data structure* (continued).**

Field	Type	Comments
pdate	DATE *	Pointer to date
pbstrVal	BSTR *	Pointer to BSTR
ppunkVal	IUnknown **	Pointer to an IUnknown pointer
ppdispVal	IDispatch **	Pointer to a dispatch interface pointer
pvarVal	VARIANT *	Pointer to a VARIANT
byref	void *	Any pointer

Table 2.17 VARIANT types.

Type	Meaning	Ordinary Field	ByRef Field
VT_EMPTY	No data present	N/A	N/A
VT_NULL	NULL value	N/A	N/A
VT_I2	2-byte integer (signed)	iVal	piVal
VT_I4	4-byte integer (signed)	lVal	plVal
VT_R4	4-byte real value	fltVal	pfltVal
VT_R8	8-byte real value	dblVal	pdblVal
VT_CY	Currency	cyVal	pcyVal
VT_DATE	Date	date	pdate
VT_BSTR	BSTR	bstrVal	pbstrVal
VT_DISPATCH	IDispatch	pdispVal	ppdispVal
VT_ERROR	Error code	scode	pscode
VT_BOOL	Boolean	bool	pbool
VT_VARIANT	VARIANT	N/A	pvarVal
VT_UNKNOWN	IUnknown	punkVal	ppunkVal
VT_UI1	Unsigned character	iVal	iVal
VT_ARRAY	SAFEARRAY	parray	N/A
VT_BYREF	Adds with other VT_ types to indicate passing by reference	N/A	N/A

ActiveX also provides some more mundane macros to simplify **VARIANT** manipulation (see Table 2.18). You may use these instead of directly manipulating the **VARIANT** structure in most cases. Recent versions of Visual C++ also support the **_variant_t** type for manipulating variants.

Table 2.18 VARIANT macros.

Macro	Meaning
VariantClear	Clears the VARIANT and sets the type to VT_EMPTY; attempts to free the existing contents (unless the original type is VT_VARIANT)
VariantCopy	Copies one VARIANT to another; the code first clears the destination VARIANT (see VariantClear, above)
VariantCopyInd	Copies a VT_BYREF VARIANT to an ordinary VARIANT
VariantInit	Sets vt to VT_EMPTY and zeros all reserved fields

Back To Invoke

Armed with information about **BSTR**s, **SAFEARRAY**s, and **VARIANT**s, we can return to examining **IDispatch::Invoke**. The **Invoke** method requires eight parameters:

- A **DISPID** that identifies the method or property the client wants to use
- A **GUID** that has no meaning; always use **IID_NULL**
- A locale ID to specify the current language in use
- A flag that specifies the operation (see Table 2.19)
- A pointer to a **DISPPARAMS** structure (Table 2.20) that identifies the arguments for this call
- A pointer to a **VARIANT** that will receive the result, if any (may be **NULL)**
- A pointer to a structure that receives error information in the event that a **DISP_E_EXCEPTION** error occurs
- A pointer to an unsigned integer that receives the index of the parameter that caused a **DISP_E_TYPEMISMATCH** or **DISP_E_PARAMNOTFOUND** error

The **DISPPARAMS** structure requires a little explanation. This structure identifies all of the arguments for the call. Of course, to read a simple property, you don't need any arguments. However, to set a simple property requires one argument. An indexed property access may need many arguments. A method call may not require any arguments, or it may need several.

Table 2.19 Operation flags.

Flag	Meaning
DISPATCH_METHOD	Perform a function call
DISPATCH_PROPERTYGET	Read a property
DISPATCH_PROPERTYPUT	Set a property
DISPATCH_PROPERTYPUTREF	Set a property by reference

Table 2.20 The DISPPARAMS structure.

Field	Meaning
rgvarg	Pointer to array of VARIANTS
rgdispidNamedArgs	Named argument DISPIDs (see text)
cArgs	Number of total arguments
cNamedArgs	Number of named arguments

The first field in the **DISPPARAMS** structure points to an array of **VARIANTS** (the **rgvarg** field). This is the argument list. There are three kinds of arguments you may encounter: positional arguments, named arguments, and optional arguments. Although some arguments are optional, the **Invoke** function always receives the entire set of arguments. If the client wishes to omit an optional parameter, the corresponding **VARIANT** will have a type of **VT_ERROR** or **VT_EMPTY**. If the client uses **VT_ERROR** (the preferred method) it also sets the **scode** field to **DISP_E_PARAMNOTFOUND**.

Named arguments each have a unique **DISPID** (from the type information). The client sets the **DISPPARAMS** structure's **rgdispidNamedArgs** field to point to an array that contains the named argument's **DISPIDs** (if any). The length of the array (and therefore, the number of named arguments) appears in the **cNamedArgs** field. If that value is zero, there are no named arguments.

If there are any named arguments, they appear first (in a random order) in the **rgvarg** array. The positional arguments follow in reverse order. Consider the following call (from a Visual Basic program):

```
rv=ActiveXObject.Go(p1=30, p2="RESET", 14, "Command")
```

This call has two named arguments (named **p1** and **p2**) and two positional arguments. You can easily parse arguments out of the **DISPPARAMS** structure by calling the **DispGetParam** functions. This function accepts the **DISPPARAMS** structure, a proper index (that is, zero is the first argument, not the last), and a type you want that argument to be. The function automatically pulls the correct parameter from the **rgvarg** array and coerces it to the proper type. Because your type information knows about argument types, you can also call **ITypeInfo::Invoke** to magically coerce all of the **VARIANTs** in the argument list. You can also get a similar effect by calling the global function **DispInvoke**.

From the client's point of view, it is often more convenient to work with names instead of **DISPIDs** for properties, methods, and named parameters. That's why the **IDispatch::GetIDsOfNames** function exists. Using this function, the client can convert the simple names of things into **DISPIDs**.

Simplifying IDispatch

Remember, like many members of the interface bestiary, ActiveX doesn't really do much for **IDispatch**. It is a protocol that you implement on the server side of your code and use on the client side. If you do a good job, your client can use any server and any client can use your server.

One way to create an **IDispatch** interface easily is to allow ActiveX to aggregate your object with a standard dispatcher. All you need to do is load your type information (see the example under **IProvideClassInfo**) and call **CreateStdDispatch**.

However, there is an easier way. MFC has good support for creating objects that support **IDispatch**. If you want to create such an object, run AppWizard and be sure to select the Automation checkbox (Automation is another term for ActiveX scripting, which means objects that support **IDispatch**).

If you are creating an EXE program, you can add **IDispatch** to your document object. Usually, you'll be creating a DLL. In that case, you need to create an object derived from **CCmdTarget**. This object will serve as the **IDispatch**-aware object. Select Add Class from the Class Wizard dialog to add a new class. In the dialog that appears, derive a new class from **CCmdTarget**. Be sure to check the Automation radio button (refer back to Figure 2.15).

Once you have an object, select Class Wizard's Automation tab (see Figure 2.17). This tab will allow you to add methods or properties. MFC supports the idea of common properties (like background color) for ActiveX controls. These are stock properties and have predefined names and semantics. However, in a general-purpose automation object, there are no stock properties.

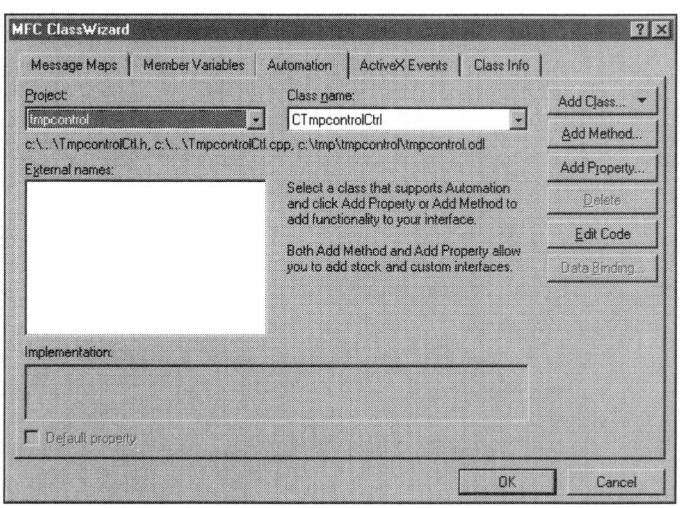

Figure 2.17 Adding methods and properties.

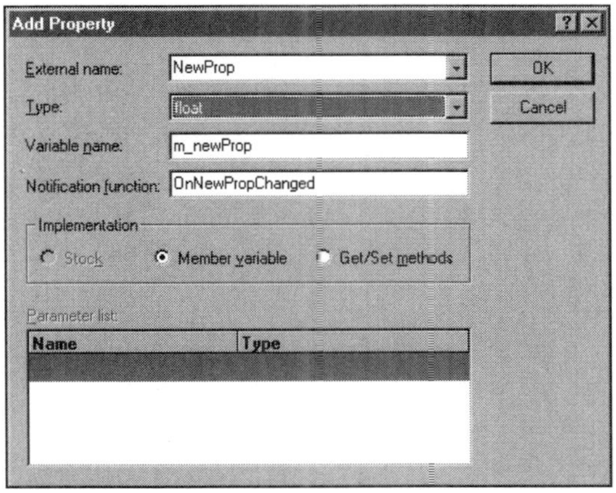

Figure 2.18 Creating a property.

To define a property, fill in its name and type (see Figure 2.18). If you want to map this property to a variable in your code, make sure the Member Variable radio button is on and provide the name of the variable in the Variable Name field. Class Wizard will automatically add this variable to your class. If you like, you can add a function in the Notification Function field that MFC will call any time another program changes your property.

Some properties don't map directly to variables. For example, suppose you want a property in centimeters, but you represent it internally in pixels. Then you might elect to select the Get/Set Methods radio button instead of the Member Variable button. This enables you to specify functions that MFC will call when a program attempts to read or write the property. You can take whatever action you require in these functions. If you need a variable, in this case, you'll have to define it yourself. If you want a read-only property, don't supply a write function. If you want a write-only property (as odd as that sounds), don't supply a read function.

MFC's implementation of **GetIDsOfNames** uses the name of the property. If you use MFC, you don't need to care about the **DISPID**s. You supply the names, and MFC will automatically assign and convert appropriate **DISPID**s.

Adding methods is very similar. The Class Wizard dialog (see Figure 2.19) enables you to select an external name (used in **GetIDsOfNames**) and an internal name (the name of your function). These names may be the same, if you like. In addition, select a return type and any arguments you want the method to accept (up to 16 arguments are possible). Again, Class Wizard knows about stock methods, but this is only legal for ActiveX controls.

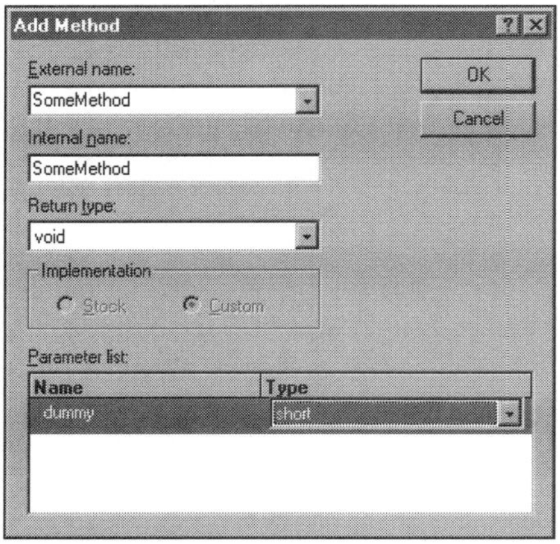

Figure 2.19 Adding a method.

The other related tab in Class Wizard is the ActiveX Events tab. This is useful only for ActiveX controls.

As you can see, building an **IDispatch** object with MFC is almost trivial. You use Class Wizard to do all the work. MFC provides a class factory and an implementation of **IDispatch** based on your input to Class Wizard. Better still, the MFC's code is quite efficient. You can read more about MFC's **IDispatch** implementation in the MFC technotes (specifically, look at notes 38 and 39).

Just to illustrate how simple this is with MFC, look at Listings 2.16 and 2.17. They show a simple **IDispatch** object that has a property and a method. The property selects a type of beep (the default is -1) and the method beeps using the selected type (by calling **MessageBeep** from the standard API).

It is amazing how little of this code did not come from MFC. I added a single line to the constructor to set the property variable to -1. I also wrote the **Beep** function (although Class Wizard already had a stub in place for me). Furthermore, I had to add the **DECLARE_OLECREATE** line in the header and the **IMPLEMENT_OLECREATE** line in the CPP file. That's it. The rest of the code is from AppWizard or Class Wizard.

If you register the class appropriately (see Listing 2.18), you can easily use this object from Visual Basic or any other language that can act as an automation controller or ActiveX script language. You can also use Visual C++ and MFC to write controllers. Simply ask Class Wizard to add a class from a type library and select the automation object's DLL, EXE, or TLB file. This will cause Class Wizard to create a class that stands in for the automation object. It writes simple functions that call **Invoke** with the correct arguments for each case.

Listing 2.16 An IDispatch example.

```
// Dispatcher.cpp : implementation file
//

#include "stdafx.h"
#include "dispatch.h"
#include "Dispatcher.h"

#ifdef _DEBUG
#define new DEBUG_NEW
#undef THIS_FILE
static char THIS_FILE[] = __FILE__;
#endif

/////////////////////////////////////////
// CDispatcher

IMPLEMENT_DYNCREATE(CDispatcher, CCmdTarget)
// Add to Class Factory
IMPLEMENT_OLECREATE(CDispatcher,"Beeper",
   0x8755aa4, 0xd365,0x11cf, 0xa7, 0xb2, 0x44,
   0x45, 0x53,0x54, 0x0, 0x0)

CDispatcher::CDispatcher()
   {
   EnableAutomation();
   m_beepType=-1;  // default
   }

CDispatcher::~CDispatcher()
   {
   }


void CDispatcher::OnFinalRelease()
   {
   CCmdTarget::OnFinalRelease();
   }


BEGIN_MESSAGE_MAP(CDispatcher, CCmdTarget)
   //{{AFX_MSG_MAP(CDispatcher)
   //}}AFX_MSG_MAP
END_MESSAGE_MAP()
```

```
BEGIN_DISPATCH_MAP(CDispatcher, CCmdTarget)
//{{AFX_DISPATCH_MAP(CDispatcher)
DISP_PROPERTY(CDispatcher,"BeepType", m_beepType, VT_I4)
DISP_FUNCTION(CDispatcher,"Beep", Beep, VT_EMPTY, VTS_NONE)
//}}AFX_DISPATCH_MAP
END_DISPATCH_MAP()

// {08755AA4-D365-11CF-A7B2-444553540000}
static const IID IID_IDispatcher =
   { 0x8755aa4, 0xd365, 0x11cf, { 0xa7,
     0xb2, 0x44, 0x45, 0x53, 0x54, 0x0, 0x0 } };

BEGIN_INTERFACE_MAP(CDispatcher, CCmdTarget)
INTERFACE_PART(CDispatcher, IID_IDispatcher, Dispatch)
END_INTERFACE_MAP()

/////////////////////////////////////////
// CDispatcher message handlers

void CDispatcher::Beep()
  {
  MessageBeep(m_beepType);
  }
```

Listing 2.17 The Dispatch Object header.

```
// dispatch.h : main header file for the DISPATCH DLL
//

#ifndef __AFXWIN_H__
#error include 'stdafx.h' before including this file
#endif

#include "resource.h"       // main symbols

/////////////////////////////////////////
// CDispatchApp
// See dispatch.cpp for the implementation of this class
//

class CDispatchApp : public CWinApp
   {
   public:
      CDispatchApp();

   // Overrides
```

```
// ClassWizard generated virtual function overrides
   //{{AFX_VIRTUAL(CDispatchApp)
   public:
      virtual BOOL InitInstance();
   //}}AFX_VIRTUAL

   //{{AFX_MSG(CDispatchApp)
   //}}AFX_MSG
DECLARE_MESSAGE_MAP()
};

/////////////////////////////////////////
```

Listing 2.18 Registry entries.

```
REGEDIT4

[HKEY_CLASSES_ROOT\CLSID\{08755AA4-D365-11CF-A7B2-444553540000}]

[HKEY_CLASSES_ROOT\CLSID\{08755AA4-D365-11CF-A7B2-
444553540000}\InProcServer32]
@="c:\\activex\\dispatch\\debug\\dispatch.dll"

[HKEY_CLASSES_ROOT\CLSID\{08755AA4-D365-11CF-A7B2-444553540000}\ProgID]
@="Beeper"

[HKEY_CLASSES_ROOT\Beeper\CLSID]
@="{08755AA4-D365-11CF-A7B2-444553540000}"
```

You'll find the code that Class Wizard creates for the sample dispatch class in Listing 2.19. Notice how each stub identifies the argument types and uses a **DISPID**.

Listing 2.19 Class Wizard-generated code.

```
// Machine generated IDispatch wrapper
// class(es) created with ClassWizard

#include "stdafx.h"
#include "dispatch.h"

#ifdef _DEBUG
#define new DEBUG_NEW
#undef THIS_FILE
static char THIS_FILE[] = __FILE__;
#endif
```

```
/////////////////////////////////////////
// IDispatcher properties

long IDispatcher::GetBeepType()
   {
   long result;
   GetProperty(0x1, VT_I4, (void*)&result);
   return result;
   }

void IDispatcher::SetBeepType(long propVal)
   {
   SetProperty(0x1, VT_I4, propVal);
   }

/////////////////////////////////////////
// IDispatcher operations

void IDispatcher::Beep()
 {
 InvokeHelper(0x2, DISPATCH_METHOD, VT_EMPTY,
   NULL, NULL);
 }
```

Armed with this wrapper class, it is a simple matter to create and use this automation class. Listing 2.20 shows a simple program that displays a dialog. When you press OK, it creates an automation object and asks it to beep. Notice that MFC's AppWizard wrote most of the code. The only original lines are the **include** for the dispatch class and the code that handles the OK case in **InitInstance**.

Listing 2.20 An automation controller.

```
// User.cpp : Defines the class behaviors
// for the application.
//

#include "stdafx.h"
#include "User.h"
#include "UserDlg.h"
#include "dispatch.h"

#ifdef _DEBUG
#define new DEBUG_NEW
#undef THIS_FILE
static char THIS_FILE[] = __FILE__;
#endif
```

```
////////////////////////////////////////
// CUserApp

BEGIN_MESSAGE_MAP(CUserApp, CWinApp)
   //{{AFX_MSG_MAP(CUserApp)
   //}}AFX_MSG
   ON_COMMAND(ID_HELP, CWinApp::OnHelp)
END_MESSAGE_MAP()

////////////////////////////////////////
// CUserApp construction

CUserApp::CUserApp()
   {
   // TODO: add construction code here,
   // Place all significant initialization in InitInstance
   }

////////////////////////////////////////
// The one and only CUserApp object

CUserApp theApp;

////////////////////////////////////////
// CUserApp initialization

BOOL CUserApp::InitInstance()
   {
   // Initialize OLE libraries
   if (!AfxOleInit())
      {
      AfxMessageBox(IDP_OLE_INIT_FAILED);
      return FALSE;
      }

#ifdef _AFXDLL
   Enable3dControls();
#else
   Enable3dControlsStatic();
#endif

   // Parse the command line
   if (RunEmbedded() || RunAutomated())
      {
```

```
        COleTemplateServer::RegisterAll();
        return TRUE;
        }

    COleObjectFactory::UpdateRegistryAll();

    CUserDlg dlg;
    m_pMainWnd = &dlg;
    int nResponse = dlg.DoModal();
    if (nResponse == IDOK)
        {
        IDispatcher disp;
        disp.CreateDispatch("Beeper");  // ProgID
        disp.Beep();
        }
    else if (nResponse == IDCANCEL)
        {
// No action
        }

    return FALSE;
    }
```

Binding Time And Efficiency

If the **IDispatch** protocol seems like a lot of trouble, then you've been paying attention. The advantage is that you can perform *late binding*. That is, you can ask an object to do something without knowing anything about the object or what it does at compile time. You find out those things at runtime (later, hence, late binding). Early binding is what C++ normally does. Sure, you can manipulate objects, but only if you have detailed knowledge of the object at compile time. For that matter, ordinary ActiveX objects are about the same way. You can find interfaces at runtime, but you have to know what those interfaces do at compile time, in general.

Of course, constructing a **DISPPARMS** structure, converting strings to **DISPIDs**, and unpacking and coercing **VARIANTs** all take time (even if you let MFC do it for you). If you need late binding, then this is as good an answer as any. However, what happens if you only need late binding on occasion? At other times, clients will know exactly what they want to do at compile time.

There are many possible answers to this dilemma. You could provide an **IDispatch** interface and custom interfaces. Clients would select whichever they wanted to use. Another approach is to define a dual interface. A *dual interface* is an interface that derives (in the proper sense) from **IDispatch**. The dual interface's first functions are identical to **IDispatch**. The remaining functions implement whatever interface you like. Clients may elect to use **IDispatch::Invoke** to use your interface or call functions directly using your custom interface (which happens to be the same as your **IDispatch** interface).

Creating a dual interface is as simple as creating the appropriate functions and marking the interface with the **dual** keyword in the ODL file. Each member must return an **HRESULT** and all arguments must be scripting compatible (that is, something that fits in a **VARIANT**). Unfortunately, there is no simple way to create dual interfaces in MFC.

New Frontiers: COM+

Windows 2000 adds significant enhancements to COM and ActiveX. To distinguish these changes from traditional COM, Microsoft refers to Win2000 COM as COM+. Everything you know about COM applies to COM+, but there are new features you can use to simplify certain tasks.

At the heart of COM+ is the traditional COM or ActiveX framework. **IUnknown** and all the interfaces that you love to hate are still present. COM+ also integrates the Microsoft Transaction Server (MTS) into COM so that it is no longer a separate piece.

MTS allows clients to define transactions that can span multiple servers. The client can roll back or undo the entire transaction easily. MTS can also pool resources so that clients don't need to create and destroy scarce assets. For example, instead of each client opening and destroying a database connection, a database server object can pool several connections and reuse them for multiple clients.

COM+ provides applications with the COM+ catalog. This catalog partially replaces the registry as a central location for information about components. You can alter the catalog using a series of new COM interfaces or using the COM+ explorer.

One key problem with using standard COM remotely (sometimes called DCOM for Distributed COM) is that clients must specifically request services from a particular server. If you wanted to balance client requests among different servers, you had to figure out how to do that manually. With COM+, it is possible to call **CoCreateInstanceEx** and specify a router machine instead of an actual server. The router determines which of a cluster of servers has the lightest load (by default, it determines the minimum response time, although you can use a custom algorithm instead) and forwards the request to the appropriate server. This process is transparent to clients.

COM+ load balancing has a few problems, but it is still better than previous alternatives. For example, the router machine is a single bottleneck in the system. If the router fails, the system will fail. Another problem is that the default algorithm for determining load is not always appropriate. Still, COM+ load balancing is better than nothing, and you can still implement a custom solution if you need more.

Other major changes to COM+ include many differences in how multithreaded applications can use COM. Conventional COM often uses the apartment threading model where each object receives calls from one thread. You can still utilize this threading model, but you can also mark objects as thread neutral. A thread neutral object receives calls from multiple threads (like the freethreading model) but does not have the restrictions that a freethreaded object incurs.

Other thread-related changes include ways to synchronize between threads including **CoWaitForMultipleHandles** (a COM-aware version of **WaitForMultipleObjects**). You can finally make calls to other threads without blocking.

Finally, COM+ allows you to transparently work with the Microsoft Message Queue (MSMQ). MSMQ allows you to send messages to objects on servers that might not be available. MSMQ buffers the work until the server is available later. Before Windows 2000, you had to make specific calls to the MSMQ API. Now, you can simply specify transparent queuing and COM+ takes care of the rest.

Summary

If that seems like a lot of material about ActiveX, that's because it is. However, this chapter only scratches the surface of ActiveX. You can read entire books about ActiveX (including my *Developing ActiveX Web Controls*).

However, ActiveX is rapidly becoming less an area of specialization, and more of an object-oriented method to provide new application programming interfaces. More and more Microsoft technology relies on ActiveX interfaces. If you can't use the interfaces, you can't take advantage of these new technologies.

Although ActiveX has a reputation as a difficult technique to master, much of this reputation isn't completely deserved. Sure, writing ActiveX objects that coexist with other objects in a complex system can be difficult. But a simple ActiveX object is actually quite straightforward.

The other reason ActiveX often seems difficult is a result of how many ActiveX objects have to meet certain expectations. For example, if you want to create an object that can appear inside an OLE container (like Microsoft Word, for instance), then it is necessary to understand the interfaces you must supply and the interfaces that the container will provide for you. These are often complicated protocols, but they still use the same simple method of providing interfaces.

Immediate Solutions

ActiveX In A Nutshell

If you aren't already familiar with ActiveX concepts, you should really read the main body of this chapter. However, in case you don't want to right away, or if you think you just need a refresher, here's the condensed version of this chapter:

ActiveX, at its core, is nothing more than a standard for creating binary objects. Objects, certainly no stranger to the modern programmer, are usually a source-code phenomenon. Think about it. If you write an object in C++, it isn't likely to be very useful to a Visual Basic or Pascal programmer. You can't even share C++ objects among different libraries or compilers. But with ActiveX, you can construct objects that are source-code independent.

Not only does that mean you can mix languages, but it also means that you can use objects that don't include their source code. How is this possible? It is actually quite easy. First, consider the goals for a typical object-oriented programming system.

An object-oriented programming system has three main goals: encapsulation, reuse, and polymorphism. *Encapsulation* is how objects hide their implementations. If you hide your implementation, other programs can't depend on it. For example, if you write a phone book object that uses a flat file, you would like to be able to change it to use a database without affecting the programs that use the object.

Reuse, of course, is the art of building your objects with other existing objects. You assume the existing objects work well. However, if they don't, you can replace them, thanks to encapsulation.

Polymorphism is just a long word that means you want to be able to treat objects as though they were more generic objects. For example, suppose you have truck, car, and motorcycle objects. It would be nice to have a way to treat them all as vehicles when it is convenient to do so. That's polymorphism.

Notice that inheritance is not a goal of object-oriented programming. It is the way C++ (and other languages) make reuse and polymorphism work.

An *ActiveX object* is any piece of code that exposes at least one (and possibly more than one) table of function pointers. The object and its users agree on what operation each function performs. These tables are *interfaces*.

Because the only access any code has to an object is via the interface, you automatically have encapsulation. So long as the interface function performs as promised, it doesn't matter how the object works internally. Of course, if an object uses another object internally, that's one form of reuse (known as *containment*).

Polymorphism is a bit trickier; it requires a small detail that I haven't shared with you yet. Every interface defines the first three functions as having the same purpose. These functions together make up the **IUnknown** interface. Because every interface begins with these three functions, you can treat any interface as though it were an **IUnknown** interface.

All by itself, this constitutes a form of polymorphism—every interface is an **IUnknown** interface. However, it isn't very general-purpose. True polymorphism hinges on the purpose of one of the **IUnknown** functions.

The three functions in the **IUnknown** interface (and therefore, in all interfaces) are **AddRef**, **Release**, and **QueryInterface**. Of course, these names are fictions, because they are really just pointers in a function table. Still, it is customary to call the functions by their names.

AddRef and **Release** simply add and subtract from a running usage count maintained for the entire object (regardless of the interface, in most cases). When the count drops to zero, the object destroys itself. Anytime you make a copy of an interface pointer that might live longer than the original, you call **AddRef**. When you are done with a copy, you call **Release**.

The real hero of **IUnknown** is **QueryInterface**. **QueryInterface** is deceptively simple. It enables you to ask an interface if its object supports a particular interface. Why is this so important? For one thing, it enables you to work with objects of any type, because you can always treat an interface as **IUnknown**. You can receive any kind of interface pointer and query it until you find an interface you know about (or until you give up).

The other important aspect to **QueryInterface** is that you can handle objects by any of their interfaces. Suppose you have an object that has a Car interface and a Vehicle interface. Then you can work with either interface, thanks to **QueryInterface**. If it suits your needs, you can handle the object as a Car or a Vehicle.

So what happens if you have an object that has Truck and Vehicle interfaces? You can work with either of these interfaces, too. That means that the objects are polymorphic. In fact, any objects that have common interfaces are polymorphic.

Notice that unlike C++, an object can be polymorphic with many other unrelated classes. For example, if the Car and Truck objects also have a Database interface, they are polymorphic with all other objects that have a similar interface. Also, ActiveX polymorphism doesn't imply reuse. You may have a Vehicle interface, but you still have to implement it. Of course, you could contain a Vehicle object that does the work for you, but you must do so explicitly.

So, by using ActiveX, you can construct binary objects that exhibit encapsulation, reuse, and polymorphism. You can use any language you choose and can work with objects from other languages.

For more specifics, you'll have to read this chapter. However, this will at least give you enough of a picture of ActiveX to tackle the topics that require it later in this book.

Understanding The Registry

The Registry stores a great deal of configuration information, including the location of ActiveX servers and information about the objects they contain. The Registry is almost, but not quite, like a file system. The Registry consists of a number of keys (similar to directories). Just as a directory can contain subdirectories, a key can contain subkeys. A key can also contain any number of name/value pairs. These are similar to files (names) and their contents (values).

One place where this analogy breaks down is that keys can have a default value. This would be like if a directory could contain files and subdirectories, but could also contain data of its own, like a file.

To uniquely identify many parts of ActiveX (including servers and interfaces), you need a UUID (a Universally Unique ID, sometimes known as a GUID or Globally Unique ID). A UUID is a 128-bit number generated so that when you create one, it is very unlikely that anyone else will ever generate the same one. You can create GUIDs with a command line tool, but most of the modern programming environments automatically generate them for you.

When you use a GUID to refer to an ActiveX class, it is a CLSID. If you use a GUID to refer to an interface, it is an IID. You'll use these IDs to refer to either object unambiguously. Because it is so awkward to deal with 128-bit numbers, the Registry also contains a short text name for each class. You can also use this (the PROGID) in some cases, but you should select PROGIDs that are unlikely to collide with other people's choices. For example, using a PROGID of **COUNTER** would be a bad idea because that is a common name. **AWC.COUNTER** is a little better because you wouldn't expect too many people to use my company name in a PROGID.

You can manipulate the Registry with a variety of calls (refer back to Table 2.1). You can also change it manually using REGEDIT or REGEDT32. In addition, REGEDIT enables you to assemble REG files that it can import into the Registry automatically.

Guide To Common Interfaces

You can define any interface you like. However, there is no assurance that anyone will want to use it. Normally, you wind up implementing interfaces that another program expects. Other times, you will expect certain interfaces from other objects.

The **IMalloc** interface (refer back to Table 2.6) enables you to ask another object to allocate or free memory. This is especially important when you must allocate memory in that other object's address space.

The **IDispatch** interface (refer back to Table 2.12) is particularly versatile. It enables programs to use objects via late binding. That is, you can use an object that implements **IDispatch** even if you don't have any knowledge about it beforehand. Objects that have an **IDispatch** interface are automation objects. Other programs (like the Visual Basic design-time interface, for example) can query the **IDispatch** interface to learn what properties, methods, and events the object supports.

There is no such thing as an **IEnum** interface (refer back to Table 2.8), but it is still handy to refer to it. In reality, there are many **IEnum** interfaces, each one enabling you to enumerate the items in a particular kind of list. The return type of the enumerator depends, of course, on the type of item that particular enumerator handles.

Using MFC For IDispatch

MFC has special facilities for handling **IDispatch**. Any class that derives from **CCmdTarget** (including **CWnd**, **CDocument**, and most other interesting classes) can have an **IDispatch** interface. When you create classes with Class Wizard, it will give you the option to add an **IDispatch** interface.

Once you have an object with an **IDispatch** interface, you can use Class Wizard to add properties and methods to the class. Class Wizard will write skeletal code for you and maintain the type library information that other programs use to learn the interface's capabilities.

Using MFC For Ordinary Interfaces

You can hijack MFC's **IDispatch** mechanisms to simplify the construction of generic interfaces. The idea is simple: Create an **IDispatch** interface for an object and take away the things that are specific to **IDispatch**. Then you can add the items you require for your interface. Of course, the object has to derive from **CCmdTarget**. You can find complete details in this chapter (see the "MFC Techniques" section).

About ATL

You may prefer to use Microsoft's Active Template Library (ATL) to realize ActiveX interfaces. This library provides a lightweight framework for constructing ActiveX objects. You'll find more about ATL in Chapter 10.

Chapter 3

Processes, Threads, And Fibers

If you need an immediate solution to:	*See page:*
Running A New Program—The Easiest Way	144
Running A New Program—A Little Harder	144
Running A New Program—The Macho Way	144
Waiting For A Program To Complete, Setting (Or Reading) The Exit Code	145
Creating A New Thread With The Windows API	146
Creating A New Thread With The C++ Library	146
Using Threads And MFC	146
Creating An MFC Worker Thread	147
Creating An MFC UI Thread	148
Making Windows And Message Boxes Appear On Top	148
Obtaining Process And Thread Handles	149
Waiting For A Thread To Complete, Setting (Or Reading) The Thread Exit Code	149
Manipulating MFC Threads	150
Learning The Return Value With MFC	151
A Complete MFC Example	152
Using Thread Local Storage	158
Using Fibers	159
Using Alternatives To Threading	159

In Depth

Is it just me, or have people gotten less polite than in times past? I won't even mention all the strange people you hear about on the news. It seems like the crimes just get stranger and stranger. Maybe I'm just naive, but I don't remember things being so—well, strange when I was a kid.

I blame the phone company for most of life's modern problems. Ever wonder why people seem less well-adjusted? More violent? More disturbed? It's the phone company. Think about it. You pick up the phone to call someone. As your finger pushes that last button, you hear: brammp, brammp, brammp...busy! Hmmm...that person is too busy to talk to *me*. Call again. Still busy.

As though that wasn't bad enough, now you have to deal with call waiting. Talking to someone? Wait! Someone more important is calling now. You'll have to wait. What a blow to your ego.

I think that's one of the best things about the Internet (and computers in general). When you try to connect to a Web site, you rarely get a busy signal. Sure, sometimes a site is down, or swamped, but that is fairly unusual. Of course, if an Internet provider gives you a busy signal, that's the ultimate sin.

One of the reasons computers are never busy is that modern machines multitask. Windows 2000 has several forms of multitasking. Of course, Windows can run multiple programs at one time. Each program has at least one thread of execution, but it might have more than one thread that appears to execute simultaneously with the other threads in the system. You can also create fibers if you want to control multiple threads of execution within one process.

In real life, of course, a computer with a single processor does only one thing at a time. Even a computer with more than one processor can't do an unlimited number of things at once. Still, the computer is so fast, that even juggling many things at once, it can seem like it is doing several things at once.

Other Operating Systems

If you have experience with other operating systems (like Unix, for example), you might find Windows multiprocessing confusing. That's because while Windows uses many of the same terms that other operating systems use, the meanings are often quite different.

When you start a program under Windows, you create a process. That is similar to many other operating systems, right? Not really. Under Windows, a process owns memory, open files, and other resources. However, a process does not execute. Instead, each process starts with a single thread. This thread (which is really just a set of processor registers) has a point in the program it is executing, and a stack pointer (and therefore its own local variables).

So what's the difference if the process executes or if threads execute? Nothing, as long as there is one thread per process. However, the thread can create more threads. And those threads might create even more threads. While a process can't share anything with another process unless it uses special techniques, threads in a single process share almost everything.

Another difference between Windows and Unix is how you create a new process. In Unix, to create a new process, you call **fork**. The **fork** call clones the current process, creating another that is practically an exact duplicate of the first. The new process has its own private copy of the original's variables. Most of the time, you follow a call to **fork** with a call to **exec**. This causes the operating system to load a new executable file into the duplicate process. However, sometimes it is useful to make a copy of a process, and then have both processes continue without starting a new program. For example, after a program loads and processes some data, let's say you want to run three "what-if" scenarios. With Unix, you could **fork** three new processes to work on the data. Each new process would have its own copy of the pertinent data.

With Windows, you really don't have this option. You can call **CreateProcess** to start a new program. That is most similar to a **fork** and an **exec**. The new process is completely new and has very little in common with the original process. You could, of course, start three threads to perform the "what-ifs." However, if the threads change the data, they will all see the changes. The data the threads access is not private.

This isn't to say that there is no solution for this problem. You could place the data in shared memory and allow the processes to make their own copies, for example. You could even store the data in a file. It is just a different philosophy and requires a different way of looking at things.

Win32 multitasking is also different from 16-bit Windows. In Windows 3.1, programs had to cooperate to multitask. When a program asked the system for a message (or performed a handful of other operations), the system might elect to put that program to sleep and run other programs. However, if any program fails to ask the system for messages, everything grinds to a halt. Win32, of course, can yank the rug out from any program at any time.

That's a good thing, isn't it? Well, from some perspectives it is a great idea. A bad program can't lock up the entire system by failing to yield to other programs. Slow programs don't slow down the whole system, either. However, with Windows-style multitasking (known as pre-emptive multitasking), you have a new set of problems to deal with as a programmer.

With Windows 3.1, you could assume that you had complete control of the machine unless you made one of the system calls that might yield to Windows. However, with pre-emptive multitasking, you can't make this assumption. Suppose you open a file and start writing a message to it. Windows may pre-empt you in favor of another thread in the middle of the operation. What happens if another thread tries to open the same file so it can write a message, too? If your thread has the file open for exclusive access, the second thread can't open it.

To prevent these kinds of problems, you need to pay special attention to your program's design. You may also need to use various types of synchronization and interprocess communications (see Chapters 4 and 6).

Of course, if you have experience programming other operating systems that pre-emptively multitask, this doesn't seem surprising. But if you are used to older versions of Windows, it might take some getting used to.

Processes

When you want to run a new program, you need to create a new process. The basic call you'll need to use is **CreateProcess**. However, **CreateProcess** has quite a few arguments that you have to fill in just to get things started. If you just want to run WordPad to display README.TXT, you might want to use something simpler.

What calls can you use? **WinExec** is very simple to use. The Microsoft documentation says you should use **CreateProcess** instead of **WinExec**, but if **WinExec** suits your needs, why not use it? **WinExec** could hardly be simpler. Besides, it calls **LoadModule** (another obsolete call) which simply calls **CreateProcess** with default arguments. You name the application you want to run (either a complete path name, or the file has to be on the system path). You also supply an argument to indicate how you would like the program to appear. This is one of the constants from **ShowWindow** (**SW_SHOW**, **SW_HIDE**, etc.). Of course, the program may choose to ignore this request and start the way it wants to anyway.

The return value of the **WinExec** call is either less than 32 if an error occurs, or if successful, the instance handles the new program (which is never less than 32). **WinExec** returns to your program immediately; it doesn't wait for the program to end.

Another simple call for starting a program is **ShellExecute**. This call is similar to **WinExec**, but it respects the shell's file type associations. So if you use **ShellExecute** on a TXT file, it will open Notepad (or whatever program you use for text files). You pass **ShellExecute** a window handle (in case there are any error dialogs) and an operation string (open, print, or explore). You can also pass the operation string as **NULL**, which causes the call to open the file. You also pass the name of the file you want to use and any command line parameters (usually **NULL**). The final arguments are the current directory, and the **ShowWindow** constant (just like **WinExec**).

The return value is also the same as **WinExec**'s. You'll usually use only the command line and the **ShowWindow** constant parameters if you are specifying an executable file to start. For document files (like TXT or DOC) you'll usually set these parameters to **NULL**.

You can use **ShellExecute** to open the root directory like this:

```
ShellExecute(handle, "open"  "c:\\", NULL, NULL, SW_SHOWNORMAL);
```

Change "open" to "explore" if you want to run the explorer view instead. Of course, you can pass any directory name you want.

Another related call is **ShellExecuteEx**. This call is just about the same as **ShellExecute**, but it takes a structure of parameters that are mostly the same as **ShellExecute**'s parameters. You can also ask the call to fill in key information about the new process (including the process handle) in the structure when it returns.

Using **WinExec** and **ShellExecute** is quite easy. You'll find an example console program in Listing 3.1 that opens a text file using two different methods. Listing 3.1 uses **WinExec** and explicitly names Notepad as the program that should open the file. Then it uses **ShellExecute** to open the text file (which probably starts WordPad, depending on how you have your system set).

Listing 3.1 Opening a text file.

```
#include <windows.h>
#include <iostream.h>

void main(int argc, char *argv[])
{
   cout<<"Opening with WinExec\n";
   // Open our source file
   if (WinExec("notepad readme.txt",SW_SHOW)<32)
      MessageBox(NULL,"Can't WinExec",NULL,MB_OK);
   cout<<"Press Enter\n";
```

```
    MessageBox(NULL,"Press OK to continue","Program Launched",MB_OK);
    cout<<"Opening with ShellExecute\n";
    if (ShellExecute(NULL,"open",
       "readme.txt",NULL,NULL,SW_SHOW)<(HANDLE)32)
          MessageBox(NULL,"Can't ShellExecute\n",NULL,MB_OK);
}
```

CreateProcess

Calls like **ShellExecute** and **WinExec** are great for simple jobs. If you want complete control over a new process, of course, you have to use **CreateProcess**. You can find the arguments that **CreateProcess** expects in Tables 3.1 and 3.2.

The **lpStartupInfo** argument is a **STARTUPINFO** structure. It enables you to set the console title, the starting size and position for the new window, and redirect the standard I/O. The new program can usually ignore most of these items if it chooses to do so. You specify flags in the structure to indicate what pieces of information you want to set. Sometimes you don't want to set any of it, but you'll still need to pass a valid pointer to an empty structure (be sure to set the size into **cb** and set the **dwFlags** member to 0).

The **lpProcessInformation** member returns the process and thread handles to you. It also contains the process and thread IDs. The handles have the access you specify in the **lpProcessAttributes** and **lpThreadAttributes** arguments.

Table 3.1 CreateProcess arguments.

Argument	Description
lpApplicationName	Name of program (or NULL if program name is in command line)
lpCommandLine	Command line string
lpProcessAttributes	Security attributes for returned process handle
lpThreadAttributes	Security attributes for returned thread handle
bInheritHandles	Indicates if new process inherits this process's handles
dwCreationFlags	Options for creation
lpEnvironment	Environment strings (or NULL to inherit current environment)
lpCurrentDirectory	Current directory (or NULL to inherit current)
lpStartupInfo	Startup information structure
lpProcessInformation	Returned process and thread handle and ID

Table 3.2 Creation options.

Flag	Meaning
CREATE_DEFAULT_ERROR_MODE	Do not inherit current error mode (see SetErrorMode)
CREATE_NEW_CONSOLE	Create a new console
CREATE_NEW_PROCESS_GROUP	Create a new process group
CREATE_SEPARATE_WOW_VDM	Run 16-bit application in its own address space
CREATE_SHARED_WOW_VDM	Run 16-bit application in a shared address space
CREATE_SUSPENDED	Create in a suspended state (use ResumeThread)
CREATE_UNICODE_ENVIRONMENT	The environment strings are UNICODE
DEBUG_PROCESS	Start process as a debugged process
DEBUG_ONLY_THIS_PROCESS	Prevent current debugger from debugging the new process
DETACHED_PROCESS	Detaches console application

You'll notice that some of the arguments to **CreateProcess** are specific to console applications. Others are useful for all kinds of programs. In many cases, you don't really need to fill in the **STARTUPINFO** structure, but you still have to supply one anyway. The return value is a Boolean, but the really interesting return values arrive in a structure that you pass as an argument (a **PROCESS_INFORMATION** structure). **CreateProcess** returns the process ID and handle, as well as the initial thread ID and handle in this structure. You can communicate the IDs to other processes or use the handles to control the new process.

You'll notice that when you call **CreateProcess**, you can arrange for the new process to inherit several things, including open file handles that are inheritable. However, this isn't very useful except for enabling console applications to share their standard inputs and outputs. That's because the standard I/O files have predefined handle values. Even if your new process has an open file handle, how can it know what the value is unless it is predefined? Sure, you could pass the handle in the command line or the environment variables, but that isn't very clean.

Given a process handle, you can manipulate the process with the calls in Table 3.3. You can also use several methods to determine if the process ends. One way is to call **GetExitCodeProcess**. This call returns either **STILL_ACTIVE** or the process exit value (if the process is complete). The return value requires a pointer to a variable that the call fills in for you. You can learn the current process handle with **GetCurrentProcess**. To manipulate a process from another process, you need to call **OpenProcess** with the process ID. You also need sufficient security to open the process for the desired access. Of course, the process that creates the new process already has the handle (from the **PROCESS_INFORMATION** structure).

Table 3.3 Process calls.

Call	Purpose	Required Security
CreateRemoteThread	Creates a thread in another process	PROCESS_CREATE_THREAD
GetExitCodeProcess	Retrieves the process exit code	PROCESS_QUERY_INFORMATION
GetGuiResources	Determines how many USER or Graphical Device Interface (GDI) objects are in use	PROCESS_QUERY_INFORMATION
SetPriorityClass	Sets the base priority for the process	PROCESS_SET_INFORMATION
GetPriorityClass	Gets base priority for the process	PROCESS_QUERY_INFORMATION
SetProcessAffinityMask	Determines which CPUs the process prefers	PROCESS_SET_INFORMATION
GetProcessAffinityMask	Sets the preferred CPUs for the process	PROCESS_QUERY_INFORMATION
SetProcessPriorityBoost	Allows or disallows Windows from dynamically changing priority of the process	PROCESS_SET_INFORMATION
GetProcessPriorityBoost	Reads the priority boost status	PROCESS_GET_INFORMATION
SetProcessShutDownParameters	Determines what order the system closes processes during system shutdown	N/A (must call from inside process)
GetProcessShutDownParameters	Reads the shutdown parameters	PROCESS_QUERY_INFORMATION N/A (must call from inside process)
SetProcessWorkingSetSize	Sets the minimum and maximum physical memory usage for the process	PROCESS_SET_INFORMATION
GetProcessWorkingSetSize	Reads the working set	PROCESS_GET_INFORMATION
TerminateProcess	Terminates the process gracefully	PROCESS_TERMINATE
ExitProcess	Terminates process abruptly	N/A (must call from inside process)
GetProcessVersion	Determines what version of Windows a process expects	N/A (uses process ID)
GetProcessTimes	Gets CPU usage for process	PROCESS_GET_INFORMATION
GetStartUpInfo	Gets startup structure as passed to CreateProcess	N/A (must call from inside process)

Another way to determine if a process is active is to use **WaitForSingleObject**, a call you will use for many other purposes in Chapter 4. The purpose of **WaitForSingleObject** is to determine if a handle is in the signaled state. A process handle signals when the process ends. When you call **WaitForSingleObject**, you specify the process handle and a timeout value (in milliseconds). If the timeout is 0, the call returns right away and you can determine the state of the process. If the timeout is the constant **INFINITE**, then the call will not return until the target process exits. Of course, you can also specify a timeout value that causes the call to wait that amount of time for the process to end. If the process ends before the timeout expires, the call returns and indicates that the handle is in the signaled state. Otherwise, it returns with a negative response.

No matter which state the handle is in, **WaitForSingleObject** will return success provided there were no errors (the handle remaining unsignaled is not an error). To determine the state of the process, you'll need to compare the return value with **WAIT_OBJECT_0** (signaled) and **WAIT_TIMEOUT** (unsignaled). A real error returns **WAIT_FAILED**. There is another possible return value (**WAIT_ABANDONED**), but you should never see it when dealing with processes (see Chapter 4 for more about **WaitForSingleObject**). To wait for a process, you must have its open handle with **SYNCHRONIZE** privileges.

Remember, a process ID isn't the same thing as a process handle. You can't simply pass handles from one process to another. That means you can't directly manipulate a process from outside the process unless you have the handle. However, the **OpenProcess** call will allow any program (with sufficient security privileges) to convert a process identifier (that you can communicate to other processes) into a process handle. You can also learn the current process identifier by calling **GetCurrentProcessId**. This can be useful if you want to share your process ID with another unrelated process so that it can open your process handle.

When calling **OpenProcess**, you can request certain access to the process. You may or may not have the security access to open the process for each type of access, so try to ask for just what you need. For example, if you want to learn the process exit code, you need **PROCESS_QUERY_INFORMATION** access. To terminate the process, you must have **PROCESS_TERMINATE** access. You can find the list of access types in Table 3.3. You can also request all access using **PROCESS_ALL_ACCESS**.

Speaking of security, if your program has the correct privilege (**SE_TCB_NAME**, to be exact), you can call **LoginUser** to find the token for a logged in user. With that token, you can use **CreateProcessAsUser** to run a program on behalf of any user that is logged in.

Listings 3.2 and 3.3 show two simple console applications. The first program (MASTER) launches the second one (SLAVE) and goes to sleep. The SLAVE program reads the original program's Process Identifier (PID) from its command line and waits for the MASTER program to terminate. You can specify the entire path name of the SLAVE program on MASTER's command line.

These programs illustrate several important techniques:

- Using **CreateProcess**
- Using **OpenProcess**
- Using **WaitForSingleObject**

You'll also notice that because MASTER doesn't use most of **CreateProcess**'s arguments, you could easily use **WinExec** instead (see the comments in Listing 3.2).

Listing 3.2 The MASTER program.

```
#include <windows.h>
#include <iostream.h>
#include <stdio.h>
#include <string.h>

void main(int argc, char *argv[])
{
    char cmd[128];
   if (argc!=1)
      strcpy(cmd,argv[1]);
   else
      strcpy(cmd,"slave.exe");
   int pid=GetCurrentProcessId();
   sprintf(cmd+strlen(cmd)," %d",pid);
   cout<<"Master: Starting:" << cmd << "\n";
   cout.flush();
// In this case, might just as well use WinExec
   //   if (WinExec(cmd,SW_SHOW)<32)
// Otherwise, you need all of this for CreateProcess
   STARTUPINFO info;
   memset(&info,0,sizeof(info));
   info.cb=sizeof(info);
   PROCESS_INFORMATION pinfo;

   if (!CreateProcess(NULL,cmd,NULL,NULL,FALSE,NORMAL_PRIORITY_CLASS,
      NULL,NULL,&info,&pinfo))
   {
      cout<<"Master: Slave process did not start\n";
      cout<<"Master: Try naming slave process on the command line\n";
```

```
    }
    cout<<"Master: Sleeping\n";
    cout.flush();
    Sleep(15000);
    cout<<"Master: Exiting\n";
    exit(0);
}
```

Listing 3.3 The SLAVE program.

```
#include <windows.h>#include <iostream.h>#include <stdio.h> void main(int
argc,char *argv[]){   if (argc!=2)
    {
        cerr<<"Slave: Please run MASTER.EXE instead.\n";
        exit(1);
    }

    int pid=atoi(argv[1]);
    HANDLE
process=OpenProcess(PROCESS_QUERY_INFORMATION|SYNCHRONIZE,FALSE,pid);
    if (!process) cout<<"Slave: Error opening process\n";
    cout<<"Slave: Waiting for master to finish\n";
    cout.flush();
    if (WaitForSingleObject(process,INFINITE)==STATUS_WAIT_0)
        cout<<"Slave: Master completed\n";
    else
        cout<<"Slave: Unexpected error\n";
    exit(0);
}
```

Jobs And Working Sets

Usually, Win2000 automatically assigns a working set to each process. The working set determines how much physical memory the memory manager inside Windows attempts to keep active for the process. The working set specifies the minimum number of pages and the maximum number of pages. You can learn the current size by calling **GetProcessWorkingSetSize**. The system may violate your working set limits if memory is low.

If you have the correct privileges, your program can change its working set size by calling **SetProcessWorkingSetSize**. Setting both limits to 0xFFFFFFFF, Windows will swap the program completely out to disk.

Windows 2000 introduces another way to manage processes: the job. A *job* is a group of related processes. You can create a job object using **CreateJobObject**, or open an existing job (using **OpenJobObject**). Armed with the job handle, you can add any process to the job by calling **AssignProcessToJobObject**.

Why would you want to group processes into jobs? There are several reasons. For example, you can terminate an entire job at one time (use **TerminateJobObject**). You can also set the working set for the whole job (and many other parameters) using the **SetInformationJobObject** call. In addition, you can use **SetInformationJobObject** to set limitations on the processes in the job. For example, you can prevent the job from calling **ExitWindows**, accessing the clipboard, or using user handles (like window handles, for example) from other processes. If you do prohibit the job from using user handles, a process that doesn't belong to the job can grant access to a user handle by calling **UserHandleGrantAccess**.

Another thing you can do with a job is determine statistics about all the processes in the job. Simply call **QueryInformationJobObject**. You can use this call to learn how much CPU time the job is consuming and similar information. You can also find the settings that **SetInformationJobObject** sets using this call.

Threads

Each process starts out with one initial thread. The only thing special about this thread is that it is the first one. It can create new threads, and then those new threads can create more threads. The process remains active until every thread exits (or something causes the whole process or job to terminate—a **TerminateProcess** call, for example).

What use is a thread? Threads have many uses, including the obvious one of making a task run in the background of your main program. For example, you might use a thread to do background printing. Another possible use for a thread is to handle something that might block (like serial I/O, for example) without stopping your main program.

The underlying call for threads is **CreateThread**. However, you'll rarely call this directly. Why? Because if you create a thread with **CreateThread**, your library (for example, the C runtime library or MFC) can't operate in a bare thread.

When you write a program using a tool like C++ or a library like MFC, the tool adds its own code that executes when the program starts. This code is essential to enable the library to function properly. When you call **CreateThread**, it is possible that the library won't work properly.

To counteract this, most libraries provide some other way to create a thread. With the ordinary C++ library, you can use **_beginthread** or **_beginthreadex** to start a new thread (**_beginthreadex** takes a few extra arguments that allow you to create the thread in the suspended state and learn the thread's handle). For

MFC, you'll use **AfxBeginThread**. You'll probably also have to call special functions to end the thread, too. This ensures that the library also has a chance to close down gracefully. For the C++ library, you can use **_endthread** or **_endthreadex** (depending on which function you used to start the thread). MFC, on the other hand, lets you terminate a thread in several ways (you'll see more in the Immediate Solutions section of this chapter).

If you are using **_beginthread** or any of the similar calls, you need to change the project settings to use the multithreading library. This option appears on the C/C++ tab, in the Code Generation settings. The option title is Use Run-Time Library.

Don't forget: Windows doesn't multitask processes. It multitasks threads. Every thread in the system runs independently. Exactly how much time each thread gets depends on several factors. First, the process has a base priority that applies to all of its threads. Then, each thread has a priority that adds to the base priority. Finally, Windows can dynamically adjust the priority of a thread if it thinks there is a benefit in doing so. For example, if the system notices that a thread has input waiting for it, it will boost that thread's priority.

Windows provides many calls for manipulating threads. You'll find a summary of these calls in Table 3.4.

Table 3.4 Thread-related calls.

Function	Required Access	Description
AttachThreadInput	N/A	Attaches a thread's input processing to another thread's allowing, among other things, the capability to set focus to each other's windows and share input state
CreateRemoteThread	PROCESS_CREATE_THREAD	Create a thread in another process
CreateThread	N/A	Create a thread in current process
ExitThread	N/A	Exit current thread
TerminateThread	THREAD_TERMINATE	Terminate a thread without proper clean up
GetCurrentThread	N/A	Get current thread handle
GetCurrentThreadId	N/A	Get current thread ID
GetExitCodeThread	THREAD_QUERY_INFORMATION	Get thread's exit code
SetThreadPriority	THREAD_SET_INFORMATION	Set thread priority
GetThreadPriority	THREAD_QUERY_INFORMATION	Read thread priority

(continued)

Table 3.4 Thread-related calls **(continued).**

Function	Required Access	Description
SetThreadPriorityBoost	THREAD_SET_INFORMATION	Enable or disable dynamic priority boosts for this thread
GetThreadPriorityBoost	THREAD_QUERY_INFORMATION	Read the state of dynamic priority boosting for this thread
GetThreadTimes	THREAD_QUERY_INFORMATION	Determine time thread was created, destroyed, and how much process time was used
SuspendThread	THREAD_SUSPEND_RESUME	Suspends a thread
ResumeThread	THREAD_SUSPEND_RESUME	Resumes thread (must call once for each call to SuspendThread)
SetThreadAffinityMask	THREAD_SET_INFORMATION	Determines which processors a thread may run on
SetThreadIdealProcessor	THREAD_SET_INFORMATION	Sets which processor a thread prefers to run on
SwitchToThread	N/A	Yields the processor to another thread (you don't get to choose which one)

An Example

Have you ever noticed how annoying user interfaces are in the movies? Usually, if there is something critical going on, the computer accompanies its reports with a mind-numbing alarm signal which would surely panic and fluster the hero in real life.

Not to be outdone, take a look at Listing 3.4. This simple program brings up a message box while beeping once per second. The beeping is handled in a separate thread.

Listing 3.4 Red Alert!

```
#include <windows.h>
#include <process.h>  // req'd for _beginthread

HANDLE mainthread;

void beepthread(void *)
{
   DWORD xitcode;
   while (GetExitCodeThread(mainthread,&xitcode)&&xitcode==STILL_ACTIVE)
   {
```

```
        MessageBeep(-1);
        Sleep(1000);
    }
}

void main()
{
    mainthread=GetCurrentThread();
    _beginthread(beepthread,0,NULL);
    MessageBox(NULL,"Red Alert","Alert",MB_OK);
}
```

The main program stores its thread handle in a global variable. This enables the beeping thread to determine when the main thread terminates. The beeping thread terminates also when it determines this is the case.

Of course, you could use **WaitForSingleObject** to find when the thread quit. But for this simple case, the **beepthread** routine calls **GetExitCodeThread**. If the return value is **STILL_ACTIVE**, the beep thread continues looping.

What happens if you don't check to see if the main thread terminates? In this case, nothing. Try it. Change the **while** loop in Listing 3.4 to read **while(1)**. Everything still works. The reason for this is that when the **main** routine ends, the C runtime library calls **exit**, and **exit** calls **ExitProcess**, which terminates all threads, anyway.

Speaking of the C runtime library, there isn't really a compelling reason to use **_beginthread** in this program. Because the thread doesn't do any C library calls, you could use **CreateThread** just as easily.

MFC And Threads

If you are an MFC programmer, you'll use **AfxBeginThread** to make a new thread. This call is actually two calls in one (thanks to function overloading). One variant of the call simply starts a new function in a thread. This type of thread is similar to the ones you create with **_beginthread** and is known as a worker thread.

However, worker threads don't have any event loops, and therefore can't create windows (they can, however, create message boxes and modal dialogs). If you want to create a thread with a user interface, you'll use Class Wizard to derive an object from **CWinThread**. Then, another version of **AfxBeginThread** will use this class to create your new thread. You'll see examples of both calls to **AfxBeginThread** in the Immediate Solutions section of this chapter.

You have to be careful using threads with MFC. MFC makes extensive use of thread local storage (discussed later in this chapter). Therefore, many MFC objects work only within the thread that created them. In general, any object that has a map can't access that map from another thread. A **CWnd** object, for example, will only perform the simplest operations unless it is in its original thread.

There are several possible answers to this problem. One is to divide your program so that different threads don't require access to each other's objects. Another way is to avoid passing MFC objects between threads. Instead, pass the underlying handle and convert it to an MFC object in the thread.

For example, suppose thread A creates a **CWnd** object. Instead of passing the object to thread B, thread A might instead pass the **m_hWnd** member of the object. Then, thread B can call **CWnd::FromHandle** to create a temporary **CWnd** object. If thread B needs a more permanent connection, it could use the **Attach** method to make a permanent association between the window and its **CWnd** object.

Another MFC issue is thread safety. MFC objects do not automatically arbitrate between different threads. So if two threads both try to access the same **CString** at the same time, havoc will likely result. It is up to you to prevent your threads from fighting over MFC objects. Usually this will require synchronization objects (see Chapter 4).

Thread Local Storage

Sometimes it is handy to have storage that is specific to a particular thread, but is not a local variable. Suppose you have some sort of network server. Each of the server's clients has its own thread. The threads call a function (say, **DoWork**) to perform some action on behalf of the client. For one reason or another, you want to limit the number of calls to **DoWork** by any one thread (that is, one client) to 10.

How can you keep track of this count? A global variable won't work. If you use a global, you'll increment the count any time any thread calls the function. This would limit you to 10 requests for all threads total. A local variable won't work either. Every time you call **DoWork**, a local variable will start from scratch.

There are, of course, many possible answers. One would be to have each thread reserve a private workspace and pass a pointer to it to **DoWork**. That's fine for a simple problem like this, but if you needed a great deal of data throughout the thread, it would quickly grow unwieldy.

But suppose you create a table with two columns. The first column contains a thread ID, and the second column has a 32-bit number. Each time a thread calls **DoWork**, you learn its thread ID (using **GetCurrentThreadID**) and search for it in the table. If you find it, great. If not, you make a new entry for the ID. Either way, you end up with the table index that corresponds to your thread. Now you can store the counter in the second column of the table. Later, when the thread terminates, you find the table index again, and clear the entire table row, leaving it free for another thread to use.

This is exactly what thread local storage (TLS) does. TLS uses a set of internal tables for each process. Windows promises to provide at least 64 tables per process, and thus you could have 64 separate TLS variables. When you call **TlsAlloc**, Windows reserves one of the tables for you. Then you use **TlsSetValue** and **TlsGetValue** to set or read the data. These operations locate your thread's slot in the table and manipulate the data for you. If you ever decide you don't want the table anymore, you call **TlsFree**. The data you place in the table can be any 32-bit number, but it is usually a pointer to a class or data structure that contains all the variables the thread needs.

Of course, TLS is not the only way to handle this problem. You could roll your own solution that works like TLS, for example. Another possibility is to simply pass each function a pointer to a workspace that it can use.

Listing 3.5 shows an example of two methods. The main program spawns two threads (**t_1** and **t_2**). These threads pick a random number of times to call (**f1** and **f2**). The **f1** function keeps track of the number of times you call it by using a TLS table (the **main** function allocates the table). The program uses the **getf1count** routine to read the count from TLS.

The **f2** function also tracks the number of calls it receives. However, it does so in a local variable passed to it as an argument. This method is satisfactory if there is a main thread function that can create the local variable.

Listing 3.5 Using TLS.

```
#include <windows.h>
#include <iostream.h>
#include <process.h>
#include <stdlib.h>
#include <time.h>

volatile int t1done=0;
volatile int t2done=0;

DWORD index;
```

```
void display(char *display,int f1,int f2)
{
   cout<<display<<" f1="<<f1<<" f2="<<f2<<"\n";
}

int getf1count()
{
   return (int)TlsGetValue(index);
}

void f1()
{
   int ct=(int)TlsGetValue(index);
   TlsSetValue(index,(void *)++ct);
   // presumably do some real work here
}

void f2(int &ctr)
{
   ctr++;
   // maybe some real work here
}


// main thread
void t_1(void *)
{
   int callf1=0;
   int callf2=0;
   int n1,n2;
   srand( (unsigned)time( NULL ) +100);
   n1=rand()%9+1;  // 1 to 10 times
   n2=rand()%9+1;  // and again
   display("T1: Calling",n1,n2);
   while (n1--) f1();
   callf1=getf1count();
   while (n2--) f2(callf2);
   display("T1: Results",callf1,callf2);
   t1done=1;
}


void t_2(void *)
{
   int callf1=0;
```

```
   int callf2=0;
   int n1,n2;
   srand( (unsigned)time( NULL )+245 );
   n1=rand()%9+1;  // 1 to 10 times
   n2=rand()%9+1;  // and again
   display("T2: Calling",n1,n2);
   while (n1--) f1();
   callf1=getf1count();
   while (n2--) f2(callf2);
   display("T2: Results",callf1,callf2);
   t2done=1;

}

void main()
{
    index=TlsAlloc();
   _beginthread(t_1,0,NULL);
   _beginthread(t_2,0,NULL);
   while (t1done==0||t2done==0);
   TlsFree(index);
   cout.flush();

   MessageBox(NULL,"Done","Debug",MB_OK);
}
```


Fibers

Threads multitask pre-emptively. When the system decides your time is up, it yanks the CPU away from your thread and schedules another thread. However, sometimes you want more control. That's where fibers come into play.

You can convert a thread into a fiber by calling **ConvertThreadToFiber**. From that point on, when the system schedules this ex-thread, it runs the current fiber for that thread.

Of course, to begin with, this has no real effect. The code that was part of the thread is now part of the fiber. However, if you add more fibers (using **CreateFiber**) you can switch among them by using **SwitchToFiber**.

What's the point? Fibers are little more than a sophisticated form of long jump (like the **longjmp** call in the C library). However, for certain systems this makes sense (especially if you are porting code from Unix or a similar operating system that simulates threads within a process).

As far as the system is concerned, each fiber is really the thread that is executing it at the moment. The only difference is that the fibers control which fiber they switch to when they yield. Note that ordinary scheduling is still in force. The fibers control only which fiber executes in the hosting thread. All other threads still execute as they normally would.

Listing 3.6 shows a simple example that uses fibers. The **main** thread converts itself to a fiber and then creates three other fibers. The main fiber then switches to each fiber in turn. Each fiber switches back to the main fiber when it is done.

Unless you have a very specific need to control the order of execution of different pieces of code, you should probably avoid fibers. Normally, threads are of much more use.

Listing 3.6 Using fibers.

```
#include <windows.h>
#undef MessageBox
#define MessageBox(s) MessageBoxA(NULL,s,"Fiber Demo",MB_OK)

void *fiber[4];

void fiber0(void *) // main fiber
{
   while (1)
   {
      for (int i=1;i<4;i++)
         SwitchToFiber(fiber[i]);
   }
}


void CALLBACK fiber1(void *)
{
   while (1)
   {
      MessageBox("Fiber 1");
      SwitchToFiber(fiber[0]);
   }
}

void CALLBACK fiber2(void *)
{
   while (1)
   {
      MessageBox("Fiber 2");
```

```
      SwitchToFiber(fiber[0]);
   }
}


void CALLBACK fiber3(void *)
{
   while (1)
   {
      MessageBox("Fiber 3");
      SwitchToFiber(fiber[0]);
   }
}



void main()
{
   fiber[0]=ConvertThreadToFiber(NULL);
   fiber[1]=CreateFiber(0,fiber1,NULL);
   fiber[2]=CreateFiber(0,fiber2,NULL);
   fiber[3]=CreateFiber(0,fiber3,NULL);
   fiber0(NULL);
}
```


APCs

The Windows executive supports a strange beast known as an *Asynchronous Procedure Call (APC)*. The APC is a function a thread calls asynchronously. This sounds great until you find out the limitations that Win32 places on APCs.

The system can never easily decide when it might interrupt a thread. Running user code at any time might cause synchronization and other problems. To prevent these problems, the system will allow only user APCs to execute when a thread is in an alertable wait.

So in practice, you can set an APC on a thread that will execute when the thread becomes alertable. This occurs only when the thread makes calls to **SleepEx**, **SignalObjectAndWait**, **WaitForSingleObjectEx**, **WaitForMultiple ObjectsEx**, and **MsgWaitForMultipleObjectsEx**. APCs can also execute when the thread begins execution (implying that another thread registered the APC before the thread started).

APCs are important because several other parts of Windows make use of them (overlapped I/O in Chapter 5, for example). However, if you need to use them yourself, you can call **QueueUserAPC**. This call takes a function pointer, a thread handle, and data to pass to the APC function.

Making the **QueueUserAPC** call simply places the APC in a queue waiting for the thread to become alertable. Once this occurs, the thread executes every function in the queue.

Listing 3.7 shows a simple program that exercises the **QueueUserAPC** function. The **main** function starts a thread and then sleeps for a bit to make sure the thread is running. Then it calls **QueueUserAPC**. This causes the secondary thread to call a special function when it enters **SleepEx** (but not **Sleep**). However, if you don't wait for the new thread to begin execution, it is possible that the APC will start before the thread runs (comment the **Sleep** call in **main** to see this happen).

Listing 3.7 Queuing a user APC.

```
#include <windows.h>
#include <iostream.h>

volatile int waiting=0;

void CALLBACK apcfunc(DWORD)
{
   waiting=1;
}


DWORD CALLBACK t1(LPVOID)
{
   cout<<"Thread started\n";
   cout.flush();
   Sleep(15000);
   cout<<"Going alertable\n";
   cout.flush();
   SleepEx(10000,TRUE); // alertable
   MessageBox(NULL,"T1 terminating","Debug",MB_OK);
   return 0;

}

void main()
{
   HANDLE thread;
   DWORD tid;
   thread=CreateThread(NULL,0,t1,0,0,&tid);
```

```
    Sleep(5000); // make sure thread starts
    QueueUserAPC(apcfunc,(HANDLE)thread,0);
    while (waiting==0);
    MessageBox(NULL,"Thread now waiting","Debug",MB_OK);
}
```

Are APCs useful? Probably not to most programmers. However, you need to understand APCs if you want to get the most out of overlapped I/O, a topic you'll read more about in Chapter 5.

Summary

If you have nothing else to compare it to, Windows' idea of threads, processes, fibers, and APCs probably doesn't seem very strange. But if you are used to other operating systems, you may find Windows' methods a bit peculiar.

It takes a bit of an effort to get used to partitioning your program into separate threads. However, once you do, the payoff can be tremendous. Multithreading leads to natural solutions for many problems. It also can improve performance, especially on multiprocessor machines.

Several of the topics you read about in this chapter will crop up again. APCs, for example, are widely used in overlapped I/O. Calls such as **WaitForSingleObject** have wide application, especially for synchronizing threads and processes.

Immediate Solutions

Running a New Program—The Easiest Way

Although Microsoft considers it outdated, there are many times when the simple **WinExec** function is the best way to run a new program. Simply pass the command line as the first argument. You also need a second order to decide how you want to show the program (which the program may ignore). Usually, you'll set this to **SW_SHOW**, but you can also try **SW_MINIMIZED** or **SW_MAXIMIZED**. Look up **ShowWindow** to see all the possible choices.

WinExec doesn't allow you all the options you get with **CreateProcess**, but it sure is simple. The return value is less than 32 if the function fails. Otherwise, it returns the new program's instance handle. You can find some example code in Listing 3.1.

Running A New Program—A Little Harder

Another outdated call that sometimes is handy is **ShellExecute**. This call makes a request for the shell to open, explore, or print a document or folder. Although you can run a program with **ShellExecute**, usually you'll just send it the name of a document and let the shell decide which program to run.

Another time that **ShellExecute** is useful is when you want to open a directory folder. You can find an example of calling **ShellExecute** in Listing 3.1.

Running A New Program—The Macho Way

There are two reasons you might call **CreateProcess** to run a new program. Perhaps you need the extra control this call provides. Or, you might just like to do things the hard way.

CreateProcess requires a program name and a command line (or you can pass the program name as part of the command line). It also requires two **SECURITY_ATTRIBUTES** structures to provide information about the process and thread handles it will return. These structures determine if the call creates process and thread handles that future child processes can inherit. The structures also determine what access these handles will allow. For example, if you want to synchronize with the child process (that is, wait for it to complete), you need **SYNCHRONIZE** access.

You also supply several flags to control **CreateProcess**'s behavior, the environment strings, the current directory, and a structure where the call leaves the new process, thread handles, and IDs.

All this is a good bit of work if you just want to run Notepad to display README.TXT, or some other trivial task. Be sure to consider **WinExec** or **ShellExecute** in lieu of **CreateProcess** if you don't need all of its power. You can find discussions about these two calls earlier in this Immediate Solutions section. If you want to use **CreateProcess**, check out the program in Listing 3.3.

Waiting For A Program To Complete, Setting (Or Reading) The Exit Code

There are at least two ways to wait for another program to terminate. First, you can call **GetExitCodeProcess**. The intent of this call is to determine the process exit code. This is simply a number the process can set, usually to indicate success or failure.

The process can set the exit code as it terminates by calling **ExitProcess** or **TerminateProcess**. Of course, you can also call **exit** from a console program, or return a value from **main** or **WinMain**. In addition, an unhandled exception can set the exit code.

GetExitCodeProcess reads the exit code from a terminated process (you must have **PROCESS_QUERY_INFORMATION** access for the process handle). However, if the process is still running, the call returns **STILL_ACTIVE** instead of the exit code.

Another way to wait for a program to terminate is to call **WaitForSingleObject** on the process handle (**SYNCHRONIZE** access required). The wait call can test and return, wait for a predefined interval, or wait forever, depending on your needs. You can find an example of using this call in Listing 3.3.

There are many other ways you can manipulate processes. You'll find a summary of calls in Table 3.3.

Creating A New Thread With The Windows API

To create a new thread of execution, the lowest level call is **CreateThread**. However, when you make this call, any library you are using (including the standard C++ library, or MFC) won't be prepared for multiple threads. That's why you will usually use a call from your library to create a new thread.

However, if you need to use **CreateThread**, it is certainly straightforward. You can see an example in Listing 3.7. You can find a variety of calls available to manipulate threads in Table 3.4.

Creating A New Thread With The C++ Library

If you want to make C++ library calls (but not MFC calls), you can use **_beginthread** and **_beginthreadex**. When you make these calls, you ensure that the C++ library is able to handle multiple threads. You also need to change the project settings to use a multithreading library. (Look on the C/C++ tab under Code Generation. You'll find a combo box marked Use Run Time Library. Select any of the multithreaded libraries.)

The only reason to use **_beginthreadex** is if you want to start the thread in its suspended state, specify security attributes, or obtain the thread ID.

To terminate a thread you started with **_beginthread**, call **_endthread**. Use **_endthreadex** for threads that started with **_beginthreadex**. If you use **_endthreadex**, you'll need to close the thread handle explicitly (using **CloseHandle**), but **_endthread** automatically closes the handle for you. Both calls return the thread handle in case you want to use any thread-related calls.

Using Threads And MFC

MFC uses the **CWinThread** object to represent all threads. It even uses an object derived from **CWinThread** to represent your program's main thread. If you look closely, you'll see that **CWinApp**, the class that represents your program, is derived from **CWinThread**.

If you need a thread that has its own event loop, you'll have to derive a class from **CWinThread**, too. You can override **InitInstance** and **ExitInstance** to handle the thread's initialization and termination. If you don't need an event loop (that is, you won't use any windows except, perhaps, modal dialogs and message boxes), then you can use **CWinThread** just like it is. A thread with no event loop is often called a *worker thread*. In either case, you don't directly create a **CWinThread** object—you use **AfxBeginThread** instead.

Creating An MFC Worker Thread

The simplest form of thread is a worker thread. These threads execute an ordinary global (or static member) function independently. The **AfxBeginThread** call takes several arguments in this case:

- The name of a function that returns a **UINT** and takes an **LPVOID** argument. Even if you don't care about the return value or argument, you still have to write the function as though you did. The function can't be a proper member variable. It can be a static member of a class, or you can just use a global function.
- A void pointer argument to pass to the function.
- The priority level for the thread.
- The stack size for the thread.
- A zero if you want the thread to run right away, or use **CREATE_SUSPENDED** to begin the thread in a suspended state.
- The security attributes for the thread. The default is **NULL**, which is normally what you want anyway.

You must supply the first two parameters, but the others are optional.

Once you call **AfxBeginThread**, it will return a pointer to the **CWinThread** object that it creates. You can use this object to manipulate the thread. You can also use the object to retrieve the normal Windows thread handle and manipulate that just like any other thread.

The **CWinThread** object automatically destroys itself when the thread terminates. This can be a problem if you want to read information from the object. Think about it. If the thread terminates before you get a chance to look at the object, the object will already be gone.

To prevent this problem, it is a good idea to create the thread in the suspended state. Then you know the object is valid. You can read what you want before calling **ResumeThread**, or set the **m_bAutoDelete** flag to false. Of course, if you set the flag to false, you'll need to delete the object yourself when you no longer need it.

Creating An MFC UI Thread

AfxBeginThread comes in two flavors: The first one creates worker threads (as you already know) and the other version creates a class that you derive from **CWinThread**. This second version is useful when you want to create a thread that has a user interface. In other words, if your thread requires an event loop, you need to derive a new class from **CWinThread**.

The arguments for this version of **AfxBeginThread** are similar to the worker thread version. However, instead of a function name and an argument, you supply the runtime class (usually using the **RUNTIME_CLASS** macro). All the other arguments remain the same.

A good place to find an example of deriving a class from **CWinThread** is the MFC source code. After all, **CWinApp** is just a thread (sure, it's the first thread, but it is still just a thread).

At the very least, you'll need to override **InitInstance** to create your main window. Don't forget to set **m_pMainWnd** to point to the thread's main window. When App Wizard creates your application object, it takes care of that automatically, but when you do your own class, you need to be aware of these details.

You can derive your new class using Class Wizard. **AfxBeginThread** returns a pointer to a **CWinThread** object, but the object is actually whatever type you specified. If you need to work with any custom members, you'll need to cast the pointer to the appropriate type.

To terminate a thread with an event loop, call **PostQuitMessage**. The argument to this call becomes the return value of the thread that other threads can read.

Making Windows And Message Boxes Appear On Top

Windows has a notion of a foreground thread (the thread that owns the foreground window for a process). When other threads create new windows, they may appear at the bottom of the window stack instead of the top.

To correct this, you can call **SetForegroundWindow** to pop the new window to the top. This presents a special problem for message boxes, however. You can't find the window handle for a message box because Windows creates it and destroys it without your code having a chance to execute. Therefore, when creating a message box, you can use the **MB_SETFOREGROUND** flag to force the box to the top.

Some libraries (like MFC) take care of these details. For those libraries, making these calls yourself is harmless, but superfluous.

Obtaining Process And Thread Handles

When you want to manipulate a process or a thread, you need a handle. Also, you need a handle with the appropriate security access. The easiest way to get these handles is to call **CreateProcess**. That call returns both the process handle and the initial thread handle to the calling program.

What if you need to control a process, but you didn't create it? Then you'll need to open the process ID using **OpenProcess**. You specify the access that you want, and the call returns a handle You can't simply pass a known process handle to another process; you must open it where you want to use it.

Threads are a bit different. To allow another process to use your thread handle, you must make two calls. First, you get the special thread handle by calling **GetCurrentThread**. Then you pass this handle to **DuplicateHandle** to create a handle that you can pass to other processes.

Waiting For A Thread To Complete, Setting (Or Reading) The Thread Exit Code

There are at least two ways to wait for another thread to terminate. First, you can call **GetExitCodeThread**. The intent of this call is to determine the process exit code. This is simply a number the thread can set, usually to indicate success or failure.

The thread can set the exit code as it terminates by calling **ExitThread** or **TerminateThread**. Of course, it may also be the return a value from the thread's function.

GetExitCodeThread reads the exit code from a terminated thread (you must have **THREAD_QUERY_INFORMATION** access for the thread handle). However, if the process is still running, the call returns **STILL_ACTIVE** instead of the exit code.

Another way to wait for a program to terminate is to call **WaitForSingleObject** on the thread handle (**SYNCHRONIZE** access required). The wait call can test and return, wait for a predefined interval, or wait forever, depending on your needs. You can find an example of using this call in Listing 3.3.

There are many other ways you can manipulate threads. You'll find a summary of calls in Table 3.4.

Manipulating MFC Threads

CWinThread has several useful members (see Table 3.5). By default, the **m_b AutoDelete** flag is **TRUE**. That means that when your thread terminates, MFC automatically destroys the object. This is handy if you are just creating a thread to do independent work, but a problem if you want to interact with the object.

Table 3.5 CWinThread members.

Member	Definition
CreateThread	Creates the thread; use AfxCreateThread instead
m_pMainWnd	Main window for thread
m_pActiveWnd	Current active window
m_bAutoDelete	If true, delete thread object when thread terminates; true is the default
m_hThread	Windows thread handle (can also cast CWinThread to HTHREAD)
m_nThreadID	Thread ID
GetThreadPriority	Gets thread's priority level
SetThreadPriority	Sets thread's priority level
SuspendThread	Suspends thread
ResumeThread	Resumes thread (call once for each call to SuspendThread)
PostThreadMessage	Posts a message to the thread's event queue
InitInstance	Override to provide initialization code for the thread
Run	Override to customize the thread's message loop
PreTranslateMessage	Filters messages and processes accelerator keys
PumpMessage	Low-level message pump
OnIdle	Called when no messages are pending
IsIdleMessage	Checks for special MFC idle messages
ExitInstance	Override to provide code on thread termination
ProcessWndProcException	Processes unhandled exceptions
ProcessMessageFilter	Filters messages
GetMainWnd	Returns main window

Suppose you have a user interface thread object derived from **CWinThread**. The new thread's job is to read a command from a serial port. There are many ways you could communicate this command to the rest of the program. However, for the sake of illustration, assume you decide to put a member variable in the thread object that contains the command string.

Assuming that everything goes well, this isn't a bad idea. The main program starts the thread using **AfxBeginThread**, casts the pointer returned to the correct type, and accesses the variable to find out the current command. You would need some other variables, too. For example, you would probably want a flag to indicate a valid command, and a member to clear the command and wait for the next one.

The problem occurs if the thread terminates unexpectedly. Then the object is no good and the pointer is invalid. This will cause major problems.

So the answer, obviously, is to set **m_bAutoDelete** to **FALSE**. But there is still a problem. What happens if the thread terminates almost immediately? In other words, what happens if by the time you try to set the flag, the object is already gone? You can't assume that the object will be valid for any length of time.

The solution is to create the thread in a suspended state. Remember the **CREATE_SUSPENDED** flag you can pass to **AfxCreateThread**? You can pass this flag and MFC will create the thread in a dormant condition. Then you can set the **m_bAutoDelete** flag or do anything else you want before calling **ResumeThread** to start execution.

Speaking of **ResumeThread**, you should know that **SuspendThread** and **ResumeThread** have to balance. In other words, if you call **SuspendThread** three times, the thread will not run again until you also call **ResumeThread** three times.

Learning The Return Value With MFC

You can set a worker thread's return value by returning it from the controlling function or passing it to **AfxEndThread**. You can set a user interface thread's return value using **PostQuitMessage**.

If your program needs to read another thread's return value, it needs the thread's handle. This is available in the **CWinThread** object (the **m_hThread** variable). You use the handle in a call to **::GetExitCodeThread**. This function requires the handle as the first argument, and a pointer to a **DWORD** result as the second argument. If the thread is still active, the function places the constant

STILL_ACTIVE in the **DWORD** result. Otherwise, the function sets the **DWORD** to reflect the exit code of the specified thread.

A Complete MFC Example

Have you ever wanted to call an MFC user interface from some other program? It is very tempting to design a DLL that has a single entry point that starts what is essentially an entire MFC program.

There are several ways you might accomplish this, but a very easy and useful way is to use a thread. Your DLL simply spawns a new thread and this thread corresponds closely with an ordinary MFC application.

In this section, you'll see a simple console application that computes a large quantity of even numbers. Since this may take awhile, the application places a dialog box on the screen that enables the user to cancel the operation. Obviously, the console application can't use a modal dialog box because it must continue processing. However, because the console application doesn't have an event loop, it can't use a modeless dialog either.

The solution is to define an MFC DLL that handles the dialog box. This presents two challenges. First, the console application must have some way to start the MFC portion. Second, the console application and the MFC abort dialog must communicate. In particular, the console program must detect that the user wants to abort, and the MFC dialog has to close down when the console program no longer needs it.

Making an exported C function is not hard. This function can create a **CWinThread**-derived class that starts the dialog box. Listing 3.8 shows the main DLL code (including the exported function **AbortBox**). Listing 3.9 contains the thread code, and Listing 3.10 shows the dialog box. Listing 3.11 shows the simple console program that uses the MFC DLL.

Listing 3.8 The abort DLL.

```
// abortdll.cpp : Defines the initialization routines for the DLL.
//

#include "stdafx.h"
#include "abortdll.h"
#include "abortthread.h"
#include "abortdlg.h"
```

```
#ifdef _DEBUG
#define new DEBUG_NEW
#undef THIS_FILE
static char THIS_FILE[] = __FILE__;
#endif

//
//   Note!
//
//      If this DLL is dynamically linked against the MFC
//      DLLs, any functions exported from this DLL that
//      call into MFC must have the AFX_MANAGE_STATE macro
//      added at the very beginning of the function.
//
//      For example:
//
//      extern "C" BOOL PASCAL EXPORT ExportedFunction()
//      {
//         AFX_MANAGE_STATE(AfxGetStaticModuleState());
//         // normal function body here
//      }
//
//      It is very important that this macro appear in each
//      function, prior to any calls into MFC.  This means that
//      it must appear as the first statement within the
//      function, even before any object variable declarations
//      as their constructors may generate calls into the MFC
//      DLL.
//
//      Please see MFC Technical Notes 33 and 58 for additional
//      details.
//

/////////////////////////////////////
// CAbortdllApp

BEGIN_MESSAGE_MAP(CAbortdllApp, CWinApp)
   //{{AFX_MSG_MAP(CAbortdllApp)
      // NOTE - the Class Wizard will add and remove mapping macros here.
      //    DO NOT EDIT what you see in these blocks of generated code!
   //}}AFX_MSG_MAP
END_MESSAGE_MAP()

/////////////////////////////////////
// CAbortdllApp construction
```

```
CAbortdllApp::CAbortdllApp()
{
   // TODO: add construction code here,
   // Place all significant initialization in InitInstance
}

///////////////////////////////////
// The one and only CAbortdllApp object

CAbortdllApp theApp;


extern "C" {
   __declspec(dllexport) BOOL AbortBox(char *text,char *event);
   }

__declspec(dllexport) BOOL AbortBox(char *text, char *event)
   {
   AFX_MANAGE_STATE(AfxGetStaticModuleState( ));
   CAbortThread *t=(CAbortThread *)
      AfxBeginThread(RUNTIME_CLASS(CAbortThread),
         THREAD_PRIORITY_NORMAL,0,CREATE_SUSPENDED);
   if (!t)
      {
      ::MessageBox(NULL,"Can't spawn thread",NULL,MB_OK);
      return FALSE;
      }
   // Set up parameters
   t->text=text;
   t->eventname=event;
   t->ResumeThread();
   return TRUE;
   }
```

Listing 3.9 The abort thread.

```
// AbortThread.cpp : implementation file
//

#include "stdafx.h"
#include "abortdll.h"
#include "AbortThread.h"
#include "Abortdlg.h"

#ifdef _DEBUG
#define new DEBUG_NEW
```

```
#undef THIS_FILE
static char THIS_FILE[] = __FILE__;
#endif

/////////////////////////////////////
// CAbortThread

IMPLEMENT_DYNCREATE(CAbortThread, CWinThread)

CAbortThread::CAbortThread()
{
}

CAbortThread::~CAbortThread()
{
}

BOOL CAbortThread::InitInstance()
{
   CAbortDlg dlg;
   m_pMainWnd=&dlg;
   event=new CEvent(FALSE,TRUE,eventname);
   dlg.m_text=text;
   dlg.Thread=this;
   dlg.DoModal();
   delete event;
   return FALSE;
}

int CAbortThread::ExitInstance()
{
   // TODO:  perform any per-thread cleanup here
   return CWinThread::ExitInstance();
}

BEGIN_MESSAGE_MAP(CAbortThread, CWinThread)
   //{{AFX_MSG_MAP(CAbortThread)
      // NOTE - the Class Wizard will add and remove mapping macros here.
   //}}AFX_MSG_MAP
END_MESSAGE_MAP()

/////////////////////////////////////
// CAbortThread message handlers
```

If you really study the code, it is amazingly unremarkable. The dialog is just a regular dialog box. The **CAbortThread** class (created with Class Wizard) is very closely related to an ordinary **CWinApp** object and serves the same purpose. The DLL code is certainly ordinary.

The only special part of the **AbortBox** code is the communication between the main program and the abort thread. The calling program creates an event using any name it chooses. It then passes this name as one of the arguments to **AbortBox**. The abort thread also opens the event. You'll read more about events in Chapter 4.

The *event* serves two purposes. First, if the user aborts, the MFC code signals the event. This enables the creating thread to know when an abort occurs. Second, if the original code signals the event, the MFC code takes that as a sign to shut down.

Listing 3.10 The abort dialog box.

```
// AbortDlg.cpp : implementation file
//

#include "stdafx.h"
#include "abortdll.h"
#include "AbortThread.h"
#include "AbortDlg.h"

#ifdef _DEBUG
#define new DEBUG_NEW
#undef THIS_FILE
static char THIS_FILE[] = __FILE__;
#endif

/////////////////////////////////////
// CAbortDlg dialog


CAbortDlg::CAbortDlg(CWnd* pParent /*=NULL*/)
   : CDialog(CAbortDlg::IDD, pParent)
{
   //{{AFX_DATA_INIT(CAbortDlg)
   m_text = _T("");
   //}}AFX_DATA_INIT
}
```

```
void CAbortDlg::DoDataExchange(CDataExchange* pDX)
{
   CDialog::DoDataExchange(pDX);
   //{{AFX_DATA_MAP(CAbortDlg)
   DDX_Text(pDX, IDC_TEXT, m_text);
   //}}AFX_DATA_MAP
}


BEGIN_MESSAGE_MAP(CAbortDlg, CDialog)
   //{{AFX_MSG_MAP(CAbortDlg)
   ON_WM_TIMER()
   //}}AFX_MSG_MAP
END_MESSAGE_MAP()

/////////////////////////////////////
// CAbortDlg message handlers



void CAbortDlg::OnOK()
{
   Thread->event->SetEvent();
   CDialog::OnOK();
}

BOOL CAbortDlg::OnInitDialog()
{
   CDialog::OnInitDialog();

   SetTimer(1,500,NULL); // Timer every 1/2 second
   return TRUE;  // return TRUE unless you set the focus to a control
                 // EXCEPTION: OCX Property Pages should return FALSE
}

void CAbortDlg::OnTimer(UINT nIDEvent)
{
   CSingleLock lock(Thread->event,FALSE);
   if (lock.Lock(0))
      {
      CDialog::OnOK();
      }
}
```

Other than the event and the custom **CWinThread** object, this could be any MFC program. Because **AbortBox** is just an ordinary exported function, you could call it from almost any program. Of course, **AbortBox** is overly simple, but you can easily apply the same concepts to more difficult tasks.

Listing 3.11 A console program to test the DLL.

```
#include <stdio.h>
#include <windows.h>

// DLL Function
extern "C" {
   BOOL AbortBox(char *string,char *eventname); // DLL function
   }

void main()
   {
   HANDLE event;
   unsigned int ct=0;
   event=CreateEvent(NULL,TRUE,FALSE,"CONABORTEVENT");
   AbortBox("Press the Abort button to terminate the console"
      " application","CONABORTEVENT");
   while (WaitForSingleObject(event,0)==WAIT_TIMEOUT&&ct<100000)
      {
      printf("%d\n",ct);
      ct+=2;
      }
   if (WaitForSingleObject(event,0)==WAIT_TIMEOUT)
      {
      SetEvent(event); // make sure AbortBox gets the message
      ::MessageBox(NULL,"Done","Operation Complete",MB_OK|MB_SETFOREGROUND);
      }
   // No message if aborted by AbortBox
   CloseHandle(event);
   }
```

Using Thread Local Storage

Thread local storage (TLS) is a system that enables threads to have private variables. Windows reserves at least 64 tables in each process to serve as TLS variables. You reserve a table with the **TlsAlloc** function. This function reserves an index that you store in a global variable. This index identifies a value that is global, yet unique for each thread.

When a thread wants to access a variable, it calls **TlsSetValue** or **TlsGetValue** with the index that **TlsAlloc** returns. That means that you call **TlsAlloc** only once near the beginning of your code. Then each thread uses the same index value for a particular TLS variable.

When you no longer need a TLS variable, you can reclaim its table by passing the index to **TlsFree**. This enables the system to reuse that table for another variable in the future. If you want to see an example of TLS in action, check out Listing 3.5.

Using Fibers

If you want to make threads cooperate, you need synchronization methods (see Chapter 4). However, sometimes it would be easier if you could use things that look like threads, but which can handle their scheduling among themselves. That's the purpose of fibers.

You can't create a new fiber directly. Instead, you convert a thread into a fiber by calling **ConvertThreadToFiber**. From that point forward, the thread is really a fiber. When Windows schedules the thread, the active fiber (initially the code the thread would run anyway) gains control.

The new fiber can create more fibers (by calling **CreateFiber**). The active fiber remains active until it calls **SwitchToFiber**. This makes a new fiber active. The newly activated fiber will remain active until it calls **SwitchToFiber**.

There are a few other calls that you can use with fibers: **DeleteFiber** destroys a fiber; **GetCurrentFiber** tells you which fiber is currently active; and **GetFiberData** returns the argument passed to the main fiber function. You can find a fiber example in Listing 3.6.

Using Alternatives To Threading

Although threading is very useful for background processing, it isn't the only game in town. If you have operations that don't interact much, you could always write them as separate programs. Windows provides many methods for such programs to communicate, although not at the high bandwidth afforded to threads.

Another option you should consider in some cases is idle processing. In a regular C program, you can do idle processing by modifying your event loop. Just change the usual call to **GetMessage** to utilize **PeekMessage** instead. If **PeekMessage** indicates you have no messages, you are free to do a small amount of idle processing.

MFC programmers will find their application object has an **OnIdle** member that MFC calls when there are no messages pending for the thread. Of course, you have to be careful not to do too much during idle time processing. It wouldn't be a good idea to wait for serial port input during **OnIdle**, for example. However, for background printing or similar tasks, it is a viable option. It also has the advantage of working on 16-bit Windows, which doesn't support threads.

Yet another way to avoid multithreading is by using overlapped I/O. You'll learn more about overlapped I/O in Chapter 5.

Chapter 4

Synchronization

If you need an immediate solution to:	*See page:*
Selecting A Synchronization Method	187
Avoiding Deadlock	189
Using Events	189
Using Mutexes	190
Using Critical Sections	190
Using Semaphores	191
Waiting For Multiple Objects	191
Using Interlocked Variables	191
Understanding MFC And Synchronization	192

In Depth

Anyone that knows me will tell you I love jokes. I suppose I got this from my father. He always had a joke or silly story. Too bad dad didn't have better material, because he was a good joke teller. He just usually had really corny jokes.

Regardless, I wound up with a great love of jokes. I like to think I have better material than my father did (meaning I steal my jokes from funnier comedians). I do write a bit of my own stuff from time to time, and I've even done a few minutes of schtick in front of an audience (just as an amateur). That can be pretty addictive (if you don't think so, watch the movie *Punchline* with Tom Hanks and Sally Fields).

Ask anyone who tells jokes what's important and you'll get a different answer each time. The truth is comedy is personal. What works for one person might not work for another. Some people do physical comedy (such as Gallagher or Sam Kinnison). Some do thought-provoking jokes (George Carlin and Robert Klein, for instance). Impressions are very popular (I've always wanted to see someone do an impression of Rich Little). I'm more of a storyteller, myself.

So, what do I think is important when telling jokes? I think the most important thing is memory. There's nothing worse than someone telling you a joke that goes like this: "Ummm...there was this guy...he, um, went to the store...no wait...it was a lady...so she went to the store and...let's see...." You have to remember your jokes. The second most important thing, for storytelling anyway, is to have a variety of voices. There are several stories I like to tell that are funny only because of the silly voices I do with them.

If you tell other kinds of jokes, a different set of skills might be important. However, everyone that loves jokes tells the occasional short, quick, joke (called a one-liner). So what's important to the one-liner?

Henny Youngman, the king of the one-liners, always wanted someone to ask him something. He might say, "Ask me what's a Grecian Urn." When the unwitting straightman would ask the question, Henny would rattle off, "About $4 an hour!" Of course, next time, it might be a henway (4 to 5 pounds).

Of course, my favorite Henny Youngman question went like this:

Henny: Ask me what's the most important skill for a comedian.

Dupe: What's the most important—

Henny: Timing!

Timing is important to comedians. It is also important to computer programs. This is especially true if you are writing programs that use multiple threads or multiple processes. It is important that threads perform operations in the correct sequence. That's why Windows provides several forms of synchronization to help you make threads work the way they should.

Defining The Problem

There are several reasons it might be important to synchronize threads. There are several different tools you can use to fit the specific situation.

Scenario #1

Suppose you have a program that performs "what-if" calculations on a set of data. Maybe you are trying to maximize profits, find the shortest way through a maze, or optimize a schedule. You might have one thread set up the initial data set. Then, when the thread is done, other threads might each try a different algorithm against the data. Finally, when all the computation threads complete their calculations, the **main** thread would report the results.

To write a program like this, you might start all the threads right away. This allows the computation threads to do any initialization they might need while the **main** thread is preparing the data. However, you need a way to prevent the computation threads from accessing the data until it is ready. So, the threads need to wait (or block) until the data-gathering thread is ready.

Windows provides an object called an *event* to handle this type of situation. An event does not have anything to do with a Windows message, nor is it asynchronous in any way. A better name for an event might be *shared flag*. The calculating threads could wait for an event that the **main** thread sets when it is ready. There are several types of events, each of which has its own use.

You also need a method to know when the calculation threads finish. You could use an event for that, too. Of course, you could also just detect when the threads exit using **GetExitCodeThread**, **WaitForSingleObject**, or **WaitForMultipleObjects** (see Chapter 3). That's possible in this case, because once the threads complete their calculations, they no longer need to run.

Scenario #2

Perhaps you are writing a set of programs that all write error information to a common log file. What happens if one program opens the file, begins writing, and then Windows pre-empts it? Windows schedules a new program, which tries to open the error file and write to it also. This won't work correctly. Exactly what happens depends on how the original program opens the file. Assuming it opens the file for exclusive access, the second program fails to open the file. If the file is shareable, however, the two programs' output may interleave, causing confusion.

The answer here is to maintain a flag that programs must test and set before opening the file. If the flag is already set, the program must wait until it is clear. So step-by-step, each program performs the following:

1. Reads the flag's value.
2. If the flag is set, goes back to Step 1.
3. Sets the flag.
4. Opens the file.
5. Writes the error messages.
6. Closes the file.
7. Clears the flag.

This sounds great, but what if Windows pre-empts one program after Step 1 but before Step 2? Another program might then execute the same steps while the first program is sleeping. The second program, then, has the flag set. But when the first program resumes, it is still examining the old copy of the flag. It will then set the flag and continue. On multiple-processor systems, this doesn't even require pre-emption, since the two threads might be executing on different processors.

Somehow, you need a way to test and set the flag in one uninterruptable operation. Windows provides several primitives that allow just that (for example, **InterlockedIncrement**). However, you'll rarely use this call, because Win32 provides higher-level constructs to do the same job.

Usually, you'll manage a situation like this using a *mutex* (short for mutual exclusion). When a thread asks to own a mutex, Windows will allow it only if it is currently unowned. Once a thread owns the mutex, other threads can't own it until the original thread releases it. There is no opportunity for the threads to conflict and both acquire the mutex.

Scenario #3

Imagine a database client program that makes requests of a network server. One of your design goals is to prevent any one workstation from flooding the server with requests. You decide to limit the number of outstanding network requests from one machine to three. Each request is in a different thread, so you can't use a simple counter.

There are many ways you might do this. You could, for example, have three mutexes. A thread that wants to make a request would have to gain ownership of one mutex. However, a better approach is to use semaphores. A *semaphore* is a synchronization object that contains a count (for example, three). Each time a thread requests access to the semaphore, the count goes down by one. When the count reaches zero, the semaphore is not available.

You could easily limit the workstation traffic using a semaphore. Before you make a request of the server, you must acquire a count from the semaphore. When the semaphore runs out of counts, you'll have to wait.

More About Synchronization

As you can see from the previous three examples, there are many reasons you might need to make threads cooperate. For any situation, there are usually several ways you might synchronize, and Windows provides methods to accommodate you.

When you start trying to cooperate between threads, you run a risk of causing deadlocks. Suppose a thread attempts to open file A and file B. Another thread opens file B and later opens file A. It is possible that when the first thread tries to open file B, it will already be open (by the other thread). Conversely, when the second thread tries to open file A, the first thread may already have it open, too. This can happen if the operating system pre-empts the threads at inopportune times, or if the threads are running on different processors.

If neither thread releases any resources (open files, in this case), the threads will deadlock. Neither will ever be able to open the files it requires. There are many possible solutions to this problem. A simple one is to release all your resources if you can't get all of them. Later, you can try to open them all again. Of course, a mutex could work here as well. In this very simple case, it would suffice to make sure the threads always open file A before file B (however, that isn't always easy to arrange).

Deadlock isn't a new idea. You can find discussions of it in any operating system text. Just a little common-sense design can go a long way toward preventing deadlock.

Synchronization Details

All of the main synchronization objects (events, mutexes, and semaphores) have a great deal in common. There are also a few other objects that perform similar functions you'll see a bit later, but for now, focus on these main three objects.

Usually, one thread calls a special function to create a synchronization object (for example, **CreateEvent**). If you are working only with threads inside the same process, you don't need to name the object. However, if you want to share the object between processes, it is customary to name it. The name is case-sensitive and can't contain the backslash character. All the object types share the same names. So you can't name an event **Coriolis**, and then name a semaphore the same thing. If you don't name the object, other processes can access it only via inheritance.

The creation call will return a handle. Any thread in the same process can share the same handle. Other processes may inherit the handle, although this is awkward. That's because you also have to inform the child process of the handle value via a command line argument, environment variable, or similar device. Otherwise, the new process has no way to know what handle the object uses. A better idea is to let the other process call an open call (like **OpenEvent**) using the same name the creating thread assigned the object. This call returns a handle the caller can use.

Sometimes, it is difficult to know which thread will execute first. In those cases, it is a good idea to call the create call from each thread. If you try to create an object that already exists, the create call works like an open call. In other cases, you definitely want the program to know if the object doesn't already exist. In those cases, you'll want to stick with the open call.

Given you have a handle (either from a create call, an open call, or inheritance) you can determine if the object is in the signaled state. Exactly what this means depends on the object. An event is in this state when it is set. Mutexes signal when they don't have an owner (and finding that out, they make your thread the owner). Semaphores signal if their count is greater than zero, and checking decreases the count.

To determine the state, you'll usually call **WaitForSingleObject**. This call lets you specify how long you will wait for the object to signal. You specify the time in milliseconds. If the time is zero, the call will not wait at all. If you specify **INFINITE**, the call will never return until the object signals.

While your thread waits, it consumes practically no processor time. This makes it very efficient to wait for an object to signal. Sometimes you want to wait for any of a number of objects. Then you can use **WaitForMultipleObjects**. There are a few other calls you'll see later that can wait for an object.

WaitForSingleObject may return several different values depending on what it finds. If the object is in the signaled state, it returns **WAIT_OBJECT_0**. If the call times out without finding the object signaled, it returns **WAIT_TIMEOUT**.

Also, if a process that is holding a mutex terminates with the mutex open, the system will assign your waiting thread the mutex and return **WAIT_ABANDONED**.

When you no longer want to own a mutex, you call **ReleaseMutex**. If you don't need the semaphore count you reserved earlier, you call **ReleaseSemaphore**. This isn't the same as closing the object (via **CloseHandle**). It just releases your claim to the mutex, or increments the semaphore count by one. After you make these calls, you can no longer access the resource the object protects. For example, if a mutex indicates you are using a shared file, you should not write to that file after calling **ReleaseMutex**.

If you absolutely don't need an object anymore, you call **CloseHandle**. Of course, **CloseHandle** isn't just for synchronization objects; it will close any handle your process has access to.

The Interlocked Calls

Windows provides several interlocked calls that enable you to access variables without fear of pre-emption by the operating system. You'll find these calls in Table 4.1. Although you can use these calls, you'll find that events, mutexes, and semaphores are much more useful.

The interlocked calls in Table 4.1 operate on a 32-bit value. This variable must be aligned on a 32-bit boundary. If you are attempting to synchronize threads, you can use an ordinary global variable. If you want to work between processes, you'll need to put the variable in some form of shared memory (see Chapter 6).

Perhaps the most generally useful call is the **InterlockedCompareExchange** call. This call compares the variable to a given value. If the variable and the value are equal, the function swaps the variable with another variable of your choice. All this occurs in a way that prevents any other thread from accessing the variable at the same time.

Table 4.1 Interlocked calls.

Call	Purpose
InterlockedDecrement	Subtracts one from the interlocked variable
InterlockedIncrement	Adds one to the interlocked variable
InterlockedExchange	Exchanges the value of the interlocked variable with another variable
InterlockedExchangeAdd	Adds a value to an interlocked variable
InterlockedCompareExchange	Compares the interlocked variable with a value, and exchanges it with another value if the comparison is true

If you had a variable **tflag**, and you wanted to set it to 1, but only if it was already zero, you might write:

```
. . .
PVOID var=(PVOID)&tflag;
PVOID newval=(PVOID)1;
PVOID compare=(PVOID)0;
InterlockedCompareExchange(&var,newval,compare);
if (newval==1)  . . . ;  // did not compare
else {
   // flag was 0, now is 1
. . .
```


Events In Detail

You can find the calls related to events in Table 4.2. When you create an event, you specify if it is a manual event or a single event. A *manual event* is no more than a shared flag. Any thread can set it (signal it) with **SetEvent** or clear it with **ResetEvent**. Once signaled, the event remains in that state no matter how many threads wait for it. You can also call **PulseEvent**. Making this call causes any threads currently waiting for the event to succeed (in other words, the **WaitForSingleObject** call succeeds, and the thread can continue). Once all the waiting threads continue, the system resets the event.

Sometimes, this isn't what you want. You might want only one thread to go each time there is an event. That's the purpose of a single event. When you set a *single event* (again, using **SetEvent**), exactly one waiting thread will succeed. Then the system automatically resets the event. If there are no threads waiting, the event remains signaled until one thread does wait for it (unlike **PulseEvent**, which resets immediately).

Which event is right for you? That depends on exactly what you want to accomplish. In the Scenario #1 example earlier in this chapter, you would want a manual event. After you set the event all threads are free to go.

What if your program had to multiply many large matrices together (maybe for circuit analysis, wind tunnel simulation, or image processing)? Assuming the order didn't matter, you might start several threads, each reading a matrix from disk. When the first matrix is ready, it sets a single event. Every other thread waits for the event before it does its multiplication. Then it sets the event again. In this way, each thread would have to wait until the one before it finishes.

Table 4.2 Event calls.

Call	Purpose
CreateEvent	Creates an event or opens an existing one
OpenEvent	Opens an existing event
SetEvent	Signals the event
ResetEvent	Resets the event
PulseEvent	Signals the event until all waiting threads unblock; then, resets the event

Listing 4.1 shows a simple test program that demonstrates a single event. First run the program with no arguments. This will cause the program to wait for the event. Next, run the program again, but this time supply a command line argument (it doesn't matter what). This causes the program to set the event, and therefore releases the first invocation of the program.

Because the event is a single event, try running several copies with no command line arguments. Then, each time you run the program with the command line argument, a single instance of the program that is waiting will complete.

Listing 4.1 Event test.

```
#include <windows.h>
#include <iostream.h>

void main(int argc,char *argv[])
{
   // create or open event
   HANDLE ev=CreateEvent(NULL,FALSE,FALSE,"nt5bbevent");
   if (argc==1)
   {
      cout<<"Waiting for event!\n";
      cout.flush();
      WaitForSingleObject(ev,INFINITE);
      cout<<"Event fired!\n";
      cout.flush();
   }
   else
   {
      cout<<"Setting event\n";
      SetEvent(ev);
   }
   CloseHandle(ev);

}
```

Mutexes In Detail

When your thread owns a mutex, it has exclusive use of the resource that the mutex protects. While your thread owns the mutex, no other thread can acquire it. However, the owning thread can acquire the mutex multiple times. It has to release the mutex as many times as it owns it. See Table 4.3 for a list of mutex-related calls.

This behavior, at first glance, seems counterintuitive. But with a little more reflection, you'll see that it makes sense. Suppose you have a mutex protecting an error log file. You have a function that reports an error named **E1**. The **E1** function acquires the mutex, outputs its message (to the already open file handle), and releases the mutex. Further imagine that the **E2** function also outputs an error, but as part of its work, it calls **E1**. Of course, it also acquires (and releases) the mutex.

If thread A calls **E2**, and thread B calls **E1** a little later, B has to wait until A releases the mutex. That's what you would expect. However, what happens when **E2**, while executing within thread A, calls **E1**? If the current thread couldn't own the mutex multiple times, you would be in big trouble. The thread would deadlock on itself. **E1** couldn't execute until **E2** completes, but **E2** couldn't complete until **E1** executes.

Luckily, mutexes don't allow this situation to occur. When **E1** (on behalf of thread A) requests the mutex, Windows realizes that the thread already owns the mutex, so it allows **E1** to acquire the mutex again. When **E1** releases the mutex, Windows is smart enough to realize that function **E2** still has a lock on the mutex, so thread A still owns it until **E2** also releases.

It is important to realize that mutexes are traffic cops with no authority. If a mutex protects an open file, it does so only because you always check that you own the mutex before you write to the file. Windows doesn't enforce anything. As far as the system knows, the mutex is just a shared object that you can signal or unsignal depending on the calls you make. What it means is up to you.

Sometimes you need the functionality of a mutex for several threads in one process, but not between processes. You can use a mutex in these cases, but you'll

Table 4.3 Mutex calls.

Call	Purpose
CreateMutex	Creates a new mutex or opens an existing one
OpenMutex	Opens an existing mutex
ReleaseMutex	Releases ownership of a mutex, making it available to other threads

probably get better performance if you can use a critical section. A *critical section* is a form of mutex that only works inside one process. A critical section has other limitations that you'll read about later in this chapter.

Listing 4.2 shows a simple program that exercises the essential mutex functions. Run the program and note that it acquires the mutex and displays a message box. Do not dismiss the message box yet. Then run another copy of the program. The new copy will be unable to acquire the mutex until the first copy completes. In other words, each new copy must wait until you dismiss the message box that is currently active. If you run several copies, only one copy at a time will display the message box.

Listing 4.2 Mutex test program.

```
#include <windows.h>
#include <iostream.h>

void main()
{
   HANDLE mtx=CreateMutex(NULL,FALSE,"NT5BBMTX");
   cout<<"Attempting mutex\n";
   cout.flush();
   WaitForSingleObject(mtx,INFINITE);
   cout<<"Mutex acquired!\n";
   cout.flush();
   MessageBox(NULL,"Acquired mutex","MUTEX",MB_OK);
   ReleaseMutex(mtx);
   CloseHandle(mtx);
}
```


Semaphores In Detail

If you understand events and mutexes, semaphores are quite straightforward. When you create a semaphore, you specify an initial count. Table 4.4 shows the calls you will use with semaphores. There's no big secret to working with semaphores. Every time a wait succeeds, the semaphore's count decreases by one. When the count reaches zero, the semaphore is no longer signaled.

Table 4.4 Semaphore calls.

Call	Purpose
CreateSemaphore	Creates a new semaphore or opens an existing one
OpenSemaphore	Opens an existing semaphore
ReleaseSemaphore	Adds a number of counts to the semaphore (usually 1) to make it available for more threads

If a thread waits on a semaphore twice, it consumes two counts from the semaphore's pool. This is different from mutexes, which count multiple accesses from the same thread as if they were one access.

Listing 4.3 is a simple program that tests semaphores. The program attempts to acquire a semaphore count before showing a message box. Once three message boxes are active, the fourth (and subsequent) invocations of the program will block. When you dismiss a message box, one of the waiting programs will continue.

Listing 4.3 Semaphore demo.

```
#include <windows.h>
#include <iostream.h>

void main()
{
   HANDLE sem=CreateSemaphore(NULL,3,3,"nt5bbsem");
   cout<<"Attempting semaphore\n";
   cout.flush();
   WaitForSingleObject(sem,INFINITE);
   cout<<"Got semaphore\n";
   cout.flush();
   MessageBox(NULL,"Acquired semaphore","Semaphore",MB_OK);
   ReleaseSemaphore(sem,1,NULL);
   CloseHandle(sem);
}
```


Secure Synchronization

There is a slight security problem intrinsic with synchronization. Suppose you are writing a program to control a nuclear missile silo. You have multiple processes: one for handling missile maintenance, another for navigation programming, a third for status reporting, and a fourth for fire control. You don't want to confuse the missile, so each process (thread, actually) has to acquire a mutex before it communicates with the missile. Your design prevents any process from holding the mutex open for very long.

To facilitate this scheme, you create a named mutex within each process. In reality, only the first process to run creates the mutex; the others simply open the existing one. Suppose an enemy agent, however, learns the name of your mutex. The agent writes a clever program that opens the mutex and holds it open forever. Until you figure out what's happening and kill the enemy process, you can't operate the missile.

One possible answer to this problem is to avoid naming the mutex. Suppose you have one program that creates a nameless mutex and then executes the other processes, allowing them to inherit the open mutex handle. Of course, the new processes won't know what the handle's value is, so the main program can pass the value on the command line to the new programs.

Now each program can access the mutex. But even if a hostile program learned the handle value, the enemy process would not have access to the handle. Of course, there are other ways you might secure the handles (using normal security, for example). Still, this method has the virtue of simplicity. Of course, no method is invulnerable to attack, but for a small amount of effort, inheriting nameless handles is actually quite secure.

Using WaitForMultipleObjects

Sometimes you want to wait for any of several objects. That's when **WaitForMultipleObjects** is useful. This call takes an array of object handles. When any one of the handles signals, the call returns and tells you which object is ready. Like the usual wait call, you can specify any timeout you like (including 0 and **INFINITE**).

The **WaitForMultipleObjects** call, of course, implements a logical **OR**. Any object can satisfy the wait. What if you want a logical **AND**? Easy. Just set the **bWaitAll** parameter to **TRUE**.

Another call you can use to wait for multiple objects is the **MsgWaitForMultipleObjectsEx** call. This call enables you to wait for any one object to signal. However, it will also exit if certain types of messages occur. You can use this to wait for something and still respond to **WM_PAINT** messages, for example.

You can also instruct **MsgWaitForMultipleObjectsEx** to wait for all the objects to signal, including the messages you specify. Of course, if you wait for all objects and events, you still won't process events until all of the objects signal, which largely defeats the purpose of using this call.

When a **WaitForMultipleObjects** call succeeds, it returns a value in a range to indicate which object signaled (if it is only waiting for one object). If you are waiting for all objects, the exact value is unpredictable, but will be in the range. The range for successful completion is from **WAIT_OBJECT_0** to **WAIT_OBJECT_0** plus the number of items in the array. **WAIT_ABANDON_0** (the same as **WAIT_ABANDON**) marks the start of the range for an abandoned mutex. Of course, **WAIT_TIMEOUT** is always just that. There is no need for the call to return a range of values for a timeout condition.

Alertable Waits

There are three additional calls you can use to wait on a handle: **WaitForSingleObjectEx**, **MsgWaitForMultipleObjectsEx**, and **WaitForMultipleObjectsEx**. The difference between these functions and their non-Ex counterparts? These waits have a Boolean parameter that enables you to specify that they are alertable.

What's alertable? When a program is in an alertable wait, it can process asynchronous procedure calls (APCs). Usually, these calls happen as a result of asynchronous I/O (see Chapter 5). Another way to queue an APC is with the **QueueUserAPC** call (see Chapter 3). When an APC is pending on a thread, the APC doesn't execute until the thread is waiting and in an alertable state. That means it must be executing one of the three calls mentioned or **SleepEx** (which may also cause an alertable state to occur). You can learn more about APCs in Chapter 3.

Waitable Timers

Another way to cause an APC is via an alertable timer. You use **CreateWaitableTimer** or **OpenWaitableTimer** in a similar fashion to the other synchronization objects. The timer signals when its timeout period expires. However, you can also use it to queue an APC when the timer expires. Like all APCs, the timer APC doesn't actually execute until the target thread is in an alertable wait state.

It may seem confusing, but you can't wait on a timer and expect it to deliver APCs to the same thread. That's because when the timer signals, the thread is no longer waiting, and therefore unable to process the APC.

Using **CreateWaitableTimer** or **OpenWaitableTimer** returns a handle to the timer. To actually begin a timing period, you call **SetWaitableTimer**. You specify the time as a **LARGE_INTEGER** in 100-nanosecond units. However, your hardware probably doesn't really support timing with 100-nanosecond resolution. If the time is positive, it indicates an absolute time period. Negative values refer to a relative time. You can also specify if you want the timer to fire once and quit, or fire over and over again at predefined intervals.

When the timer expires, it signals. It also can call a completion routine as an APC. You can stop the timer by calling **CancelWaitableTimer**.

Critical Sections

Usually, if you want to prevent programs from using a resource at the same time, you'll use a mutex. What if you have a function that you want only one thread to call at any one time? You could use a mutex for this purpose, of course. Each thread has to acquire the mutex before it calls the function.

This will work, but a mutex has a great deal of overhead for this simple (and common) task. To help this situation, Windows supports critical sections (see Table 4.5). A *critical section* uses a simple variable in your process as a flag that prevents multiple threads from executing the same piece of code.

To protect a piece of code, define a **CRITICAL_SECTION** variable and pass its address to **InitializeCriticalSection**. You only need to make this call from one thread (usually your **main** thread). Then, the critical function starts with a call to **EnterCriticalSection**. If another thread is inside the protected function, this call will block until the first thread completes. If you don't want to block, you can call **TryEnterCriticalSection** instead. If the call succeeds, you may proceed into the protected code. If the call fails, the thread has to do something else, and call **TryEnterCriticalSection** again.

TryEnterCriticalSection will continue to fail (and **EnterCriticalSection** will continue to block) until the thread inside the protected function calls **LeaveCriticalSection**. A typical function looks like this:

```
void one_at_a_time_please()
  {
  EnterCriticalSection(&section);  // assume Init somewhere else
  // Do protected things here
  LeaveCriticalSection(&section);
  }
```

Or:

```
BOOL only_one_at_a_time()
  {
  if (!TryEnterCriticalSection(&section))  // assume Init somewhere else
      return FALSE;  // operation busy right now
  // do protected things here
  LeaveCriticalSection(&section);
   return TRUE;  // we did it
  }
```

When you no longer need a critical section, you can call **DeleteCriticalSection** to destroy it. This frees resources associated with the critical section.

There is another call that first appeared in NT 4.0 Service Pack 3 that can initialize critical sections. This call (**InitializeCriticalSectionAndSpinCount**) works just like **InitializeCriticalSection** if it executes on a single-processor machine.

Table 4.5 Critical section calls.

Call	Purpose
InitializeCriticalSection	Sets up a CRITICAL_SECTION variable
InitializeCriticalSectionAndSpinCount	Sets up a CRITICAL_SECTION variable and initializes the spin count (see text)
EnterCriticalSection	Enters a critical section, blocking if another thread is in the section
TryEnterCriticalSection	Attempts to enter a critical section, returns an error if another thread is in the section
LeaveCriticalSection	Leaves a critical section, allowing other threads to enter
SetCriticalSectionSpinCount	Sets the spin count (see text)
DeleteCritcalSection	Destroys a CRITICAL_SECTION variable

However, when the computer has multiple processors, it has a slight efficiency advantage. In these cases, if a thread finds the critical section in use, it waits (spins) for a small amount of time, determined by the spin count. If the critical section remains unavailable for that time, then the thread does a more expensive wait operation (similar to **WaitForSingleObject**). You can set the spin count for any critical section using **SetCriticalSectionSpinCount**. On a single processor system, these calls have no effect, because there must be a thread switch before the critical section can become available, anyway.

A Major Example

It isn't uncommon to use several different synchronization methods in a single program—it just depends on what you need. Figure 4.1 shows a simple console-based video game. What makes it unusual is that it is highly-threaded and uses most of the major synchronization objects (events, semaphores, mutexes, and critical sections). It also uses the **InterlockedIncrement** call.

The premise of the game is simple. You control a firing base with the left and right arrow keys. Bad guys move across the top of the window either from right to left or left to right. You can fire a shot at the bad guys by pressing the spacebar. You can shoot up to three shots at once. Every second, the game may (or may not) create a new bad guy. The likelihood of a bad guy appearing increases as the game continues. Also, the bad guys travel faster as play continues.

You score a point for each bad guy you hit. When a bad guy escapes, that counts as a miss. Once you've missed 30 bad guys, the game is over. You can keep track of the score by looking at the game's title bar.

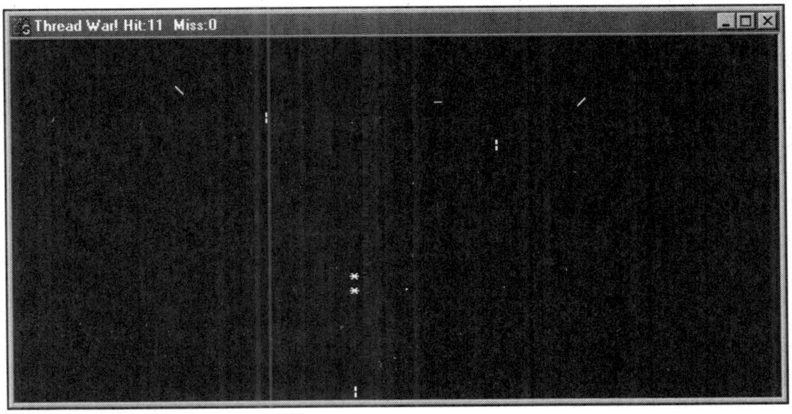

Figure 4.1 Thread War.

When the game starts, you should maximize the console window (double-clicking on the title bar works well). Bad guys don't appear until you press one of the arrow keys (left or right). However, if you don't press an arrow key within 15 seconds, the bad guys will start coming anyway.

The program is much simpler than you might expect (see Listing 4.4). This is due largely to the heavy use of threads. The **main** thread handles the drawing of the firing base and the keyboard input. The **main** thread also starts a new thread that handles generating bad guys. Each bad guy is also a thread. When you fire a shot, the shot becomes a new thread, too.

Listing 4.4 Thread War.

```
// Thread War
// Simple video game
// Use left/right arrow keys to move your fire base
// spacebar fires
// When 30 bad guys leave the screen unshot, you lose
// Score points for each bad guy you hit

#include <windows.h>
#include <process.h>
#include <stdlib.h>
#include <time.h>
#include <stdio.h>

// sync objects
HANDLE screenlock;  // only one thread changes the screen
HANDLE bulletsem;   // max 3 shots at a time
HANDLE startevt;   // Wait for arrow key before starting
```

```
HANDLE conin,conout; // console handles
HANDLE mainthread;  // The main thread
CRITICAL_SECTION gameover;

CONSOLE_SCREEN_BUFFER_INFO info; // info about the console
// our hit and miss counters
long hit=0;
long miss=0;
long delayfactor=7;  // bad guy delay factor


// Create a random number from n0 to n1
int random(int n0,int n1)
{
   if (n0==0&&n1==1) return rand()%2; // special case
   return rand()%(n1-n0)+n0;
}

// Clear console screen
void cls()
{
   COORD org={0,0};
   DWORD res;
   FillConsoleOutputCharacter(conout,
      ' ',info.dwSize.X*info.dwSize.Y,org,&res);
}


// write a character at the given x and y
void writeat(int x,int y,char c)
{
   // Lock screen mutex
   WaitForSingleObject(screenlock,INFINITE);
   COORD pos={x,y};
   DWORD res;
   WriteConsoleOutputCharacter(conout,&c,1,pos,&res);
   ReleaseMutex(screenlock);
}

// Get a key (repeat count in ct)
int getakey(int &ct)
{
   INPUT_RECORD input;
   DWORD res;
   while (1)
```

```
   {
      ReadConsoleInput(conin &input,1,&res);
// ignore non key events
      if (input.EventType!=KEY_EVENT) continue;
// ignore key up events
      if (!input.Event.KeyEvent.bKeyDown) continue;
      ct=input.Event.KeyEvent.wRepeatCount;
      return input.Event.KeyEvent.wVirtualKeyCode;
   }
}

// Handle ^C, ^Break, etc.
BOOL WINAPI ctrl(DWORD type)
{
   exit(0);
   return TRUE; //not reached
}

// Find character at screen position
int getat(int x,int y)
{
   char c;
   DWORD res;
   COORD org={x,y};
// Lock console, so no changes until we are done
   WaitForSingleObject(screenlock,INFINITE);
   ReadConsoleOutputCharacter(conout,&c,1,org,&res);
   ReleaseMutex(screenlock);  // unlock
   return c;
}

// display score in title bar and check for end
void score(void)
{
   char s[128];
   sprintf(s,"Thread War! Hit:%d  Miss:%d",hit,miss);
   SetConsoleTitle(s);
   if (miss>=30)
   {
      EnterCriticalSection(&gameover);
      SuspendThread(mainthread);  // stop main thread
      MessageBox(NULL,"Game Over!","Thread War",
         MB_OK|MB_SETFOREGROUND);
      exit(0);  // never leave critical section
   }
```

```
    if ((hit+miss)%20==0)
       InterlockedDecrement(&delayfactor);  // should be ilock
}

char badchar[]="-\\|/";
// this is the badguy thread
void badguy(void *_y)
{
   int y=(int)_y; // random y coordinate
   int dir;
   int x;
// odd y starts at left, even y starts at right
   x=y%2?0:info.dwSize.X;
// set the direction depending on left or right
   dir=x?-1:1;
// as long as you aren't at the screen edge
   while ((dir==1&&x!=info.dwSize.X)||(dir==-1&&x!=0))
   {
      int dly;
      BOOL hitme=FALSE;
      //  hit test here (bullet?)
      if (getat(x,y)=='*') hitme=TRUE;
// write the character
      writeat(x,y,badchar[x%4]);
      // check for bullet again
      if (getat(x,y)=='*') hitme=TRUE;
      // do small waits testing for bullets all the while
      if (delayfactor<3) dly=3;
      else dly=delayfactor+3;
      for (int i=0;i<dly;i++)
      {
         Sleep(40);
         if (getat(x,y)=='*')
         {
            hitme=TRUE;
            break;
         }
      }
      writeat(x,y,' ');
// one more bullet test
      if (getat(x,y)=='*') hitme=TRUE;
      if (hitme)
      {
         // hit me!
         MessageBeep(-1);
```

4. Synchronization

```
            InterlockedIncrement(&hit);
            score();
            _endthread();
         }
         x+=dir;
      }
      // count escaped!
      InterlockedIncrement(&miss);
      score();
   }

   // this thread generates bad guy threads
   void badguys(void *)
   {
      // wait for starting event or 15 seconds
      WaitForSingleObject(startevt,15000);
      // make random bad guys
      // every 5 seconds there is a chance of
      // making a new bad guy at a y coordinate of 1 to 10
      while (1)
      {
         if (random(0,100)<(hit+miss)/25+20)  // more likely all the time
            _beginthread(badguy,0,(void *)(random(1,10)));
         Sleep(1000);  // every 1 seconds
      }
   }

   // This is the bullet thread
   // each shot is a separate thread
   void bullet(void *_xy_)
   {
      COORD xy=*(COORD *)_xy_;
      if (getat(xy.X,xy.Y)=='*') return;  // already there so wait
      //  Check bullet semaphore
      // if the semaphore is at 0, give up
      if (WaitForSingleObject(bulletsem,0)==WAIT_TIMEOUT) return;
      while (--xy.Y)
      {
         writeat(xy.X,xy.Y,'*'); // write shot
         Sleep(100);
         writeat(xy.X,xy.Y,' ');  // erase shot
      }
      // shot done, so add 1 to semaphore
      ReleaseSemaphore(bulletsem,1,NULL);
   }
```

```
// The main program
void main()
{
   HANDLE me;
   // Set up global variables
   conin=GetStdHandle(STD_INPUT_HANDLE);
   conout=GetStdHandle(STD_OUTPUT_HANDLE);
   SetConsoleCtrlHandler(ctrl,TRUE);
   SetConsoleMode(conin,ENABLE_WINDOW_INPUT);
   me=GetCurrentThread(); // not a real handle
// change current thread pseudo handle to real handle
   DuplicateHandle(GetCurrentProcess(),me,GetCurrentProcess(),
      &mainthread,0,FALSE,DUPLICATE_SAME_ACCESS);
   startevt=CreateEvent(NULL,TRUE,FALSE,NULL);
   screenlock=CreateMutex(NULL,FALSE,NULL);
   InitializeCriticalSection(&gameover);
   bulletsem=CreateSemaphore(NULL,3,3,NULL);
   GetConsoleScreenBufferInfo(conout,&info);
   // Init score display
   score();
   // Randomize random # generator
   srand( (unsigned)time( NULL ) );
   cls(); // not really needed
// set initial position for fire base
   int y=info.dwSize.Y-1;
   int x=info.dwSize.X/2;
// start the badguys thread; won't do anything until
// I set the event (or 15 seconds pass)
   _beginthread(badguys,0,NULL);
// main game loop
   while (1)
   {
      int c,ct;
      writeat(x,y,'|');  // draw fire base
      c=getakey(ct);     // read character
      switch (c)
      {
      case VK_SPACE:     // fire
         {
            static COORD xy;
            xy.X=x;
            xy.Y=y;
            _beginthread(bullet,0,(void *)&xy); //ignore repeat
            Sleep(100); // give bullet time to get away
            break;
```

```
        }
      case VK_LEFT:       // move left
        SetEvent(startevt);  // let badguys start
        writeat(x,y,' ');     // clear fire base
        while (ct--)        // and move
          if (x) x--;
        break;
      case VK_RIGHT:       // move right; same logic
        SetEvent(startevt);
        writeat(x,y,' ');
        while (ct--)
          if (x!=info.dwSize.X-1) x++;
        break;
      }


    }



}
```


This threaded approach allows each routine to be very simple. Each shot worries only about itself, for example. The same code handles all the bad guys no matter how many or how few are active.

The program uses several synchronization objects. The **screenlock** mutex prevents threads from simultaneously accessing the screen. A semaphore (**bulletsem**) ensures there are only three shots active at once. The **startevt** event stops bad guy generation until you press a key or 15 seconds elapses. Finally, the **gameover** critical section stops the game over message from appearing more than once.

When the **main** function starts, it initializes many items, including the synchronization objects. It stores its thread handle so that when the game ends, the **score** routine can suspend the input processing. Notice that the thread handle that **GetCurrentThread** returns isn't really a handle. It is a special value that indicates to act against the current thread. So if you store this fake handle, and then call **SuspendThread**, you will automatically suspend the thread that makes the call. To get the actual handle, **main** calls **DuplicateHandle** to make a copy of the current thread handle.

Just before **main** begins looping for input, it starts the **badguys** function as a thread. This function waits for the **startevt** event or 15 seconds, whichever comes first. The **WaitForSingleObject**'s timeout parameter makes this easy to accomplish.

With all the setup out of the way, the **main** function loops, looking for keyboard input and drawing the firing base. The left and right arrow keys are simple to handle, and the spacebar just creates a new thread with the **bullet** function.

The **badguy** thread randomly decides if it should create a new bad guy and then sleeps for a second before checking again. If it decides to make a new bad guy, it generates a random y-axis value and starts a **badguy** thread.

The **badguy** thread does a little more work than most of the other threads. It decides if the bad guy moves left to right or right to left and then begins moving it. As it moves the bad guy, it frequently checks to see if any bullet has hit its mark. If it has, the thread records the hit and calls **score** to update the score. If a bad guy escapes, the thread records that and also calls **score**. The **score** function not only updates the title bar, it also checks for the end of game condition.

The game uses **InterlockedIncrement** to update the **hit** and **miss** variables. This ensures that if two **badguy** threads try to update the variable at once, everything works.

When the game is over, the **score** routine passes through the **gameover** critical section, which ensures that the game doesn't report the game being over more than once. It also stops the **main** thread and calls **exit** to end the game, after the user acknowledges the end of game.

The **bullet** thread checks to see if it is legal to fire. One case where **bullet** ends quickly is when there is already a bullet on the screen at the exact location. This can occur if the player fires rapidly. Another thing the routine tests is the **bulletsem** semaphore. This semaphore must have a count to allow the gun to fire. This enforces the three shot rule. If **bullet** can't immediately acquire a semaphore count, it returns. This prevents firing a fourth shot much later. If you try to fire a fourth shot, the game ignores the request.

This is certainly not the only way to write this program. However, you have to admit, the threaded nature of this code lends a certain elegance to the program. Each routine is quite concise and easy to understand. However, this would be much harder to do without synchronization.

Other Waitable Handles

There are several other types of objects that **WaitForSingleObject** and its related calls will work with. Although these are not really synchronization objects *per se*, this is as good a time as any to talk about them. Of course, in Chapter 3 you saw these calls in programs that determined when a process (or thread) terminated. It is fair to say that process and thread handles signal when the associated entity terminates.

Change Notifications

A *change notification* is a special object that can detect when you make a change to a directory. To create a change notification, you call **FindFirstChange-Notification**. This function requires a directory name and two flag words. The first flag determines if the notification is for a single directory or the entire directory tree starting with the named directory. The second flag determines what events you want to watch for (for example, any change in a file, a change in file size, a change in the write time for any file, and so on).

When any of the specified events occur, the handle signals. You can, of course, watch for that using **WaitForSingleObject**, or any related call. To reset the handle so that it is no longer signaled, call **FindNextChangeNotification**. When you no longer care, call **FindCloseChangeNotification**.

Listing 4.5 shows a simple program that monitors the **C:\SPOOLMSG** directory. If you drop a file into that directory (or erase or rename one), it pops up a dialog box that reports the change. Of course, a more ambitious program would locate the file (using **FindFirst** and its related calls), display the contents in some way, and then delete the file.

Listing 4.5 Using change notifications.

```
#include <windows.h>

void main()
{
   HANDLE spool=FindFirstChangeNotification("c:\\spoolmsg",
      FALSE,FILE_NOTIFY_CHANGE_FILE_NAME);   while(1) {
      WaitForSingleObject(spool,INFINITE);
      MessageBox(NULL,
         "Spool directory changed","SPOOLMSG",MB_OK);
      FindNextChangeNotification(spool);
   }
}
```

Console Handles

A console handle signals when it has input waiting for your program to read. You can get the standard input handle in several different ways, which include calling **CreateFile** with the file name of CONIN$, or calling **GetStdHandle**.

At first, this may not seem very useful. After all, you hope the normal C++ library blocks when there is no input pending. However, when you read about overlapped I/O in Chapter 5, you'll see that you can have an event signal when there is input from a serial port (among other things).

This suggests a useful technique for a dumb terminal program. You could set up overlapped input on the serial port and wait for either the serial port's event to signal or the console handle to signal (using **WaitForMultipleObjects**). Of course, this isn't the only possible way to write such a program, but it certainly is one way.

Summary

If you aren't taking advantage of using cooperating processes and threads, you aren't taking full advantage of Windows. It is true that these techniques take a little time to master, but Windows provides a nice set of operations to help you synchronize multiple threads.

The missing piece of the puzzle, for now, is how to share memory and otherwise communicate with other processes. That will have to wait for Chapter 6. Meanwhile, Chapter 5 will introduce you to overlapped I/O, another way to exploit multiple threads of execution for I/O processing.

Immediate Solutions

Selecting A Synchronization Method

Often, using a synchronization method is less difficult than selecting one. The three main synchronization objects are events, mutexes, and semaphores. Each has its own special properties that make it appropriate for various tasks.

Events are little more than a shared flag. They are most useful when one thread needs to signal another thread that it is ready. A manual event remains set until your program explicitly resets it. Single events reset as soon as a single thread detects the event. You can also call **PulseEvent** to cause an event to signal any threads currently waiting for the event, and then immediately reset.

Mutexes imply the ownership of some resource. Only a single thread owns a mutex at any one time. If a thread owns a mutex, it can successfully attempt to own the mutex any number of times. The thread will continue to own the mutex until it makes the same number of **ReleaseMutex** calls. The system will deny ownership of the mutex to all other threads, until the owning thread makes the final **ReleaseMutex** call.

Sometimes you want behavior like a mutex, but only inside one process. While you can use a mutex in a single process, you might gain better efficiency by using a critical section instead. A critical section uses a special variable in your program (of type **CRITICAL_SECTION**) to act as a traffic cop. When one thread calls **EnterCriticalSection**, it gains ownership of the critical section. If another thread calls **EnterCriticalSection**, it will block until the owning thread calls **LeaveCriticalSection**. Threads that don't want to block in this case can call **TryEnterCriticalSection** instead.

Semaphores also imply ownership of a resource. However, a resource that a semaphore protects usually can handle more than one owner. The semaphore has a maximum count associated with it. Each time a thread successfully waits for the semaphore, the semaphore's count decreases by one. When the count reaches zero, threads attempting to wait for the semaphore will block (at least, until a thread calls **ReleaseMutex** and makes a count available for use).

Which synchronization object is best? It depends on what you want to do. If you need to signal threads that input data is available, you would probably use an event. To prevent more than one thread from attempting to write to a file, you would use a mutex (or a critical section if you know all the threads are in one process). To limit the number of network requests a single workstation makes, you could use a semaphore.

Except for critical sections, all the synchronization objects work in a similar fashion. You call a creation call (like **CreateMutex**). This call either creates the object or opens an existing object with the name you specify. If you want only to open existing objects, you can call an open call (for example, **OpenMutex**). In either event, you receive a handle. You don't need to name the object if you don't plan to share it with unrelated processes. A nameless object is useful within the creating process, and you may pass it to child processes.

The first argument you supply to a synchronization object's **Create** call is a security attribute (a **SECURITY_ATTRIBUTE**) structure. This simple structure contains a flag to determine if child processes will inherit this handle, and an optional pointer to a security descriptor. The descriptor specifies what access the process has from that pointer. If you want the defaults, you can specify **NULL**. You can also specify **NULL** for the security attribute if you don't mind the default for the security descriptor and the inheritance flag. If you must set the security descriptor, use **InitializeSecurityDescriptor** along with calls that set the various access settings.

To share an object with any arbitrary process, you'll need to assign it a name. The name is case-sensitive and can't contain backslashes. All objects share the same name space, so you can't make a mutex and a semaphore with the same name.

The basic way to access an object is by making the **WaitForSingleObject** call. This call returns when the object signals. For an event, that means the event is set. For a mutex or semaphore, it implies that the calling thread now owns the mutex (or a count of the semaphore). You can ask **WaitForSingleObject** to wait indefinitely, not wait at all, or wait for a particular time period before giving up.

There are other calls you can use instead of **WaitForSingleObject**. **WaitForMultipleObjects** enables you to wait for multiple objects. Depending on the arguments, this call will wait until all the objects signal, or any one of the group signals. There are variations on these calls, which you can use, but all of them essentially work the same as these two basic calls.

With an event, you can set or clear the state at will. Mutexes and semaphores, however, have the notion of an owning thread. You need to call **ReleaseMutex** or **ReleaseSemaphore** to give up ownership of the object.

Avoiding Deadlock

Anytime you use multiple threads that cooperate or share resources, you introduce the possibility of deadlock (or deadly embrace). In simple terms, *deadlock* is the state when two threads are in the blocked state waiting for each other.

Suppose two threads need to acquire two mutexes (**MTXA** and **MTXB**). The first thread waits on **MTXA** and becomes its owner. The second thread acquires **MTXB**. Now when the threads attempt to acquire the other mutex, they will block. Also, they will block forever if you allow it, because neither can get what it needs.

Of course, you can easily envision more complex scenarios. Suppose thread **X** waits for thread **Y**, thread **Y** waits for thread **Z**, and thread **Z** waits for thread **X**. The possibilities are endless.

Any good operating systems textbook will have at least one chapter devoted to deadlock. However, a little common sense goes a long way toward preventing the situation. One good rule is to put a timeout value in any wait. If a wait fails, release all the objects you currently own, wait a bit, and try again. Of course, in the simple **MTXA** and **MTXB** example, you could make sure the threads always wait for the objects in the same order. That would also prevent deadlock.

Using Events

If you want to use an event with multiple threads, you can simply create a nameless event. Use **CreateEvent** and fill in its four arguments. The first argument specifies the security attributes. You will usually pass **NULL** to indicate that you want the defaults. The second and third arguments specify if the event is manual or single and the initial state of the event. For an explanation of the different types of events, see "*Selecting A Synchronization Method*" earlier in this Immediate Solutions section. The final argument specifies the event's name (**NULL** if you don't want a name).

If you plan to share an event with other processes, you'll usually give it a name. The name is case-sensitive and can't contain a backslash. You can have each process call **CreateEvent**, or have one process call **CreateEvent** and the others call **OpenEvent**. If more than one process calls **CreateEvent** with the same name, all but the first process opens the event handle.

To read the state of an event, you call a wait function (for example, **WaitForSingleObject**). See "*Selecting A Synchronization Method*" for more details.

To signal an event, you can call **SetEvent** or **PulseEvent**. **PulseEvent** signals the event long enough for waiting threads to see the event and then causes the event to reset. Manual events remain set until a call to **ResetEvent**. When you no longer need an event, you call **CloseHandle**. You can find a simple example of an event in Listing 4.1, earlier in this chapter.

Using Mutexes

Use **CreateMutex** to create a mutex and **OpenMutex** to open an existing one by name. Like other objects, you need only name the mutex if you plan on sharing it. **CreateMutex** requires a security attribute (usually **NULL**), a flag to determine if the creating thread owns the mutex, and an optional name.

If a thread wants to own the mutex, it must call **WaitForSingleObject**, or a similar **wait** function. On a successful return, the thread owns the mutex, and only the exact same thread may wait on the mutex again successfully.

When the thread no longer needs the mutex, it calls **ReleaseMutex**. If the thread called a wait function for this mutex more than once, it must call **ReleaseMutex** the same number of times. When the thread no longer requires the mutex, it calls **CloseHandle**. Listing 4.2, earlier in this chapter, shows an example of a program that uses a mutex.

Using Critical Sections

Critical sections are similar to mutexes, but they do not work across process boundaries. While this limits their usefulness, it also makes them more efficient. If you need a mutex that only threads in one process will use, you should try a critical section instead.

To use a critical section, create a **CRITICAL_SECTION** variable in global memory, then have one thread call **InitializeCriticalSection** one time. When you have code that you want only one thread to execute, call **EnterCriticalSection**. After the code completes, call **LeaveCriticalSection**. Once one thread calls **EnterCriticalSection**, all other threads that call it will block. When the initial thread calls **LeaveCriticalSection**, one waiting thread will return from **EnterCriticalSection**. Of course, if no threads are waiting, then the next thread to call **EnterCriticalSection** will succeed.

Sometimes you want to know if you can acquire the critical section, but you don't want to block. In that case, call **TryEnterCriticalSection**. If it returns successfully, you own the critical section. If it returns an error, you do not own the critical section, and must not execute the protected code.

When you no longer need a critical section, call **DeleteCriticalSection**. Obviously, you only need to call this call and **InitializeCriticalSection** once.

Using Semaphores

Semaphores are like mutexes that allow a certain number of threads to own a resource before they close the gate. Call **CreateSemaphore** or **OpenSemaphore**. As usual, **CreateSemaphore** opens an existing object or creates a new one. **OpenSemaphore** will work only if the object already exists.

When you create a semaphore, you specify the security attributes, the initial count, the maximum possible count, and the optional name. Each wait on the semaphore consumes a count until the count reaches zero. At that time, waits will not succeed until a thread calls **ReleaseSemaphore**.

The **ReleaseSemaphore** call is a bit odd. You specify how many counts you want to add back to the semaphore (usually one). You can also find out how many counts the semaphore had before you added your value to it. You can find an example of using a semaphore in Listing 4.3, earlier in this chapter.

Waiting For Multiple Objects

Usually, you'll use **WaitForSingleObject** to wait for a synchronization object. However, what if you need to wait for more than one object? That's what **WaitForMultipleObjects** is for. This call takes an array of object handles and a flag that indicates if you want to wait for all the objects or just any one object.

There are other variations of the wait calls that you can read about in this chapter. However, these two calls form the basis for all the other calls.

Using Interlocked Variables

Windows enables you to manipulate the contents of a variable in such a way that no other thread can access the variable at the same time. You can accomplish this with the interlocked calls. For example, **InterlockedIncrement** adds 1 to a 32-bit integer and returns the previous value. You can be sure no other thread altered the value at the same time.

Of course, if you use an ordinary variable, the only threads that could alter the variable are ones in your process, anyway. However, shared memory variables may need protection from threads in other processes.

The calls that work this way include **InterlockedCompareExchange**, **InterlockedDecrement**, **InterlockedExchange**, **InterlockedExchangeAdd**, and **InterlockedIncrement**. You won't often use these calls because the higher-level synchronization objects are often more useful.

Understanding MFC And Synchronization

MFC provides objects to wrap the major synchronization objects (**CEvent**, **CMutex**, and **CSemaphore**). These objects are all derived from **CSyncObject**. There is also a **CSyncObject**-derived class for critical sections (**CCritical-Section**). You can create these objects just as you would any other MFC object.

When you want to wait for a synchronization object, you create a **CSingleLock** object. The constructor takes a pointer to a **CSyncObject** (in other words, a pointer to any of the three synchronization objects). You can also ask for the lock to acquire (wait) for the object right away.

Once you have a **CSingleLock** object, you can call **Lock**, **Unlock**, and **IsLocked**. **CMultiLock** is a similar object that corresponds to **MsgWaitFor-MultipleObjects**.

The **CSingleLock** and **CMultiLock** objects lend a C++ flavor to using the synchronization objects. However, they don't make synchronization significantly easier, in my opinion. While you can use these objects, you might just as well use the regular handle-based calls in an MFC program, if you wish.

Another alternative is to use the MFC synchronization objects directly instead of using **CSingleLock** and **CMultiLock**. All **CSyncObject**-derived classes have **Lock** and **Unlock** functions so that you can manipulate them directly. Of course, if you want to wait on multiple objects, you'll want to use **CMultiLock** or simply use the standard Windows functions.

Listing 4.6 shows a simple MFC dialog that acquires a mutex using a **CSingleLock** object. When the main program creates the dialog object, it initializes the mutex as part of its constructor code. When the dialog initializes, it creates a **CSingleLock** object on the heap using **new**. This is important, because the program never blocks for the mutex. This allows it to continue processing messages.

During initialization, the dialog attempts to acquire the mutex. If it is successful, it displays a success message in a static control and waits for the user to dismiss it. If the mutex is not available, the dialog sets up a timer and informs the user that the mutex is not available. On each timer tick, the dialog checks the mutex again and informs the user when the mutex is available.

The MFC synchronization objects, by the way, require the **AFXMT.H** file. If you are using them in your program, you might as well include **AFXMT.H** in your **STDAFX.H** file. This way, the compiler will precompile the header with the other system headers.

Listing 4.6 MFC mutex.

```
// mfcmtxDlg.cpp : implementation file
//

#include "stdafx.h"
#include "mfcmtx.h"
#include "mfcmtxDlg.h"

#ifdef _DEBUG
#define new DEBUG_NEW
#undef THIS_FILE
static char THIS_FILE[] = __FILE__;
#endif

//////////////////////////////////////////////////////////////////////////////
/
// CAboutDlg dialog used for App About

class CAboutDlg : public CDialog
{
public:
   CAboutDlg();

// Dialog Data
   //{{AFX_DATA(CAboutDlg)
   enum { IDD = IDD_ABOUTBOX };
   //}}AFX_DATA

   // ClassWizard generated virtual function overrides
   //{{AFX_VIRTUAL(CAboutDlg)
```

```
    protected:
    virtual void DoDataExchange(CDataExchange* pDX);    // DDX/DDV support
    //}}AFX_VIRTUAL

// Implementation
protected:
    //{{AFX_MSG(CAboutDlg)
    //}}AFX_MSG
    DECLARE_MESSAGE_MAP()
};

CAboutDlg::CAboutDlg() : CDialog(CAboutDlg::IDD)
{
    //{{AFX_DATA_INIT(CAboutDlg)
    //}}AFX_DATA_INIT
}

void CAboutDlg::DoDataExchange(CDataExchange* pDX)
{
    CDialog::DoDataExchange(pDX);
    //{{AFX_DATA_MAP(CAboutDlg)
    //}}AFX_DATA_MAP
}

BEGIN_MESSAGE_MAP(CAboutDlg, CDialog)
    //{{AFX_MSG_MAP(CAboutDlg)
        // No message handlers
    //}}AFX_MSG_MAP
END_MESSAGE_MAP()

//////////////////////////////////////////////////////////////////////////////
/
// CMfcmtxDlg dialog

CMfcmtxDlg::CMfcmtxDlg(CWnd* pParent /*=NULL*/)
    : CDialog(CMfcmtxDlg::IDD, pParent), mtx(FALSE,"MFCMTX")
{
    //{{AFX_DATA_INIT(CMfcmtxDlg)
        // NOTE: the ClassWizard will add member initialization here
    //}}AFX_DATA_INIT
    // Note that LoadIcon does not require a subsequent DestroyIcon in Win32
    m_hIcon = AfxGetApp()->LoadIcon(IDR_MAINFRAME);
}

void CMfcmtxDlg::DoDataExchange(CDataExchange* pDX)
```

4. Synchronization

```
{
   CDialog::DoDataExchange(pDX);
   //{{AFX_DATA_MAP(CMfcmtxDlg)
      // NOTE: the ClassWizard will add DDX and DDV calls here
   //}}AFX_DATA_MAP
}

BEGIN_MESSAGE_MAP(CMfcmtxDlg, CDialog)
   //{{AFX_MSG_MAP(CMfcmtxDlg)
   ON_WM_SYSCOMMAND()
   ON_WM_PAINT()
   ON_WM_QUERYDRAGICON()
   ON_WM_TIMER()
   //}}AFX_MSG_MAP
END_MESSAGE_MAP()

////////////////////////////////////////////////////////////////////////////
/
// CMfcmtxDlg message handlers

BOOL CMfcmtxDlg::OnInitDialog()
{
   CDialog::OnInitDialog();
   lock=new CSingleLock(&mtx,FALSE);
   if (lock->Lock(0)==0)
   {
      SetDlgItemText(ID_STATUS,"Mutex in use");
      SetTimer(1,1000,NULL);
   }
   else
      SetDlgItemText(ID_STATUS,"Mutex acquired");

   // Add "About..." menu item to system menu.

   // IDM_ABOUTBOX must be in the system command range.
   ASSERT((IDM_ABOUTBOX & 0xFFF0) == IDM_ABOUTBOX);
   ASSERT(IDM_ABOUTBOX < 0xF000);

   CMenu* pSysMenu = GetSystemMenu(FALSE);
   if (pSysMenu != NULL)
   {
      CString strAboutMenu;
      strAboutMenu.LoadString(IDS_ABOUTBOX);
      if (!strAboutMenu.IsEmpty())
      {
```

4. Synchronization

```
            pSysMenu->AppendMenu(MF_SEPARATOR);
            pSysMenu->AppendMenu(MF_STRING,
                                 IDM_ABOUTBOX, strAboutMenu);
        }
    }

    // Set the icon for this dialog.  The framework does this automatically
    //  when the application's main window is not a dialog
    SetIcon(m_hIcon, TRUE);         // Set big icon
    SetIcon(m_hIcon, FALSE);      // Set small icon

    // TODO: Add extra initialization here

    return TRUE;  // return TRUE  unless you set the focus to a control
}

void CMfcmtxDlg::OnSysCommand(UINT nID, LPARAM lParam)
{
    if ((nID & 0xFFF0) == IDM_ABOUTBOX)
    {
        CAboutDlg dlgAbout;
        dlgAbout.DoModal();
    }
    else
    {
        CDialog::OnSysCommand(nID, lParam);
    }
}

// If you add a minimize button to your dialog, you will need the code below
//  to draw the icon.  For MFC applications using the document/view model,
//  this is automatically done for you by the framework.

void CMfcmtxDlg::OnPaint()
{
    if (IsIconic())
    {
        CPaintDC dc(this); // device context for painting

        SendMessage(WM_ICONERASEBKGND, (WPARAM) dc.GetSafeHdc(), 0);

        // Center icon in client rectangle
        int cxIcon = GetSystemMetrics(SM_CXICON);
        int cyIcon = GetSystemMetrics(SM_CYICON);
        CRect rect;
        GetClientRect(&rect);
```

```
      int x = (rect.Width() - cxIcon + 1) / 2;
      int y = (rect.Height() - cyIcon + 1) / 2;

      // Draw the icon
      dc.DrawIcon(x, y, m_hIcon);
   }
   else
   {
      CDialog::OnPaint();
   }
}

// The system calls this to obtain the cursor to display while the user
      drags
//  the minimized window.
HCURSOR CMfcmtxDlg::OnQueryDragIcon()
{
   return (HCURSOR) m_hIcon;
}

void CMfcmtxDlg::OnTimer(UINT nIDEvent)
{
   if (!lock->Lock(0)) return;
// Mutex is available! Kill timer and tell user
   KillTimer(1);
   SetDlgItemText(ID_STATUS,"Mutex now available");
   CDialog::OnTimer(nIDEvent);
}

BOOL CMfcmtxDlg::DestroyWindow()
{
   if (lock)
   {
      lock->Unlock();  // may not be us, but if not... who cares?
      delete lock;
   }
   return CDialog::DestroyWindow();
}
```

Chapter 5

File I/O

If you need an immediate solution to:	See page:
Opening A File	225
Reading Or Writing A File Synchronously	226
Detecting EOF (Synchronous)	226
Duplicating File Handles	226
Closing A File	227
Using Methods For Asynchronous I/O	227
Using Asynchronous I/O With Threads	228
Starting Overlapped I/O	230
Completing Asynchronous I/O	230
Detecting EOF (Asynchronous)	231
Using ReadFileEx And WriteFileEx	231
Using Completion Ports	232
Memory Mapping Files	232

In Depth

There are few things you take for granted as much as your hearing. Yet most of us would be in trouble if it were suddenly gone. Not long ago, I had an experience that really made me think about that.

As part of my consulting business, I travel to different parts of the country and deliver seminars on programming. Once, as I was setting up a class at a client's site, a young lady who had enrolled in the course came in to speak to me. She informed me that because she was deaf, two sign language interpreters would be coming to sit with her.

In the past, I had worked with foreign language students who had used only one interpreter, so I wondered why she needed two. I soon found out. The reason had to do with the fact that there are two common forms of sign language. One form, often called finger spelling, requires the signer to spell each word, letter by letter. A more convenient method is American Sign Language (ASL), in which a gesture represents an entire word—so a certain sign means "drink" and another means "happy." Obviously, ASL has much higher bandwidth than finger spelling.

When I asked one of the translators if they used ASL, she told me that they couldn't use it much because many of the technical terms have no ASL gesture assigned to them. Each translator would last about an hour doing finger-spelling before suffering a complete overload, so one would rest while the other one signed.

Think about the student (who did quite well in the class, by the way). She had to endure the entire four-day class having the whole thing spelled letter by letter. Amazing.

While I'm not deaf, I am a bit hard of hearing. My wife, Pat, always snickers when she sees a particular TV commercial that features an older couple in a restaurant. The announcer says, "This man takes his hearing aid everywhere he goes." After the waiter tells them the specials, the man turns to his wife and says, "What did he say?" It turns out the man's "hearing aid" is his wife.

Apparently, my wife thinks I have something in common with the man on TV. It is true that my hearing isn't what it used to be. But I've noticed something: I think most of my hearing loss is caused by nosiness rather than noisiness.

If I am sitting in a quiet room, I can hear most anything, but in a crowded restaurant, I am almost completely deaf. I think my brain, while trying to eavesdrop on and sort out all the different conversations, succeeds in hearing nothing. On the other hand, random noise seems to kill my hearing, too, so maybe my nosiness theory is wrong. Still, I suspect focusing on one single sound would help me a great deal.

One of the strengths of Windows (and many other modern operating systems) is that it can carry on lots of simultaneous conversations. This capability makes network servers, among other things, feasible. The Web wouldn't be nearly as popular if it worked like a phone, would it? If it did, you might try to search on AltaVista, but the line would probably be busy because someone else is searching.

In Chapter 3, you saw that multiple processes and threads can enable the computer to look like it is doing many things at once. That's great when you want to do different things. But what happens when you want to do the same thing (like serve a Web page) over and over? Sure, you can still use threads, but you might find you run into problems with that approach.

Why Asynchronous I/O?

Suppose you want to design a Web server. Each time a client requests a page, you create a new thread, and that thread handles the request. That will certainly work. However, creating a thread is somewhat expensive in terms of system resources. Also, there is some practical limit on how many threads you can create. Sure, for a small server this isn't a problem. But major Web sites can get thousands of hits at once. It might be a better idea to service these requests with a pool of threads that share the load. That's one purpose of asynchronous I/O.

Another problem arises when you want to handle multiple I/O sources at the same time. Suppose you are writing a terminal program. You need a way to read from the serial port and the keyboard without waiting for either one. You want to react to any input immediately. Again, asynchronous I/O is the answer.

Before you tackle the various forms of I/O, it is a good idea to understand how Windows handles file and device I/O. If you are familiar with **CreateFile** and its use, you might want to skip ahead to the "Using Threads" section of this chapter.

File I/O Review

Most of the time if you want to open a file, you use some library routine (like **fopen**, for example). Most languages provide a very convenient, high-level way to manipulate files. However, sometimes you need to open a file directly at the operating system level and bypass higher-level processing. One reason you might want to do this is to perform some types of asynchronous I/O.

The system call that you'll use to open a file is **CreateFile**. This is perhaps the worst-named API call of all. **CreateFile** might actually create a file on disk. On the other hand, it might not. It depends on the flags you pass to the call. A better name for **CreateFile** would be **CreateFileHandle**, because that is what it really does. It creates a file handle you can use to work with a file. That file may already exist, or the call might create the file.

CreateFile takes several arguments (see Table 5.1). Of course, you must supply a file name. You also need to specify how you want to access the file (for reading, writing, or both), if you will allow sharing of the file and the security attributes. Next, specify two sets of flags. The first set tells the call if it should create the file, or open only existing files. The second set of flags sets a variety of options and tells what attributes the file should have if Windows creates it. The final argument is a handle to a template file. If you supply this handle and the call creates a file, the new file will have the same attributes as the template file.

The really interesting argument to **CreateFile** is the second set of flags. These flags let you set a number of interesting options (see Table 5.2). You can ask the system to delete the file when you close it or specify overlapped access (the principal way to do asynchronous I/O). You can also control how the system caches files using these flags.

Table 5.1 Arguments for CreateFile.

Argument	Description
lpFileName	Pointer to the file or device name.
DesiredAccess	Specifies the type of access to the object. An application can obtain read access, write access, read-write access, or device query access. A 0 indicates that the program wants to determine if it can access the object. Otherwise, you'll use GENERIC_READ, GENERIC_WRITE, or both (joined with a | operator).
dwShareMode	Set of bit flags that specifies how the object can be shared. If dwShareMode is 0, the object cannot be shared. Subsequent open operations on the object will fail, until the handle is closed. If you want to share the file, use any combination of FILE_SHARE_DELETE, FILE_SHARE_READ, or FILE_SHARE_WRITE.
lpSecurityAttributes	Pointer to a SECURITY_ATTRIBUTES structure that determines whether the returned handle is inheritable by child processes. If lpSecurityAttributes is NULL, the handle cannot be inherited.

(continued)

Table 5.1 Arguments for CreateFile (continued).

Argument	Description
dwCreationDisposition	Specifies how to create (or not create) the file. Specify CREATE_NEW, CREATE_ALWAYS, OPEN_EXISTING, OPEN_ALWAYS, or TRUNCATE_EXISTING.
dwFlagsAndAttributes	Specifies the file attributes and flags for the file. For example, use FILE_ATTRIBUTE_HIDDEN to make the file hidden if the call creates it. You may also set any of a number of parameters (see Table 5.2). You may also specify special flags here for named pipes.
hTemplateFile	Specifies a handle with GENERIC_READ access to a template file. The template file supplies file attributes and extended attributes for the file being created.

Table 5.2 Flags to CreateFile.

Flag	Meaning
FILE_FLAG_WRITE_THROUGH	Instructs the system to write through any intermediate cache and go directly to disk. Windows can still cache write operations, but cannot lazily flush them.
FILE_FLAG_OVERLAPPED	Instructs the system to initialize the object so that it performs overlapped I/O (see text).
FILE_FLAG_NO_BUFFERING	Instructs the system to open the file with no intermediate buffering or caching. When combined with FILE_FLAG_OVERLAPPED, the flag gives maximum asynchronous performance, because the I/O does not rely on the synchronous operations of the memory manager. However, some I/O operations will take longer, because data is not being held in the cache. An application must meet certain requirements when working with files opened with FILE_FLAG_NO_BUFFERING (including strict limits on the starting offset, block transfer size, and the address of data buffers).
FILE_FLAG_RANDOM_ACCESS	Indicates that the file is accessed randomly. The system can use this as a hint to optimize file caching.
FILE_FLAG_SEQUENTIAL_SCAN	Indicates that the file is to be accessed sequentially from beginning to end. The system can use this as a hint to optimize file caching. If an application moves the file pointer for random access, optimum caching may not occur; however, the system still assures correct operation.

(continued)

Table 5.2 Flags to CreateFile (continued).

Flag	Meaning
FILE_FLAG_DELETE_ON_CLOSE	Indicates that the operating system is to delete the file immediately after all of its handles have been closed, not just the handle for which you specified FILE_FLAG_DELETE_ON_CLOSE. Subsequent open requests for the file will fail, unless FILE_SHARE_DELETE is used.
FILE_FLAG_BACKUP_SEMANTICS	Indicates that the file is for a backup or restore operation. The operating system ensures that the calling process overrides file security checks, provided it has the necessary privileges (SE_BACKUP_NAME and SE_RESTORE_NAME).
FILE_FLAG_POSIX_SEMANTICS	Accesses the file according to POSIX rules. This includes allowing multiple files with names, differing only in case, for file systems that support such naming. Use care when using this option because files created with this flag may not be accessible by applications written for DOS or Windows.
FILE_FLAG_OPEN_REPARSE_POINT	Specifying this flag inhibits the reparse behavior of NTFS reparse points. When the file is opened, a file handle is returned, whether the filter that controls the reparse point is operational or not. This flag cannot be used with the CREATE_ALWAYS flag.
FILE_FLAG_OPEN_NO_RECALL	Indicates that the file data is requested, but it should continue to reside in remote storage. This flag is intended for use by remote storage systems or the Hierarchical Storage Management system.

There is one other oddity about **CreateFile**: Suppose you attempt to access a file on a removable drive (like a floppy) and the device is not ready. By default, the system will bring up an ugly error box prompting the user to retry or fail the operation. If you don't want this (and that's usually the case), you need to call **SetErrorMode**. Passing the **SEM_FAILCRITICALERRORS** flag to this call will prevent the system from showing the dialog.

Once you have an open file handle, you usually access it with **ReadFile** and **WriteFile**. These calls work as you would expect: They take a file handle, a buffer, the length of the buffer, and a pointer where you want to store the number of bytes the call processed. They also take an **OVERLAPPED** structure that is only for overlapped I/O. For normal files, this structure is always **NULL**. Later, you'll see how this structure signals an overlapped I/O request.

When you no longer want to keep a file open, simply call **CloseHandle**. Of course, **CloseHandle** operates on many types of handles, not just file handles.

Listing 5.1 shows a simple, straightforward program that uses the file operations to print one or more files to the screen. The **CreateFile** call opens the file for input, while a call to **GetStdHandle** retrieves the standard output handle. Then calls to **ReadFile** and **WriteFile** transfer data in 4K blocks until the end of the file.

Listing 5.1 NTCAT2.

```
// NTCAT - Cat files on NT or Win2000
// Doesn't do nice error handling
// Any error causes the program to exit
// even though some other files might still work

#include <windows.h>

// Just a dumb wrapper around MessageBox:
void MB(char *s)
{
   MessageBox(NULL,s,NULL,MB_OK|MB_ICONSTOP);
}

// This routine does all the real work:
void docat(char *fname)
{
   HANDLE f=CreateFile(fname,GENERIC_READ,0,NULL,OPEN_EXISTING,0,NULL);
   HANDLE out=GetStdHandle(STD_OUTPUT_HANDLE);
   if (f==INVALID_HANDLE_VALUE)
   {
      MB("Can't open file");
      exit(1);
   }
   char buf[4096];
   unsigned long n;
   do
   {
     unsigned long wct;
     if (!ReadFile(f,buf,sizeof(buf),&n,NULL)) break;
     if (n) WriteFile(out,buf,n,&wct,NULL);
   } while (n==sizeof(buf));  // if EOF this is not true
   CloseHandle(f);
}

void main(int argc,char *argv[])
{
   if (argc==1)
   {
      MB("Usage: ntcat FILENAME [FILENAME ....]");
```

5. File I/O

```
        exit(9);
    }
    // Do all named files
    while (--argc) docat(*++argv);
    exit(0);
}
```

So that's how you work with a file using the bare Win32 API. Normally, when you call **ReadFile** or **WriteFile**, your thread stops until the I/O operation is complete. What happens if you don't want that? Then you need some form of asynchronous I/O.

You can achieve asynchronous I/O in several ways. The simplest way is to start a new thread and do your I/O from within that thread. You can also use overlapped I/O or I/O completion ports.

Using Threads

By far, the simplest way to prevent a thread from stopping for I/O is to let another thread stop for I/O. In a console-based terminal program, for example, you could have a thread dedicated to reading the serial port and another thread that reads the keyboard. Both threads deposit any input into a circular buffer. A third thread waits for a character to appear in one of the buffers and takes the appropriate action.

There is one problem with this simplistic approach. The third thread must constantly examine the circular buffer pointers to determine if a character is ready. A more sophisticated solution might employ an event (see Chapter 4). When one of the I/O threads receives a character, it signals the event. That way the third thread could wait for the events using **WaitForMultipleObjects** and consume very little unnecessary processor time. Of course, console handles signal when they have input pending, so you could wait for an event or the console handle and use only two threads.

If the terminal program has a message loop (which a console application usually does not have), you could consider another approach. You could cause the I/O threads to post user-defined messages to the program's main window. Then the main program would respond to the messages as it would any other event.

These strategies have the virtue of simplicity. However, they are not terribly efficient. Creating threads can be an expensive operation, and there is some limit to the number of threads the system can support (albeit a large limit). For a simple terminal program, these aren't big concerns, but for a program that expects to do a lot of asynchronous I/O, threads may be unacceptable. You'll find an example of thread-based I/O in the Immediate Solutions section of this chapter (see Listing 5.6 in the "Using Asynchronous I/O with Threads" section).

Overlapped I/O

The most common way to implement asynchronous I/O under Windows is via overlapped I/O. Windows provides this facility for practically all types of files: disk files, communication ports, named pipes, and network sockets. In general, if you can use **ReadFile** and **WriteFile** with something, you can perform overlapped I/O with it as well.

Before you can use a file in overlapped mode, you must open it with the **FILE_FLAG_OVERLAPPED** flag (using **CreateFile**). If you don't specify this flag, no overlapping is possible. If you do set this flag, then you can't use the file as a normal file. You must perform overlapped I/O on the file.

When you call **ReadFile** or **WriteFile**, you must supply an **OVERLAPPED** structure. The system uses the first two 32-bit words of this structure internally. The next two enable you to set a 64-bit offset. This offset is where you want to read or write in the file. Because the I/O occurs asynchronously, you can't be sure the operations will complete in sequence. Therefore, there is no concept of a current position. You always specify an offset for file operations. With streams (like a COM port or a socket), there is no way to seek a particular offset, so the system ignores the offset in those cases.

The final entry in the **OVERLAPPED** structure is an optional event handle. You'll see how you can use that later. For now, assume that this handle is **NULL**.

When you call one of the I/O functions, the system may be able to complete it immediately. For example, you might ask to read a byte from a serial device, and the buffer has 30 bytes waiting. In this case, the call returns normally, and you never notice you are using overlapped I/O. This is an important point: If the call returns a nonzero value, that means that the I/O completed and everything worked just as it would have if you hadn't used overlapped I/O.

The asynchronous part of overlapped I/O occurs when the call returns **FALSE**. Then, you have one of two possible situations. Either the call is still pending, or there was a legitimate error. To decide which case applies, you must call **GetLastError**. If this call returns **ERROR_IO_PENDING**, the I/O is still in progress. This isn't really an error, of course. Any other return value indicates an actual error.

Completing The I/O

When there is an asynchronous I/O request pending, you eventually want to know that it completed. For a read, the input buffer is not valid until the I/O completes. For a write, you'll want to know that the write was successful. There are several ways to do this.

The most direct method is to call **GetOverlappedResult**. This call requires the file handle, the **OVERLAPPED** structure that you used in the original call, a pointer to a byte count, and a flag that determines if the call waits. If the I/O is complete, the call returns a nonzero value and fills in the byte count variable. If the I/O is not complete and the wait flag is **TRUE**, the call will wait until the I/O does complete or there is an error. If the wait flag is **FALSE**, the call returns an error (a zero return value).

Once again, if you get an error return (and the wait flag is **FALSE**), you'll need to call **GetLastError**. A value of **ERROR_IO_INCOMPLETE** indicates that the I/O is still in progress. Any other value informs you that there was an actual error.

Another way to complete I/O is to cancel it. You can call **CancelIo** to cancel all I/O the current thread started on a given file handle. Notice that you can't cancel a single transaction. You must stop all I/O that is pending on that file. This call doesn't affect I/O initiated by other threads. This call only works for overlapped I/O, of course. If a thread starts regular I/O, it would never have the chance to call **CancelIo** until the operation finished anyway. A canceled I/O request completes with an error return (via **GetLastError**) of **ERROR_OPERATION_ABORTED**.

The **ReadFile** function may fail and return **ERROR_INVALID_USER_BUFFER** or **ERROR_NOT_ENOUGH_MEMORY** whenever there are too many outstanding asynchronous I/O requests. I've never personally seen this happen, but it is a good idea to complete your I/O as soon as possible.

Using Events

Using **GetOverlappedResult** is straightforward, but it almost defeats the purpose of using overlapped I/O to begin with. After all, if you wanted to wait for the I/O, you might as well use the regular I/O calls. Repeatedly checking for I/O completion is not much better for most programs. One answer is to use the optional event in the **OVERLAPPED** structure.

When you pass **ReadFile** or **WriteFile** an **OVERLAPPED** structure, you can include a manual event handle (see Chapter 4) in the last field. If the I/O has to wait, the system resets the event. When the I/O finally completes, the system will signal the event.

Is this any better? It can be. Imagine that you are writing a program to read two serial ports. When you detect input on one port, you write the same data to the second port. If data arrives from the second port, you duplicate it to the first port. This might be the basis for a data monitor application, for example.

A clever way to implement this would use overlapped I/O and events. You could read data from both ports until they both raise an **ERROR_IO_PENDING** error. Then you could use **WaitForMultipleObjects** to efficiently wait for either port to present input. This would be much better than repeatedly calling **Get OverlappedResult** and wasting processor time.

Using ReadFileEx And WriteFileEx

Another way to wait for an I/O operation to complete is to use **ReadFileEx** and **WriteFileEx**. These calls are only for overlapped I/O. They take an extra parameter that specifies a function to call when the I/O operation finishes.

This sounds great, but there is a catch. The system uses APCs (see Chapter 3) to call the completion function. That means you must be in an alertable wait state for the call to occur. In practice, that means you have to call **WaitFor SingleObjectEx** (or a related call) or **SleepEx** to get a call to the completion function.

If this seems unsatisfying to you, you are not alone. Overlapped I/O works in several important cases, but it really isn't as asynchronous as you would like it to be. To truly have asynchronous I/O, you need to implement regular I/O in separate threads. I/O completion ports (which I'll discuss shortly) offer another alternative that might be appropriate for some programs.

EOF Detection

There is a slight difference in how overlapped I/O calls signal EOF. A regular **ReadFile** call signals end of file by setting the number of bytes read to zero. Overlapped calls to **ReadFile** return an error when they reach EOF. The code that **GetLastError** returns is **ERROR_HANDLE_EOF**. This error may occur when you call **ReadFile**, or it may occur when you call **GetOverlappedResult**.

If you think about it, this is natural. The system may encounter EOF when you make the **ReadFile** call or later, as it processes the request. You just need to remember to check for EOF in the appropriate way depending on what type of I/O you are using.

I/O Completion Ports

Obviously, overlapped I/O has its limitations. High-volume servers, in particular, are hard to implement with overlapped I/O. For a low-volume server, starting a new thread for each client is a good approach. However, creating threads for a large number of clients might not be efficient. On the other hand, it would be nice if you could service clients with multiple threads. Each thread might handle more than one client.

This strategy is difficult to implement with overlapped I/O. However, it is exactly the sort of thing that I/O completion ports excel at.

The idea behind an I/O completion port is similar to a queue. This queue holds notifications that I/O has completed. Any thread can check the queue and process the I/O. To use an I/O completion port, you must first create the port using **CreateIoCompletionPort** and specifying an overlapped file handle that the port handles. Once you attach the file handle to the completion port, you can't use **ReadFileEx** and **WriteFileEx** on that file. You should also avoid sharing the handle with other processes.

Once a file handle attaches to a completion port, each successful I/O will post a notification in the completion port's queue. You can use the same call to attach a file to an existing completion port.

Each call to **CreateIoCompletionPort** enables you to specify a key. This is simply a 32-bit number that the system includes with each completion notification associated with the specified file. You can use any 32-bit number that has meaning to your program.

The other parameter you can specify when calling **CreateIoCompletionPort** enables you to control approximately how many threads the call will allow to proceed at one time. Usually, you will set this argument to zero so that any thread waiting on a port can proceed when data is available. However, you can request that the port allow only a certain number of threads to proceed at once. This number is not absolute, because there are conditions that can cause the number of threads to exceed this number.

Threads can retrieve available completion data by calling **GetQueuedCompletionStatus**. This call returns the number of bytes transferred, the completion key (the 32-bit value you sent to **CreateIoCompletionPort**), and the **OVERLAPPED** structure that the original call received. You can elect to wait indefinitely for a completed I/O. You can also force the I/O to time out in a specified number of milliseconds, or time out immediately if there is no I/O completion notification ready.

It is possible to create an I/O completion port without an attached file handle, by the way. This may be useful if you want to use a completion port as a signal between different threads in a single process. A thread can enqueue a notification using **PostQueuedCompletionStatus**. The calling thread sets all the information, including the number of processed bytes, the completion key, and the **OVERLAPPED** structure that **GetQueuedCompletionStatus** returns.

I/O completion ports are not for every program. Still, when you need them, they are indispensable.

An Example Application

Listing 5.2 shows a simple application of overlapped I/O. This program enables you to chat by using a named pipe between a client and a server. If you run it with no command line arguments, it becomes a server. If you name a machine on the command line, you start in client mode and connect to that server. You can use a single dot if you want to connect to a server on your own machine.

You'll find out more about named pipes in Chapter 6. For now, just think of a named pipe as a Star Trek-style wormhole—when you put data in either side of the pipe, it pops out the other side. When the pipe isn't connected to two processes, the pipe returns an **ERROR_PIPE_LISTENING** error. Once there is a connection between two processes, the named pipe works about the same as any file. There are other ways you can access a named pipe, but those will wait for Chapter 6. For now, just pretend it is a file.

Listing 5.2 The Talk program.

```
#include <windows.h>
#include <iostream.h>
#include <string.h>
#include <stdio.h> // sprintf

BOOL server=FALSE;



HANDLE OpenTalkPipe(char *host)
{
   HANDLE rv;
   if (!server)
   {
      char fn[1024];
      sprintf(fn,"\\\\%s\\pipe\\talkpipe_awc",host);
      cerr<<"Opening "<<fn<<"\n";
```

```
        rv=CreateFile(fn,GENERIC_READ|GENERIC_WRITE,FILE_SHARE_READ|
                FILE_SHARE_WRITE,NULL,OPEN_EXISTING,FILE_FLAG_OVERLAPPED,NULL);
    }
    else
    {
        // we are the server
        SECURITY_ATTRIBUTES sa;
        SECURITY_DESCRIPTOR sd;
        // allow all access
        InitializeSecurityDescriptor(&sd,SECURITY_DESCRIPTOR_REVISION);
        sa.bInheritHandle=FALSE;
        sa.lpSecurityDescriptor=&sd;
        sa.nLength=sizeof(sa);
        rv=CreateNamedPipe("\\\\.\\pipe\\talkpipe_awc",
           PIPE_ACCESS_DUPLEX|FILE_FLAG_OVERLAPPED,
           PIPE_TYPE_BYTE|PIPE_READMODE_BYTE,1,1024,1024,1000,&sa);

    }
    return rv;
}

void main(int argc, char *argv[])
{
    if (argc==1) server=TRUE;
    HANDLE pipe=OpenTalkPipe(server?".":argv[1]);
    HANDLE console=GetStdHandle(STD_INPUT_HANDLE);
    HANDLE pipeevent=CreateEvent(NULL,TRUE,FALSE,NULL);
    OVERLAPPED over;
    char pipebuf;
    DWORD inlen;
    DWORD err;
    if (pipe==INVALID_HANDLE_VALUE)
    {
        err=GetLastError();
        cout<<"Error opening pipe ("<<err<<")\n";
        exit(9);
    }
    over.Internal=over.InternalHigh=over.Offset=over.OffsetHigh=0;
    over.hEvent=pipeevent;
    if (!SetConsoleMode(console,0))
    {
        cerr<<"Error: can't set console mode\n"<<GetLastError();
        exit(4);
    }
    cout<<"Waiting to connect\n";
```

```
cout.flush();
//read pipe
do {
while (ReadFile(pipe,&pipebuf,1,&inlen,&over)) cout<<pipebuf;
err=GetLastError();
} while (err==ERROR_PIPE_LISTENING);  // wait for client
cerr<<"Connected (^C to disconnect)\n";
if (err!=ERROR_IO_PENDING)
{
   cerr<<"Error reading pipe ("<<err<<")\n";
   exit(3);
}
// Enter wait
HANDLE waits[2];
DWORD obj;
waits[0]=pipeevent;
waits[1]=console;
while (1)
{
   obj=WaitForMultipleObjects(2,(void **)&waits,FALSE,INFINITE);
   // if wait ended for console, read console and send
   if (obj==WAIT_OBJECT_0-1)
   {
      char inbuf; // ANSI only
      OVERLAPPED dummy;
      INPUT_RECORD irec;
      dummy.hEvent=NULL;
            dummy.Offset=dummy.OffsetHigh=dummy.Internal=
                  dummy.InternalHigh=0;
      DWORD inlen;
      // Using ReadConsole here never unsignals console!
      ReadConsoleInput(console,&irec,1,&inlen);
      if (irec.EventType==KEY_EVENT&&
                        irec.Event.KeyEvent.bKeyDown&&
irec.Event.KeyEvent.uChar.AsciiChar!='\0')
      {
         inbuf=irec.Event.KeyEvent.uChar.AsciiChar;
         if (inbuf=='\003')
         {
            // quit
            CloseHandle(pipe);
            CloseHandle(pipeevent);
            exit(0);
         }
         WriteFile(pipe,&inbuf,1,&inlen,&dummy);
```

5. File I/O

```
            // echo
            cout<<((inbuf=='\r')?'\n':inbuf);
            cout.flush();
         // Wait for write to complete so we don't get confused
            if (!GetOverlappedResult(pipe,&dummy,&inlen,TRUE))
               cout<<"Unknown pipe write error!\n";

         }
      }
// if wait ended for pipe, dump character to console and issue another read
      if (obj==WAIT_OBJECT_0)
      {
         DWORD len;
         // Get the result, even though we know what it is
         if (!GetOverlappedResult(pipe,&over,&len,TRUE))
         {
            cout<<"!Unknown pipe error!\n";
            exit(3);
         }
         do
         {
            if (pipebuf=='\r') cout<<'\n'; else cout<<pipebuf;
         } while (ReadFile(pipe,&pipebuf,1,&inlen,&over));
         DWORD err=GetLastError();
         if (err!=ERROR_IO_PENDING)
         {
            cerr<<"Error reading pipe\n";
            exit(3);
         }
         cout.flush();
      }
   }
}
```

Both the client and the server open the pipe for overlapped I/O. However, they leave the console input stream as it is. That's because the console handle signals when it has input anyway, so using overlapped I/O with it isn't necessary in this case.

The main program enters a loop, reading data from the pipe as long as it keeps getting **ERROR_PIPE_LISTENING** errors. These errors indicate that the pipe is not connected yet. Eventually, either a real character will appear (in which case the program prints it), or the I/O will be pending. In the latter case, the program knows that the overlapped event (**pipeevent**) will signal when input is ready. The program therefore enters an efficient wait state by using **WaitForMultipleObjects** to wait for the pipe's event or the console handle to signal.

When the wait returns, the program determines what caused it to finish. If it is the console handle that signaled, the program reads the input (using **ReadConsoleInput**) and sends it to the pipe. Because this is a simple program, I don't want to have to track multiple writes in an overlapped way, so I call **GetOverlappedResult** if the write doesn't succeed immediately. This essentially converts the asynchronous I/O to synchronous. Writes usually occur very quickly, so this isn't a big issue for this program.

When the pipe's event signals, the program issues a **GetOverlappedResult** so that it can check for any errors. Finding no errors, the program writes the data to the console (again, no need for asynchronous operation in this case). Then the program issues another **ReadFile** against the pipe.

Notice that there is some chance that the pipe will have data right away. Then the program must be careful to write that data and issue another read. That's why the code to print a character is inside a **do** loop like this:

```
do
{
   if (pipebuf=='\r') cout<<'\n'; else cout<<pipebuf;
} while (ReadFile(pipe,&pipebuf,1,&inlen,&over));
```

The first time in the loop the program is dealing with data from the asynchronous read that was pending. If the loop executes more than once, it is because the **ReadFile** call in the **while** clause returned data immediately. Once there is no more data available at the moment, **ReadFile** will return **FALSE**, breaking the loop. At that point, you have to call **GetLastError** to decide if it is simply waiting (**ERROR_IO_PENDING**) or an error.

A Completion Port Example

Listing 5.3 shows a program very similar to the one in Listing 5.2, except it uses completion ports. This is not very useful in this case, unless the program also needs to do some other processing while waiting for I/O.

To understand why this is the case, consider how the original code in Listing 5.2 works. If the pipe has no input and the console has no input, the original program goes into an efficient wait state (using **WaitForMultipleObjects**). This enables the operating system to attend to other things until data is available.

Although a thread can block on a completion port, it can't block on the completion port and wait for some other event at the same time (like console input). That's the problem with the program in Listing 5.3: It must continuously poll the completion port and the console, never blocking on either one.

Of course, you could start another thread to wait for the completion port, but again, that implies that the thread has something else to do. Otherwise, it could simply block and dispense with overlapped I/O anyway.

Nevertheless, the code in Listing 5.3 is an interesting contrast to the earlier code. With a completion port, it is no longer necessary to use an event to determine when the overlapped I/O completes. The program runs in a loop, polling both the completion port and the console handle.

Other than this trivial change, the program works about the same as it did before. One interesting point is that you receive completion notification packets for each completed read and write. That means the code that prints the incoming characters must differentiate between these two different notifications.

At first, you would think the completion's key might be useful for this. However, you assign the key when you attach the port to the file handle. It doesn't matter if you are reading or writing to the file, the completion key is the same.

The answer, it turns out, is the **OVERLAPPED** structure. The code can compare the pointer to the **OVERLAPPED** structure the completion port returns to the pointer passed to **WriteFile**. If the addresses match, the completion notification refers to a write, so the program just skips it. If you omit this check, you will get a garbage character after your press each key.

Listing 5.3 Using a completion port.

```
#include <windows.h>
#include <iostream.h>
#include <string.h>
#include <stdio.h> // sprintf

BOOL server=FALSE;



HANDLE OpenTalkPipe(char *host)
{
   HANDLE rv;
   if (!server)
   {
      char fn[1024];
      sprintf(fn,"\\\\%s\\pipe\\talkpipe_awc",host);
      cerr<<"Opening "<<fn<<"\n";
      rv=CreateFile(fn,GENERIC_READ|GENERIC_WRITE,FILE_SHARE_READ|
  FILE_SHARE_WRITE,NULL,OPEN_EXISTING,FILE_FLAG_OVERLAPPED,NULL);
   }
```

```
    else
    {
        // we are the server
        SECURITY_ATTRIBUTES sa;
        SECURITY_DESCRIPTOR sd;
        // allow all access
        InitializeSecurityDescriptor(&sd,SECURITY_DESCRIPTOR_REVISION);
        sa.bInheritHandle=FALSE;
        sa.lpSecurityDescriptor=&sd;
        sa.nLength=sizeof(sa);
        rv=CreateNamedPipe("\\\\.\\pipe\\talkpipe_awc",
            PIPE_ACCESS_DUPLEX FILE_FLAG_OVERLAPPED,
            PIPE_TYPE_BYTE|PIPE_READMODE_BYTE,1,1024,1024,1000,&sa);

    }
    return rv;
}

void main(int argc, char *argv[])
{
    if (argc==1) server=TRUE;
    HANDLE pipe=OpenTalkPipe(server?".":argv[1]);
    HANDLE console=GetStdHandle(STD_INPUT_HANDLE);
    OVERLAPPED over;
    OVERLAPPED dummy;
    HANDLE port= CreateIoCompletionPort(pipe,NULL,1,0);
    char pipebuf;
    DWORD inlen;
    DWORD err;
    if (pipe==INVALID_HANDLE_VALUE||port==INVALID_HANDLE_VALUE)
    {
        err=GetLastError();
        cout<<"Error opening pipe or port ("<<err<<")\n";
        exit(9);
    }
    over.Internal=over.InternalHigh=over.Offset=over.OffsetHigh=0;
    over.hEvent=NULL;
    if (!SetConsoleMode(console,0))
    {
        cerr<<"Error: can't set console mode\n"<<GetLastError();
        exit(4);
    }
    cout<<"Waiting to connect\n";
    cout.flush();
    //read pipe
```

5. File I/O

```
do {
while (ReadFile(pipe,&pipebuf,1,&inlen,&over)) cout<<pipebuf;
err=GetLastError();
} while (err==ERROR_PIPE_LISTENING);  // wait for client
cerr<<"Connected (^C to disconnect)\n";
if (err!=ERROR_IO_PENDING)
{
   cerr<<"Error reading pipe ("<<err<<")\n";
   exit(3);
}
// Enter wait
while (1)
{

   if (WaitForSingleObject(console,0)==WAIT_OBJECT_0)
   {
      char inbuf; // ANSI only
      INPUT_RECORD irec;
      dummy.hEvent=NULL;
      dummy.Offset=dummy.OffsetHigh=
                  dummy.Internal=dummy.InternalHigh=0;
      DWORD inlen;
      // Using ReadConsole here never unsignals console!
      ReadConsoleInput(console,&irec,1,&inlen);
      if (irec.EventType==KEY_EVENT&&
                        irec.Event.KeyEvent.bKeyDown&&
         irec.Event.KeyEvent.uChar.AsciiChar!='\0')
      {
         inbuf=irec.Event.KeyEvent.uChar.AsciiChar;
         if (inbuf=='\003')
         {
            // quit
            CloseHandle(pipe);
            exit(0);
         }
         WriteFile(pipe,&inbuf,1,&inlen,&dummy);
         // echo
         cout<<((inbuf=='\r')?'\n':inbuf);
         cout.flush();

      }
   }
// if wait ended for pipe, dump character to console and issue another read
      DWORD rsiz,key;
      OVERLAPPED *o;
```

```
      if (GetQueuedCompletionStatus(port,&rsiz,&key,&o,0))
      {
         if (o==&dummy) continue; // was a write
         do
         {
            if (pipebuf=='\r') cout<<'\n'; else cout<<pipebuf;
         } while (ReadFile(pipe,&pipebuf,1,&inlen,&over));
         DWORD err=GetLastError();
         if (err!=ERROR_IO_PENDING)
         {
            cerr<<"Error reading pipe\n";
            exit(3);
         }
         cout.flush();
      }
   // Presumably we have something else we want to do here....

   }
}
```


Another Way To Access Files

Another exotic technique possible with Windows 2000 is memory-mapped files. This prevails on the virtual memory manager to make an entire file appear as though it is in memory. Of course, it really isn't. The virtual memory manager swaps pages of the file in and out of memory. On a Pentium, these pages are 4K in length, but that isn't necessarily true on every processor. You'll read more about the virtual memory manager in Chapter 7, but for now, you can use it without knowing much about it.

To page a file, open it with **CreateFile** and then use the file handle with **CreateFileMapping**. This generates a file mapping object. Windows uses these file mapping objects for shared memory, too (see Chapter 6). If you are using the object to share memory, you'll want to give it a name so other processes can access it. However, for simple file access, there's no reason to name the object. When you are ready to actually access the file, call **MapViewOfFile**. This function retrieves a pointer to the file's contents.

This pointer is just an ordinary pointer to memory and you can use it any way you like. So if you treat the pointer as a pointer to an array of characters, the first element is the file's first byte, the second element is the second byte in the file, and so on. Of course, you can also treat the pointer as a pointer to integers, or structures, or anything else you like.

When you map the file, you specify the number of bytes you want to work with as an argument to **CreateFileMapping**. You can pass 0 to request the entire file. You can also pass a number that is either larger or smaller than the actual file size, if you want. However, once you set the size, you can't change it. That makes it tough to use file mapping for files you expect to make larger (although, in that case, you could close the file mapping and create another).

When you no longer need the file mapping, call **UnmapViewOfFile**. Then call **CloseHandle** twice to dispose of the file mapping object and the actual file handle.

An Example

So let's put this theory into practice. As a simple example program, I decided to implement a console application that duplicates the function of the Unix **cat** command. For those who didn't take a turn on Unix, **cat** simply takes a list of file names and copies them, one at a time, to the standard out stream. You can use this command to join multiple files or display a single file. Of course, under Unix, **cat** also will copy standard input, but this program doesn't do that.

This is a classic example program to write with STDIO functions or C++ I/O streams. Listing 5.1 shows a version that uses the raw Windows file I/O calls. How does it look with mapped files?

You can find the completed program in Listing 5.4. It is really quite simple. Armed with a pointer to the file in memory, a single call to **cout.write** dumps the entire file to the output. You'll notice that the program asks the mapping to automatically make its size the same as the file's size. However, it still has to read the file size to know what number to pass to **write**. Also, the code doesn't attempt to handle files larger than 4 gigabytes.

Is using a file mapping better in any tangible way? Well, it is certainly elegant, but that's hardly a tangible quality. How about performance? Listing 5.5 shows two different implementations of **cat** (their **#if** statements differ). One method uses the old reliable **getc** and **putchar** calls. The other uses **fread** and **fwrite** with a 4K block size (because the MMU uses 4K pages).

The results were not very surprising. The mapped file version chewed through a 200K file in about 56.7 seconds. The version that uses **fread** was quite comparable at 56.6 seconds (well within my margin of error). Using **putchar**, of course, was a losing proposition. That version took about 1 minute and 20 seconds to display the same file.

Subjectively, there was an interesting result. Although the mapped file and the **fread** version took about the same amount of time, the mapped file seemed smoother. The **fread** version seemed jerky as it processed the 4K blocks of data. I didn't take the trouble to quantify this, but it certainly appeared to be true.

So in the final analysis, there doesn't seem to be much advantage or disadvantage to using file mapping over well-crafted I/O code. Of course, Listing 5.5 uses a memory buffer that the original code didn't use. Also, I just think the file mapping code is elegant by comparison to the file I/O versions.

Listing 5.4 Memory mapping version of NTCAT.

```
// NTCAT - Cat files on NT/Win2000
// Doesn't do nice error handling
// Any error causes the program to exit
// even though some other files might still work

#include <windows.h>
#include <iostream.h>

// Just a dumb wrapper around MessageBox:
void MB(char *s)
{
   MessageBox(NULL,s,NULL,MB_OK|MB_ICONSTOP);
}

// This routine does all the real work:
void docat(char *fname)
{
   HANDLE file; // file
   HANDLE map;  // file mapping
   char *base; // pointer to starting position
   int n; // size of file
   // Open the file for exclusive access/read only/no create
   file=CreateFile(fname,GENERIC_READ,0,NULL,
         OPEN_EXISTING,0,NULL);
      if (file==INVALID_HANDLE_VALUE
      {
            MB("Can't open file");
            exit(1);
      }
   // Assume size must be <4GB
   n=GetFileSize(file,NULL); // need size to know when to stop
   // Create mapping read only -- no sharing, so don't name it
   map=CreateFileMapping(file,NULL,PAGE_READONLY,0,0,NULL);
   if (!map)
      {
         MB("Can't open map");
```

```
            exit(2);
        }
        // Convert to pointer
        base=(char *)MapViewOfFile(map,FILE_MAP_READ,0,0,0);
        if (!base)
        {
            MB("Can't resolve map");
                exit(3);
    }
    // Dump characters:
    // could use cout<<base[i] in a loop or use puchar
    // but cout.write should be more efficient
    cout.write(base,n);
    // Undo everything
    UnmapViewOfFile(base);
    CloseHandle(map);
    CloseHandle(file);
}

void main(int argc,char *argv[])
{
    if (argc==1)
    {
         MB("Usage: ntcat FILENAME [FILENAME ....]");
         exit(9);
        }
        // Do all named files
        while (--argc) docat(*++argv);
        exit(0);
}
```


Listing 5.5 Normal version of NTCAT.

```
// NTCAT - Cat files on NT/Win2000
// Doesn't do nice error handling
// Any error causes the program to exit
// even though some other files might still work

#include <windows.h>
#include <stdio.h>

// Just a dumb wrapper around MessageBox:
void MB(char *s)
{
   MessageBox(NULL,s,NULL,MB_OK|MB_ICONSTOP);
}
```

```
// This routine does all the real work:
void docat(char *fname)
{
   FILE *f=fopen(fname,"r");
   if (!f)
   {
        MB("Can't open file");
        exit(1);
   }
#if 1 // select method
   int c;
   while ((c=getc(f))!=EOF) putchar(c);
#else
   char buf[4096];
   int n;
   while (!feof(f))
   {
        n=fread(buf,1,sizeof(buf),f);
        if (n) fwrite(buf,1,n,stdout);
   }
#endif
   fclose(f);
}

void main(int argc,char *argv[])
{
   if (argc==1)
   {
        MB("Usage: ntcat FILENAME [FILENAME ....]");
        exit(9);
   }
   // Do all named files
   while (--argc) docat(*++argv);
   exit(0);
}
```

Summary

Do you have to use **CreateFile** and the related calls to work with Windows files? Not at all. If you just need ordinary file I/O, you can continue to use **fopen**, MFC **CFiles**, C++ streams, or whatever you usually use. However, if you want special effects (like overlapped I/O), you'll probably have to use **CreateFile** because most libraries don't offer advanced Windows-specific features.

Of course, you won't use overlapped I/O every day, either. Usually, it is most useful when you want to read or write to a source that may not be ready (like a serial port, named pipe, or a socket). It can also be useful when you need to handle data from multiple sources at the same time. Programs that require very high I/O throughput are also candidates.

Immediate Solutions

Opening A File

To open a file using a direct call to Windows, call **CreateFile**. This is a poorly named API function because it might create a file, or it might open an existing one, depending on how you call it. The name should actually be **CreateFile-Handle**, but it isn't.

When calling **CreateFile**, you pass in a variety of arguments (refer back to Table 5.1) that control the operation. The return value is a handle to the open file.

The first argument you supply to **CreateFile** is the file name. Next, you specify how you want to access the file by using either **GENERIC_READ**, **GENERIC_WRITE**, or both values joined with the bit-wise "|" operator (which signifies "or"). The next argument is usually zero, unless you want to share the file with other processes.

The next argument is a pointer to a **SECURITY_ATTRIBUTES** structure (usually **NULL**). If you supply this parameter, it will determine if child processes can inherit the file, and what security options the file uses.

After the security attributes, you'll supply an argument that determines if the call actually creates the file (**CREATE_NEW** or **CREATE_ALWAYS**), or will open only an existing file (**OPEN_EXISTING**). After that, you provide a set of flags. These flags enable you to set special modes (like overlapped I/O; refer back to Table 5.2). You can also provide information here about how you want the system to create the file, if it creates it at all. For example, you can specify that the new file has the hidden attribute. This doesn't affect files that already exist.

The final argument, which is usually **NULL**, provides the handle of an open file that you want to use as a template file. If you supply this template, and the call creates a new file, the new file will have the same attributes (hidden, read-only, etc.) as the template file.

Although there are quite a few arguments to this call, you won't use many of them often. Usually, you'll supply the file name, **GENERIC_READ** or **GENERIC_WRITE** (or perhaps both), zero for file sharing, a **NULL** for the security attributes, **CREATE_NEW** or **OPEN_EXISTING**, flags of zero, and a **NULL** template file.

You should always check the return value of **CreateFile** because there are so many things that might go wrong. If the call fails, it will return **INVALID_HANDLE_VALUE**. Of course, you can call **GetLastError** to find out why the call failed.

Reading Or Writing A File Synchronously

If you create a file with **CreateFile**, you'll need to use **ReadFile** to read from the file and **WriteFile** to write to it. These calls could hardly be simpler. Each takes the file handle, the address of a data buffer, and the number of bytes to process as arguments. They also require a pointer to a **DWORD** where the call stores the actual number of bytes processed. Each call also takes a pointer to an **OVERLAPPED** structure. For normal synchronous I/O, this parameter is always **NULL**. You only supply this parameter when doing overlapped, or asynchronous, I/O (covered in several sections later in this Immediate Solutions section).

The calls return 0 if they do not succeed. You then can use **GetLastError** to determine why. Listing 5.1, earlier in this chapter, shows an example of synchronous I/O.

Detecting EOF (Synchronous)

When you read a file synchronously (that is, without providing an **OVERLAPPED** structure), it is easy to tell when you are at the end of the file. If **ReadFile** encounters the end of the file, it returns whatever it managed to read. Another call to **ReadFile** will also succeed, but the returned count of characters will be zero.

It is important to realize that this method does not work for overlapped files. You'll see a method for detecting EOF asynchronously in the "Detecting EOF (Asynchronous)" section later in this Immediate Solutions section.

Duplicating File Handles

If you have a handle, you might want to duplicate it so that it has different properties than the original. You can duplicate nearly any kind of handle with **DuplicateHandle**. This call requires the source process handle and the process handle that will use the new handle. These can be the same if you aren't planning on sharing the new handle (use **GetCurrentProcess** to learn your process handle).

Additional arguments to **DuplicateHandle** enable you to change the access to the handle or control whether child processes inherit it or not. You can also tell the call not to change the access to the handle or to close the original handle after duplication.

Closing A File

When you are done with a file, you'll want to close it. If you open the file with **CreateFile**, close it with **CloseHandle**. Of course, **CloseHandle** will close any handle, not just a file handle.

Using Methods For Asynchronous I/O

There are many cases where it is useful to ask the system to perform I/O, but you don't want your program to wait if there is no data available at the moment. This is asynchronous I/O.

Windows provides several different techniques for performing asynchronous I/O, including:

- Blocking I/O in a separate thread
- Overlapped (nonblocking) I/O with explicit completion
- Overlapped I/O with event-based completion
- Overlapped I/O with callbacks
- Overlapped I/O with completion ports

Each of these techniques has advantages and disadvantages. Using a separate thread, for example, is simple and provides the most flexibility. However, it isn't necessarily very efficient. Ultimately, the best choice depends on your particular situation and what you want to achieve.

Using Asynchronous I/O With Threads

Using a separate thread is by far the easiest way to do asynchronous I/O. You simply start a thread, do regular I/O from inside that thread, and somehow communicate the results to the rest of your program.

Of course, a natural idea is to use a circular buffer to communicate with the main thread. This isn't hard to implement, although you should use a synchronization method (like a critical section) to protect the buffer's data structure.

You can find an example of just this sort of circular buffer in Listing 5.6. This simple program uses a circular buffer (protected with a critical section) and a single event. When the I/O thread adds characters to the buffer (from the console), it signals the event. This enables the program to wait efficiently for characters, if it wants to wait at all.

It would be moderately simple to add another thread to read from a serial port, and convert this into a simple dumb terminal program. The main program could wait on both events and take the appropriate action when characters appeared from either source.

Listing 5.6 Thread-based I/O.

```
#include <windows.h>
#include <iostream.h>
#include <process.h>


HANDLE comevent;
HANDLE console;
CRITICAL_SECTION csection;

int head=0,tail=0;
char buf[32];  // circular buffer

void addbuf(char c)
{
    EnterCriticalSection(&csection);
    buf[head++]=c;
    if (head>=sizeof(buf)) head=0;
    SetEvent(comevent);
    // you had better get characters out before overflow
    LeaveCriticalSection(&csection);
}

char getbuf(void)
{
```

```
    char c;
    if (head==tail) return (char)0;
    EnterCriticalSection(&csection);
    c=buf[tail++];
    if (tail>=sizeof(buf)) tail=0;
    LeaveCriticalSection(&csection);
    return c;
}

BOOL bufdataready(void)
{
    return head!=tail;
}

void comthread(void *)
{
    char cbuf;
    DWORD inlen;
    while (1)
    {
      if (!ReadFile(console,&cbuf,1,&inlen,NULL)) continue;
      if (inlen) addbuf(cbuf);
    }
}


void main()
{
    char c;
    DWORD len;
    HANDLE consoleout;
    InitializeCriticalSection(&csection);
    console=GetStdHandle(STD_INPUT_HANDLE);
    SetConsoleMode(console,0);
    consoleout=GetStdHandle(STD_OUTPUT_HANDLE);
    comevent=CreateEvent(NULL,FALSE,FALSE,NULL);
    _beginthread(comthread,0,NULL);
    while (1)
    {
        if (WaitForSingleObject(comevent,INFINITE)==WAIT_OBJECT_0)
        {
            c=getbuf();
            WriteFile(consoleout,&c,1,&len,NULL);
        }
        // Presumably do something else here
    }
}
```

Starting Overlapped I/O

To perform any type of overlapped I/O, you must use **CreateFile** with the **FILE_FLAG_OVERLAPPED** parameter. If you provide this parameter, you must use overlapped I/O calls to work with the file. If you do not pass **FILE_FLAG_OVERLAPPED**, then you must not use overlapped calls. For the most part, overlapped calls have a pointer to an **OVERLAPPED** structure that is not **NULL**.

The simplest calls you can make are **ReadFile** and **WriteFile**. These calls work as they usually do, except you must supply a pointer to an **OVERLAPPED** structure. This structure has five fields. The system reserves the first two fields, so I'll discuss only the last three. Two of these fields store the high and low 32 bits of the offset you want to read from (or write to). That means you can perform your read or write anywhere in a file even if it is larger than 4GB. If you are working with a socket, named pipe, or a device (like a COM port), the system ignores this field.

The last field of the **OVERLAPPED** structure can be zero, but if it isn't, the system treats it as a manual event handle. You'll see how this event handle works in the next section.

When you issue an overlapped read or write, it may be that the system has the data available right away. This could be because the data is already in the disk cache or a device (or socket) has data queued up waiting.

When this happens, the call returns success, and there is no difference between overlapped I/O and regular I/O. However, if the I/O requires you to wait, the call returns **FALSE**. This normally means the operation failed. However, in this case, you must call **GetLastError**. If it returns **ERROR_IO_PENDING**, then it isn't really an error. It means that the call did not complete immediately, and that the system is still working on it.

If the I/O call returns **ERROR_IO_PENDING**, you'll have to check back later to see when (and if) the call really completed. You'll find out how to do so in the next section.

Completing Asynchronous I/O

If your I/O call returns a nonzero value, then the call completed without waiting. But if it returns **FALSE**, and calling **GetLastError** returns **ERROR_IO_PENDING**, then you'll have to wait. There are several ways you can complete the I/O call. The least useful way is to call **CancelIo**. This completes it by terminating the operation (not what you usually want).

Another way to complete the I/O is by calling **GetOverlappedResult**. You can specify if you want this call to wait indefinitely. If you tell it to wait indefinitely, it will return when the operation completes or when an error occurs. Otherwise, it will return if either condition is true, or it will return **FALSE** immediately. If you call **GetLastError**, and the operation is pending, the call will return **ERROR_IO_INCOMPLETE**. This doesn't terminate the operation; it notifies you that the operation is still in progress.

A third way to complete an overlapped I/O operation is to specify a manual event handle in the **OVERLAPPED** structure. When the I/O request returns **ERROR_IO_PENDING** to your program, it resets the event. Then, when the operation completes, it signals the event. This provides a handy way to wait on multiple I/O operations (refer back to the example in Listing 5.2).

These three methods are the basic techniques you'll use to complete overlapped I/O. However, you can also use **ReadFileEx**, **WriteFileEx**, and completion ports. You'll read about these techniques shortly.

Detecting EOF (Asynchronous)

Asynchronous (or overlapped) I/O makes it harder to detect the end of file condition. That's because the system might detect the EOF when you call **ReadFile**, or it might not detect it until you complete the I/O.

It would be unpleasant if you had to have two special cases to worry about. Luckily, the system makes the two different cases seem the same. When you call **ReadFile** or **GetOverlappedResult**, and the file is at EOF, the call returns **FALSE** (that is, it fails). When you call **GetLastError**, it returns **ERROR_HANDLE_EOF** in either case.

Using ReadFileEx And WriteFileEx

When using overlapped I/O, you may find it useful to employ **ReadFileEx** and **WriteFileEx** instead of their more common cousins. Unlike **ReadFile** and **WriteFile**, these two calls are only for overlapped I/O.

These calls work much like the regular **ReadFile** and **WriteFile** calls, but they accept an extra parameter. This parameter specifies a callback function that the system calls when the I/O completes.

This seems ideal. However, there is a catch. The system calls the callback function as an APC (asynchronous procedure call; see Chapter 3). These calls can occur only when your thread is in an alertable wait state. You can find out more about this in Chapter 3, but the short story is that you won't get APC calls unless you call **SleepEx**, **WaitForSingleObjectEx**, or **WaitForMultipleObjectsEx**. This limits the usefulness of these calls.

Using Completion Ports

Another way to wait for overlapped I/O to complete is by using I/O completion ports. You open the overlapped file as usual, but then call **CreateIoCompletionPort**, specifying the file handle and a 32-bit key number (which can have any value you like).

When the corresponding file handle completes any I/O, it will post a notification in the completion port. You can think of the port as a queue of notifications. Any thread that queries the port (using **GetQueuedCompletionStatus**) will get the next available notification.

Completion ports are most useful when you are trying to implement a design where a pool of threads handles your I/O (for example, a Web server with a fixed number of threads). You can find a simple example of using completion ports in Listing 5.3, earlier in this chapter.

Memory Mapping Files

Another way to access files is to map them into memory. To do this, open the file with **CreateFile**, then use the file handle with **CreateFileMapping**. This generates a file mapping object. When you are ready to actually access the file, call **MapViewOfFile**. This function retrieves a pointer to the file's contents. You can use this pointer in any way you like.

When you no longer need the pointer, call **UnmapViewOfFile**, then call **Close Handle** twice to close the file mapping object and the file. You can find a complete example in Listing 5.4, earlier in this chapter.

Mapped files are handy, especially for reading files. They are a bit less useful for writing because you have to fix the size when you create the mapping. Windows also uses mapped files as shared memory, as you will see in Chapter 6.

Chapter 6

Interprocess Communications

If you need an immediate solution to:	*See page:*
Summary Of IPC Methods	322
Using **WM_COPYDATA**	323
Using DLLs For Shared Memory	324
File Mapping Shared Memory	325
Using Anonymous Pipes	325
Using Named Pipes	326
Replacing A Standard Handle With A Pipe	327
Using Mailslots	327
Using Sockets	328
Using RPCs	329
Understanding When To Use Obsolete Or Little-Used IPC Methods	330

In Depth

My Dad gave me a priceless gift when I was very young. It all started when he introduced me to a fascinating hobby: shortwave radio listening. Apparently, before I was born, he had built an Allied Radio regenerative receiver. One of his friends was trying to get an amateur radio license at the time, and Dad thought he would do it, too.

I don't know what ever happened to that old radio, because family responsibilities didn't allow enough time for Dad to continue his radio hobby. But when I was about six or seven, Dad told me a bit about it and it really sparked my imagination. He told me how he would listen to the Vatican, China, and London—exotic places to a six-year-old in those days.

I got so interested in the whole thing that he and my Mom bought me an Eico shortwave receiver. It wasn't top of the line or anything, but I loved it. I would spend hours listening to London, Ecuador, Canada, South Africa, and most anyplace in Europe. It was even fun to listen to the constant propaganda coming from Radio Moscow, and the equally ridiculous counter-propaganda from the Voice of America.

Later, I took the plunge and earned my amateur radio license. My radio hobby led me to a career in electronics, and later computers. I made many lifelong friends and learned a lot of geography. What a great hobby for a child.

So there must be a lot of young radio hobbyists today, right? Sadly, the answer is no. Today's young people couldn't care less. Want to listen to news from faraway places? Watch CNN. Want to talk to people who belong to different cultures? Get on the Internet. There's no challenge, but most people want results, not challenges.

The world is smaller today, thanks to modern telecommunications infrastructure. When my grandfather passed away, we sent a telegram to my uncle, who was in Japan with the United States Navy. You couldn't pick up the phone and call Japan without a bevy of operators and a fat bank account. Nowadays, Candice Bergen and her colleagues all but beg us to call Japan (or anywhere else) direct, for mere pennies.

Of course, another outgrowth of this technology (and some related ones) is the beloved and maligned Internet. Today, most computers participate, at least part time, on the Internet. There are many cases where scientists distribute experimental results, pictures, and telemetry in realtime over the Net to investigators all over the world. It won't be long until your phone, your TV, your car, and maybe your toaster all talk over the Net (or whatever replaces it).

This puts a whole new importance on interprocess communications. At one time, interprocess communications meant moving punched cards from a card punch's output tray to the card reader's hopper so the next program could read them. Later, as operating systems grew in sophistication, interprocess communications (or IPC) took on more sophisticated forms, too. On a single machine, IPC might take the guise of shared memory, or a pipe. For a long time, IPC largely occurred between processes on the same machine.

However, networking adds a new twist to the picture. As more and more computers connect, there is a strong temptation to communicate between processes that might be on different computers. This is particularly thorny when one machine is a VAX and the other is a PC, for example.

Each operating system evolution introduces new IPC mechanisms. The older methods, however, usually have some merit, so they don't disappear. That means that a modern operating system like Win2000 includes many features that you can class as IPC technologies. Not every one is appropriate in every situation, of course.

Why The Big Deal?

If you are used to thinking about programming one program at a time, the idea of IPC might seem strange. After all, you could certainly write data to a file, and let another program read the data from there, right? Well, in a way, using a file like this is a very crude form of IPC. However, files are usually slow because they depend on some form of magnetic media. Besides, files make it difficult to carry on realtime conversations. Ideally, you would like to have one program send some data to another program, wait for a response, and then send some more data.

The situation becomes even more complex when you want the programs to reside on different machines. Then you have client/server architecture. It is especially important to have ways that a server can handle more than one client at a time.

So if you have IPC, what can you do with it? Well, one IPC application you probably use every day is the World Wide Web (and the Internet in general). When your browser views a Web page, it connects to a remote server, and these two very different programs communicate. The server may not even be a Windows program (many Web servers run under Unix), but it doesn't matter. Using the right IPC mechanism can smooth out the differences.

Other large-scale examples include any system that has a remote database server or a system with many distributed workstations. Online transaction processing systems like those found in banks, large retailers, and airline reservations systems fit this model. None of these would be possible without some kind of IPC.

These large-scale examples seem obvious, but what can you use IPC for in more mundane settings? IPC is essential if you want to build any application that has functionality distributed across several programs. Simulations are a classic example of this. For example, if you wanted to model the stock market, you might use separate programs to model buyers and sellers.

You can find a simpler example in any ordinary Unix shell. Unix has a history of letting you join little programs together to make larger ones easily and quickly. Consider the DOS **DIR** command that you might run from a command prompt. It has lots of options that let you pause its output and sort the listing by various criteria. The Unix **ls** command (which is similar to **DIR**) doesn't have any of these options. Does that mean that **ls** is not as powerful as **DIR**? Absolutely not.

The **ls** command doesn't include paging and sorting functions, because it doesn't have to provide them. Other programs provide those features. Want to see a directory listing one page at a time? Use a pipe and the **more** program:

```
ls | more
```


How about a sorted list, one page at a time? Try this with your choice of options to the **sort** program:

```
ls | sort | more
```

Sure, you can do this from a DOS prompt, too, but in Unix it isn't just a feature, it is the entire design philosophy. This philosophy has many advantages. Often small programs combine in ways that surprise their authors to produce powerful results. Also, programs are simpler because they reuse other programs instead of reinventing the wheel. Finally, each function is free for other programs to use. For example, suppose you have a list of kids on your Little League team in the Team1.TXT and Team2.TXT files. If you want to sort that list, you could write:

```
cat Team1.TXT Team2.TXT | sort
```

Of course, **cat** is similar to the DOS **TYPE** command (although **cat** can do things that **TYPE** can't). The sort program couldn't care less if it is sorting a directory listing, a team roster, or your grocery list.

Of course, you don't absolutely have to use IPC to get this effect. DOS has had pipes for years, and it doesn't support multiple processes, much less IPC, right? Not exactly. DOS uses files for its IPC. Consider this command line:

```
DIR | SORT | MORE
```

What does DOS do to process this line? First it runs **DIR**, redirecting its output to a temporary file. Once **DIR** is completely finished, DOS runs **SORT**, redirecting its input to the temporary file and creating a second temporary file to catch the output. When **SORT** exits, DOS runs **MORE**, allowing it to read from the second temporary file.

Not only does this waste disk space, but it means that each intermediate program must run to completion before any output appears. With Unix, all three programs (**ls**, **sort**, and **more**) run simultaneously. The IPC pipes that connect them let data flow immediately between programs. This is economical and provides speedy results.

Partitioning problems into multiple programs is often a difficult habit to develop. Once you get used to it, however, it is hard to switch back to thinking about one large monolithic program. Of course, another way to partition programs is to use threads. How does this fit in with IPC?

Threads And IPC

In reality, IPC should be interthread communication. Processes don't communicate, threads do. However, threads in the same process don't need IPC. They can work together using simple variables. The only time you'll use IPC is when you have threads in different processes that need to communicate.

This leads to a basic design question: When do you use threads, and when do you use processes? The answer is sometimes very obvious. For example, if you are writing a Web browser, and you plan to connect with a server over the Internet, you will definitely need IPC. Other times the answer is less clear. For example, what if you set out to write the stock market simulation I mentioned earlier in this chapter? Would it be better to represent the traders as threads or as processes?

This is not always an easy choice. In my mind, the tradeoff is between efficiency and safety. Representing traders as threads is very efficient. Threads have the maximum possible communications bandwidth. However, threads are not very safe. If one thread goes crazy, it can easily sabotage the entire program. Of course, for this program, that might not be a problem. Other programs may be more sensitive, however.

Implementing traders as processes is certainly safer. It is harder for one trader process to crash another. It isn't impossible, however. Windows promises you that unrelated processes won't crash your process, but once you start communicating with another process, you don't have as strong a promise. For example, suppose you read an array index from another process and then use that index to read from some shared memory. If the index is invalid, and you don't check it first, you could crash. On the other hand, an errant thread can easily bring other threads to their knees no matter how much checking is in place. The downside is that IPC is more complex and must be less efficient than communications between threads in the same process.

Sometimes, a particular design goal will dictate which method you choose. For example, what if you wanted to add new traders dynamically? That might make separate processes a good choice. You could write each trader separately (even using different languages, perhaps) and add them in dynamically at any time. A buggy trader wouldn't crash the simulation if you program defensively.

Overview of Windows 2000 IPC Mechanisms

Here's the short list of IPC mechanisms you'll find in Windows:

- ***WM_COPYDATA***—Passes a block of memory between two processes.
- *The clipboard*—The clipboard is perhaps the most rudimentary form of Windows IPC. However, because the user usually manipulates the clipboard, it is considered rude for programs to use it unless the user requests it.
- *DLLs*—Odd as it may seem, DLLs have the power to share memory between processes.
- *Shared memory*—Win32's version of shared memory is somewhat unusual. The official way to share memory between processes is to use a mapped file (see Chapter 5). When a process maps a file, it uses a file mapping object to page that file directly into its virtual address space. Processes on the same machine can share the file mapping object to get a synchronized view of the file. If you only want to share memory, you can create a file mapping object without the file.
- *Anonymous pipes*—These are similar to pipes you use at the DOS and Unix command lines. These have limited usefulness for most Windows programs.
- *Named pipes*—Named pipes are a powerful way for two programs to communicate using a client/server model even when they are on different computers. In recent years, sockets have eclipsed named pipes in many programs, but you may still find named pipes handy for certain purposes.

- *Mailslots*—Mailslots are an odd way for programs to accept messages from other programs. Mailslots are one-way only, so for bidirectional communications, you'll need two of them. Mailslots' biggest claim to fame is that you can broadcast a message to related mailslots over a local area network in one operation.
- *Dynamic Data Exchange (DDE)*—At one time, DDE was a popular protocol for communicating between programs. Many Microsoft programs (even the Windows Program Manager) offered support for it. Today DDE support is largely for backward compatibility. There isn't anything wrong with DDE per se, but Microsoft decided to promote OLE (which became ActiveX) at the expense of other technologies that might compete with OLE. DDE was one of those technologies.
- *NetBios*—For many years, NetBios reigned as the PC network protocol. Today, Windows still supports NetBios, but mostly this support is to ensure compatibility with older programs.
- *Sockets*—Considered the workhorses of the Internet, sockets are a standard way to communicate over large networks. Few computers today don't offer some socket interface. Windows' excellent support for sockets is very similar to the socket libraries you'll find on other operating systems. If you already know how to program sockets under Unix, for example, you'll have little trouble using them with Windows.
- *Remote Procedure Calls (RPCs)*—RPCs are another widely available standard. RPC isn't so much an IPC method as it is a wrapper over a more traditional IPC method. The idea is to allow a server to expose an actual function that a client apparently calls directly. RPC enables this process to work transparently. The client makes an ordinary function call, and the server receives an ordinary function call. RPC provides the magic that makes the network part of this operation invisible.
- *ActiveX*—ActiveX can do many things. Recall from Chapter 2 that ActiveX is really just a way to create binary objects. However, one purpose for which you can use these objects is IPC. Microsoft defines an interface, **IDataObject**, just for this purpose. The Distributed Component Object Model (DCOM) is another ActiveX technology that can help facilitate IPC. DCOM is essentially a marriage between ActiveX and RPC.
- *Microsoft Message Queue (MSMQ)*—MSMQ is a protocol that enables applications to send messages to each other. What makes MSMQ different from other forms of IPC is that it is possible to send a message to a process that is not currently available (the server is down or there is a network problem, for example). MSMQ queues the message until it can deliver it at a later time.

Purists may classify some of these as parts of networking. This is true, but what is networking other than really high-powered IPC? Notice too that I didn't include synchronization methods in this list, because they don't transfer data (see Chapter 4). However, in some cases they serve to transmit information between processes.

Is it hard to decide what IPC method to use? You bet! The good news is that most IPC methods are not hard to use.

Simple IPC

The simplest way to communicate with other processes is via the **WM_COPYDATA** message. The **WM_COPYDATA** message isn't used often, but it is sometimes all you need. When you send this message to a window in another process, you supply a **COPYDATASTRUCT** (see Table 6.1), and you must use **SendMessage** (not **PostMessage**). Windows takes care of transforming the structure so that the receiving process can read it. This doesn't, of course, enable both processes to access the data simultaneously. Instead, it is like sending a friend a photocopy of a document. You won't see any changes your friend makes, nor will any changes you make later be reflected in your friend's copy.

The **COPYDATASTRUCT** has a 32-bit value that the receiving process can read. It also contains a pointer to some data and the length of that data in bytes. You must not change the data until your **SendMessage** call returns. Also, the receiving process can access only the pointer while it is processing this message.

Although **WM_COPYDATA** is simple, it has the same limitation that nearly all IPC methods have: You can't be sure that both processes will see the shared data at the same address. Therefore, you should avoid putting addresses that point to shared memory in shared memory.

Suppose you allocate a block of memory, and then you build a linked list of structures, where each structure contains a pointer to the next structure. This works fine, until you try to send this data to another process. When the second process receives **WM_COPYDATA**, there is no way to know if the address will be the

Table 6.1 The COPYDATASTRUCT structure.

Field	Definition
dwData	32-bit integer to pass between processes
cbData	Number of bytes to transfer
lpData	Pointer to bytes (size in cbData)

6. Interprocess Communications

same. If it isn't (and that is quite likely to be the case), the linked list's pointers will contain invalid addresses (or worse, valid addresses that have nothing to do with the linked list).

So, does this mean you can't pass complex data structures using IPC? Not at all. But you do have to be careful not to use addresses. One solution might be to store an offset from the beginning of the list instead of an absolute address. Then each routine that accesses the list has to remember to add the start address (which might differ between processes) before actually using the address. This is similar to the steps you would need to take if you were writing the structure out to a file.

A WM_COPYDATA Example

Listings 6.1 through 6.3 show two programs that communicate via **WM_COPYDATA**. Listing 6.1 is a simple console mode program. It searches for the other program's window by calling **FindWindow** and looking for the correct title. When it finds the window, it takes your input, packages it in a **COPYDATASTRUCT**, and sends it along to the window.

Listing 6.1 The transmitter.

```
#include <stdio.h>
#include <windows.h>
#include <string.h>

void main()
{
   char s[256];
   HWND w=FindWindow(NULL,"WM_COPYDATA Reader");
   COPYDATASTRUCT data;
   printf("enter quit to end program\n");
   do {
     gets(s);
     strcat(s,"\r\n");
       data.cbData=strlen(s);
     data.lpData=s;
     printf("addr=%x\n",(int)s);
     SendMessage(w,WM_COPYDATA,(WPARAM)GetFocus(),(LPARAM)&data);
   } while (strcmp(s,"quit\r\n"));
}
```

The second program is a simple MFC program that uses a **CFormView** (similar to a dialog). Listing 6.2 shows the main frame class, which embodies the program's main window. This is the window that receives the **WM_COPYDATA** message since the **FindWindow** call in Listing 6.1 finds only main windows. The window processes the message with a standard MFC message map, which delivers the message to the **OnCopyData** routine.

Listing 6.2 The receiver frame.

```
// MainFrm.cpp : implementation of the CMainFrame class
//

#include "stdafx.h"
#include "copyrcvr.h"

#include "MainFrm.h"

#ifdef _DEBUG
#define new DEBUG_NEW
#undef THIS_FILE
static char THIS_FILE[] = __FILE__;
#endif

/////////////////////////////
// CMainFrame

IMPLEMENT_DYNCREATE(CMainFrame, CFrameWnd)

BEGIN_MESSAGE_MAP(CMainFrame, CFrameWnd)
   //{{AFX_MSG_MAP(CMainFrame)
   ON_WM_CREATE()
   ON_WM_COPYDATA()
   //}}AFX_MSG_MAP
END_MESSAGE_MAP()

static UINT indicators[] =
{
   ID_SEPARATOR,           // status line indicator
   ID_INDICATOR_CAPS,
   ID_INDICATOR_NUM,
   ID_INDICATOR_SCRL,
};

/////////////////////////////
// CMainFrame construction/destruction

CMainFrame::CMainFrame()
{
   // TODO: add member initialization code here

}

CMainFrame::~CMainFrame()
```

```
{
}

int CMainFrame::OnCreate(LPCREATESTRUCT lpCreateStruct)
{
   if (CFrameWnd::OnCreate(lpCreateStruct) == -1)
      return -1;

   if (!m_wndToolBar.Create(this) ||
      !m_wndToolBar.LoadToolBar(IDR_MAINFRAME))
   {
      TRACE0("Failed to create toolbar\n");
      return -1;      // fail to create
   }

   if (!m_wndStatusBar.Create(this) ||
      !m_wndStatusBar.SetIndicators(indicators,
        sizeof(indicators)/sizeof(UINT)))
   {
      TRACE0("Failed to create status bar\n");
      return -1;      // fail to create
   }

   // TODO: Remove this if you don't want tool tips or a resizeable toolbar
   m_wndToolBar.SetBarStyle(m_wndToolBar.GetBarStyle() |
      CBRS_TOOLTIPS | CBRS_FLYBY | CBRS_SIZE_DYNAMIC);

   // TODO: Delete these three lines if you don't want the toolbar to
   //  be dockable
   m_wndToolBar.EnableDocking(CBRS_ALIGN_ANY);
   EnableDocking(CBRS_ALIGN_ANY);
   DockControlBar(&m_wndToolBar);

   return 0;
}

BOOL CMainFrame::PreCreateWindow(CREATESTRUCT& cs)
{
    cs.style&=~FWS_ADDTOTITLE;
   return CFrameWnd::PreCreateWindow(cs);
}

////////////////////////////////
// CMainFrame diagnostics
```

6. Interprocess Communications

```
#ifdef _DEBUG
void CMainFrame::AssertValid() const
{
   CFrameWnd::AssertValid();
}

void CMainFrame::Dump(CDumpContext& dc) const
{
   CFrameWnd::Dump(dc);
}

#endif //_DEBUG

//////////////////////////////
// CMainFrame message handlers

BOOL CMainFrame::OnCopyData(CWnd* pWnd, COPYDATASTRUCT* pCopyDataStruct)
{
// delegate to view
   GetActiveView()->
          SendMessage(WM_COPYDATA,
          (WPARAM)pWnd->m_hWnd,(LPARAM)pCopyDataStruct);
   return CFrameWnd::OnCopyData(pWnd, pCopyDataStruct);
}
```


Listing 6.3 The receiving view.

```
// copyrcvrView.cpp : implementation of the CCopyrcvrView class
//

#include "stdafx.h"
#include "copyrcvr.h"

#include "copyrcvrDoc.h"
#include "copyrcvrView.h"

#ifdef _DEBUG
#define new DEBUG_NEW
#undef THIS_FILE
static char THIS_FILE[] = __FILE__;
#endif

//////////////////////////////
// CCopyrcvrView
```

```
IMPLEMENT_DYNCREATE(CCopyrcvrView, CFormView)

BEGIN_MESSAGE_MAP(CCopyrcvrView, CFormView)
   //{{AFX_MSG_MAP(CCopyrcvrView)
   ON_WM_COPYDATA()
   //}}AFX_MSG_MAP
   // Standard printing commands
   ON_COMMAND(ID_FILE_PRINT, CFormView::OnFilePrint)
   ON_COMMAND(ID_FILE_PRINT_DIRECT, CFormView::OnFilePrint)
   ON_COMMAND(ID_FILE_PRINT_PREVIEW, CFormView::OnFilePrintPreview)
END_MESSAGE_MAP()

//////////////////////////////
// CCopyrcvrView construction/destruction

CCopyrcvrView::CCopyrcvrView()
   : CFormView(CCopyrcvrView::IDD)
{
   //{{AFX_DATA_INIT(CCopyrcvrView)
   m_text = _T("");
   //}}AFX_DATA_INIT
   // TODO: add construction code here

}

CCopyrcvrView::~CCopyrcvrView()
{
}

void CCopyrcvrView::DoDataExchange(CDataExchange* pDX)
{
   CFormView::DoDataExchange(pDX);
   //{{AFX_DATA_MAP(CCopyrcvrView)
   DDX_Text(pDX, IDC_EDIT1, m_text);
   //}}AFX_DATA_MAP
}

BOOL CCopyrcvrView::PreCreateWindow(CREATESTRUCT& cs)
{
   // TODO: Modify the Window class or styles here by modifying
   //  the CREATESTRUCT cs

   return CFormView::PreCreateWindow(cs);
}
```

```
//////////////////////////////
// CCopyrcvrView printing

BOOL CCopyrcvrView::OnPreparePrinting(CPrintInfo* pInfo)
{
   // default preparation
   return DoPreparePrinting(pInfo);
}

void CCopyrcvrView::OnBeginPrinting(CDC* /*pDC*/, CPrintInfo* /*pInfo*/)
{
   // TODO: add extra initialization before printing
}

void CCopyrcvrView::OnEndPrinting(CDC* /*pDC*/, CPrintInfo* /*pInfo*/)
{
   // TODO: add cleanup after printing
}

void CCopyrcvrView::OnPrint(CDC* pDC, CPrintInfo*)
{
   // TODO: add code to print the controls
}

//////////////////////////////
// CCopyrcvrView diagnostics

#ifdef _DEBUG
void CCopyrcvrView::AssertValid() const
{
   CFormView::AssertValid();
}

void CCopyrcvrView::Dump(CDumpContext& dc) const
{
   CFormView::Dump(dc);
}

CCopyrcvrDoc* CCopyrcvrView::GetDocument() // non-debug version is inline
{
   ASSERT(m_pDocument->IsKindOf(RUNTIME_CLASS(CCopyrcvrDoc)));
   return (CCopyrcvrDoc*)m_pDocument;
}
#endif //_DEBUG
```

```
////////////////////////////
// CCopyrcvrView message handlers

BOOL CCopyrcvrView::OnCopyData(CWnd* pWnd, COPYDATASTRUCT* pCopyDataStruct)
{
   CString s=(char *)pCopyDataStruct->lpData;
   CString addr;
   addr.Format("(%x)",(int)pCopyDataStruct->lpData);
   m_text+=s+addr;
   UpdateData(FALSE);
   return TRUE;
}
```

The only problem is that the frame isn't in a good position to update the text in the form view. The answer is simple. The **OnCopyData** routine in Listing 6.2 delegates the message by resending it to the view (see Listing 6.3). **WM_COPYDATA** messages don't have to be between processes.

I added a few lines of code to print the address each program sees for the data. Of course, the transmitting console program always uses the same address. The receiving program uses a different address. Try running multiple copies of the transmit program at the same time and notice the different address the receive program uses.

Using DLLs For Shared Memory

DLLs are the core of Windows. Usually, you think of DLLs as a way to package code for dynamic linking. However, you can also use them to map shared variables into multiple process spaces. Like **WM_COPYDATA**, you can't be sure every process will see the memory at the same address, however.

When a Win32 DLL declares a variable, it may make it shared or private. If it is private, each process that attaches to the DLL receives its own copy of the variable. If the DLL marks a variable shared, then all processes will use the same physical memory for that variable.

DLLs have an address they prefer to load at (you set this at link time). If an attaching process has this space available, the DLL will load there. However, if the linear address space is otherwise occupied, Windows will relocate the DLL to a different address. When this happens, the shared memory winds up at a different address, too.

Exactly how to mark variables as shared or private depends on the compiler you use. For Microsoft Visual C++, the default is to make DLL variables private. If you want to share them, you'll need to use some pragmas.

DLL Details

The key question for using DLLs as an IPC mechanism is: Who owns a global variable in a DLL? For Win32, the answer isn't clear-cut. By default, a Microsoft DLL always gives each program a private copy of global variables. Consider this partial code from a DLL:

```
int threshold;
void set_thresh(int n) // export this function
  {
  threshold=n;
  }

int get_thresh(void)  // export this function
  {
  return threshold;
  }
```

If multiple processes use this DLL (compiled with Visual C++), they will all have a private copy of the **threshold** variable. If you compile the DLL with Borland's compiler and use it from multiple processes, all processes will share the **threshold** variable (unless you specify **MULTIPLE** in the DEF file). With Microsoft's compiler, follow these steps to get the same effect.

1. Mark the variable with a special pragma. This places the variable in a data section.
2. Make certain that the variable has an initial value.
3. Use the linker options (or the DEF file) to set the attributes for the data section that holds the variable.

Here's the same variable declaration with the sharing pragma:

```
#pragma data_seg(".ASHARE")
int threshold=0;
// more shared data could go here
#pragma data_seg()
```

Be sure to initialize all shared variables. If you don't, the variable will wind up in the uninitialized variable pool and won't share. That's why **threshold** has an initial value of zero explicitly set.

The section name can be any legal identifier that is eight characters or fewer, preceded by a period. The actual name you use doesn't really matter. Of course, you can't use section names the compiler already uses for something else (for example, **.CODE**, **.DATA**, **.BSS**, etc.).

Next, you need a special option passed to the linker. You can set this in the project settings (exactly where depends on what version of Visual C++ you are using). The setting dialog doesn't have a special place for the option you need; you'll have to modify the command line (at the bottom of the dialog). If you can't change it, make sure you have either Debug or Release build selected, but *not* both. If both are selected, Visual C++ won't allow you to edit the command line. Here's what you need:

```
/SECTION:.ASHARE,RWS
```

Of course, if you called your section something else, use that name instead of ASHARE. The RWS means Read, Write, and Shared. Shared is what makes IPC possible.

If you prefer, you can create a **DEF** file and put a **SECTIONS** line in it, instead of using the **/SECTION** option:

```
LIBRARY DLL
SECTIONS
  .ASHARE READ,WRITE SHARED
```

If you use this method, be sure to add the **DEF** file to your project. MSVC doesn't use **DEF** files by default, but it will use one if you include it into the project.

If you want to share everything, just set the **.DATA** and **.BSS** sections to shared using one of the above techniques (that is, the **/SECTION** option or a **DEF** file).

That's it. Now you can share memory without any trouble. You can also share memory in a way that is compatible between Win16 and Win32. This can be important if you still maintain 16-bit versions of your program. But remember: Under Win32, DLLs don't have to load at the same address for different processes. You shouldn't take the address of a shared variable and pass it to another process. Specifically, don't put the address of a shared variable in a shared variable:

```
// Bad
#pragma data_seg(".ASHARE")
char buf[100]="";
char *bufp=&buf;  // bad!
#pragma data_seg()
```

This works for Windows 95—the DLL must load at the same address for each process. In Windows NT or Windows 2000, it can (and probably will) fail.

You can find a complete example in Listings 6.4 (the DLL) and 6.5 (the program). This program is a simple console mode program. To see it in action, run two (or more) copies. You can set variables in one copy of the program and read the same value in the other copy.

Listing 6.4 A shared DLL.

```
#pragma data_seg(".ASHARE")
int sharedarray[100] = { 0, 0}; // some init
#pragma data_seg()

__declspec(dllexport) int getvalue(int index)
{
   return sharedarray[index];
}

__declspec(dllexport) void setvalue(int index,int v)
{
   sharedarray[index]=v;
}

__declspec(dllexport) void *getaddr(void)
{
   return (void *)sharedarray;
}
```


Listing 6.5 Using the shared DLL.

```
#include <stdio.h>
#include <string.h>

__declspec(dllimport) int getvalue(int index);
__declspec(dllimport) void setvalue(int index,int v);
__declspec(dllimport) void *getaddr(void);


void main()
{
   char buf[256];
   int index,v;
   printf("Enter quit to exit\nTo set value: xx=vv\nTo read value: ?xx\n");
   printf("Array address=%x\n",(long)getaddr());
```

```
    do {
       gets(buf);
       if (sscanf(buf,"%d=%d',&index,&v)==2)
       {
          setvalue(index,v);
          printf("Set!\n");
       }
       else if (sscanf(buf,"?%d",&index)==1)
          printf("%d\n",getvalue(index));
       else if (strcmp(buf,"cuit"))
          printf("Huh? Type cuit to quit.\n");
    } while (strcmp(buf,"quit"));
}
```

Another Shared Memory Technique

The official way to create shared memory with Win32 is to use mapped files (see Chapter 5 and Tables 6.2 and 6.3). Of course, any two processes can share a file with a file mapping object, and that enables them to communicate. But you usually don't want the performance penalty associated with file I/O when you are using shared memory. That's not a problem, however. When you create a file mapping object, you can specify **(HANDLE)0xFFFFFFFF** for the file handle you want to map. This tells Windows that you really just want shared memory.

Table 6.2 Arguments to CreateFileMapping.

Argument	Type	Definition
hFile	HANDLE	File handle to use (use 0xFFFFFFFF for simple shared memory)
lpFileMappingAttributes	LPSECURITY_ATTRIBUTES	Security attribute structure (controls inheritance and access)
flProtect	DWORD	Sets protection (read-only, reserved, or committed, etc.)
dwMaximumSizeHigh	DWORD	Top 32 bits of the 64-bit size of this mapping
dwMaximumSizeLow	DWORD	Low 32 bits of the 64-bit size of this mapping
lpName	LPCTSTR	Name of this file mapping object

Table 6.3 Arguments to MapViewOfFile.

Argument	Type	Definition
hFileMappingObject	HANDLE	Handle to file mapping object
dwDesiredAccess	DWORD	Requests read or write access
dwFileOffsetHigh	DWORD	Top 32 bits of the 64-bit starting position
dwFileOffsetLow	DWORD	Low 32 bits of the 64-bit starting position
dwNumberOfBytesToMap	DWORD	Number of bytes to map (0 for entire file)

Of course, when you call **MapViewOfFileEx**, you can specify an address where you would like to map the file. However, there is no way to be sure this address will be available. The safest course is to set the address to **NULL** (or call **MapViewOfFile**) and let Windows pick an address. Of course, that means that once again you can't be sure what address each process will use.

To create a shared memory region, follow these steps:

1. Call **CreateFileMapping**; specify **(HANDLE)0xFFFFFFFF** or **INVALID_HANDLE_VALUE** for the file handle and specify a unique name so that other processes can access the memory.
2. Call **MapViewOfFile** (or **MapViewOfFileEx**) to obtain a pointer that you can use to access the memory.
3. When done, call **UnmapViewOfFile** to invalidate the pointer.
4. To release the shared memory, call **CloseHandle** on the handle found in Step 1.

To access the shared memory with other processes, follow these steps:

1. Call **OpenFileMapping** to open the shared memory area by name.
2. Use one of the **MapViewOfFile** calls to obtain a pointer.
3. When done, call **UnmapViewOfFile** to invalidate the pointer.
4. To release the shared memory, call **CloseHandle** on the handle found in Step 1.

This works, of course, even if you specify a file. However, if you do specify a file, the memory will persist (just like a file). Also, if you specify a networked file, only processes on the same machine will really share data.

Anonymous Pipes

Anonymous pipes are similar to the pipes you use at the DOS command prompt (or a Unix shell). They are very efficient, but not very flexible. They don't work over a network, nor can you use overlapped I/O with them. Data flows in one direction only. Another limitation is that you usually can't use them between just any two processes. The usual way to get an anonymous pipe is to create it or inherit it from your parent process. That's because they are—well—anonymous. You can send one end of an anonymous pipe to another process via shared memory or another IPC method, but that is unusual, because that implies the processes are already talking via another method.

What does this mean in practice? Any process can create an anonymous pipe. The pipe consists of two handles, one for reading and one for writing. The only meaningful way the process can use the pipe is if it passes one of the handles to a child process via inheritance. Of course, the child process has no way of knowing what the handle value is unless you pass it as part of the command line, in the environment, or some other method. Of course, you can also use the pipe to replace the child's standard input or standard output. The child may, of course, pass the handle along to its children.

To create a pipe, call **CreatePipe**. This call requires two pointers to handles, a suggested buffer size (usually set to zero for the default), and a **SECURITY_ATTRIBUTES** structure. You'll usually use this structure so you can make the handles inheritable. The alternative is to call **DuplicateHandle** to make a copy of the handle you want to make inheritable. The call places the handles (one for reading and one for writing) in the pointers you supply.

After you have both ends of the pipe in place, one process writes to the pipe and the other reads using **ReadFile** and **WriteFile**. If the pipe buffer fills up, the **WriteFile** call will block. **ReadFile** blocks if there is no data available. Of course, if the pipe closes, the calls will return an error. You can't use overlapped I/O, so you have little choice but to wait.

One common use for anonymous pipes is to replace a child's standard input or output. Doing this is a bit tricky. First, you call **GetStdHandle** and store away the existing handle (either input or output). Next, you use **SetStdHandle** to replace your standard handle with the appropriate pipe handle. Create the new process (usually with **CreateProcess**). Be sure to set the flag that allows the child to inherit handles. After the child process is running, you can close the pipe handle that the child is using (call **CloseHandle**). Finally, you'll want to reset your standard handle to its previous value with another call to **SetStdHandle**.

There is at least one other way to accomplish the same task. When you call **CreateProcess**, you can specify new standard I/O handles in the **STARTUPINFO** structure. You still have to set the handles for inheritance. You also have to set the **STARTF_USESTDHANDLES** in the **dwFlags** member of the **STARTUPINFO** structure.

The simple program in Listing 6.6 generates Fibonacci numbers (a particular mathematical sequence that occurs often in nature). The program creates its output with each number on a separate line. This makes the output hard to read.

To simplify the formatting of the program's output, the main program runs a filter (**xmore** in Listing 6.7) that reformats its standard input. The main program uses a pipe to deliver its output to the filter's standard input.

This is a pleasing arrangement, because the main program worries only about creating output. The filter, on the other hand, worries only about formatting. Changing the format (for example, to HTML) would require only changing **xmore**. Don't forget to put **xmore** somewhere where the main program can find it (usually the current directory or a directory on the path).

Listing 6.6 Fibonacci numbers.

```
#include <windows.h>
#include <stdio.h>
#include <string.h>

void main()
{
   // temporary redirect of STDIN
   HANDLE pipein,pipeout;
   SECURITY_ATTRIBUTES sa;
   STARTUPINFO si;
   PROCESS_INFORMATION pi;
   sa.nLength=sizeof(sa);
   sa.lpSecurityDescriptor=NULL;
   sa.bInheritHandle=TRUE;
   if (!CreatePipe(&pipein,&pipeout,&sa,0))
   {
      printf("Can't create pipe\n");
      exit(1);
   }
   memset(&si,0,sizeof(si));
   si.cb=sizeof(si);
   si.dwFlags=STARTF_USESTDHANDLES;
   si.hStdInput=pipein;
   si.hStdOutput=GetStdHandle(STD_OUTPUT_HANDLE);
   si.hStdOutput=GetStdHandle(STD_ERROR_HANDLE);
   if (!CreateProcess(NULL,"xmore",NULL,NULL,TRUE,0,NULL,NULL,&si,&pi))
   {
      int err=GetLastError();
```

6. Interprocess Communications

```
      if (err==2)
      printf(
    "Can't find xmore, move it to the path or current directory\n");
      else
         printf("Can't run xmore error:%lx\n",GetLastError());
      exit(1);
   }
   CloseHandle(pipein);
   char buf[32];
   unsigned long dw;
// Calculate fibonacci numbers up to 100000
   int last0=0;
   int last1=1;
   for (int i=1;i<100000;i=last0+last1)
   {
      last0=last1;
      last1=i;
      sprintf(buf,"%d\n",i);
       WriteFile(pipeout,buf,strlen(buf),&dw,NULL);
   }
   *buf=(char)26;  // Control+Z
   WriteFile(pipeout,buf,1,&dw,NULL);
   CloseHandle(pipeout);
   exit(0);
}
```

Listing 6.7 The xmore filter.

```
// Really dumb more replacement
#include <stdio.h>
#include <string.h>
void main()
{
   char buf[80];
   while (fgets(buf,80,stdin))
   {
      char *p=strchr(buf,'\n');
      if (p) *p='\0';
      strcat(buf,",");
      printf("%s",buf);
   }

}
```

Named Pipes

The alternatives to anonymous pipes are named pipes. Because these pipes have names, they are easier to share among processes. They are also more powerful in general because they work well over networks and support overlapped I/O. In addition, you can transfer data over named pipes in both directions if you create them for bidirectional access.

To create a named pipe, call **CreateNamedPipe**. It is possible to create more than one instance of a pipe so that the pipe can handle multiple clients at once.

When you create a named pipe, you specify a UNC network name of the form: //./pipe/*anyname*. The *anyname* part of the pipe name can be anything you want (up to 256 characters), and the name isn't case-sensitive. You also specify if you want the pipe to be one-way or two-way. You can select a byte-mode pipe or a pipe that is optimized for transferring packets of data. Other parameters set the suggested buffer sizes, the default timeout period, and the maximum number of instances allowed. Of course, you also have the usual **SECURITY_ATTRIBUTES** structure, and you can also create the pipe for overlapped I/O.

Using A Pipe

Once the server creates a pipe, it can wait for a connection on the pipe with **ConnectNamedPipe**. It is possible to use overlapped I/O to connect even if you didn't open the pipe for overlapped I/O. Clients connect to a pipe by using a UNC file name with **CreateFile**. The UNC specifies the server and the pipe name. So if a server named DarkStar creates a pipe with the UNC //./pipe/spock, clients connect to it using //DarkStar/pipe/spock. A client running on the DarkStar machine can substitute a dot for the server name. You can use **WaitNamedPipe** to see if a pipe instance is available.

With an established connection, the server can use ordinary **ReadFile** and **WriteFile** calls to read and write the pipe if it uses the byte-transfer mode. The pipe client uses the same calls to read and write data.

Message Mode Pipes

Pipes that carry blocks of data are more likely to use the message mode instead of the byte-oriented mode. Then you'll want to use **TransactNamedPipe** for both sides of the transfer. You can set the mode when you create the pipe, or change it with **SetNamedPipeHandleStatus**. You can read its status with **GetNamedPipeHandleStatus**.

Another way to use a message-oriented pipe is to call **CallNamedPipe**. This function opens a pipe (possibly waiting, if necessary), sends a message, reads a reply message, and closes the pipe all in one operation.

Miscellaneous Pipe Calls

Another way to find information about a named pipe is by calling **GetNamedPipeInfo**. This returns the state of the pipe and also tells you about the buffer sizes in effect.

When a server wants to disconnect from a client, it can call **DisconnectNamedPipe**. This call terminates the connection so that the next client access returns an error. The client still should call **CloseHandle** on its handle. You'll usually want to make sure the client has read all the data in the pipe before disconnecting it. This is easy to do; just call **FlushFileBuffers** with the pipe handle. This call will not return until the pipe is empty.

Sometimes, it is useful to examine what the pipe contains without actually removing the data from the pipe. That's the purpose of the **PeekNamedPipe** function. It enables you to examine data in the pipe without removing it and without waiting. You can also use this call to learn how much data is waiting in the pipe for you to read.

You can find an example of using a named pipe in Chapter 5 (see Listing 5.2). This program uses named pipes with overlapped I/O to enable two users to chat over the network.

Mailslots

Mailslots are a simple one-way protocol based on datagrams. Because *datagrams* are network packets that don't ensure reliable delivery, mailslots are not fail-safe, either. If you need reliable communications, you will probably prefer named pipes. However, mailslots let you broadcast a message to all related mailslots on your local area network.

You can only create a mailslot on your local machine. To do so, simply call **CreateMailSlot** (see Table 6.4). This function requires a name in the form of \\.\mailslot*anyname* (where you can use anything you like for *anyname*). You also supply the maximum size of any single message, the timeout period in milliseconds, and the ubiquitous **SECURITY_ATTRIBUTES** structure. If you set the size to zero, it really means that you will accept messages of any size. The timeout determines how long a **ReadFile** call will block before returning if there is no data available. If you want **ReadFile** to block indefinitely, you can specify **MAILSLOT_WAIT_FOREVER**. The function returns a handle that you use with **ReadFile**. Because the mailslot is one-way only, you can't write to the handle.

Table 6.4 Calling CreateMailSlot.

Argument	Type	Definition
lpName	LPCTSTR	Name of mailslot
nMaxMessageSize	DWORD	Maximum size of message (0 for any size; broadcasts limited to 400 bytes regardless of this parameter)
lReadTimeout	DWORD	Time to wait for input (in milliseconds; 0 for no wait; MAILSLOT_WAIT_FOREVER for infinite)
lpSecurityAttributes	LPSECURITY_ATTRIBUTES	Security attributes structure

When another program wants to send the mailslot a message, it uses **CreateFile** to open the mailslot using the machine name. For example, to send a message to the SYSMESSAGE mailbox on the DarkStar machine, you would open \\darkstar\mailslot\SYSMESSAGE for writing. Be sure to specify **FILE_SHARE_READ** and **OPEN_EXISTING** in the call to **CreateFile**. Then you would use **WriteFile** as usual.

Although a mailslot looks a lot like a file, it actually exists in memory. That means, among other things, that the buffer is not persistent like a real file.

Suppose you have a domain named *Enterprise* . You could send a message to all the SYSMESSAGE mailslots on the domain by opening \\Enterprise\mailslots\SYSMESSAGE. You can also send a message to all the SYSMESSAGE mailsots on the primary domain by using * as the domain name. One thing to keep in mind: When you broadcast a message, it must be 400 bytes or less or you will receive an error, even if the mailslot is set to accept larger messages.

You can change the mailslot's message size and read timeout value at any time by calling **SetMailslotInfo**. **GetMailslotInfo** returns these values and also tells you the size of the next message and the total number of messages waiting.

Listing 6.8 shows a simple MFC program that listens for messages in the sysmsg mailslot. The program uses a mailslot with no timeout (in other words, **ReadFile** will return immediately if there is no data). Then, the program uses a timer to check the slot periodically. It displays any messages for you to see.

Listing 6.9 contains a program that enables you to send messages to this mailslot. You can run the programs on one machine or across a network. When specifying a delivery address, you can use a domain name or another imprecise name. You may see the transmitted message more than once, depending on how your network identifies machines.

Listing 6.8 Listening to a mailslot.

```
// sysmsgView.cpp : implementation of the CSysmsgView class
//

#include "stdafx.h"
#include "sysmsg.h"

#include "sysmsgDoc.h"
#include "sysmsgView.h"

#ifdef _DEBUG
#define new DEBUG_NEW
#undef THIS_FILE
static char THIS_FILE[] = __FILE__;
#endif

////////////////////////////////
// CSysmsgView

IMPLEMENT_DYNCREATE(CSysmsgView, CFormView)

BEGIN_MESSAGE_MAP(CSysmsgView, CFormView)
   //{{AFX_MSG_MAP(CSysmsgView)
   ON_WM_SIZE()
   ON_WM_TIMER()
   //}}AFX_MSG_MAP
END_MESSAGE_MAP()

////////////////////////////////
// CSysmsgView construction/destruction

CSysmsgView::CSysmsgView()
   : CFormView(CSysmsgView::IDD)
{
   //{{AFX_DATA_INIT(CSysmsgView)
   m_msg = _T("");
   //}}AFX_DATA_INIT
   // TODO: add construction code here
   mailslot=INVALID_HANDLE_VALUE;

}

CSysmsgView::~CSysmsgView()
{
   if (mailslot!=INVALID_HANDLE_VALUE)
```

6. Interprocess Communications

```
        CloseHandle(mailslot);
}

void CSysmsgView::DoDataExchange(CDataExchange* pDX)
{
   CFormView::DoDataExchange(pDX);
   //{{AFX_DATA_MAP(CSysmsgView)
   DDX_Control(pDX, IDC_MSG, m_msgctl);
   DDX_Text(pDX, IDC_MSG, m_msg);
   //}}AFX_DATA_MAP
}

BOOL CSysmsgView::PreCreateWindow(CREATESTRUCT& cs)
{
   // TODO: Modify the Window class or styles here by modifying
   //  the CREATESTRUCT cs

   return CFormView::PreCreateWindow(cs);
}

/////////////////////////////
// CSysmsgView diagnostics

#ifdef _DEBUG
void CSysmsgView::AssertValid() const
{
   CFormView::AssertValid();
}

void CSysmsgView::Dump(CDumpContext& dc) const
{
   CFormView::Dump(dc);
}

CSysmsgDoc* CSysmsgView::GetDocument() // non-debug version is inline
{
   ASSERT(m_pDocument->IsKindOf(RUNTIME_CLASS(CSysmsgDoc)));
   return (CSysmsgDoc*)m_pDocument;
}
#endif //_DEBUG

/////////////////////////////
// CSysmsgView message handlers

void CSysmsgView::OnSize(UINT nType, int cx, int cy)
```

```
{
   CFormView::OnSize(nType, cx, cy);

    if (IsWindow(m_msgctl.m_hWnd)) m_msgctl.MoveWindow(0,0,cx,cy);
}

void CSysmsgView::OnInitialUpdate()
{
   CRect r;
   CFormView::OnInitialUpdate();
   GetClientRect(&r);
   m_msgctl.MoveWindow(&r);
   mailslot=CreateMailslot("\\\\.\\mailslot\\sysmsg",128,0,NULL);
   if (mailslot==INVALID_HANDLE_VALUE)
      MessageBox("Can't open mailslot!");
   SetTimer(1,1000,NULL);
}

void CSysmsgView::OnTimer(UINT nIDEvent)
{
    // Check Mailslot
   char buf[128];
   DWORD rlen;
   ReadFile(mailslot,buf,sizeof(buf),&rlen,NULL);
   if (rlen)
   {
      m_msg+=buf;
      m_msg+="\r\n";
      UpdateData(FALSE);
   }
   CFormView::OnTimer(nIDEvent);
}
```

Listing 6.9 Sending to the mailslot.

```
// xmitmsgView.cpp : implementation of the CXmitmsgView class
//

#include "stdafx.h"
#include "xmitmsg.h"

#include "xmitmsgDoc.h"
#include "xmitmsgView h"

#ifdef _DEBUG
```

6. Interprocess Communications

```
#define new DEBUG_NEW
#undef THIS_FILE
static char THIS_FILE[] = __FILE__;
#endif

//////////////////////////////
// CXmitmsgView

IMPLEMENT_DYNCREATE(CXmitmsgView, CFormView)

BEGIN_MESSAGE_MAP(CXmitmsgView, CFormView)
   //{{AFX_MSG_MAP(CXmitmsgView)
   ON_BN_CLICKED(IDC_SEND, OnSend)
   //}}AFX_MSG_MAP
END_MESSAGE_MAP()

//////////////////////////////
// CXmitmsgView construction/destruction

CXmitmsgView::CXmitmsgView()
: CFormView(CXmitmsgView::IDD)
{
   //{{AFX_DATA_INIT(CXmitmsgView)
   m_host = _T("");
   m_msg = _T("");
   //}}AFX_DATA_INIT
   // TODO: add construction code here

}

CXmitmsgView::~CXmitmsgView()
{
}

void CXmitmsgView::DoDataExchange(CDataExchange* pDX)
{
   CFormView::DoDataExchange(pDX);
   //{{AFX_DATA_MAP(CXmitmsgView)
   DDX_Control(pDX, IDC_MSG, m_msgctl);
   DDX_Text(pDX, IDC_HOST, m_host);
   DDX_Text(pDX, IDC_MSG, m_msg);
   DDV_MaxChars(pDX, m_msg, 128);
   //}}AFX_DATA_MAP
}
```

```
BOOL CXmitmsgView::PreCreateWindow(CREATESTRUCT& cs)
{
   // TODO: Modify the Window class or styles here by modifying
   //  the CREATESTRUCT cs

   return CFormView::PreCreateWindow(cs);
}

/////////////////////////////
// CXmitmsgView diagnostics

#ifdef _DEBUG
void CXmitmsgView::AssertValid() const
{
   CFormView::AssertValid();
}

void CXmitmsgView::Dump(CDumpContext& dc) const
{
   CFormView::Dump(dc);
}

CXmitmsgDoc* CXmitmsgView::GetDocument() // non-debug version is inline
{
   ASSERT(m_pDocument->IsKindOf(RUNTIME_CLASS(CXmitmsgDoc)));
   return (CXmitmsgDoc*)m_pDocument;
}
#endif //_DEBUG

/////////////////////////////
// CXmitmsgView message handlers

void CXmitmsgView::OnSend()
{
   HANDLE mailslot;
   DWORD wlen;
   CString fn="\\\\";
   UpdateData(TRUE); // read controls
   fn+=m_host;
   fn+="\\mailslot\\sysmsg";
   mailslot=CreateFile(fn,
    GENERIC_WRITE,FILE_SHARE_READ,NULL,OPEN_EXISTING,FILE_ATTRIBUTE_NORMAL,NULL);
   if (mailslot==INVALID_HANDLE_VALUE)
   {
      CString msg;
      msg.Format("%s: %x Can't open mailslot!",fn,GetLastError());
```

6. Interprocess Communications

```
        MessageBox(msg);
    }
    else
    {
        WriteFile(mailslot,(const char *)m_msg,
                m_msg.GetLength()+1,&wlen,NULL);
        CloseHandle(mailslot);
        m_msg="";
        m_msgctl.SetFocus();
        UpdateData(FALSE);

    }
}
```

Another Example—Serial Numbers

Because you can broadcast to all mailslots simultaneously, they make it simple to implement network-wide protocols. Consider a common case where you want to make sure that licensed software runs only on one computer at a time. If each program broadcasts its serial number and computer name over the network, the program can detect if another copy is running simultaneously.

Listing 6.10 shows a simple console program that implements this idea. The program reads its serial number from the command line. In real life, you'd need a way to brand each program with a separate serial number and make it difficult for the user to change the serial number. Many commercial installation packages can do this. Other schemes include encrypting the serial number or making serial numbers pass some checksum-type calculation so that random serial numbers are invalid.

When the program starts, it reads the computer name (using **GetComputerName**). Then it opens two handles. The first handle is the mailslot on the local computer. The second handle is the one the program will use to broadcast to all similar mailslots across the LAN.

Once the handles are in order, the program starts a thread (the **checksn** function) that listens to the mailslot. Finally, the main program broadcasts a string to all the mailslots. This string contains the machine name, a colon, and the serial number followed by a new line.

With these tasks complete, the program goes on to do its work (in this case, printing a palindrome—hopefully you have something more useful to do). While the program works, the thread monitors data from the mailslot.

When data arrives from the mailslot, the thread looks at the machine name. If the name matches the local machine's name, the thread ignores the message. If the serial number doesn't match, the thread still ignores the message. However, if the computer name is different but the serial number is the same, then the thread prints an error message and exits the program.

There are other ways you could use this program. For example, if you add the program's instance handle to the mailslot string, you could detect multiple programs running on the same computer. Another idea: when the program detects a second copy, it could rebroadcast its serial number to make sure the other program shuts down too.

Listing 6.10 Serial number checking with mailslots.

```
// serialnum.cpp : Defines the entry point for the console application.
//

#include "stdafx.h"
#include <stdio.h>
#include "process.h"


int sn=1;  // Serial number
char machname[128];

// This routine runs in a thread and listens for other programs
void checksn(void *h)
{
    HANDLE mh=(HANDLE)h;
    unsigned long n;
    char imsg[128],*p;
    while (1) {
            if (ReadFile(mh,imsg,sizeof(imsg),&n,NULL)) {
                    p=strchr(imsg,'\n');
                    if (!p) continue; // bad packet
                    *p='\0';
                    p=strchr(imsg,':');
                    if (!p) continue; // bad packet?
                    *p='\0';
// check for message from myself
                    if (!stricmp(machname,imsg)) continue;
                    // Someone else sent us a message
                    if (sn==atoi(p+1))
                    {
                            // someone else is using our serial number!
                            printf("Unauthorized copy started... exiting\n");
```

```
                                exit(100);
                        }
                }
        }
}

int main(int argc, char* argv[])
{
    unsigned long n;
// Just for debug purposes, we read the serial number from the command line
    if (argc>1) sn=atoi(argv[1]);

        SECURITY_ATTRIBUTES sa;
        SECURITY_DESCRIPTOR sd;
// allow all access
        InitializeSecurityDescriptor(&sd,SECURITY_DESCRIPTOR_REVISION);
        sa.bInheritHandle=FALSE;
        sa.lpSecurityDescriptor=&sd;
        sa.nLength=sizeof(sa);

    unsigned long sz=sizeof(machname);
    GetComputerName(machname,&sz);

// Create mailslot and open for broadcast writing too
    HANDLE
h=CreateMailslot("\\\\.\\mailslot\\serial.box",128,MAILSLOT_WAIT_FOREVER,&sa);
    if (!h) { printf("Can't open mailslot\n"); exit(1); }
    HANDLE
w=CreateFile("\\\\*\\mailslot\\serial.box",GENERIC_WRITE,0,NULL,OPEN_ALWAYS,0,NULL);
    if (!w) { printf("Can't open broadcast mailslot\n"); exit(2); }
// Listen for other serial numbers
    _beginthread(checksn,0,(void *)h);

// broadcast our sn
    char msg[128];
    wsprintf(msg,"%s:%d\n",machname,sn);
    WriteFile(w,(LPCVOID)msg,strlen(msg),&n,NULL);
    CloseHandle(w);

// Do something until someone stops us!
    printf("Working...\n");
    while (1) {
            printf("Rats live on no evil star -- a palindrome!\n");
    }
    return 0;
}
```

About Sockets

The NCHECKER program (see Figure 6.1) is a simple checker game. You click on a piece to select it and then click on an empty square to move the piece. If you right-click on a piece it changes to a king. If the piece is already a king, the program removes it from the board. If you click on an empty square, you can create a new piece (left-click for red, right-click for black).

All by itself, this is unremarkable. What makes it interesting is that you can set up one copy of the program to be a server on the network, and then connect another copy of the program to the server. When connected, the two checkerboards stay synchronized—you can easily play checkers across the network.

Windows sockets make the network communications possible. If you are familiar with Unix sockets (I'm an old Unix guy from way back), you'll find Windows sockets are 99 percent compatible with BSD-style sockets. Why not 100 percent? You'll see why shortly. If you are already familiar with BSD sockets, you might want to skip the next section and go right to the "Windows Sockets" section that follows.

Sockets

Sockets are like the wormholes on *Star Trek*. When you write to a socket, the data magically appears at the other end. The other end might be another process running on the same machine, or it could be halfway around the world. You don't know or care. The data might flow over phone lines, Ethernet, a token ring net-

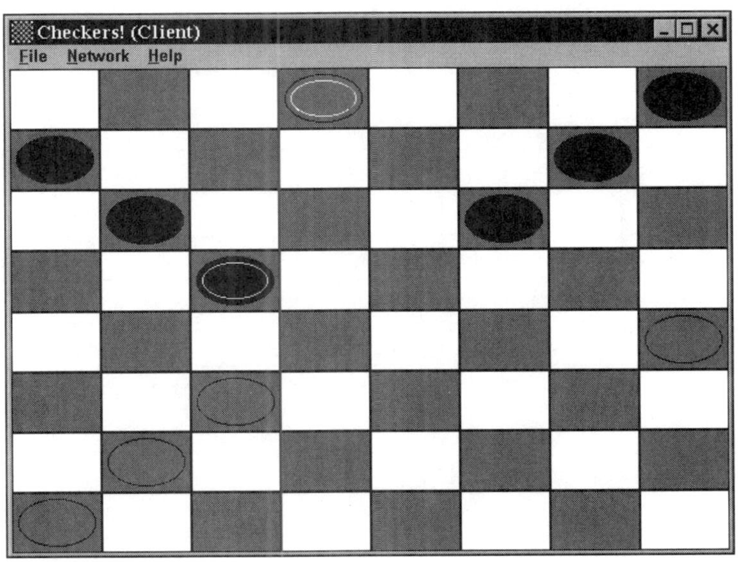

Figure 6.1 The NCHECKER program.

work, or X.25 satellite links—again, you don't care. If you create the socket the right way, the system will guarantee that the data appears correctly, and in the same sequence you sent it. The program on the other end of the socket reads the data. Sockets are two-way wormholes. Both sides can send data across to the other end. You'll find a summary of standard socket calls in Table 6.5.

Table 6.5 Standard socket calls.

Call	Description
Socket	Create a socket
getsockopt	Get socket options
setsockopt	Set socket options
ioctlsocket*	Control socket flags
recv	Read data from socket
recvfrom	Read data from specific address
send	Send data to socket
sendto	Send data to specific address
bind	Associate a socket with a network address
listen	Ready a socket to accept connections
accept	Accept a connection request from a client
connect	Connect to a server's socket
select	Determine the status of one or more sockets
shutdown	End connection without closing socket
closesocket*	Close socket
getpeername	Retrieve socket partner's address
getsockname	Retrieve local socket address
htonl	Convert long from host (native) to network format
ntohl	Convert long from network to host (native) format
htons	Convert short from host (native) to network format
ntohs	Convert short from network to host (native) format
inet_addr	Convert a string with a dotted address to an address structure
inet_ntoa	Convert an address structure to a dotted address string
gethostbyaddr	Find host name from address
gethostbyname	Find host address from name
gethostname	Retrieve local host name
getprotobyname	Retrieve protocol by name

(continued)

***Table 6.5 Standard socket calls* (continued).**

Call	Description
getprotobynumber	Retrieve protocol by port number
getservbyname	Retrieve protocol and port number by service name
getservbyport	Retrieve protocol and service name by port number

** Windows name (see text)*

Under Unix, sockets appear like files from the programmer's point of view (in fact, nearly everything under Unix appears to be a file). This was a problem for Windows 3.1 because DOS provides support for files and it doesn't know anything about sockets. In the next section, you'll see how that affects your programs. Win32 programs can treat sockets as ordinary handles—but it still has the additional baggage for compatibility with Windows 3.1.

Sockets use an address and a port number. Usually, you'll use a host name (**desktop.al-williams.com**, for example) to specify a connect address. The port number is an arbitrary number that identifies a particular service on a host. You'll see more about managing addresses and ports later.

Another important issue is number formats. Some machines store integers with their most significant bytes first; others store the least significant bytes first. To combat this, the network system provides calls to convert native integers to canonical format—the network's idea of how to order integers. On some systems, this call does nothing. On others, it reverses the bit order. When you specify integer portions of addresses, they must be in canonical format. For example, when specifying a port number, you'll need to use the **htons()** (host to network short) function. To go the other way, you would use **ntohs()** (network to host short). There is a similar pair of functions for converting longs.

Socket-oriented programs act as servers or clients. A server creates a socket and listens for a connection. The server usually has a well-known port number and name. Clients can use the server's address and port number to connect to it. When a client makes a connection, the system assigns a private socket for the connection so that the server can continue to listen for other clients with the original socket.

Starting A Server

Follow these steps to prepare a socket for connection to a typical server:

1. Call **socket()** to create a socket. You must specify the type of socket you want. For typical applications, you'll use this call to create a socket with an

Internet-style address that guarantees correct delivery (a TCP socket as opposed to a UDP socket):

```
SOCKET sock;
       /* Use SOCK_STREAM for TCP or
          SOCK_DGRAM for UDP */
              sock=socket(PF_INET,SOCK_STREAM,0);
              if (sock==INVALID_SOCKET) error();
```

2. Set up a **SOCKADDR_IN** structure to specify the port number, and indicate willingness to accept any address:

```
SOCKADDR_IN sockaddr;
sockaddr.sin_family=AF_INET; sockaddr.sin_addr.s_addr=INADDR_ANY;
sockaddr.sin_port=htons(port_number);
```

3. Call **bind()** to associate the **SOCKADDR_IN** structure from Step 2 with the socket from Step 1:

```
if (bind(sock,(PSOCKADDR)&sockaddr,
   sizeof(SOCKADDR_IN))) error();
```

4. Wait for a connection by calling **listen()**:

```
/* Queue up to 10 connections */
listen(sock,10);
```

5. Call **accept()** to allow a connection. The function returns a new socket for the connection. If you want to know the address of the client, you can pass a **SOCKADDR_IN** structure (and its length) to **accept()**. If you don't care, pass **NULL** and zero for these arguments:

```
newsocket=accept(sock,NULL,0);
```

Starting A Client

Starting a client is much easier. Here are the steps:

1. Call **socket()** to create a socket (this is exactly what the server does).
2. Set up a **SOCKADDR_IN** structure to specify the host address and port number. Here's an example of converting a host name to an address:

```
SOCKADDR_IN sockaddr;
PHOSTENT phe;
phe=gethostbyname(host_name);
memcpy((char FAR *)&(sockaddr.sin_addr,
  phe->h_addr,phe->h_length);
sockaddr.sin_family=AF_INET; sockaddr.sin_port=htons(port_number);
```

3. Call **connect()** to connect to the host:

```
connect(sock,(PSOCKADDR)&sockaddr,sizeof(sockaddr));
```

If the **accept()** or **socket()** call fails, the call returns **INVALID_SOCKET**. Most other calls return **SOCKET_ERROR** if they fail. Once you have a good connection, you can use calls like **send()** and **recv()** to transfer data on the socket. When you no longer need the connection, you should close the socket.

This is a simple example of how to use sockets. In this case, any socket operation that may take awhile (like **connect()** or **accept()**) will block the program. Under Unix and Windows 2000, this isn't a problem because other programs will still run. Under Windows 3.1, the socket system will try to allow other programs to run, but it can cause reentrancy problems.

A better way to manage sockets is to force them not to block. Then, calls that would ordinarily block will return an error instead of blocking. You can retry the offending call whenever you like until it succeeds. In the next section, you'll see that Windows has an even better way to handle nonblocking sockets.

Windows Sockets

The Windows socket library is almost the same as the Unix socket library. However, if you port code from Unix, you may run into a few problems.

In theory, Unix programs should check for return values of **INVALID_SOCKET** when calling **accept()** or **socket()**. However, many of them assume that constant is -1 and test accordingly. Under Windows, this assumption isn't true. Again, if you are porting code it is something to check. If you are writing new code, just use **INVALID_SOCKET**.

Because Windows 3.1 can't treat a socket handle as an ordinary file handle, some calls are different under Windows. In a Unix program, for example, you would call **close()** to close a file handle or a socket. For Windows, you need to call **closesocket()** to close a socket. The same thing is true for **ioctl()**, which becomes **ioctlsocket()**. Of course, under Windows NT or Win2000, you should be able to use either call. However, Windows 3.1 and Windows 95/98 may still require the Windows-specific calls.

Another thing to watch for when porting is the use of far pointers. To ensure compatibility, all Winsock calls require far addresses. Of course, on Windows 2000, this isn't an issue. There are a few other porting issues. For example, Unix code that uses the **select()** call (which I won't talk about in this chapter) often needs an argument reformatted.

Error codes are also slightly different under Windows. Because the Unix operating system manages sockets directly, any error code appears in the standard **errno** variable. For Windows, you need to call **WSAGetLastError()** to find the error codes. Under Windows 2000, this is the same as a call to **GetLastError()**, but it is a special function under Windows 3.1.

Windows provides many nonstandard socket calls that begin with "WSA" (see Table 6.6). There are a few special calls like **WSAGetLastError()** and calls to set up and close down the library (**WSAStartup()** and **WSACleanup()**). Most of the **WSA** calls correspond to ordinary calls that can block. The **WSA** calls do not block, but take a user-defined message and a window handle as arguments. When the call completes, the system sends the message to the corresponding window. For instance, the **gethostbyname()** call (which may block) corresponds to the Windows-specific **WSAAsyncGetHostByName()** function. The checker game example uses one of these nonblocking calls, **WSAAsyncSelect()**, to receive notifications when there is data to process.

Table 6.6 Windows-specific socket calls.

Call	Description
WSAStartup	Start up Winsock
WSACleanup	Shut down Winsock
WSAGetLastError	Retrieve last error code
WSAAsyncSelect	Windows version of select
WSAIsBlocking	Returns TRUE if a network call is already blocking
WSACancelBlockingCall	Abort a blocked socket call
WSAAsyncGetHostByAddr	Windows version of gethostbyaddr
WSAAsyncGetHostByName	Windows version of gethostbyname
WSAAsyncGetProtoByName	Windows version of getprotobyname
WSAAsyncGetProtoByNumber	Windows version of getprotobynumber
WSAAsyncGetServByName	Windows version of getservbyname
WSAAsyncGetServByNumber	Windows version of getservbynumber
WSASetBlockingHook	Specifies function to call while blocking
WSAUnhookBlockingHook	Reset blocking hook

More Sockets

That's not all there is to sockets—I've only scratched the surface. You can send raw data, use a secondary data channel (out of band data), or broadcast data to multiple sockets. You can register services with unique IDs and search for them. You'll have to look in the Winsock specification (available on the Web) to find out more about these things.

Inside Checkers

How does all this relate to checkers? The checker program has three source files. **CHECKER.C** (see Listing 6.11) contains all the ordinary checkerboard code. **CHECKNET.C** (see Listing 6.12) handles network-specific code. The final source file, **CHECKDLG.C**, contains dialog callbacks. The **CHECKER** code has two core routines that manipulate the checkerboard: **move()** and **setcell()**. The **move()** function moves a piece from one cell to another. The **setcell()** function adds and removes pieces from the board. It also changes ordinary pieces to kings.

Listing 6.11 CHECKER.C.

```
/* Net Checkers -- Williams */
#include <windows.h>
#include <commdlg.h>
#include <stdio.h>
#include <string.h>
#include <stdlib.h>
#include "checker.h"


/* Fresh board */
STATE newboard[8][8]=
  {
   {CELL_EMPTY,CELL_BLACK,CELL_EMPTY,CELL_BLACK,
     CELL_EMPTY,CELL_BLACK,CELL_EMPTY,CELL_BLACK},
   {CELL_BLACK,CELL_EMPTY,CELL_BLACK,CELL_EMPTY,
     CELL_BLACK,CELL_EMPTY,CELL_BLACK,CELL_EMPTY},
   {CELL_EMPTY,CELL_EMPTY,CELL_EMPTY,CELL_EMPTY,
     CELL_EMPTY,CELL_EMPTY,CELL_EMPTY,CELL_EMPTY},
   {CELL_EMPTY,CELL_EMPTY,CELL_EMPTY,CELL_EMPTY,
     CELL_EMPTY,CELL_EMPTY,CELL_EMPTY,CELL_EMPTY},
   {CELL_EMPTY,CELL_EMPTY,CELL_EMPTY,CELL_EMPTY,
     CELL_EMPTY,CELL_EMPTY,CELL_EMPTY,CELL_EMPTY},
   {CELL_EMPTY,CELL_EMPTY,CELL_EMPTY,CELL_EMPTY,
     CELL_EMPTY,CELL_EMPTY,CELL_EMPTY,CELL_EMPTY},
   {CELL_EMPTY,CELL_RED,CELL_EMPTY,CELL_RED,
     CELL_EMPTY,CELL_RED,CELL_EMPTY,CELL_RED},
```

```
   {CELL_RED,CELL_EMPTY,CELL_RED,CELL_EMPTY,
     CELL_RED,CELL_EMPTY,CELL_RED,CELL_EMPTY}
   };

/* Current board */
STATE board[8][8];


POINT selectp;                /* Selected cell */
BOOL selected;                /* TRUE when selection active */

HWND       hWnd;              /* Handle to main window */
HINSTANCE  hInst;             /* Handle to instance data*/

/* File open filter */
char filefilter[]="Checker file\0*.chk\0All files\0*.*\0";

/* Make new board */
void new_board(HWND hWnd)
  {
  memcpy(board,newboard,sizeof(board));
  selected=FALSE;
  InvalidateRect(hWnd,NULL,FALSE);
  }


int PASCAL WinMain(HINSTANCE hInstance, HINSTANCE hPrevInstance,
                   LPSTR lpCmdLine, int nCmdShow)
  {
  MSG msg;

  if (!hPrevInstance)
    if (!InitApplication(hInstance))
       return (FALSE);

  if (!InitInstance(hInstance, nCmdShow))
       return (FALSE);

  while (GetMessage(&msg, NULL, 0, 0))
    {
    TranslateMessage(&msg);
    DispatchMessage(&msg);
    }
  return (msg.wParam);
  }
```

```
BOOL InitApplication(HINSTANCE hInstance)
   {
   WNDCLASS wc;
   wc.style = 0;
   wc.lpfnWndProc = MainWndProc;
   wc.cbClsExtra = 0;
   wc.cbWndExtra = 0;
   wc.hInstance = hInstance;
   wc.hIcon = LoadIcon(hInstance, MAKEINTRESOURCE(APPICON));
   wc.hCursor = LoadCursor(NULL, IDC_ARROW);
   wc.hbrBackground = (HBRUSH)(COLOR_WINDOW+1);
   wc.lpszMenuName ="Checker";
   wc.lpszClassName = "CheckerClass";
   return (RegisterClass(&wc));
   }


BOOL InitInstance(HINSTANCE hInstance, int nCmdShow)
   {
   RECT r;
/* Setup board */
   memcpy(board,newboard,sizeof(board));
   hInst = hInstance;
   r.top=r.left=0;
   r.right=600;
   r.bottom=400; /* force to 600x400 client area */
   AdjustWindowRect(&r,WS_OVERLAPPEDWINDOW,TRUE);
   hWnd = CreateWindow(
        "CheckerClass",
        "Checkers! ",
        WS_OVERLAPPEDWINDOW,
        CW_USEDEFAULT,
        CW_USEDEFAULT,
        r.right-r.left,
        r.bottom-r.top,
        NULL,
        NULL,
        hInstance,
        NULL
        );

    if (!hWnd)
        return (FALSE);

    ShowWindow(hWnd, nCmdShow);
    UpdateWindow(hWnd);
```

```
   return (TRUE);
   }


LRESULT CALLBACK MainWndProc(HWND hWnd,
  UINT message, WPARAM wParam, LPARAM lParam)
   {
   switch (message)
     {
     case WM_PAINT:
       return Paint(hWnd);

     case WM_LBUTTONDOWN:
       selecting(hWnd,LOWORD(lParam),HIWORD(lParam));
       break;

     case WM_RBUTTONDOWN:
       action(hWnd,LOWORD(lParam),HIWORD(lParam));
       break;

     case WM_COMMAND:
           switch (wParam)
             {
             case IDM_NEW:
               if (MessageBox(hWnd,
                 "Starting a new game will destroy"
                 " the current game and network connection. "
                 "Do you really want a new game?",
                 "Notice",MB_YESNO|MB_ICONSTOP)==IDNO) break;
               netclose(hWnd);
               new_board(hWnd);
               break;

             case IDM_OPEN:
               {
               char fn[_MAX_PATH];
               FILE *f;
               *fn='\0';
               if (MessageBox(hWnd,
                 "Opening a new game will destroy"
                 " the current game and network connection. "
                 "Do you really want a new game?",
                 "Notice",MB_YESNO|MB_ICONSTOP)==IDNO) break;
               if (get_file(hWnd,fn,_MAX_PATH,
                 "Open File",filefilter,FALSE)||
```

```
    !(f=fopen(fn,"rb")))
      {
      MessageBox(hWnd,
        "Can't open file",NULL,MB_OK|MB_ICONSTOP);
      break;
      }
  netclose(hWnd);
  fread(&board,sizeof(board),1,f);
  fclose(f);
  InvalidateRect(hWnd,NULL,FALSE);
  break;
  }

case IDM_SAVE:
  {
  char fn[_MAX_PATH];
  FILE *f;
  *fn='\0';
  if (get_file(hWnd,fn,_MAX_PATH,
    "Save As",filefilter,TRUE)||
    !(f=fopen(fn,"w")))
    {
    MessageBox(hWnd,"Can't open file",
      NULL,MB_OK|MB_ICONSTOP);
    break;
    }
  fwrite(&board,sizeof(board),1,f);
  fclose(f);
  break;
  }


case IDM_SERVER:
  server(hWnd);
  break;

case IDM_CLIENT:
  client(hWnd);
  break;

case IDM_QUIT:
  if (MessageBox(hWnd,
    "Do you really want to close the connection?",
    "Confirm",MB_YESNO)==IDYES)
     netclose(hWnd);
```

```
                    break;

                case IDM_EXIT:
                    DestroyWindow(hWnd);
                    break;


                case IDM_ABOUT:
                     MessageBox(hWnd,"Checkers! by Al Williams",
                         "About",MB_OK|MB_ICONEXCLAMATION);
                     break;
              }

          break;  /* End WM_COMMANDs */

/* User defined message -- handle action from network partner */
              case WM_TRANSACT:
                   UpdateWindow(hWnd);
                   transact(hWnd,lParam);
                   break;

        case WM_DESTROY:
                   netclose(hWnd);
                   PostQuitMessage(0);
                   break;

        default:
              return (DefWindowProc(hWnd, message,
                wParam, lParam));
        }
     return 0;
  }


/* Drawing code */
long Paint(HWND w)
  {
  PAINTSTRUCT ps;
  HDC dc;
  RECT r;
  HBRUSH wht,gry,br,red,blk,selbrush;
  HPEN whtpen,oldpen;
  LONG x,y;
  dc=BeginPaint(w,&ps);
  GetClientRect(w,&r);
```

6. Interprocess Communications

```
  wht=CreateSolidBrush(RGB(0xFF,0xFF,0xFF));
  gry=CreateSolidBrush(RGB(0x80,0x80,0x80));
  red=CreateSolidBrush(RGB(0xFF,0,0));
  blk=CreateSolidBrush(RGB(0,0,0));
  selbrush=CreateSolidBrush(RGB(0,0xFF,0xFF));
  whtpen=CreatePen(1,PS_SOLID,RGB(0xFF,0xFF,0xFF));
  br=SelectObject(dc,wht);
/* For each cell... */
  for (y=0;y<8;y++)
    for (x=0;x<8;x++)
      {
/* compute bounds */
      int x0=x*75,y0=y*50,x1=(x+1)*75,y1=(y+1)*50;
      BOOL notempty=TRUE;
/* Pick white or grey brush */
      SelectObject(dc,x%2==y%2?wht:gry);
/* Unless selected, then pick selected brush */
      if (selected&&selectp.x==x&&selectp.y==y)
        SelectObject(dc,selbrush);
/* Draw cell */
      Rectangle(dc,x0,y0,x1,y1);
/* Draw piece */
      switch (board[y][x])
        {
        case CELL_RED:
        case CELL_REDKING:
          SelectObject(dc,red);
          break;

        case CELL_BLACK:
        case CELL_BLACKKING:
          SelectObject(dc,blk);
          break;

        default:
          notempty=FALSE;
        }
       if (notempty)
        {
        Ellipse(dc,x0+5,y0+5,x1-5,y1-5);
 /* Draw kings */
        if (board[y][x]==CELL_REDKING||board[y][x]==CELL_BLACKKING)
          {
          oldpen=SelectObject(dc,whtpen);
          Ellipse(dc,x0+10,y0+10,x1-10,y1-10);
```

```
            SelectObject(dc,oldpen);
            }
          }
        }
    SelectObject(dc,br);
    DeleteObject(blk);
    DeleteObject(wht);
    DeleteObject(red);
    DeleteObject(gry);
    DeleteObject(selbrush);
    DeleteObject(whtpen);
    EndPaint(w,&ps);
    return 0;
    }

/* Handle movement between two cells */
void move(HWND w,LONG x0,LONG y0,LONG x1,LONG y1,BOOL send)
  {
  board[y1][x1]=board[y0][x0];
  board[y0][x0]=CELL_EMPTY;
  InvalidateCell(w,x0,y0);
  InvalidateCell(w,x1,y1);
/* If this isn't a network transaction, send it to
   network partner */
  if (send)
    {
    Send(MOVE,x1,y1,x0,y0,0);
    }
  }

/* Set a cell to a new state */
void setcell(HWND w,LONG x,LONG y,STATE s,BOOL send)
  {
  board[y][x]=s;
  InvalidateCell(w,x,y);
/* If necessary, pass info to net partner */
  if (send)
    {
    Send(SET,x,y,0,0,s);
    }
  }

/* Select a cell */
void selecting(HWND w,LONG x,LONG y)
  {
```

```
  PixToCell(&x,&y);  /* Convert to cell */
  if (selected)  /* Move existing selection? */
    {
    selected=FALSE;
    if (selectp.x==x&&selectp.y==y)
      {
      InvalidateCell(w,x,y); /* no move */
      return;
      }
    move(w,selectp.x,selectp.y,x,y,TRUE);
    }
  else
    {   /* new selection or new red piece */
    if (board[y][x]==CELL_EMPTY)
      {
      setcell(w,x,y,CELL_RED,TRUE);
      return;
      }
    selected=TRUE;
    selectp.x=x;
    selectp.y=y;
    InvalidateCell(w,x,y);
    }
  }

/* Mark cell as dirty for painting */
void InvalidateCell(HWND w,LONG x,LONG y)
  {
  RECT r;
  CellToPix(&x,&y);
  r.left=x;
  r.top=y;
  r.right=x+75;
  r.bottom=y+50;
  InvalidateRect(w,&r,FALSE);
  }

/* Convert cell coordinates to pixel coordinates */
void CellToPix(LONG *x,LONG *y)
  {
  *x*=75;
  *y*=50;
  }

/* Convert pixel coordinates to cell coordinates */
void PixToCell(LONG *x,LONG *y)
```

```
  {
  *x/=75;
  *y/=50;
  }

/* Perform a right click action */
void action(HWND w,LONG x,LONG y)
  {
  PixToCell(&x,&y);
  if (board[y][x]==CELL_EMPTY)
    {
    setcell(w,x,y,CELL_BLACK,TRUE);     /* Set black cell */
    return;
    }
/* If cell is a king empty it, else make it a king */
  if (board[y][x]==CELL_REDKING||board[y][x]==CELL_BLACKKING)
    setcell(w,x,y,CELL_EMPTY,TRUE);
  else
    setcell(w,x,y,board[y][x]+2,TRUE);
  }

/* Get a file name with common dialog */
int get_file(HWND parent,char *fn,int sz,
  char *title,char *filter,BOOL flag)
  {
  OPENFILENAME of;
  char ft[_MAX_PATH],dir[_MAX_PATH],*p;
  strcpy(dir,fn);
  p=strrchr(dir,'\\');
  if (p) *p='\0'; else *dir='\0';
  memset(&of,0,sizeof(of));
  of.lStructSize=sizeof(of);
  of.hwndOwner=parent;
  of.hInstance=hInst;
  of.lpstrFilter=filter;
  of.nFilterIndex=1;
  of.lpstrFile=fn;
  of.lpstrFileTitle=ft;
  of.nMaxFile=sz;
  of.nMaxFileTitle=_MAX_PATH;
  of.lpstrTitle=title;
  of.lpstrInitialDir=dir;
  if (flag)
    {
    of.Flags=OFN_HIDEREADONLY|OFN_OVERWRITEPROMPT;
```

```
    if (!GetSaveFileName(&of)) return 1;
    }
  else
    {
    of.Flags=OFN_FILEMUSTEXIST|OFN_HIDEREADONLY;
    if (!GetOpenFileName(&of)) return 1;
    }
  return 0;
  }
```

The **CHECKER** code has minimal knowledge of the network. It depends on five functions in **CHECKNET.C**: **client()**, **server()**, **Send()**, **transact()**, and **netclose()**. The first two functions set up operations as a client or server. The **Send()** function transmits a data structure (a **PLAYREC**—see Table 6.7) over the network. When the **PLAYREC** arrives at the other end, it generates a **WM_TRANSACT** message (a user-defined message). The **CHECKER** code calls **transact()** to handle the message. Finally, **netclose()** closes down the network.

Table 6.7 The PLAYREC structure (32-bit).

Field	Type	Description
cmd	PLAYCMD	One of: MOVE or SET
x	LONG	X coordinate
y	LONG	Y coordinate
x0	LONG	Starting X coordinate (used only for MOVE)
y0	LONG	Starting Y coordinate (used only for MOVE)
state	STATE	Cell state (used only for SET)

Listing 6.12 CHECKNET.C.

```
/* Net Checkers network code */
#include <windows.h>
#include <winsock.h>
#include "checker.h"

/* The socket */
SOCKET sock=INVALID_SOCKET;

/* Port and host name */
DWORD portnr;
char hostname[128];
```

```
/* Reports network errors -- could use some work */
static void neterror(LPSTR s)
  {
  int err=WSAGetLastError();
  char title[65];
  sprintf(title,"Network Error %x!",err);
  MessageBox(NULL,s,title,MB_OK|MB_ICONSTOP);
  if (sock!=INVALID_SOCKET) closesocket(sock);
  sock=INVALID_SOCKET;
  WSACleanup();
  PostQuitMessage(-1);
  }


/* Sets the menu state so you can't connect twice */
static void setmenu(HWND w,UINT state)
  {
  HMENU menu=GetMenu(w);
  EnableMenuItem(menu,IDM_CLIENT,MF_BYCOMMAND|state);
  EnableMenuItem(menu,IDM_SERVER,MF_BYCOMMAND|state);
  if (state==MF_ENABLED)
    state=MF_GRAYED;
  else
    state=MF_ENABLED;
  EnableMenuItem(menu,IDM_QUIT,MF_BYCOMMAND|state);
  }

/* Shutdown network operations */
void netclose(HWND w)
  {
  SendMessage(w,WM_SETTEXT,0,(DWORD)"Checkers!");
  if (sock!=INVALID_SOCKET)
    if (closesocket(sock)) neterror("Close");
  sock=INVALID_SOCKET;
  setmenu(w,MF_ENABLED);
  WSACleanup();
  }


/* Send a transaction */
void Send(PLAYCMD c,LONG x1,LONG y1,LONG x0,LONG y0,STATE s)
  {
  PLAYREC play;
  if (sock==INVALID_SOCKET) return;
  play.cmd=c;
```

6. Interprocess Communications

```
  play.x=x1;
  play.y=y1;
  play.x0=x0;
  play.y0=y0;
  play.state=s;
/***** Send PLAYREC over network */
  if (send(sock,(LPSTR)&play,sizeof(PLAYREC),0)==SOCKET_ERROR)
    neterror("Send");
  }

/* Handle a network transaction */
void transact(HWND w,LPARAM lParam)
  {
  PLAYREC play;
/* Check for partner quitting */
  if (WSAGETSELECTEVENT(lParam)==FD_CLOSE)
    {
        netclose(w);
        MessageBox(w,"Your partner quit",
          "Game Over",MB_OK|MB_ICONSTOP);
        return;
        }
/* Otherwise, data is ready, so read the PLAYREC */
  if (recv(sock,(LPSTR)&play,sizeof(PLAYREC),0)==SOCKET_ERROR)
    neterror("Recv");
/* Process command in PLAYREC */
  switch (play.cmd)
    {
        case MOVE:
          move(w,play.x0,play.y0,play.x,play.y,FALSE);
          break;

        case SET:
          setcell(w,play.x,play.y,play.state,FALSE);
          break;

        default:
          MessageBox(w,"Unknown network transaction",
            NULL,MB_OK|MB_ICONSTOP);
        }
  }

/* Start as server */
void server(HWND w)
  {
```

6. Interprocess Communications

```
  SOCKADDR_IN saddr;
  SOCKET sock1;
  WSADATA data;
  new_board(w);      /* make sure game is clean */
  if (WSAStartup(0x101,&data)) /* Start WinSock */
    neterror("Init");
/* Get our host name to show user */
  if (gethostname(hostname,sizeof(hostname)))
    neterror("GetHost");
/* Prompt for port number */
  if (DialogBox(hInst,"SERVERDLG",w,ServerDlg)==IDCANCEL)
    return;
/* Change title */
  SendMessage(w,WM_SETTEXT,0,
    (DWORD)"Checkers! (Waiting for connection)");
/* Create socket */
  sock=socket(PF_INET,SOCK_STREAM,0);
  if (sock==INVALID_SOCKET)
    neterror("Socket");
/* Bind to assigned port number */
  saddr.sin_family=AF_INET;
  saddr.sin_addr.s_addr=INADDR_ANY;
/* Convert port # to canonical format */
  saddr.sin_port=htons(portnr);
  if (bind(sock,(PSOCKADDR)&saddr,sizeof(SOCKADDR_IN)))
    neterror("Bind");
/* Disallow more client/server requests */
  setmenu(w,MF_GRAYED);
/* Might block, so make sure window is OK */
  UpdateWindow(w);
/* Wait for connect */
  if (listen(sock,1))
    neterror("Listen");
  sock1=accept(sock,NULL,0);
  if (sock1==INVALID_SOCKET)
    neterror("Accept");
/* Close original socket (only 1 connect allowed) */
  if (closesocket(sock))
    neterror("close");
/* Use new socket */
  sock=sock1;
/* Change title again */
  SendMessage(w,WM_SETTEXT,0,
    (DWORD)"Checkers! (Server)");
/* Ask for WM_TRANSACT message when data available or
```

```
    socket closes */
   if (WSAAsyncSelect(sock,w,WM_TRANSACT,FD_READ|FD_CLOSE))
     neterror("Select");
/* Notify user */
   MessageBox(w,"Connection made.","Success",
     MB_OK|MB_ICONEXCLAMATION);
   }

/* Set up as client */
void client(HWND w)
   {
   PHOSTENT phe;
   SOCKADDR_IN saddr;
   WSADATA data;
   new_board(w);  // Start with clean game
/* Init WinSock */
   if (WSAStartup(0x1C1,&data))
     neterror("Init");
/* Get my host name (used as default) */
   if (gethostname(hostname,sizeof(hostname)))
     neterror("GetHost");
/* Prompt user for host/port */
   if (DialogBox(hInst,"CLIENTDLG",w,ClientDlg)==IDCANCEL)
     return;
/* Change title */
   SendMessage(w,WM_SETTEXT,0,
     (DWORD)"Checkers! (Connecting to server)");
/* Make new socket */
   sock=socket(PF_INET,SOCK_STREAM,0);
   if (sock==INVALID_SOCKET)
     neterror("Socket");
   saddr.sin_family=AF_INET;
/* Convert hostname to address */
   phe=gethostbyname(hostname);
   memcpy((char FAR *)&(saddr.sin_addr),phe->h_addr,phe->h_length);
/* Convert port # to canonical format */
   saddr.sin_port=htons(portno);
/* Update menus */
   setmenu(w,MF_GRAYED);
/* Might block, so make sure window is OK */
   UpdateWindow(w);
/* Connect! */
   if (connect(sock,(FSOCKADDR)&saddr,sizeof(saddr)))
     neterror("Connect");
/* Change title again */
```

```
  SendMessage(w,WM_SETTEXT,0,(DWORD)"Checkers! (Client)");
/* Ask for WM_TRANSACT when data available or
   partner closes socket */
  if (WSAAsyncSelect(sock,w,WM_TRANSACT,FD_READ|FD_CLOSE))
    neterror("Select");
/* Notify user */
  MessageBox(w,"Connection made.","Success",MB_OK|MB_ICONEXCLAMATION);
  }
```

The **move()** and **setcell()** functions are key to maintaining the checkerboard. Each takes a flag argument. If the flag is **TRUE**, the functions automatically call **Send()** to update the network partner. Then, the partner's **transact()** function makes the exact same call to **move()** or **setcell()** with the flag set to **FALSE**.

The **server()** call shows you your computer's host name, and prompts you for a port number. By convention, port numbers greater than 5000 are available for your use. The system automatically assigns numbers between 1024 and 5000. The system reserves port numbers below 1024 for well-known services (e.g., Telnet, FTP, etc.). In a typical application, you would make an entry for the service in the system's services file. Then you would use **getservbyname()** to convert the service name to a port number. However, specifying the port number directly lets you play without any configuration file changes. The client must specify the server's host name and the same port number to make the connection.

Because the server handles only one game at a time, the server calls **listen()** with an argument of 1. When **accept()** returns a socket, the program closes the original socket and uses the new socket to communicate.

When the server or client gets a valid, connected socket, it calls **WSAAsyncSelect()**. This automatically sets the socket to nonblocking mode and posts a message when certain conditions occur. The checker code asks for a **WM_TRANSACT** message whenever there is data to read or the socket closes. The **transact()** function then either shuts down the connection or reads data, as is appropriate.

The remainder of the checker code is not exceptional. The checkerboard is a simple array of enumerated types. The window processes mouse messages to handle selecting a piece, moving a piece, and so on.

Special Considerations

I originally wrote this code under Windows NT. I wanted to make sure it would work under Windows 3.1. When I made the port, I found an interesting portability issue. I've always been suspicious of enumerated types. After all, you can do the same thing with the preprocessor. With C++ there are some advantages, but under C, there doesn't seem to be a compelling reason to use them. With this project, I used an enum to store the command in the **PLAYREC** structure and another to store the cell state—why not?

As I moved the code to 16 bits, I found out why not. An enumerated type is always the size of an integer. Under 16-bit Windows, that size is 16 bits. Under 32-bit Windows, it is, of course, 32 bits. This size difference prevents 16-bit clients from working with 32-bit servers and vice versa. There is no way to change the size. In the end, I simply made the enumerated fields **DWORD**s under Windows 3.1. This would have been much uglier under C++, because C++ enforces strict type checking.

Another special concern is the state of the board. Because the client and server assume their boards are the same when they connect, it is a good idea to force a new game before the connection. This ensures that the boards are the same. There are no checks to keep you from loading a new board from a file while playing, however. Besides, both players could agree to load a file before starting a game.

Improvements

If you are adventurous, you might try modifying the checkers game. There are several improvements you can make:

- Let the user specify the address as a numerical address or a host name. You could also resolve symbolic port names using **getservbyname()**.
- The user interface is simplistic. As long as you continue to call **setcell()** and **move()**, you can change the user interface as much as you like and the network code won't change.
- It would be useful if the players could "chat" during a game. To keep things simple, you could collect data in an edit control and then display it using a message box or simple dialog. You could send a special **PLAYREC** that contains the number of bytes in the message. Then, you could read the data during the next transaction. Alternatively, you could send the message as out of band data.
- It would be very simple to show the client's address information when you connect. The **accept()** call will fill in an address structure, if you provide it.
- Error handling is complete, but simplistic. You could easily improve it.
- I made no effort to detect legal moves, automatically handle jumps, or automatically change pieces to kings, although that would not be difficult. Slightly more ambitious would be to make the computer play checkers (an auto-server mode).

- You might want to fix the program to play a regulation game of checkers with three rows of checkers on each side instead of two rows.

MFC Sockets

The checkers game used ordinary C along with the standard Winsock library. But what about MFC? MFC has support for sockets in several forms.

I thought it would be interesting to contrast MFC's sockets with garden-variety sockets. However, I won't do checkers this time. Instead I'll use MFC sockets to construct a game reminiscent of a board game my son Patrick likes to play.

The game (see Figure 6.2) pits two army commanders against one another. In the first phase of the game, you place your pieces (a tank, a missile carrier, etc.) on the board. Once the board is full, one player enters the host mode and the other connects to the host. (To test it out, you can run both sides on one machine). Next, the players take turns using the mouse to bomb the board. The computer reports all hits and misses.

About CSocket

MFC's easiest-to-use socket class is the **CSocket** class. This class wraps up all the messy details inherent in using sockets. You don't need to know about

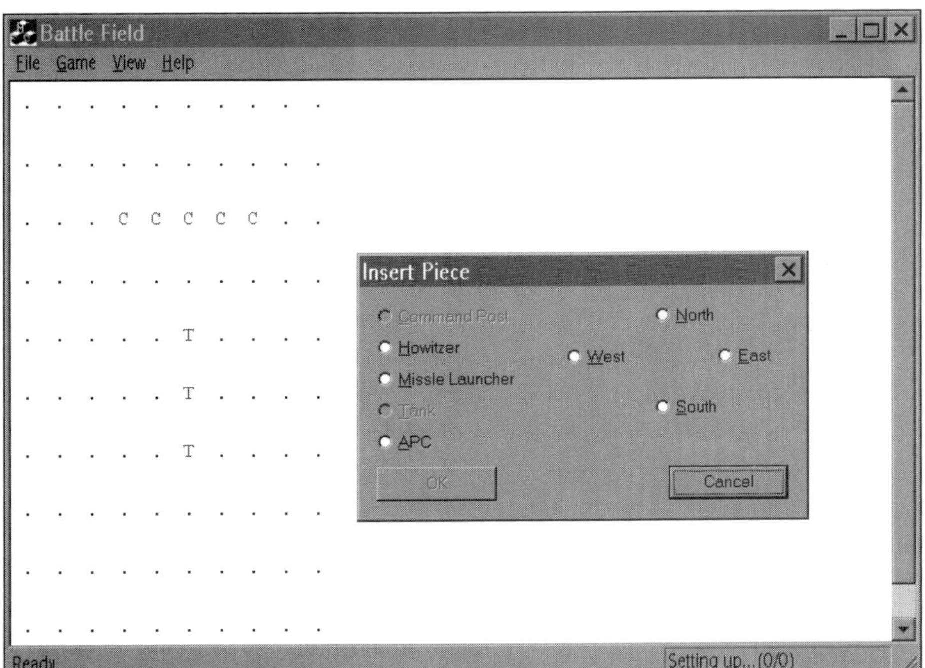

Figure 6.2 The BField program.

network byte ordering, host name resolution, or address families. Hosts and clients use **CSockets** differently (see Tables 6.8 and 6.9). If you want to act as a client, you simply create the **CSocket**, then call **Connect**, passing the host name and port number.

Servers are a bit more complicated. First, you create the socket with the port number you want, then you call **Listen**. Finally, you call **Accept** to wait for a connection. There's one catch: You pass **Accept** an uninitialized **CSocket** object. This is the object that you use to carry on the conversation with the client.

Why do you need two sockets? The answer lies in the way most servers operate. Consider a Web server. By convention, the server listens on port 80. That way, when a client wants to connect, it knows to use port 80. But if a client really connected with port 80, other clients couldn't connect until the first client closed its connection, which wouldn't be a good idea. So, servers listen with a socket with a well-known port number (like 80). When a client tries to connect to the port, the server actually redirects the request to some other random port and assigns a new socket. This leaves the well-known socket free to make more connections.

At this point, you can use a **CSocket** directly to pass data back and forth between the two sockets. These sockets are reliable. Assuming the network is up, the data you put in one socket will appear at the other socket, correctly and in the proper order. You can create connectionless sockets, too, but then you can't be sure the data will appear without errors and in the correct order. Why use sockets that aren't reliable? Perhaps you are writing a program that has its own protocol for

Table 6.8 Using CSocket as a client.

Step	Code	Description
1	CSocket socket;	Create an empty, uninitialized socket
2	socket.Create();	Initialize socket; use any port
3	socket.Connect("ahost",100);	Connect to host "ahost" on port 100

Table 6.9 Using CSocket as a host.

Step	Code	Description
1	CSocket hostsocket	Create a socket to listen with
2	hostsocket.Create(100);	Initialize socket and use port 100
3	hostsocket.Listen();	Open up for connections
4	CSocket socket;	Create a socket to use for connection
5	hostsocket.Accept(socket);	Handle incoming connection with socket

correcting errors and ordering data. In that case, duplicating the effort at the socket level is a waste, and an unreliable socket is more efficient.

Although you can use the sockets directly at this point, all they will do is exchange raw data. What happens if you want to pass C++ objects from one side of the connection to the other? MFC enables you to serialize objects across a socket connection. Just as you serialize objects to a file and load them later, you can write your objects across the network and reconstitute them on the other side of the network.

Using Archives With CSocket

The trick to transporting objects across the network is to attach your **CSocket** object to a **CSocketFile**. By itself, this object isn't very useful. However, you can attach the **CSocketFile** to a **CArchive** object. Then, you can serialize objects using the **CArchive** object. You'll find the exact steps in Table 6.10.

Remember, **CArchive** objects can read objects or write objects, but not both at the same time. However, it is perfectly permissible to create two **CArchive** objects that both refer to the same socket. Then, you can read objects from one archive and write them to the other.

One other thing: You can't use unreliable sockets in a **CArchive**. That makes sense. The **CArchive** object treats the socket as a file, and files are reliable.

Going Deeper—CAsyncSocket

If you are familiar with socket programming, you might not like MFC doing so much work for you. You can use **CAsyncSocket** instead (see your online help for details about **CAsyncSocket**). This class (which is the base class for **CSocket**, by the way) allows you more direct access to sockets. However, if you use **CAsyncSocket**, you'll have to do a lot more work. For example, using a **CAsyncSocket** requires you to order your bytes in network order. Also, you can't use these sockets in archives. In nearly every case, you'll want to use **CSocket** instead of **CAsyncSocket**.

Table 6.10 Connecting a CArchive and a CSocket.

Step	Code	Description
1	CSocketFile file(&socket);	Create CSocketFile connected to socket
2	CArchive input(&file,CArchive::load);	Attach socket to inbound archive
3	CArchive output(&file,CArchive::store);	Attach socket to outbound archive

Still, there are times where you'll want to use **CAsyncSocket**. In particular, **CSocket** can sometimes block and cause your program to apparently lock up while waiting for some network event to call.

Blocking Calls

One big difference between using a file-based archive and one that uses sockets is the potential for latency. If you read an object from a file, it is either in the file or it isn't. However, with a socket, you can't be sure if the data is available. If you try to read an object, your program may come to an abrupt halt until the object is available.

What's the answer? You could make these blocking calls in a thread. However, in some cases you can use special virtual functions to take care of this problem.

For example, the **OnReceive** function executes when the socket has data available. Of course, to override this function, you have to derive your own class from **CSocket**. **CAsyncSocket** also provides overrides for connections, but you can't use these with **CSocket**. **CSocket** connections either fail or succeed. If the connection fails, it is up to you to try again later if you want to.

The Example

Now that you know about **CSockets** and how to attach them to **CArchives**, think of how this can apply to the battlefield game. It is easy to create a class that contains information to send across the network (see Table 6.11). You can easily write a serialize function for this simple packet. Although it isn't strictly necessary in this case, you should derive classes you plan to serialize from **CObject**.

In the case of battlefield, communication follows a strict protocol. The host sends a **CMD_CLICK** packet. The client then replies with a **CMD_REPLY**. Then, it is the client's turn to send a **CMD_CLICK** and receive a **CMD_REPLY** packet. Instead of a **CMD_CLICK** packet, the program can send a **CMD_RESIGN** command to end the game.

Table 6.11 CPacket.

Member	Description
cmd	Integer describing command (CMD_CLICK, CMD_REPLY, CMD_RESIGN)
x	X coordinate (not used for CMD_RESIGN)
y	Y coordinate (not used for CMD_RESIGN)
data	Character representing state of cell at (x,y) (not used for CMD_CLICK or CMD_RESIGN)
Serialize	Function writes packet to CArchive

Having the packet, of course, isn't enough to play the game. You also need a user interface. That shouldn't be a big deal, but blocking network calls can require a bit of special attention.

The Basic Framework

The program is an ordinary MFC document-view program that uses **CScrollView**. Nothing special there. The document object handles most of the work (see Listing 6.13). It contains a 3D array (**grid**). This is really two 10x10 2D arrays. The first one contains the local computer's board. The other 2D array holds what you know about your opponent's board.

Listing 6.13 The BFIELD document object.

```
// Doc.cpp : implementation of the CBfieldDoc class
// Battlefield document -- most real work is here

#include "stdafx.h"
#include "bfield.h"
#include "insert.h"
#include "bsocket.h"
#include "Doc.h"
#include "ConnDlg.h"
#include "HostDlg.h"
#include "packet.h"
#include "mainfrm.h"


#ifdef _DEBUG
#define new DEBUG_NEW
#undef THIS_FILE
static char THIS_FILE[] = __FILE__;
#endif

////////////////////////
// CBfieldDoc

IMPLEMENT_DYNCREATE(CBfieldDoc, CDocument)

BEGIN_MESSAGE_MAP(CBfieldDoc, CDocument)
        //{{AFX_MSG_MAP(CBfieldDoc)
        ON_COMMAND(IDM_CONNECT, OnConnect)
        ON_COMMAND(IDM_HOST, OnHost)
        ON_UPDATE_COMMAND_UI(IDM_CONNECT, OnUpdateConnect)
        ON_UPDATE_COMMAND_UI(ID_TURN, OnUpdateTurn)
        ON_UPDATE_COMMAND_UI(IDM_HOST, OnUpdateHost)
```

```
        ON_COMMAND(IDM_RESIGN, OnResign)
        ON_UPDATE_COMMAND_UI(IDM_RESIGN, OnUpdateResign)
        //}}AFX_MSG_MAP
END_MESSAGE_MAP()

///////////////////////
// CBfieldDoc construction/destruction

CBfieldDoc::CBfieldDoc()
{
        sockfile=NULL;
        xmit=NULL;
        rcv=NULL;
        MyTurn=FALSE;
}

CBfieldDoc::~CBfieldDoc()
{
    NetClose();
}

BOOL CBfieldDoc::OnNewDocument()
{
        if (!CDocument::OnNewDocument())
                return FALSE;
        NetClose();
    // empty grids
        for (int i=0;i<2;i++)
                for (int x=0;x<10;x++)
                        for (int y=0;y<10;y++)
                                grid[i][x][y]='.';
        mode=0;
        placed=0;
        HitCt[0]=0;
        HitCt[1]=0;
        MyTurn=FALSE;
        return TRUE;
}

///////////////////////
// CBfieldDoc serialization -- not used

void CBfieldDoc::Serialize(CArchive& ar)
{
        if (ar.IsStoring())
```

```
        {
                // TODO: add storing code here
        }
        else
        {
                // TODO: add loading code here
        }
}

////////////////////////
// CBfieldDoc diagnostics

#ifdef _DEBUG
void CBfieldDoc::AssertValid() const
{
        CDocument::AssertValid();
}

void CBfieldDoc::Dump(CDumpContext& dc) const
{
        CDocument::Dump(dc);
}
#endif //_DEBUG

////////////////////////
// CBfieldDoc commands

// Get state based on current mode
char CBfieldDoc::GetState(int x,int y)
{
   return grid[mode][x][y];
}

// Handle mouse click from view
void CBfieldDoc::OnClick(int x,int y)
{
if (grid[mode][x][y]!='.'||x>9||y>9)
        {
        AfxMessageBox("Please click a blank square");
        return;
        }
if (mode==0)  // setup
        {
        int q,step=1;
        CInsert dlg;
```

```
        if (placed==0x1F)
            {
            AfxMessageBox("You have placed all your pieces");
            return;
            }
// set up placement dialog
        dlg.m_placed=placed;
        dlg.m_x=x;
        dlg.m_y=y;
// call dialog
        int res=dlg.DoModal();
        if (res==-1) return;
        if (res=='.') return; // shouldn't happen
// check for piece sticking over edge
        if ((dlg.m_Dir==DIR_WEST && x-dlg.m_Len<-1)||
            (dlg.m_Dir==DIR_EAST && x+dlg.m_Len>10)||
            (dlg.m_Dir==DIR_NORTH && y-dlg.m_Len<-1)||
            (dlg.m_Dir==DIR_SOUTH && y+dlg.m_Len>10))
                {
                AfxMessageBox(
                  "The piece must completely fit on the board");
                return;
                }
// Now check for overlapping pieces
        if (dlg.m_Dir==DIR_WEST||dlg.m_Dir==DIR_NORTH) step=-1;
        if (dlg.m_Dir==DIR_EAST||dlg.m_Dir==DIR_WEST)
                {
                for (q=0;q<dlg.m_Len;q++)
                        if (grid[0][x+step*q][y]!='.')
                          {
                          AfxMessageBox(
                            "The piece overlaps another piece!");
                          return;
                          }
// set it up
                for (q=0;q<dlg.m_Len;q++)
                   grid[0][x-step*q][y]=res;
                }
        else
                {
                for (q=0;q<dlg.m_Len;q++)
                        if (grid[0][x][y+step*q]!='.')
                          {
                          AfxMessageBox(
                            "The piece overlaps another piece!");
```

```
                        return;
                        }
                for (q=0;q<dlg.m_Len;q++)
                    grid[0][x][y+step*q]=res;
                }
// mark it as placed and redraw
        placed|=dlg.m_Piece;
        UpdateAllViews(NULL);
        }
else  // not in setup mode -- hostile click!
        {
        CPacket pkt;
        if (!MyTurn) return; // no cheating
// build outbound packet
        pkt.cmd=CMD_CLICK;
        pkt.x=x;
        pkt.y=y;
        pkt.Serialize(*xmit);
        xmit->Flush();  // make sure to send it
// get reply -- might block for a bit
// but assuming everything works, no big deal
        pkt.Serialize(*rcv);
        if (pkt.cmd!=CMD_REPLY)
                {
                AfxMessageBox("Bad reply");
                return;
                }
// update board
        grid[1][pkt.x][pkt.y]=pkt.data;
// count our hits
        if (pkt.data!='X') HitCt[0]++;
// check for win!
        if (HitCt[0]==17)
                {
                AfxMessageBox("You win!");
                NetClose();
                OnNewDocument();
                UpdateAllViews(NULL);
                }
        UpdateAllViews(NULL);
        MyTurn=FALSE;
        }
}

int CBfieldDoc::GetMode(void)
{
```

```
   return mode;
}


// Come here to connect to host
// Host must be ready
void CBfieldDoc::OnConnect()
{
     CConnDlg dlg;
         if (dlg.DoModal()==IDCANCEL) return;
         mode=-1;
         UpdateStatus();
         if (!socket.Create())
                 {
                 err(socket.GetLastError());
                 return;
                 }

         if (!socket.Connect(dlg.m_Host,dlg.m_Port))
                 if (socket.GetLastError()!=WSAECONNREFUSED)
                   {
                   mode=0;
                   err(socket.GetLastError());
                   socket.Close();
                   return;
                   }
                 else
                   {
                   // Host not ready yet
                   mode=0;
                   AfxMessageBox("Host not available");
                   socket.Close();
                   return;
                }
         sockfile=new CSocketFile(&socket);
         xmit=new CArchive(sockfile,CArchive::store);
         rcv=new CArchive(sockfile,CArchive::load);
         mode=1;
         UpdateStatus();
         UpdateAllViews(NULL);
}

//Here to set up as host
void CBfieldDoc::OnHost()
{
```

```
        CHostDlg dlg;
        if (dlg.DoModal()==IDCANCEL) return;
        mode=-1;
        UpdateStatus();
        if (!hostsocket.Create(dlg.m_Port))
                {
                err(GetLastError());
                return;
                }
        if (!hostsocket.Listen())
                {
                err(GetLastError());
                return;
                }
      // wait for connection or error -- blocks
      while (!hostsocket.Accept(socket) &&
             !hostsocket.GetLastError());
      if (hostsocket.GetLastError())
          {
          err(hostsocket.GetLastError());
          return;
          }
        hostsocket.Close(); // no more connections
        sockfile=new CSocketFile(&socket);
        xmit=new CArchive(sockfile,CArchive::store);
        rcv=new CArchive(sockfile,CArchive::load);
        mode=1;
        UpdateStatus();
        UpdateAllViews(NULL);
        MyTurn=TRUE;
        AfxMessageBox("Connected: It is your turn");
        }

// Enable connect menu
void CBfieldDoc::OnUpdateConnect(CCmdUI* pCmdUI)
  {
  pCmdUI->Enable(mode==0&&placed==0x1F);
  }

// Enable host menu
void CBfieldDoc::OnUpdateHost(CCmdUI* pCmdUI)
{
pCmdUI->Enable(mode==0&&placed==0x1F);
}
```

6. Interprocess Communications

```
// Resign game
void CBfieldDoc::OnResign()
{
  CPacket pkt;
  if (AfxMessageBox(
     "Do you really want to quit?",MB_YESNO)==IDNO)
        return;
  pkt.cmd=CMD_RESIGN;
  pkt.Serialize(*xmit);
  NetClose();
  OnNewDocument();
  UpdateAllViews(NULL);
  }

// Enable Resign
void CBfieldDoc::OnUpdateResign(CCmdUI* pCmdUI)
{
  pCmdUI->Enable(mode==1&&MyTurn);
}

// Very bad general error routine
void CBfieldDoc::err(int ern)
{
  CString s;
  s.Format("%x-%x",ern,GetLastError());
  AfxMessageBox(s);
}

// Close network connection
void CBfieldDoc::NetClose()
{
  if (xmit) delete xmit;
  if (rcv) delete rcv;
  if (sockfile) delete sockfile;
  socket.Close();
  sockfile=NULL;
  xmit=NULL;
  rcv=NULL;
  mode=0;
  placed=0;
}

void CBfieldDoc::OnCloseDocument()
{
        NetClose();
```

```
        CDocument::OnCloseDocument();
}


// CBattleSocket calls this when data is available
void CBfieldDoc::GoAhead(void)
{
  CPacket pkt;
  CPacket outgoing;
  UpdateStatus();
  pkt.Serialize(*rcv);  // get packet
  if (pkt.cmd==CMD_RESIGN) // quitter?
        {
        AfxMessageBox("Your opponent resigned");
        NetClose();
        OnNewDocument();
        UpdateAllViews(NULL);
        return;
        }
  if (pkt.cmd!=CMD_CLICK)
        {
        AfxMessageBox("Unexpected error");
        return;
        }
// prepare reply
  outgoing.data=grid[0][pkt.x][pkt.y];
  outgoing.cmd=CMD_REPLY;
  outgoing.x=pkt.x;
  outgoing.y=pkt.y;
  if (outgoing.data=='.') // convert our . to outbound X
    outgoing.data='X';
  else
      HitCt[1]++;  // He hit us!
// send it
  outgoing.Serialize(*xmit);
  xmit->Flush();
// check for loss
  if (HitCt[1]==17)
        {
        AfxMessageBox("You lose!");
        NetClose();
        OnNewDocument();
        UpdateAllViews(NULL);
        }
  MyTurn=TRUE;
  CString msg;
```

```
  if (outgoing.data!='X')
    msg.Format("Opponent hit: %c. ",outgoing.data);
  msg=msg+"It is your turn";
  AfxMessageBox(msg);
}

BOOL CBfieldDoc::GetTurn()
{
  return MyTurn;
}

// Helper function to update status bar
void CBfieldDoc::UpdateStatus(void)
{
  CMainFrame *fw=(CMainFrame *)AfxGetMainWnd();
  fw->UpdateStatus();
}

// We are ready if all pieces are placed (0x1F)
BOOL CBfieldDoc::GetReady(void)
{
  return placed==0x1F;
}

// This updates the status bar pane
void CBfieldDoc::OnUpdateTurn(CCmdUI* pCmdUI)
{
  int mode=GetMode();
  BOOL turn=GetTurn();
  CString s;
  if (!mode)
        {
        if (placed==0x1F)
          s="Ready to connect";
        else
          s="Setting up...";
        }
   else
     {
     if (mode==-1) s="Connecting...";
     if (turn)
       s="Your turn";
     else
       s="Waiting...";
     }
```

```
    CString counts;
    counts.Format("(%d/%d)",HitCt[0],HitCt[1]);
    s+=counts;
    pCmdUI->SetText(s);
    pCmdUI->Enable(TRUE);
}
```

The only important functions in the view are the ones that draw the board and handle mouse clicks. The **OnDraw** function (see Listing 6.14) queries the document object to learn the contents of each cell. All the logic that colors different squares and spaces them in the scrolling view is in this function.

Listing 6.14 The BFIELD view object.

```
// View.cpp : implementation of the CBfieldView class
//

#include "stdafx.h"
#include "bfield.h"

#include "bsocket.h"
#include "Doc.h"
#include "View.h"

#ifdef _DEBUG
#define new DEBUG_NEW
#undef THIS_FILE
static char THIS_FILE[] = __FILE__;
#endif

////////////////////////
// CBfieldView

IMPLEMENT_DYNCREATE(CBfieldView, CScrollView)

BEGIN_MESSAGE_MAP(CBfieldView, CScrollView)
        //{{AFX_MSG_MAP(CBfieldView)
        ON_WM_LBUTTONDOWN()
        //}}AFX_MSG_MAP
END_MESSAGE_MAP()

////////////////////////
// CBfieldView construction/destruction

CBfieldView::CBfieldView()
{
```

6. Interprocess Communications

```
        // TODO: add construction code here

}

CBfieldView::~CBfieldView()
{
}

BOOL CBfieldView::PreCreateWindow(CREATESTRUCT& cs)
{
        // TODO: Modify the Window class or styles here by modifying
        //  the CREATESTRUCT cs

        return CScrollView::PreCreateWindow(cs);
}

///////////////////////
// CBfieldView drawing

void CBfieldView::OnDraw(CDC* pDC)
{
        CBfieldDoc* pDoc = GetDocument();
        ASSERT_VALID(pDoc);
        TEXTMETRIC tm;
        COLORREF clr,curcolor;
        pDC->SelectStockObject(ANSI_FIXED_FONT);
        pDC->GetTextMetrics(&tm);
// Change default color based on mode (setup/hits)
        clr=pDoc->GetMode()?RGB(0xFF,0,0):RGB(0,0x80,0);
        for (int x=0;x<10;x++)
                for (int y=0;y<10;y++)
                  {
                  char piece[2];
                  piece[1]='\0';
                  piece[0]=pDoc->GetState(x,y);
                  curcolor=clr;
                  // custom colors
                  if (piece[0]=='.') curcolor=RGB(0,0,0);
                  if (piece[0]=='X') curcolor=RGB(0,0,0xFF);
                  pDC->SetTextColor(curcolor);
                  pDC->TextOut(
                    x*tm.tmAveCharWidth*3+
                      tm.tmAveCharWidth,
                    y*tm.tmHeight*3+
                      tm.tmAveCharWidth,piece);
```

6. Interprocess Communications

```
                    }

 }

 void CBfieldView::OnInitialUpdate()
 {
         CScrollView::OnInitialUpdate();
         CSize sizeTotal;
         // TODO: calculate the total size of this view
         CDC *dc=GetDC();
         TEXTMETRIC tm;
         dc->SelectStockObject(ANSI_FIXED_FONT);
         dc->GetTextMetrics(&tm);
// allow for 3 characters per cell plus a border character
         sizeTotal.cx = 31*tm.tmAveCharWidth;
         sizeTotal.cy = 31*tm.tmHeight;
         SetScrollSizes(MM_TEXT, sizeTotal);
// While this code should work, it has problems with the
// new style windows
//       GetParentFrame()->RecalcLayout(TRUE);
//       ResizeParentToFit();

}

////////////////////////
// CBfieldView diagnostics

#ifdef _DEBUG
void CBfieldView::AssertValid() const
{
        CScrollView::AssertValid();
}

void CBfieldView::Dump(CDumpContext& dc) const
{
        CScrollView::Dump(dc);
}

CBfieldDoc* CBfieldView::GetDocument() // non-debug version is inline
{
        ASSERT(m_pDocument->IsKindOf(RUNTIME_CLASS(CBfieldDoc)));
        return (CBfieldDoc*)m_pDocument;
}
#endif //_DEBUG
```

6. Interprocess Communications

```
///////////////////////
// CBfieldView message handlers

void CBfieldView::OnLButtonDown(UINT nFlags, CPoint point)
{
        CDC *dc;
        CPoint scrollpos;
        int x,y;
        CBfieldDoc *doc=GetDocument();
        // convert to X,Y
        dc=GetDC();
        TEXTMETRIC tm;
        dc->SelectStockObject(ANSI_FIXED_FONT);
        dc->GetTextMetrics(&tm);
// Account for scrolling
        scrollpos=GetDeviceScrollPosition();
        point+=scrollpos;
        x=(point.x-tm.tmAveCharWidth)/(3*tm.tmAveCharWidth);
        y=(point.y-tm.tmHeight)/(3*tm.tmHeight);
// Pass to Document
        doc->OnClick(x,y);
}
```

The mouse event handler computes the x and y coordinates in terms of the 10×10 playing grid. It then passes this information directly to the document.

The document not only tracks the playing board contents, but it also knows the current mode. Mode 0 is when the player is setting up the board. This later becomes mode -1 when the game attempts to connect to its counterpart. When the connection is successful, the game is in progress and the document records this as mode 1.

In mode 0, the document tracks what pieces are already on the board. This serves two purposes: First, you can't place a piece twice, and second, you can't connect until your pieces are all on the board.

When your pieces are in place, you can set up as a host or connect to a host. The **OnHost** function handles the first case. **OnConnect** takes care of the second. You can find both functions in Listing 6.13. If you want to be a host, you need only specify the port number you want to use. Clients must specify the host name and the port. If you want to run both sides on the same machine, use **localhost** as the host name (or use TCP/IP address 127.0.0.1).

While your host waits for a connection, your application appears locked up. The code is at fault here, because MFC would return an error if the call would block.

However, battlefield keeps trying until the call is successful. It wouldn't be hard to put in some timeout mechanism here. A bit more difficult would be to have a timer event keep trying the connection until it is successful. More difficult still, you could handle the connection sequence in a separate thread. For a simple game like battlefield, I decided it was not a problem if the program freezes while waiting for a connection.

Once the game is underway, the document keeps track of whose turn it is in the **MyTurn** variable. The host player gets to go first. Nothing really happens until the host player clicks on an empty square. This causes the document to send a packet to the other player.

My first version of the battlefield program simply tried to read from the socket archive each time it wanted data. This has the unpleasant side effect that if your computer is waiting for a response, your program appears to lock up. The advantage of this approach is that you can use the standard **CSocket** class with no modifications. However, the fact that it was locking up during 50 percent of the game was too annoying, so I decided to fix things by using a custom socket class.

Adding A Custom Socket

I had to derive a new class from **CSocket** so that I could override the **OnReceive** function. **CSocket** calls this function when data is available. Therefore, you can issue a read and be certain it will succeed without delay from this routine. Class Wizard won't help you create a **CSocket** subclass; you'll have to do it the old-fashioned way. You can find the source code for **CBattleSocket** in Listing 6.15. Notice that I tried to avoid putting any code that contains game-related logic in **CBattleSocket**. Instead, **CBattleSocket** simply finds the current document and calls the document's **GoAhead** function. This function reads the data and processes it.

Listing 6.15 CBattleSocket's CPP file.

```
// BattleField Socket
// Simple override of CSocket
// Delegates receive to document->GoAhead function
#include "stdafx.h"
#include "bfield.h"
#include "bsocket.h"
#include "mainfrm.h"
#include "doc.h"

void CBattleSocket::OnReceive(int n)
        {
        if (!n)
```

```
        {
        CMainFrame *frm=(CMainFrame *)
                AfxGetMainWnd();
        CBfieldDoc *doc=(CBfieldDoc *)
                frm->GetActiveDocument();
        doc->GoAhead();
        }
}
```

Although **CAsyncSocket** provides overrideable functions for other events, **CSocket** doesn't seem to support these. Also, **CSocket** supposedly dispatches **WM_PAINT** messages while blocking, but I could find no evidence that this works. The MFC source code contains code that clearly thinks it is doing something (see **OnMessagePending** in the MFC source file **SOCKCORE.CPP**). However, if you set a breakpoint in **OnMessagePending**, **CSocket** apparently never calls it.

The document object has two member variables for sockets. The first (**socket**) is for the active connection. This has to use **CBattleSocket**. The other socket is **hostsocket**. The document uses this socket only to listen for requests. Therefore, this can remain an ordinary **CSocket**. The program never reads data from it, so there is no need for the special code.

Other Considerations

The only other tricky part is displaying messages in the status bar. Ordinarily, this isn't a big deal—all you have to do is write an **ON_UPDATE_COMMAND_UI** handler in your message map. In the associated function, you set the status bar pane's text and enable it. MFC routes the associated message just as it routes menu messages, so you can put the handler in any message map.

Class Wizard won't write these handlers for the status bar. However, you can fool it. The key is to realize that Class Wizard will write **ON_UPDATE_COMMAND_UI** handlers for menu items. Simply create a handler for a menu item that you don't already have an **ON_UPDATE_COMMAND_UI** handler for—**IDM_ABOUT**, perhaps. Be sure to select the class you want to handle the status message. When Class Wizard prompts you to name the function **OnUpdateAbout**, pick something else that describes your real intentions (maybe **OnUpdateStatus**). Finally, edit the class that contains the handler. You'll find an entry in the message map that looks like this:

```
ON_UPDATE_COMMAND_UI(IDM_ABOUT, OnUpdateStatus)
```

Change this line to use the ID of your status bar pane instead of **IDM_ABOUT**.

The only problem is that when your socket is blocking, the update messages cease. One possible answer is to update the status bar manually just before you expect the socket to block. That's what battlefield does. The main frame class contains a simple function to force the status bar to repaint. Here's the code:

```
void CMainFrame::UpdateStatus(void)
{
  CWnd *sb=GetMessageBar();
  sb->SendMessage(WM_IDLEUPDATECMDUI);
  sb->UpdateWindow();
}
```

You have to find the **CWnd** that corresponds to the status bar, send it a **WM_IDLEUPDATECMDUI** message, and call **UpdateWindow**. Of course, **WM_IDLEUPDATECMDUI** is a private MFC message, so you have to include **AFXPRIV.H** to use it.

Socket Wrapup

So, what's the verdict on MFC sockets? That depends. Using **CSocket** is certainly much easier than directly calling the Winsock API. Combined with MFC's archive facility, **CSocket** enables you to write some very powerful network programs. However, **CSocket** falls short when it comes to notifying you asynchronously about events. To do that, you'll have to use **CAsyncSocket**. Frankly, using **CAsyncSocket** may be a step above calling Winsock, but not by much.

Of course, many of **CSocket**'s shortcomings go away if you apply multithreading. By performing socket operations in a separate thread, you can avoid the hassle of polling sockets or missing events.

About RPCs

RPCs (Remote Procedure Calls) are a part of the Open Software Foundation's Distributed Computing Environment (OSF/DCE). They are a standard way for client code to call functions on a server without much (or any) knowledge of networking issues.

RPC is a topic that could fill an entire book. Luckily, for most purposes, you need only a few function calls. Basic RPC is easy.

RPC Theory

The idea behind RPC is really quite simple. Suppose there is a function—**GetMOTD**—that resides on a server and returns a message of the day string. You want to call it from a client on another machine. You could modify the function so that it used, for example, sockets, or a named pipe. However, this might be tricky. First, you would have to worry about all the issues involved in writing a server: blocking, waiting for connections, and handling multiple connections. Second, different machines on the network might have different formats for strings, numbers, and other data types. You would have to write code to convert data into a canonical format so that each machine interprets data correctly.

What if you could write a special function (a stub) named **GetMOTD** that lived on the client computer? This function would package up its arguments and send them across the network to another special function (a proxy or server stub). The proxy unpacks the arguments, converting them to the proper format. Then, it calls the real **GetMOTD** function. When **GetMOTD** returns, the proxy bundles up the return values and passes them back to the client's stub function. The stub then unpacks the return values and returns them to the original caller.

The net effect? The client calls an ordinary function named **GetMOTD**. The server has a function called **GetMOTD** that receives an ordinary function call (apparently from a local caller). All the network issues occur in the proxy and stub.

So what? That just moves the tricky parts of the code out of the client and server code and moves them to the proxy and stub, right? Not exactly. By using a special (and simple) script, the RPC tools will automatically generate the proxy and stub for you. That's good, because the proxy and the stub could be difficult to write. For example, to pass a string to the server, the stub has to transmit the bytes in the string to the stub, which then reconstructs the string on the server.

RPC In Practice

Is that all there is to it? Almost. The only thing you have to do is tell the proxies where to look for the server and how to talk to it. You can also leave the clients alone and put all the work on the server in some cases. Another issue is to make sure both the client and server agree on what the functions look like.

RPC identifies *interfaces*, which are groups of functions a server makes available via RPC. Each interface has its own UUID (Universally Unique Identifier), which is a 128-bit number in the same format as an ActiveX CLSID (see Chapter 2). If you change an interface, you change its UUID, too.

Locating a server and a protocol requires a *binding handle*, which is nothing more than a magic cookie that RPC assigns to a client. This handle identifies the server and the required protocol. In certain cases, you can make the server register itself with a central database so clients don't need to worry about anything but the function name they want to call. However, if you want to maintain information between calls, or use a specific server (in cases where there might be more than one server), you'll need to manage binding handles in the client code. This isn't hard to do, thankfully.

There are two ways to manage binding handles in a function. First, you can explicitly pass a binding handle as an argument to each call. This is obtrusive because it requires you to add an alien parameter to each call.

A nicer way is to use an implicit handle. Essentially, this is a global handle that you set up once in your code. After that, all RPC calls you make use the implicit handle. This is probably the best choice for most applications.

RPC Step-By-Step

The first step to writing an RPC application is to plan. You must know what functions will make up your interface (or interfaces, if you are using more than one group of functions). After the planning is complete, you can get the RPC routines to write a great deal of the required code for you.

The only code you need to write is the actual client program and the server functions. You'll also supply an IDL (Interface Definition Language) file. This looks suspiciously like a C-language header file, but has some extra information about the function parameters you are using. There is also a file you will probably supply with the ACF (Application Configuration File) extension. This file sets options for the entire interface that the IDL file defines. Using the IDL and ACF files, the RPC compiler (MIDL under Windows) will create most of the code you need.

As an example, consider the simple server I mentioned earlier: MOTD. This server has one function, **GetMOTD**, which has no return value, but which does take two arguments. The first argument is a pointer to a string where the function is to write the message. The second argument is the maximum length of the first argument.

Follow these steps to write an RPC application:

1. Run **UUIDGEN** with the **/I** option to generate an empty IDL file with a new UUID. You'll use the **/o** option to generate a particular file name. Don't put a space between the **/o** and the file name. For example: "UUIDGEN /I /omotd.idl".
2. Edit the resulting IDL file to look like Listing 6.16. Replace **INTERFACENAME** with **MOTD** (the name of the interface).
3. Inside the empty curly braces, add a line to define the **GetMOTD** function, like this:

```
void GetMOTD([out, string, max_is(ct)] char *msg,[in] unsigned char ct);
```

4. Create a new file named MOTD.ACF. It contains a line that creates an implicit handle that **GetMOTD** will use. Put the contents of Listing 6.17 in the file to define a handle with the name **MOTDHandle**.
5. Run MIDL with the argument **MOTD.IDL**. This causes the IDL compiler to create motd.h (a header file you can include for the interface declarations), motd_c.c (the stubs you link with the client code), and motd_s.c (the proxies you link with the server code).
6. Finish writing the server and client code (I wrote client.c and server.c; see Listings 6.18 and 6.19). You'll need to include two functions in both the server and client that RPC will use to allocate memory (**midl_user_allocate** and **midl_user_free**). You can almost always call **malloc** and **free** from these functions.
7. Compile your client code and your server code. You'll need to link the client code with motd_c.c and rpcrt4.lib (the runtime library for RPC). The server requires motd_s.c and rpcrt4.lib. You can construct a makefile, or use an IDE project. For a simple project like MOTD, I just wrote a batch file (see Listing 6.20).

Of course, if you intend to have the client or server on another type of machine, you might not need to do everything here. For example, you might only compile the client on Windows and then move to a VAX to write the server (ignoring the client code on the VAX). Each machine has slightly different steps to follow, but the same IDL will work across platforms.

Listing 6.16 The IDL file.

```
[
uuid(e02e2ede-e5e9-11d1-996c-00400526dbea),
version(1.0)
]
interface MOTD
{
  void GetMOTD([out, string, max_is(ct)] char *msg,[in] unsigned char ct);
}
```

Listing 6.17 The ACF file.

```
[implicit_handle (handle_t MOTDHandle)]
   interface MOTD {}
```

Listing 6.18 The client program.

```
#include <stdlib.h>
#include <stdio.h>
```

```
#include <ctype.h>
#include "motd.h"
void main(int argc, char *argv[]) {
    RPC_STATUS status;
    unsigned char * pszUuid             = NULL;
    unsigned char * pszProtocolSequence = "ncacn_np";
    unsigned char * pszNetworkAddress   = NULL;
    unsigned char * pszEndpoint    = "\\pipe\\MOTD";
    unsigned char * pszOptions          = NULL;
    unsigned char * pszStringBinding    = NULL;
    unsigned long ulCode;
    char msg[100];
/* Use network address if supplied on command line */
    if (argc==2) pszNetworkAddress=argv[1];

    status = RpcStringBindingCompose(pszUuid,
                                     pszProtocolSequence,
                                     pszNetworkAddress,
                                     pszEndpoint,
                                     pszOptions,
                                     &pszStringBinding);
    if (status) {
        printf("Error binding to RPC\n");
        exit(status);
        }
    status = RpcBindingFromStringBinding(pszStringBinding,
                                         &MOTDHandle);
    if (status) {
        printf("Error binding to RPC\n");
        exit(status);
        }
    RpcTryExcept {
        GetMOTD(msg,sizeof(msg));
        }
    RpcExcept(1) {
        ulCode = RpcExceptionCode();
        printf("Runtime reported exception 0x%lx = %ld\n", ulCode, ulCode);
        }
    RpcEndExcept
    printf("From server: %s\n",msg);
   status = RpcStringFree(&pszStringBinding);
   if (status)  {
     exit(status);
     }
   status = RpcBindingFree(&MOTDHandle);
```

```
    if (status) {
         exit(status);
         }
    exit(0);
    }


void __RPC_FAR * __RPC_USER midl_user_allocate(size_t len){
     return(malloc(len));
     }

void __RPC_USER midl_user_free(void __RPC_FAR * ptr)  {
     free(ptr);
     }
```

Listing 6.19 The server program.

```
#include <stdlib.h>
#include <stdio.h>
#include <string.h>
#include <ctype.h>
#include "motd.h"
void main() {
     RPC_STATUS status;
     unsigned char * pszProtocolSequence = "ncacn_np";
     unsigned char * pszSecurity     = NULL; /*Security not implemented */
     unsigned char * pszEndpoint    = "\\pipe\\MOTD";
     unsigned int    cMinCalls           = 1;
     unsigned int    cMaxCalls           = 20;
     unsigned int    fDontWait           = FALSE;
     status = RpcServerUseProtseqEp(pszProtocolSequence,
                                    cMaxCalls,
                                    pszEndpoint,
                                    pszSecurity);
     if (status) {
          exit(status);
          }
     status = RpcServerRegisterIf(MOTD_v1_0_s_ifspec,
                                  NULL,
                                  NULL);
     if (status) {
        exit(status);
        }
     status = RpcServerListen(cMinCalls,
                              cMaxCalls,fDontWait);
```

6. Interprocess Communications

```
    if (status) {
        exit(status);
     }
   }

static char *motd[]=
  {
  "Yawn a more Roman way",
  "Rats live on no evil star.",
  "If I had a hi-fi",
  "Rise to vote sir",
  "Evil Olive",
  "Never odd or even",
  "No lemons, no melon"
  };

/* The function */
void GetMOTD(
     unsigned char __RPC_FAR *msg,
    unsigned char ct)
    {
    static int n=0;
     char tmp[1024];
    sprintf(tmp,"%d: %s",++n,motd[n%(sizeof(motd)/sizeof(char *))]);
    strncpy(msg,tmp,ct);
    }


void __RPC_FAR * __RPC_USER midl_user_allocate(size_t len){
    return(malloc(len));
    }

void __RPC_USER midl_user_free(void __RPC_FAR * ptr)  {
    free(ptr);
    }
```

Listing 6.20 The build batch file.

```
midl motd.idl
cl client.c motd_c.c rpcrt4.lib
cl server.c motd_s.c rpcrt4.lib
```

Inside The IDL File

Notice that the line you added in Step 3 (above) looks suspiciously like a C function declaration (you can find the entire file in Listing 6.16). If you remove the parts in square brackets, it looks exactly like a C function declaration. The parts in the square brackets tell the IDL compiler how to handle the argument that follows. For example, **[out, string, max_is(ct)]** indicates that the **msg** parameter is an output from the function that contains a zero-terminated string. The maximum size of the string is in the **ct** variable (which the IDL file marks as an input).

You can make parameters both inputs and outputs, but don't do this unless you really need data flow in both directions. Remember that RPC has to copy data back and forth over the network. In this case, there is no point to copying the string from the client to the server because the server never examines the string. It probably contains garbage anyway.

There are many other attributes you can use to specify other types of parameters (like arrays, for instance). You can also define your own types. The online help for the IDL compiler explains all the various attributes you can use.

Writing The Client

The client code (see Listing 6.18) must make a few simple calls before it can issue RPC requests. First, it uses **RpcStringBindingCompose** to build an RPC string that defines the connection. This call requires the UUID of the interface you want (**NULL** if you don't care to specify it), a network address, and a protocol sequence string. This protocol string determines how the network connection operates. For example, to use named pipes, use **ncacn_np**. For TCP sockets, use **ncacn_nb_tcp**. You can find a complete list in the online help. If you are working across platforms, be sure to select something both sides support.

To some extent, the network name depends on the protocol you select. For example, **ncan_nb_tcp** is for TCP sockets with a named host, whereas **ncan_ip_tcp** requires an IP address. The function also requires an endpoint that depends on the protocol. For a named pipe, this is the name of the pipe. For a socket, it is the port number. If you set the machine name to **NULL**, RPC will use the local machine.

There is also an options string that you may use, depending on the protocol. Many times, you'll simply set the options to **NULL**. However, you may use the option string with certain protocols. For example, Windows 2000 supports **ncacn_http**,which uses the option string to specify a proxy server, if applicable.

For the sample client, I set the machine name to **NULL** or to the command line argument, if there is one. This enables you to test on your own machine (with no arguments) or over the network by supplying a machine name. The code uses named pipes (you'll find a TCP version on the companion CD-ROM).

Once you have a binding string, you can call **RpcStringBindingCompose** to transform the string into a binding handle. Because the code uses the implicit handle (defined in MOTD.ACF), it initializes that handle.

All that is left is to call **GetMOTD**, which you can do directly. The sample code calls it inside an **RpcTryExcept** block so that it can catch any RPC exceptions. Finally, the code frees the binding string that RPC allocated by calling **RpcStringFree**.

The only other detail is to supply **midl_user_allocate** and **midl_user_free**. As you can see in Listings 6.18 and 6.19, these are simply wrappers around **malloc** and **free**.

Writing The Server

The server is also simple to construct (see Listing 6.19). The server calls **RpcServerUseProtseqEp** to register its protocol and endpoint. (You can use other calls to register multiple methods, but for this example you won't need those.) Then the server registers what interfaces it supplies by calling **RpcServerRegisterIf**. The MIDL-generated variable **MOTD_v1_0_s_ifspec** contains the UUID.

The last step the server needs to take is to call **RpcServerListen**. This causes the server to wait for requests from clients. You can tell the server not to block waiting for clients, but for this example that isn't necessary. Even in a larger RPC server that shouldn't block, it is probably best to use a separate thread and allow it to block just like this example.

Of course, you also have to write the **GetMOTD** function. My simple version returns an integer counter and a simple message (composed of palindromes). You also need to supply the simple **midl_user_allocate** and **midl_user_free** functions.

Finishing Touches

It is easy to test this system on a single machine. Just run the server and allow it to keep running. If you are working from a command prompt, use START to run the server in its own window. Otherwise, just use the Run menu command from the Start menu. Once the server is running, you can execute client.exe to see the results.

This example, of course, is exceedingly simple. You can define types in the IDL file (using **typedef**). You can also register the server so that clients that don't care which server processes a request don't need to build a binding handle at all. Instead, the indiscriminate client may use what's called an *auto binding handle*.

It is customary to have a server function named **Shutdown** that clients can call to request an orderly shutdown of the server. The server should call **RpcMgmtStopServerListening** and **RpcServerUnregisterIf**. Of course, this also requires an addition to the IDL file to register the new function.

More Than Meets The Eye

There is much more to RPC, if you really want to get into it. You can define your own types, make calls asynchronously, and more. You can use IDL to define many things, including functions that take arrays, counted strings, or just about any data type that you can envision.

However, if you can write the MOTD server (and its client) you can probably tackle 95 percent of the RPC programs you'll want to write. For the other five percent, you shouldn't have any trouble if you spend a few minutes reading the online help.

Microsoft Message Queue (MSMQ)

The Microsoft Message Queue is a new form of RPC aimed at communicating over a large network. As you might expect, MSMQ enables applications to send messages to another application. The queue part comes into play if the target application is not available. Perhaps its server is not running, or the network connection is down.

If MSMQ sees that it can't deliver a message right away, it queues the message until it can deliver it. The sending program doesn't have to worry about the message's ultimate delivery.

There are two ways you can use MSMQ. Probably the hardest way is to call the API that Microsoft provides. However, MSMQ also exposes its functions via a set of ActiveX controls that may be more convenient. Of course, the ActiveX controls are also handy for use in Visual Basic and programs written with similar languages.

Like named pipes and mailslots, a queue has a file like name. If your server is named STARFLEET, and you have a private queue called SUBSPACE, the name of the queue is \\STARFLEET\PRIVATE$\SUBSPACE. If the queue were public, it would be \\STARFLEET\SUBSPACE. However, programs that want to send a public queue a message will probably search for a type of queue. For example, a client program might ask to open a printer queue (a queue with the **PRINTER_SERVICE_TYPE** type).

Creating a queue with the ActiveX control is simple (use the **MSMQQueueInfo** object). Simply fill in any attributes that you want the queue to have and call the object's **Create** method. The only attribute you must supply is the **PathName** property. All others are optional.

The **MSMQQueueInfo** object is also useful if you are looking for a particular kind of queue. In that case, you'll create an **MSMQQuery** object and call

LookupQueue. This function takes a string that sets the search criteria. For example, if you were looking for a queue named AWC-QUEUE, you would supply this search string:

```
Label:="AWC-QUEUE"
```

The **LookupQueue** method returns an **MSMQQueueInfos** object, which is a simple enumeration object. You should call **Reset** on this object before you do anything else. Then, call **Next** repeatedly. Each call to **Next** returns an **MSMQQueueInfo** object (or **NULL** if there are no more queues that match). Here is an example of searching for a queue.

```
mqQInfos = mqQuery->LookupQueue(NULL,NULL,"SomeQueue"); // search for queue
mqQInfos->Reset();
mqQInfo = mqQInfos.Next();
If (!mqQinfo) // not found ;
//Open the queue (a MSMQ.MSMQQueue object) with Send access.
mqTXQueue = mqQInfo->Open(MQ_SEND_ACCESS, MQ_DENY_NONE);
```

After you have found a queue you want to work with, call the **MSMQQueueInfo** object's **Open** method. This returns an **MSMQQueue** object that you use to interact with the queue. To send a message, you can create an **MSMQ.MSMQMessage** object, set its **Body** and **Label** properties, and then use the **Send** method to transmit the message to a queue. The **Send** method requires the queue object as an argument. Here is ome sample code:

```
//Send some message
//mqTXmsg is a MSMQ.MSMQMessage
  mqTXmsg->Body = "Body string";
  mqTXmsg->Label = "Label string";

  mqTXmsg->Send(mqTXQueue);
```

It is also possible to use Windows 2000's COM+ architecture to set up an MSMQ-aware proxy. This proxy behaves like a normal ActiveX proxy, but it records each method call until the program releases the underlying ActiveX object. Then the recorder uses MSMQ to replay the methods to the server via an MSMQ queue.

Summary

The number of IPC methods available under Windows is truly bewildering. However, after a little thought, you can usually prune your number of choices considerably (see the Immediate Solutions section for more selection advice, as well).

Often you won't have a choice anyway, because you will be talking to some other system that requires one method or another. For example, if you are working with an IBM mainframe, you may have to use RPC. Many systems employ sockets today, so sometimes that's your only choice.

If you get a choice about which methods you can use for IPC, however, you'll find that IPC really falls into two categories: those that can cross the network and those that can't. Once you decide to use a method that is network-capable (or not network-capable), the other choices are largely a personal preference. There probably isn't anything you can do with one IPC method that you can't do with the other similar methods—it's just that some methods are easier than others for certain purposes.

Immediate Solutions

Summary Of IPC Methods

- ***WM_COPYDATA***—Passes a block of memory between two processes.
- *The clipboard*—The clipboard communicates between processes, but it is really for the user and not very useful as an IPC method for programs.
- *DLLs*—DLLs can share global memory between processes.
- *Shared memory*—Win32's official way to share memory between processes is to use a mapped file, but without a file.
- *Anonymous pipes*—Anonymous pipes are similar to pipes you use at the DOS and Unix command line. They have limited usefulness for most Windows programs.
- *Named pipes*—Named pipes are a powerful way for two programs to communicate using a client/server model, even when they are on different computers.
- *Mailslots*—Mailslots are one way for programs to accept messages from other programs. Mailslots are one-way only, so for bidirectional communications, you'll need two of them. Mailslots enable you to broadcast a message to related mailslots over a local area network in one operation.
- *Dynamic Data Exchange (DDE)*—Today, DDE support is largely for backward compatibility. There isn't anything wrong with DDE per se, but Microsoft decided to promote OLE (which became ActiveX).
- *NetBios*—Windows supports NetBios, but mostly this support is to ensure compatibility with older programs.
- *Sockets*—Considered the workhorses of the Internet, sockets are a standard way to communicate over large networks. Few computers today don't offer some socket interface. Windows' excellent support for sockets is very similar to the socket libraries you'll find on other operating systems.
- *Remote Procedure Calls (RPCs)*—RPCs are another widely available standard. RPC isn't so much an IPC method as it is a wrapper over a more traditional IPC method. The idea is to allow a server to expose an actual function that a client apparently calls directly. RPC enables this process to work transparently. The client makes an ordinary function call, and the server receives an ordinary function call. RPC makes the network part of this operation invisible.

- *ActiveX*—ActiveX can do many things. Recall from Chapter 2 that ActiveX is really just a way to create binary objects. However, one purpose you can use these objects for is IPC. Microsoft defines an interface, **IDataObject**, just for this purpose. The Distributed Component Object Model (DCOM) is another ActiveX technology that can help facilitate IPC. DCOM is essentially a marriage between ActiveX and RPC. ActiveX and DCOM could (and do) fill another book. However, be aware that you can use them for IPC.
- *Microsoft Message Queue (MSMQ)*—MSMQ is a protocol that enables applications to send messages to each other. What makes MSMQ different is that it is possible to send a message to a process that is not currently available (the server is down or there is a network problem, for example). MSMQ queues the message until it can deliver it at a later time. You can work with MSMQ using a special API, or you can use ActiveX controls that make the calls for you, if you prefer.

In general, if you are talking over a network, you'll be thinking about named pipes, DCOM, RPCs, or sockets. You might also use MSMQ if you need that level of functionality. If you are communicating between processes on the same machine, you'll want to think about DLLs, **WM_COPYDATA**, anonymous pipes, or shared memory (although any of the other methods will also work).

Using WM_COPYDATA

The simplest way to send a block of data from one process to another is by using the **WM_COPYDATA** message. You send this message to a window using the usual **SendMessage** call.

WM_COPYDATA takes a pointer to a **COPYDATASTRUCT** structure as the **lParam** parameter (see Table 6.1). You also pass a window handle that belongs to the calling process as the **wParam** parameter. The **COPYDATASTRUCT** structure contains a 32-bit value (**dwData**) and a pointer to the data to pass (**lpData**). You'll also fill in the count of the bytes you are passing in the **cbData** member. If the target window belongs to a different process, Windows translates the data pointer so that the receiving process can read it. Of course, this translation will very likely alter the address, so don't assume that both processes will see the same address. By the same token, the data you pass in the **lpData** pointer shouldn't contain pointers, because these won't be usable in the target process.

You can find an example of using **WM_COPYDATA** in Listings 6.1 through 6.3. Of course, **WM_COPYDATA** is one of the simplest methods of communicating between processes. You'll often want to use one of the other methods discussed in this chapter.

Using DLLs For Shared Memory

DLLs are useful for a variety of purposes, but you can also use them for interprocess communication. This is possible because you can make global variables in a DLL shared between processes.

By default, if you use the Microsoft C++ compiler, each process that uses a DLL gets its own private copy of any global variables. However, using a special technique, it is possible to make any (or all) variables shared.

The trick is to use a pragma to move the variables to a separate region of memory and then instruct the linker to share that region. You can name this region of memory anything you like as long as the name starts with a period.

```
#pragma data_seg(".ASHARE")
int sharevalue=0;
// more shared data could go here
#pragma data_seg()
```

You must initialize the variable, or else the sharing won't work. Next, you'll need to share the **.ASHARE** segment. There are two ways to do this. Perhaps the easiest is to set a command line option for the compiler. For the preceding example, add this line to the existing option string:

```
/SECTION:.ASHARE,RWS
```


This line sets the **.ASHARE** region of memory so that it is available for reading, writing, and sharing. You can also prepare a **DEF** file, define the segment in this file, and add it to the list of files that you build. You can find more details about using a **DEF** file in the In Depth section of this chapter.

One interesting aspect of using a DLL as a shared memory device is that it works on 16-bit versions of Windows and 32-bit versions of Windows. On 16-bit Windows platforms, all memory is shared all the time, so using a DLL really isn't necessary, but you can use it anyway. With Windows NT, Windows 2000, and Windows 95, however, you must do something to share memory, and a DLL is as good as anything. Sure, you can use another method (like file mapping shared memory, discussed next), but that won't work on the 16-bit Windows platforms. DLLs make a neat solution that works in either case.

Each process may see the DLL's shared memory at different addresses. Be careful not to store addresses to shared memory in shared memory.

File Mapping Shared Memory

Surprisingly, the same mechanism that maps files into your memory space can also create shared memory. The file mapping object (see Chapter 5) normally allows you to access files as though they were in memory. When one process creates a file mapping object, other processes may open it and share a consistent view of the file. That is, each process shares the file, each seeing changes made by other processes.

Obviously, this is a form of shared memory, but it relies on an underlying file. Or does it? You can specify an invalid file handle for the underlying file, and Windows will share a memory region between the processes.

For this to work, you create a file mapping object using **CreateFileMapping** or open one with **OpenFileMapping**. Then each process uses the resulting handle in a call to **MapViewOfFile**. This returns an address (which may be different for each process). When you no longer need the shared memory, call **UnmapViewOfFile** and use **CloseHandle** to dispose of the file mapping handle.

You can find a complete example of using mapped files in Chapter 5. Although the NTCAT program doesn't share the mapped file, the use of the file mapping object wouldn't be any different if it did.

Using Anonymous Pipes

An anonymous pipe is, not surprisingly, a pipe with no name. Because it has no name, an anonymous pipe is most useful when used between a process and a child process. The child process can inherit the anonymous pipe handle from its parent. The most common use of an anonymous pipe is to read the standard output from a child process or feed input to a child. These pipes are similar to pipes you use at the DOS command prompt. They transfer data in one direction only.

When you call **CreatePipe**, you receive two handles. One handle is for reading from the pipe and the other is for writing to the pipe. You'll usually pass a **SECURITY_ATTRIBUTES** structure to **CreatePipe** because you'll want to allow a child process to inherit the pipe handle.

After each process has a pipe handle, one uses **WriteFile** to write to the pipe and **ReadFile** to read from the pipe. Obviously, only one process will write and the other will read. A simple call to **CloseHandle** will terminate the pipe.

You can find a complete example in the In Depth section of this chapter. The code in Listing 6.6 generates a list of numbers and filters the output through a formatting program (see Listing 6.7).

Using Named Pipes

Named pipes are more flexible than anonymous pipes. Because they have names, it is easier to share them between unrelated processes. In fact, you can even use named pipes over a network. One process creates a pipe by calling **CreateNamedPipe**. To create a named pipe with the name **xyz**, you'll use a name in the form of \\.\pipe\xyz. You can only create a named pipe on the current machine, so you'll use the period as the machine name.

Another problem you may encounter with named pipes is security. The default security attributes will not allow any process to open the pipe. You may want to set explicit security, or you can set an empty security descriptor (not a **NULL** security attribute) to allow everyone to access the pipe. Here's a bit of code that will create a descriptor you can use to allow all access:

```
SECURITY_ATTRIBUTES sa;
SECURITY_DESCRIPTOR sd;
// allow all access
InitializeSecurityDescriptor(&sd,SECURITY_DESCRIPTOR_REVISION);
sa.bInheritHandle=FALSE;
sa.lpSecurityDescriptor=&sd;
sa.nLength=sizeof(sa);
```


Programs that want to use the named pipe open it with a simple call to **CreateFile**, using the entire name, possibly substituting a host name for the period.

There are many ways you can use a pipe (see the In Depth section of this chapter). However, the simplest way is to use **ReadFile** and **WriteFile**. The pipe is bidirectional, so data you put in one end appears on the other end, and vice versa.

It is possible to use named pipes as the foundation for client/server programming. You can create multiple instances of pipes so that a single server can handle multiple clients. You can find more about these techniques in the In Depth section of this chapter. You'll also find a pipe example program in Chapter 5 (see Listings 5.2 and 5.3).

Replacing A Standard Handle With A Pipe

One very important technique you'll often use with pipes is substituting an anonymous or named pipe for a program's standard input or output. There are several ways you can do this. One way is to set the **STARTUPINFO** structure in the call to **CreateProcess**. Using this structure, it is possible to set the standard input or output (among other things) to anything you want.

An alternate method is to save your existing standard handle and reset it to the pipe's handle (using **GetStdHandle** and **SaveStdHandle**). Then call **CreateProcess**, enabling the child process to inherit the standard input and output handles. Then, after the new process is running, the original process can reset its handles to the original value. You'll find an example of this technique in the example for anonymous pipes (see Listings 6.6 and 6.7).

Using Mailslots

Mailslots are similar to a special file where a process can read messages sent to it by other processes. One process creates the mailslot (using the **CreateMailSlot** call) and reads only from the handle. Other processes open the mailslot using **CreateFile** and write to the handle (using **WriteFile**) to pass data to the receiving process.

To create a mailslot named *FrankPoole*, the owning process calls **CreateMailSlot** using \\.\mailslot\FrankPoole. Other processes use the host name instead of the period (unless, of course, you are opening a mailslot on the same machine, in which case you can use the period if you like).

Another feature of mailslots is that you can use a domain name instead of a host name when you open the mailslot handle for writing. When you do this, writing to the handle broadcasts to all the mailslots of the specified name on all machines on the domain. If you want to use the local domain, use an asterisk for the domain name. One thing to be aware of is that Windows does not assure delivery of messages to a mailslot. Any number of factors may prevent delivery of a message. Another limitation is that broadcast messages can't exceed 400 bytes. When you create the mailslot, you can limit the message size to less if you want. You can also specify a message size greater than 400 bytes, but broadcast messages still can't exceed 400 bytes.

When you open a mailslot for writing, be sure to specify the correct flags. You must set **FILE_READ_SHARE** and **OPEN_EXISTING** or the call to **CreateFile** will fail.

You'll find more details about mailslots in the In Depth section of this chapter. You'll also find programs that use mailslots in Listings 6.8 and 6.9.

Using Sockets

Sockets are a standard way for programs to communicate across networks. Sockets form the basis for the Internet, and most computers now support them. A complete discussion of sockets would take an entire book (there are, in fact, many books on nothing but socket programming). However, here's the condensed version.

Each socket has a unique port number. The system reserves some port numbers for well-known sockets. For example, by convention, a Web server uses port 80. Other servers like FTP and Telnet use other well-known numbers.

Servers create a socket with the well-known port number. Next, the server listens for connections on the socket. A client creates a socket with a generic port number assigned at random by the system. The client uses this socket to connect to the server's socket.

It would seem that the client socket then connects to the well-known socket on the server, but this is not exactly the case. The system intercepts the request to connect to the well-known socket, and prevents it from actually happening. Instead, the system automatically creates a new socket (with a random, generic port number) on the server and connects it to the client's socket. The client doesn't care, and this leaves the server's socket free for further connections.

Many servers start a new process or thread to handle each connection. This enables the code to be very clean, because each process (or thread) handles only one client, yet the overall server can handle many requests at the same time.

It is also possible to create sockets that don't work with a connection. Using these sockets allows for greater efficiency, but they don't assure correct delivery of data. If you are implementing a protocol that has its own error correcting built-in, you may benefit from using sockets without connections.

The In Depth section of this chapter contains two examples of using sockets. One (the checker game in Listings 6.11 and 6.12) uses sockets directly. The other (a battlefield game in Listings 6.13 and 6.14) uses MFC wrapper classes that simplify using sockets.

Using RPCs

The idea behind RPC is for a client to make a local call that actually winds up executing on a server. This is possible because RPC creates a local function (a stub) that stands in for the server function. When the program calls the stub, the stub transmits its arguments to another function (the proxy) on the server. The proxy unpacks the arguments and calls the actual function.

When the function returns to the proxy, the proxy bundles up the return values and sends them to the stub. The stub unpacks the return values and sends them to the original caller. The client thinks it made a local call and the server thinks it received a local call. Only the RPC proxy and stub understand that something else happened.

Using RPC for basic clients and servers is actually relatively simple. First, you design an interface that consists of all the functions a server will supply to clients. Then, you describe this interface in an IDL file. The IDL file is similar to a C header file, but it contains a bit of extra information.

The MIDL compiler transforms this IDL file (and an ACF file that is even simpler) into several C source files: a header that defines the interface, as well as two C files (one links with the server and the other links with the client). Both programs also need to link with RPCRT4.LIB to satisfy references to the RPC API.

RPC centers around a binding handle. You can think of a binding handle as similar to a file handle, but it specifies a server, not a file. The client creates a string that specifies the server's name and the network protocol to use (named pipe, TCP/IP, or a host of other methods). You also specify the endpoint, which depends on the protocol you are using. For example, named pipes require a name and TCP/IP requires a port number. Usually, the client creates this string with the **RpcStringBindingCompose** function, although you can build it manually, if you prefer.

Armed with the string, the client calls **RpcBindingFromStringBinding** to set up the binding handle. The examples in this chapter use the ACF file (Listing 6.17) to specify a global binding handle that all the RPC calls use. The client code (in Listing 6.18) initializes this global handle. There are other ways to satisfy the requirement for a binding handle that you can read about in the In Depth section of this chapter.

The server (Listing 6.19) makes three calls:

- The **RpcServerUseProtseqEp** function informs the RPC system what network transport and endpoint the server will use.

- The **RpcServerRegisterIf** function tells the RPC system what interface (or interfaces) this server supports.
- Finally, a call to **RpcServerListen** starts the server listening for incoming requests from clients.

You can find a complete RPC example in Listings 6.16 through 6.19. This example is a simple client that reads and prints a message of the day from a server.

Understanding When To Use Obsolete Or Little-Used IPC Methods

Some IPC methods are not used often and are mainly for compatibility. Other IPC methods, like the clipboard, are not suitable for use in most programs. (The clipboard is for the user, not for programs, to communicate.) Another odd way to communicate between programs is via the global atom table.

Windows will support DDE (Dynamic Data Exchange) and NetBios. However, both of these protocols are not widely supported anymore. If you need them for backward compatibility, they are there. However, you shouldn't use them for new development.

Chapter 7

Memory Management

If you need an immediate solution to:	*See page:*
When To Use **VirtualAlloc**	345
Using **VirtualAlloc** And **VirtualFree**	345
Setting Page Protection	346
Reading Page Protection	347
Responding To Exceptions	347
Creating A New Heap	348
Finding The Default Heap	349
Allocating And Freeing Heap Data	349
Compacting A Heap	350
Debugging A Heap	350
Heap Performance Considerations	351

In Depth

Are you adventurous? I used to be, I think. But I'm afraid there's some kind of inverse relationship between age and adventure. I'm not even talking about big adventures, like sky diving or climbing Everest. Just the simple little everyday adventures seem to become less attractive as the years pass.

I've come to the realization that at some time in the past I became a creature of habit. Take restaurants, for example. There are literally thousands of restaurants in Houston and hundreds near where I live. Yet when we go out to eat, we always go to the same 9 or 10 places. Worse still, I'm pretty likely to order the same thing I had there last time.

Granted, going to a new restaurant isn't the kind of adventure you see in a Bruce Willis movie. But between you and me, I never was any good at leaping ahead of explosions in my undershirt. (Besides, when has a computer guy been at the center of adventure? Even in *Mission Impossible* the computer guy just sat in the elevator shaft.)

Habits are tough to break. Try switching text editors, for example. I was pleased to finally get Emacs for Windows so I could use the same keystrokes from Windows or Linux—well, almost.

Programmers can form habits, too. Not that they are necessarily bad habits at the time. But sometimes they become bad habits down the road. This sometimes gives newer programmers an advantage over old-timers like me—they don't have old habits.

Breaking old habits is a particular problem if you've been working with Windows for a long time. The earlier you started programming for Windows, the more accumulated baggage you probably have to lose. Programming for Windows is a lot different than programming for, say, Windows 2.0. Of course, there are a lot more features to choose from, but also, some things just work differently.

With the release of Windows 2000, it is time to break some old habits—at least when it comes to memory management.

Why Bother With Memory Management?

You might wonder why you would care about directly managing memory. After all, the C library has **malloc** and C++ offers **new**, so why not use those? Well, most of the time that is exactly what you want to do. But there are times you might want more control over allocating memory.

For example, suppose you are writing a program to capture video. You might need a lot of contiguous memory (say, 50MB) to store five minutes of video. On the other hand, the user might record only 30 seconds of video. Why waste the time and resources to allocate 50MB for a short clip?

You might try to solve this problem by allocating a little memory at a time. But what's to guarantee that memory is contiguous? Another subroutine (or another thread) might allocate memory and prevent expansion of the allocation. You certainly don't want **remalloc** moving around 25MB blocks of memory.

Windows can accommodate this requirement by enabling you to reserve memory with little expense. Then, you can allocate some or all of the reserved memory at a later time.

Other reasons you might directly access Windows memory management include creating read-only memory or implementing sparse arrays.

Memory Paging

At the core of all modern computer architectures is a memory management unit (MMU) of some kind. On a Pentium, the MMU is an integral part of the CPU chip. The MMU translates linear addresses to actual physical addresses.

The MMU makes a variety of techniques possible. When a program accesses location zero, for example, the MMU can relocate the access to location 16384. Because each process has its own MMU translation, each process can believe it has a private memory space starting at location 0 and extending to location 4G.

If the MMU could remap every byte to a different byte, its data tables would be huge. Instead, MMUs translate blocks of memory (called pages) together. On the Pentium, the MMU works with 4K pages (other processors may use a different size; call **GetSystemInfo** to find out). So if location 0 maps to physical address 16384, then location 1 maps to address 16385, and so on. Location 4096, however, could map to some completely different address because it is in another page.

You can also instruct the MMU to mark an entire page as absent. This is the basic mechanism that allows virtual memory. When the MMU informs the operating system that a program accessed an absent page, the OS can load that page from disk and let the program try again. Of course, this might require the OS to move other pages out to disk and mark them as absent as well.

Marking a page as absent has another possible use: sparse arrays. Suppose you have a very large matrix of floating point numbers that consumes 10MB. What's more is that most of the matrix actually contains zeros (or some other constant value). Matrices of this sort are common in engineering problems.

Instead of blowing 10MB on the array, why not partition it into MMU-sized pages? Mark any page that contains all zeros as absent. Then, when the MMU reports the page as absent, you can assume the value is really zero.

Using VirtualAlloc

The call that makes it possible to manipulate the MMU is **VirtualAlloc**. This call can behave differently depending on how you call it.

In its simplest form, you pass **VirtualAlloc** a **NULL** as its first argument. This enables it to select the starting address for the allocation (which will lie on a page boundary). You also specify the number of bytes you want. Windows internally rounds up this number to a whole number of pages. The next argument is a flag specifying **MEM_COMMIT**, and the protection you want for the allocated pages (see Table 7.1). Obviously, it doesn't make much sense to specify some attributes (like **PAGE_READONLY**) here, because the memory is uninitialized.

Table 7.1 Protection constants.

Flag	Meaning
PAGE_READONLY	The pages are read-only.
PAGE_READWRITE	Read and write access to the pages.
PAGE_WRITECOPY	Causes a new copy of the page to replace the page upon write (useful only with shared memory or mapped files).
PAGE_EXECUTE	Allows execution of program code.
PAGE_EXECUTE_READ	Allows execution and reading.
PAGE_EXECUTE_READWRITE	Enables execute, read, and write access.
PAGE_GUARD	Pages in the region become guard pages. Attempting to read from or write to a guard page causes the operating system to raise a STATUS_GUARD_PAGE exception and turn off the guard page status. Guard pages thus act as a one-shot access alarm. Use this with another flag (any flag except PAGE_NOACCESS).
PAGE_NOACCESS	Disables all access to the committed region of pages. Any access causes a general protection (GP) fault.
PAGE_NOCACHE	Disallows caching of the pages (not recommended). Use this with another flag (any flag except PAGE_NOACCESS).

Using **VirtualAlloc** this way causes Windows to allocate the desired amount of actual memory, almost as if you had called **malloc**. This might be useful if you need memory aligned on a page boundary, want special protection attributes, or you want to be sure you could easily free the memory. This can be a concern if your library doesn't actually return freed memory to the operating system.

If you want to alter the protection for any or all of the allocated pages, call **VirtualProtect**. You can use any of the attributes in Table 7.1. **VirtualProtectEx** is a similar function but allows you to change attributes of memory for a specified process. Of course, this assumes you have the correct security privileges to operate on the process. When you no longer need the memory, call **VirtualFree** to dispose of it.

The really interesting use of **VirtualAlloc**, however, occurs when you pass **MEM_RESERVE** instead of **MEM_COMMIT**. This causes **VirtualAlloc** to reserve the requested amount of linear address space. However, it doesn't place actual memory or swap file space in those pages. The memory is reserved, but not committed.

When you actually want to use this memory, call **VirtualAlloc** with the address and the **MEM_COMMIT** flag. You don't have to commit the entire allocation at once. At this point, you incur the overhead required to find space for the pages you commit.

VirtualAlloc In Practice

To get an idea about the relative speed when calling the various versions of **VirtualAlloc**, take a look at Listing 7.1. This contrived program allocates a large amount of memory in three different ways. By default, the program uses a 75MB block, which is large enough to be substantial, but not too large for most modern PCs. If you want a different size, just specify it (in MB) on the command line.

Select 1 from the menu. The program will commit and deallocate the block of memory, which should take no more than a few seconds on most modern machines. Windows has to build page table entries, scramble around for some physical memory, and marshal some swap file pages, too (unless you have a lot of memory, in which case try a higher number).

After you have selected option 1 from the menu a few times, try allocating the same amount of memory with a simple reservation (option 2). This happens so fast that you can't tell it happened (at least on my machine). Of course, the memory isn't useful, because it doesn't really exist until you commit it.

That's where option 3 comes into play. Try it. This option reserves the entire block and then commits a single megabyte. It models the situation where you might need a lot of memory in some cases, but mostly you just need a little bit. You'll see that this set of calls is also practically instantaneous. Sometimes you can make your programs appear faster, just by spreading out the work. In other words, even if you had to commit the entire 10MB a megabyte at a time, the user might perceive it as faster because the program doesn't stop responding for any single long period of time.

Listing 7.1 Testing **VirtualAlloc.**

```
#include <windows.h>
#include <iostream.h>

char *p=NULL;
#define MEGABYTE 1048576
#define MSIZE 75


void main(int argc, char *argv[])
{
   char choice;
   int msize=0;
   if (argc>1) msize=atoi(argv[1]);
   if (!msize) msize=MSIZE;
   do
   {
      int valid=1;
      if (p)
      {
         cout<<"\nFreeing memory\n";
         VirtualFree(p,0,MEM_RELEASE);
         p=NULL;
         cout<<"Done\n";
      }
      cout<<"1 - Allocate " <<msize<< "MB Committed\n";
      cout<<"2 - Allocate " <<msize<<"MB Reserved\n";
      cout<<"3 - Allocate " <<msize<<"MB Reserved & commit 1MB\n";
      cout<<"4 - Quit\n";
      cout<<"Your choice: ";
      cin>>choice;
      switch (choice)
      {
      case '1':
         cout<<"\nAllocating committed\n";
```

```
         p=(char *)VirtualAlloc(NULL,msize*MEGABYTE,
                   MEM_COMMIT,PAGE_READWRITE);
         break;
      case '2':
         cout<<"\nAllocating reserved\n";
         p=(char *)VirtualAlloc(NULL,msize*MEGABYTE,
                   MEM_RESERVE,PAGE_READWRITE);
         break;
      case '3':
         cout<<"\nAllocating with partial commit\n";
         p=(char *)VirtualAlloc(NULL,msize*MEGABYTE,
                   MEM_RESERVE,PAGE_READWRITE);
         cout<<"\nCommitting\n";
         VirtualAlloc(p,MEGABYTE,MEM_COMMIT,PAGE_READWRITE);
         break;
      case '4':
         exit(0);
      default:
         cout<<"\nHuh?\n";
         valid=0;
      }
      if (p&&valid)
              cout<<"Memory block @ "<<hex<<(unsigned int)p<<"\n";
      if (!p&&valid) cout<<"Allocation failed!\n";
   } while (1);
}
```

Working With Page Attributes

Certainly one advantage to using **VirtualAlloc** is that you can alter the page access type, either when you allocate the memory or later (with **VirtualProtect**). Judicious use of this feature can enhance many programs.

For a simple example, consider the code in Listing 7.2. This is a library routine that returns a pointer to a static string. In real life, this probably would reside in a DLL. For this exercise, however, the main program is in the same file.

Listing 7.2 Passing a static string read-only.

```
#include <stdio.h>
#include <malloc.h>
#include <string.h>

#if 0  // normal library version
char *getmsg()
```

```
{
  static char *msg;
  if (msg==NULL)
  {
      char tmp[1024];
      FILE *f;
      f=fopen("strings.txt","r");
      if (!f) return NULL;
      fgets(tmp,sizeof(tmp),f);
      msg=(char *)malloc(strlen(tmp)+1);
      strcpy(msg,tmp);
      fclose(f);
  }
  return msg;
}

#else
// Win32 version
#include <windows.h>

char *getmsg()
{
    static char *msg;
    if (msg==NULL)
    {
      char tmp[1024];
      DWORD oldprot;
      FILE *f;
      f=fopen("strings.txt","r");
      if (!f) return NULL;
      fgets(tmp,sizeof(tmp),f);
// Allocates an entire page, which is OK for this example
      msg=(char
*)VirtualAlloc(NULL,strlen(tmp)+1,MEM_COMMIT,PAGE_READWRITE);
      strcpy(msg,tmp);
      fclose(f);
// make memory read only (actually makes entire page read only)
      VirtualProtect(msg,strlen(msg)+1,PAGE_READONLY,&oldprot);
    }
  return msg;
}
#endif

void main()
{
```

```
    char *m=getmsg();
    try {
    printf("Entire string: %s\n",m);
    m=strtok(m," \t");
    printf("token1=%s\n",m);
    m=getmsg();
    printf("Entire string: %s\n",m);
    }
    catch (...)  // catch all exceptions
    {
      printf("Exception caught!\n");
    }
    getchar();  // wait for debugging
}
```

The main program asks for the static string and then calls **strtok** to break it apart. However, this causes the program to fail the next time it asks for the string. Why? Because **strtok** modifies the string you pass it. Sure, you can tell the compiler that the string is **const**, but a persistent programmer may just cast that away.

A better answer is to put the string in a read-only page. Of course, you can't make the page read-only until you set the initial data. Also, every time the routine wants to change the string it has to use **VirtualProtect** to make the page temporarily writeable.

The code in Listing 7.2 catches the protection exception (actually, it catches all exceptions), so when using **VirtualAlloc**, the program terminates cleanly with an error. If you omit the **try** block that handles the exception, the program will terminate with a rude system error.

What stops the main program from calling **VirtualProtect**? Absolutely nothing. However, that is a much more deliberate act than casting a pointer. Also, the program would need to know the correct starting address, which might not be the same as the pointer it receives (although it is in this case). Besides, it is hard to imagine how an errant program would accidentally call **VirtualProtect** with the correct address.

Sparse Memory Techniques

If you attempt to access a page that is not committed, you'll generate an exception. You can also generate an exception by setting the **PAGE_GUARD** attribute (although this exception occurs only once). Using one of these techniques, you can notice when the program tries to access certain pages. Why is this useful? One idea would be to make a region of reserved pages and automatically commit more pages when you reach the end of the current allocation. Another possibility is to implement efficient sparse tables.

Suppose you have an array where nearly all the values are the same. Engineering calculations often use such arrays, for example. The idea is to store only the 4K pages that contain distinct values. Any page that contains, say, all zeros doesn't need to take up physical RAM. Instead, you can mark the page as no access (or leave it uncommitted) and catch the exception Windows generates when you read the page. When you see the exception, you can return zero (or whatever the appropriate value is).

There are several ways to catch exceptions in C and C++. C's **__try** and **__except** statements are not too hard to use, but they don't do well with C++ constructs. For C++, you should use the standard **try** and **catch** keywords.

There is a slight catch when using **try** and **catch**, however. By default, Windows' standard exceptions don't show up in exception handlers that use **catch**. The key is to use the **_set_se_translator** function to set a user-defined function that translates C-style exceptions (like those Windows throws) into C++ exceptions. This can be a very simple routine—just throwing the integer exception code—if you like.

Once you catch an exception that indicates a missing page, you can commit the underlying page, return a default value, or do anything else you feel is appropriate. When you access an uncommitted page, you'll trigger an 0xc0000005 exception.

Examine the code in Listing 7.3. It shows a simple library that provides a buffer for a main program (again, the so-called library is really in the same source file for the sake of clarity). When the main program calls **getbuffer**, the library allocates 1,010 pages of memory, but does not commit them (on an Intel machine this is over 4MB of memory, because each page is 4K). Initially however, the buffer has no pages with actual memory in them. The pages are simply reserved.

When the main program wants to write a byte into the buffer, it calls **putbuffer**. This function is simple at its core. It really only contains one important line that assigns the value to the buffer. If there is memory at the destination address, this is the only line of code that does anything.

Things are more interesting, however, when the program attempts to access an empty page (for example, on the first access). The **putbuffer** code catches the 0xc0000005 exception and commits the single page required to allow the access to proceed. Then it retries the operation by making a recursive call to itself. Of course, the exception handler gets all exceptions, so it is important to make sure that the exception code is correct, and that the address in question is valid.

Because the exception is invisible to a normal C++ exception handler, the **_set_se_translator** function installs a simple routine to convert C exceptions to an **unsigned int** C++ exception. The **_set_se_translator** function returns the previous translator function's address, so **putbuffer** restores it before it returns. The **typedef** for **_se_translator_function** (in eh.h) makes it easier to create variables that hold these function pointers.

Armed with this library, the main program is simple. It allocates the buffer, writes into it using any order it likes, and everything works. The main program is oblivious to the fact that advanced Windows memory management is at work behind the scenes.

Listing 7.3 An endless buffer.

```
#include <windows.h>
#include <stdio.h>
#include <eh.h>  // convert C exception to C++ exception


static int maxindex;

char *getbuffer()
{
    SYSTEM_INFO info;
    // read real page
    GetSystemInfo(&info);

    char *rv;
    rv=(char *)VirtualAlloc(NULL,maxindex=info.dwPageSize*1010,
      MEM_RESERVE,PAGE_READWRITE);
    return rv;
}

void cppexcept( unsigned int u, _EXCEPTION_POINTERS* pExp )
{
    throw u;
}

void putbuffer(char *p,int index, char value)
{
    _se_translator_function oldhandler=_set_se_translator(cppexcept);
    try {
      p[index]=value;
    }
    catch (unsigned int code)
    {
     printf("Code=%x @%d\n",code,index);
     if (code!=0xC0000005)
```

```
        {
                printf("Unexpected exception!\n");
                exit(1);
        }
 // make sure index is in range
        if (index>=maxindex)
        {
            printf("Attempt to access outside buffer limit\n");
            exit(2);
        }
 // commit one byte so only the current page gets committed
 // in reality, the system will commit the whole page
        VirtualAlloc(p+index,1,MEM_COMMIT,PAGE_READWRITE);
        _set_se_translator(oldhandler);
 // try again
        putbuffer(p,index,value);
       }
   _set_se_translator(oldhandler);

}


void freebuffer(char *p)
{
    VirtualFree(p,0,MEM_RELEASE);
}


// Main program (probably should be outside the library)

void main()
{
    char *p=getbuffer();
    for (int i=0;i<4000000;i++)
    {
        putbuffer(p,i,i&0xFF);
    }
    freebuffer(p);
    printf("Pass #2\n");
    p=getbuffer();
    // now backwards for variety
    for (int j=4000000-1;j>=0;j--)
    {
        putbuffer(p,j,j&0xFF);
    }
    freebuffer(p);
}
```

Using Heaps

VirtualAlloc has its uses, but it is a bit too low-level for some purposes. As usual, Windows provides programmers with as much or as little control as they could want. If you don't want to use **VirtualAlloc**, your obvious choice is to manipulate the heap using calls like **malloc** or **new**—the standard memory allocation functions for C or C++.

If your program uses a lot of dynamic memory, you may find that the heap managed by **malloc** or **new** is not completely satisfactory. For one thing, the heap can fragment. This is a particular problem when you allocate many small items on the heap, and then free some of them. When you attempt to allocate larger memory, Windows may have to compact the heap or expand it to satisfy your request.

What if you could use multiple heaps in your program? If one heap handled only allocations of a 128-byte structure, then fragmentation would not be an issue. Freeing one structure would leave a hole just big enough for the next allocation. This can lead to efficiency that would be hard to attain with a conventional heap.

Windows supports multiple heaps using the calls in Table 7.2. Your process has one automatic heap (call **GetProcessHeap** to learn the handle of this heap). This is the heap that calls like **malloc** use. However, you can create any number of heaps using **HeapCreate**.

The **HeapCreate** call allows you to create a fixed-size heap by specifying a number of bytes as the third argument. If you set this size to 0, then the heap can grow without bounds. Fixed-size heaps also have an upper limit on how large a single item can be (a bit more than 512K).

Once you have a heap handle, you can allocate using **HeapAlloc** and free memory with **HeapFree**. You can also lock and unlock the heap to restrict access to the heap to a single thread. This normally happens automatically on a per call basis, but you may wish to lock the heap before doing a series of operations to enhance performance.

Another possible reason to create heaps is to improve multithreading performance. Normally, Windows synchronizes access between threads by locking the heap before performing operations. However, if your thread has a private heap, you can prevent this serialization by specifying **HEAP_NO_SERIALIZE**. This can improve performance, but be certain that no other thread attempts to access a non-serialized heap.

Most of the time, you won't need to use private heaps. However, in cases where you need the fastest performance, heaps can help you squeeze that last bit of performance from your programs.

Table 7.2 Heap-related calls.

Function	Description
HeapCreate	Creates a new heap
HeapAlloc	Allocates a block on a heap
HeapCompact	Compacts a heap
HeapDestroy	Destroys a heap
HeapFree	Frees blocks in a heap
GetProcessHeap	Learns default process heap handle
GetProcessHeaps	Gets handles for all heaps
HeapLock	Locks out other threads for a heap
HeapUnlock	Resumes normal heap serialization after HeapLock
HeapRealloc	Reallocates a block on the heap
HeapSize	Determines the actual size of an allocated block
HeapValidate	Tests the heap's validity
HeapWalk	Enumerates the blocks in a heap

Summary

It is possible to go your entire life and use only **malloc**, **new**, or whatever mechanism your language provides for memory allocation. However, to truly take best advantage of Windows' memory management features, you'll eventually have to turn to **VirtualAlloc**.

Of course, for many purposes, using a library-supplied memory allocation routine is the best idea. But there are many special cases where you are better off using Windows' core memory allocation routine. For example, you might want to make certain pages read-only. Another possibility is to implement sparse memory management for large arrays. There are many things you can do if you know how to use **VirtualAlloc** and its related calls.

Immediate Solutions

When To Use **VirtualAlloc**

When you want to allocate memory, you usually think of using **malloc** or **new** (or some other construct provided by the library and language you are using). For many cases this is fine, and you should use those calls. However, by taking advantage of special features in the Windows operating system, you may be able to achieve better performance by managing memory at a lower level.

VirtualAlloc is the primary way Win32 programs allocate memory. You may want to use this call in the following circumstances:

- You want to make sure when you no longer need the memory that the operating system recovers the allocated memory.
- You want to have some of the memory reserved, but not actually allocated until a later time. Perhaps you plan on allocating it all in small chunks, or you may want to implement sparse arrays so that they have certain regions that you never allocate.
- Some or all of the allocation requires a special attribute (such as read-only).

For whatever reason, you usually don't want to call **VirtualAlloc** to get small bits of memory. This call works only on pages of memory. For an Intel machine, the page size is 4K, but other machines may use even larger page sizes (use **GetSystemInfo** to find out).

Using **VirtualAlloc** And **VirtualFree**

VirtualAlloc requires four arguments:

- *The linear address of the allocation*—This will be **NULL** if you want any available address. Windows will round the value down to the nearest page boundary.
- *The size of the allocation in bytes*—Windows rounds this up so that it equals the number of bytes in the nearest whole number of pages. In other words, on an Intel machine, asking for 1 byte actually allocates 4K. Asking for 4,100 bytes results in an 8K allocation.

- *The allocation type*—This may be **MEM_COMMIT** (normal allocation) or **MEM_RESERVE** (reserve memory but don't allocate physical memory or swap space). You can add **MEM_TOPDOWN** to either of these to indicate that Windows should select addresses from the highest address possible. When you reserve memory, you will probably call **VirtualAlloc** again later with a specific address to commit some or all of the reserved allocation.
- *The page protection*—See Table 7.1. You will usually specify **PAGE_READWRITE** here so you can initialize the contents of the memory. You might then change the protection by using **VirtualProtect**.

It is perfectly legal to call **VirtualAlloc** to commit pages that you already committed. However, you may not reserve a page more than once. The function returns the address that corresponds to the beginning of the allocation.

You can also call **VirtualAlloc** later with the **MEM_RESET** allocation type. This informs Windows that the contents of the page are no longer important. This means that Windows can discard the memory instead of swapping it out, if it needs to swap.

When you no longer need the memory region, you can call **VirtualFree**. **VirtualFree** requires an address, a size (in bytes), and a flag to request a particular operation. If the flag is **MEM_RELEASE**, the address must be the start of a region previously allocated with **VirtualAlloc**, and the size argument must be zero. Then, **VirtualFree** completely releases the allocation.

The other possible value for the flag, **MEM_DECOMMIT**, causes the specified area of memory to revert to the reserved state. **VirtualFree** rounds the starting address down and the size up, if necessary, so that you always operate on a whole number of pages. It is not an error to decommit pages that are not currently committed.

Setting Page Protection

Once you have pages initialized, you might want to change their protection attributes (see Table 7.1). For example, you might want to make a page read-only, or set it to be unavailable. You can easily do this with the **VirtualProtect** call. This call requires four parameters. The first is an address that specifies the start of the pages you want to alter. Next, you supply the number of bytes you want to affect. Of course, calling **VirtualProtect** really changes the protection for an entire page (or group of pages). If you try to affect one byte, you'll really change the protection for the entire page that contains the byte.

The next argument specifies the new protection attribute you want to set. The final argument is a pointer to a **DWORD**. This **DWORD** will receive the previous protection attribute that was in force. If you are working with multiple pages, the returned protection level is the one that applied to the first page. Even if you don't care what the previous protection attribute was, you must supply this pointer.

Reading Page Protection

On occasion, it is useful to find out what protection attributes a page (or set of pages) already has. If you need this information, make a call to **VirtualQuery**. You provide a base address, a pointer to a **MEMORY_BASIC_INFORMATION** structure, and the size in bytes of the structure.

When the call returns, the **MEMORY_BASIC_INFORMATION** structure will contain the base allocation address that the supplied address belongs to (**AllocationBase**). You'll also find flags that indicate the page's initial protection, its current protection, and its current state (**MEM_COMMIT**, for example). Another flag (**Type**) shows if the page belongs to a file mapping, is part of an executable image, or is private memory. The structure also contains the number of bytes that have the same attributes.

Responding To Exceptions

When working with memory, it is a common situation to run into an exception. When Windows generates an exception (for example, an access exception or a page guard exception), it expects you to handle the exception with structured exception handling (SEH). However, SEH is not easy to use, so the C compiler provides **__try** and **__except** keywords that will handle it just as well.

With C++, however, you should use the standard **try** and **catch** keywords. Not only are these more convenient, but they also understand C++ object semantics so that destructors, for example, properly execute.

C++ exception handlers, however, don't normally receive Windows exceptions. Luckily, you can work around this by writing a translator function. This function (which returns **void**) receives the exception code and an **_EXCEPTION_POINTERS** pointer. These arguments give you details about the exception. Your job is to throw a corresponding C++ exception.

If you want, you can create an exception object (perhaps derived from **CException** if you are using MFC), initialize the object with information from the two arguments you receive, and throw the object. However, it is usually sufficient to just throw the error code. That means that your translator function can be this simple:

```
void cppexcept( unsigned int u, _EXCEPTION_POINTERS* pExp )
{
    throw u;
}
```

Once you have your translator function ready, you must call **_set_se_translator** to register your translator. The call returns the pointer for the old translator. Store it away in a **_se_translator_function** variable and restore it when you are done handling exceptions, if you don't want to be permanently responsible for handling exceptions. You'll find a complete example in Listing 7.3.

Creating A New Heap

HeapCreate allows you to build new heaps. The call returns a handle to the heap and requires three arguments. The first argument allows you to set options. The **HEAP_GENERATE_EXCEPTIONS** flag causes Windows to throw an exception if the call fails. Without this flag, **HeapCreate** returns a **NULL** handle to indicate failure. The other flag you can specify is **HEAP_NO_SERIALIZE**. This flag indicates that Windows should not use a mutual exclusion to prevent multiple threads from accessing the heap simultaneously. These flags set the default options for the heap, although you can also set these flags in most of the other heap calls if you don't set them here.

The second argument you specify is the initial size of the heap. The system rounds this value to the nearest whole-number multiple of a page size. On Intel-architecture systems, a page is 2K long, so requesting 4000 bytes will result in a 4096 byte allocation, for example. You can learn the page size on the current system by calling **GetSystemInfo**.

The final argument to **HeapCreate** is the maximum size for the heap. This value is also rounded so that it matches a page boundary. However, you'll often specify zero so that the heap has no maximum size. If you set a size, the maximum single allocation in the heap may not exceed 0x7FFF8 bytes in size. **HeapCreate** will reserve (but not commit) the entire maximum amount.

If you don't set a heap size, the heap can grow until you run out of virtual address space. In this case there is no preset maximum allocation size.

If you do select a maximum size, don't forget that the system uses some of the memory for heap management. That means that a 64K heap doesn't really have 64K available to you, but instead provides a bit less memory. When you no longer need a heap, you can call **HeapDestroy**.

Finding The Default Heap

Every program has a default heap that it uses. If you ever need this handle, call **GetProcessHeap**. Keep in mind that you should never call **HeapDestroy** on this heap handle.

Allocating And Freeing Heap Data

Once you have a handle to a heap, it is easy to use **HeapAlloc** to all ocate memory from the heap. The function requires a heap handle, a flag argument,and the size (in bytes) of the allocation you want. The flags can be **HEAP_GENERATE_EXCEPTIONS**, **HEAP_NO SERIALIZE**,or **HEAP_ZERO_MEMORY**. The **HEAP_GENERATE_EXCEPTIONS** and **HEAP_NO_SERIALIZE** flags operate in the same way that they do for **HeapCreate**. **HEAP_ZERO_MEMORY** causes Windows to set the memory block to zero before returning.

Don't forget that if the heap has a fixed size, you can't allocate items larger than 0x7FFF8 bytes. Once you allocate an item, you can learn its actual size (which may be more than you requested) by calling **HeapSize**.

You can resize an element in the heap by using **HeapReAlloc**. This function allows you to set several flags including the familiar **HEAP_GENERATE_EXCEPTIONS**, **HEAP_NO_SERIALIZE**, and **HEAP_ZERO_MEMORY**. You may also specify **HEAP_REALLOC_IN_PLACE_ONLY** to indicate that the reallocation should fail if it must move the memory block. This is an issue only if you are making the block larger, since shrinking a block never moves it.

When you no longer need an allocated memory block, you can release it by calling **HeapFree**. You can specify **HEAP_NO_SERIALIZE** as an argument to prevent serialization.

Compacting A Heap

Once you have used a heap for awhile, it may become fragmented. You can call **HeapCompact** to force Windows to gather together free space in the heap as well as decommit pages that are no longer in use. This function requires a handle to a heap and a flag argument that can specify **HEAP_NO_SERIALIZE**.

Debugging A Heap

There are several ways you can check to see if a heap is corrupt. Your program might corrupt a heap by writing past the end of an allocation, or writing to a block that you already freed. An easy way to check that a heap is valid is to call **HeapValidate**. You can use this function to check a specific block of memory, or the entire heap (by specifying 0 as the address to check).

The **HeapWalk** function allows you to enumerate the blocks in a heap. It returns information about each block in a **PROCESS_HEAP_ENTRY** structure (see Table 7.3). Each call returns information about the next block until you've processed all the blocks. If you want to call **HeapValidate** on the blocks that **HeapWalk** returns, you should know that **HeapValidate** will fail any block that is not allocated. Therefore, you should only pass **HeapValidate** blocks that have their **PROCESS_HEAP_ENTRY_BUSY** flag set.

Table 7.3 PROCESS_HEAP_ENTRY structure.

Field	Type	Description
lpData	PVOID	Pointer to data
cbData	DWORD	Size of block
cbOverhead	BYTE	Number of bytes used to manage this block
iRegionIndex	BYTE	Index of memory region
wFlags	WORD	Indicates status of region
hMem	HANDLE	Handle to allocated memory region
Region.dwCommittedSize	DWORD	Number of bytes committed
Region.dwUnCommittedSize	DWORD	Number of bytes uncommitted
Region.lpFirstBlock	LPVOID	First valid block pointer
Region.lpLastBlock	LPVOID	Pointer to first invalid block pointer

Heap Performance Considerations

Using heaps allows you to handle several special cases that can improve performance, if you use them carefully. One of the obvious ways to improve performance is to use separate heaps for structures and objects of different sizes. This reduces the penalty you pay for fragmentation. Each time you free data in a heap, you'll leave a space just big enough for another allocation.

Another way to improve performance is to disable serialization in heaps that do not require it. If you only access a heap from a single thread, you don't really need serialization. This can also work if your threads already use some method to synchronize themselves. Just be sure that there is no way for multiple threads to access the heap at the same time.

Chapter 8

Windows Security

If you need an immediate solution to:	*See page:*
Learning An Object's Owner	374
Converting A SID To A Name	375
Converting A Name To A SID	376
Creating A Descriptor	376
Converting Between Absolute And Self-Relative Descriptors	377
Using The Default Security Descriptor	377
Using A Universal Security Descriptor	378
Using A Specific Security Descriptor	378
Using Private Security	379

In Depth

When I used to work for the government, I occasionally had to visit a very secure government facility (I won't mention exactly which one). This site was crucial to national security (this was, after all, during the cold war). When we arrived, the very serious guards would search us, check inside our van, and open every container larger than a soda can. One guard would even look under the van with a mirror on a long shaft in case there was a bomb underneath.

This routine would happen every time we arrived. Every time, that is, except on Sundays. On Sundays, the guard would just wave us in. It always struck me as ludicrous that the military guards apparently thought enemy saboteurs were members of a union that prevented them from blowing things up on Sunday.

Like physical security, computer security depends on the vigilance of the guards. It also shouldn't depend on the actions of the people who want to gain entrance. In other words, programs that want to access a secure resource shouldn't have to do anything special to trigger security—only programs that want to guard something need any code for security. This is good news because many programs don't require any security code at all.

For the sake of convenience, I'll call programs that want to secure something *servers*, and programs that want to access the secure item *clients*. Many times, the securing program will actually be a network server, and the clients will be programs accessing the server over a network. However, this isn't always the case. In reality, any program that wants to prevent certain users from accessing something uses security even if there's no network involved.

TIP: *For the purposes of this chapter, an object is anything that the security system controls. For example, a file, a named pipe, a registry key, and an event are all securable objects.*

Goals Of Security

The security system has only two objectives. The first is to verify that a user has access to a particular object. If the user isn't allowed to access a system object, the offending call will fail with an "access denied" error. In your own programs, you can react in any way you feel is appropriate. For example, you might have a database with information about employees. Suppose one of the many fields in the database contains sensitive information (like the employee's salary). The database server might check to see if each request originates from a user who has permission to view this data. If the user doesn't have the appropriate permission, the server might return asterisks in the salary field. In other words, what you do when you detect a security error in your own code is up to you. Usually, you'll just return an "access denied" error (like Windows itself), but you don't have to do so.

The second function that security performs is, optionally, to audit access to objects. This simply means that security can write into a log file when a user attempts to access particular objects. Administrators can turn auditing on and off, and also select if they want to audit all accesses to an object or merely unsuccessful ones.

Security seems complicated because it appears throughout the operating system. It appears that every important call you make requires some sort of security descriptor. The good news is that unless you want to interact specifically with security, you can generally use the default descriptor by passing **NULL** for these arguments.

Privileges And Rights

Security tracks who can perform certain actions in two fundamental ways: by privileges and by rights. Privileges pertain to the user and the system as a whole. You might have the privilege to log on to the computer, for example. Backing up disks, formatting disks, and debugging programs are other examples of privileges. You'll find a list in Table 8.1.

Table 8.1 Privileges.

Privilege	Privilege Required In Order To...
SE_ASSIGNPRIMARYTOKEN_NAME	Assign the primary token of a process.
SE_AUDIT_NAME	Generate audit log entries. Give this privilege to secure servers.
SE_BACKUP_NAME	Perform backup operations.
SE_CHANGE_NOTIFY_NAME	Receive notifications of changes to files or directories. This privilege also causes the system to skip all traversal access checks. It's enabled by default for all users.
SE_CREATE_PAGEFILE_NAME	Create a paging file.
SE_CREATE_PERMANENT_NAME	Create a permanent object.
SE_CREATE_TOKEN_NAME	Create a primary token.
SE_DEBUG_NAME	Debug a process.
SE_INC_BASE_PRIORITY_NAME	Increase the base priority of a process.

(continued)

***Table 8.1 Privileges* (continued).**

Privilege	Privilege Required In Order To...
SE_INCREASE_QUOTA_NAME	Increase the quota assigned to a process.
SE_LOAD_DRIVER_NAME	Load or unload a device driver.
SE_LOCK_MEMORY_NAME	Lock physical pages in memory.
SE_PROF_SINGLE_PROCESS_NAME	Gather profiling information for a single process.
SE_REMOTE_SHUTDOWN_NAME	Shut down a system using a network request.
SE_RESTORE_NAME	Perform restore operations. This privilege enables you to set any valid user or group SID as the owner of an object.
SE_SECURITY_NAME	Perform a number of security-related functions, such as controlling and viewing audit messages. This privilege identifies its holder as a security operator.
SE_SHUTDOWN_NAME	Shut down a local system.
SE_SYSTEM_ENVIRONMENT_NAME	Modify the nonvolatile RAM of systems that use this type of memory to store configuration information.
SE_SYSTEM_PROFILE_NAME	Gather profiling information for the entire system.
SE_SYSTEMTIME_NAME	Modify the system time.
SE_TAKE_OWNERSHIP_NAME	Take ownership of an object without being granted discretionary access. This privilege allows the owner value to be set only to those values that the holder may legitimately assign as the owner of an object.
SE_TCB_NAME	Identify its holder as part of the trusted computer base. Some trusted protected subsystems are granted this privilege. This privilege is required to call the LogonUser function.
SE_UNSOLICITED_INPUT_NAME	Read unsolicited input from a terminal device.
SE_MACHINE_ACCOUNT_NAME	Create a machine account.

The other type of security is by right. Rights are part of some object (a file on an NTFS volume, for example). A particular user might have the right to read a file, but not the right to write it. Rights may be negative, as well. A right may deny a user read access to, for example, a named pipe. In addition, a right may apply to a group instead of an individual user.

Because rights are part of an object, the system stores them with the objects. This is why files on FAT disks can't use most security functions. Implementing security by rights is a good idea because changes to the rights associated with an object need only to worry about the object, not hundreds of users scattered over a network.

Filling In The NULL

If you've been programming under Windows for any length of time, you probably just automatically put a **NULL** everywhere you see a **SECURITY_ATTRIBUTES** structure in an API call. But what if you want to fill it in? You can find the fields in Table 8.2.

In previous chapters, you've seen one case where you have to fill in at least part of the structure: inheritance. When you want a child process to inherit a handle, you'll usually pass a **SECURITY_ATTRIBUTES** structure to the call that creates the handle. You need to set only two members of the structure in this case: **nLength** (the size of the structure in bytes) and **bInheritHandle**. If you aren't interested in security, you can set the remaining field, **lpSecurityDescriptor**, to **NULL**.

You may be surprised to find that the internal structure of the **SECURITY_DESCRIPTOR** structure isn't documented. The pointer in the **SECURITY_ATTRIBUTES** structure is simply a void pointer. Presumably, if you knew what was in a **SECURITY_DESCRIPTOR**, you might be able to subvert security, so you don't have access to that information.

If you've ever worked in a high-security area, you might have had an "orphan Annie badge"—a card you swiped to get into particular doors. You can think of a **SECURITY_DESCRIPTOR** as a badge reader. Your badge is a **SID**, or Security ID. Each user (and group of users) has a unique SID. When you attempt to access an object that has a **SECURITY_DESCRIPTOR**, you're swiping your SID through the **SECURITY_DESCRIPTOR**. If you have the right card, the system grants you access. If not, you aren't allowed to use the object.

Security descriptors store several important pieces of information:

- The SID of the object's owner
- The SID of the object's owner's primary group
- The discretionary access control list (DACL)
- The system access control list (SACL)

Table 8.2 The SECURITY_ATTRIBUTES structure.

Field	Description
nLength	Length of structure
lpSecurityDescriptor	Security Descriptor that controls access to the object
bInheritHandle	Allows the associated handle to pass from parent to child

- Control information (for example, flags pertaining to how the descriptor's ACLs pass information to child descriptors)

The DACL controls who can (and can't) access the object. The SACL determines what actions generate log file entries.

If you don't know the format of a **SECURITY_DESCRIPTOR**, how can you create one? Just use the call **InitializeSecurityDescriptor**. This function requires a pointer to a **SECURITY_DESCRIPTOR** and a **DWORD** that contains the revision number for the structure. Just pass **SECURITY_DESCRIPTOR_REVISION** for that argument.

It's interesting to note that calling **InitializeSecurityDescriptor** creates an absolute descriptor. An absolute descriptor contains pointers to different things inside itself. This result is usually what you want. However, what happens if you want to write a security descriptor to disk? When you read it back in, the pointers will be invalid.

To combat this problem, Windows allows you to convert descriptors to self-relative format and back again. Usually, you'll convert to self-relative form only when you're about to write out the descriptor, and convert it back to absolute form when you read it back. Calls that modify the descriptor will require an absolute descriptor to work with.

Making the conversions is as simple as calling **MakeSelfRelativeSD** and **MakeAbsoluteSD**. It's simple to convert to self-relative form. However, converting to absolute requires you to specify several memory buffers, so **MakeAbsoluteSD** is tedious to call.

Inside SIDs

You'll use two primary functions to manipulate SIDs: **LookupAccoutName** and **LookupAccountSid**. These functions allow you to transform SIDs to names and names to SIDs.

If you're in a networked environment, you can run these functions on remote machines. This capability is important if you're a server attempting to work with a remote user, for example. Both functions will allow you to pass **NULL** as the machine name if you want to examine local users.

In addition to the name or the SID, these functions also return an enumerated type that tells you what the SID is for (see Table 8.3). The **SID_NAME_USE** variable can tell you exactly what kind of SID you're dealing with.

Incidentally, if you just need to know the name of the user, it's easy to find. Use **GetUserName** to retrieve the name. Then you could call **LookupAccountSid** to convert that name to a SID.

Not all SIDs have names. When you log on, for example, the system assigns you an arbitrary SID to represent the current session. That SID has no name.

Other SID functions you may find useful are **AllocateAndInitializeSid**, **InitializeSid**, **FreeSid**, **CopySid**, **IsValidSid**, **GetLengthSid**, and **EqualSid**.

ACEs And ACLs

An Access Control Element (ACE) is a record that specifies whether a particular user (or group) is allowed a particular right. You may commonly encounter three kinds of ACEs: **ACCESS_ALLOWED_ACE_TYPE**, **ACCESS_DENIED_ACE_TYPE**, and **SYSTEM_AUDIT_ACE_TYPE**. The first two grant or deny a right to a user (or group of users), whereas the third type marks an audit requirement.

An access control list is just a list of ACEs. The DACL contains **ACCESS_ALLOWED_ACE_TYPE** and **ACCESS_DENIED_ACE_TYPE** ACEs. The **SACL** contains **SYSTEM_AUDIT_ACE_TYPE** records.

Each access-type ACE has a 32-bit **ACCESS_MASK**. This mask is a set of bits that determines what rights the ACE grants or denies. Exactly what each bit means depends on the object in question. Semaphores, for example, have different rights than files. However, the following four generic access bits always mean the same thing for every object: **GENERIC_READ**, **GENERIC_WRITE**, **GENERIC_EXECUTE**, and **GENERIC_ALL**.

Table 8.3 The SID_NAME_USE type.

Name	Description
SidTypeUser	Ordinary user
SidTypeGroup	Ordinary group
SidTypeDomain	Domain name
SidTypeAlias	Alias
SidTypeWellKnownGroup	Well-known group
SidTypeDeletedAccount	Old account
SidTypeUnknown	Unknown

When you're working with system objects or files, the system automatically stores the ACLs for you. However, in some cases you may need to build your own ACLs and store them to protect data the system doesn't know about.

Types Of Security Objects

Security can influence several types of objects. Each object has its own calls for accessing the associated security descriptor (see Table 8.4).

Files are by far the most common object you'll deal with in a security context. However, in some cases, you'll be interested in private objects. Windows doesn't really understand these objects, but you want to secure them anyway.

For example, suppose you have a database that contains payroll information. You might want to maintain your own ACL that determines who has access to the payroll data. If you receive a query from an unauthorized source, you might log it, deny it completely, or return data with sensitive materials replaced with asterisks.

Using The Default

Of course, most of the time you don't supply security descriptors when you create an object. So what does that mean? The answer depends on exactly what kind of object you're using.

For example, consider what happens when you create a file without specifying a security descriptor. As you might guess, the new file inherits the security settings

Table 8.4 Security objects and their calls.

Object Type	Examples	Calls
Files	NTFS files, named pipes	GetSecurity, SetSecurity
Kernel	Process and thread handles, file mapping objects, synchronization handles	GetKernelObjectSecurity, SetKernelObjectSecurity
User	Windows, menus	GetUserObjectSecurity, SetUserObjectSecurity
Registry	Keys	RegGetKeySecurity, RegSetKeySecurity
Services	Any service	QueryServiceObjectSecurity, SetServiceObjectSecurity
Private	User-defined	CreatePrivateObjectSecurity, GetPrivateObjectSecurity, SetPrivateObjectSecurity, DestroyPrivateObjectSecurity

of its parent directory. Users expect this behavior, and Windows does the correct thing with no intervention on your part. Registry keys, which have a similar organization to the file system, behave the same way.

What about synchronization objects and other kernel objects, such as file mappings? They don't have any parent to inherit from. In this case, Windows creates the object with a **NULL** ACL. This action effectively allows anyone to do anything to the object.

What about things that resemble file handles (like mailslots or named pipes)? You'd think they would be similar to synchronization objects, but they aren't. Instead, they receive the default ACL from your login SID. You may have inadvertently discovered this fact in Chapter 5 if you set the security attributes to **NULL** and then tried to run the named pipe chat program as two different users. The default ACL grants all access to you and other members of your group. Other users have no access—not what you usually want!

Finally, you might wonder about user objects. You might even find it surprising that they have anything to do with security. In fact, you rarely (if ever) set their security. The calls dealing with windows and menus don't accept security attributes or any other security data.

The answer to this puzzle is that user objects receive the same security as their desktop and window station. In fact, these are the only objects you can actually pass to **GetUserObjectSecurity** and **SetUserObjectSecurity**.

Building SDs

Consider the named pipe example from Chapter 5. Suppose you wanted to use the pipe between unrelated users (which makes sense). You'll have to supply a security descriptor when you create the pipe.

If you want everyone to have full access to the pipe, you can take a cue from the kernel objects and create a **SECURITY_DESCRIPTOR** with a **NULL** ACL. The alternative, of course, is to create a new ACL that gives you full control over access to the pipe.

In either case, you wind up with a **SECURITY_DESCRIPTOR** that you can pass in **CreateNamedPipe**'s **SECURITY_ATTRIBUTES** argument.

Creating a **SECURITY_DESCRIPTOR** with a **NULL** ACL is relatively simple. Here's the code:

```
SECURITY_ATTRIBUTES sa;
SECURITY_DESCRIPTOR sd;
```

```
sa.nLength=sizeof(sa);
sa.bInheritHandle=TRUE;  // or whatever you like

InitalizeSecurityDescriptor(&sd,SECURITY_DESCRIPTOR_REVISION);
SetSecurityDescriptorDacl(&sd,TRUE,NULL,FALSE);
sa.lpSecurityDescriptor=&sd;
rv=CreateNamedPipe("\\\\.\\pipe\\talkpipe_awc",
  PIPE_ACCESS_DUPLEX|FILE_FLAG_OVERLAPPED,
  PIPE_TYPE_BYTE|PIPE_READMODE_BYTE,1,1024,1024,1000,&sa);
```

If this were a different type of object, the procedure would be essentially the same (with a different call replacing **CreateNamedPipe**, of course).

You might wonder if allowing everyone access to a named pipe is a security hazard. That depends. In this case, it's probably good that everyone can use the pipe. But suppose the pipe's job was to read a file name and return the file's contents to the client.

You might find it unacceptable that anyone can ask the hypothetical file server pipe for a file and get it. This easy access might allow users to subvert file system security. The answer is relatively simple: The pipe code can call **Impersonate NamedPipeClient**. This call effectively makes my server code pretend that it's the client. The security system checks the client's SID against any ACLs it checks, instead of the server's SID.

It's important to realize that using a **NULL** ACL isn't the same as making an ACL with no entries. An ACL that's empty denies all access to everyone. A **NULL** ACL grants all access to everyone.

Tokens And Impersonations

Impersonation is an important part of Windows security. A server with the correct authority can impersonate a user to prevent the user from operating at the server's security level. When the server wants to remove its mask, it calls **RevertToSelf**. A few calls require an impersonation token even if you only want to know about yourself. For these cases, there's the **ImpersonateSelf** call.

Of course, it's more common to impersonate someone else. Usually you'll call **ImpersonateLoggedOnUser**. You can use the **LogonUser** function to learn the user's token if you have their user ID and password.

What's a token? The security system refers to entities such as processes and threads by their tokens. Some tokens are also impersonation tokens. The system understands that an impersonation token is one process or thread pretending to be another.

You usually get tokens from the **OpenProcessToken** and **OpenThreadToken** calls. For most purposes, you won't care much about these tokens, but if you're implementing private security (covered later in this chapter) you'll find you must use them.

Building Arbitrary ACLs

The previous example with the named pipe is overly simple, because it allows everyone to access the named pipe with no restrictions. What happens if you want to allow certain users to have certain access rights, but you want to deny other rights to other users? Then you'll have to build an ACL from scratch.

An ACL is nothing more than a region of memory that contains an **ACL** header and zero or more ACEs. An ACE, in turn, consists of an **ACE_HEADER**, and then either an **ACCESS_ALLOWED_ACE** or **ACCESS_DENIED_ACE** structure. When you build an ACL in NT 4.0 (or earlier versions) it is up to you to add the **ACCESS_DENIED_ACE** entries before other entries so that the system rejects users with a negative ACE even if there is another ACE that grants them a right.

One of the problems with building an ACL is that you have to calculate the size of the ACL. The ACL must be large enough to contain all of the ACEs. Since ACEs can vary in size, this is not always an easy task.

The size of an ACE depends on its type, and the length of the SID that it contains. For an access-allowed ACE, the length is:

```
L=  sizeof(ACCESS_ALLOWED_ACE) - sizeof(ACCESS_ALLOWED_ACE.SidStart) +
    GetLengthSid((PSID)ace.SidStart);
```

This code simply adds the length of the header (minus the dummy placeholder for the first part of the SID) and the actual length of the SID.

The length of an ACL, then, is the length of the ACL structure plus the sum of the lengths of the ACEs within the list. Often, you'll be tempted to treat ACLs like you often handle file names: Simply allocate a large buffer and assume it will have enough space. It's acceptable to have an ACL that's larger than necessary.

Once you have a large enough buffer, you can initialize the ACL by calling **InitializeAcl**. Next, you can add ACEs by calling **AddAccessDeniedAce** and **AddAccessAllowedAce**. These calls require a pointer to the ACL buffer, the **ACL_REVISION** constant, the rights you're granting or denying, and a pointer to a SID. This SID specifies a user or group that the ACE refers to. You'll usually get the SID by calling **LookupAccountName**.

Don't forget to add the ACEs that deny access first. Otherwise, Windows NT 4.0 and earlier versions of NT may not behave correctly when there are contradictory ACEs. For example, suppose I'm a member of the TECH group and a member of the USERS group. If an ACE denies the USERS group access to a file but grants access to the TECH group, I shouldn't have access to the file (because I belong to a group expressly prohibited from using the file). This ACE structure won't work properly in some versions of NT if you don't put all the negative ACEs before the affirmative ones.

Once the ACL is ready, you can use **SetSecurityDescriptorDacl** to install it into the **SECURITY_ATTRIBUTES** structure you pass to **CreateFile** or whatever API call you're using. This is the same call the first code fragment used, but now you'll pass a real ACL instead of a **NULL** pointer.

Listing 8.1 shows the named-pipe program again, but this time the pipe is fully accessible by everyone except those in the GUEST group. Even though users in the GUEST group are also members of the EVERYONE group, the explicit denial of access to GUEST prohibits them from using the pipe.

In this example, I used **GENERIC_ALL** as the access right, but you could use more specific rights if you wanted to further limit rights. For example, you might limit some users to write-only access or prevent them from deleting a file.

Listing 8.1 Security-aware named pipe talk program.

```
#include <windows.h>
#include <iostream.h>
#include <string.h>
#include <stdio.h> // sprintf

BOOL server=FALSE;



HANDLE OpenTalkPipe(char *host)
{
   HANDLE rv;
   if (!server)
   {
      char fn[1024];
      sprintf(fn,"\\\\%s\\pipe\\talkpipe_awc",host);
      cerr<<"Opening "<<fn<<"\n";
      rv=CreateFile(fn,GENERIC_READ|GENERIC_WRITE,FILE_SHARE_READ|
      FILE_SHARE_WRITE,NULL,OPEN_EXISTING,FILE_FLAG_OVERLAPPED,NULL);
   }
   else
```

```
   {
      // we are the server
        SECURITY_ATTRIBUTES sa;
        SECURITY_DESCRIPTOR sd;
        sa.nLength=sizeof(sa);
        sa.bInheritHandle=TRUE;
        InitializeSecurityDescriptor(&sd,SECURITY_DESCRIPTOR_REVISION);
        SetSecurityDescriptorDacl(&sd,TRUE,NULL,FALSE);
        sa.lpSecurityDescriptor=&sd;
      rv=CreateNamedPipe("\\\\.\\pipe\\talkpipe_awc",
                     PIPE_ACCESS_DUPLEX|FILE_FLAG_OVERLAPPED,
         PIPE_TYPE_BYTE|PIPE_READMODE_BYTE,1,1024,1024,1000,&sa);

   }
   return rv;
}

void main(int argc, char *argv[])
{
   if (argc==1) server=TRUE;
   HANDLE pipe=OpenTalkPipe(server?".":argv[1]);
   HANDLE console=GetStdHandle(STD_INPUT_HANDLE);
   HANDLE pipeevent=CreateEvent(NULL,TRUE,FALSE,NULL);
   OVERLAPPED over;
   char pipebuf;
   DWORD inlen;
   DWORD err;
   if (pipe==INVALID_HANDLE_VALUE)
   {
      err=GetLastError();
      cout<<"Error opening pipe ("<<err<<")\n";
      exit(9);
   }
   over.Internal=over.InternalHigh=over.Offset=over.OffsetHigh=0;
   over.hEvent=pipeevent;
   if (!SetConsoleMode(console,0))
   {
      cerr<<"Error: can't set console mode\n"<<GetLastError();
      exit(4);
   }
   cout<<"Waiting to connect\n";
   cout.flush();
   //read pipe
   do {
   while (ReadFile(pipe,&pipebuf,1,&inlen,&over)) cout<<pipebuf;
```

```
err=GetLastError();
} while (err==ERROR_PIPE_LISTENING);  // wait for client
cerr<<"Connected (^C to disconnect)\n";
if (err!=ERROR_IO_PENDING)
{
   cerr<<"Error reading pipe ("<<err<<")\n";
   exit(3);
}
// Enter wait
HANDLE waits[2];
DWORD obj;
waits[0]=pipeevent;
waits[1]=console;
while (1)
{
   obj=WaitForMultipleObjects(2,(void **)&waits,FALSE,INFINITE);
   // if wait ended for console, read console and send
   if (obj==WAIT_OBJECT_0+1)
   {
      char inbuf; // ANSI only
      OVERLAPPED dummy;
      INPUT_RECORD irec;
      dummy.hEvent=NULL;
      dummy.Offset=dummy.OffsetHigh=dummy.Internal=
                      dummy.InternalHigh=0;
      DWORD inlen;
      // Using ReadConsole here never unsignals console!
      ReadConsoleInput(console,&irec,1,&inlen);
      if (irec.EventType==
                     KEY_EVENT&&irec.Event.KeyEvent.bKeyDown&&
         irec.Event.KeyEvent.uChar.AsciiChar!='\0')
      {
         inbuf=irec.Event.KeyEvent.uChar.AsciiChar;
         if (inbuf=='\003')
         {
            // quit
            CloseHandle(pipe);
            CloseHandle(pipeevent);
            exit(0);
         }
         WriteFile(pipe,&inbuf,1,&inlen,&dummy);
         // echo
         cout<<((inbuf=='\r')?'\n':inbuf);
         cout.flush();
      // Wait for write to complete so we don't get confused
```

```
            if (!GetOverlappedResult(pipe,&dummy,&inlen,TRUE))
               cout<<"Unknown pipe write error!\n";

         }
      }
// if wait ended for pipe, dump character to console and issue another read
      if (obj==WAIT_OBJECT_0)
      {
         DWORD len;
         // Get the result, even though we know what it is
         if (!GetOverlappedResult(pipe,&over,&len,TRUE))
         {
            cout<<"!Unknown pipe error!\n";
            exit(3);
         }
         do
         {
            if (pipebuf=='\r') cout<<'\n'; else cout<<pipebuf;
         } while (ReadFile(pipe,&pipebuf,1,&inlen,&over));
         DWORD err=GetLastError();
         if (err!=ERROR_IO_PENDING)
         {
            cerr<<"Error reading pipe\n";
            exit(3);
         }
         cout.flush();
      }
   }
}
```

Using AccessCheck

What if you want to check for a particular access right in an ACL yourself? For example, you might have private data you want to protect. The answer is to use **AccessCheck**. In theory, this is a simple call: Tell **AccessCheck** who's asking, what they're asking for, and which ACL you want to check against. **AccessCheck** answers yes or no, depending on what it finds in the ACL.

In practice, this call is fairly difficult to use. First, you can't pass in a real security token. Instead, you must use an impersonation token (even if that means calling **ImpersonateSelf**). Next, you can't ask for any of the generic access rights (like **GENERIC_READ** or **GENERIC_ALL**), because those bits don't really mean anything—they map to other bits.

If you have a table that maps generic rights to specific ones, you can call **MapGenericMask** to convert generic rights into real ones. This call uses the **GENERIC_MAPPING** structure, which simply has fields for each generic access right (**GenericRead**, **GenericWrite**, **GenericExecute**, and **GenericAll**). These fields store the actual right bits for each generic case.

In practice, you won't use **AccessCheck** very often, because for system objects, calls you make either succeed or fail with little intervention from you. However, if you're writing a server that wants to protect data, you'll call **AccessCheck**. You'll also want to create a private security object.

Private Security

For those cases where Windows doesn't protect something but you need to subject it to security, you can use a private security object. This isn't very hard to do: You'll simply call **CreatePrivateObjectSecurity** and receive a new security descriptor.

What's in this new descriptor? The new descriptor can inherit rights from the object's parent (like a parent directory), from another descriptor that you specify, or from the process' default security. Of course, it's up to you to specify the parent object, the creating process, or the descriptor, because Windows has no opinions about this private object. You also have to specify the **GENERIC_MAPPING** structure to help Windows convert generic rights to specific rights.

Once you have the descriptor from **CreatePrivateObjectSecurity**, you can call **AccessCheck** with it to validate a particular user's access rights. You'll find an example in Listing 8.2.

The code in Listing 8.2 returns a database record. Usually, you'd think of this program as being part of a server, but for simplicity, it's just a function call. The main code requests data by record number. The private object is set up so that guests can't see the data at all. It also grants a custom right (**2**) to those in the MANAGER group so they can see the payroll data. Everyone else just has right **1**, which causes the payroll data to show up as asterisks. When the program no longer needs the private object, it calls **DestroyPrivateObjectSecurity**.

Listing 8.2 Private security.

```
#include <windows.h>
#include <iostream.h>

// Custom rights
#define DB_ACCESS_ALL 3
#define DB_ACCESS_PAY 2
```

```
#define DB_ACCESS_INFO 1

// Single "database" record
struct record
{
  char name[32];
  char phone[32];
  char wage[32];
} rec = { "Nick Rivers", "555-1212", "$32/hour" };


void err(char *s)
{
    cerr<<s<<" "<<GetLastError();
    exit(1);
}

HANDLE getMyToken()
{
  HANDLE rv;
  if (!ImpersonateSelf(SecurityImpersonation))
    err("Can't impersonate");
  if (!OpenThreadToken(GetCurrentThread(),TOKEN_ALL_ACCESS,FALSE,&rv))
    err("Token error");
  return rv;
}

GENERIC_MAPPING mapping= { 1, 0, 3, 3 };

void AcctToSID(char *name,PSID sid,DWORD siz)
{
    char dom[64];
    SID_NAME_USE use;
    DWORD domsiz=sizeof(dom);
    if (!LookupAccountName(NULL,name,sid,&siz,dom,&domsiz,&use))
        err("Name lookup error");
}

void createACL(PACL acl,DWORD asiz)
{
   BYTE everyone[512];
   BYTE admin[512];
   BYTE guests[512];



   if (!InitializeAcl(acl,asiz,ACL_REVISION))
```

```
        err("Can't init ACL");
// find group names
    AcctToSID("Everyone",(PSID)everyone,sizeof(everyone));
    AcctToSID("Administrators",(PSID)admin,sizeof(admin));
    AcctToSID("Guests",(PSID)guests,sizeof(guests));
// Add rights
    if (!AddAccessDeniedAce(acl,ACL_REVISION,GENERIC_ALL,(PSID)guests))
        err("Can't set Guests rights");
    if (!AddAccessAllowedAce(acl,ACL_REVISION,3,(PSID)admin))
        err("Can't set admin rights");
    if (!AddAccessAllowedAce(acl,ACL_REVISION,1,(PSID)everyone))
        err("Can't set everyone rights");


}

void buildSecurityObject(PSECURITY_DESCRIPTOR *privsd,HANDLE token)
{
    SECURITY_DESCRIPTOR sd;
    BYTE aclbuf[1024];

    if (!InitializeSecurityDescriptor(&sd,SECURITY_DESCRIPTOR_REVISION))
        err("Can't init SD");



    // Create Dacl
    createACL((PACL)aclbuf,sizeof(aclbuf));

    if (!SetSecurityDescriptorDacl(&sd,TRUE,(PACL)aclbuf,NULL)) // set DACL
        err("Can't set DACL");

    if (!CreatePrivateObjectSecurity(NULL,&sd,privsd,FALSE,token,&mapping))
        err("Can't create private SD");
}

record getRecord()
{
    BOOL accessallowed;
    PSECURITY_DESCRIPTOR privsd=NULL;
    HANDLE token;
    PRIVILEGE_SET pset;
    DWORD len;
    DWORD amask;
    record rv;
```

```
   token=getMyToken();

// get ready to return data
   strcpy(rv.name,rec.name);
   strcpy(rv.phone,rec.phone);

// Let's see if this guy has access
   buildSecurityObject(&privsd,token);

   len=sizeof(pset);
   if (!AccessCheck(privsd,token,DB_ACCESS_ALL,&mapping,&pset,&len,&amask,
        &accessallowed)||!accessallowed)
      if
(!AccessCheck(privsd,token,DB_ACCESS_INFO,&mapping,&pset,&len,&amask,
           &accessallowed)||!accessallowed)
      {
         DWORD errnum=GetLastError();
         if (errnum!=5&&errnum!=0)
       {
           cerr<<GetLastError()<<"\n";
       }

// no access granted at all
       strcpy(rv.name,"********* NOT ALLOWED *********");
       strcpy(rv.phone,rv.name);
       strcpy(rv.wage,rv.name);
       accessallowed=FALSE; // in case error caused this
      }
   if (accessallowed&&(amask&2)==0)
       strcpy(rv.wage,"******************************");
   else if (accessallowed)
       strcpy(rv.wage,rec.wage);
   if (privsd) DestroyPrivateObjectSecurity(&privsd);
   return rv;
}

void main(int argc,char *argv[])
{
    record r=getRecord();
    cout<<r.name<<"\n"<<r.phone<<"\n"<<r.wage<<"\n";

}
```

Privileges

Usually, privileges are less interesting to programmers than rights. However, for completeness, you should know that the system identifies privileges with a locally unique identifier (LUID). You can convert between privilege names and LUIDs using the **LookupPrivilegeValue**, **LookupPrivilegeName**, and **LookupPrivilegeDisplayName** functions.

Once you know the LUIDs for particular privileges, you can call **AdjustTokenPrivileges** to enable or disable a process' privileges (you can't, however, add new privileges). The **GetTokenInformation** call can provide information on existing privileges. The **SetTokenPrivileges** sets only the default ACL, the owner, or the default group for a process.

Kerberos

Windows 2000 supports the same Kerberos security system that many other operating systems provide (Internet RFC 1510 spells out the exact requirements). Kerberos is a method that allows a secure Key Distribution Center (KDC) to track all users and passwords. Only the KDC and the user know the actual passwords.

When a Kerberos application wants to use a Kerberos-aware server, it asks the KDC for a ticket. The KDC issues tickets only to users who have correct passwords. The application then sends the ticket (not its password) to the server it wants to access. The server calls the KDC to validate the ticket.

The KDC is like a bank, in a way, and tickets are like ATM cards. When you pay for something with an ATM card, you assume that the bank will deduct only what you owe for the transaction, and the merchant assumes the bank will really deduct the money. In other words, both parties trust the bank. You wouldn't tell the gas station attendant: "Here's my ATM card and password. Run it through, and I'll be right back." Nor would the gas station allow you to enter your purchase price without knowing what you were doing.

Kerberos is much the same. The user doesn't want to give some unknown server the password. But the server doesn't want to let the user in without one. But because they both trust the KDC, it's possible for both parties to do business.

Starting with Windows 2000, Kerberos is integrated with normal Windows security. When you log in to a domain, you receive a Kerberos ticket. The normal security checks take Kerberos into account. From a programmer's point of view, nothing could be easier. The encrypted data in the Kerberos ticket is the Windows SIDs that specify the user's identity and the associated group memberships. Windows can use this data in the ticket to determine access rights and privileges.

Summary

Security isn't usually very important for most programs. However, if you're creating shared resources or acting as a server in some other way, you'll need to at least think about security and how it will affect you.

The security API lacks convenience. It's tedious to build ACLs and keep all the data structures straight. Building user interfaces to let users maintain ACLs is even worse. Of course, for files—the most common objects of interest—you don't need to do much, because the system handles files entirely.

Immediate Solutions

Learning An Object's Owner

Occasionally it's important to know who owns an object. If you're the administrator (or have similar privileges), it can be important to assume ownership of an object, too, because the object's owner can change the security on the object. In other words, if you own a file, and it's marked read-only, you can change the ACL so that you can write to it as well—but only because you're the owner (or you've become the owner).

Finding the security descriptor requires a call that depends on the type of object. For example, for a file, you can call **GetFileSecurity** (see Table 8.4 for a representative list). The simple console program in Listing 8.3 determines the owner of a file whose name you provide on the command line.

Listing 8.3 File ownership.

```
#include <iostream.h>
#include <windows.h>

void err(char *s)
{
    cerr<<s<<" "<<GetLastError();
    exit(1);
}

void main(int argc, char *argv[])
{
  SECURITY_DESCRIPTOR *sd;
  DWORD sdsiz=256;
  DWORD siz;
  SID *sid;
  BOOL def;
  char acct[256];
  DWORD acctsiz=sizeof(acct);
  char dom[256];
  DWORD domsiz=sizeof(dom);
  SID_NAME_USE use;
```

```
  sd=(SECURITY_DESCRIPTOR *)malloc(256);
// error 122 means you don't have a big enough buffer
  if (!GetFileSecurity(argv[1],
    OWNER_SECURITY_INFORMATION|GROUP_SECURITY_INFORMATION,
    sd,
    256,
    &siz)) err("GetFileSecurity Error");
  if (!GetSecurityDescriptorOwner(sd,(void **)&sid,&def))
      err("GetSecurityDescriptorOwner Error");
  if (!LookupAccountSid(NULL,sid,acct,&acctsiz,dom,&domsiz,&use))
      err("LookupAccountSid Error");
  cout<<"Owner is "<<acct<<"\n";
  cout<<"Domain is "<<dom<<"\n";


  exit(0);
}
```

As you can see, the program really only consists of three calls: **GetFileSecurity** retrieves the security descriptor, **GetSecurityDescriptorOwner** finds the SID of the owner, and **LookupAccountSid** converts the SID into a legible name.

You can also use similar functions to pick apart the other fields in a descriptor. For example, **GetSecurityDescriptorGroup** and **GetSecurityDescriportDacl** are just two of the calls you can use.

Of course, you can reverse the whole process and call **SetFileSecurity** to change the owner of a file.

Converting A SID To A Name

If you have a SID, you can easily find out the name associated with it by calling **LookupAccountSid**. This call takes seven arguments: the name of the machine of interest, the SID, two character buffers for outputs, the lengths of those buffers, and an output variable that tells you what kind of SID you have. The output buffers will contain the user's name and the user's primary domain.

You can find an example of calling **LookupAccountSid** in Listing 8.3. This program retrieves a file's owner using **GetFileSecurity** and **GetSecurityDescriptorOwner**. It returns the owner's SID, and **LookupAccountSid** converts it into a name for display purposes.

Converting A Name To A SID

Converting a name to a SID is almost as easy as converting the other way around: You simply call **LookupAccountName**. This call basically takes the same arguments as **LookupAccountSid** (see the previous topic). The only difference is that for this call the SID is an output (with an associated length), and the account name is an input. Remember, the name may be a username or a group name.

You can find an example of calling **LookupAccountName** in the LOOKUP example program (see Listing 8.2). This program builds an ACL, and therefore needs the SIDs for several groups.

Creating A Descriptor

Security descriptors contain information about a secured object. This information includes the object's owner, the object's DACL, the object's SACL, and the owner's primary group. The DACL controls what access is allowed for particular users (and groups of users). The SACL determines what actions generate log entries for the system administrator to review.

The descriptor also contains information about the descriptor itself. For example, in Windows 2000, you can mark a descriptor to cause the ACLs to automatically propagate ACEs to child descriptors (this feature isn't available in NT 4 and earlier).

When you create a security descriptor, you'll usually call **InitializeSecurityDescriptor**. This function sets up the descriptor to be essentially empty. It also makes the descriptor absolute. Absolute descriptors contain pointers to other data within the descriptor, and that's what most functions want. However, if you want to write a descriptor out to a file or otherwise move it, you can't expect the pointers to remain valid. For those cases, you'll want to convert to a self-relative descriptor (see the next topic).

Once you have a descriptor, it's fairly simple to set its various members by calling functions like **SetSecurityDescriptorDacl** and **SetSecurityDescriptorGroup**. You can find examples in Listing 8.1 (the TALK example program).

Converting Between Absolute And Self-Relative Descriptors

If you have an absolute security descriptor (which is usually what you want), you may have occasion to convert it to self-relative form. This conversion changes all the pointers in the structure into offsets from the beginning of the descriptor, making the descriptor suitable for writing to a file or any other place you want to store it.

To convert a descriptor to self-relative form, call **MakeSelfRelativeSD**. You can also call **MakeAbsoluteSD** to reverse the process, although you have to provide many arguments that indicate where you want the portions of the descriptor to reside.

Using The Default Security Descriptor

Usually, you pass a **NULL** to calls that expect a security descriptor. The documentation tells you that **NULL** gives you the default descriptor. What does that mean, exactly?

Well, the answer depends on what object you create. For example, consider what happens when you create a file without specifying a security descriptor. Not surprisingly, the new file inherits the security settings of its parent directory. Registry keys, which have a similar organization to the file system, behave the same way.

Synchronization objects and other kernel objects (such as file mappings) don't have any parent to inherit from. In this case, Windows creates the object with a **NULL** ACL, which effectively allows anyone to do anything to the object.

Some things resemble file handles (like mailslots or named pipes) but don't have real parent directories. You'd think they would be similar to synchronization objects, but they aren't. Instead, these receive the default ACL from your login SID. The default ACL grants all access to you and other members of your group. Other users have no access.

Using A Universal Security Descriptor

What happens if you want to make a named pipe, or other similar object, that's universally accessible? You need to create a security descriptor with a **NULL** discretionary ACL. Here's an example of setting a named pipe's descriptor to have a **NULL** ACL, thereby allowing everyone access to the pipe:

```
SECURITY_ATTRIBUTES sa;
SECURITY_DESCRIPTOR sd;

sa.nLength=sizeof(sa);
sa.bInheritHandle=TRUE;  // or whatever you like

InitalizeSecurityDescriptor(&sd,SECURITY_DESCRIPTOR_REVISION);
SetSecurityDescriptorDacl(&sd,TRUE,NULL,FALSE);
sa.lpSecurityDescriptor=&sd;
rv=CreateNamedPipe("\\\\.\\pipe\\talkpipe_awc",
  PIPE_ACCESS_DUPLEX|FILE_FLAG_OVERLAPPED,
  PIPE_TYPE_BYTE|PIPE_READMODE_BYTE,1,1024,1024,1000,&sa);
```

Using A Specific Security Descriptor

Creating a more specific descriptor requires a bit more work. You need to initialize the descriptor (just like in the previous example), but you also need to create an ACL to insert into the descriptor.

Creating an ACL requires several steps. First, you call **InitializeAcl** to set the ACL's data structures to their default values. Then you need to deny and grant rights to users and groups. To do this, you call **AddAccessDeniedAce** and **AddAccessAllowedAce** with the correct SIDs and the rights affected. These calls add access control elements (ACEs) to the ACL. The SIDs, of course, specify which users or groups you want to affect.

In NT 4 and earlier, you should make sure that all calls to **AddAccessDeniedAce** precede any calls to **AddAccessAllowedAce**. Doing so ensures that the system obeys the proper semantics when searching the ACL.

Armed with an ACL that describes who can and can't access the file, it's a simple matter to call **SetSecurityDescriptorDacl** to set the descriptor's ACL. You can pass this descriptor to a call that creates an object, and that object will respect your ACL. You'll find an example of this in the TALK and LOOKUP samples (Listings 8.1 and 8.2).

Using Private Security

Sometimes you want to secure an object that the system doesn't know about (a database field, for example). Windows allows you to create a private security object (using **CreatePrivateSecurityObject**). This object is like any other secure object, but it has no meaning to the operating system. You can call **AccessCheck** to determine if a program has the requested access to your private object.

Using private security is moderately difficult, but you won't have to do it very often. You'll find an example of using private security to protect a database field in the main portion of this chapter (see Listing 8.2).

Chapter 9

Registry And Logging

If you need an immediate solution to:	*See page:*
Opening A Registry Key	412
Finding Subkeys	412
Finding Values	412
Using The Registry Instead Of INI Files	413
Creating REG Files	414
Creating INF Files	415
Creating A Message DLL	416
Registering A Message DLL	416
Logging Events	417
Converting Errors To Messages	418

In Depth

You may have noticed that two things are really simple: things that are truly simple, and things that are incredibly complex. Think about travelling over water. I suspect the first sailor was probably a caveman. By accident, or perhaps on purpose, he grabbed a log and floated downstream. How simple can you get?

Next thing you know, our nautical caveman lashed a few logs together so he and his possessions didn't get wet. A great idea, and still pretty simple. Of course, soon he wanted to go upstream on the water, too. So he adds an oar—then a rudder.

Things get progressively more complicated. When the sailors get tired of rowing, they invent the sail, pulleys, and windlasses. It takes a good bit of knowledge to handle a boat under sail effectively not to mention navigate.

Then things become even more involved—and, paradoxically, easier to use. Motors of various kinds made boats independent of wind and muscle power (although not fuel). Navigational aids allow you to navigate with practically no knowledge of the stars or higher mathematics. Autopilots let even giant ships run with a very small crew.

Eventually, you can imagine boarding a ship, telling it where you want to go, and being taken there automatically. What could be simpler than that? Of course, the technology behind that simple ship is not itself simple.

Technology leads to problems when things don't work. You might argue that our hypothetical automated ship is even simpler than the caveman's log to use. But when the caveman saw his log rotting, he knew how to fix it. If your robotic boat stalls in the middle of the ocean, what will you do? It's probably too complex for the average passenger to fix.

PCs have a similar evolution. There wasn't much to early computing devices like slide rules (the computer analog to a tree trunk in the water). But things rapidly got more complicated. Adding machines were a mechanical nightmare, and some of my early computers required you to punch in arcane hex or binary codes with switches to run any programs.

Sure, it took some skill to set up and use, say, an MS-DOS system. However, most people learned quickly that the autoexec.bat and config.sys files were the keys to managing the system. A bit complicated, but not as bad as manually entering boot loaders in hex. If something went wrong, you had a pretty good idea where to look.

Most people would agree that Windows 3.x was simpler for most users to operate than MS-DOS. However, when something went wrong, there were many more places to search for the problem. In particular, a myriad of INI files contained vital system information.

Windows 2000, Windows NT, and Windows 95 began phasing out INI files, however, in favor of the system Registry. The system Registry is a centralized repository that contains configuration data for the operating system and other applications.

Luckily, the Registry isn't hard to use in programs (although it isn't as easy to use as INI files). The Registry database resembles a file system with directories (keys) and files (values). You use special APIs to create, manipulate, and destroy these items. If you can navigate the hard disk on your computer, you can learn to use the Registry.

This chapter will show you how to manipulate the Registry via user-level tools and programming APIs. You'll also see a bit about what the Registry contains.

Give Up INI Files?

Giving up INI files causes most programmers to experience a slight panic. INI files are friendly. They're easy to use, easy to modify, and well understood. However, INI files have a few limitations:

- INI files can't exceed 64K on some platforms.
- Adding entries to win.ini and system.ini quickly clutters those files and may push them past 64K.
- Accessing a large INI file can be slow, because Windows performs a linear search for the item. So, even systems that could support large INI files shouldn't do so.
- INI files aren't easily protected or remotely administered over a network.
- Data in INI files is untyped—you must store the data as a string and convert it in your program.

The Registry addresses all of these problems. In essence, it's a hierarchical database. You access a key and obtain its values. Keys may have subkeys as well as values. This arrangement is very similar to the file system—think of a key as a directory and values as files. The Registry has been around for a while. Most programs didn't use it until recently, however. Traditionally, only OLE programs and the old Program Manager used the Registry. Now, however, most new Windows features (the advanced shell, ActiveX, and so on) rely on it.

Have INI files gone away? No, not at all. You can still use the INI file calls if you like. However, to interact with the shell, get Windows logo compliance, or be a good Win32 citizen, you'll want to use the Registry. Also, an administrator may set the system so that when you think you're using an INI file, you're really using the Registry (see the Immediate Solutions). Once you use the Registry a few times, you'll find that it's an improvement over INI files.

The Registry: Up Close And Personal

Figures 9.1 and 9.2 show the Registry editors you can use with Windows 2000. REGEDIT is the same as the standard Windows 95 Registry editor of the same name. REGEDT32 is the NT/Windows 2000 version that understands key security. As you can see, the Registry resembles a file system with folders and files. The root of this pseudo file system contains several items: HKEY_CLASSES_ROOT, HKEY_CURRENT_USER, HKEY_LOCAL_MACHINE, HKEY_USERS, and HKEY_CURRENT_CONFIG. These items loosely segregate the various entries in broad categories.

Suppose you want to work with a value called PATH in the HKEY_CURRENT_USER\SOFTWARE\AWC\REALFAST\1.0 key. You have several choices. The best plan is to open the HKEY_CURRENT_USER\SOFTWARE\ AWC\REALFAST\1.0 key and then modify the PATH subkey. However, you could simply open the

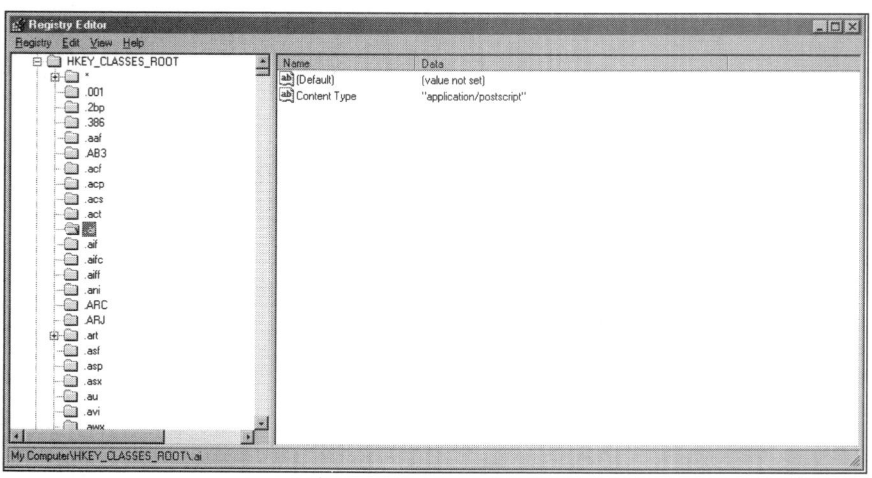

Figure 9.1 The Windows REGEDIT program.

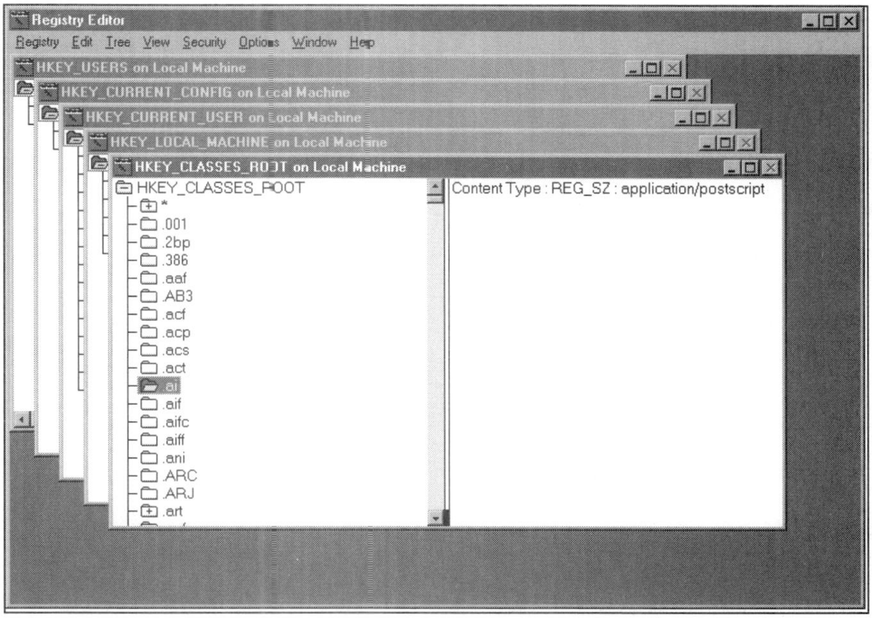

Figure 9.2 The REGEDT32 program.

HKEY_CURRENT_USER key and work with the SOFTWARE\AWC\REALFAST\1.0 subkey. However, you may have security issues with the last method, so it's best to open the most specific key possible.

You'll use an **HKEY** variable (key handle) to refer to an open Registry key. You can obtain an **HKEY** with **RegOpenKeyEx** or **RegCreateKeyEx** (see Table 9.1 for a list of Registry-related calls). These calls present a chicken and egg problem: The first argument required is an **HKEY**! However, you can use a constant to refer to any of the root entries (like HKEY_CLASSES_ROOT). For example, you might write:

```
HKEY key;
RegCreateKeyEx(HKEY_CURRENT_USER,
  "SOFTWARE\AWC\REALFAST\1.0",0,
  NULL,REG_OPTION_NON_VOLATILE,
  KEY_ALL_ACCESS,NULL,&key,NULL);
```

Once you have an open key, you can read a value (**RegQueryValueEx**), change the value (**RegSetValueEx**), delete the key (**RegDeleteKey**), or enumerate the subkeys (**RegEnumKeyEx**). You can also enumerate all of the named values for a given key (**RegQueryValue**). Once you're done, you need to close the open **HKEY** using **RegCloseKey**. Table 9.1 shows the details of Registry-related calls.

Table 9.1 Selected Registry calls.

Function	Description
RegCloseKey	Closes an open Registry key
RegConnectRegistry	Connects to a remote Registry
RegCreateKeyEx	Creates a new subkey
RegDeleteKey	Deletes a key
RegDeleteValue	Deletes a value
RegEnumKeyEx	Enumerates subkeys (returns a different key on each call)
RegEnumValue	Enumerates values (returns a different value on each call)
RegFlushKey	Flushes (write) key values (required only if you demand immediate update)
RegLoadKey	Loads a key from a special file (see RegSaveKey)
RegOpenKeyEx	Opens a key
RegQueryInfoKey	Queries key information
RegQueryValueEx	Reads a value
RegReplaceKey	Replaces a key after a system restart
RegSaveKey	Saves a key to a file
RegSetKeySecurity	Sets key security
RegSetValueEx	Sets a value
RegUnloadKey	Unloads a set of entries

Windows 2000 includes advanced security features to protect portions of the Registry (see Chapter 8). A particular program may not have access rights to work with every Registry key on the system.

Registry Oddities

A few things about the Registry don't work the way you'd expect. Here, in no particular order, are the unusual things I've noticed.

RegEnumValue

RegEnumValue has a peculiar property. The documentation says that this function walks through the values for a particular key. If the key has only a default value, the function returns it. However, if the key has non-default values, this function will return them, but not the default value. That means if you want to be sure to get all the values, you'll need to get the default value explicitly (**RegQueryValue**) and then enumerate. If you retrieve the default value during enumeration (it will have an empty string as its name), just discard it.

RegDeleteKey

If you attempt to delete a key that has subkeys under Windows 2000, the **RegDeleteKey** call will fail. Under Windows 95 and 98 the call succeeds and wipes out the key and all subkeys. This result can be very dangerous. In particular, you can get into lots of trouble under Windows 95 with code like this:

```
char subkey[100];
GetSubKeyName(subkey); // this fails—subkey is NULL
RegDeleteKey(HKEY_CLASSES_ROOT,subkey);
// if subkey is NULL, the entire HKEY_CLASSES_ROOT
// branch is now gone!
```

Error Returns

Don't depend on **GetLastError** to check for error values from the Registry functions. These functions all return the error code directly. Calling **GetLastError** will simply return whatever error some other API call generated earlier in your program.

Typed Data

If you browse the help files, you'll see that the Registry can contain many exotic data types (see Table 9.2). The system doesn't pay attention to these types in any real way. For example, the **REG_EXPAND_SZ** type is for strings that should have environment variables expanded in-line. Don't think that the Registry will do this expansion for you. The flag implies that you should do the expansion yourself (use the Win32 function **ExpandEnvironmentStrings**).

There are a few exceptions. For example, Windows 95 and 98 will add a terminating zero to a **REG_SZ** string if you forget to do it. Windows 2000, however, won't add the zero. Neither system adds the extra **NULL** to **REG_MULTI_SZ** or **REG_EXPAND_SZ** types.

Table 9.2 Registry data types.

Type	Description
REG_BINARY	Binary data in any form
REG_DWORD	A 32-bit number (often used to hold a byte, a word, or even a bit)
REG_DWORD_LITTLE_ENDIAN	A 32-bit number in Intel-style format
REG_DWORD_BIG_ENDIAN	A 32-bit number in Motorola-style format
REG_EXPAND_SZ	A null-terminated string that contains unexpanded references to environment variables (for example, "%PATH%")

(continued)

***Table 9.2 Registry data types* (continued).**

Type	Description
REG_LINK	A Unicode symbolic link
REG_MULTI_SZ	An array of null-terminated strings, terminated by two null characters
REG_NONE	No defined value type
REG_RESOURCE_LIST	A device-driver resource list
REG_SZ	A null-terminated string

MFC Program Example

Figure 9.3 shows a simple MFC program that manipulates the Registry (REGDEMO). You can create a new key, delete keys, and view the keys and values that are present. Be careful when deleting keys, especially if you're running Windows 95 or 98. When you start the program, it may take a minute to read and sort every key in the Registry.

Because this code is just for illustration, I took a few shortcuts with the user interface. You'll notice each key's default value appears after it (preceded by an equal sign). This arrangement can cause strange behavior if a key or value has an equal sign in it already. In practice, this behavior doesn't seem to be a problem. If you want to view a key's values, delete the key, or create a new subkey, just double-click on the line you want to alter. A dialog box will appear that shows the values and allows you to delete the key or create a new subkey. The program doesn't let you alter or add values (such functionality would be easy to add, and a worthwhile exercise if you'd like to try your hand at some Registry programming). If you really need to modify the Registry, just use REGEDIT or REGEDT32.

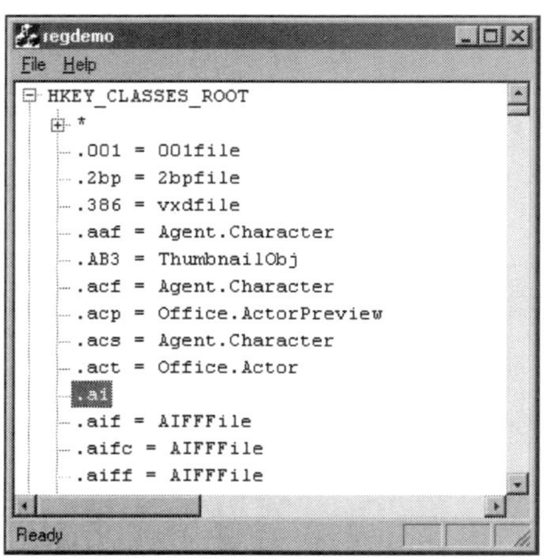

Figure 9.3 REGDEMO.

The code in Listing 9.1 shows the highlights of the Registry manipulation code. Of course, a great deal of code on the CD handles the user interface of the program. The functions you'll want to examine are all in RegDemoView.cpp (Listing 9.1). Look closely at **DoUpdateRegView**. This function opens each top-level key, one at a time. It then inserts a text string to represent the key into the tree view. Next, it calls **InsertReg**. This function recursively adds each subkey to the tree. Finally, the program closes the top-level key before moving on to the next root key. **InsertReg** examines the key passed in by the caller and enumerates each subkey. It adds the key (and its value) to the tree and then calls itself to add the new key's subkeys.

The only other interesting function (concerning the Registry, anyway) is **OnDblClick**. As you might expect, this function executes when the user double-clicks on an entry. Don't be distracted by the **FindFullKey** function—it simply pulls the names back out of the tree view. The action occurs when the call to **DoModal** returns. If the user decided to delete or create (you can tell by the **m_cmd** variable), the code takes the appropriate action.

Listing 9.1 RegDemoView.cpp.

```
// regdemoView.cpp : implementation of the CRegdemoView class
//

#include "stdafx.h"
#include "regdemo.h"
#include "winreg.h"
#include "regdialog.h"
#include "waitdlg.h"
#include "promptdlg.h"

#include "regdemoDoc.h"
#include "regdemoView.h"

#ifdef _DEBUG
#define new DEBUG_NEW
#undef THIS_FILE
static char THIS_FILE[] = __FILE__;
#endif

//////////////////////////////////////
// CRegdemoView

IMPLEMENT_DYNCREATE(CRegdemoView, CTreeView)

BEGIN_MESSAGE_MAP(CRegdemoView, CTreeView)
   //{{AFX_MSG_MAP(CRegdemoView)
```

```
   ON_NOTIFY_REFLECT(NM_DBLCLK, OnDblclk)
   //}}AFX_MSG_MAP
// Standard printing commands
ON_COMMAND(ID_FILE_PRINT, CTreeView::OnFilePrint)
ON_COMMAND(ID_FILE_PRINT_DIRECT, CTreeView::OnFilePrint)
ON_COMMAND(ID_FILE_PRINT_PREVIEW, CTreeView::OnFilePrintPreview)
END_MESSAGE_MAP()

//////////////////////////////////////
// CRegdemoView construction/destruction

CRegdemoView::CRegdemoView()
   {
   // TODO: add construction code here

   }

CRegdemoView::~CRegdemoView()
   {
   }

BOOL CRegdemoView::PreCreateWindow(CREATESTRUCT& cs)
   {
   // TODO: Modify the Window class or
   //  styles here by modifying the CREATESTRUCT cs

   return CTreeView::PreCreateWindow(cs);
   }

//////////////////////////////////////
// CRegdemoView drawing

void CRegdemoView::OnDraw(CDC* pDC)
   {
   CRegdemoDoc* pDoc = GetDocument();
   ASSERT_VALID(pDoc);

   // TODO: add draw code for native data here
   }

void CRegdemoView::OnInitialUpdate()
   {
   CTreeView::OnInitialUpdate();
   fixedfont.CreatePointFont(100,"Courier New");
   GetTreeCtrl().SetFont(&fixedfont);
```

```
    GetTreeCtrl().ModifyStyle(0,
        TVS_HASLINES|TVS_LINESATROOT|TVS_HASBUTTONS,0);
    UpdateRegView();
    }

/////////////////////////////////////////////
// CRegdemoView printing

BOOL CRegdemoView::OnPreparePrinting(CPrintInfo* pInfo)
    {
    // default preparation
    return DoPreparePrinting(pInfo);
    }

void CRegdemoView::OnBeginPrinting(CDC*, CPrintInfo*)
    {

    }

void CRegdemoView::OnEndPrinting(CDC*, CPrintInfo*)
    {
    // TODO: add cleanup after printing
    }

/////////////////////////////////////////////
// CRegdemoView diagnostics

#ifdef _DEBUG
void CRegdemoView::AssertValid() const
    {
    CTreeView::AssertValid();
    }

void CRegdemoView::Dump(CDumpContext& dc) const
    {
    CTreeView::Dump(dc);
    }

// non-debug version is inline
CRegdemoDoc* CRegdemoView::GetDocument()
    {
    ASSERT(m_pDocument->IsKindOf(
        RUNTIME_CLASS(CRegdemoDoc)));
    return (CRegdemoDoc*)m_pDocument;
    }
```

```
#endif //_DEBUG

////////////////////////////////////////
// CRegdemoView message handlers

void CRegdemoView::UpdateRegView(LPCSTR s)
   {
   CWaitDlg dlg;
   if (s) dlg.message=s;
   dlg.Create(CWaitDlg::IDD);  // create wait dialog
   DoUpdateRegView();          // update view
   dlg.DestroyWindow();        // kill wait dialog
   }

void CRegdemoView::DoUpdateRegView()
   {
   HKEY root;
   CTreeCtrl &tree=GetTreeCtrl();
   HTREEITEM parent;
   // Kill everything already there
   tree.DeleteAllItems();

   // Start with HKEY_CLASSES_ROOT
   if (RegOpenKeyEx(HKEY_CLASSES_ROOT,NULL,0,
      KEY_READ,&root)!=ERROR_SUCCESS)
   return;
   // Insert string to represent the root key
   parent=tree.InsertItem("HKEY_CLASSES_ROOT",
     TVI_ROOT,TVI_LAST);
   tree.SetItem(parent,TVIF_PARAM,NULL,0,0,0,0,
      (LPARAM)HKEY_CLASSES_ROOT);

   // Recursively add subkeys
   InsertReg(root,tree,parent,TVI_LAST);
   tree.SortChildren(parent);
   // Finished with key
   RegCloseKey(root);

   // Repeat for other root keys
   if (RegOpenKeyEx(HKEY_CURRENT_USER,NULL,0,
      KEY_READ,&root)!=ERROR_SUCCESS)
   return;
   parent=tree.InsertItem("HKEY_CURRENT_USER",
     TVI_ROOT,TVI_LAST);
   tree.SetItem(parent,TVIF_PARAM,NULL,0,0,0,0,
```

```
        (LPARAM)HKEY_CURRENT_USER);
    InsertReg(root,tree,parent,TVI_LAST);
    tree.SortChildren(parent);
    RegCloseKey(root);
    if (RegOpenKeyEx(HKEY_LOCAL_MACHINE,NULL,0,
        KEY_READ,&root)!=ERROR_SUCCESS)
    return;
    parent=tree.InsertItem("HKEY_LOCAL_MACHINE",
      TVI_ROOT,TVI_LAST);
    tree.SetItem(parent,TVIF_PARAM,NULL,0,0,0,0,
        (LPARAM)HKEY_LOCAL_MACHINE);
    InsertReg(root,tree,parent,TVI_LAST);
    tree.SortChildren(parent);
    RegCloseKey(root);
    if (RegOpenKeyEx(HKEY_USERS,NULL,0,
        KEY_READ,&root)!=ERROR_SUCCESS)
    return;
    parent=tree.InsertItem("HKEY_USERS",TVI_ROOT,TVI_LAST);
    tree.SetItem(parent,TVIF_PARAM,NULL,
        0,0,0,0,(LPARAM)HKEY_USERS);
    InsertReg(root,tree,parent,TVI_LAST);
    tree.SortChildren(parent);
    RegCloseKey(root);

    }

void CRegdemoView::InsertReg(HKEY key,CTreeCtrl &tree,
    HTREEITEM parent,HTREEITEM last)
    {
    int i=0;
    char subkeyname[1024];
    HTREEITEM nextparent;
    HKEY nextkey;
    DWORD siz;
    while (1)
        {
        // Enumerate each subkey
        siz=sizeof(subkeyname);
        if (RegEnumKeyEx(key,i,subkeyname,&siz,NULL,
            NULL,NULL,NULL)!=ERROR_SUCCESS)
        break;
        i++;
        if (RegOpenKeyEx(key,subkeyname,0,KEY_READ,
            &nextkey)==ERROR_SUCCESS)
            {
```

9. Registry And Logging

```
            char val[256];
            DWORD type,siz=sizeof(val);
            // Ask key for default value
            if (RegQueryValueEx(nextkey,NULL,NULL,&type,
               (BYTE *)val,&siz)==ERROR_SUCCESS)
               {
               if (siz&&*val)
                  {
                  strcat(subkeyname," = ");
// no need to check type because default key is always string
                  strcat(subkeyname,val);
                  }
               }
            nextparent=tree.InsertItem(subkeyname,parent,TVI_LAST);
            InsertReg(nextkey,tree,nextparent,TVI_LAST);
            RegCloseKey(nextkey);
            }
      }
   }



void CRegdemoView::OnDblclk(NMHDR* pNMHDR, LRESULT* pResult)
   {
   // Find full name of key
   CString name;
   HTREEITEM sel=GetTreeCtrl().GetSelectedItem();
   HKEY rootkey;
   if (FindFullKey(sel,name,rootkey))
      {
      CRegDialog dlg(rootkey,name);

      if (dlg.DoModal()==IDOK)
         {
         CString msg;
         // Windows 95 will delete no matter what
         if (dlg.m_cmd==-1)
            {
            if (RegDeleteKey(rootkey,name)==ERROR_SUCCESS)
               msg="Delete sucessful";
            else
               msg="Delete failed";
            }
         else // create new subkey
            {
```

```
            CPromptDlg pdlg;
            pdlg.Prompt="Enter name of subkey";
            if (pdlg.DoModal()!=IDOK) return;

            msg="Create failed";
            HKEY newroot,newkey;
            if (RegOpenKeyEx(rootkey,name,0,KEY_WRITE,
             &newroot)==ERROR_SUCCESS)
               {
               if (RegCreateKeyEx(newroot,pdlg.Result,0,NULL,
                0,KEY_READ,NULL,&newkey,NULL)==ERROR_SUCCESS)
                  {
                  RegCloseKey(newkey);
                  msg="Create successful";
                  }
               RegCloseKey(newroot);
               }
            }
         UpdateRegView(msg+"\nPlease wait...");
         }
      }

   *pResult = 1;
   }

BOOL CRegdemoView::FindFullKey(HTREEITEM sel,CString &name,
   HKEY &rootkey)
   {
   // This algorithm may break if a
   // key with no value contains an = sign
   CString raw;
   HTREEITEM next;
   CTreeCtrl &tree=GetTreeCtrl();
   TV_ITEM item;
   name="";
   do
      {
      next=tree.GetParentItem(sel);
      if (next)
         {
         int n;
         raw=tree.GetItemText(sel);
         n=raw.ReverseFind('=');
         if (n!=-1)
            name="\\"+raw.Mid(0,n-1)+name;
```

```
         else
            name="\\"+raw+name;
         sel=next;
         }
      } while (next);
   item.mask=TVIF_PARAM;
   item.hItem=sel;
   tree.GetItem(&item);
   rootkey=(HKEY)item.lParam;
   name=(LPCSTR)name+1;
   return TRUE;
   }
```

You'll also find some code concerning values in Listing 9.2 (RegDialog.cpp). The **OnInitDialog** call first generates a readable name for the key. Then it opens the key and enumerates each value. This is a good place to use the debugger to see that default values enumerate only if no other values are present. To prevent confusion, the program itself filters out default values by testing the **val** variable.

Listing 9.2 RegDialog.cpp.

```
// RegDialog.cpp : implementation file
//

#include "stdafx.h"
#include "regdemo.h"
#include "winreg.h"
#include "RegDialog.h"

#ifdef _DEBUG
#define new DEBUG_NEW
#undef THIS_FILE
static char THIS_FILE[] = __FILE__;
#endif

///////////////////////////////////////
// CRegDialog dialog


CRegDialog::CRegDialog(HKEY root,CString &nam,
   CWnd* pParent /*=NULL*/)
: CDialog(CRegDialog::IDD, pParent)
   {
      //{{AFX_DATA_INIT(CRegDialog)
      m_key = _T("");
      //}}AFX_DATA_INIT
```

```
    rootkey=root;
    name=nam;
    }


void CRegDialog::DoDataExchange(CDataExchange* pDX)
    {
    CDialog::DoDataExchange(pDX);
        //{{AFX_DATA_MAP(CRegDialog)
        DDX_Control(pDX, IDC_LIST, m_listbox);
        DDX_Text(pDX, IDC_KEY, m_key);
        //}}AFX_DATA_MAP
    }


BEGIN_MESSAGE_MAP(CRegDialog, CDialog)
    //{{AFX_MSG_MAP(CRegDialog)
    ON_BN_CLICKED(IDC_Create, OnCreate)
    //}}AFX_MSG_MAP
END_MESSAGE_MAP()

/////////////////////////////////////////////////////////////////////
// CRegDialog message handlers


BOOL CRegDialog::OnInitDialog()
    {
    CDialog::OnInitDialog();
    m_key="\\";
    switch ((DWORD)rootkey)
        {
        case (DWORD)HKEY_CLASSES_ROOT:
            m_key+="HKEY_CLASSES_ROOT";
            break;
        case (DWORD)HKEY_LOCAL_MACHINE:
            m_key+="HKEY_LOCAL_MACHINE";
            break;
        case (DWORD)HKEY_CURRENT_USER:
            m_key+="HKEY_CURRENT_USER";
            break;
        case (DWORD)HKEY_USERS:
            m_key+="HKEY_USERS";
            break;
        default:
            m_key+="<<Unknown>>";
```

```
        break;
      }
   m_key+="\\";
   m_key+=name;
   UpdateData(FALSE);

   m_listbox.ResetContent();
   m_listbox.SetTabStops(154);

   //Enumerate all values
   HKEY curkey;
   char val[256],data[1024];
   DWORD siz=sizeof(val),datasiz=sizeof(data),type;
   RegOpenKeyEx(rootkey,name,0,KEY_READ,&curkey);
   for (int i=0;
      RegEnumValue(curkey,i,val,&siz,
        NULL,&type,(BYTE *)data,&datasiz)==ERROR_SUCCESS;
      i++)
      {
      CString lbval;
      CString num;
      if (*val)
         lbval=val;
      else
         continue; // don't show default
      lbval+="\t";
      switch (type)
         {
         case REG_SZ:
            lbval+=data;
            break;
         case REG_DWORD:
            num.Format("0x%08x",*(DWORD *)data);
            lbval+=num;
            break;
         case REG_BINARY:
            lbval+="<Binary data>";
            break;
         default:
            lbval+="<Unknown>";
            break;
         }
     m_listbox.AddString(lbval);
     }
   RegCloseKey(curkey);
```

```
   return TRUE;
   }

void CRegDialog::OnOK()
   {
   m_cmd=-1;
   CDialog::OnOK();
   }

void CRegDialog::OnCreate()
   {
   m_cmd=0;
   CDialog::OnOK();
   }
```

Values have a type flag associated with them. This program checks for **REG_SZ** (strings), **REG_DWORD** (32-bit binary), and **REG_BINARY** (series of bytes). There are other types (see Table 9.2), but the system doesn't actually deal with them. They're for your program to interpret. Default values, by the way, are always **REG_SZ**. This type dates back to when there was no support for multiple values or multiple data types in the Registry.

If you need to get a specific value from the Registry, you can use **RegQuery ValueEx**. Pass a **NULL** value name for the default. You can create new values with **RegSetValueEx** or delete them with **RegDeleteValue**.

Are you wondering why some of these functions have an "Ex" in their name while others don't? Microsoft has changed the Registry in many ways since its first release. All the older calls are there, but you should use the "Ex" call when you program under Win32. Doing so allows you to control issues like security, multiple values, and value data types. In some cases, the calls haven't changed, and you still use the original call (always very confusing when coding late at night).

That's It?

Is that all there is to manipulating the Registry? Yes and no. Physically working with the Registry is just this easy. However, you also need to know what goes where so that other programs (and Windows) can work with the information you provide. The API is like an alphabet. Even if you know all the letters, you can't communicate without words.

You can store data in many standard places in the Registry. For example, you can register a file type so that the shell can display custom icons, context menus, and so forth for your files. Another example is profile information (what you used to store in INI files). You should put your profile information in HKEY_CURRENT_USER\SOFTWARE*company_name\product_name\version_number* if it applies to the current user, or under the HKEY_LOCAL_MACHINE\SOFTWARE*company_name\product_name\version_number* key if it applies to the machine.

What's In There?

So what's actually in the Registry? Lots of things that belong to lots of different programs. Of course, the most important parts are those that Windows uses to control its own configuration.

Unfortunately, there's no one single place that seems to have all the data about everything that might go in the Registry. The Windows Resource Kit contains some of the information, and a variety of books talk about the Registry's contents, but none have everything. Sometimes there's no substitute for a little detective work.

From a programmer's perspective, one of the most interesting things you can do with the Registry is to register file types. Suppose you have a text file (a file with a .txt extension). When you click (or double-click, depending on your system) on the file, what happens? Notepad or some similar program opens the file, right? Also, the file displays an icon different from that of other files. If you ask for the file's properties, the text description also includes the file's type.

All of this is because of certain entries in the system Registry. You can easily create your own file types if you know how. If you want to create ActiveX servers to extend the shell, you can create very sophisticated file types: For example, you might have a word-processing program that marks document icons with their creator's initials. However, for simple static file types, it's easy to create your own types.

Building REG Files

If you need only to add Registry entries or alter existing ones, you can use a REG file (and REGEDIT) to make the necessary changes. A REG file is simply the file format that REGEDIT exports and imports. The files are simple ASCII and you can view and change them with Notepad or any editor. Of course, if you make up your own file, REGEDIT won't know the difference. The only limitation is that you can't use REG files to delete entries from the Registry.

It's quite simple to build a REG file. You simply start with a line that reads **REGEDIT4**. Then you put each key you want to work with in square brackets on a line by itself. After each key, you can put name/value pairs (use the special name "@" for the default value). All names and values (except "@") should be in double quotes. You can find an example in Listing 9.3.

Listing 9.3 A sample REG file.

```
REGEDIT4[HKEY_CLASSES_ROOT\aspfile]"EditFlags"=hex:00,00,01,00@="Active
Server Document"[HKEY_CLASSES_ROOT\aspfile\CLSID]@="{bd70c020-2d24-11d0-
9110-00004c752752}"

[HKEY_CLASSES_ROOT\aspfile\DefaultIcon]
@="E:\\Program Files\\Microsoft FrontPage\\bin\\fpexplor.exe,6"

[HKEY_CLASSES_ROOT\aspfile\shell]

[HKEY_CLASSES_ROOT\aspfile\shell\edit]
@="Edit"

[HKEY_CLASSES_ROOT\aspfile\shell\edit\command]
@="E:\\Program Files\\Microsoft FrontPage\\bin\\fpeditor.exe \"%1\""
```

A few things you should know. At least some versions of REGEDIT fail to process the last line if it doesn't end in a new line. REGEDIT doesn't complain—it simply discards the line. Be sure your REG files have at least one new line at the very end. I usually just insert several blank lines at the bottom to be sure.

Another interesting problem arises with backslashes. REGEDIT requires you to use double backslashes to get a single backslash in value names. However, if you forget and put only one, REGEDIT doesn't complain: It just quietly discards the entire value. Of course, a newer version of REGEDIT may fix this problem and report the error, but I wouldn't wait for it. Be sure to double your backslashes.

Once you have a REG file, how do you import it? The brute-force method is to use the Registry menu in REGEDIT. If you want to automate things from a program or a script file, you can run REGEDIT with the name of the REG file on the command line. This technique has the annoying habit of displaying a dialog box telling you that it performed the import, however. If you don't want to see that dialog box, you can use the **/S** option on the REGEDIT command line.

Another alternative to creating registry entries is the INF file. These files are usually used for installing device drivers. However, you can use them to add and delete registry entries with very little effort.

INF Files

INF files are similar to old-fashioned INI files because they use sections delimited by square brackets. The file must begin with a version section that contains a signature of $CHICAGO$. The **DefaultInstall** section provides instructions to the system installer. There are many things you can ask the installer to do, but the two things of interest here are the **AddReg** and **DelReg** commands. These commands point to user-named sections that specify registry keys to add or delete.

Instead of spelling out the root key names, INF files allow you to use **HKCR** for **HKEY_CLASSES_ROOT**, **HKCU** for **HKEY_CURRENT_USER**, **HKLM** for **HKEY_LOCAL_MACHINE**, and **HKU** for **HKEY_USERS**. You'll find an example INF file in the Immediate Solutions Listing 9.7.

To make the INF file perform its duties, you can right-click on it and select Install from the context menu. This executes the command:

```
C:\WINDOWS\rundll.exe setupx.dll,InstallHinfSection DefaultInstall 132 %1
```

where C is your system drive, and %1 represents the INF file name.

Inside A File Type

All of the entries relating to file types reside in the HKEY_CLASSES_ROOT Registry key. File types aren't the only things in that key, by the way. ActiveX server registration entries are also present under HKEY_CLASSES_ROOT.

The first entry is a subkey that has the same name as the file's extensions (including the dot). The value of this key is a short string that the user never sees. Of course, it needs to be unique, but it can be anything you want. For a text file, here's what my Registry shows:

```
.txt = txtfile
```

This entry doesn't appear very useful at first. However, you'll also find another subkey named txtfile under HKEY_CLASSES_ROOT. It looks like this:

```
txtfile = Text Document
```

This line is the reason that when you ask for the properties of a TXT file, the properties dialog box shows that the file is a "Text Document."

You might wonder why the .txt key doesn't simply supply the string. The reason is simple: There might be more than one extension associated with a particular file type. For example, on my machine, .dic, .exc, .log, .scp, and .wtx all share the txtfile entries.

When you click (or double-click) on a text file, Notepad opens. You can also set other menu items to appear when you right-click on the file. Doing so requires more entries under the file type subkey (txtfile, in this example). Again, using my Registry as an example, I found the following:

```
txtfile\shell\open =  &Open
txtfile\shell\open\command = %SystemRoot%\system32\NOTEPAD.EXE %1
```

```
txtfile\shell\print = &Print
txtfile\shell\print\command = %SystemRoot%\system32\NOTEPAD.EXE /p %1
```

You can omit the menu names (&Open and &Print) and Windows will still do the right thing. However, you could make the menu more verbose, such as changing &Open to &Open With Notepad, for example.

Sometimes you want to run a program for certain classes of files. Windows provides several file-type keys that don't correspond to a particular extension; you can use them for this purpose. For example, you might want to run a checksum program against any file (the * subkey). Or you might have a program that applies to audio CDs (AudioCD) or directories (Directory). The Unknown subkey handles items for types the shell doesn't recognize.

Of course, you won't want to have a custom file type without assigning it a custom icon, right? That's easy to do. Here's the line from my Registry:

```
txtfile\DefaultIcon = %SystemRoot%\system32\shell32.dll,-152
```

The value of this key is the name of an executable or DLL and the icon's ID within that file.

The final element of a custom file type is the shell's New menu. When you right-click on a shell window (or the desktop), you'll see a New menu item. This item cascades to another menu that presents many types of documents. Selecting a document creates an empty document in that folder.

The first thing you should know about the shell New menu Registry entries is that none of them will work unless your file type also has an Open menu command (under the shell\open keys as described above for text files). If you have the Open command in place, you'll have no problems.

The second interesting point about the New menu entries is that they appear under the extension key (for example, .txt), not the usual file-type key (like txtfile). Why? Because Windows needs to know what extension to use for the new file. On my machine, for example, a txtfile might have a .txt extension or it might use .log. By placing the entries under the extension key, there's no doubt which one to use.

To allow the shell to create new documents for you, place a ShellNew key under the extension key. The key doesn't need a value. However, you can put one name/value pair under the key to specify the contents of your new document.

If you place a value named NullFile in the key, the shell will simply create a zero-byte file for your new document (the name/value pair needs no actual value, in this case). Using a binary value of Data causes the binary data in this Registry entry to become the new file's contents. You can also use FileName to specify a template file to copy to the new location. Finally, you can specify Command, which runs a program to initialize the new file.

Logging

Many programs need to enter messages into some sort of log file. This task is especially common for unattended servers or when something really bad happens. However, it's annoying for system administrators to deal with logs in a variety of formats for different programs.

To solve this problem, Windows 2000 provides a centralized logging service that any program can use. This logging service (which the operating system also uses) provides a standard file format, along with standard viewers for the logged data.

Applications can log five types of events, listed in Table 9.3. Not all of these events indicate an error—some are simply informational messages. Of course, it's bad form to flood a log with uninteresting messages. For example, many servers make a log entry to indicate when they start (using the Information event type). However, it would be a bad idea if, for example, Microsoft Word left the same sort of event every time it started.

The Registry contains a key that corresponds to each log file in use (usually the application log, the system log, and the security log). The keys appear under \HKEY_LOCAL_MACHINE\SYSTEM\Current Control Set\Services\EventLog. The subkeys for each log file contain information about the file name that contains the log, the maximum size of the log, and how long to retain entries in the log. Usually, ordinary programs use the application log. Device drivers and other portions of the operating system use the system log, and the security system uses the security log.

Table 9.3 Event types.

Type	Description	Value (decimal)
EVENTLOG_ERROR_TYPE	Error event	1
EVENTLOG_WARNING_TYPE	Warning event	2
EVENTLOG_INFORMATION_TYPE	Information event	4
EVENTLOG_AUDIT_SUCCESS	Success Audit event	8
EVENTLOG_AUDIT_FAILURE	Failure Audit event	16

Event Sources

Other entries under the log subkeys store information about programs that generate events. You can add your program to this list using **RegisterEventSource**. When you call **RegisterEventSource**, you provide the event logging system with files that describe the events you want to generate. You also indicate which event types you might generate (from Table 9.3). You can also provide files that categorize your events. For example, you might have some events in the Signon category and others in the Process Failed category. What you call your categories is up to you, but you'll refer to them by numbers starting at 1 and increasing consecutively.

All the events and categories you generate will be by number. The files you set in **RegisterEventSource** convert those numbers to strings (which may be localized for particular languages). In a message file, you can use %*n* (where *n* is an integer greater than or equal to 1) to insert variable strings into your messages. You can also use %%*n* to insert strings from a parameter file that you set when you call **RegisterEventSource**.

Why not use the strings directly? The idea is to allow a high degree of support for multiple languages. Suppose a French-speaking user is using software written in Germany. The program logs an event (which is really just some numbers). When the user examines the log, the messages appear in French. However, if the user emails the log to Germany, the support staff there will see the events in Deutsche (German). The strings you insert into a message shouldn't depend on language. Usually the strings are file names, user IDs, or other items that refer to an entity the program was trying to work with when it generated the event.

Creating Message Files

The message files (and the related category and parameter files) are actually DLLs. To prepare one, you start with a C source file that contains one function: **DllMain**. It can simply return **TRUE**. Since the default **DLLMain** does this, you can generally omit this function when using Visual C++. You compile this file in the usual way to produce an OBJ file.

Next you write a message source file and compile it with MC, the message compiler. Doing so generates three files: an RC file, a BIN file, and a header you can use in your program. Use RC to compile the RC file into a RES file and link the resulting RES file with the OBJ file to produce the DLL. It's simpler than it sounds.

The MC file's format is straightforward. It's simply an ASCII text file that contains comments, directives, and strings. Directives take the form of $a = b$ where a and b stand for some directive key and its value. You can use a semicolon to start a comment. If you have a comment by itself on a line, MC will convert it to a C++

comment in the generated header file. Directive names aren't case sensitive, and any white space after the value (including new lines) ends the current directive.

The first entries in an MC file make up the header (which is optional). The header can contain any of the statements listed in Table 9.4. If you're programming only in English, the defaults will probably work fine for you. If you're working with multiple languages, you'll want to specify them with the **LanguageNames** directive. Usually, the defaults are fine for the other values in either case.

After the header, you'll begin a block that defines an individual message. The first line of this block must be the **MessageId** directive. The value of this directive is the message ID number for this string. You can also specify the number relative to the last message by using the plus sign in front of the number.

Other lines in the block determine the severity and facility codes (just like that in a standard **HRESULT**). Use the **Severity** and **Facility** keywords to set the values. If you omit these directives, MC uses the last values you set. The **Symbolic Name** directive sets the name of the **#define** that MC will include in the header file. Finally, the **OutputBase** directive sets the radix to decimal (10) or hexadecimal (16).

After the block of directives, you'll begin a message using the **Language** directive along with a value to specify the language that this message uses. On the following line, you can place a message using any format you like. End the message with a line that contains only a period. You can use several escapes in the text, if you like (see Table 9.5).

After the period, you can add more strings, start a new message, or end the file. The MC compiler uses this data to generate a header, a binary resource, and a resource script. The message file is just a DLL that contains these resources.

If you need to retrieve a string at runtime from the DLL, just open the event source Registry key (using **RegOpenKey** or **RegOpenKeyEx**). Then get the name of the DLL using **RegQueryValueEx** to find the value of the **EventMessageFile** entry. Armed with the name of the DLL, it's a simple matter to call **LoadLibraryEx** and then **FormatMessage** to extract and format the message text from the DLL.

Table 9.4 Message header statements.

Statement	Purpose	Default
MessageIdTypeDef	Sets typedef to use for message ID	none (default integer)
SeverityNames	Sets severity code values	Success=0; Informational=1; Warning=2; Error=3
FacilityNames	Defines possible facility codes	System=0xFF; Application=0xFFF
LanguageNames	Lists known language IDs and associated file name	English=1:MSG00001

Table 9.5 Message escapes.

Escape	Meaning
%0	Terminates message without a new line
%*n*	(*n*=1 to 99) Inserts a string passed to FormatMessage (optionally followed by a printf-specifier surrounded by exclamation points)
%%	A percent sign
%\	Hard line break
%r	Carriage return (no line feed)
%b	Blank space
%.	A period (used to start a line with a period)
%!	Exclamation point

System Messages

Once you make a message file and examine the header it produces, you may find it looks familiar. That's because it will have the same format as the standard winerror.h file that Windows uses. If you're guessing that you can get system error strings using **FormatMessage**, you're correct.

Look at Listing 9.4. It shows a simple program that attempts to open a bad file name. When the program detects an error, it calls **FormatMessage** to decode the message number that **GetLastError** returns. Because the program doesn't specify a particular language, the system selects one that's appropriate.

Listing 9.4 Displaying an error message.

```
#include <windows.h>void main(int argc, char *argv[]){    HANDLE h;    char
*fn="z?x";    if (argc>=2) fn=argv[1];
h=CreateFile(fn,GENERIC_READ,0,NULL,OPEN_EXISTING,0,NULL);
    if (h==INVALID_HANDLE_VALUE)
    {
        void *buf;
        FormatMessage(FORMAT_MESSAGE_ALLOCATE_BUFFER |
                      FORMAT_MESSAGE_FROM_SYSTEM |
                      FORMAT_MESSAGE_IGNORE_INSERTS,
                      NULL,GetLastError(),0,
                      (LPTSTR) &buf,0,NULL);

        MessageBox(NULL, (LPTSTR)buf, NULL, MB_OK | MB_ICONINFORMATION);
// Free the buffer
        LocalFree(buf);
    }
}
```

Try running the program with files that don't exist or bad network file names and note the different errors you receive. The program is a little more complicated than it has to be, but it does ignore insert strings for the sake of brevity. If you scan winerror.h for percent signs, you'll see that not many common messages have insert strings, anyway.

This program is extra complex because it asks **FormatMessage** to allocate a buffer for the string (by passing the **FORMAT_MESSAGE_ALLOCATE_BUFFER**). As a result, the program doesn't need to know how long the buffer should be. However, you have to call **LocalFree** to return the buffer memory to the system. If you wanted to simplify things, you could pass a buffer of known length and its length, and remove the **FORMAT_MESSAGE_ALLOCATE_BUFFER** parameter.

Operating On A Log

A handful of functions work with logs; they're listed in Table 9.6. You can open a log with the **OpenEventLog** or **RegisterEventSource** calls. Normally, if you want to write to the log, you'll use **RegisterEventSource**. **OpenEventLog** is appropriate for administering a log (for example, clearing it or backing up).

In most cases, all you'll need to do is call **RegisterEventSource**, and then call **ReportEvent** and later **DeregisterEventSource**. The **ReportEvent** call requires the event type and the message ID, along with any categories and strings to include in the message. You can also attach binary data to the event, although the event viewer will show it only as a hex dump without interpreting it.

Table 9.6 Log functions.

Function	Description
RegisterEventSource	Sets up to report events (may be to a remote machine)
ReportEvent	Reports an event
DeregisterEventSource	Stops reporting events
OpenEventLog	Opens a log for administration (may be on a remote machine)
CloseEventLog	Closes a log
BackupEventLog	Backs up a log
OpenBackupEventLog	Creates a backup log (use with BackupEventLog)
ClearEventLog	Clears a log
NotifyChangeEventLog	Requests notification when a log changes
GetOldestEventLogRecord	Gets the oldest record
GetNumberOfEventLogRecords	Gets the number of records
ReadEventLog	Reads entries

Normally, you won't care much about administering a log file, because perfectly good tools do that already. However, if you need to do it, the process is straightforward. You simply open the log file and use the calls to do what you want. You could write your own replacement for the standard event viewer, for example, which understood custom data that you stored with the events. Of course, you'd also have to have the correct privileges to do things like clear a log.

Logging Example

Listings 9.5 and 9.6 show a simple example of logging. The messages are in Listing 9.5. The three messages include one to note the program starting, one for when the program ends, and another that reports the user's name and age. This last message requires two parameters.

Listing 9.5 An MC file.

```
MessageID=100
Severity=Success
Facility=Application
SymbolicName=StartMsg
Language=English
The Message Demo program started.
.
MessageID=101
SymbolicName=EndMsg
Language=English
The Message Demo program ended.
.
MessageID=102
SymbolicName=DataMsg
Language=English
Operator name is:%1 age is %2.
.
```

Listing 9.6 Reporting a logged event.

```
#include <windows.h>
#include <iostream.h>
#include "..\message.h"

void main()
{
    char *strings[2];
    char name[256];
    char age[33];
    strings[0]=name;
    strings[1]=age;
```

```
    HANDLE mhandle=RegisterEventSource(NULL,"MsgPgm");
    ReportEvent(mhandle,EVENTLOG_AUDIT_SUCCESS,0,
       StartMsg,NULL,0,0,NULL,NULL);

    cout<<"What's your name?";
    cin>>name;
    cout<<"How old are you?";
    cin>>age;

    ReportEvent(mhandle,EVENTLOG_AUDIT_SUCCESS,0,
       DataMsg,NULL,2,0,(const char **)strings,NULL);
    ReportEvent(mhandle,EVENTLOG_AUDIT_SUCCESS,0,
       EndMsg,NULL,0,0,NULL,NULL);
    DeregisterEventSource(mhandle);
}
```

MC compiles the messages into a resource file, and it's trivial to build these resources into a DLL. To notify the system that this DLL exists, you need a few Registry entries in the following location:

```
HKEY_LOCAL_MACHINE
    SYSTEM
     CurrentControlSet
       Services
         EventLog
          Application
              AppName
```

Of course, you'll substitute your event source name for *AppName*. The values (not subkeys) under this key can specify the name of the DLL that handles the messages and also the names of any optional categories or parameters. You may also specify what types of events this source can provide. Table 9.7 shows the possible entries.

Table 9.7 Event log Registry entries.

Value	Meaning
EventMessageFile	Specifies the path for the event message file. You can list multiple files, separated by semicolons.
CategoryMessageFile	Specifies the path for the category message file. You can list multiple files, separated by semicolons.
ParameterMessageFile	Specifies the path for the parameter message file. You can list multiple files, separated by semicolons.
CategoryCount	Specifies the number of event categories supported.
TypesSupported	Specifies a bitmask of supported types (see Table 9.3).

Once the system knows about the DLL, you can easily produce events in the application log using the code from Listing 9.6. This simple console program prompts the user for a first name and an age and logs it in the application log.

To see what the program does, you'll need to open the event viewer (see Figure 9.4). Once the event viewer is open, select the Application Log to see the messages.

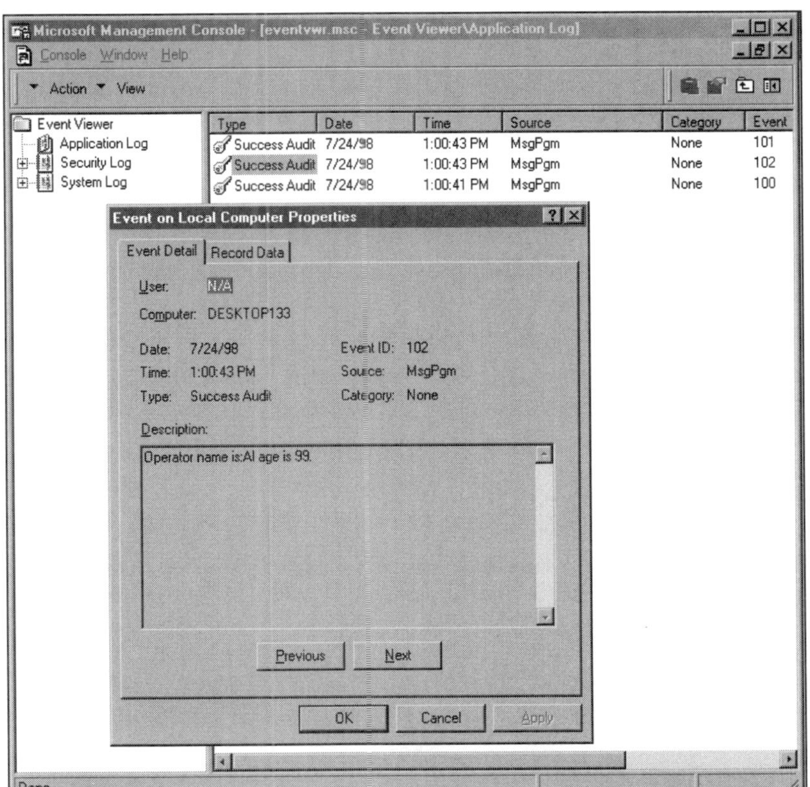

Figure 9.4 Viewing the events using Event Viewer.

Immediate Solutions

Opening A Registry Key

Before you can work with a Registry key, you need an open **HKEY**. To open an existing key, you call **RegOpenKeyEx**. To create a new key, you call **RegCreate KeyEx**. Both of these functions return an **HKEY**, but they also require an **HKEY**.

How can this be possible? Windows provides several **HKEY**s that are always open. These keys are HKEY_CLASSES_ROOT, HKEY_CURRENT_USER, HKEY_LOCAL_MACHINE, HKEY_USERS, and HKEY_CURRENT_CONFIG. Of course, if you have another key open already, you can start with it instead. However, the root keys give you someplace to start.

To open a key, you supply the root key, the name of the subkey you wish to open, any options you want to supply, the access you want, and a pointer to an **HKEY** variable that will receive the result. **RegCreateKeyEx** takes similar arguments, but it also accepts a key class name and security attributes.

Finding Subkeys

Of course, if you have the name of a subkey, you can open it using the techniques outlined in the last section. However, sometimes it's useful to search for subkeys without having prior knowledge of the key's name. In that case, the **RegEnumKeyEx** function is handy. This call takes an open key handle and a **DWORD** index. By altering the index, you can easily walk through all the top-level subkeys of a given key. You can find an example of using this function in Listing 9.1.

Finding Values

When you want to retrieve a name/value pair, you can do so by name, or you can enumerate through all the pairs. To retrieve a value by name, call **RegQueryValueEx**. If you want to enumerate through all the pairs, call **RegEnumValue**.

There is one peculiarity you should watch for when using **RegEnumValue**. If the key has only a default value, the function will return that default value. However, if the key has other name/value pairs, **RegEnumValue** returns these, and does not return the default value.

Using The Registry Instead Of INI Files

When programs read or write INI files, they nearly always use one of the standard API functions (like **GetPrivateProfileInt** or **WritePrivateProfileString**). However, you can redirect these calls to force them to use the Registry instead of an actual INI file.

Doing so is good if you want to have the benefit of the Registry with older programs. However, if a program tries to open an INI file directly (say, using **CreateFile** or **fopen**), this method will cause the program to fail or become confused.

The key, of course, is an entry in the Registry. In particular, HKEY_LOCAL_MACHINE\Software\Microsoft\Windows NT\CurrentVersion\IniFileMapping is the key that controls this behavior.

When you call one of the standard profile functions under Windows 2000, the system uses the following logic to search for the correct entry:

1. Look in the Registry for the name of the initialization file, say xxx.ini, in

   ```
   HKEY_LOCAL_MACHINE\Software\Microsoft\Windows NT\
        CurrentVersion\IniFileMapping\xxx.ini
   ```

2. Look for the section name specified by the call. It will be a named value under xxx.ini or a subkey of xxx.ini, or it won't exist.
3. If the section name specified by the call is a named value under xxx.ini, then that value specifies where in the Registry you'll find the keys for the section.
4. If the section name specified by the call is a subkey of xxx.ini, then named values under that subkey specify where in the Registry you'll find the keys for the section. If the key you're looking for doesn't exist as a named value, then there will be an unnamed value (shown as "<No Name>") that specifies the default location in the Registry where you'll find the key.

5. If the section name specified doesn't exist as a named value or as a subkey under xxx.ini, then there will be an unnamed value (shown as "<No Name>") under xxx.ini that specifies the default location in the Registry where you'll find the keys for the section.
6. If there's no subkey for xxx.ini, or if there's no entry for the section name, then look for the actual xxx.ini on the disk and read its contents.

When looking at values in the Registry that specify other Registry locations, several prefixes change the behavior of the mapping:

- *!*—Forces all writes to go both to the Registry and to the INI file on disk.
- #—Causes the Registry value to be set to the value in the Windows 3.1 INI file when a new user logs in for the first time after setup.
- @—Prevents any reads from going to the INI file on disk if the requested data isn't found in the Registry.
- *USR*—Stands for HKEY_CURRENT_USER, and the text after the prefix is relative to that key.
- *SYS*—Stands for HKEY_LOCAL_MACHINE\SOFTWARE, and the text after the prefix is relative to that key.

If you examine your system Registry, you'll find some entries already present that redirect some system INI files (like clock.ini, for example). You can use these entries as examples to create your own.

Creating REG Files

REG files are simple ASCII text files that REGEDIT creates to represent the registry. Of course, you can also create these ASCII files yourself and use REGEDIT to import your data into the registry.

In Listing 9.3 you'll notice that the first line contains the keyword **REGEDIT4**. This simply marks the version of REGEDIT that created the file (or in this case that you want to simulate).

After this first line, you can name keys in square brackets. After each key, you can place name value pairs. Use the @ sign to indicate the default key. Be sure to use double quotes around all strings and to use double backslashes in the file. Also, the file requires a carriage return before the end of file or it will fail to import the last line of the file.

Creating INF Files

INF files are another way that you can manipulate the registry. The system setup program uses INF files to install, among other things, device drivers. However, creating a file to manipulate the registry is easy enough.

Each INF file requires a version section. This is the first portion of the file in Listing 9.7. The only required piece of data here is the signature which is **$CHICAGO$**. This simply serves to identify the INF file as one that belongs to Windows.

The next section's name is DefaultInstall. This is the section the default installer will use to determine what to do. There are many possible actions, but the ones you'll want to use for manipulating the registry are the **AddReg** and **DelReg** commands. These commands simply name another section of the file that determines what to add and delete. In the example, I used AddRegKey and DelRegKey, but you could use any names you wanted.

The sample INF file adds the HKEY_CLASSES_ROOT\.000 key if it doesn't exist. If the key does exist, the INF file also deletes the name/value pair that has the name "book". The lines beneath the AddRegKey section all require several fields of data (many of which are optional). First is the abbreviated root key name. Following this field is the subkey name, if any. Next, if you are using a name/value pair, you'll supply the name. The final two fields are some option flags (usually 0) and the value you want to set.

If you want to manipulate the default value, leave the name blank. The most useful flag, **FLG_ADDREG_NOCLOBBER**, allows you to not overwrite existing entries.

The lines that delete keys are also simple. You just name the key and optionally a value. While this file both adds and deletes keys, you don't have to do both in every file.

The sample file adds only one key and deletes one key, but you can append additional lines to each section if you need to work with multiple keys.

Listing 9.7 A sample INF file.

```
[version]
signature=$Chicago$

[DefaultInstall]
DelReg=DelRegKey
AddReg=AddRegKey
```

```
[AddRegKey]
HKCR, .000,,,"A test extension"

[DelRegKey]
HKCR, .000,book
```

To execute the commands in the INF file, simply right-click it and select Install. You won't get any error messages though, so you have to be sure you have your syntax correct without help from the computer.

Creating A Message DLL

To create a message DLL, you need only create a Win32 DLL project using your environment. You can insert a blank C or C++ source file into the project. The compiler will provide the DLL's startup routine. Although the default routine doesn't do anything, it's adequate for this purpose.

The real action for a message DLL is in the MC file. This is a file of message directives and messages (you can learn more about message directives in the main portion of this chapter). You'll compile the MC file using the MC compiler. This compilation will generate an RC file, a BIN file, and an H file.

You can use the H file in your program to refer to messages by symbolic names. The RC file becomes the resources for the DLL (you'll need to add the RC file to the project). The RC file refers to the BIN file, so you don't need to include the BIN file explicitly.

Once you've set up the resources, you can build the DLL. The DLL doesn't contain any code, but it does contain the message strings in its resources. With the proper Registry entries, the system will use these strings for interpreting logged messages.

Registering A Message DLL

To make the system recognize a message DLL, you need the right entries in the system Registry. If your application is named AWC, the entries belong in

```
HKEY_LOCAL_MACHINE
    SYSTEM
     CurrentControlSet
```

```
Services
  EventLog
   Application
       AWC
```

The values under this key set the DLL file name and other important parameters (see Tables 9.2 and 9.3).

Logging Events

If you want your program to report events, you must first call **RegisterEventSource**. This call takes two arguments: a machine name and an application name. If you're logging on the local machine, you can set the machine name argument to **NULL**. The application name is the same name you placed in the Registry for the message DLL (see the previous topic).

RegisterEventSource returns a handle you can use in calls to **ReportEvent**. **ReportEvent** takes many arguments, but you won't always use all of them. The arguments are as follows:

- The event source handle
- The event type
- The category, if you're using categories
- The message ID
- The security ID (used only for security logging)
- The number of strings to replace in the message (may be zero)
- The number of bytes of raw data to include (may be zero)
- A pointer to an array of replacement strings
- A pointer to the raw data

You can find an example of calling **ReportEvent** with and without replacement strings in Listing 9.6.

When you no longer want to report events, you can call **DeregisterEventSource** and pass it the handle from **RegisterEventSource**. Doing so ends your program's access to the event log.

Converting Errors To Messages

You can convert the normal Windows error codes (the kind that **GetLastError** returns) into language-appropriate messages using **FormatMessage**. This call is usually used to format user-defined messages. However, by specifying a special flag (**FORMAT_MESSAGE_FROM_SYSTEM**), the call will search the system's error messages.

FormatMessage can allocate a buffer large enough to hold the resulting text, or you can supply a predefined buffer. You'll find an example in Listing 9.4. If you allow the function to allocate its own buffer, you'll need to free it yourself when you no longer need it.

Chapter 10

Shell Tricks With ATL

If you need an immediate solution to:	*See page:*
About Shell Extensions	470
Resolving Shortcuts	470
Creating A Shortcut	471
Writing Icon Tray Programs	472
Miscellaneous Shell Calls	473
About MMC	473
Writing MMC Snap-ins	473

In Depth

In the paper today I read that scientists have found more evidence that dinosaurs evolved into birds. Imagine the changes required to transform the killers you saw in *Jurassic Park* into the pretty robin perched on your bird feeder. Perhaps they should sell dino-feeders, instead. The time it takes for evolution of this sort to take place is mind-boggling.

User interfaces also have a way of evolving. Of course, no computerized user interface is old enough to really evolve from a velociraptor to a wren. However, there are better examples in the world around us that are much more recent. For example, consider the television. When the TV first appeared, it had very little in common with the entertainment complex of today. An old Dumont, with its small dial, tiny screen, and heavy wood cabinet, looked more like a radio than a modern TV.

Of course, TVs became more complex. Every year manufacturers added new features: remote control, on-screen display, channel labels, sleep timers, parental lock out. How far will it go? We already have computers merging with TVs. It won't be long before you'll be able to change channels by voice command, or program your built-in VCR over the Internet from work.

The telephone is another everyday instrument with a long evolutionary history. The evolution of the phone was glacially slow for years. The Bell phone monopoly and the FCC wouldn't allow anyone but the phone company to make phone equipment. The real explosion in phone technology started when the FCC opened the door for third parties to hook up devices to the phone lines. The result? Inexpensive answering machines, speakerphones, and a host of other devices that you take for granted today. The phone company (on purpose or not) greatly increased the value of the phone system by allowing other people to add things to it.

I've always believed that the best computer user interfaces are extensible, too. One reason that Unix has a die-hard following is that it's easy to extend the interface using shell scripts, C programs, PERL, and a variety of other techniques.

The Windows shell (and several other parts of Windows) has become more extensible over time. In Chapter 9, you saw how simple Registry entries could inform the shell about your custom file types. However, by using ActiveX interfaces, it's possible to make even more sophisticated modifications. In addition, it isn't too hard to write programs that become part of the icon bar (the so-called system tray).

Other parts of Windows are now also more extensible. Prior to Windows 2000, you had to use a variety of programs to manage Windows. You used the Control Panel (and its myriad interfaces), the Internet Information Server's management program, and several custom programs to do all administration.

With Windows 2000, a single program—the MMC or Microsoft Management Console—can administer everything. MMC can administer anything because it doesn't do anything by itself. Instead, it relies on MMC snap-ins (special ActiveX objects) to provide all the smarts. Microsoft provides many snap-ins, but you can also write your own so that administrators can use MMC to configure your program just as they configure other parts of the system.

Shell Extensions

When the Windows shell prepares to perform certain operations, it consults the Registry to see what to do. This happens frequently. For example, when the shell displays the icon for a file, it first consults the Registry for that file type. The Registry contains a key (under the HKEY_CLASSES_ROOT entry) that corresponds to the file's extension. This key's value indicates the file type. So for the .txt extension, for example, the file type might be TXTFILE. This TXTFILE entry directs the shell to further examine the Registry (again under HKEY_CLASSES_ROOT) to find further information about the file type. While this process seems confusing, it allows multiple extensions (like .txt and .asc, for example) to refer to the same file type.

Once the shell locates the TXTFILE key (to continue the example), it locates the subkey DefaultIcon. Normally, this key's value specifies the location of the icon. For a TXTFILE, the key's value might be c:\windows\notepad.exe,0 for example. This value instructs the shell to pull the first icon from the NOTEPAD.EXE program and use that icon. You can find more details about Registry-based file types in Chapter 9.

This technique works well if you want a static icon (the usual case). But what happens if you want an icon that doesn't appear the same for all files of a single type? For example, what if you want to define a file type that showed one icon for files that start with the letters A through M and another icon for those starting with N through Z? You can't really set the DefaultIcon key so that al.xxx has one icon and zip.xxx has another.

If you need this sort of capability, you'll have to write a custom ActiveX server known as a *shell extension*. Shell extensions can enhance the shell in a number of ways, including specifying icons dynamically. Other types of extensions can modify context menus, add property sheets, and manage drag-and-drop operations. A shell extension that supplies icons is called an *icon handler*.

If you've read Chapter 2, you may find the idea of writing an ActiveX server daunting. You could write such an object many ways, including raw C++ and MFC. However, most ActiveX programmers prefer to use the ActiveX Template Library (ATL) that Microsoft ships with Visual C++. ATL uses some clever classes and templates to make ActiveX server development easier. Unfortunately, ATL's tools don't readily handle shell extensions. With a few tricks, however, you can get the job done.

To successfully write an icon handler, you must supply the shell an ActiveX object that implements the **IPersistFile** and **IExtractIcon** interfaces defined by Microsoft (see Tables 10.1 and 10.2). The **IExtractIcon** interface is where all the real work occurs. **IPersistFile** is a standard interface with several complex functions. However, for an icon handler, you need only to supply one **IPersistFile** function (**Load**). The rest of the functions can simply return an error code and won't require any significant programming. (Note that all interfaces include the **IUnknown** functions.)

Other Shell Extensions

Table 10.3 shows the set of shell extensions that Windows supports. You can find the interfaces required in the same table. Most extensions rely on **IPersistFile** for initialization. However, the context menu and property sheet extensions use a different interface—**IShellExtInit**—to receive instructions from the shell. This interface has only one significant function: **Initialize**. It's straightforward to implement any of these shell extensions using ATL or MFC and the techniques outlined earlier.

Table 10.1 The IPersistFile interface.

Function	Description
GetClassID	Not required; return E_NOTIMPL
IsDirty	Not required; return E_NOTIMPL
Load	The shell passes a filename to this function; convert the Unicode filename to ANSI and store it
Save	Not required; return E_NOTIMPL
SaveCompleted	Not required; return E_NOTIMPL
GetCurFile	Not required; return E_NOTIMPL

Table 10.2 The IExtractIcon interface.

Function	Description
GetIconLocation	Returns the name of the file that contains the icon and its index in that file
ExtractIcon	Returns an icon by handle

Table 10.3 Shell extensions.

Name	Description	Interfaces
Icon	Supplies the dynamic icon for a file type	IExtractIcon, IPersistFile
Context menu	Adds context menus or drag-and-drop menus (resulting from right-click or right-drag)	IContextMenu, IShellExtInit
Property sheet	Adds custom property sheets	IShellPropSheetExt, IShellExtInit
Copy hook	Manages file operations	ICopyHook
Drop target	Reacts when an object is dropped on another	IDropTarget, IPersistFile
Data object	Supplies a data object for drag and drop or copy and paste	IDataObject, IPersistFile
Quick view	Parses a file for Quick Viewer	IFileViewer, IPersistFile
Briefcase reconcile	Combines multiple versions of a file into one file	IReconcilableObject, IPersistFile

Essential ATL

A full treatment of ATL is beyond the scope of this book. However, if you understand ActiveX (see Chapter 2) you can easily use ATL for simple tasks like creating shell extensions.

Starting an ATL project is just like starting any other project. Select New|Projects and select ATL COM AppWizard to open a single-page Wizard. For a shell extension, you'll want a DLL project. You don't need to select any of the options, unless you want to use MFC (the example later in this chapter does use MFC). Should you use MFC? In this case, it probably doesn't matter. If you use ATL to create Internet controls, you may not want the overhead introduced by MFC. However, shell extensions will reside only on the local machine, so the MFC overhead isn't significant in most cases.

Once your project is ready, you might wonder where the ActiveX object is. The answer is nowhere, yet. The Wizard simply creates an empty project that has the capacity to become an ActiveX server.

To create an object, you'll choose the Insert|New ATL Object menu item. Doing so starts the ATL Object Wizard; select Simple Object from the Objects area, as shown in Figure 10.1, and click on Next. The resulting dialog box requires a few simple entries. In the Names tab, you can select a Short Name. The dialog box will generate other names (like file names) based on what you type in this field. You can accept the defaults.

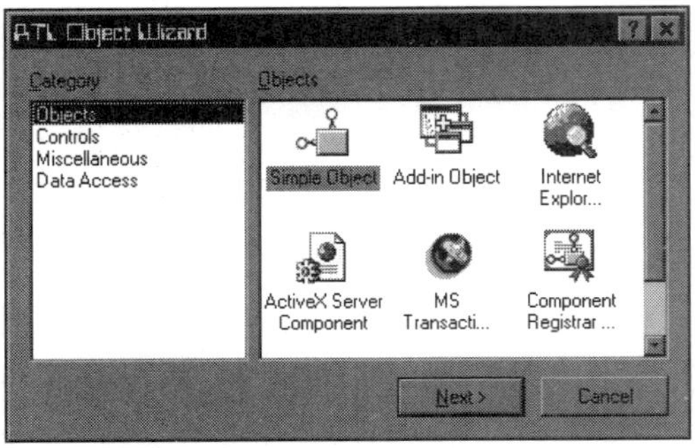

Figure 10.1 Inserting a new ATL object.

Before you dismiss this dialog box, you'll need to make some changes on the Attributes tab. Specifically, you should check the Apartment Threading Model option, and clear all the check boxes (these are the defaults anyway). Also select the Custom Interface radio button and turn off support for Aggregation.

When you dismiss this dialog box, ATL will create a C++ object (using the names you selected). This object will implement a custom ActiveX interface, which that at this moment has no functions except for the standard **IUnknown** functions.

Normally, when you're implementing a predefined interface (like **IExtractIcon**), you'll right-click on this class in the Class View window and select Implement Interface from the context menu that appears. However, this step assumes that you have a type library that describes the interface. For the shell extensions, you won't easily find such a type library.

Of course, you could construct your own type library, but doing so isn't very handy. An easier way to proceed is to simply right-click on your custom interface (in the Class View window) and select Add Method from the context menu that appears. You'll have to add the exact members found in Table 10.2 and in the same order. ATL will insert stubs for the function, update the header file, and also generate the correct Interface Definition Language (IDL) statements. This process is easier than manually wrestling with the IDL syntax yourself.

Although shell extension type libraries aren't readily available, other interfaces do have type libraries (in various TLB files or bound into their DLL files). To implement these interfaces, you can simply right-click on the object, select Implement Interface, and select the correct type library. Once the library is available, you'll see the interfaces in the library. You can check the ones you want, to automatically add all the correct stubs and IDL for the interface in one step.

If you use this strategy to implement an icon handler, you'll have a slight problem. When you're done, your object exposes **IPersistFile** and a custom interface that mimics exactly **IExtractIcon**. The problem is, the interface *isn't* **IExtractIcon**. You can resolve this problem several ways. The easiest way is to add an entry in the object's COM map that establishes an equivalence between the custom interface and **IExtractIcon**.

You can locate the COM map in the object's header file. ATL uses this map to automatically handle **QueryInterface** calls. If your class name is **IAtlIco**, then this line will do the trick:

```
COM_INTERFACE_ENTRY_IID(IID_IExtractIconA,IAtlIco)
```

You can also consider removing the entry that refers to the custom interface, because you really aren't using it. If you prefer, you can open the IDL file and replace the IID (Interface ID) for your custom interface with the **IExtractIcon** IID. However, you don't want to name your custom interface **IExtractIcon** because doing so will cause duplicate definitions when you include standard headers that define the real **IExtractIcon**. Luckily, COM (and therefore the shell) doesn't care what the name of your interface is—it only looks at the IID.

An Example Icon Handler

Listing 10.1 shows a simple example of an icon handler. This handler displays one icon for file names that begin with A through M, a different icon for files that start with N through Z, and a third icon for other files. Which file extensions the handler will apply to depends on the Registry entries you create. Figure 10.2 shows the icon handler working for files with the type .00x. Of course, in the figure the Windows Explorer is hiding the file extensions (since you've registered the file type).

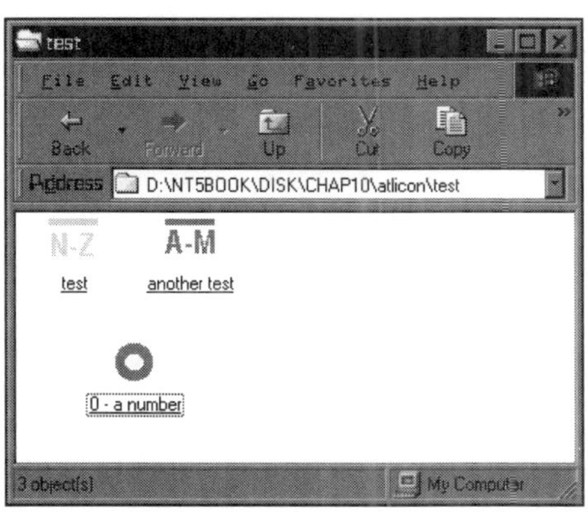

Figure 10.2 The icon handler at work.

By following the steps outlined in the previous section, it's easy to get stubs for all the **IExtractIcon** and **IPersistFile** functions. Of course, then you'll need to fill out these stubs to contain useful code.

For **IPersistFile**, writing this code is simple because you need only one function: **Load**. When the shell creates the icon handler, it calls **IPeristFile::Load** to initialize the object. If you need to analyze the contents of the file, you could open it here. However, this handler just looks at the file name, so it's sufficient to store the file name away for later use.

When the shell calls **IExtractIcon::GetIconLocation**, the handler calculates which of its icons it should use. It also locates the DLL file that contains the server code, thereby allowing the routine to return a file name and an index to the shell.

In our example, returning this information is adequate for the task. However, some programs might want to provide the actual icon. For example, suppose you wanted your handler to draw a custom icon based on information in the file, rather than selecting one of several static icons. A word processor, for example, might put the author's initials in the icon.

In such a case, the handler must return **GIL_NOTFILENAME** in the flags sent back to the shell, indicating that the icon location has meaning only to the handler. Therefore, the shell makes a further call to **IExtractIcon::Extract**, allowing the handler to return two icon handles: one for large icons and the other for small icons. Because the example program doesn't need to return an icon handle, it's permissible for this function to simply return **S_FALSE**.

Listing 10.1 The Icon handler.

```
// AtlIco.h : Declaration of the CAtlIco

#ifndef __ATLICO_H_
#define __ATLICO_H_

#include "resource.h"       // main symbols

/////////////////////////////////////////////////
// CAtlIco
class ATL_NO_VTABLE CAtlIco :
   public CComObjectRootEx<CComSingleThreadModel>,
   public CComCoClass<CAtlIco, &CLSID_AtlIco>,
   public IExtractIconATL,
   public IPersistFile
{
public:
```

```
    CAtlIco()
    {
        fn=NULL;
    }

    ~CAtlIco()
    {
        if (fn) free(fn);
    }

DECLARE_REGISTRY_RESOURCEID(IDR_ATLICO)
DECLARE_NOT_AGGREGATABLE(CAtlIco)

DECLARE_PROTECT_FINAL_CONSTRUCT()

BEGIN_COM_MAP(CAtlIco)
    COM_INTERFACE_ENTRY(IExtractIconATL)
            // A different way to do the same thing...
    //COM_INTERFACE_ENTRY_IID(IID_IExtractIconA,IAtlIco)
    COM_INTERFACE_ENTRY(IPersistFile)
END_COM_MAP()

// IAtlIco  -- see ATLICO.CPP for the GetIconLocation function
public:
    char * fn;
    STDMETHOD(Extract)(LPCSTR pszFile, UINT nIconIndex,
           HICON *lg, HICON *sm,UINT iconsize);
    STDMETHOD(GetIconLocation)(UINT flags, LPSTR szIconFile,
           int cchMax, int * piIndex, UINT *pwFlags);
// IPersistFile
    STDMETHOD(IsDirty)()
    {
        return E_NOTIMPL;
    }
    STDMETHOD(Load)(LPCWSTR pszFileName, ULONG dwMode)
    {
        USES_CONVERSION;
        fn=strdup(W2A(pszFileName));
        return NOERROR;
    }
    STDMETHOD(Save)(LPCOLESTR pszFileName, BOOL fRemember)
    {
        return E_NOTIMPL;
    }
    STDMETHOD(SaveCompleted)(LPCWSTR pszFileName)
    {
```

```
      return E_NOTIMPL;
   }
   STDMETHOD(GetCurFile)(LPWSTR * ppszFileName)
   {
      if (ppszFileName == NULL)
         return E_POINTER;

      return E_NOTIMPL;
   }
   STDMETHOD(GetClassID(CLSID __RPC_FAR *pClassID))
   {
       return E_FAIL;
   }
};

#endif //__ATLICO_H_
```

Using MFC Instead Of ATL

Writing an ActiveX inproc (or in process) server (just a DLL, remember) isn't hard, but you have to handle a lot of details. Luckily, MFC will do some of this work for you if you ask. If you search for ActiveX support in App Wizard, however, you won't find it directly. The trick is to create an ActiveX automation object (a special form of ActiveX object) and cut away everything you don't need.

Before you try this technique, let's look at some of the support MFC provides that your object will need. MFC supports objects with multiple interfaces in an odd way. If you think that a COM interface sounds like a C++ Virtual Table (VTBL), you're right. MFC uses virtual functions to create interfaces. The VTBL then directly acts as an ActiveX interface. To support multiple interfaces, MFC creates nested objects (by default, their names start with an *X*). For example, here's what a class for an OLE object with two interfaces, **I1** and **I2**, might look like:

```
class myobject: public CCmdTarget
     {
      .
      .
      class XI1
           {
           // functions for I1
  // (including AddRef,
  // Release, and
  //QueryInterface)
     .
```

```
.
  .
    STDMETHODIMP f1(void);
     };
  class XI2
    {
      // functions for I2
      .
      .
      .
      STDMETHODIMP f2(void);
     };
       } // end of myobject
```

All ActiveX objects derive from **CCmdTarget** (the base class for any MFC object that has maps). This base class provides default implementations for **AddRef**, **Release**, and **QueryInterface**. Good thing, too: **AddRef** and **Release** are more complex than they appear, because they must be thread safe. Here's an example of what **I1**'s **AddRef** function might look like:

```
STDMETHODIMP_(ULONG) myobject::XI1::AddRef()
{
        METHOD_PROLOGUE(myobject,I1)
        return pThis->ExternalAddRef();
}
```

Notice that you use the *X* in the class name for the function declaration, but not in the **METHOD_PROLOGUE** macro. This macro allows you to access the outer class (**myobject**) using the predefined **pThis** pointer.

You don't write the nested classes directly. Instead, you use the **BEGIN_INTERFACE_PART** and **END_INTERFACE_PART** macros in the header file. Omit the *X* from the nested class names when using these macros. Between the macros, you'll name the functions that interface supports (the **IUnknown** triplets—**AddRef**, **Release**, and **QueryInterface**—appear automatically when you use the macros). The actual definition for **myobject** could look like this:

```
class myobject : public CCmdTarget
  {
   DECLARE_DYNCREATE(myobject,CCmdTarget);
// class factory
   DECLARE_OLECREATE(myobject);
   myobject();
```

```
    DECLARE_MESSAGE_MAP()
    BEGIN_INTERFACE_PART(myobject,I1)
          STDMETHOD (f1)();
    END_INTERFACE_PART(I1)
    BEGIN_INTERFACE_PART(myobject,I2)
          STDMETHOD (f2)();
    END_INTERFACE_PART(I2)
};
```

MFC's support for ActiveX is mainly in the form of macros (such as **BEGIN_INTERFACE_PART**). Here are the most important macros:

- ***DECLARE_INTERFACE_MAP***—Appears in your class' header file. It creates an interface map. This map designates which nested class corresponds to a particular COM interface.
- ***BEGIN_INTERFACE_MAP***—Creates the interface map in the class' CPP file.
- ***INTERFACE_PART***—Takes three arguments: the main class name, the interface IID, and the nested class name (without the leading *X*). Use this macro after the **BEGIN_INTERFACE_MAP** macro to define the particular map entries.
- ***END_INTERFACE_MAP***—Ends the interface map.
- ***DECLARE_OLE_CREATE***—Declares a class factory. Use this macro in your H file.
- ***IMPLEMENT_OLE_CREATE***—Corresponds to ***DECLARE_OLE_CREATE*** but appears in the CPP file. It takes the class name, an external name, and the object's **CLSID**.
- ***STDMETHOD***—Declares a COM interface function that returns an **HRESULT**.
- ***STDMETHODIMP***—Implement a COM function that returns an **HRESULT**.
- ***STDMETHOD_***—Declares a COM interface function that returns something other than an **HRESULT**.
- ***STDMETHODIMP_***—Implements a COM function that doesn't return an **HRESULT**. (See the **AddRef** code earlier for an example.)
- ***METHOD_PROLOGUE***—Appears in member functions of the nested classes that implement each interface. It creates a variable, **pThis**, that points to the main class. See the earlier code fragment for **AddRef** for an example.

An MFC ActiveX Object Step-By-Step

To get MFC to create a COM object, you'll need to create an automation DLL and then remove the portions that relate to automation. Here are the steps to follow to coax MFC to generate an inproc COM server:

1. Use App Wizard to create an OLE automation DLL.
2. Use Class Wizard to derive a class from **CCmdTarget** that uses OLE automation.
3. Delete the lines that relate to the dispatch map from the new class.
4. Delete the call to **EnableAutomation()** in the constructor.
5. Delete the **OnFinalRelease()** function from the header and the CPP file.
6. Remove the **BEGIN_INTERFACE_PART** macro that defines the **IDispatch** interface. Replace it with as many **BEGIN_INTERFACE_PART** macros as you need to define all the interfaces you want to create.
7. Add **DECLARE_OLECREATE** and **IMPLEMENT_OLECREATE** macros to the H and CPP files.
8. Include any headers you might need (for shell extensions, you'll want WINNETWK.H, SHLOBJ.H, and WINNLS.H).
9. Write the interface functions you need (including, the **IUnknown** functions).

When you look up the interface functions in the online help, you'll see that each function has an initial **this** pointer. When using C++, the compiler automatically adds this parameter, so don't include it explicitly.

The Icon Handler In Detail

Now that you have some idea of how to create a COM server, what good is it? Look at Table 10.3. Notice that an icon handler requires a COM object that has two interfaces: **IPersistFile** and **IExtractIcon**. If you create an inproc server that supplies objects with these interfaces (and inform the shell about it) you can create code that provides customizable icons for a file type.

Don't forget: If you simply want a static icon, just change the Registry. An icon handler works best for icons that change based on some file attribute or on some other dynamic condition.

Tables 10.1 and 10.2 show the functions that the icon handler needs to implement. You can see that most of them are simple stubs. The **IPersistFile::Load** function passes your object a Unicode file name. The shell wants you to provide an icon for this file. Usually, you'll convert the file name to ANSI (unless you're working with Unicode anyway) and store it away for later use.

The two functions that provide an icon (**IExtractIcon::GetIconLocation** and **IExtractIcon::Extract**) are complementary. You usually implement only **GetIconLocation**. This function allows you to return a file name and an icon number. It's often convenient to use **GetModuleFileName** to learn the name of your DLL. Then you can use the icons inside the DLL. You can also use **Extract** to return an **HICON** for the file. Doing so is useful if you want to draw the icon (using an image list, perhaps) from scratch. The arguments to **Extract** include the file name and icon number set in **GetIconLocation** (if any).

Listing 10.2 shows the important excerpts from the example icon handler. This icon handler supplies two icons: one for files less than 1,024 bytes long and another for files larger than that size. Both icons are in the DLL, so the handler only needs to determine which icon to use.

Providing the icon handler isn't enough. You also need to tell the shell about it. Suppose you wanted to use this icon handler for .viz files. You'd need the following Registry entries:

```
[HKEY_CLASSES_ROOT\.VIZ]="VIZFile"

[HKEY_CLASSES_ROOT\VIZFile]="Visual Developer File"

[HKEY_LOCAL_MACHINE\SOFTWARE\Classes\CLSID\{your CLSID here}]
      ="VIZFILE Icon Ext"

[HKEY_LOCAL_MACHINE\SOFTWARE\Classes\CLSID\{your CLSID here}\InProcServer32]
      ="vizicon.dll"
"ThreadingModel"="Apartment"

[HKEY_CLASSES_ROOT\VIZFile\shellex\IconHandler]="{your CLSID here}"

[HKEY_CLASSES_ROOT\VIZFile\DefaultIcon]="%1"
```

Listing 10.2 The MFC icon handler.

```
// IconHandler.cpp : implementation file
//

#include "stdafx.h"
#include "vizicon.h"
#include "winnetwk.h"
#include "shlobj.h"
#include "winnls.h"
#include "IconHandler.h"
```

```
#ifdef _DEBUG
#define new DEBUG_NEW
#undef THIS_FILE
static char THIS_FILE[] = __FILE__;
#endif

//////////////////////
// CIconHandler

IMPLEMENT_DYNCREATE(CIconHandler, CCmdTarget)

CIconHandler::CIconHandler()
{
}

CIconHandler::~CIconHandler()
{
}



BEGIN_MESSAGE_MAP(CIconHandler, CCmdTarget)
        //{{AFX_MSG_MAP(CIconHandler)
// NOTE - the ClassWizard will add and remove mapping macros here.
        //}}AFX_MSG_MAP
END_MESSAGE_MAP()

// Note: This is the GUID used for your icon handler
// {D9FB7760-5CAC-11CF-A7B2-444553540000}
static const IID IID_IIconHandler =

{ 0xD9FB7760, 0x5CAC, 0x11CF,
  { 0xA7,0xB2,0x44,0x45,0x53,0x54,0x00,0x00 } };

IMPLEMENT_OLECREATE(CIconHandler,"AlIconHandler",
  0xD9FB7760,0x5CAC,0x11CF,
  0xA7,0xB2,0x44,0x45,0x53,0x54,0x00,0x00);

BEGIN_INTERFACE_MAP(CIconHandler, CCmdTarget)
        INTERFACE_PART(CIconHandler, IID_IPersistFile, PersistFile)
        INTERFACE_PART(CIconHandler, IID_IExtractIcon, Icon)
END_INTERFACE_MAP()


STDMETHODIMP_(ULONG) CIconHandler::XPersistFile::AddRef()
```

```
{
        METHOD_PROLOGUE(CIconHandler,PersistFile)
        return pThis->ExternalAddRef();
}

STDMETHODIMP_(ULONG) CIconHandler::XPersistFile::Release()
{
        METHOD_PROLOGUE(CIconHandler,PersistFile)
        return pThis->ExternalRelease();
}

STDMETHODIMP CIconHandler::XPersistFile::QueryInterface
   (REFIID iid,void FAR * FAR *pObj)
{
        METHOD_PROLOGUE(CIconHandler,PersistFile)
                return (HRESULT)pThis->ExternalQueryInterface(&iid,pObj);
}

STDMETHODIMP CIconHandler::XPersistFile::IsDirty()
{
   return E_NOTIMPL;
}

STDMETHODIMP CIconHandler::XPersistFile::Load(LPCOLESTR pszFileName,DWORD)
{
        METHOD_PROLOGUE(CIconHandler,PersistFile);
        WideCharToMultiByte(CP_ACP,0,(LPCWSTR)pszFileName,-1,
                pThis->m_szFile,sizeof(pThis->m_szFile),
                NULL,NULL);
        return NOERROR;
}

STDMETHODIMP CIconHandler::XPersistFile::Save(LPCOLESTR,BOOL)
{
        return E_NOTIMPL;
}

STDMETHODIMP CIconHandler::XPersistFile::SaveCompleted(LPCOLESTR)
{
        return E_NOTIMPL;
}

STDMETHODIMP CIconHandler::XPersistFile::GetCurFile(LPOLESTR FAR *)
{
        return E_NOTIMPL;
```

```
}

STDMETHODIMP CIconHandler::XPersistFile::GetClassID(LPCLSID)
{
        return E_NOTIMPL;
}

STDMETHODIMP_(ULONG) CIconHandler::XIcon::AddRef()
{
        METHOD_PROLOGUE(CIconHandler,Icon)
        return pThis->ExternalAddRef();
}

STDMETHODIMP_(ULONG) CIconHandler::XIcon::Release()
{
        METHOD_PROLOGUE(CIconHandler,Icon)
        return pThis->ExternalRelease();
}

STDMETHODIMP CIconHandler::XIcon::QueryInterface(REFIID iid,
   void FAR * FAR *pObj)
{
        METHOD_PROLOGUE(CIconHandler,Icon)
                return (HRESULT)pThis->ExternalQueryInterface(&iid,pObj);
}

STDMETHODIMP CIconHandler::XIcon::GetIconLocation(UINT uFlags,
  LPSTR szIconFile,

                         UINT cchMax,int *piIndex,

                         UINT *pwFlags)
{
        METHOD_PROLOGUE(CIconHandler,Icon);
//TODO: Supply icon file & index here
// - if you need the file name use pThis->m_szFile
//      OR return S_FALSE and supply an HICON below
        ::GetModuleFileName(AfxGetInstanceHandle(),szIconFile,cchMax);
        HANDLE f=CreateFile(
                     pThis->m_szFile,GENERIC_READ,
                     FILE_SHARE_READ|FILE_SHARE_WRITE,
         NULL,OPEN_EXISTING,0,NULL);
      DWORD siz=
        GetFileSize(f NULL);
      CloseHandle(f);
```

```
        *piIndex=siz>1024?1:0;
        *pwFlags|=GIL_PERINSTANCE;
        return S_OK;
}

STDMETHODIMP CIconHandler::XIcon::Extract(LPCSTR,UINT,HICON *,HICON *,UINT)
{
        METHOD_PROLOGUE(CIconHandler,Icon);
//TODO: Supply HICON here -- if you need the file name use pThis->m_szFile
//      OR return S_FALSE and provide an icon file (see above)
        return S_FALSE;
}

///////////////////////// CIconHandler message handlers
```

ATL Vs. MFC

As you can see, you can do the same job in ATL or MFC. Which is better? That depends on what you consider important. The ATL extension doesn't require the MFC DLLs, so an ATL program will be smaller to distribute (especially important over the Internet). The ATL program has more of the flavor of ActiveX, which will appeal to you if you're experienced with ActiveX and may not appeal to you if you're more comfortable with MFC.

In the end, only you can decide which method you like best. Of course, it's possible to build MFC support into an ATL program and use both. However, this approach always strikes me of getting the worst of both worlds.

Icon Tray Programs

Another way you can customize the shell is by adding icons to the Taskbar. The Taskbar contains a small area (the icon or system tray) in which your programs can display information to the user. (This area often contains a clock, modem indicators, and similar items.) Luckily, it isn't hard to create programs that take advantage of the icon tray.

The key is to register your program using **Shell_NotifyIcon**. This call requires two arguments: a function code and a pointer to a **NOTIFYICONDATA** structure. The function code can be **NIM_ADD** to register your program, **NIM_DELETE** to unregister, or **NIM_MODIFY** to change your program's settings. The structure contains the window handle that you want to control the icon tray, a user-defined message, an icon handle, and a tip string.

When you call **Shell_NotifyIcon** the shell will place the icon you specify on the Taskbar. In addition, when the user floats the mouse cursor over the icon, the tip string appears in a balloon window. The shell also forwards mouse messages directed to the icon to your controlling window. To do this, it sends you the user-defined message of your choice along with the mouse information. The shell passes the mouse message (**WM_LBUTTONDOWN**, for instance) in **lParam** and the ID you've assigned the icon in the **NOTIFYICONDATA** structure.

What you do with the mouse data is up to you. However, here are some suggestions from Microsoft:

- When the user clicks on the icon, your application should display a window with additional information
- When the user clicks on the icon with the right mouse button, your application should display the shortcut menu.
- When the user double-clicks on the icon, your application should execute the default shortcut menu command.

If you want to change the icon, the tip string, or the message you receive, you can call **Shell_NotifyIcon** with the **NIM_MODIFY** command. You can also set flags in the **NOTIFYICONDATA** structure to indicate which parts you want to modify, thereby making it possible to change the tip string without modifying the icon.

When you no longer want to display the icon, you call **Shell_NotifyIcon** again with the **NIM_DELETE** parameter. If you fail to do this, your icon may remain on the Taskbar for a while before the shell notices your program is no longer present.

You can find a contrived example in Listing 10.3. This simple MFC program installs an icon on the Taskbar during its **OnInitialUpdate** handler. Initially, there's no tip string, but the user can set one using the simple user interface. The program responds to mouse clicks with a message box.

While this example isn't very practical, it shows the basic steps that all icon handlers must take. You can easily add the same steps to practically any program and make it work with the Taskbar.

Listing 10.3 A tray application.

```
// trayappView.cpp : implementation of the CTrayappView class
//
#include "stdafx.h"
#include "shellapi.h"
#include "trayapp.h"
#include "trayappDoc.h"
#include "trayappView.h"
#ifdef _DEBUG
```

```
#define new DEBUG_NEW
#undef THIS_FILE
static char THIS_FILE[] = __FILE__;
#endif
////////////////////////////////////////
// CTrayappView
IMPLEMENT_DYNCREATE(CTrayappView, CFormView)
BEGIN_MESSAGE_MAP(CTrayappView, CFormView)
   //{{AFX_MSG_MAP(CTrayappView)
   ON_BN_CLICKED(IDC_SET, OnSet)
   ON_WM_DESTROY()
   //}}AFX_MSG_MAP
   ON_MESSAGE(WM_USER,OnTrayMsg)
END_MESSAGE_MAP()

////////////////////////////////////////
// CTrayappView construction/destruction

CTrayappView::CTrayappView()
   : CFormView(CTrayappView::IDD)
{
   //{{AFX_DATA_INIT(CTrayappView)
   m_tip = _T("");
   //}}AFX_DATA_INIT
   // TODO: add construction code here

}

CTrayappView::~CTrayappView()
{
}

void CTrayappView::DoDataExchange(CDataExchange* pDX)
{
   CFormView::DoDataExchange(pDX);
   //{{AFX_DATA_MAP(CTrayappView)
   DDX_Text(pDX, IDC_Tip, m_tip);
   DDV_MaxChars(pDX, m_tip, 63);
   //}}AFX_DATA_MAP
}

BOOL CTrayappView::PreCreateWindow(CREATESTRUCT& cs)
{
   // TODO: Modify the Window class or styles here by modifying
   //  the CREATESTRUCT cs

   return CFormView::PreCreateWindow(cs);
```

```
}

///////////////////////////////////////
// CTrayappView diagnostics

#ifdef _DEBUG
void CTrayappView::AssertValid() const
{
   CFormView::AssertValid();
}

void CTrayappView::Dump(CDumpContext& dc) const
{
   CFormView::Dump(dc);
}

CTrayappDoc* CTrayappView::GetDocument() // non-debug version is inline
{
   ASSERT(m_pDocument->IsKindOf(RUNTIME_CLASS(CTrayappDoc)));
   return (CTrayappDoc*)m_pDocument;
}
#endif //_DEBUG

///////////////////////////////////////
// CTrayappView message handlers

void CTrayappView::OnSet()
{
   UpdateData(TRUE);
   // This code updates the tip
   NOTIFYICONDATA icond;
   icond.cbSize=sizeof(icond);
   icond.hWnd=m_hWnd;
   icond.uID=1;
   icond.uFlags=NIF_TIP;
   strcpy(icond.szTip,m_tip);
   Shell_NotifyIcon(NIM_MODIFY,&icond);

}

void CTrayappView::OnInitialUpdate()
{
   CFormView::OnInitialUpdate();
   NOTIFYICONDATA icond;
   icond.cbSize=sizeof(icond);
   icond.hWnd=m_hWnd;        // Give this window the message
```

```
    icond.uID=1;              // Only 1 so that's OK
    icond.uFlags=NIF_ICON|NIF_MESSAGE|NIF_TIP;
    icond.uCallbackMessage=WM_USER;
    icond.szTip[0]='\0';      // No tip to start with
    // load the icon
     icond.hIcon=AfxGetApp()->LoadIcon(IDR_TRAYAPTYPE);
    // This tells the shell we are ready
     Shell_NotifyIcon(NIM_ADD,&icond);
}

void CTrayappView::OnDestroy()
{
   CFormView::OnDestroy();
   // Get rid of the icon handler
   NOTIFYICONDATA icond;
   icond.cbSize=sizeof(icond);
   icond.hWnd=m_hWnd;
   icond.uID=1;
   icond.uFlags=0;
   Shell_NotifyIcon(NIM_DELETE,&icond);

}

// This message fires when a mouse action occurs over
// our icon... the mouse message is in lParam
// the ID is in wParam (always 1 for us)
UINT CTrayappView::OnTrayMsg(WPARAM wParam,LPARAM lParam)
{
  if (lParam==WM_LBUTTONDOWN||
      lParam==WM_RBUTTONDOWN) MessageBox("Don't click me, man!");
  return 0;
}
```

About Smart Pointers

When you write a shell extension, you usually don't deal with any ActiveX objects—you simply supply them. However, with shortcuts and MMC (topics just around the corner), you'll have to deal with interfaces provided by the shell or MMC. It's often handy to use ATL smart pointers to deal with these interfaces.

The basic smart pointer is a template class, **CComPtr**. This object wraps an interface pointer, calling **AddRef** and **Release** as appropriate. So to wrap a pointer to an **IPersistFile** interface named **pipf**, for example, you could write:

```
CComPtr<IPersistFile> ptr(pipf);
```

This code assumes that **pipf** is already an **IPersistFile** pointer. If you didn't have an **IPersistFile** pointer, you'd have to call **QueryInterface** to obtain the object's **IPersistFile** interface. This step is so common that another class—**CComQIPtr**—does it automatically. Suppose you have a pointer to an **IUnknown** pointer (**p**) and you want to make a smart pointer to an **IPersistFile**. You could write:

```
CComQIPtr<IPersistFile,&IID_IPersistFile> ptr(p);
```

This code creates a pointer that queries for the correct interface. In either case, when the pointer goes out of scope, the smart pointer automatically releases the interface.

Shortcuts

In Unix, it's possible for a file to have more than one name. Each separate name is a hard link and refers to the same actual area of disk storage. A similar device known as a *soft link* or a *symbolic link* is simply a file that points to another file. When you attempt to open a symbolic link, the operating system opens the real file instead.

This mechanism has great utility. It can make network files appear local, for example. However, the reason it's so useful is because it's part of the operating system. Windows has a similar facility known as *shortcuts*. A shortcut is very similar to a symbolic link except in one important area: The operating system doesn't know anything about shortcuts.

If the operating system doesn't understand shortcuts, then what does? The shell is responsible for managing shortcuts. In fact, a shortcut is a special ActiveX object managed by the shell.

You use shortcuts all the time. Every entry in your Windows Start menu is a shortcut to the actual application somewhere on your disk. Most icons on your desktop are probably shortcuts.

Try this experiment. Create a text file (with a .txt extension) anywhere on your hard drive. Then right-click on your desktop and create a new shortcut to the text file. Now start Microsoft Word (or a similar word processor) and ask it to open a file. Navigate the file open dialog box to your desktop folder and select the LNK file that represents the shortcut on your desktop. Most word processors will correctly resolve this link and read the actual TXT file. However, try to open the same file with Notepad. Until Microsoft fixes Notepad, it will open up the binary shortcut instead of the text file!

The point is that a program has to be aware of shortcuts in order to use them. This makes them less attractive than a true symbolic link that would work at the operating system level.

The good news is that most programs that use the standard open dialog box will automatically resolve shortcuts. If you don't specify **OFN_NODE-REFERENCELINKS** in the standard dialog box's options, the dialog box will automatically resolve the shortcut and return the correct file name.

This approach is fine if you're using the standard open file dialog box, but it isn't much help if you need to read file names from the command line or a file. To resolve shortcuts, you'll need to ask the shell for an ActiveX object, load the object from disk (the LNK file), and then query the object about its state.

Creating A Shortcut

Suppose you want to create a shortcut from within a program. There is no easy way to do this. You must follow these steps (assuming you've already initialized ActiveX by calling **CoInitialize**):

1. Use **CoCreateInstance** to request an ActiveX object from the shell. This object will present the **IShellLink** interface.
2. Use the object's functions (for example, **SetPath**, **SetDescription**, and **SetIcon**) to initialize the shortcut so that it meets your requirements. You'll most often call **SetPath** with a complete path name, so **GetFullPathName** may be helpful.
3. Make sure the LNK file name is in Unicode, not ANSI (for example, call **MultiByteToWideChar**). This step isn't a problem if your program already uses Unicode.
4. Call **QueryInterface** to learn the object's **IPersistFile** interface. This interface is a standard one supported by all objects that can save themselves to disk.
5. Call the **IPersistFile** interface's **Save** function, passing it the Unicode file name for the .LNK file.
6. Call **Release** on both interfaces to free the shell's object (not required if you're using smart pointers).

The idea is that you obtain an uninitialized object from the shell. You use the available functions to initialize the object and then save it to disk. Why so complicated? Who knows? However, it's simple to write this code once, wrap it in a function or class, and never have to write it again. You can find a function you can use in Listing 10.4. Notice that this function uses ATL smart pointers so it doesn't have to worry about details like **AddRef** and **Release**.

Listing 10.4 Creating a shortcut.

```
HRESULT CreateShellLink(PCSTR lpszPathObj,
    PSTR lpszPathLink, PSTR lpszDesc)
{
    HRESULT hres;
   CComPtr<IShellLink> psl;
   char fullname[2048];
   char *_8x3name;
   GetFullPathName(lpszPathObj,sizeof(fullname),fullname,&_8x3name);
    lpszPathObj=fullname;
    // Get a pointer to the IShellLink interface.
    hres = CoCreateInstance(CLSID_ShellLink, NULL,
        CLSCTX_INPROC_SERVER, IID_IShellLink,(void **) &psl);
    if (SUCCEEDED(hres)) {
        CComQIPtr<IPersistFile> ppf(psl);
        WORD wsz[MAX_PATH];

        // Set the path to the shortcut target, and add the
        // description.
        psl->SetPath( lpszPathObj);
        psl->SetDescription( lpszDesc);


            // Ensure that the string is ANSI.
            MultiByteToWideChar(CP_ACP, 0, lpszPathLink, -1,
                wsz, MAX_PATH);

            // Save the link by calling IPersistFile::Save.
            hres = ppf->Save( wsz, TRUE);
        }
    return hres;
}
```

Resolving Shortcuts

As you might expect, resolving a shortcut is the exact opposite of creating one. You still obtain the blank object from the shell, but you load it from a disk file to initialize it. Then you can use several functions to examine the contents of the link before you release it. Here are the steps:

1. Call **CoCreateInstance** to retrieve the shell object that supports **IShellLink**.
2. Call **QueryInterface** to find the **IPersistFile** interface.
3. Call **IPersist::Load** to read the disk file that holds the shortcut (the LNK file). Make sure the file name is in Unicode format.

4. Call **IShellLink::Resolve** to make sure the system searches for the target file if it moves.
5. Call the functions that allow you to examine the shortcut's data. Usually, you'll want to use **GetPath**, at least.
6. Call **Release** on both interfaces (not required if you're using smart pointers).

Again, you'll probably write a function once to do this. Better still, you can borrow the function that appears in Listing 10.5. Interestingly, Windows CE provides simple functions to create and resolve shortcuts (**SHGetShortcutTarget** and **SHCreateShortcut**), but other versions of Windows apparently don't.

Listing 10.5 Resolving a shortcut.

```
HRESULT ResolveShellLink(LPSTR lpszPath, LPCSTR lpszLinkFile)
{
    HRESULT hres;
   CComPtr<IShellLink> psl;
    char szGotPath[MAX_PATH];
    char szDescription[MAX_PATH];
    WIN32_FIND_DATA wfd;

    *lpszPath = 0; // assume failure

    // Get a pointer to the IShellLink interface.
    hres = CoCreateInstance(CLSID_ShellLink, NULL,
            CLSCTX_INPROC_SERVER, IID_IShellLink,(void **) &psl);
    if (SUCCEEDED(hres)) {
        // Get a pointer to the IPersistFile interface.
      CComQIPtr<IPersistFile,&IID_IPersistFile> ppf(psl);
        WORD wsz[MAX_PATH];

            // Ensure that the string is Unicode.
            MultiByteToWideChar(CP_ACP, 0, lpszLinkFile, -1, wsz,
                MAX_PATH);

            // Load the shortcut.
            hres = ppf->Load(wsz, STGM_READ);
            if (SUCCEEDED(hres)) {

                // Resolve the link.
            // may prompt the user so should have an hWnd, but I used NULL
                hres = psl->Resolve(NULL, SLR_UPDATE);
                if (SUCCEEDED(hres)) {
```

```
                    // Get the path to the link target.
                    hres = psl->GetPath( szGotPath,
                        MAX_PATH, (WIN32_FIND_DATA *)&wfd,
                        SLGP_SHORTPATH );
                    if (!SUCCEEDED(hres))
                {
errrel:
                        return hres;
                }

                    // Get the description of the target.
                    hres = psl->GetDescription(szDescription, MAX_PATH);
                    if (!SUCCEEDED(hres))
                        goto errrel;
                    lstrcpy(lpszPath, szGotPath);
                 }
              }
          }
    return hres;
}
```

The shell has other features you've already seen in previous chapters. For example, the **ShellExecute** function (Chapter 3) causes the shell to run a program or open a document for you.

The shell also supports drag and drop (via the **DragAcceptFiles** and related functions). You can use this feature to allow users to drag files directly into your application. In addition, the shell supports application bars, which are similar to the system Taskbar but can contain buttons and controls that work with your program.

Another area for which the shell provides calls is file manipulation. For example, you can copy a file using the shell instead of the more traditional **CopyFile** call. Using the shell displays the animated progress screen and provides more user feedback than using **CopyFile**.

You can find a brief list of shell-related calls in Table 10.4. Many of these calls are useful only in special situations. Others, like **SHAddToRecentDocs**, are common and easy to use. The shell also provides a set of calls to access the Registry, but you're usually as well off to use the ordinary Registry calls in all but the simplest cases.

Table 10.4 Shell calls.

Call	Description
SHAddToRecentDocs	Adds a file to the recent document menu (or clears the list)
SHAppBarMessage	Sends application bar messages to the system
SHBrowseForFolder	Displays a dialog box to select a shell folder
SHChangeNotify	Notifies the shell that the program has made a change that may change the state of the shell (for example , it created or deleted a file)
SHEmptyRecycleBin	Empties the recycle bin on the specified drive
SHQuer yRecycleBin	Deter mines infor mation about the recycle bin on the specified drive
SHFileOperation	Copies, moves, renames, or deletes file
SHFreeNameMappings	Frees data retur ned by ShFileOperation
SHGetInstanceExplorer	Retur ns the IUnknown interface for the shell
SHGetDesktopFolder	Retur ns the IShellF older interface for the desktop folder
SHGetFileInfo	Retur ns infor mation about the specified file
SHGetMalloc	Retrieves the IMalloc interface used by the shell
SHGetSettings	Retrieves the shell' s options (for example , the option to hide extensions or use HTML)
SHGetSpecialF olderLocation	Retur ns an ID List for a special folder (for example , the recycle bin or the program files director y)
SHGetSpecialF olderPath	Retur ns the path to a special folder
SHGetDataF romIDList	Reads extended property data from a shell folder
SHGetPathF romIDList	Retur ns the path of a shell folder
SHLoadInProc	Creates an ActiveX object in the shell' s process

MMC

ATL can also make life easier when you're creating a snap-in for the Microsoft Management Console (MMC). The MMC is an administrative tool that allows a system administrator to build custom views of various administration tools (see Figure 10.3 which shows a custom snap-in running in MMC). However, MMC can display more than one snap-in at a time. For example, if you have snap-ins that monitor free disk space and network connections, you can assemble them into a custom MMC document. Opening this document will recall the tools you want to use. You might have one set of tools for monitoring network usage and another for gauging database performance, for example.

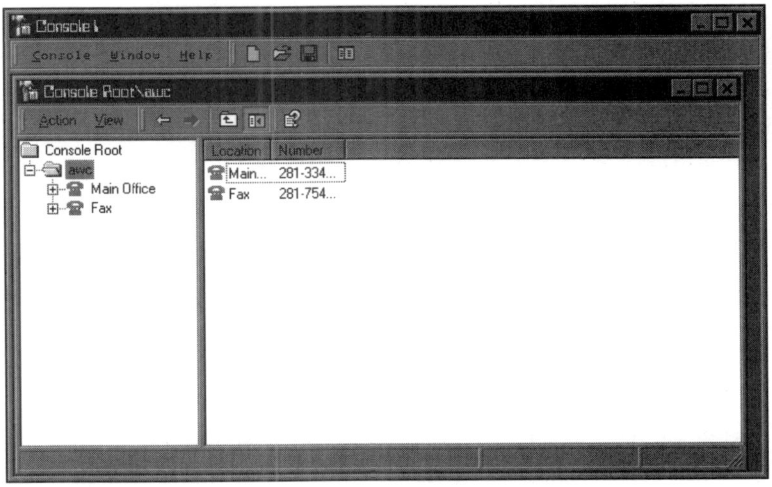

Figure 10.3 The MMC with a custom snap-in.

MMC's display is in two parts. The left portion of the window is the scope pane; it corresponds to a directory listing in the Windows Explorer, except in this case the folders are actually snap-ins. On the right side of the MMC window is the result pane, which shows the contents of each snap-in pseudo folder. The contents may be more pseudo folders (which add to the scope pane) or a view of some actual data. You can think of the MMC window as analogous to the standard explorer, but it explores MMC snap-ins rather than a file system. Your snap-in interfaces primarily with the MMC node manager, which loads and initializes snap-ins. It also provides services to snap-ins (primarily via **IConsole**). Most snap-ins must supply an **IComponentData** interface that informs MMC about the general nature of the snap-in and provides for persistence. In addition, each result pane view requires an object that implements the **IComponent** interface. The only snap-ins that don't require these interfaces are those that don't use the result pane (some snap-ins extend other snap-ins and don't directly use the result pane).

When the user adds your snap-in to an instance of the MMC, your snap-in appears as a folder, or node, in the scope pane. Nodes fall into three categories: built-in, static, and enumerated. Built-in nodes are handled by MMC itself (for example, Web pages or shortcuts). Snap-ins create static or enumerated nodes. Static nodes contain information that doesn't change (for example, a configuration dialog box). Enumerated nodes appear as a list. You assign your nodes a GUID (Globally Unique Identifier), just like an ActiveX object; MMC identifies your nodes using this GUID.

To support persistence (that is, saving and loading from an MSC file), the snap-in may provide an **IPersistStorage**, **IPersistStream**, or **IPersistStreamInit** interface. MMC provides the actual file, and the snap-in is never actually aware of the file—only the ActiveX structured storage or stream.

Snap-ins may supplement other snap-ins. A snap-in that requires other snap-ins to work is called an *extension* snap-in. A snap-in that's independent of other snap-ins is a *standalone* snap-in. Some snap-ins, known as *dual-mode* snap-ins, can provide certain functions of an extension snap-in, but will function as a standalone snap-in if the required additional snap-ins aren't present.

When you insert an ATL object, one of the choices the Wizard offers is an MMC snap-in object. This option sounds ideal, because you'd expect the Wizard to do the bulk of the work required. Unfortunately, this isn't really the case.

What The ATL Wizard Does

When you instruct the ATL Wizard to insert an MMC object, it creates a simple MMC snap-in. However, this snap-in has no hierarchical structure—it's simply an empty folder that will show up in the scope pane.

In real life, this snap-in isn't very useful. It is, however, a starting point. The problem is that ATL offers no support for any further automated customization. To add more subfolders or any scope pane items, you must manually add classes. That means you have to understand the architecture the Wizard uses so you can extend it.

The main class you'll be interested in is the **CxxxData** class (where **xxx** is the name you supplied the Wizard). This class is similar to the view class in a standard MFC program. However, don't forget that you don't have complete control of the view—the MMC program enforces a certain look and feel.

The main function in this class that you'll change is **Notify**. The framework calls **Notify** when MMC asks your snap-in a question. The default code uses a giant switch statement to separate the various questions. In the **MMCN_SHOW** case, you set up the result pane. **MMCN_EXPAND** allows you to modify the scope pane. The only other function you might want to alter is **GetResultPaneColInfo**, which lets you set the data for the different columns in the result pane when the pane is displaying data in a columnar format.

What The Wizard Doesn't Do

The biggest problem with the ATL Wizard is that each separate node in the result pane requires a data object. However, the Wizard creates only one object and there's no simple way to add more. The quickest way to resolve this issue is to resort to cut and paste. Here's the basic strategy:

1. Open the header file and copy the **CxxxData** class definition. Change the name of the class and also change the references to the name in the templates and the constructor name. In other words, change the name of the class everywhere it appears in the copy. You can use any unique name you like.

2. Open the CPP file and copy everything from the line that begins "static const GUID" to the end of the **GetResultPaneColInfo** function. In the copy, change all the references to the class name to the new class name you used in Step 1.
3. Generate a new GUID for this class. You can use the command line program UUIDGEN or use the Project|Add To Project|Components And Controls menu item to insert the GUID Generator component (from the Visual C++ Components gallery). This isn't really a component—it's just a tool that places a GUID on the clipboard.
4. Change the name of the node type GUID in the copy (in the CPP file). Replace the existing GUID with the one generated in Step 3. You'll also need to change the same name in the next line and change the Registry-format GUID stored in **m_SZNODETYPE** so that it matches the new GUID. You'll probably also want to change the **m_SZDISPLAYNAME** variable. All of these definitions are at the very top of the block you copied into the CPP file.

You can repeat these four steps to create each node that you need. When you're done, you should do a dry-run compile to make sure you changed everything correctly.

The ATL Wizard uses **CComQIPtr** to provide access to the various interfaces MMC passes to your code. That means you don't have to worry about managing the interfaces or using **QueryInterface** directly. Just remember that smart pointers are objects, so using the dot operator (**.**) will access members of the smart pointer class. To access the interface members, use the arrow operator (**->**).

Fleshing Out The Code

In each object's **MMCN_EXPAND** handler, you inform MMC what you want in the scope view. For any node that has children, you call the child's **GetScopePaneInfo** function, which will fill in a **SCOPEDATAITEM** structure. You can pass this structure to the **InsertItem** method of the **IConsoleNameSpace** interface (see Table 10.5). MMC V1.1 supports an extended interface—**IConsoleNameSpace2**—that has all the same functions and adds two new functions: **Expand** and **AddExtension**. The Wizard's boilerplate code provides you with a pointer to this interface.

If you have more than one child, of course, you'll have to call **InsertItem** multiple times. It isn't unusual to make the call inside a loop if you've stored your children in an array. You only insert your immediate children. Presumably, the children call **InsertItem** as appropriate to add their children. Of course, a node that has no children doesn't need to do anything.

Table 10.5 The IConsoleNameSpace and IConsoleNameSpace2 interfaces.

Method	Description
InsertItem	Adds a new item to the scope view
DeleteItem	Removes a scope view item
SetItem	Sets the attributes of an existing item
GetItem	Finds a particular scope view item
GetChildItem	Finds the first child item
GetNextItem	Enumerates items
GetParentItem	Finds the parent item
Expand	Expands an item without altering the scope pane (IConsoleNameSpace2)
AddExtension	Adds a dynamic extension to an item (IConsoleNameSpace2)

The **MMCN_SHOW** handler lets you set the result pane (the right side of the MMC window). The Wizard arranges for you to have a pointer to the **IResultData** interface (see Table 10.6). You can insert columns, set column widths, set the description bar, and even control the view's mode (iconic, columnar, and so on).

When you insert items into either view, you'll set the text to **MMC_CALLBACK**—a special value that causes MMC to call your **GetResultPaneColInfo** function to retrieve the actual text.

Table 10.6 The IResultData interface.

Method	Description
InsertItem	Inserts a new item
DeleteItem	Deletes an item
FindItemByLParam	Finds items by a user-defined number
DeleteAllRsltItems	Deletes all items
SetItem	Sets a single item
GetItem	Gets an item
GetNextItem	Enumerates items
ModifyItemState	Modifies the state (selected, focused, and so on)
ModifyViewStyle	Modifies the view style (single selection, sorted, and so on)
SetViewMode	Sets the view mode (iconic , list, report, and so on)

(continued)

Table 10.6 The IResultData interface **(continued).**

Method	Description
GetViewMode	Returns the current view mode
UpdateItem	Redraws an item
Sort	Sorts the result pane
SetDescBarText	Sets the description bar text
SetItemCount	Sets the number of items to preallocate memory or implement virtual lists managed by the snap in

The Wizard also creates a component object that serves—in a way—as the snap-in's document object. That is to say, this object handles persistence to a file and provides the description strings to MMC. The descriptions, by the way, are in the snap-in's resource table, so it's very easy to modify them to reflect your company name and information. If you need to save and restore the state, you add code to the component's **Load** and **Save** methods.

An ATL MMC Snap-In

Listings 10.6 and 10.7 and Figure 10.3 show an example snap-in. This simple snap-in provides technical support numbers for a make-believe vendor so that this information can be put in the MMC view.

Of course, the first step to creating this snap-in is to create a new ATL project. The project should reside in a DLL. Armed with an empty project, you can use the ATL Object Wizard (Insert|ATL Object) to add an MMC snap-in object.

When you select MMC Snap-In Object in the ATL Object Wizard, a dialog box will open. Some of the choices in this dialog box might require a little explanation. The Wizard uses the short name to build names for the other fields. Usually you can leave the names alone; however, if you want to change any of them, you can.

The other page of the dialog box contains options about the type of snap-in you'll create. The Extension checkbox allows you to write a snap-in that extends an existing snap-in. You can also support the **ISnapInAbout** interface (recommended), or provide interfaces for control bars, property sheets, or context menus. You can also specify whether you want your snap-in to support persistence (that is, save state information to a file). If it does, you can elect to use a stream, a storage, or the **IPersistStreamInit** interface (a special case of the **IPersistStream**).

This particular example snap-in has two node types (even though the root node may have multiple phone numbers, each phone number is an instance of the same class). So the first changes you'll perform are the four steps to copy the nodes (see Listings 10.6 and 10.7). The original node is the **CawcData** object, and the new node is the **CawcNumData** object. In Listing 10.6, you can see the new class easily because its code begins and ends with a comment marking it as the new class.

The root node now has to enumerate the child nodes. Because all the phone numbers are the same, it makes sense to use an array for this item. The root object (**CawcData**) has a **Notify** function in which you can make the correct calls. For the root object, the correct call is **InsertItem**.

You'll also want to modify the root object to show a result pane. In this case, the result pane is a columnar list of all the phone numbers in the child nodes. To accomplish this list, you simply need to add two columns using **InsertColumn**.

You'll need to make similar changes to the new class (**CawcNumData** in the example). The scope pane requires no code because the phone number objects have no children. In the result view, the program sets up two columns and adjusts their widths. It also sets some helpful text in the description bar (which may not appear if the user has the bar turned off).

Because the phone number nodes need to set their phone number as the column text, it's important to change the **GetResultPaneColInfo** function as well. Each phone object stores the number in an instance variable, and this function just returns the correct string on request from MMC.

Another nice touch is to make double-clicking on the node dial the associated phone number. I didn't include the code to dial the phone; however, you could use TAPI (Microsoft's Telephony API) to do that easily. The **Notify** function checks for the **MMCN_DBLCLICK** notification and displays a message box.

Of course, you can do many more things with a snap-in like this. It's easy enough to change the images both in the resources and for each node. The Wizard's code is pretty easy to follow in that respect. If you make the proper selections in the Wizard, it's also simple to add property pages and context menus.

Listing 10.6 The MMC snap-in.

```
#include "stdafx.h"
#include "Awcsnap.h"
#include "awc.h"

///////////////////////
// CawcComponentData
static const GUID CawcGUID_NODETYPE =
{ 0x60db2ef, 0x949, 0x11d3,
 { 0x9f, 0x15, 0x44, 0x45, 0x53, 0x54, 0x0, 0x0 } };
const GUID*  CawcData::m_NODETYPE = &CawcGUID_NODETYPE;
```

```
const OLECHAR* CawcData::m_SZNODETYPE =
   OLESTR("060DB2EF-0949-11D3-9F15-444553540000");
const OLECHAR* CawcData::m_SZDISPLAY_NAME = OLESTR("awc");
const CLSID* CawcData::m_SNAPIN_CLASSID = &CLSID_awc;

HRESULT CawcData::GetScopePaneInfo(SCOPEDATAITEM *pScopeDataItem)
{
   if (pScopeDataItem->mask & SDI_STR)
      pScopeDataItem->displayname = m_bstrDisplayName;
   if (pScopeDataItem->mask & SDI_IMAGE)
      pScopeDataItem->nImage = m_scopeDataItem.nImage;
   if (pScopeDataItem->mask & SDI_OPENIMAGE)
      pScopeDataItem->nOpenImage = m_scopeDataItem.nOpenImage;
   if (pScopeDataItem->mask & SDI_PARAM)
      pScopeDataItem->lParam = m_scopeDataItem.lParam;
   if (pScopeDataItem->mask & SDI_STATE )
      pScopeDataItem->nState = m_scopeDataItem.nState;

   // TODO : Add code for SDI_CHILDREN
   return S_OK;
}

HRESULT CawcData::GetResultPaneInfo(RESULTDATAITEM *pResultDataItem)
{
   if (pResultDataItem->bScopeItem)
   {
      if (pResultDataItem->mask & RDI_STR)
      {
         pResultDataItem->str =
            GetResultPaneColInfo(pResultDataItem->nCol);
      }
      if (pResultDataItem->mask & RDI_IMAGE)
      {
         pResultDataItem->nImage = m_scopeDataItem.nImage;
      }
      if (pResultDataItem->mask & RDI_PARAM)
      {
         pResultDataItem->lParam = m_scopeDataItem.lParam;
      }

      return S_OK;
   }

   if (pResultDataItem->mask & RDI_STR)
   {
```

```
        pResultDataItem->str = GetResultPaneColInfo(
                    pResultDataItem->nCol);
    }
    if (pResultDataItem->mask & RDI_IMAGE)
    {
        pResultDataItem->nImage = m_resultDataItem.nImage;
    }
    if (pResultDataItem->mask & RDI_PARAM)
    {
        pResultDataItem->lParam = m_resultDataItem.lParam;
    }
    if (pResultDataItem->mask & RDI_INDEX)
    {
        pResultDataItem->nIndex = m_resultDataItem.nIndex;
    }

    return S_OK;
}

HRESULT CawcData::Notify( MMC_NOTIFY_TYPE event,
     long arg,
     long param,
    IComponentData* pComponentData,
    IComponent* pComponent,
    DATA_OBJECT_TYPES type)
{
    // Add code to handle the different notifications.
    // Handle MMCN_SHOW and MMCN_EXPAND to enumerate children items.
    // In response to MMCN_SHOW you have to enumerate both the scope
    // and result pane items.
    // For MMCN_EXPAND you only need to enumerate the scope items
    // Use IConsoleNameSpace::InsertItem to insert scope pane items
    // Use IResultData::InsertItem to insert result pane items.
    HRESULT hr = E_NOTIMPL;


    _ASSERTE(pComponentData != NULL || pComponent != NULL);

    CComPtr<IConsole> spConsole;
    CComQIPtr<IHeaderCtrl, &IID_IHeaderCtrl> spHeader;
    if (pComponentData != NULL)
        spConsole = ((Cawc*)pComponentData)->m_spConsole;
    else
    {
        spConsole = ((CawcComponent*)pComponent)->m_spConsole;
```

```
   spHeader = spConsole;
}

switch (event)
{
case MMCN_SHOW:
   {
      CComQIPtr<IResultData,
                &IID_IResultData> spResultData(spConsole);
      // TODO : Enumerate the result pane items
      if (arg)
      {
         hr=spHeader->InsertColumn(0,L"Location",
                        LVCFMT_LEFT,MMCLV_AUTO);
         hr=spHeader->InsertColumn(1,L"Number",
                        LVCFMT_LEFT,MMCLV_AUTO);
      }
      else
         hr=spResultData->DeleteAllRsltItems();

      break;
   }
case MMCN_EXPAND:
   {
      CComQIPtr<IConsoleNameSpace,
            &IID_IConsoleNameSpace> spConsoleNameSpace(spConsole);
      // TODO : Enumerate scope pane items
      hr = S_OK;
      if (arg) {
         SCOPEDATAITEM sdi;
         for (int i=0;i<2;i++) {
            memset(&sdi,0,sizeof(sdi));
            sdi.mask=SDI_STR|SDI_PARAM|
                           SDI_IMAGE|SDI_OPENIMAGE|SDI_PARENT;
            num[i]->GetScopePaneInfo(&sdi);
            sdi.displayname=MMC_CALLBACK;
            sdi.relativeID=param;
            hr=spConsoleNameSpace->InsertItem(&sdi);
         }
      }
      break;
   }
case MMCN_ADD_IMAGES:
   {
      // Add Images
```

```
            IImageList* pImageList = (IImageList*) arg;
            hr = E_FAIL;
            // Load bitmaps associated with the scope pane
            // and add them to the image list
            // Loads the default bitmaps generated by the Wizard
            // Change as required
            HBITMAP hBitmap16 = LoadBitmap(
                         _Module.GetResourceInstance(),
                         MAKEINTRESOURCE(IDB_AWC_16));
            if (hBitmap16 != NULL)
            {
               HBITMAP hBitmap32 = LoadBitmap(
                               _Module.GetResourceInstance(),
                                MAKEINTRESOURCE(IDB_AWC_32));
               if (hBitmap32 != NULL)
               {
                  hr = pImageList->ImageListSetStrip
                                 ((long*)hBitmap16,
                  (long*)hBitmap32, 0, RGB(0, 128, 128));
                  if (FAILED(hr))
                     ATLTRACE(_T("IImageList::ImageListSetStrip failed\n"));
               }
            }
            break;
         }
      }
      return hr;
   }

   LPOLESTR CawcData::GetResultPaneColInfo(int nCol)
   {
      if (nCol == 0)
         return m_bstrDisplayName;
      // TODO : Return the text for other columns
      return OLESTR("Override GetResultPaneColInfo");
   }

   // *** Begin new class (phone number)




   static const GUID CawcNumGUID_NODETYPE =
   { 0x6e391881, 0xc57, 0x11d3,
      { 0x9f, 0x15, 0x44, 0x45, 0x53, 0x54, 0x0, 0x0 } };
   const GUID*  CawcNumData::m_NODETYPE = &CawcNumGUID_NODETYPE;
```

```
const OLECHAR* CawcNumData::m_SZNODETYPE =
   OLESTR("{6E391881-0C57-11D3-9F15-444553540000}");
const OLECHAR* CawcNumData::m_SZDISPLAY_NAME = OLESTR("awc Number");
const CLSID* CawcNumData::m_SNAPIN_CLASSID = &CLSID_awc;

HRESULT CawcNumData::GetScopePaneInfo(SCOPEDATAITEM *pScopeDataItem)
{
   if (pScopeDataItem->mask & SDI_STR)
      pScopeDataItem->displayname = m_bstrDisplayName;
   if (pScopeDataItem->mask & SDI_IMAGE)
      pScopeDataItem->nImage = m_scopeDataItem.nImage;
   if (pScopeDataItem->mask & SDI_OPENIMAGE)
      pScopeDataItem->nOpenImage = m_scopeDataItem.nOpenImage;
   if (pScopeDataItem->mask & SDI_PARAM)
      pScopeDataItem->lParam = m_scopeDataItem.lParam;
   if (pScopeDataItem->mask & SDI_STATE )
      pScopeDataItem->nState = m_scopeDataItem.nState;

   // TODO : Add code for SDI_CHILDREN
   return S_OK;
}

HRESULT CawcNumData::GetResultPaneInfo(RESULTDATAITEM *pResultDataItem)
{
   if (pResultDataItem->bScopeItem)
   {
      if (pResultDataItem->mask & RDI_STR)
      {
         pResultDataItem->str =
                      GetResultPaneColInfo(pResultDataItem->nCol);
      }
      if (pResultDataItem->mask & RDI_IMAGE)
      {
         pResultDataItem->nImage = m_scopeDataItem.nImage;
      }
      if (pResultDataItem->mask & RDI_PARAM)
      {
         pResultDataItem->lParam = m_scopeDataItem.lParam;
      }

      return S_OK;
   }

   if (pResultDataItem->mask & RDI_STR)
   {
      pResultDataItem->str = GetResultPaneColInfo(
```

```
                pResultDataItem->nCol);
    }
    if (pResultDataItem->mask & RDI_IMAGE)
    {
        pResultDataItem->nImage = m_resultDataItem.nImage;
    }
    if (pResultDataItem->mask & RDI_PARAM)
    {
        pResultDataItem->lParam = m_resultDataItem.lParam;
    }
    if (pResultDataItem->mask & RDI_INDEX)
    {
        pResultDataItem->nIndex = m_resultDataItem.nIndex;
    }

    return S_OK;
}

HRESULT CawcNumData::Notify(MMC_NOTIFY_TYPE event,
     long arg,
     long param,
    IComponentData* pComponentData,
    IComponent* pComponent,
    DATA_OBJECT_TYPES type)
{
    // Add code to handle the different notifications.
    // Handle MMCN_SHOW and MMCN_EXPAND to enumerate children items.
    // In response to MMCN_SHOW you have to enumerate both the scope
    // and result pane items.
    // For MMCN_EXPAND you only need to enumerate the scope items
    // Use IConsoleNameSpace::InsertItem to insert scope pane items
    // Use IResultData::InsertItem to insert result pane items.
    HRESULT hr = E_NOTIMPL;

    _ASSERTE(pComponentData != NULL || pComponent != NULL);

    CComPtr<IConsole> spConsole;
    CComQIPtr<IHeaderCtrl, &IID_IHeaderCtrl> spHeader;
    if (pComponentData != NULL)
        spConsole = ((Cawc*)pComponentData)->m_spConsole;
    else
    {
        spConsole = ((CawcComponent*)pComponent)->m_spConsole;
        spHeader = spConsole;
    }
```

```
switch (event)
{
 case MMCN_DBLCLICK:
   // Really would need phone dial code here....
   ::MessageBox(NULL,mynum,"Debug",MB_OK);
   hr=S_OK;
   break;

case MMCN_SHOW:
   {
      CComQIPtr<IResultData,
                  &IID_IResultData> spResultData(spConsole);

      if (arg)
      {
         RESULTDATAITEM rdi;

         hr=spHeader->InsertColumn(
                         0,L"Location",LVCFMT_LEFT,MMCLV_AUTO);
         hr=spHeader->InsertColumn(
                         1,L"Number",LVCFMT_LEFT,MMCLV_AUTO);
         spHeader->SetColumnWidth(0,100);
         spHeader->SetColumnWidth(1,90);
         memset(&rdi,0,sizeof(rdi));
         rdi.mask=RDI_STR|RDI_PARAM|RDI_IMAGE;
         GetResultPaneInfo(&rdi);
         rdi.str=MMC_CALLBACK;
         hr=spResultData->InsertItem(&rdi);
         spResultData->SetDescBarText(
                          OLESTR("Double click to dial"));
// useless in this case but interesting
      //   spResultData->SetViewMode(MMCLV_VIEWSTYLE_ICON);
      }
      else
      {
         hr=spResultData->DeleteAllRsltItems();
      }

      break;
   }
 case MMCN_EXPAND:
   {
      CComQIPtr<IConsoleNameSpace,
            &IID_IConsoleNameSpace> spConsoleNameSpace(spConsole);
```

```
            // TODO : Enumerate scope pane items
            hr = S_OK;
            break;
         }
      case MMCN_ADD_IMAGES:
         {
            // Add Images
            IImageList* pImageList = (IImageList*) arg;
            hr = E_FAIL;
            // Load bitmaps associated with the scope pane
            // and add them to the image list
            // Loads the default bitmaps generated by the Wizard
            // Change as required
            HBITMAP hBitmap16 = LoadBitmap(
                          _Module.GetResourceInstance(),
                          MAKEINTRESOURCE(IDB_AWC_16));
            if (hBitmap16 != NULL)
            {
               HBITMAP hBitmap32 = LoadBitmap(
                             _Module.GetResourceInstance(),
                             MAKEINTRESOURCE(IDB_AWC_32));
               if (hBitmap32 != NULL)
               {
                  hr = pImageList->ImageListSetStrip(
                                 (long*)hBitmap16,
                  (long*)hBitmap32, 0, RGB(0, 128, 128));
                  if (FAILED(hr))
                     ATLTRACE(_T("IImageList::ImageListSetStrip failed\n"));
               }
            }
            break;
         }
      default:
         ATLTRACE(_T("unknown event (num)\n"));
         return hr;
   }
   return hr;
}

LPOLESTR CawcNumData::GetResultPaneColInfo(int nCol)
{
   USES_CONVERSION;
   if (nCol == 0)
      return m_bstrDisplayName;
   if (nCol==1)
```

```
      return A2OLE(mynum);
}
//*** End of new class


HRESULT Cawc::Initialize(LPUNKNOWN pUnknown)
{
   HRESULT hr = IComponentDataImpl<Cawc,
        CawcComponent >::Initialize(pUnknown);
   if (FAILED(hr))
      return hr;

   CComPtr<IImageList> spImageList;

   if (m_spConsole->QueryScopeImageList(&spImageList) != S_OK)
   {
      ATLTRACE(_T("IConsole::QueryScopeImageList failed\n"));
      return E_UNEXPECTED;
   }

   // Load bitmaps associated with the scope pane
   // and add them to the image list
   // Loads the default bitmaps generated by the Wizard
   // Change as required
   HBITMAP hBitmap16 = LoadBitmap(_Module.GetResourceInstance(),
         MAKEINTRESOURCE(IDB_AWC_16));
   if (hBitmap16 == NULL)
      return S_OK;

   HBITMAP hBitmap32 = LoadBitmap(_Module.GetResourceInstance(),
        MAKEINTRESOURCE(IDB_AWC_32));
   if (hBitmap32 == NULL)
      return S_OK;

   if (spImageList->ImageListSetStrip((long*)hBitmap16,
      (long*)hBitmap32, 0, RGB(0, 128, 128)) != S_OK)
   {
      ATLTRACE(_T("IImageList::ImageListSetStrip failed\n"));
      return E_UNEXPECTED;
   }
   return S_OK;
}
```

Listing 10.7 The MMC snap-in header file.

```
#ifndef __AWC_H_
#define __AWC_H_
#include "resource.h"
#include <atlsnap.h>

// "New class"
class CawcNumData : public CSnapInItemImpl<CawcNumData>
{
public:
   static const GUID* m_NODETYPE;
   static const OLECHAR* m_SZNODETYPE;
   static const OLECHAR* m_SZDISPLAY_NAME;
   static const CLSID* m_SNAPIN_CLASSID;

private:
   char *myname;
   char *mynum;
public:
   CComPtr<IControlbar> m_spControlBar;

   CawcNumData(char *nam,char *num)
   {
      // Image indexes may need to be modified depending on the images
      specific to
      // the snapin.
      myname=strdup(nam);
      mynum=strdup(num);
      m_bstrDisplayName=myname;
      memset(&m_scopeDataItem, 0, sizeof(SCOPEDATAITEM));
      m_scopeDataItem.mask = SDI_STR | SDI_IMAGE | SDI_OPENIMAGE |
         SDI_PARAM;
      m_scopeDataItem.displayname = MMC_CALLBACK;
      m_scopeDataItem.nImage = 0;        // May need modification
      m_scopeDataItem.nOpenImage = 0;    // May need modification
      m_scopeDataItem.lParam = (LPARAM) this;
      memset(&m_resultDataItem, 0, sizeof(RESULTDATAITEM));
      m_resultDataItem.mask = RDI_STR | RDI_IMAGE | RDI_PARAM;
      m_resultDataItem.str = MMC_CALLBACK;
      m_resultDataItem.nImage = 0;       // May need modification
      m_resultDataItem.lParam = (LPARAM) this;
   }

   ~CawcNumData()
   {
```

```
      if (myname) free(myname);
      if (mynum) free(mynum);
   }

   STDMETHOD(GetScopePaneInfo)(SCOPEDATAITEM *pScopeDataItem);

   STDMETHOD(GetResultPaneInfo)(RESULTDATAITEM *pResultDataItem);

   STDMETHOD(Notify)(MMC_NOTIFY_TYPE event,
      long arg,
      long param,
      IComponentData* pComponentData,
      IComponent* pComponent,
      DATA_OBJECT_TYPES type);

   LPOLESTR GetResultPaneColInfo(int nCol);
};

class CawcData : public CSnapInItemImpl<CawcData>
{
public:
   static const GUID* m_NODETYPE;
   static const OLECHAR* m_SZNODETYPE;
   static const OLECHAR* m_SZDISPLAY_NAME;
   static const CLSID* m_SNAPIN_CLASSID;

   CawcNumData *num[2];
   CComPtr<IControlbar> m_spControlBar;

   CawcData()
   {
      // Image indexes may need to be modified depending on the images
      specific to
      // the snapin.
      memset(&m_scopeDataItem, 0, sizeof(SCOPEDATAITEM));
      m_scopeDataItem.mask =
                SDI_STR | SDI_IMAGE | SDI_OPENIMAGE | SDI_PARAM;
      m_scopeDataItem.displayname = MMC_CALLBACK;
      m_scopeDataItem.nImage = 0;        // May need modification
      m_scopeDataItem.nOpenImage = 0;     // May need modification
      m_scopeDataItem.lParam = (LPARAM) this;
      memset(&m_resultDataItem, 0, sizeof(RESULTDATAITEM));
      m_resultDataItem.mask = RDI_STR | RDI_IMAGE | RDI_PARAM;
      m_resultDataItem.str = MMC_CALLBACK;
      m_resultDataItem.nImage = 0;      // May need modification
```

```
        m_resultDataItem.lParam = (LPARAM) this;
        num[0]=new CawcNumData("Main Office","800-555-1212");
        num[1]=new CawcNumData("Fax","888-555-1212");
    }

    ~CawcData()
    {
        delete num[0];
        delete num[1];
    }

    STDMETHOD(GetScopePaneInfo)(SCOPEDATAITEM *pScopeDataItem);

    STDMETHOD(GetResultPaneInfo)(RESULTDATAITEM *pResultDataItem);

    STDMETHOD(Notify)(MMC_NOTIFY_TYPE event,
        long arg,
        long param,
        IComponentData* pComponentData,
        IComponent* pComponent,
        DATA_OBJECT_TYPES type);

    LPOLESTR GetResultPaneColInfo(int nCol);
};



class CawcComponent;

class Cawc : public CComObjectRootEx<CComSingleThreadModel>,
public CSnapInObjectRoot<1, Cawc>,
    public IComponentDataImpl<Cawc, CawcComponent>,
    public IPersistStreamInit,
    public CComCoClass<Cawc, &CLSID_awc>
{
public:
    Cawc()
    {
        m_pNode = new CawcData;
        _ASSERTE(m_pNode != NULL);
        m_pComponentData = this;
    }

    ~Cawc()
    {
```

```
        delete m_pNode;
        m_pNode = NULL;
    }

BEGIN_COM_MAP(Cawc)
    COM_INTERFACE_ENTRY(IComponentData)
    COM_INTERFACE_ENTRY(IPersistStreamInit)
END_COM_MAP()

DECLARE_REGISTRY_RESOURCEID(IDR_AWC)

DECLARE_NOT_AGGREGATABLE(Cawc)

    STDMETHOD(GetClassID)(CLSID *pClassID)
    {
        ATLTRACENOTIMPL(_T("Cawc::GetClassID"));
    }

    STDMETHOD(IsDirty)()
    {
        ATLTRACENOTIMPL(_T("Cawc::IsDirty"));
    }

    STDMETHOD(Load)(IStream *pStm)
    {
        ATLTRACENOTIMPL(_T("Cawc::Load"));
    }

    STDMETHOD(Save)(IStream *pStm, BOOL fClearDirty)
    {
        ATLTRACENOTIMPL(_T("Cawc::Save"));
    }

    STDMETHOD(GetSizeMax)(ULARGE_INTEGER *pcbSize)
    {
        ATLTRACENOTIMPL(_T("Cawc::GetSizeMax"));
    }

    STDMETHOD(InitNew)()
    {
        ATLTRACE(_T("Cawc::InitNew\n"));
        return S_OK;
    }

    STDMETHOD(Initialize)(LPUNKNOWN pUnknown);
```

```
    static void WINAPI ObjectMain(bool bStarting)
    {
       if (bStarting)
          CSnapInItem::Init();
    }
};


class CawcComponent : public CComObjectRootEx<CComSingleThreadModel>,
   public CSnapInObjectRoot<2, Cawc >,
   public IPersistStreamInit,
   public IComponentImpl<CawcComponent>
{
public:
BEGIN_COM_MAP(CawcComponent)
   COM_INTERFACE_ENTRY(IComponent)
   COM_INTERFACE_ENTRY(IPersistStreamInit)
END_COM_MAP()

public:
   CawcComponent()
   {
   }

   STDMETHOD(Notify)(LPDATAOBJECT lpDataObject,
         MMC_NOTIFY_TYPE event, long arg, long param)
   {
      if (lpDataObject != NULL)
         return IComponentImpl<CawcComponent>
                      ::Notify(lpDataObject, event, arg, param);
      // TODO : Add code to handle notifications
      // that set lpDataObject == NULL.
      return E_NOTIMPL;
   }

   STDMETHOD(GetClassID)(CLSID *pClassID)
   {
      ATLTRACENOTIMPL(_T("CawcComponent::GetClassID"));
   }

   STDMETHOD(IsDirty)()
   {
      ATLTRACENOTIMPL(_T("CawcComponent::IsDirty"));
   }
   STDMETHOD(Load)(IStream *pStm)
```

```
    {
       ATLTRACENOTIMPL(_T("CawcComponent::Load"));
    }

    STDMETHOD(Save)(IStream *pStm, BOOL fClearDirty)
    {
       ATLTRACENOTIMPL(_T("CawcComponent::Save"));
    }

    STDMETHOD(GetSizeMax)(ULARGE_INTEGER *pcbSize)
    {
       ATLTRACENOTIMPL(_T("CawcComponent::GetSizeMax"));
    }

    STDMETHOD(InitNew)()
    {
       ATLTRACE(_T("CawcComponent::InitNew\n"));
       return S_OK;
    }

};


class ATL_NO_VTABLE CawcAbout : public ISnapinAbout,
    public CComObjectRoot,
    public CComCoClass< CawcAbout, &CLSID_awcAbout>
{
public:
    DECLARE_REGISTRY(CawcAbout, _T("awcAbout.1"), _T("awcAbout.1"),
             IDS_AWC_DESC, THREADFLAGS_BOTH);

    BEGIN_COM_MAP(CawcAbout)
       COM_INTERFACE_ENTRY(ISnapinAbout)
    END_COM_MAP()

    STDMETHOD(GetSnapinDescription)(LPOLESTR *lpDescription)
    {
       USES_CONVERSION;
       TCHAR szBuf[256];
       if (::LoadString(_Module.GetResourceInstance(), IDS_AWC_DESC,
                 szBuf, 256) == 0)
          return E_FAIL;

       *lpDescription = (LPOLESTR)CoTaskMemAlloc((lstrlen(szBuf) + 1)
```

```
                    * sizeof(OLECHAR));
    if (*lpDescription == NULL)
       return E_OUTOFMEMORY;

    ocscpy(*lpDescription, T2OLE(szBuf));

    return S_OK;
}

STDMETHOD(GetProvider)(LPOLESTR *lpName)
{
   USES_CONVERSION;
   TCHAR szBuf[256];
   if (::LoadString(_Module.GetResourceInstance(), IDS_AWC_PROVIDER,
    szBuf, 256) == 0)
      return E_FAIL;

   *lpName = (LPOLESTR)CoTaskMemAlloc((lstrlen(szBuf) + 1) *
   sizeof(OLECHAR));
   if (*lpName == NULL)
      return E_OUTOFMEMORY;

   ocscpy(*lpName, T2OLE(szBuf));

   return S_OK;
}

STDMETHOD(GetSnapinVersion)(LPOLESTR *lpVersion)
{
   USES_CONVERSION;
   TCHAR szBuf[256];
   if (::LoadString(_Module.GetResourceInstance(),
            IDS_AWC_VERSION, szBuf, 256) == 0)
      return E_FAIL;

   *lpVersion = (LPOLESTR)CoTaskMemAlloc((
            lstrlen(szBuf) + 1) * sizeof(OLECHAR));
   if (*lpVersion == NULL)
      return E_OUTOFMEMORY;

   ocscpy(*lpVersion, T2OLE(szBuf));

   return S_OK;
}
STDMETHOD(GetSnapinImage)(HICON *hAppIcon)
```

```
   {
      if (!hAppIcon) return E_POINTER;
      *hAppIcon = (HICON)::LoadImage(_Module.GetResourceInstance(),
                  MAKEINTRESOURCE(IDI_TEL),IMAGE_ICON,0,0,LR_DEFAULTCOLOR);
      return S_OK;
   }

   STDMETHOD(GetStaticFolderImage)(HBITMAP *hSmallImage,
      HBITMAP *hSmallImageOpen,
      HBITMAP *hLargeImage,
      COLORREF *cMask)
   {
      *hSmallImageOpen = ::LoadBitmap(_Module.GetResourceInstance(),
                  MAKEINTRESOURCE(IDB_AWC_16));
      *hLargeImage = ::LoadBitmap(_Module.GetResourceInstance(),
                  MAKEINTRESOURCE(IDB_AWC_16));
      *hLargeImage = ::LoadBitmap(_Module.GetResourceInstance(),
                  MAKEINTRESOURCE(IDB_AWC_32));
      return S_OK;
   }
};

#endif
```

Summary

Microsoft has certainly created plenty of opportunities for you to customize the user's working environment. By manipulating the Registry you can make many common changes, but ActiveX shell extensions provide for the ultimate in flexibility.

Besides shell extensions, you can customize the icon tray and write MMC snap-ins. You can even take full control of shell links (also known as shortcuts) by using ActiveX technology.

Of course, too much customization can be a bad thing. Imagine if every time you rented a car, you needed a 30-minute orientation lecture so you could drive it. That wouldn't be a good idea. You have an expectation that all cars work about the same—car makers know that and don't alter the basic layout of things too much. The same thing applies to customizing the shell. If you go too far, users won't appreciate it.

Immediate Solutions

About Shell Extensions

Shell extensions are ActiveX objects that add functionality to the Windows shell. You can find a list of the possible extensions in Table 10.1. Shell extensions allow you to write code to determine context menus, specify icons, add property sheets, and perform other useful functions.

Keep in mind that for simple extensions you don't need anything more than a few Registry entries. For example, changing a file's icon to a fixed icon doesn't require a shell extension. Setting the icon so that it contains the initials of the file's creator probably does require a shell extension.

Like all ActiveX objects, shell extensions require information in the system Registry so that the system can locate them. In addition, you have to make Registry entries to inform the shell that you want to use the extension.

You can use any method that you normally use to create ActiveX objects to create a shell extension. The example earlier in this chapter uses MFC, but you could easily use straight C++, ATL (the ActiveX Template Library), or any other scheme that produces ordinary ActiveX objects.

Writing an extension is a big job. However, you will find two complete examples in Listings 10.1 and 10.2. Listing 10.1 uses ATL (a template library that somewhat simplifies ActiveX object creation). Listing 10.2 uses MFC's built-in ActiveX support.

Resolving Shortcuts

Shortcuts (or shell links) are files that have an .lnk extension. These files contain a special ActiveX object that points to another file. Normally, when you open an LNK file, you really open the file that it points to.

If you use the standard file open dialog box, you never have to worry about resolving a shortcut. The file open dialog box does it for you (unless you specify the **OFN_NODEREFERNCELINKS** option).

What happens, however, if you need to resolve a shortcut yourself? Then you have to resort to ActiveX. The trick is to obtain a shell link object from the shell (using **CoCreateInstance**). The object you want to create has the CLSID (**CLSID_ShellLink**) and you want the **IID_IShellLink** interface. Both of these constants appear in SHLOBJ.H. Of course, before you make any ActiveX calls, you must call **CoInitialize** to set up ActiveX.

Once you have a shell link object, you can learn its **IPersistFile** interface by calling **QueryInterface**. This is the standard interface provided by all objects that read and write files. You can call **Load** on this interface to initialize the object from the LNK file. The file name you pass to **Load** must be a Unicode string. If you're programming with ANSI characters, you can use the **MultiByteToWideChar** call or the MFC **A2W** macro.

At this point, the object has the same state it had the last time someone saved it. However, the target file may not be in the same place at this time. For example, what if you create a shortcut, rename the target file, and then try to resolve the shortcut? To prevent this problem, you should call **IShellLink::Resolve**. This function performs a simple search that may locate the file under certain circumstances. If it can't find a good match for the file, it can prompt the user to locate the target file.

Finally, you can call members of the **IShellLink** interface to learn the target file's name (**GetPath**), its icon (**GetIconLocation**), and find other information about the shortcut.

You can find a simple function that is useful for resolving shortcuts in Listing 10.5. As it stands, the function returns only the path of the target file. However, it would be easy to extend the function to return any values your program needs. Notice that this program uses ATL smart pointers so it doesn't have to worry about details like **AddRef** and **Release**.

Creating A Shortcut

Creating a shortcut is essentially the reverse of resolving one. You still retrieve the shell link object (using **CoCreateInstance**), but this time you initialize it and save it to disk.

To initialize the object, you use calls like **SetPath** and **SetIconLocation**. When you're ready to save, you pass the Unicode file name to the **IPersistFile::Save** function.

You can find a simple function that performs these steps in Listing 10.4. Once you have a function like this that meets your needs, you no longer need to worry about the ActiveX objects.

Writing Icon Tray Programs

Many popular programs place icons in the system tray (the area next to the Taskbar that usually contains things like a clock, a speaker icon, and other icons to control programs). Any program can install an icon in this tray area. The shell will notify you when the icon receives mouse events so that you can take appropriate action.

The key function to make this technique work is **Shell_NotifyIcon**. You pass this call a function code and a pointer to a **NOTIFYICONDATA** structure. To register, use **NIM_ADD** as the function code. You can also use **NIM_MODIFY** to change your icon data or **NIM_DELETE** to remove the icon.

In addition to an icon, you can specify tip text that appears when the mouse pointer floats over the icon. You can set this text in the **NOTIFYICONDATA** structure (see Table 10.7) when you add the icon, and you can change it later. By setting the **uFlags** member of the structure, you can selectively change the tip text (or the icon) without disturbing the other item(s).

If **uFlags** contains the **NIF_MESSAGE** bit, it tells the shell to get a user-defined message from the **uCallbackMessage** field. The shell will send this message to the owner window whenever it sees a mouse event occur over the icon. The **wParam** of the message will be the same as the icon's ID (from the **uID** field), and the **lParam** will contain the particular mouse event that occurred.

Table 10.7 The NOTIFYICONDATA structure.

Type	Field	Description
DWORD	cbSize	Size of this structure
HWND	hWnd	Window handle that owns this icon
UINT	uID	ID of this icon (make up any ID; distinguishes multiple icons that belong to the same window)
UINT	uFlags	Tells which of the following fields in the structure are valid (NIF_ICON, NIF_MESSAGE, NIF_TIP)
UINT	uCallbackMessage	User-defined message that the shell will send to hWnd if there's a mouse event to process
HICON	hIcon	The icon to display
char	szTip[64]	The tip text to display

Listing 10.3 shows a tray icon program. This simple program has a normal user interface, which is perfectly legitimate. However, some tray icon programs will hide their main window, providing the illusion that the program is simply an icon on the tray. Others will hide their user interface until the user double-clicks on the icon.

Miscellaneous Shell Calls

You can use myriad calls to work with the shell. You can find a list in Table 10.4. Here's a summary of the more useful calls:

- ***SHAddToRecentDocs***—Takes a flag (nearly always **SHARD_PATH**) and the name of a file to place on the recently opened menu.
- ***SHChangeNotify***—Allows well-behaved programs to notify the shell when they take actions that might require the shell to update its views of folders. For example, if you create, rename, or delete a file (or a folder), you can use this function to notify the shell.
- ***SHQueryRecycleBin***—Returns a **SHQUERYRBINFO** structure that tells you how many items and bytes are in the specified drive's recycle bin.
- ***SHEmptyRecycleBin***—Empties the recycle bin for a given drive.

About MMC

The Microsoft Management Console (MMC) provides a unified interface for system administration tasks. Microsoft and other providers supply snap-ins—ActiveX programs that perform the desired task.

Users (typically administrators) can create documents that consist of several related snap-ins and save these to disk. Doing so allows the user to reload the tools as a group at a later time.

Writing MMC Snap-ins

Creating an MMC snap-in is somewhat simplified by the ATL Object Wizard. You'll find complete details earlier in this chapter (see Listings 10.6 and 10.7). The Wizard creates an object that represents a single node in the MMC. You'll have to cut and paste to create more nodes.

Each object (that is, each node) will handle various notifications in the **Notify** method. Particularly, the **MMCN_SHOW** and **MMCN_EXPAND** notifications are very important. **MMCN_EXPAND** allows the node to enumerate its children. **MMCN_SHOW** allows the snap-in to populate the result pane (the right part of the window).

Chapter 11

Internet And Network Programming

If you need an immediate solution to:	*See page:*
Working With Internet Shortcuts	532
Methods Of Internet Communications	532
Using Resource URLs	533
Inside Internet Explorer	534
Using The Scripting Object Model	534
Using HTML Dialog Boxes	535
Using MFC's Internet Support	535

In Depth

Winston Churchill once said,

"Pessimism is the cleverness of the weak. It is cheap, and it is always at least partly true. But optimism—ah, optimism is the courage of the clever."

In technology businesses, it's hard to be too optimistic. Even the most enthusiastic techno-supporter can grossly underestimate how much things will grow and change.

Bill Gates, certainly a supporter of technology, remarked in 1981: "640K ought to be enough for anybody." Hmm, my video card and printer both have around four times that amount of memory. My PC at the moment has 96MB.

Mr. Gates has good company, though. History is littered with famous statements like this. The President of Digital Equipment Corp stated in 1977: "There is no reason why anyone would want to have a computer in their home." In 1943, IBM's chairman postulated a world market for five computers. A bit earlier, in 1941, *Popular Mechanics* told its readers that "Computers in the future will weigh no more than 1.5 tons."

However, one of my favorite statements is from a city official (whose name escapes me) who received a demonstration of the brand-new telephone device. He was so impressed, he estimated that one day every town would have one!

Honestly, who could foresee the enormous infrastructure that the phone system would create? Internet access, pagers, cell phones, and fax machines, have overburdened the phone number system in many parts of the country (kind of like running out of your 640KB of memory). I doubt even Bell himself could imagine it.

Networking is a bit like a telephone for computers. I'm guilty of the same limited thinking about networks that many people had about telephones. I've always worked with networks, but for years, I thought of it as a specialty—not part of mainstream programming.

Boy, was I wrong! Many homes and small offices now have their own networks. My house, of course, is wired with Ethernet for the computers in my office and my son's room, and in the electronics lab (well, OK, my garage). But the real explosive growth in networking technology is, of course, the Internet.

If you didn't have to work with networking before the Internet took off, it's a good bet you do now. At its core, the Internet is just good old-fashioned TCP/IP programming. Most ordinary networking topics—such as sockets, RPCs (Remote Procedure Calls), and mailslots—appear in Chapter 6. In this chapter, you'll see some newer technologies designed for exploiting the Internet as well as an overview of some more advanced networking techniques.

Internet Shortcuts

In Chapter 10, you saw that the shell manages *shortcuts*—files that refer to other files. These files are really ActiveX objects saved to disk. Windows also supports the same idea for a file that points to an Internet URL. Oddly enough, these files are plain text files (see Listing 11.1). However, Windows still provides an ActiveX object interface that allows you to manipulate these Internet shortcuts.

Listing 11.1 An Internet shortcut.

```
[InternetShortcut]
URL=http://www.al-williams.com/
Modified=A021BE1D15E3BD0152
```

In practice, I suppose you could choose to manipulate these shortcuts as plain text files (or INI files, which have the same format). However, Microsoft might change the underlying file format at any time. It's unlikely that the ActiveX interface will change.

Suppose you wanted to convert a bunch of Internet shortcuts into a Web page. If you had a program like that, you'd be able to publish your favorites list on the Web easily.

I decided to use MFC's **CEditView** class to make a simple text editor, and then add code to convert a directory full of URLs into HTML. The conversion code places the HTML in the editor so you can tweak it, copy it to the Clipboard, or save it as a file. You can see the results in Figures 11.1 and 11.2.

Getting Started

As usual, you start an MFC project using the App Wizard. At the end of the Wizard's questions, you'll need to change the view base class to **CEditView**. Once you make that selection, you can generate the project.

The program must scan through the URLs it is converting. Originally, I put the scanning logic in the view's **OnInitialUpdate** routine (see Listing 11.2). However, doing so prevents you from seeing the main window until everything is done. For a large scan, this can be worrisome.

Listing 11.2 The URL converter.

```
// url2htmlView.cpp :
// implementation of the CUrl2htmlView class
//
#include "stdafx.h"
#include "url2html.h"
#include "dirdlg.h"

#include "url2htmlDoc.h"
#include "url2htmlView.h"
#include <intshcut.h>   // internet shortcut
#include <afxpriv.h>
#include <shlobj.h>
#include <initguid.h>
#include <shlguid.h>
#include <afxtempl.h>

#ifdef _DEBUG
#define new DEBUG_NEW
#undef THIS_FILE
static char THIS_FILE[] = __FILE__;
#endif

#pragma comment( lib, "url" )   // link library!
////////////////////////////////////////
// CUrl2htmlView

IMPLEMENT_DYNCREATE(CUrl2htmlView, CEditView)

BEGIN_MESSAGE_MAP(CUrl2htmlView, CEditView)
   //{{AFX_MSG_MAP(CUrl2htmlView)
   //}}AFX_MSG_MAP
   // Standard printing commands
   ON_COMMAND(ID_FILE_PRINT, CEditView::OnFilePrint)
   ON_COMMAND(ID_FILE_PRINT_DIRECT,CEditView::OnFilePrint)
   ON_COMMAND(ID_FILE_PRINT_PREVIEW, CEditView::OnFilePrintPreview)
   ON_MESSAGE(WM_USER,DoScan)
END_MESSAGE_MAP()

////////////////////////////////////////
// CUrl2htmlView construction/destruction

CUrl2htmlView::CUrl2htmlView()
{
   // TODO: add construction code here
```

```
}

CUrl2htmlView::~CUrl2htmlView()
{
}

BOOL CUrl2htmlView::PreCreateWindow(CREATESTRUCT& cs)
{
   //  the CREATESTRUCT cs

   BOOL bPreCreated = CEditView::PreCreateWindow(cs);
   cs.style &= ~(ES_AUTOHSCROLL|WS_HSCROLL);   // Enable word-wrapping

   return bPreCreated;
}

/////////////////////////////////////////////
// CUrl2htmlView drawing

void CUrl2htmlView::OnDraw(CDC* pDC)
{
   CUrl2htmlDoc* pDoc = GetDocument();
   ASSERT_VALID(pDoc);

}

/////////////////////////////////////////////
// CUrl2htmlView printing

BOOL CUrl2htmlView::OnPreparePrinting(CPrintInfo* pInfo)
{
   // default CEditView preparation
   return CEditView::OnPreparePrinting(pInfo);
}

void CUrl2htmlView::OnBeginPrinting(CDC* pDC, CPrintInfo* pInfo)
{
   // Default CEditView begin printing.
   CEditView::OnBeginPrinting(pDC, pInfo);
}

void CUrl2htmlView::OnEndPrinting(CDC* pDC, CPrintInfo* pInfo)
{
   // Default CEditView end printing
```

```
    CEditView::OnEndPrinting(pDC, pInfo);
}

/////////////////////////////////////////
// CUrl2htmlView diagnostics

#ifdef _DEBUG
void CUrl2htmlView::AssertValid() const
{
    CEditView::AssertValid();
}

void CUrl2htmlView::Dump(CDumpContext& dc) const
{
    CEditView::Dump(dc);
}

CUrl2htmlDoc* CUrl2htmlView::GetDocument() // non-debug version is inline
{
    ASSERT(m_pDocument->IsKindOf(RUNTIME_CLASS(CUrl2htmlDoc)));
    return (CUrl2htmlDoc*)m_pDocument;
}
#endif //_DEBUG

/////////////////////////////////////////
// CUrl2htmlView message handlers

void CUrl2htmlView::OnInitialUpdate()
{
    CEditView::OnInitialUpdate();
    PostMessage(WM_USER);  // kick off processing
}


void CUrl2htmlView::CalcWindowRect(LPRECT lpClientRect,
    UINT nAdjustType)
{
    CEditView::CalcWindowRect(lpClientRect, nAdjustType);
}

// This is the "core engine" that
// scans directories
int CUrl2htmlView::scan(CString dir)
{
    WIN32_FIND_DATA fdata;
```

```
   HANDLE h;
    IMalloc *pMalloc;
   CList<CString,CString &> stack;  // directory stack
   int urls=0;

   int l;
   dir+="\\*.*";   // form wildcard
    SHGetMalloc(&pMalloc);   // get shell's malloc
// Begin finding files
   h=FindFirstFile(dir,&fdata);
   if (h==INVALID_HANDLE_VALUE)
   {
      MessageBox("No files found");
      pMalloc->Release();
      return 0;
   }
   do {  // for each file
// ignore ., .., and files that start with hyphen
      if (!strcmp(fdata.cFileName,".")
          ||!strcmp(fdata.cFileName,"..")
          ||*fdata.cFileName=='-')
         continue;

// Store directories in stack
      if (fdata.dwFileAttributes&FILE_ATTRIBUTE_DIRECTORY)
      {
         CString tmp=fdata.cFileName;
         stack.AddTail(tmp);
         stack.AddTail(dir.Left(dir.GetLength()-3)+fdata.cFileName);
      }
// Any file that ends with .URL
      l=strlen(fdata.cFileName);
      if (!stricmp(".url",fdata.cFileName+l-4))
      {
        CString link;
        TCHAR ffname[1024];  // full file name
        LPTSTR url;
        CString surl;
        CString shortname;
        IUniformResourceLocator *iurl;
        IPersistFile *pfile;
        USES_CONVERSION;
// Create ActiveX object
        if (FAILED(CoCreateInstance(CLSID_InternetShortcut,
           NULL,CLSCTX_INPROC_SERVER,
```

11. Internet And Network Programming

```
              IID_IUniformResourceLocator,(void **)&iurl)))
           {
              MessageBox("Can't create Internet Shortcut");
              return -1;
           }
// Find IPersistFile interface
           iurl->QueryInterface(IID_IPersistFile,(void **)&pfile);
           strcpy(ffname,dir);
           char *p=strrchr(ffname,'\\');
           strcpy(p+1,fdata.cFileName);
           if (FAILED(pfile->Load(A2W(ffname),0)))
           {
              MessageBox("Can't open shortcut");
              return -1;
           }
// Find URL
           if (SUCCEEDED(iurl->GetURL(&url)))
           {
            surl=url;
            pMalloc->Free(url);  // Free storage
           }
           iurl->Release();
           pfile->Release();
           shortname=fdata.cFileName;
// chop off .URL and make HTML
           shortname=shortname.Left(shortname.GetLength()-4);
           link.Format("<P><A HREF='%s'>%s</A></P>\r\n",surl,shortname);
           AddString(link);
           urls++;
        }
     } while (FindNextFile(h,&fdata));  // keep searching
     // process directories after all files
     while (!stack.IsEmpty())
     {
        CString &nam=stack.RemoveHead();
        CString &sdir=stack.RemoveHead();
        int selst,selend;
        GetEditCtrl().GetSel(selst,selend);
        AddString("<BLOCKQUOTE><H2>");
        AddString(nam);
        AddString("</H2>\r\n");
        if (usehr) AddString("<HR>\r\n");
        if (scan(sdir)>0)
           AddString("</BLOCKQUOTE>\r\n");
        else
```

```
        {
// undo this directory heading since it had no files!
            CEdit &ctrl=GetEditCtrl();
            ctrl.SetSel(selst,-1);
            ctrl.Clear();
        }
    }

    pMalloc->Release();
    return urls;
}

// Put a string in the edit control
void CUrl2htmlView::AddString(const char * s)
{
     CEdit &ctrl=GetEditCtrl();
     ctrl.ReplaceSel(s,FALSE);
     ctrl.SetSel(-1,0);
}

// User interface to scan()
LRESULT CUrl2htmlView::DoScan(WPARAM w, LPARAM l)
{
    CDirDlg dlg;
    CString dir;
    if (FAILED(CoInitialize(NULL)))
    {
        MessageBox("Can't initialize COM!");
        return -2;
    }
    if (dlg.DoModal()==IDCANCEL) return -1;
    dir=dlg.m_path;
// headings
    AddString("<HTML><HEAD><TITLE>\r\n");
    AddString(dlg.m_title+"</TITLE>\r\n");
    AddString("</HEAD><BODY><H1>");
    AddString(dlg.m_title+"</H1>\r\n");
    usehr=dlg.m_hr;
    scan(dir);  // do the work
    AddString("</BODY></HTML>\r\n");  // end tags
    CoUninitialize();
    return 0;
}
```

I finally decided to simply post a user-defined message during **OnInitialUpdate**. Because I used **PostMessage** (instead of **SendMessage**), the **OnInitialUpdate** can complete. Then, a user-defined message handler (**DoScan**) takes control.

Class Wizard doesn't handle user-defined messages. To handle an arbitrary message (like **WM_USER**), you'll need the following line in your message map:

```
ON_MESSAGE(WM_USER,DoScan)
```

Another issue: Class Wizard has no idea what arguments **WM_USER** requires (because **WM_USER** is completely user defined). As a result, the **DoScan** function must look like this:

```
LRESULT CUrl2htmlView::DoScan(WPARAM w, LPARAM l)
  {
  }
```

In this case, the program doesn't use the arguments, nor does it return anything meaningful. However, it still must return something and accept the arguments because that is the nature of **WM_USER**.

The **DoScan** function simply brings up a dialog box to collect options. Then it calls **scan** to do the actual work. This step is important, because **scan** will call itself recursively to process directories. If the work occurred in **DoScan**, recursion would be a problem because each pass would bring up the dialog box.

In reality, **scan** performs two major functions: It scans directories, and it selects URL files and processes them. The scanning function is just a classic loop using **FindFirstFile** and **FindNextFile**. These Win32 functions search for files in a directory and fill in a **WIN32_FIND_DATA** structure. This structure contains the long and short names for each file, along with the file's attributes. The code automatically skips **.** (the current directory) and **..** (the parent directory). The loop also skips any file that starts with a hyphen, so you can make private shortcuts that don't appear in the generated HTML file.

When the software identifies a URL file, it adds the file name to the path to form the full file name. Next, it uses the ActiveX call **CoCreateInstance** to instantiate an **InternetShortcut** object (the definitions for all this are in intshcut.h).

The shortcut has an **IPersistFile** interface that you can find by calling **QueryInterface** on the original object. You use the **IPersistFile::Load** function to read the file's contents into the nascent object. However, the **Load** function requires the file name to be in Unicode, and my program uses ANSI (or ASCII) characters.

Unicode characters are the 16-bit characters that allow you to form strings using practically any character. This system is especially popular with non-English users, because nearly every conceivable character exists in Unicode. Even for English programs, Unicode allows you to use many symbols and special characters that are otherwise unavailable.

There are several ways to convert ANSI characters to Unicode. For example, the function **MultiByteToWideChar** will do the conversion. However, for this project, I opted to use the simplified macros that MFC provides. Using **A2W** converts the ANSI string to Unicode. However, you have to place the **USES_CONVERSION** macro in your function to make this technique work.

Once the shortcut is ready, you can call **InternetShortcut::GetURL** to retrieve the actual URL for the shortcut. The program copies this URL to a **CString** and frees the original string. The shortcut uses the ActiveX memory allocator to reserve space for the string. However, the calling program is responsible for deleting the memory. For that purpose, the code uses **SHGetMalloc** to find the **IMalloc** interface for the shell. This interface has a **Free** function that releases the memory. Once all the ActiveX work is done, the program releases both interfaces, also freeing the object.

Handling directories is a bit different. The program uses an MFC **CList** to create a simple stack. **CList** is one of the fundamental MFC template-based containers. To use it, you have to instantiate a **CList** object and provide template arguments for it. For example, the line of code

```
CList<CString,CString &> stack;
```

creates a list that contains **CString** objects. When you extract an element from the list, however, it will use a **CString** reference, which is more efficient.

When the code encounters a directory, it places the directory on the stack for later processing. Doing so allows the contents of a directory to appear before its subdirectories. Once all the files in a directory are complete, the code works back through the stack, processing directories.

Processing directories requires the program to emit a bit of HTML with the name of each directory. Then it recursively calls **scan**. The **scan** function returns the number of URLs processed. If this number is zero, the directory-processing code deletes the HTML title for the directory because it was empty.

Using CEditView

In this program, I'm using **CEditView** as though it were a text output stream, more or less. This isn't difficult to do, but I made it even easier by creating an

AddString member in the view class. This simple function just inserts a string at the current selection point (using **ReplaceSel**) and then sets the selection to the end of the text.

This is often a nice solution when you need to output some text. After all, the user has several choices: She can change the text easily, copy some or all of it to the Clipboard, or save the text. Best of all, most of the functionality comes from the AppWizard, so it's very little work for the programmer. Just remember that if you want a newline character in the text, you'll need to use **\r\n**, not just **\n**.

Using Internet Explorer

Because this is a programming book, you might be surprised to find a section on using Internet Explorer (IE). The truth is that IE is really not the program that users think it is. If you examine the IE executable, you'll find that it's quite small. The program that users think of as IE is little more than a shell around an ActiveX control (contained in shdocvw.dll). This ActiveX control (along with additional helper controls) does most of the work. Each type of document has its own helper control. For example, the MSHTML control is the engine that parses and displays HTML.

If you want to display a Web page (either locally or over a network), you could do all the work yourself (a formidable task). A better idea is to reuse the same ActiveX control that IE uses. Why not? It performs a bewildering array of tasks—everything from handling proxy servers and JavaScript to maintaining history and cookies. Parsing simple HTML is a chore, but the control handles dynamic HTML (DHTML) and a host of extensions like style sheets.

You can use IE two ways. First, you can run IE as a separate program and control it via ActiveX automation. This approach is useful if you want IE to look like it always does. However, it's generally more useful to conceal IE within your own program. You can do so by creating the ActiveX control that IE uses (technically, an ActiveX document). Containing an ActiveX document is moderately complex, but MFC provides a special class—**CHtmlView**—that takes care of all the details for you.

Automation

If you want to run IE as a separate application, you simply create an instance of the **InternetExplorer** object and obtain the **IWebBrowser2** interface (see Table 11.1). The interface allows you to control the Web browser. This technique requires very little overhead in the calling program. Initially, the browser is invisible; if you want to show it, you'll need to retrieve the window handle (using **get_HWND**) and use the standard **ShowWindow** call.

Table 11.1 The IWebBrowser2 interface.

IWebBrowser2 Method	Description
GoBack	Returns to the previous item in the history list
GoForward	Moves to the next item in the history list
GoHome	Navigates to the current start page
GoSearch	Loads the current search page
Navigate	Navigates to a URL
Refresh	Reloads the current page
Refresh2	Reloads the current page and optionally prevents the "pragma:nocache" header from being sent
Stop	Stops opening a page
get_Application	Returns an application object representing the application that contains the current instance of the Internet Explorer application
get_Parent	Returns the parent object
get_Container	Returns the container of the WebBrowser control
get_Document	Returns the active document
get_TopLevelContainer	Indicates if the current object is the top-level container of the WebBrowser control
get_Type	Returns the type name of the document object
get_Left	Returns the screen coordinate of the left edge
put_Left	Sets the left edge coordinate
get_Top	Returns the top coordinate
put_Top	Sets the top coordinate
get_Width	Returns the browser's width
put_Width	Sets the browser's width
get_Height	Returns the browser's height
put_Height	Sets the browser's height
get_LocationName	Returns the name of the page that the WebBrowser control is currently displaying
get_LocationURL	Returns the URL of the current page
get_Busy	Indicates if a download or other activity is still in progress
Quit	Closes the browser +
ClientToWindow	Converts the client coordinates of a point to window coordinates +
PutProperty	Sets the value of a property associated with the given object +

(continued)

Table 11.1 The IWebBrowser2 interface (continued).

IWebBrowser2 Method	Description
GetProperty	Retrieves the current value of a property associated with the given object +
get_Name	Returns the name of the object that contains the WebBrowser control used by Internet Explorer +
get_HWND	Returns the window handle to the Internet Explorer main window +
get_FullName	Returns the full path of the file that Internet Explorer is currently displaying +
get_Path	Returns a string that evaluates to the full path of the resource that Internet Explorer is currently displaying +
get_Visible	Returns the visible status of the browser
put_Visible	Shows or hides the browser
get_StatusBar	Determines if the status bar is visible
put_StatusBar	Sets a value that determines whether the status bar is visible
get_StatusText	Returns the text of the status bar
put_StatusText	Sets the text for the status bar
get_ToolBar	Returns a value that indicates whether the toolbar is visible
put_ToolBar	Sets a value that determines whether the toolbar is visible
get_MenuBar	Returns a value that indicates whether the menu bar is visible
put_MenuBar	Sets a value that determines whether the menu bar is visible
get_FullScreen	Returns a value indicating whether Internet Explorer is in full-screen or normal window mode
put_FullScreen	Sets a value that determines whether Internet Explorer is in full-screen or normal window mode
Navigate2	Navigates to a resource identified by a pointer to an item identifier list (PIDL)
QueryStatusWB	Queries the object for status of commands
ExecWB	Executes a command
ShowBrowserBar	Shows or hides a specified browser bar
get_ReadyState	Returns a standard OLE ReadyState bindable property for the WebBrowser control
get_Offline	Returns a value that determines whether the control is offline
put_Offline	Sets a value that determines whether the control is offline
get_Silent	Returns a value indicating whether any dialog boxes can be shown

(continued)

***Table 11.1 The IWebBrowser2 interface* (continued).**

IWebBrowser2 Method	Description
put_Silent	Sets a value indicating whether any dialog boxes can be shown
get_RegisterAsBrowser	Returns a value indicating whether the WebBrowser control is registered as a top-level browser for target name resolution
put_RegisterAsBrowser	Sets a value indicating whether the WebBrowser control is registered as a top-level browser for target name resolution
get_RegisterAsDropTarget	Returns a value indicating whether the WebBrowser control is registered as a drop target for navigation
put_RegisterAsDropTarget	Sets a value indicating whether the WebBrowser control is registered as a drop target for navigation
get_TheaterMode	Retrieves a value indicating whether the WebBrowser control is in theater mode
put_TheaterMode	Sets a value indicating whether the WebBrowser control is in theater mode
get_AddressBar	Determines if the Internet Explorer object's address bar is visible
put_AddressBar	Shows or hides the Internet Explorer object's address bar
get_Resizable	Retrieves the Internet Explorer object's resizable property
put_Resizable	Sets the Internet Explorer object's resizable property

NOTE: *These items marked + are not available when browser is running as an ActiveX control.*

Once you have the browser running you'll have no problem controlling it through the **IWebBrowser2** interface. If you need to, you can even access the scripting object model (the same object model that scripts use to control the browser from C++).

Listing 11.3 shows a simple program that exercises several features of the IE application. Running IE is simple enough:

```
hr=CoCreateInstance(CLSID_InternetExplorer,NULL,CLSCTX_SERVER,
    IID_IWebBrowser2,(void **)&m_browser);
```

m_browser is an **IWebBrowser2** interface pointer. This pointer starts the browser but keeps it invisible. You could set the position of the browser and make it visible by asking for the **HWND** that the browser is using. Here's how:

```
HWND w;
m_browser->get_HWND((long *)&w);
::ShowWindow(w,SW_SHOW);
```

The only problem with using **IWebBrowser2** is that many of the calls require special ActiveX data types like variants and URL monikers. For example, to navigate to a Web page, you can use the **Navigate** method. However, this call requires a **BSTR** and several variants. All the variants are optional. However, you still have to create an error variant to indicate that you don't want to pass the argument. For example, here's some code that navigates to a particular URL:

```
COleVariant Vempty;
Vempty.vt=VT_ERROR;
Vempty.scode=DISP_E_PARAMNOTFOUND;
CString url("file://c:/test.htm");
m_browser->Navigate(url.AllocSysString(),Vempty,Vempty,Vempty,Vempty);
```

Notice that to indicate a missing optional argument, you have to set the variant's **vt** field to **VT_ERROR** and the **scode** field to **DISP_E_PARAMNOTFOUND**.

Further Control

If you want to access the scripting object model, you'll need to find the **IHTMLDocument2** interface. You need to call **get_Document** to get this pointer. However, **get_Document** returns an **IDispatch** interface, so you'll need to call **QueryInterface** to get the correct interface.

Another problem is that the browser won't have a document object until the page you're loading is at least partially loaded. Here's a snippet of code that will change the page's background color and title:

```
READYSTATE rdy;
do{
  Sleep(0);  // give browser a chance to run
  m_browser->get_ReadyState(&rdy);
  } while (rdy!=READYSTATE_COMPLETE);
IDispatch *dDoc;
hr=m_browser->get_Document(&dDoc);
IHTMLDocument2 *doc;
hr=dDoc->QueryInterface(&doc);
dDoc->Release();
COleVariant vred(0xFF0000L);
hr=doc->put_bgColor(vred);
CString titles("Greetings from C++");
doc->put_title(titles.AllocSysString());
```

Again, notice that you must construct a variant and a **BSTR** to make these calls. You'll find the complete code in Listing 11.3.

Listing 11.3 Using the browser from a program.

```
// browsebuddyView.cpp : implementation of the CBrowsebuddyView class
//

#include "stdafx.h"
#include <atlbase.h>
#include "browsebuddy.h"
#include <mshtmhst.h>

#include "browsebuddyDoc.h"
#include "browsebuddyView.h"

#include "chtmldlg.h"

#ifdef _DEBUG
#define new DEBUG_NEW
#undef THIS_FILE
static char THIS_FILE[] = __FILE__;
#endif

///////////////////
// CBrowsebuddyView

IMPLEMENT_DYNCREATE(CBrowsebuddyView, CFormView)

BEGIN_MESSAGE_MAP(CBrowsebuddyView, CFormView)
   //{{AFX_MSG_MAP(CBrowsebuddyView)
   ON_BN_CLICKED(IDC_BUTTON1, OnButton1)
   ON_BN_CLICKED(IDC_BUTTON2, OnButton2)
   //}}AFX_MSG_MAP
END_MESSAGE_MAP()

/////////////////
// CBrowsebuddyView construction/destruction

CBrowsebuddyView::CBrowsebuddyView()
   : CFormView(CBrowsebuddyView::IDD)
{
   //{{AFX_DATA_INIT(CBrowsebuddyView)
      // NOTE: the ClassWizard will add member initialization here
   //}}AFX_DATA_INIT
   // TODO: add construction code here
    m_browser=NULL;
}
```

```
CBrowsebuddyView::~CBrowsebuddyView()
{
   if (m_browser) m_browser->Release();
   OleUninitialize();
}

void CBrowsebuddyView::DoDataExchange(CDataExchange* pDX)
{
   CFormView::DoDataExchange(pDX);
   //{{AFX_DATA_MAP(CBrowsebuddyView)
      // NOTE: the ClassWizard will add DDX and DDV calls here
   //}}AFX_DATA_MAP
}

BOOL CBrowsebuddyView::PreCreateWindow(CREATESTRUCT& cs)
{
   // TODO: Modify the Window class or styles here by modifying
   //  the CREATESTRUCT cs

   return CFormView::PreCreateWindow(cs);
}

void CBrowsebuddyView::OnInitialUpdate()
{
   HRESULT hr;
   CFormView::OnInitialUpdate();
   GetParentFrame()->RecalcLayout();
   ResizeParentToFit();
   // Create slave instance of IE
   hr=OleInitialize(NULL);
   if (FAILED(hr))
   {
      MessageBox("Can't initialize ActiveX");
      return;
   }

}

////////////////////////
// CBrowsebuddyView diagnostics

#ifdef _DEBUG
void CBrowsebuddyView::AssertValid() const
```

```
{
   CFormView::AssertValid();
}

void CBrowsebuddyView::Dump(CDumpContext& dc) const
{
   CFormView::Dump(dc);
}

// non-debug version is inline
CBrowsebuddyDoc* CBrowsebuddyView::GetDocument(){
   ASSERT(m_pDocument->IsKindOf(RUNTIME_CLASS(CBrowsebuddyDoc)));
   return (CBrowsebuddyDoc*)m_pDocument;
}
#endif //_DEBUG

/////////////////////////////////////////////////////////////////////////////
// CBrowsebuddyView message handlers

void CBrowsebuddyView::OnButton1()
{
   // TODO: Add your control notification handler code here
   // Open IE
    HRESULT hr;
   hr=CoCreateInstance(CLSID_InternetExplorer,NULL,CLSCTX_SERVER,
        IID_IWebBrowser2,(void **)&m_browser);
   if (FAILED(hr))
   {
      MessageBox("Can't run IE");
      return;
   }

   // Show Browser
   HWND w;
   m_browser->get_HWND((long *)&w);
   ::ShowWindow(w,SW_SHOW);
   COleVariant Vempty;
   // Go to c:\test.htm (which of course must exist)
   Vempty.vt=VT_ERROR;
   Vempty.scode=DISP_E_PARAMNOTFOUND;
   CString url("file://c:/test.htm");
   m_browser->Navigate(url.AllocSysString(),Vempty,Vempty,Vempty,Vempty);
   // wait for browser to finish loading
   READYSTATE rdy;
    do {
```

11. Internet And Network Programming

```
        Sleep(0);
        m_browser->get_ReadyState(&rdy);
    } while (rdy!=READYSTATE_COMPLETE);

    // Get the document object
    IDispatch *dDoc;
    hr=m_browser->get_Document(&dDoc);
    IHTMLDocument2 *doc;
    hr=dDoc->QueryInterface(&doc);
    dDoc->Release();
    // change color to red
    COleVariant vred(0xFF0000L);
    hr=doc->put_bgColor(vred);
    // change title
    CString titles("Greetings from C++");
    doc->put_title(titles.AllocSysString());
    doc->Release();

}

void CBrowsebuddyView::OnButton2()
{
    //HTML Dialog Example
     CHTMLDialog dlg("HTMLDLG");
    dlg.ShowModal(this);

}
```

Using CHtmlView

Using **CHtmlView** (the MFC view that encapsulates IE) is very simple. If you're starting a new program using App Wizard, just select **CHtmlView** as the base class for your view. If you're adding a view using Class Wizard, you can select **CHtmlView** as your base class.

The **CHtmlView** class has many members (see Table 11.2). You can use them to control the browser much as you'd directly use the **IWebBrowser2** interface. You can also override certain virtual functions to handle events that the browser sends to you. (To do this without **CHtmlView** you'd have to provide a **DWebBrowserEvents2** interface.)

Although the **CHtmlView** class exposes most of the **IWebBrowser2** interface, a few of the functions don't really act the way you expect because the browser is a control, not a proper application. For example, you can't make the view display a toolbar or an address bar.

So, to use **CHtmlView** as a complete Web browser, you'll have to do a good bit of work. Usually, you'll use the view when you want to display some HTML as part of a larger application.

Table 11.2 CHtmlView members.

Member	Description
GetType	Gets type name of the document object
GetLeft	Gets the left coordinate of the browser
SetLeft	Sets the left position of the browser
GetTop	Gets the top coordinate of the browser
SetTop	Sets the top position of the browser
GetHeight	Gets the browser's height
SetHeight	Sets the browser's height
SetVisible	Sets the visible/hidden flag
GetVisible	Returns the visible/hidden flag
GetLocationName	Retrieves the name of the current page
GetReadyState	Retrieves the ready state
GetOffline	Retrieves a value that determines whether the control is offline
SetOffline	Sets a value to determine whether the control is offline
GetSilent	Indicates whether any dialog boxes can be shown
SetSilent	Sets a value to determine whether the control will display dialog boxes
GetTopLevelContainer	Retrieves a value indicating whether the current object is the top-level container of the WebBrowser control
GetLocationURL	Retrieves the URL of the current page
GetBusy	Retrieves a value indicating whether a download or other activity is still in progress
GetApplication	Retrieves an application object representing the application that contains the current instance of the browser
GetParentBrowser	Retrieves a pointer to the IDispatch interface
GetContainer	Retrieves the container of the browser
GetHtmlDocument	Retrieves the active HTML document
GetFullName	Retrieves the full name, including the path, of the resource displayed in the Web browser (the WebBrowser control ignores this member; Internet Explorer only)

(continued)

***Table 11.2 CHtmlView members* (continued).**

Member	Description
GetToolBar	Retrieves a value that determines whether the toolbar is visible
SetToolBar	Sets a value to determine whether the control's toolbar is visible (the WebBrowser control ignores this member; Internet Explorer only)
GetMenuBar	Retrieves a value that determines whether the menu bar is visible
SetMenuBar	Sets a value to determine whether the control's menu bar is visible (the WebBrowser control ignores this member; Internet Explorer only)
GetFullScreen	Indicates whether the WebBrowser control is operating in full-screen mode or in normal window mode
SetFullScreen	Sets a value to determine whether the control is operating in full-screen mode or in normal window mode (the WebBrowser control ignores this member; Internet Explorer only)
QueryStatusWB	Queries the status of a command being processed by the WebBrowser control
GetRegisterAsBrowser	Indicates whether the WebBrowser control is registered as a top-level browser for target name resolution
SetRegisterAsBrowser	Sets a value indicating whether the WebBrowser control is registered as a top-level browser for target name resolution
GetRegisterAsDropTarget	Indicates whether the WebBrowser control is registered as a drop target for navigation
SetRegisterAsDropTarget	Sets a value indicating whether the WebBrowser control is registered as a drop target for navigation
GetTheaterMode	Indicates whether the WebBrowser control is in theater mode
SetTheaterMode	Sets a value indicating whether the WebBrowser control is in theater mode
GetAddressBar	Determines if the Internet Explorer object's address bar is visible (WebBrowser control ignores this member; Internet Explorer only)
SetAddressBar	Shows or hides the Internet Explorer object's address bar (WebBrowser control ignores this member; Internet Explorer only)
GetStatusBar	Indicates whether the Internet Explorer's status bar is visible (WebBrowser control ignores this member; Internet Explorer only)
SetStatusBar	Sets a value to determine whether the Internet Explorer's status bar is visible (WebBrowser control ignores; Internet Explorer only)
GoBack	Navigates to the previous item in the history list
GoForward	Navigates to the next item in the history list

(continued)

***Table 11.2 CHtmlView members* (continued).**

Member	Description
GoHome	Navigates to the current home or start page
GoSearch	Navigates to the current search page
Navigate	Navigates to the resource identified by a URL
Navigate2	Navigates to the resource identified by a URL, or to the file identified by a full path
Refresh	Reloads the current file
Refresh2	Reloads the current file and optionally prevents the "pragma:nocache" header from being sent
Stop	Stops opening a file
PutProperty	Sets the value of a property associated with the given object
GetProperty	Retrieves the current value of a property associated with the given object
ExecWB	Executes a command
LoadFromResource	Loads a resource in the WebBrowser control
OnDraw	Called to render an image of the document for screen display, printing, or print preview
Create	Creates the WebBrowser control
OnNavigateComplete2	Called after a navigation to a hyperlink completes (on either a window or frameset element)
OnBeforeNavigate2	Called before a navigation occurs in the given WebBrowser control (on either a window or frameset element)
OnStatusTextChange	Called to notify an application that the text of the status bar associated with the WebBrowser control has changed
OnProgressChange	Called to notify an application that the progress of a download operation has been updated
OnCommandStateChange	Called to notify an application that the enabled state of a Web browser command has changed
OnDownloadBegin	Called to notify an application that a navigation operation is beginning
OnDownloadComplete	Called when a navigation operation finishes, is halted, or fails
OnTitleChange	Called to notify an application if the title of a document in the WebBrowser control becomes available or changes
OnPropertyChange	Called to notify an application that the PutProperty method has changed the value of a property

(continued)

***Table 11.2 CHtmlView members* (continued).**

Member	Description
OnNewWindow2	Called when a new window is to be created for displaying a resource
OnDocumentComplete	Called to notify an application that a document has reached the READYSTATE_COMPLETE state
OnQuit	Called to notify an application that the Internet Explorer application is ready to quit (applies to Internet Explorer only)
OnVisible	Called when the window for the WebBrowser control should be shown/hidden
OnToolBar	Called when the ToolBar property has changed
OnMenuBar	Called when the MenuBar property has changed
OnStatusBar	Called when the StatusBar property has changed
OnFullScreen	Called when the FullScreen property has changed
OnTheaterMode	Called when the TheaterMode property has changed

Resource URLs

Once you start incorporating HTML into your programs, you'll find you don't want to place the HTML into separate files. Often you'd like to display an HTML page that you store internally in your program. This is a perfect job for a resource. Visual Studio provides a special resource type just for HTML documents, and IE knows how to display resource URLs that start with the **res://** protocol.

Suppose your executable is named, for example, drum.exe and resides in the c:\drum directory. Further assume you have an HTML resource identified by the string *RESDOC*. You can point IE at **res://c:\drum\drum.exe/RESDOC** and it will display the document (assuming the resource is an HTML resource). If the resource isn't an HTML resource, you have to specify the type between another pair of slashes placed between the file name and the resource ID.

When you insert any resource, Visual Studio generates an ID for it that's really a **#define** constant that resolves into a number. Because this number is available only at compile time, IE can't find this sort of resource. If you want to use a number, you'll need to examine your resources (use the View|Resource IDs menu item) and use the decimal number, preceded by a # sign, in the URL. For example:

```
res://c:\drum\drum.exe/#233
```

You may prefer to store the resource ID as a string so you don't have to use cryptic numbers in the URL. In that case, just rename the resource and place the ID between double quotation marks. Doing so informs Visual Studio that you want to use a string ID instead of a numeric one.

If you're using **CHtmlView**, you can use the **LoadFromResource** member to load a page from your current resources. This technique is handy because the code finds the executable name and takes care of the difference between numeric and string resource IDs by supplying overloaded versions of the function.

HTML Dialog Boxes

Displaying documents from the Web is certainly useful. However, once you start showing documents from resources, it's easy to imagine using HTML for dialog boxes. What about a dialog box that contains an animated GIF file? How about a dialog box that shows Web pages in a frame? You can easily construct this sort of "dialog" box using HTML. An HTML dialog box can contain DHTML elements, style sheets, JavaScript or VBScript code, frames, and hyperlinks—anything a Web page can contain.

Of course, you don't want to start a separate copy of IE just to show a dialog box. However, the **CHtmlView** class isn't really appropriate either, especially for a modal dialog box. Luckily, the mshtml.dll file has a function that allows you to create HTML dialog boxes.

You'll need to dynamically load the library using **LoadLibrary** and **GetProcAddress**. The function's name is **ShowHTMLDialog**. Here's the code:

```
library=::LoadLibrary(TEXT("MSHTML.DLL"));
if (library)
{
        fn=(SHOWHTMLDIALOGFN *)
          ::GetProcAddress((HINSTANCE)
          library,TEXT("ShowHTMLDialog"));
        .
        .
        .
```

Of course, the smart thing to do is to wrap the HTML dialog box code into a class, as demonstrated in Listings 11.4 and 11.5. This is a useful class because it handles several tasks:

- Loading the DLL and finding the function address
- Learning the current module's file name and using it to form a **res://** URL
- Creating a URL moniker that corresponds to the URL

TIP: *According to the Microsoft documentation, you can pass various option strings to set the height and width of the HTML dialog box (among other things). However, they don't seem to work, or at least they don't work consistently.*

Listing 11.4 The HTML dialog box header.

```
class CHTMLDialog
{
private:
   void commoninit();
   static int refct;
   void ShowEngine(CWnd *parent,COleVariant *in,COleVariant *out);
protected:
   static HANDLE library;
   static void *fn;
   static CString exename;
   IMoniker *moniker;
   COleVariant inparam;
   COleVariant outparam;
   CString res;
public:
   CHTMLDialog(int id);
   CHTMLDialog(const char *id);
   ~CHTMLDialog();
   void ShowModal(CWnd *parent);
   void ShowModal(CWnd *parent, CString in);
   void ShowModal(CWnd *parent, CString in,CString &out);
};
```

Listing 11.5 The HTML dialog box source code.

```
#include "stdafx.h"
#include <afxconv.h>
#include <mshtmhst.h>
#include "chtmldlg.h"

HANDLE CHTMLDialog::library = NULL;
int CHTMLDialog::refct=0;
void * CHTMLDialog::fn;
CString CHTMLDialog::exename;

void CHTMLDialog::commoninit()
{
```

```
  refct++;
  if (!fn)
  {
     LPTSTR p;
     library=::LoadLibrary(TEXT("MSHTML.DLL"));
     if (library)
     {
        fn=(SHOWHTMLDIALOGFN *)::GetProcAddress(
                     (HINSTANCE)library,TEXT("ShowHTMLDialog"));
     }
     p=exename.GetBufferSetLength(1024);
     ::GetModuleFileName(NULL,p,1024);
     exename.ReleaseBuffer();
  }
  res="res://";
  res+=exename;
  res+="/";
}

CHTMLDialog::CHTMLDialog(int id)
{
  USES_CONVERSION;
  CString sid;
  commoninit();
  sid.Format("%d",id);
  res+="#";
  res+=sid;
  CreateURLMoniker(NULL,T2OLE(res),&moniker);
}

CHTMLDialog::CHTMLDialog(const char *id)
{
  USES_CONVERSION;
  commoninit();
  res+=id;
  CreateURLMoniker(NULL,A2W(res),&moniker);
}

CHTMLDialog::~CHTMLDialog()
{
  if (--refct==0)
  {
```

```
        ::FreeLibrary((HINSTANCE)library);
        library=NULL;
        fn=NULL;
    }
}

void CHTMLDialog::ShowEngine(CWnd *parent,COleVariant *in,COleVariant *out)
{
    SHOWHTMLDIALOGFN *_fn=(SHOWHTMLDIALOGFN *)fn;
    CString optstring;
    _fn(parent?parent->m_hWnd:NULL,moniker,in,optstring.GetBuffer(0),out);

}

void CHTMLDialog::ShowModal(CWnd *parent)
{
    ShowEngine(parent,NULL,NULL);
}

void CHTMLDialog::ShowModal(CWnd *parent,CString in)
{
    COleVariant v0;
    v0=in;
     ShowEngine(parent,&v0,NULL);
}

void CHTMLDialog::ShowModal(CWnd *parent,CString in, CString &out)
{
    COleVariant v0,v1;
    v0=in;
    ShowEngine(parent,&v0,&v1);
    out=v1.bstrVal;
}
```

You'll find a simple program that exercises the **CHTMLDialog** class in Listing 11.3. Clicking on a button in this program will launch an HTML dialog box. This simple form-based application is the same program that launches the browser if you click on the other button.

The Web Post API

The **WebPost** API is very simple and allows you to leverage Microsoft's Web Publishing Wizard. This Wizard is part of IE and is freely available on the Web.

Table 11.3 The WebPost API.

Method	Description
WpBindToSite	Obtains a pointer to an ActiveX object supporting either the IWPSite interface or the IWPProvider interface
WpCreateSite	Creates a new site entry
WpCreateSiteEx	Creates a new site entry including a user name and password
WpDeleteSite	Deletes the information for a site from the Registry
WpDoesSiteExist	Determines whether the specified site exists
WpEnumProviders	Enumerates the currently installed service providers
WpGetErrorString	Translates an error code
WpListSites	Lists the sites currently known
WpPost	Posts one or more files or directories to the specified site
WpPostEx	Posts one or more files or directories to the specified site, using a user name and password
WpPostFile	Posts one file or directory to the specified site

You can use **WebPost** two ways. The easy way is to use one of several functions that the API exposes (see Table 11.3). Often, you'll really need to use only one of these calls. The example program uses two of them: **WpListSites** and **WpPost**.

The other way you can use **WebPost** is to ask it for an ActiveX object that allows you to manipulate the Web Publishing Wizard. This approach is overkill for most applications, but if you need the functions this object provides, it's easy enough to use.

Of course, you need the magic header files wpapi.h, wpguid.h, and wpspi.h and the webpost.lib library (from the Microsoft **WebPost** SDK). You probably already have them installed with Visual C++. If not, check out **www.microsoft.com/windows/software/webpost/wpsdk/wpsdk.htm**.

Most **WebPost** programs will care only about one API call: **WpPost**. This function requires eight arguments (see Tables 11.4 and 11.5). You can omit several of them in many cases. The arguments you're most interested in are the array of files to send to the Web server and the name of the server. You can specify a friendly name or a URL. If you don't supply a URL, the call will fill in the URL for you. You can also leave both site fields **NULL** (and omit the **WPF_NO_WIZARD** flag) to let the Wizard prompt the user for a site.

Table 11.4 WpPost arguments.

Argument	Type	Comments
hWnd	HANDLE	Optional window used as parent window
cLocalPaths	DWORD	Number of files or directories to send
lppszLocalPaths	LPTSTR	Array of file or directory names
lpszSiteName	LPTSTR	Optional friendly name of a Web site
lpcbURL	LPDWORD	Pointer to the length of the URL buffer
lpszURL	LPTSTR	Optional URL of a Web site (filled on output if supplied)
dwFlags	DWORD	Flags that control operation (see Table 11.5)

Table 11.5 WpPost flags.

Flag	Meaning
WPF_FIRST_FILE_AS_DEFAULT	Take the first file specified as the file that will be shown as the default page.
WPF_NO_DIRECT_LOOKUP	Do not attempt to look up the site based on the site name. This flag has the same effect as a NULL or empty szSiteName.
WPF_NO_PROGRESS_DLGS	Do not show the "Publishing Files" progress bar during the transfer of files to the destination computer.
WPF_NO_RECURSIVE_POST	If a directory is specified, do not post files recursively.
WPF_NO_UI	Predefined combination of WPF_NO_WIZARD and WPF_NO_PROGRESS_DLGS.
WPF_NO_URL_LOOKUP	Do not attempt to look up the site based on the site URL. This flag has the same effect as a NULL or empty szSiteURL.
WPF_NO_WIZARD	Do not prompt the user for any input.
WPF_SHOWPAGE_ALL	Predefined combination of WPF_SHOWPAGE_*. WPF_NO_WIZARD overrides this flag.
WPF_SHOWPAGE_DESTSITE	Forces the Wizard to display the "Select A Web Server" page. Normally this page is skipped if the site name is specified in the call to WpPost. Note that the WPF_NO_WIZARD flag overrides this flag.
WPF_SHOWPAGE_PROVIDER	Forces the Wizard to display any pages associated with the service provider. The WPF_NO_WIZARD flag overrides this flag.
WPF_SHOWPAGE_SRCFILE	Forces the Wizard to display the "Select A File Or Folder" page. Normally this page is skipped if the path or paths to publish are specified in the call to WpPost. Note that the WPF_NO_WIZARD flag overrides this flag.
WPF_SHOWPAGE_WELCOME	Forces the Wizard to display the initial page. Normally this page is skipped if the only other page being displayed is the Finish page. Note that the WPF_NO_WIZARD flag overrides this flag.

Table 11.6 WPSITEINFO.

Member	Type	Description
dwSize	DWORD	Size of the structure
fdwFlags	DWORD	Flags regarding this site
lpszSiteName	LFTSTR	Name of the site
lpszSiteURL	LFTSTR	Root URL for the site

It would be nice to let users pick friendly names of Web sites they've already entered. That's easy to do, too: You can use the **WpListSites** call to get a list. This function accepts a buffer, the size of the buffer, and a pointer to a **DWORD**. On return, the buffer contains a series of **WPSITEINFO** structures (see Table 11.6), the number of sites, and the number of bytes used in the buffer. If you provide a **NULL** buffer, the call will fail; but it will also fill in the number of sites and the buffer size.

A Custom Upload Program

To test the **WebPost** API, I wrote a simple MFC program that lists the available sites and allows you to upload a batch of files. Each batch is a simple text file that lists the entire path to the files in the batch, one per line.

Because this is a simple program, I used App Wizard to start an SDI application based on **CFormView**. The interface is trivially simple (see Figure 11.1). A list box holds the names of the Web sites. Clicking on a Web site places its URL in an edit control. Of course, you can modify the URL or enter an entirely new one. Another edit control allows you to specify the list of files to publish. An adjacent button allows you to fill in the edit control using a standard **CFileDialog**.

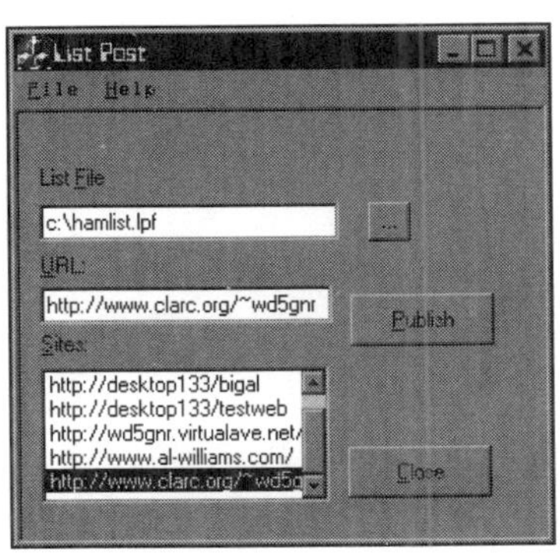

Figure 11.1 Uploading a file with the WebPost API.

All the interesting work takes place in **CListpostView::OnPublish** (see Listing 11.6). There, a simple **fopen** call parses the list file into an array of strings. The code is somewhat complicated by the use of **malloc** and **remalloc** to dynamically size the array to hold practically any number of strings.

Listing 11.6 View class for ListPost.

```
// listpostView.cpp : implementation of the CListpostView class
//

#include "stdafx.h"
#include "listpost.h"

#include "listpostDoc.h"
#include "listpostView.h"

#ifdef _DEBUG
#define new DEBUG_NEW
#undef THIS_FILE
static char THIS_FILE[] = __FILE__;
#endif

//////////////////////////////
// CListpostView

IMPLEMENT_DYNCREATE(CListpostView, CFormView)

BEGIN_MESSAGE_MAP(CListpostView, CFormView)
   //{{AFX_MSG_MAP(CListpostView)
   ON_BN_CLICKED(IDC_PUBLISH, OnPublish)
   ON_BN_CLICKED(IDC_CLOSE, OnClose)
   ON_LBN_SELCHANGE(IDC_LIST1, OnSelchangeList1)
   ON_BN_CLICKED(IDC_BROWSE, OnBrowse)
   ON_EN_CHANGE(IDC_URL, OnChangeUrl)
   //}}AFX_MSG_MAP
END_MESSAGE_MAP()

//////////////////////////////
// CListpostView construction/destruction

CListpostView::CListpostView()
   : CFormView(CListpostView::IDD)
{
   buf=NULL;
   //{{AFX_DATA_INIT(CListpostView)
   m_filename = _T("");
```

```
    m_url = _T("");
    //}}AFX_DATA_INIT
    // TODO: add construction code here

}

CListpostView::~CListpostView()
{
     if (buf) free(buf);
}

void CListpostView::DoDataExchange(CDataExchange* pDX)
{
    CFormView::DoDataExchange(pDX);
    //{{AFX_DATA_MAP(CListpostView)
    DDX_Control(pDX, IDC_PUBLISH, m_pubbtn);
    DDX_Control(pDX, IDC_LIST1, m_sitelist);
    DDX_Text(pDX, IDC_FILE, m_filename);
    DDX_Text(pDX, IDC_URL, m_url);
    //}}AFX_DATA_MAP
}

BOOL CListpostView::PreCreateWindow(CREATESTRUCT& cs)
{
    // TODO: Modify the Window class or styles here by modifying
    //  the CREATESTRUCT cs

    return CFormView::PreCreateWindow(cs);
}

void CListpostView::OnInitialUpdate()
{
    CFormView::OnInitialUpdate();
    GetParentFrame()->RecalcLayout();
    ResizeParentToFit();

    // get list of sites
    unsigned long ct,siz;

    WpListSites(&siz,NULL,&ct);  // don't check error ret!
    buf=(WPSITEINFO *)malloc(siz);
    if (WpListSites(&siz,buf,&ct)!=ERROR_SUCCESS)
       return;
    for (unsigned long i=0;i<ct;i++)
    {
```

```
        int n;
        n=m_sitelist.AddString(buf[i].lpszSiteName);
        m_sitelist.SetItemData(n,i);
    }

}

//////////////////////////////
// CListpostView diagnostics

#ifdef _DEBUG
void CListpostView::AssertValid() const
{
    CFormView::AssertValid();
}

void CListpostView::Dump(CDumpContext& dc) const
{
    CFormView::Dump(dc);
}

CListpostDoc* CListpostView::GetDocument() // non-debug version is inline
{
    ASSERT(m_pDocument->IsKindOf(RUNTIME_CLASS(CListpostDoc)));
    return (CListpostDoc*)m_pDocument;
}
#endif //_DEBUG

//////////////////////////////
// CListpostView message handlers

// Here is where all the work happens
void CListpostView::OnPublish()
{

    unsigned long flen,sitelen;
    unsigned long dummy;
    char site[256];
    char **ary;
    unsigned long maxary=0;
    UpdateData(TRUE);
    FILE *flist = fopen(m_filename,"r");
    if (!flist)
    {
        MessageBox("Can't open file");
```

```
        return;
    }
    flen=0;
    while (fgets(site,sizeof(site),flist))
    {
// assume overlap copy OK
        while (*site && isspace(*site)) strcpy(site,site+1);
          int n=strlen(site)-1;
        while (n>=0 && isspace(site[n])) site[n--]='\0';
        if (*site=='\0') continue; // blank line
        if (flen>=maxary)
        {
            maxary+=10;
            ary=(char **)(ary?
            malloc(maxary*sizeof(char **)):realloc(ary,
                  maxary*sizeof(char**)));
            if (!ary)
            {
                MessageBox("Out of memory");
                return;
            }
        }
        ary[flen]=strdup(site);
        flen++;
    }
    fclose(flist);
    sitelen=sizeof(site);
    dummy=0;
    strcpy(site,m_url);
    if (WpPost(m_hWnd,flen,ary,&dummy,
         NULL,&sitelen,site,WPF_NO_WIZARD)!=ERROR_SUCCESS)
        MessageBox("Unable to post");
    else
        MessageBox("Post complete");
    for (unsigned long i=0;i<flen;i++)
        free(ary[i]);
    free(ary);
}

void CListpostView::OnClose()
{
  AfxGetMainWnd()->PostMessage(WM_CLOSE);
}

void CListpostView::OnSelchangeList1()
```

```
{
   UpdateData(TRUE);
     m_pubbtn.EnableWindow();
   m_url=
       buf[m_sitelist.GetItemData(m_sitelist.GetCurSel())].lpszSiteURL;
   UpdateData(FALSE);
}

void CListpostView::OnBrowse()
{
  UpdateData(TRUE);
  CFileDialog dlg(TRUE,".lps",m_filename,
    OFN_HIDEREADONLY|OFN_FILEMUSTEXIST);
  if (dlg.DoModal()==IDCANCEL) return;
  m_filename=dlg.GetPathName();
  UpdateData(FALSE);
}

void CListpostView::OnChangeUrl()
{
   UpdateData(TRUE);
   m_pubbtn.EnableWindow(m_url.GetLength()!=0);
}
```

Once the array is complete, the program calls **WpPost**. Instead of specifying a friendly name, the program always uses the URL. As a result, the user can enter a URL directly or pick a friendly name (which sets the URL correctly).

The only other part of the program specific to the **WebPost** API appears in the **OnInitalUpdate** routine. Here, the program calls **WpListSites** twice. The first call simply discovers the number of sites that the second call will return. This dual call allows the program to dynamically allocate the buffer to the correct size.

The rest of the program is straightforward MFC code. Exactly three lines of code deal with posting files to the Web—a great improvement over trying to transfer the files using conventional methods. Besides, the Web Publishing Wizard can handle non-standard posting mechanisms (like CompuServe's OurWorld, for example). Web servers can provide a special URL that informs the Wizard how it should upload files to that server, resulting in great flexibility.

Another Easy Way

Actually, there's another way to use the WebPost API that might even be easier in some cases. You can directly invoke the WebPost Wizard as a separate program. This Wizard uses the WebPost API and requires no programming on your part. You can simply run wpwiz.exe using a function like **WinExec** or **CreateProcess**.

Here's the syntax for the Wizard's command line:

```
Wpwiz [-w "FriendlyName"] [-u "URL"] [-n "UserName"] [-p "password"]
    [-s "Service"] [-f [flags]] path [...]
```

Table 11.7 explains the options in more detail. You can include as many file names as you wish, but they must be full pathnames.

The ActiveX Connection

You can use ActiveX objects two ways to access the Web Publishing Wizard. First, you can call **WpBindToSite**. Of the six arguments to this call, two (**fdwFlags** and **dwReserved**) are always zero. The return value of this call is a pointer to an ActiveX object that implements the **IWPSite** interface. This value allows you to directly manipulate the Wizard using several functions. If all you need is the **PostFiles** function, you might just as well use the **WpPost** API discussed earlier.

However, in some cases you might want the extra control that **IWPSite** offers. For example, using the **IWPSite** interface, you can add steps to the existing Wizard. You can also control the specifics used to log in and log off the server and customize the progress indicator for uploading.

Table 11.7 WpWiz options.

Option	Explanation
-w "*FriendlyName*"	The friendly name to use for the site.
-u "*URL*"	The destination URL to use for the site.
-n "*UserName*"	The username to use for the site.
-p "*Password*"	The password to use for the site.
-s "*Service*"	The service provider to use for the site.
-f[*flags*]	Flags. By default, the Wizard will skip any pages for which the required information has already been provided on the command line. These flags allow you to override this default behavior and force the Wizard to show whatever pages you specify (a for all, i for introduction, s for source path, w for Web server, n for Web server name, u for URL page, or p for provider pages).
-b	Disables auto-binding. This option applies only when a new site is being created.
-i	Instructs the Wizard not to recurse into the folder being published, but rather to publish only its immediate children.

Another way to use the Web Publishing Wizard is to incorporate the file upload control, which is an ActiveX control (the control's CLSID is {886E7BF0-11CF-B1AE-00AA00A3F2C3}).

This control is also known by its **PROGID** (**MSFlUpl.Flupl.1**) or its file name (flupl.ocx).

The file upload control is primarily for use on Web pages, but you might find it useful in some C++ programs as well. The control allows the user to drag files to the control; the control then uploads them to the server. If the user simply clicks on the control, it displays a file open dialog box.

Reading The Web

Another ActiveX control of more interest to C++ programmers is the Internet Transfer control. This control allows you to download the raw contents of a document from the Internet using HTTP or FTP. At first glance, the control looks intimidating; but for simple uses, you need only one method: **OpenURL**.

Try these simple steps:

1. Create an SDI application with App Wizard, selecting **CFormView** as your view class.
2. Open the main application dialog box template. Delete the TODO label left by the App Wizard and add two edit controls and a button (see Figure 11.2). Be sure to make the lower edit control multiline and read-only.

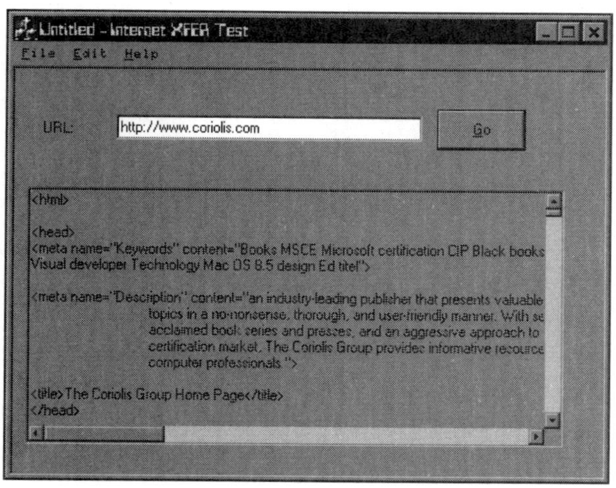

Figure 11.2 Using the Internet Transfer Control.

3. Choose Project|Add To Project|Components And Controls. Insert the Microsoft Internet Transfer Control object. Accept the default name (**CInet**).
4. Return to the dialog box template and note that the control palette now has a new item on it representing the **CInet** control. Insert a **CInet** control anywhere on your dialog box (the control is invisible).
5. Create **CString** variables for the small edit control (**m_url**) and the large edit control (**m_result**) using the Class Wizard. Also create an **m_inet** variable for the **CInet** control and an **m_gobtn** variable for the button control.
6. Create an event handler for the Go button. Here's the code you'll use:

```
   UpdateData(TRUE);  // read vars

// INet control expects variants
   COleVariant r;  // result
   COleVariant zero(0L);  // zero
   COleVariant url(m_url);  // URL

// Might take a while
   m_gobtn.EnableWindow(FALSE);
   BeginWaitCursor();
// Do it
   r=m_inet.OpenURL(url,zero);
// Convert the Variant to a string
   CString res(r.bstrVal);
// Store it
   m_result=res;
// Write vars and put all back
   UpdateData(FALSE);
   EndWaitCursor();
   m_gobtn.EnableWindow(TRUE);
```

You can find the complete code in Listing 11.7. When you're done, you'll be able to run your program, enter a URL, and click on Go. The program will fetch the raw data and display it in the lower edit control.

Of course, this functionality isn't very useful. However, once your program can read data from the Web, the possibilities are unlimited. You can create enhanced interfaces to search engines, parse stock prices, or even read hit counts from E-Bay searches.

If you were going to use this control a lot, you might consider subclassing it and hiding all the ugly **COleVariant** code. For example:

```
class CMFCInet : public CInet
  {
   CString &OpenURL(CString &url, int mode)
      {
      COleVariant res;
      COleVariant vmode(mode);
      COleVariant vurl(url);
      res=CInet::OpenURL(vurl,vmode);
      CString rv(res);
      return rv;
      }
}
```

This control can do things that are more complicated if you're willing to learn the rest of its properties and methods. You could even use it to post to some Web servers, because it can do FTP. You could also use it to write a very nice FTP program with any features you might want.

ISP Side

If you control your own Web server, you may be interested to know how WebPost knows what to do with your server. Although a complete discussion of this topic is outside the scope of this book, here's a bit of information to help you get started:

First, the default page of your Web site should have a <META> tag pointing to the posting information:

```
<META name="postinfo" content="/scripts/postinfo.txt">
```

In this case, the file is a TXT file, but it could be a CGI script or an ASP script if you need a high-degree of customization.

A typical postinfo.txt file might look like this:

```
version=1.5
[WebPost.FtpWpp]
servername="ftp.coriolis.com"
subfolder="/uploads/$USERNAME"
```

This file instructs the Wizard to connect (using FTP) to **ftp.coriolis.com** and place files in the /uploads/$USERNAME directory. Of course, $USERNAME expands to the correct name as provided to the Wizard.

You can find more about configuring servers for WebPost (including the use of ASP files to make fancy upload scripts) at **www.microsoft.com/Windows/SOFTWARE/webpost/isp.htm**.

Listing 11.7 View class for InetXTest.

```
// inetxtestView.cpp : implementation of the CInetxtestView class
//

#include "stdafx.h"
#include "inetxtest.h"

#include "inetxtestDoc.h"
#include "inetxtestView.h"

#ifdef _DEBUG
#define new DEBUG_NEW
#undef THIS_FILE
static char THIS_FILE[] = __FILE__;
#endif

//////////////////////////////
// CInetxtestView

IMPLEMENT_DYNCREATE(CInetxtestView, CFormView)

BEGIN_MESSAGE_MAP(CInetxtestView, CFormView)
   //{{AFX_MSG_MAP(CInetxtestView)
   ON_BN_CLICKED(IDC_GO, OnGo)
   //}}AFX_MSG_MAP
END_MESSAGE_MAP()

//////////////////////////////
// CInetxtestView construction/destruction

CInetxtestView::CInetxtestView()
   : CFormView(CInetxtestView::IDD)
{
   //{{AFX_DATA_INIT(CInetxtestView)
   m_result = _T("");
   m_url = _T("");
   //}}AFX_DATA_INIT
```

```
    // TODO: add construction code here

}

CInetxtestView::~CInetxtestView()
{
}

void CInetxtestView::DoDataExchange(CDataExchange* pDX)
{
    CFormView::DoDataExchange(pDX);
    //{{AFX_DATA_MAP(CInetxtestView)
    DDX_Control(pDX, IDC_GO, m_gobtn);
    DDX_Control(pDX, IDC_INET1, m_inet);
    DDX_Text(pDX, IDC_RESULT, m_result);
    DDX_Text(pDX, IDC_URL, m_url);
    //}}AFX_DATA_MAP
}

BOOL CInetxtestView::PreCreateWindow(CREATESTRUCT& cs)
{
    // TODO: Modify the Window class or styles here by modifying
    //  the CREATESTRUCT cs

    return CFormView::PreCreateWindow(cs);
}

void CInetxtestView::OnInitialUpdate()
{
    CFormView::OnInitialUpdate();
    GetParentFrame()->RecalcLayout();
    ResizeParentToFit();

}

//////////////////////////////
// CInetxtestView diagnostics

#ifdef _DEBUG
void CInetxtestView::AssertValid() const
{
    CFormView::AssertValid();
}

void CInetxtestView::Dump(CDumpContext& dc) const
```

```
{
   CFormView::Dump(dc);
}

CInetxtestDoc* CInetxtestView::GetDocument() // non-debug version is inline
{
   ASSERT(m_pDocument->IsKindOf(RUNTIME_CLASS(CInetxtestDoc)));
   return (CInetxtestDoc*)m_pDocument;
}
#endif //_DEBUG

/////////////////////////////
// CInetxtestView message handlers

void CInetxtestView::OnGo()
{
   UpdateData(TRUE);  // read vars

// INet control expects variants
   COleVariant r;  // result
   COleVariant zero(0L);  // zero
   COleVariant url(m_url);  // URL

// Might take a while
   m_gobtn.EnableWindow(FALSE);
   BeginWaitCursor();
// Do it
   r=m_inet.OpenURL(url,zero);
// Convert the Variant to a string
   CString res(r.bstrVal);
// Store it
   m_result=res;
// Write vars and put all back
   UpdateData(FALSE);
   EndWaitCursor();
   m_gobtn.EnableWindow(TRUE);
}
```

MFC Internet Support

MFC supports two different methods for using the Internet: a simple model for times you just want to read data and a more complex model if you want to write more sophisticated clients (for example, if you want to submit a form to a Web server). Both models start with **CInternetSession** (see Table 11.8). This object

Table 11.8 CInternetSession.

Member	Description
QueryOption	Reads current options (asynchronous operation, extended errors, time outs, cache control, and so on)
SetOption	Sets current options
OpenURL	Opens a URL for reading
GetFTPConnection	Opens an FTP connection, allowing you to enumerate available files, read, write, and command the remote FTP host
GetHTTPConnection	Opens an HTTP connection that allows you to post data, read files, and so on
GetGopherConnection	Opens a Gopher connection
EnableStatusCallback	Turns on asynchronous notifications
Close	Closes the session
OnStatusCallback	Handles asynchronous notifications, if enabled

represents your connection to the Internet. By using this object, you don't need to care about the dialer, using proxies, or any of the other mundane details required to connect to the Internet. The user's normal preferences will control the process.

NOTE: *The documentation and header files list **ServiceTypeFromHandle** as a member even though it doesn't actually appear in the **CInternetSession** source code. Using it will cause a link error.*

If you simply want to read data from the host, you can call the **CInternetSession**'s **OpenURL** method. This call parses a URL and returns a file object. The file object is always a **CStdioFile** or derived from **CStdioFile**. If the URL starts with **file://**, then the object is actually **CStdioFile**. If the URL begins with **http://**, MFC returns a **CHttpFile** object. FTP transfers return a **CInternetFile** object and Gopher files use **CGopherFile**. Each file type is similar to **CStdioFile** (which, in turn, bases itself on **CFile**). However, each object has its own special calls, too.

More sophisticated programs might want to actually interact with the server instead of just pulling data from it. In such cases you need a connection object to manage this interaction. For HTTP, the object is **CHttpConnection**. You can create the object by calling **CInternetSession::GetHttpConnection**.

Table 11.9 CHttpFile.

Member	Description
AddRequestHeaders	Adds headers to an outbound request
SendRequest	Sends the request to the server
QueryInfo	Reads headers from the server
QueryInfoStatusCode	Reads the status code from the server
GetVerb	Determines the method of transmission
GetObject	Gets the object name
GetFileURL	Gets the full URL of the file
Close	Closes the file
Read	Reads data
ReadString	Reads an entire string
Write	Writes data
WriteString	Writes an entire string

For FTP and Gopher, you then call **OpenFile**. For HTTP, you call **OpenRequest** followed by **SendRequest**. In either event, you'll now have a **CStdioFile**-derived class, just as before. The difference is that you can manipulate the object to interact with the server. For example, a **CHttpFile** (see Table 11.9) obtained in this way can alter the headers sent to the server by calling **AddHeaders** in between the **OpenRequest** and **SendRequest** calls.

The Link Checker

To exercise the MFC classes, I wrote a simple hyperlink checker (see Listing 11.8). Just for checking links, it's sufficient to simply read an HTTP file and parse it for further **HREF** and **SRC** links to other files. As a practical matter, you don't want to do this endlessly, because you would forever walk links between Web sites (like a Web spider program). Instead, the LINKCK program parses only the initial file for further links.

Listing 11.8 linkckview.cpp.

```
// linkckView.cpp : implementation of the CLinkckView class
//

#include "stdafx.h"
#include "linkck.h"
#include <afxinet.h>
#include "urlinput.h"
```

```
#include "linkckDoc.h"
#include "linkckView.h"

#ifdef _DEBUG
#define new DEBUG_NEW
#undef THIS_FILE
static char THIS_FILE[] = __FILE__;
#endif

////////////////////////
// CLinkckView

IMPLEMENT_DYNCREATE(CLinkckView, CFormView)

BEGIN_MESSAGE_MAP(CLinkckView, CFormView)
  //{{AFX_MSG_MAP(CLinkckView)
 ON_BN_CLICKED(IDC_SCAN, OnScan)
 ON_COMMAND(ID_FILE_PRINT_PREVIEW, OnFilePrintPreview)
 ON_COMMAND(ID_FILE_SCAN, OnScan)
 ON_LBN_DBLCLK(IDC_LB, OnScan)
 ON_UPDATE_COMMAND_UI(ID_FILE_PRINT, OnUpdateFilePrint)
 ON_UPDATE_COMMAND_UI(ID_FILE_PRINT_PREVIEW, OnUpdateFilePrint)
 //}}AFX_MSG_MAP
 // Standard printing commands
 ON_COMMAND(ID_FILE_PRINT, CFormView::OnFilePrint)
 ON_COMMAND(ID_FILE_PRINT_DIRECT, CFormView::OnFilePrint)
END_MESSAGE_MAP()

////////////////////////
// CLinkckView construction/destruction

void CLinkckView::OnFilePrintPreview()
{
        AfxGetMainWnd()->ShowWindow(SW_MAXIMIZE);
        CFormView::OnFilePrintPreview();
}

CLinkckView::CLinkckView()
        : CFormView(CLinkckView::IDD)
{
        //{{AFX_DATA_INIT(CLinkckView)
// NOTE: the ClassWizard will add member initialization here
        //}}AFX_DATA_INIT
        PrintEnable=FALSE;
```

```
}

CLinkckView::~CLinkckView()
{
}

void CLinkckView::DoDataExchange(CDataExchange* pDX)
{
        CFormView::DoDataExchange(pDX);
        //{{AFX_DATA_MAP(CLinkckView)
        DDX_Control(pDX, IDC_LB, m_lb);
        //}}AFX_DATA_MAP
}

BOOL CLinkckView::PreCreateWindow(CREATESTRUCT& cs)
{
        return CFormView::PreCreateWindow(cs);
}

////////////////////////
// CLinkckView printing

BOOL CLinkckView::OnPreparePrinting(CPrintInfo* pInfo)
{
        // default preparation
        return DoPreparePrinting(pInfo);
}

void CLinkckView::OnBeginPrinting(CDC* /*pDC*/,
         CPrintInfo* /*pInfo*/)
{
        // TODO: add extra initialization before printing
}

void CLinkckView::OnEndPrinting(CDC* /*pDC*/,
         CPrintInfo* /*pInfo*/)
{
        // TODO: add cleanup after printing
}

// Simple code to dump the results out to a printed page
void CLinkckView::OnPrint(CDC* pDC, CPrintInfo*)
{
        int i;
        int y=0,texthi;
```

```
        TEXTMETRIC tm;
        pDC->GetTextMetrics(&tm);
        texthi=tm.tmHeight+tm.tmExternalLeading;
        for (i=1;i<m_lb.GetCount();i++)
        {
          CString item;
          m_lb.GetText(i,item);
          pDC->TabbedTextOut(5,y,item,0,NULL,0);
          y+=texthi;
        }
}

///////////////////////
// CLinkckView diagnostics

#ifdef _DEBUG
void CLinkckView::AssertValid() const
{
        CFormView::AssertValid();
}

void CLinkckView::Dump(CDumpContext& dc) const
{
        CFormView::Dump(dc);
}

CLinkckDoc* CLinkckView::GetDocument()
{
   ASSERT(m_pDocument->IsKindOf(RUNTIME_CLASS(CLinkckDoc)));
   return (CLinkckDoc*)m_pDocument;
}
#endif //_DEBUG

///////////////////////
// CLinkckView message handlers

// Do a scan from user interface
void CLinkckView::OnScan()
{
  CString URL;
  CString err;
  int sel=m_lb.GetCurSel();
  if (sel==LB_ERR||sel==0||m_lb.GetItemData(sel)==-1)
  {
```

```
  // prompt if no good selection in the list box
          CUrlInput indlg;
          if (indlg.DoModal()==IDCANCEL) return;
          URL=indlg.m_url;
  }
  else
  {
          m_lb.GetText(sel,URL);
  }
// clear list box
  m_lb.ResetContent();
  m_lb.AddString("<<New URL>>");
// do real work
  DoScan(URL);
  // enable menu items
  PrintEnable=TRUE;
}

// This routine really does the work
void CLinkckView::DoScan(CString & URL, BOOL recurse)
{
        CString line;
        int item;
        CInternetSession session("Commando Link Check V1.0");
        CStdioFile *f;
        try
          {
          f=session.OpenURL(URL);
          }
        catch (...)
          {
          f=NULL;
          }
// apparently the MFC Dlls don't export
// CHttpFile's runtime class? (see text)
    if (f && f->IsKindOf(RUNTIME_CLASS(CHttpFile)))
//      if (f && !strnicmp(URL,"http",4))
        {
                DWORD stat; // http status
                CHttpFile *hf=(CHttpFile *)f;
                hf->QueryInfoStatusCode(stat);
// only codes 200-299 are good
                if (stat<200||stat>299)
                {
                        f->Close();
```

```
                        f=NULL;
                    }
                }
                if (!f)  // some problem
                {
                  CString err;
                  err=URL;
                  err+="\tError!";
                  item=m_lb.AddString(err);
                  m_lb.SetItemData(item,-1);
                  return;
                }
// go!
                item=m_lb.AddString(URL);
                m_lb.SetItemData(item,0);
// if recurse is true, then parse file
                while (recurse && f->ReadString(line))
                {
                        int n=0;
                         char *p, *e;
                        p=(char *)(LPCSTR)line;
                        do {
                          p=strchr(p,'=');    // search for =
                          if (p)    // backward search for HREF/SRC
                          {
                                  if (toupper(p[-1])!='F' ||
                                          toupper(p[-2])!='E' ||
                                          toupper(p[-3])!='R' ||
                                          toupper(p[-4])!='H')
                                          if (toupper(p[-1])!='C' ||
                                                  toupper(p[-2])!='R' ||
                                                  toupper(p[-3])!='S')
                                          {
                                                  p++;
                                                  continue;
                                          }
                                  if (p[1]=='"') // skip quotes
                                        p++;
                                         e=p+1+strcspn(p+1," \t\n>\"#");
                                         *e='\0';
// don't recurse empty URLs (e.g., HREF=#anchor)
                                         if (e!=p+1)
                                          {
                                            CString newURL;
                                            ExpandURL(newURL,p+1,URL);
```

```
                                    DoScan(newURL,FALSE);
                                 }
                              *e=' ';
                              p=e+1;
                   }
                } while (p && *p);
          } // end while
      f->Close();
}

void CLinkckView::OnInitialUpdate()
{
        CFormView::OnInitialUpdate();
        GetParentFrame()->RecalcLayout();
        ResizeParentToFit(FALSE);
}


void CLinkckView::ExpandURL(CString &result,
   CString source,CString current)
{
   CString proto,host,path,file,chost,cpath,cproto;
// break up both URLs
   ParseURL(source,&proto,&host,&path,&file);
   ParseURL(current,&cproto,&chost,&cpath,NULL);
// copy empty parts from current URL
   if (proto.IsEmpty()) proto=cproto;
   if (host.IsEmpty()) host=chost;
   if (path.IsEmpty())
     path=cpath;
   else if (path[0]!='/'&&path[0]!='\\'&&!cpath.IsEmpty())
     path=cpath+"/"+path;
   result=proto + host ;
// if path is relative, prepend current path
   if (!path.IsEmpty())
       {
       if (path[0]!='/' && path[0]!='\\')
         result+="/";
       result+= path;
       }
   if (!file.IsEmpty()) result+="/" + file;
}


// Homebrew URL parser AfxParseURL is too lazy to
// decide what is a file and what is a directory, so we
```

```
// do it ourselves (sigh)
void CLinkckView::ParseURL(CString url,CString *proto,
                           CString *host, CString *path,
                           CString *fileplus)
{

        CString _proto, _host, _path, _fileplus;
        int n;
        n=url.Find("://");
        if (n==-1) n=url.Find(":\\\\");
// get protocol
        if (n!=-1)
        {
                _proto=url.Left(n+3);
                url=url.Right(url.GetLength()-(n+3));
                n=url.FindOneOf("/\\");
                if (n==-1)
                {  // get host
                        _host=url;
                        url="";
                }
                else
                {
                        _host=url.Left(n);
                        url=url.Right(url.GetLength()-n);
                }
        }
// find path or file name
        n=url.ReverseFind('/');
        if (n==-1) n=url.ReverseFind('\\');
        if (n!=-1)
        {
                _fileplus=url.Right(url.GetLength()-n-1);
                _path=n==-1?url:url.Left(n);
                if (!_path.IsEmpty()&&(_path[0]=='/'||
                     _path[0]=='\\'))
                        _path=_path.Right(_path.GetLength()-1);
        }
        else
        {
                _fileplus=url;
        }
        // Special case heuristic
        // if host name and file provided, but no path then file
        // is probably a path if it doesn't contain a period
```

```
        if (!_host.IsEmpty() && _path.IsEmpty() &&
                !_fileplus.IsEmpty() && _fileplus.Find('.')==-1)
        {
                _path="/" + _fileplus;
                _fileplus="";
        }
        if (proto) *proto=_proto;
        if (host) *host=_host;
        if (path) *path=_path;
        if (fileplus) *fileplus=_fileplus;
}


void CLinkckView::OnEndPrintPreview(CDC* pDC, CPrintInfo* pInfo,
             POINT point, CPreviewView* pView)
{
        AfxGetMainWnd()->ShowWindow(SW_NORMAL);
        CFormView::OnEndPrintPreview(pDC, pInfo, point, pView);
}

void CLinkckView::OnUpdateFilePrint(CCmdUI* pCmdUI)
{
        pCmdUI->Enable(PrintEnable);
}
```


The parsing is somewhat tricky and not terribly robust. For example, the link checker will pick up any **SRC=** or **HREF=** line, even if it's in a comment. Also, it includes many special cases to handle relative links, links with anchors, and all the other myriad ways to express URLs. I even try to allow for forward slashes or backslashes. While my algorithm handles all the cases I could think of, I'm sure someone will find a URL that breaks it.

The key parts to the parser are the **ExpandURL** and **ParseURL** functions. **ExpandURL** takes two URLs: the URL you want to expand and the current URL. It then calls **ParseURL** twice to break down the URL into its constituent parts. Finally, it generates a new URL by using the original URL to fill in missing pieces from the new URL. These routines are very general purpose, and you might find a use for them in your own code. MFC also provides **AfxParseURL** which performs a similar function. Unfortunately, the output format of **AfxParseURL** isn't what I needed for this program, so I decided to write my own version.

The **OnScan** routine starts the show when you click on the Scan button or a menu item or double-click on a selection in the list box. If the list box has a selection, and the selection's extra data is zero, **OnScan** uses the list box's entry as the URL to scan. Otherwise, the routine displays a simple dialog box to request a URL for scanning. The user must enter a complete URL.

The real work occurs in **DoScan**. This code opens the given URL (using **OpenURL**), checks for a valid response, and, if required, parses the file for links. Note that the code assumes you're scanning an HTML file. If you point at an FTP file, for example, **DoScan** still attempts to find links in the file.

That brings up another interesting problem. Checking to see if the file exists is tricky. Suppose you request a file from a legitimate server, but the file doesn't exist. You'd expect an error or an exception, right? Wrong. **OpenURL** succeeds, but the contents of the **CHttpFile** is an error message from the server! To correctly check the result, you'd like to examine the return code. Normal return codes are in the range of 200 to 299. Missing files usually show a return of 404.

You might think that finding the status code would be easy. **CHttpFile** has a member function named **QueryInfoStatusCode** to find the return code. The problem is, **OpenURL** returns a pointer to a **CStdioFile** that may (or may not) point to a **CHttpFile**. Casting is dangerous because you don't know for sure what type of file object **OpenURL** returns.

Protecting an uncertain cast seems like a perfect job for **IsKindOf**. **CFile** derives from **CObject**, so why not use **IsKindOf** to detect a **CHttpFile**? Doing so sounds good in theory, but in practice, it looks like Microsoft forgot to export the class information for **CHttpFile** from the MFC DLLs. So if you write

```
if (f && f->IsKindOf(RUNTIME_CLASS(CHttpFile))) . . .
```

the code won't even link with the DLL version of the MFC library. If you turn on the static library option (under Project|Settings), everything works fine.

I left the code the way I wanted it to be, and assumed the project would link with the static library. However, if you prefer, you can use the commented-out code as a workaround. The only way to get a **CHttpFile** is if the URL begins with *http*, so the workaround code looks like this:

```
if (f && !strnicmp(URL,"http",4)) . . .
```

This code has the same effect in practice as the **if** statement above that uses **IsKindOf**.

Beyond that, the program isn't very interesting. **DoScan** adds all the URLs it finds to the list box. Good items appear by themselves and have an extra data word of zero. Bad URLs have a tab and the word *Error!* appended to them. They also have an extra word of -1, allowing **OnScan** to recognize the URL as bad so it won't try to scan it later.

The parsing is a mishmash of **CString** code and good old-fashioned C library string calls. Most of the **CString** manipulation functions refuse to work on portions of strings, and that makes it easier to use the ordinary calls in certain cases.

Active Directory Services Overview

If you read Chapter 6, you probably noticed that the network communications solutions you found there were all geared towards allowing two processes to communicate. What they lacked was a way for two processes to find each other among the dozens of processes on a particular machine and the thousands that might exist on a single local area network (LAN). For example, if you want to make an RPC call that retrieves a stock quote, doing so isn't too difficult. But what if you don't know the name of a stock quote server? What if you know a name, but that server isn't available? The answer is active directory services (ADS).

ADS can also find a printer for you, or even an email address. ADS encompasses several standards for finding names and relating them to unique (or distinguished) names. As a programmer, you can access ADS three ways: ADSI, LDAP, or MAPI. The most flexible way is to use ADSI, a set of ActiveX interfaces (the *I* stands for *interfaces*). These interfaces allow you to resolve names in any language from C++ to scripting languages.

If you're interested in compatibility with other platforms, you might want to use light-weight directory access protocol (LDAP; the RFC 1833 interface) or the Messaging API (MAPI). LDAP is a standard directory service, and the core that ADS uses to implement its features. The MAPI interface is strictly for compatibility with existing MAPI applications. You shouldn't use it unless you have existing code that depends on this interface. By using ADS, your program can work with LDAP, Windows, Novell Directory Services (NDS), or any other provider that supports ADS.

Terms

You need to know a few important terms to understand ADS:

- *Distinguished name*—A complete name that uniquely identifies an object
- *ADsPath*—A case-sensitive name that uniquely identifies an ADSI object
- *User principal name*—A shorthand name for a user or group
- *Virtual container*—A wrapper for an LDAP directory that places it somewhere in the ADS tree
- *Global catalog*—The global list of all directories available; useful for finding an object by attribute instead of name or browsing objects

- *Metadata*—Data or properties that belong to an ADSI object
- *Schema*—The types of objects known to the directory service

Using ADSI

Accessing ADS is fairly straightforward when you use ADSI. ADSI objects represent any item within the directory service, including users, computers, files, servers, printers, print queues, and other entities.

All ADSI objects support the **IADs** and **IADsPropertyList** interfaces. These interfaces allow access to the object's metadata by any development language. Objects also provide **IDirectoryObject** for direct access to properties by languages that can manipulate vtables (like C++). Of course, C++ (and similar languages) can use either interface (but not both at the same time). **IADs** uses caching to improve performance. On the other hand, **IDirectoryObject** supports any data type, not just automation types.

All container objects also support **IADsContainer**. Using this interface, you can create new objects, delete objects, and so forth. Specific objects may support other interfaces, but these are the most common ones; other interfaces depend on what the object actually is. For example, computers support **IADsComputer**, and objects that represent users support **IADsUser**.

An ADsPath contains the name of the provider, a colon, two slashes, and a provider-specific string. It's very similar to a normal network UNC. For example, the ADsPath

```
WINNT://AWCDomain/alw
```

refers to the user alw on the AWCDomain domain.

ADSI also provides helper functions for C++ programmers (see Table 11.10). These functions aren't strictly necessary, but they make life easier, and you'll want to use them.

Table 11.10 ADSI Functions.

Function	Description
AdsGetObject	Binds to an ADSI object using default options
AdsOpenObject	Binds to an ADSI object
AdsGetLastError	Retrieves the last error code
AdsSetLastError	Sets the error code value
AdsBuildVarArrayInt	Builds a variant array from an array of DWORDs

(continued)

***Table 11.10 ADSI Functions* (continued).**

Function	Description
AdsBuildVarArrayStr	Builds a variant array from an array of Unicode strings
AdsBuildEnumerator	Creates an enumerator object for the specified ADSI container
AdsEnumerateNext	Populates a variant array with elements retrieved from the specified enumerator
AdsFreeEnumerator	Frees an enumerator object previously created by ADsBuildEnumerator
AllocADsMem	Allocates a block of memory
FreeADsMem	Frees the memory allocated by AllocADsMem
ReallocADsMem	Reallocates memory
AllocADsStr	Allocates memory for a string
FreeADsStr	Frees the memory allocated for a string
ReallocADsStr	Replaces an existing string with a new one
AdsEncodeBinaryData	Converts binary data to the format suitable for a search filter

Summary

In today's networked world, you can't afford to ignore the Internet. The good news is there are lots of different ways you can add Internet support to your programs, so you can certainly find something that suits you. The bad news is that you have to understand these different technologies to some degree to make your selection.

Because most of these networking technologies rely on ActiveX, you don't need to worry about the internal details the way you did before ActiveX was common. Instead, you'll focus on the properties, methods, and events that comprise that control—even if the control is the entire Web browser!

Immediate Solutions

Working With Internet Shortcuts

Internet shortcuts are similar to ordinary shortcuts, but they point to Internet resources instead of local files. Internet shortcuts are ordinary text files, so you might elect to work with them just using their text structure. This structure resembles an INI file (see Listing 11.1).

The preferred way to work with Internet shortcuts, however, is to use the ActiveX interface that Microsoft provides. Doing so protects your code from future changes in the file format.

The **CLSID_InternetShortcut** object is an Internet shortcut. The **IUniformResourceLocator** interface allows you to manipulate the shortcut. However, to load (or save) the shortcut to disk, you'll need to query this interface for the **IPersistFile** interface. You can find a complete example in Listing 11.2.

Methods Of Internet Communications

You can use a dizzying array of methods to communicate over the Internet. To summarize, the techniques discussed in this chapter are as follows:

- Use Internet Explorer as an automation client.
- Use Internet Explorer as an ActiveX control.
- Use MFC's **CHtmlView** class.
- Use MFC's **CInternetSession** class (and its related classes).
- Use the Internet Transfer Control.
- Use **WebPost**.

Usually, your choice of method will depend on what you're trying to accomplish. For example, if you want to display a full-function Web browser, you'll probably opt to use Internet Explorer as an automation client. However, if you want to embed a Web browser in your program, using it as an ActiveX control might be more appropriate.

MFC programmers, of course, will generally use **CHtmlView** instead of the ActiveX control because it handles many of the details for you. If you want to simply read data and process it, the Internet Transfer Control is a good bet.

The **WebPost** API is useful only for sending files to Web servers. You can also accomplish this task—for most servers, at least—with the Internet Transfer Control. The advantage to **WebPost** is that it can accommodate nonstandard servers, as long as they adhere to the FrontPage guidelines for informing the **WebPost** system how to send files.

Using Resource URLs

When you use a Web browser in your own program, you probably want to read data from the Web. However, after a while you'll start thinking about displaying HTML that's specific to your program. The problem is, you don't want your program to depend on a lot of separate HTML files. Luckily, you can store HTML pages in your resources and display them directly from your EXE (or DLL) file that contains the resource. Visual Studio provides a special resource type just for HTML documents, and Internet Explorer knows how to display resource URLs that start with the **res://** protocol.

The URL **res://c:\drum\drum.exe/RESDOC** points to a resource named RESDOC in the c:\drum\drum.exe executable. Be sure that RESDOC has a string for a name and not a number. When you insert any resource, Visual Studio generates an ID for it that is really a **#define** constant that resolves into a number. You may prefer to store the resource ID as a string so you don't have to use cryptic numbers in the URL. In that case, just rename the resource and place the ID between double quotation marks. This formatting informs Visual Studio that you want to use a string ID instead of a numeric one.

If you prefer to use a number, that's possible, too. Because this number is only available at compile time, IE can't find this sort of resource. If you want to use a number, you'll need to examine your resources (choose View|Resource IDs) and use the decimal number, preceded by a # sign, in the URL. For example:

```
res://c:\drum\drum.exe/#233
```

If you're using **CHtmlView**, you can use the **LoadFromResource** member to load a page from your current resources. This approach is handy because the code finds the executable name and takes care of the difference between numeric and string resource IDs by supplying overloaded versions of the function.

Inside Internet Explorer

One of the most powerful tools at your disposal when adding Internet support to your programs is Internet Explorer, Microsoft's Web browser. Unless the Justice Department changes things, Internet Explorer installs with Windows, so you can assume it's present on any modern Windows machine.

You can use Internet Explorer two ways as a coordinated piece of your software. First, you can launch the browser and use ActiveX automation (sometimes known as *scripting*) to control its operation. If you prefer to incorporate the browser, you can also create an ActiveX control (or use MFC's **CHtmlView** wrapper class). The advantage is that the browser looks more like a part of your program. The disadvantage is that you're responsible for more user interface tasks (for example, the back button).

Luckily, the interface to the browser (**IWebBrowser2**) is the same in either case (see Table 11.1). However, a few of the functions are available only when the browser is running separately and you're controlling it only with scripting.

If you want to see an example of using the Web Browser directly, look at Listing 11.3. There you'll see a program that not only launches the Web Browser, but also manipulates the HTML that the browser displays.

Using The Scripting Object Model

When you use the Web Browser from your program, you can access the scripting object model just like an HTML script can. If you aren't familiar with the Scripting object model, it is a series of objects that the browser provides so that HTML scripts (and your program, too) can interact with the browser.

At the head of the object hierarchy is the **Window** object. This represents the current browser window (which could be a frame inside a larger page). Each **Window** object has a **Document** object that represents the HTML inside that window. In addition, there are objects that allow you to manipulate history, learn about the browser's capabilities and more.

To access the scripting object model, you'll need the **IHTMLDocument2** interface. A simple call to **get_Document** will return this pointer. However, **get_Document** returns an **IDispatch** interface, so you'll call **QueryInterface** to get the correct interface.

Be careful. The browser won't have a document object until the page you're loading is at least partially loaded. You can determine when the page is loaded by examining the **ReadyState** property. Here's a snippet of code that will get the correct **IHTMLDocument2** pointer (you can find the complete code in Listing 11.3):


```
READYSTATE rdy;
do {
   Sleep(0);  // give browser a chance to run
   m_browser->get_ReadyState(&rdy);
} while (rdy!=READYSTATE_COMPLETE);
IDispatch *dDoc;
hr=m_browser->get_Document(&dDoc);
IHTMLDocument2 *doc;
hr=dDoc->QueryInterface(&doc);
dDoc->Release();
```

Using HTML Dialog Boxes

The mshtml.dll file has a function (**ShowHTMLDialog**) that allows you to create HTML dialog boxes from a resource in your program. Ordinarily, you'd need to dynamically load the library and use **GetProcAddress** to get a pointer to the function. However, in Listing 11.4 and 11.5 you'll find a class wrapper that encapsulates the HTML dialog box functions for you.

To use the dialog box object, simply construct a **CHTMLDialog** object, passing the resource ID (either as a string or a number) to the constructor. Then you can call **ShowModal** with the **CWnd** pointer that corresponds to the parent window. For example:

```
CHTMLDialog dlg(IDR_HDLG);
dlg.ShowModal(this);
```

Using MFC's Internet Support

MFC supports Internet transfers through clever subclassing of the **CFile** class. Your program receives a file that corresponds to an Internet document (either from HTTP, FTP, or Gopher).

To use this file-oriented approach, you must first construct a **CInternetSession** object. Once you have this object, you can use one of two methods to access the Internet. The easiest way is to supply a URL to the **OpenURL** method. This retrieves the file and returns either a **CHttpFile** (for Web documents), a **CInternetFile** (for FTP documents), or a **CGopherFile** (for Gopher documents). From there, reading the data from the Internet is as easy as accessing any common **CFile** object. You can find an example of this technique in Listing 11.8.

An alternate method is to use **GetHttpConnection** and use the connection object it returns to call **OpenFile**, **OpenRequest**, or **SendRequest**. These methods allow you to take complete control over the transaction. For example, you can add headers to the HTTP request before sending it—something you can't do with the simplified method of calling **OpenURL**.

Of course, sometimes you want to display Web pages, not just load their data into your program. Displaying HTML requires sophisticated parsing and display management that is more than most people want to write themselves. Luckily, MFC provides **CHtmlView** to deal with this problem. This view class encapsulates Internet Explorer's ActiveX control so you can read and display HTML documents.

Chapter 12

Console Applications And Services

If you need an immediate solution to:	*See page:*
Starting A Console Program	585
Using MFC From Console Programs	585
Methods For Accessing Consoles	585
Creating A Main Console For A GUI Program	586
Creating And Using Auxiliary Consoles	587
Handling Console Events	587
Finding A Console's Window Handle	588
Inside Services	588
Accessing A Service	589
The C++ Service Base Class	589
Debugging Services	590

In Depth

The movie *Raiders of the Lost Ark* includes a classic scene in which a bad guy comes at Indiana Jones with some very fancy sword work. He pauses, and you expect the intrepid Mr. Jones to respond in kind. Instead, he pulls out a revolver and shoots his sword-wielding opponent. Sometimes the simplest approach is the best.

The same is true when you program Windows. Graphical user interfaces are great—they're certainly as flashy as fancy sword work. However, just as sometimes a quick gunshot will do better than flashy sabers, sometimes there's just no substitute for a simple character-based program.

Character-based programs are nothing new. Many programmers remember writing for MSDOS or Unix with a simple character-mode interface. C programmers fondly recall using **printf** and **scanf** (or **cout** and **cin**). With Windows 2000 you can still write applications that use standard I/O by writing a console program.

In the console application's simplest form, you can write an old-fashioned C or C++ program that performs simple character-mode I/O. However, there's more to it than just **printf** and **scanf**. You can also call the Windows API and use several special API calls to control your console application.

Creating A Simple Console Application

The simplest possible console application is just like the simplest possible C program. You can include stdio.h (or iostream.h, if you prefer) and write a "Hello World" program. Just be sure you're set to build a console application. The easiest way to do so is to select Win32 Console Application in the New Project dialog box. All this option does is creates a blank project with settings to indicate that MFC isn't in use, **_CONSOLE** is defined, and the /subsystem:console linker option is in force.

However, it's possible to include windows.h and make ordinary Windows calls. For example, Listing 12.1 uses **MessageBox** to display a message box.

Listing 12.1 A very simple console program.

```
#include <windows.h>

void main()
{
   MessageBox(NULL,"Howdy World!","Texas Demo",MB_OK);
}
```

Something More

What makes console applications special is that they can access the entire Windows API, if you know how to make them. To illustrate this technique, look at the Another Version Controller (AVC) program in Listing 12.2. This program uses the ActiveX Structured Storage System (SSS) to hold multiple versions of a file in a single storage.

Listing 12.2 The AVC program.

```
// Another Version Control System
// Uses structured storage to perform version control
#include <iostream.h>
#include <stdio.h>
#include <windows.h>
#include <string.h>
#include "avc.h"
#include "dialog.h"
// Global variables
CMD cmd;                // current cmd
char filename[1024];    // archive file name
char user[33];          // current user (if any)
int listlen;            // length of input list
char **filelist;        // input list
IStorage *archive;      // archive
int dirlen;             // length of directory
char **dir;             // directory
HANDLE hInst;           // our hInstance


// Helper to convert ANSI string to unicode
wchar_t *ucode(char *p)
  {
  static wchar_t cvt[1024];
  MultiByteToWideChar(CP_ACP,MB_PRECOMPOSED,
  p,-1,cvt,sizeof(cvt)/sizeof(wchar_t));
  return cvt;
  }

// Open archive
```

```
BOOL OpenArchive()
   {
   IStream *dirstream;
   HRESULT r;
   if (FAILED(r=StgOpenStorage(ucode(filename),NULL,
      STGM_READWRITE|STGM_SHARE_EXCLUSIVE|STGM_TRANSACTED,
      NULL,0,&archive)))
      {
      // if checking in, archive need not exist, create it
      if (r==STG_E_FILENOTFOUND)
         if (cmd!=CHECKIN||
             FAILED(StgCreateDocfile(ucode(filename),
            STGM_READWRITE|STGM_SHARE_EXCLUSIVE|
            STGM_TRANSACTED,0,&archive)))
         {
         cerr<<"Can't open "<<filename<<"\n";
         return FALSE;
         }
      }
   // Open dir stream
   r=archive->OpenStream(L"$\tDIR$",NULL,
      STGM_READWRITE|STGM_SHARE_EXCLUSIVE,0,&dirstream);
   if (FAILED(r))  // create if not present
      {
      if (FAILED(archive->CreateStream(L"$\tDIR$",
          STGM_READWRITE|STGM_SHARE_EXCLUSIVE,
          0,0,&dirstream)))
         {
         archive->Release();
         return FALSE;
         }
      dirlen=0;
      // must use malloc so we can use realloc
      dir=(char **)malloc(sizeof(char *));
      *dir=NULL;
      dirstream->Release();
      return TRUE;
      }
   dirstream->Read((void *)&dirlen,sizeof(int),NULL);
   // must use malloc so we can use realloc
   dir=(char **)malloc(sizeof(char *)*(dirlen+1));
   for (int i=0;i<dirlen;i++)
      {
      char fn[1024];
      int len;
      dirstream->Read((void *)&len,sizeof(int),NULL);
      dirstream->Read((void *)fn,len,NULL);
```

```
      fn[len]='\0';
      dir[i]=strdup(fn);
      }
   dir[dirlen]=NULL;
   dirstream->Release();
   return TRUE;
   }

// Close archive w/o commit
void CloseArchive()
   {
   archive->Release();
   }

// Write out dir
BOOL WriteDir()
   {
   IStream *dirstream;
   // Use create instead of open so we get an empty stream
   archive->CreateStream(L"$\tDIR$",STGM_WRITE|
     STGM_SHARE_EXCLUSIVE|STGM_CREATE,0,0,&dirstream);
   dirstream->Write((void *)&dirlen,sizeof(int),NULL);
   for (int i=0;i<dirlen;i++)
      {
      int len=strlen(dir[i]);
      dirstream->Write((void *)&len,sizeof(int),NULL);
      dirstream->Write((void *)dir[i],len,NULL);
      }
   dirstream->Release();
   return TRUE;
   }

// Process command line arguments
// Argument string looks like:
// avc archive[,user_name] command [file...]
// command is CHECKIN, CHECKOUT, LIST, or REMOVE (any case)
int process_args(int argc, char *argv[])
   {
   char *p;
   cmd=UNKNOWN;
   if (argc==1) return 0;
   p=strchr(argv[1],',');
   if (p)
      {
      *p='\0';
      strcpy(user,p+1);
      }
```


12. Console Applications And Services

```
    strcpy(filename,argv[1]);
    if (argc==2) return 1;
    strupr(argv[2]);
    if (!strcmp(argv[2],"CHECKIN")) cmd=CHECKIN;
    else if (!strcmp(argv[2],"CHECKOUT")) cmd=CHECKOUT;
    else if (!strcmp(argv[2],"LIST")) cmd=LIST;
    else if (!strcmp(argv[2],"REMOVE")) cmd=REMOVE;
    if (argc==3) return 2;
    filelist=argv+3;
    listlen=argc-3;
    return 3;
    }



// This routine brings up a dialog if you don't issue
// enough command line arguments
BOOL DialogArg()
   {
   if (DialogBox(hInst,MAKEINTRESOURCE(IDD_OPTIONS),NULL,
      (DLGPROC)dlgcb)==-1)
      return FALSE;
   else
      return TRUE;
   }

// Check in files
// If not successful, rollback
void checkin()
   {
   BOOL success=TRUE;
   char buf[1024];
   int siz;
   IStream *prime=NULL;
   IStream *file;
   LARGE_INTEGER off={0,0};
   int v=0;
   char ckout='Y';
   char puser[33];
   BOOL dirchange=FALSE;
   // for each file in input list
   for (int i=0;i<listlen;i++)
      {
      if (!success) break;
      BOOL found=FALSE;
      char *basename;
      // if file name begins with * then just undo checkout
```

```
strcpy(buf,filelist[i]+(filelist[i][0]=='*'));
FILE *f;
// find base name (no directory)
basename=strrchr(buf,'\\');
if (basename)
   basename++;
else
   basename=buf;
if (filelist[i][0]!='*')
   {
   f=fopen(buf,"r");  // open file
   if (!f)
      {
      cerr<<"Can't open "<<buf<<"\n";
      success=FALSE;
      continue;
      }
   }
// is filelist[i] in dir string?
for (int j=0;j<dirlen;j++)
if (!stricmp(basename,dir[j]))
   {
   found=TRUE;
   break;
   }

v=0;
ckout='Y';
*puser='\0';


if (found)
   {
   // read prime storage
   archive->OpenStream(ucode(basename),NULL,
      STGM_READWRITE|STGM_SHARE_EXCLUSIVE,0,&prime);
   prime->Read((void *)&v,sizeof(int),NULL);
   prime->Read((void *)&ckout,sizeof(char),NULL);
   prime->Read((void *)puser,sizeof(puser),NULL);
   prime->Seek(off,STREAM_SEEK_SET,NULL);
   }
else if (filelist[i][0]!='*')
   {
   // create prime storage
   archive->CreateStream(ucode(basename),
```

```
        STGM_READWRITE|STGM_SHARE_EXCLUSIVE,0,0,&prime);
    // (v=0, ckout=y, user="")

    *puser='\0';
    prime->Write((void *)&v,sizeof(int),NULL);
    prime->Write((void *)&ckout,sizeof(char),NULL);
    prime->Write((void *)puser,sizeof(puser),NULL);
    prime->Seek(off,STREAM_SEEK_SET,NULL);
    dir=(char **)realloc(dir,++dirlen*sizeof(char *));
    dir[dirlen-1]=strdup(basename);
    // check for out of memory here would be smart
    dirchange=TRUE;
    }
else  // can't undo checkout if not there
    {
    cerr<<"Can't find "<<basename<<"\n";
    success=FALSE;
    continue;
    }
// make sure checked out to this user (or no user)
if (ckout!='Y')
    {
    cerr<<basename<<" is not checked out.\n";
    success=FALSE;
    continue;
    }
if (*user && stricmp(user,puser))
    {
    cerr<<basename<<" is not checked out to you.\n";
    success=FALSE;
    continue;
    }
// increment version
if (filelist[i][0]!='*')
    {
    v++;
    // write storage for this version
    char fname[1030];
    wsprintf(fname,"%s\t%d",basename,v);
    archive->CreateStream(ucode(fname),STGM_READWRITE|
        STGM_SHARE_EXCLUSIVE,0,0,&file);
    do
        {
        siz=sizeof(buf);
        siz=fread(buf,1,siz,f);
```

```
            if (siz)
               {
               file->Write((void *)buf,siz,NULL);
               }
            } while (siz);
         fclose(f);
         file->Release();
         }
      // mark prime storage as checked in
      ckout='N';
      *puser='\0';
      prime->Write((void *)&v,sizeof(int),NULL);
      prime->Write((void *)&ckout,sizeof(char),NULL);
      prime->Write((void *)puser,sizeof(user),NULL);
      if (dirchange) WriteDir();
      }
   // if no failure, commit
   if (success)
      archive->Commit(0);
   if (prime) prime->Release();
   }


// Check out files (use file,version for specific version)
void checkout()
   {
   for (int i=0;i<listlen;i++)
      {
      BOOL found=FALSE;
      char buf[1024];
      unsigned long siz;
      IStream *prime=NULL;
      IStream *file;
      LARGE_INTEGER off={0,0};
      int v=0,v0=-1;
      char ckout='Y';
      char puser[33];
      char *p;
      char *basename;
      strcpy(buf,filelist[i]);
      p=strchr(buf,',');  // specific version?
      if (p)
         {
         v0=atoi(p+1);
         *p='\0';
```

```
   }
// find base name (no directory)
basename=strrchr(buf,'\\');
if (basename)
   basename++;
else
   basename=buf;
// is filelist[i] in dir string?
for (int j=0;j<dirlen;j++)
if (!stricmp(basename,dir[j]))
   {
   found=TRUE;
   break;
   }
// if not, error and continue
if (!found)
   {
   cerr<<"Can't find "<<basename<<"\n";
   continue;
   }
// read prime storage
archive->OpenStream(ucode(basename),NULL,
   STGM_READWRITE|STGM_SHARE_EXCLUSIVE,0,&prime);
prime->Read((void *)&v,sizeof(int),NULL);
prime->Read((void *)&ckout,sizeof(char),NULL);
prime->Read((void *)puser,sizeof(puser),NULL);
prime->Seek(off,STREAM_SEEK_SET,NULL);
// if v0>v then must be an error!
if (v0>v)
   {
   cerr<<basename<<" only contains "<<v
       <<" versions\n";
   prime->Release();
   continue;
   }
// if file is checked out, error and continue
if (ckout=='Y')
   {
   cerr<<basename<<" is already checked out\n";
   prime->Release();
   continue;
   }
// copy file to output file
char fname[1030];
FILE *f;
```

```
        f=fopen(buf,"w");
        if (!f)
            {
            cerr<<"Can't open "<<buf<<" for writing\n";
            prime->Release();
            continue;
            }
        wsprintf(fname,"%s\t%d",basename,v0==-1?v:v0);
        if (FAILED(archive->OpenStream(ucode(fname),NULL,
            STGM_READWRITE|STGM_SHARE_EXCLUSIVE,0,&file)))
            {
            cerr<<"Can't locate "<<basename<<","
                <<(v0==-1?v:v0)<<"\n";
            prime->Release();
            continue;
            }
        do
            {
            file->Read((void *)buf,sizeof(buf),&siz);
            if (siz) fwrite(buf,1,siz,f);
            } while (siz);
        fclose(f);
        file->Release();

        // mark as check out
        ckout='Y';
        strcpy(puser,user);
        prime->Write((void *)&v,sizeof(int),NULL);
        prime->Write((void *)&ckout,sizeof(char),NULL);
        prime->Write((void *)user,sizeof(user),NULL);
        prime->Release();
        }
    archive->Commit(0);
    }

// Directory list
void list()
    {
    // headers
    cout<<"file\t\t\t\tvers.\tckout?\tuser\tsize\n";
    cout<<
    "---------------------------------------------------\n";
    // work through directory
    for (int i=0;i<dirlen;i++)
        {
```

```
      char fn[1033];
      IStream *prime, *file;
      int v;
      char ckout;
      char puser[33];
      STATSTG fstatus;
      // open prime storage
      archive->OpenStream(ucode(dir[i]),NULL,
         STGM_READWRITE|STGM_SHARE_EXCLUSIVE,0,&prime);
      prime->Read((void *)&v,sizeof(int),NULL);
      prime->Read((void *)&ckout,sizeof(char),NULL);
      prime->Read((void *)puser,sizeof(puser),NULL);
      prime->Release();
      // open current version to learn size
      wsprintf(fn,"%s\t%d",dir[i],v);
      archive->OpenStream(ucode(fn),NULL,
         STGM_READWRITE|STGM_SHARE_EXCLUSIVE,0,&file);
      file->Stat(&fstatus,STATFLAG_NONAME);
      // print name, version, ckout, user, size
      cout<<dir[i]<<"\t";
      int l=strlen(dir[i]);
      // logic to tab over to column 32
      if (l<24) cout<<"\t";
      if (l<16) cout<<"\t";
      if (l<8) cout<<"\t";
      cout<<v<<"\t"<<ckout<<"\t"<<puser<<"\t"
          <<fstatus.cbSize.LowPart<<"\n";
      file->Release();
      }
   cout<<
   "-----------------------------------------------------\n";
   cout<<dirlen<<(dirlen==1?" file\n":" files\n");
   }


// remove files (use file,version for specific version)
void rm()
   {
   for (int i=0;i<listlen;i++)
      {
      BOOL found=FALSE;
      char buf[1024],fn[1024];
      IStream *prime=NULL;
      LARGE_INTEGER off={0,0};
      int v=0,v0=-1;
```

```
char ckout='Y';
char puser[33];
char *p;
strcpy(buf,filelist[i]);
p=strchr(buf,','); // specific version?
if (p)
   {
   v0=atoi(p+1);
   *p='\0';
   }
// is filelist[i] in dir string?
for (int j=0;j<dirlen;j++)
if (!stricmp(buf,dir[j]))
   {
   found=TRUE;
   break;
   }
// if not, error and roll back
if (!found)
   {
   cerr<<"Can't find "<<buf<<"\n";
   return;
   }
// read prime storage
archive->OpenStream(ucode(buf),NULL,
   STGM_READWRITE|STGM_SHARE_EXCLUSIVE,0,&prime);
prime->Read((void *)&v,sizeof(int),NULL);
prime->Read((void *)&ckout,sizeof(char),NULL);
prime->Read((void *)puser,sizeof(puser),NULL);
prime->Seek(off,STREAM_SEEK_SET,NULL);
// if v0>v then must be an error!
if (v0>v)
   {
   cerr<<buf<<" only contains "<<v<<" versions\n";
   prime->Release();
   return;
   }
// if file is checked out, error and roll back
if (ckout=='Y')
   {
   cerr<<buf<<" is already checked out\n";
   prime->Release();
   return;
   }
if (v0!=-1&&(v0!=1||v0!=v))
```

```
            {
            // delete specific version
            // unless only 1 version
            wsprintf(fn,"%s\t%d",buf,v0);
            if FAILED(archive->DestroyElement(ucode(fn)))
               {
               cerr<<"Can't remove "<<filelist[i]<<"\n";
               prime->Release;
               return;
               }
            if (v0==v) v--;
            // rewrite Prime
            prime->Write((void *)&v,sizeof(int),NULL);
            prime->Write((void *)&ckout,sizeof(char),NULL);
            prime->Write((void *)user,sizeof(user),NULL);
            prime->Release();
            }
         else
            {
            // delete all versions
            for (int k=1;k<=v;k++)
               {
               wsprintf(fn,"%s\t%d",buf,k);
               archive->DestroyElement(ucode(fn));
               }
            prime->Release();
            // Delete prime storage
            archive->DestroyElement(ucode(buf));
            // remove from dir string
            free(dir[j]);
            for (k=j;k<dirlen;k++)
            dir[k]=dir[k+1];
            dirlen--;
            // write Dir
            WriteDir();
            }
         }
      archive->Commit(0);
      }

   void main(int argc, char *argv[])
      {
      // Our console app might need its inst. handle
      hInst=(HINSTANCE)GetModuleHandle(NULL);
      // if not enough arguments, call for dialog
```

```
if (process_args(argc,argv)<2)
   if (!DialogArg()) return;
// Open archive for all commands
if (!OpenArchive()) return;
switch (cmd)
   {
   case CHECKIN:
      checkin();
   break;
   case CHECKOUT:
      checkout();
   break;
   case LIST:
      list();
   break;
   case REMOVE:
      rm();
   break;
   default:
      cerr<<"Unknown command\n";
   }
CloseArchive();          // close archive (no commit)
}
```

The AVC version control system is very simplistic. The program is primarily a command-line driven console application. However, if you don't supply enough arguments, the program will display a dialog box to collect the remaining arguments, as shown in Figure 12.1. Even though this is a console application, it can still call up a dialog box.

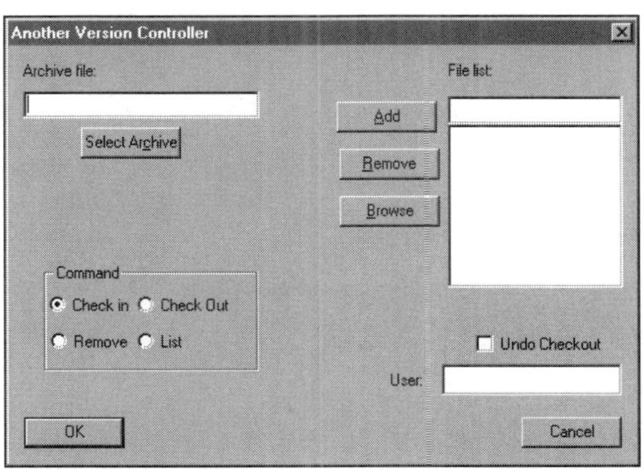

Figure 12.1 The AVC options dialog box.

In this case, it isn't important for the dialog box to have a parent window. That's good, because it's hard to find the console window (although not impossible; see the CONTEST application, later in this chapter). However, you do need the program's instance handle so that Windows can locate the dialog box resource.

Luckily, it's easy to find the instance handle. A simple call to **GetModuleHandle** suffices. The dialog box is an ordinary, old-fashioned dialog box, and it doesn't use MFC. You can find its callback routine in Listing 12.3.

Listing 12.3 The dialog box callback.

```
// Dialog for AVC
#include <windows.h>
#include "dialog.h"
#include "avc.h"



// Generic browse file routine
int browse_file(HWND parent,HWND w ,char *title,char *filter)
  {
  OPENFILENAME of;
  char fn[_MAX_PATH],ft[_MAX_PATH],dir[_MAX_PATH],*p;
  SendMessage(w,WM_GETTEXT,_MAX_PATH,(DWORD)fn);
  strcpy(dir,fn);
  p=strrchr(dir,'\\');
  if (p) *p='\0'; else *dir='\0';
  memset(&of,0,sizeof(of));
  of.lStructSize=sizeof(of);
  of.hwndOwner=parent;
  of.hInstance=hInst;
  of.lpstrFilter=filter;
  of.nFilterIndex=1;
  of.lpstrFile=fn;
  of.lpstrFileTitle=ft;
  of.nMaxFile=of.nMaxFileTitle=_MAX_PATH;
  of.lpstrTitle=title;
  of.lpstrInitialDir=dir;
  of.Flags=OFN_FILEMUSTEXIST|OFN_HIDEREADONLY;
  if (!GetOpenFileName(&of)) return 1;
  SendMessage(w,WM_SETTEXT,0,(DWORD)fn);
  return 0;
  }


// Handle WM_COMMAND messages
void command(HWND dlg,HWND ctl,UINT id,UINT code)
        {
        switch (id)
```

```
{
case IDOK:
  // make sure archive name is present
  if (SendDlgItemMessage(dlg,
    IDC_ARCHIVE,WM_GETTEXTLENGTH,0,0)==0)
    {
    MessageBox(dlg,"Please enter an archive name",
               NULL,MB_OK);
    SetFocus(GetDlgItem(dlg,IDC_ARCHIVE));
    return;
    }
  // store data
  GetDlgItemText(dlg,IDC_USER,user,sizeof(user));
  GetDlgItemText(dlg,IDC_ARCHIVE,filename,
         sizeof(filename));
  listlen=SendDlgItemMessage(dlg,
          IDC_FILELIST,CB_GETCOUNT,0,0);
  if (SendDlgItemMessage(dlg,
        IDC_CKIN,BM_GETCHECK,0,0)) cmd=CHECKIN;
  else if (SendDlgItemMessage(dlg,IDC_CKOUT,
        BM_GETCHECK,0,0)) cmd=CHECKOUT;
  else if (SendDlgItemMessage(dlg,IDC_LIST,
        BM_GETCHECK,0,0)) cmd=LIST;
  else if (SendDlgItemMessage(dlg,IDC_REM,
        BM_GETCHECK,0,0)) cmd=REMOVE;
  if (listlen==CB_ERR)
     {
     listlen=0;
     }
 else
     {
     filelist=(char **)
     malloc(sizeof(char *)*listlen);
     for (int i=0;i<listlen;i++)
        {
        char buf[1025],*bp=buf+1;
        SendDlgItemMessage(dlg,IDC_FILELIST,
             CB_GETLBTEXT,i,(LPARAM)bp);
        unsigned int data=SendDlgItemMessage(
                   dlg,IDC_FILELIST,
                   CB_GETITEMDATA,i,0);
        if (data&0x80000000 && cmd==CHECKIN)
           {
           *buf='*';
           bp=buf;
           data&=~0x80000000;
           }
```

12. Console Applications And Services

```
                if (data && cmd==CHECKOUT)
                   {
                   char vers[16];
                   wsprintf(vers,",%d",data);
                   strcat(bp,vers);
                   }
               filelist[i]=strdup(bp);
               }
           }
           EndDialog(dlg,0);
           break;
        case IDCANCEL:
                EndDialog(dlg,-1);
                break;
        case IDC_FILELIST:
                switch (code)
                        {
                        // set up CB change
                        case CBN_SELCHANGE:
                                int index=SendMessage(ctl,
                                  CB_GETCURSEL,0,0);
                                if (index==CB_ERR)
                                  {
                                  SetDlgItemText(dlg,
                                     IDC_VERSION,"");
                                  SendDlgItemMessage(dlg,
                                     IDC_STAR,BM_SETCHECK,0,0);
                                   }
                                else
                                  {
                                  unsigned int v=SendMessage(ctl,
                                      CB_GETITEMDATA,index,0);
                                  char vers[16];
                                  SendDlgItemMessage(dlg,IDC_STAR,
                                   BM_SETCHECK,v&0x80000000!=0,0);
                                  v&=~0x80000000;
                                  if (v)
                                     wsprintf(vers,"%d",v);
                                  SetDlgItemText(dlg,
                                  IDC_VERSION,v?vers:"");
                                  }
                               break;
                        }
                break;
        case IDC_ADD:
                // move combo box ec to list
                if (SendDlgItemMessage(dlg,IDC_FILELIST,
```

```
   WM_GETTEXTLENGTH,0,0)!=0)
        {
        char buf[1024];
        int index;
        unsigned v;
        SendDlgItemMessage(dlg,IDC_FILELIST,
          WM_GETTEXT,sizeof(buf),(LPARAM)buf);
        index=SendDlgItemMessage(dlg,IDC_FILELIST,
          CB_FINDSTRINGEXACT,
          (unsigned)-1,(LPARAM)buf);
        if (index==CB_ERR)
          index=SendDlgItemMessage(dlg,
            IDC_FILELIST,
            CB_ADDSTRING,0,(LPARAM)buf);
        GetDlgItemText(dlg,IDC_VERSION,
           buf,sizeof(buf));
        v=atoi(buf);
        if (SendDlgItemMessage(dlg,IDC_STAR,
            BM_GETCHECK,0,0)) v|=0x80000000;
        SendDlgItemMessage(dlg,IDC_FILELIST,
            CB_SETITEMDATA,index,v);
        SendDlgItemMessage(dlg,IDC_FILELIST,
            WM_SETTEXT,0,(LPARAM)"");
        SetDlgItemText(dlg,IDC_VERSION,"");
        SendDlgItemMessage(dlg,IDC_STAR,
            BM_SETCHECK,0,0);
        }
  break;
case IDC_REMOVE:
  // remove selected combo box item
  if (SendDlgItemMessage(dlg,IDC_FILELIST,
    CB_GETCURSEL,0,0)!=CB_ERR)
        {
        SendDlgItemMessage(dlg,IDC_FILELIST,
          CB_DELETESTRING,0,0);
        SetDlgItemText(dlg,IDC_VERSION,"");
        SendDlgItemMessage(dlg,IDC_STAR,
          BM_SETCHECK,0,0);
        }
  break;
case IDC_BROWSE:
  browse_file(dlg,GetDlgItem(dlg,IDC_FILELIST),
    "Select a file","All files\0*.*");
  break;
case IDC_ARBROWSE:
  browse_file(dlg,GetDlgItem(dlg,IDC_ARCHIVE),
   "Select an archive","AVC archives\0*.AVC");
```

```
                break;
            case IDC_LIST:
                ShowWindow(GetDlgItem(dlg,IDC_FILELIST),SW_HIDE);
                ShowWindow(GetDlgItem(dlg,IDC_FLLBL),SW_HIDE);
                ShowWindow(GetDlgItem(dlg,IDC_ADD),SW_HIDE);
                ShowWindow(GetDlgItem(dlg,IDC_REMOVE),SW_HIDE);
                ShowWindow(GetDlgItem(dlg,IDC_BROWSE),SW_HIDE);
                ShowWindow(GetDlgItem(dlg,IDC_USERLBL),SW_HIDE);
                ShowWindow(GetDlgItem(dlg,IDC_USER),SW_HIDE);
                ShowWindow(GetDlgItem(dlg,IDC_STAR),SW_HIDE);
                ShowWindow(GetDlgItem(dlg,IDC_VERSLBL),SW_HIDE);
                ShowWindow(GetDlgItem(dlg,IDC_VERSION),SW_HIDE);
                break;
            case IDC_CKIN:
            case IDC_CKOUT:
            case IDC_REM:
                int howuser=SW_SHOW;

                ShowWindow(GetDlgItem(dlg,IDC_STAR),
                    id==IDC_CKIN?SW_SHOW:SW_HIDE);
                ShowWindow(GetDlgItem(dlg,
                    IDC_VERSLBL),id==IDC_CKOUT?SW_SHOW:SW_HIDE);
                ShowWindow(GetDlgItem(dlg,IDC_VERSION),
                    id==IDC_CKOUT?SW_SHOW:SW_HIDE);


                if (id==IDC_REM) howuser=SW_HIDE;

                ShowWindow(GetDlgItem(dlg,IDC_FILELIST),SW_SHOW);
                ShowWindow(GetDlgItem(dlg,IDC_FLLBL),SW_SHOW);
                ShowWindow(GetDlgItem(dlg,IDC_ADD),SW_SHOW);
                ShowWindow(GetDlgItem(dlg,IDC_REMOVE),SW_SHOW);
                ShowWindow(GetDlgItem(dlg,IDC_BROWSE),SW_SHOW);

                ShowWindow(GetDlgItem(dlg,IDC_USERLBL),howuser);
                ShowWindow(GetDlgItem(dlg,IDC_USER),howuser);
                break;
            }
        }


BOOL CALLBACK dlgcb(HWND dlg,UINT msg,WPARAM wParam,LPARAM lParam)
        {
        switch (msg)
            {
            case WM_INITDIALOG:
                SendDlgItemMessage(dlg,IDC_CKIN,BM_SETCHECK,1,0);
```

```
                if (*filename)
                        SetDlgItemText(dlg,IDC_ARCHIVE,filename);
                if (*user)
                        SetDlgItemText(dlg,IDC_USER,user);
                return FALSE;

        case WM_COMMAND:
                command(dlg,(HWND)lParam,
                   LOWORD(wParam),HIWORD(wParam));
                break;
        default:
                return FALSE;

        }
return TRUE;
}
```


It's worthwhile to note that you can use MFC (or at least parts of it) from within a console application. Just go to the Project Settings dialog box and, on the General tab, select one of the MFC options. Then include afx.h in your source file. Doing so will allow you to use many MFC objects (including things like **CString** and **CFile**) with no problems. Of course, you're also including the large MFC library and you may not need much of it. On the other hand, if you're using the library from a DLL and you need the DLL for other programs anyway, the overall cost is probably small.

AVC Details

AVC uses a single archive file to store all versions of all files in a project. This archive is an SSS compound file. It contains a single primary stream for each file in the project. This primary stream doesn't contain the file's data; instead, it contains information about the file's status and the number of versions available. The actual file contents are in a different stream. This stream has the same name as the primary stream, followed by a tab character and the version number (in decimal).

Although an SSS function is available to make a storage enumerate its elements, Microsoft warns that it might not be efficient for compound files. Instead, AVC stores another special stream that's always named $\tDIR$. This stream just contains a list of the primary file names. For simplicity's sake, I don't store any path information with the file names.

The command line has a simple structure. The first argument is always the name of the archive file you wish to use. If you want to use a particular user name, you add a comma to the file name and follow it with your user name (no spaces allowed). The second argument is the command you want to execute. Finally, you can specify a list of files to use.

The commands are simple:

- ***CHECKIN***—Adds files to the archive or creates new versions of them. This command will create a new archive if you specify a name that doesn't exist. If you just want to mark a file as checked in without creating a new version, precede its name with an asterisk.
- ***CHECKOUT***—Checks out a file from the archive by copying it to the ordinary file system. This step prevents anyone else from checking out the file until you check it back in. It also reserves the file using your user name, if you provided one. If you want a specific version of the file, follow the name with a comma and the version number. By default, the program checks out the most recent version.
- ***REMOVE***—Removes files (or particular versions) from the archive. You can specify versions in the same way you would for the **CHECKOUT** command.
- ***LIST***—Ignores the file list and displays the contents of the archive.

In each case, you can specify a full path in the file list. However, AVC uses only the base file name internally. The **CHECKIN** command, for example, will copy a file from \files\file1 into an internal stream named file1. The **CHECKOUT** command might later specify \new\file1 to retrieve the same file to the new directory.

Because compound files allow transactioning, I decided to take advantage of it. If a **REMOVE** or **CHECKIN** command doesn't complete successfully, the entire operation fails. In other words, suppose you issue the following command:

```
AVC test.avc REMOVE f1.txt f2.txt f3.ttx
```

If f3.ttx doesn't exist, AVC removes nothing from the archive.

Learning The Console Window

AVC didn't need to know the window handle of the main window. However, many API calls do need to know this information. For example, what if you wanted to hide your console window? **ShowWindow** will easily do that, if you have the window handle.

There's no easy way to get the window handle for a console program. However, Microsoft's Knowledge Base contains an article that offers a workaround (well, honestly, a hack) that seems to work. In article Q124103, you'll find the following advice:

1. Read the console's title (using **GetConsoleTitle**).
2. Change the title to something unique (using **SetConsoleTitle**).
3. Wait for at least 40 milliseconds (using **Sleep**) to ensure the title actually had time to change.
4. Call **FindWindow** to locate a window with the given title.

5. Set the console title back to its original value.
6. Wait another 40 milliseconds.
7. Call **GetWindowText** to verify that the window's title is the same as the original console title.

You can find a simple program that does this in Listing 12.4. After the program hides itself, it also allocates several megabytes of memory (no big deal for a Windows program) and issues a message box.

Listing 12.4 A console program that determines its own window handle.

```
// Example console program -- Williams

#include <stdio.h>
#include <stdlib.h>
#include <windows.h>
#include <wincon.h>  // console API header

char title[128]="Finding window; please wait...";


BOOL __stdcall OnClose(DWORD code)
{
   // do this for all codes
   return MessageBox(NULL,
     "Really close CONTEST?",
     "Confirm",MB_YESNO)==IDNO;
}


main()
  {
  char str[128],name[64];
  HWND w;
  SetConsoleCtrlHandler(OnClose,TRUE);
  printf("What's your name? ");
  scanf("%s",name);
  printf("Thanks! Please wait.");
  // Here's a hack to get the current HWND
  // Set title to a (maybe) unique string
  GetConsoleTitle(str,sizeof(str));
  SetConsoleTitle(title);
// wait for title to "take" (MS says 40 is OK; see KB Q124103)
  Sleep(40);
  w=FindWindow(NULL,title);  // find window
  if (!w)
         {
```

```
        printf("Can't find window handle");
        return 1;
        }
  SetConsoleTitle(str); // put back
  Sleep(40); // wait again
  // make sure title changed... if not,
  // we must have found the wrong window!
  GetWindowText(w,title,sizeof(title));
  if (strcmp(title,str))
       {
       printf("Error locating window handle");
       return 2;
   }
  // end of hack

  // We'll use MessageBox for the rest of the output,
  // so hide that #*#$#! console window
  ShowWindow(w,SW_HIDE);

  // Do something we can't do in DOS
  char *big,*msg;
  big=(char *)malloc(2000000);  // 2Megabytes!
  if (big)
          msg="Allocation succeeded";
  else
          msg="Allocation failed";
  MessageBox(w,msg,"Result",MB_OK|MB_ICONEXCLAMATION);
  if (big) free(big);
  wsprintf(title,"Goodbye %s",name);
  MessageBox(w,title,"End program",MB_OK);

// Since we hid the window, we had better put it back
// If not, and you run this from DOS, the DOS window
// will disappear!
   ShowWindow(w,SW_SHOW);
  return 0;
  }
```

Special Console Calls

You can do lots of other things with a console, as shown in Table 12.1. You can even have more than one console, if you like. The catch: Only one console can be visible at a time. You can create extra consoles by using **CreateConsoleScreenBuffer**. This call returns a console handle, but the actual console won't appear until you call **SetConsoleActiveScreenBuffer**. This call, of course, makes any previously active console for this program inactive (and hence invisible).

Table 12.1 Console calls.

Calls	Purpose
AllocConsole	Creates new standard console
CreateConsoleScreenBuffer	Creates a new non-active console
FillConsoleOutputAttribute	Fills part of the console with an attribute
FillConsoleOutputCharacter	Fills part of the console with a character
FlushConsoleInputBuffer	Flushes the input buffer
FreeConsole	Frees the console (opposite of AllocConsole)
GenerateConsoleCtrlEvent	Allows you to simulate a Ctrl+C or Ctrl+Break event
GetConsoleCP	Returns the console's code page
GetConsoleCursorInfo	Gets the size and visibility of the cursor in a CONSOLE_CURSOR_INFO structure
GetConsoleMode	Retrieves the console mode
GetConsoleOutputCP	Gets the console's output code page
GetConsoleScreenBufferInfo	Returns the cursor position, default attribute, window size, and maximum window size in a CONSOLE_SCREEN_BUFFER_INFO structure
GetConsoleTitle	Returns the console's title
GetLargestConsoleWindowSize	Gets the largest possible window size
GetNumberOfConsoleInputEvents	Gets the number of input events pending
GetNumberOfConsoleMouseButtons	Gets the number of buttons on the console mouse
GetStdHandle	Gets a standard handle
PeekConsoleInput	Examines pending input without consuming it
ReadConsole	Reads the console in ANSI or Unicode as appropriate
ReadConsoleInput	Reads raw input from the console
ReadConsoleOutput	Reads data from the console's output buffer
ReadConsoleOutputAttribute	Reads attributes from the console's output buffer
ReadConsoleOutputCharacter	Reads characters from the console's output buffer
ScrollConsoleScreenBuffer	Scrolls the screen buffer
SetConsoleActiveScreenBuffer	Sets the active buffer
SetConsoleCP	Sets the code page
SetConsoleCtrlHandler	Sets the event handler (see text)
SetConsoleCursorInfo	Sets the cursor appearance
SetConsoleCursorPosition	Sets the cursor position

(continued)

***Table 12.1 Console calls* (continued).**

Calls	Purpose
SetConsoleMode	Sets the console mode
SetConsoleOutputCP	Sets the console's output code page
SetConsoleScreenBufferSize	Sets the size of the buffer
SetConsoleTextAttribute	Sets the default text attribute
SetConsoleTitle	Sets the console title
SetConsoleWindowInfo	Sets information about the window
SetStdHandle	Sets a standard handle
WriteConsole	Writes to the console in ANSI or Unicode as appropriate
WriteConsoleInput	Simulates keyboard input
WriteConsoleOutput	Writes rich data to the console
WriteConsoleOutputAttribute	Writes attributes only to the console
WriteConsoleOutputCharacter	Writes characters only to the console

Console input is usually strictly text based. However, it's possible to read mouse and window events if you enable the console for it (using **SetConsoleMode**). You can pass the **ENABLE_WINDOW_INPUT** flag if you want notifications when the console's size changes or **ENABLE_MOUSE_INPUT** if you want mouse messages. The only problem with using these flags is that the system then returns a special structure (of type **INPUT_RECORD**) and you can't obtain that structure by calling **ReadFile** or **ReadConsole**—you must call **ReadConsoleInput**. Window-resizing input is waiting for you to read it, but **ReadFile** and **ReadConsole** will return nothing even though there's input pending; so you must use **ReadConsoleInput**. **ReadFile** automatically discards mouse input. Of course, the **INPUT_RECORD** structure will also indicate when you get keyboard input; it just isn't as convenient for that purpose as using **ReadFile** or **ReadConsole**.

There are many other reasons to call **SetConsoleMode**. You can use flags to indicate that you want to see input one line at a time, to echo input, to process certain output control characters (like a bell, for example) and more.

Just as there's **ReadConsole**, there's also a **WriteConsole**. You might wonder why either of these calls is necessary when **ReadFile** and **WriteFile** already exist. The console functions work in either ANSI or Unicode mode depending on the type of the console, not on the compilation mode of your program. Otherwise, these functions are interchangeable.

However, sometimes you want to output more than just characters. For example, you might like to set the color and attributes of text you write. That's what **WriteConsoleOutput** is for. This function accepts an array of characters and attributes and transfers it to a given rectangle inside the console. The elements of the array are of type **CHAR_INFO**. This structure contains the character (in either the **UnicodeChar** or **AsciiChar** member) and an attribute (these attributes allow you to mix red, green, and blue as background or foreground colors; you can also set either foreground or background as a bright color).

You can retrieve the contents of the console using **ReadConsoleOutput** (to fill in an array of **CHAR_INFO** structures). If you don't want that much data, you can also use **ReadConsoleOutputCharacter** or **ReadConsoleOutputAttribute** to get just part of the data. You can also learn the current cursor position, the default attribute, and other similar information by calling **GetConsoleScreenBufferInfo**.

The current cursor position is also easy to set. You simply call **SetConsoleCursorPosition**. The **SetConsoleCursorInfo** function works with the size of the cursor and sets the cursor's visibility.

The size of the console is under your program's control (to an extent, anyway). You can call **GetLargestConsoleWindowSize** to learn just how big your console could be. This size is different, by the way, from the number that **GetConsoleScreenBufferInfo** returns. The number that **GetLargestConsoleWindowSize** returns is a theoretical maximum; whereas **GetConsoleScreenBufferInfo** takes the actual size of the console buffer's contents into account. Although the default is 24 lines of 80 columns of content, you can alter this size by calling **SetConsoleScreenBufferSize**. Be careful, though—you can't make the buffer smaller than the window.

If your buffer is larger than the window, you might want to programmatically scroll the window around. You can do this with **ScrollConsoleScreenBuffer**. **GetConsoleScreenBufferInfo** can tell you where the current scroll position is. Of course, the user can always scroll the console, and when you output text or move the cursor, you may trigger automatic scrolling.

Handling Events

You can use the **SetConsoleCtrlHandler** function to register a function that will respond to special events in your program. Your function should return a **BOOL** and accept a **DWORD** argument. The **DWORD** will indicate if your program receives a Ctrl+C or a Ctrl+Break, or when the user closes the program, logs off, or shuts down the system. Depending on what you return from the handler, you can prevent a shutdown or other program-closing event. You can also control this behavior with **SetProcessShutdownParameters**.

Creating Useful New Consoles

Even GUI programs can have a console if they call **AllocConsole**. This call sets the program's standard input, standard output, and standard error streams at the operating system level. However, you have to be careful: When a GUI program creates a console, the standard C library isn't aware of it. That means you won't be able to use calls like **printf** or **scanf** (or their C++ relatives) unless you manually initialize **stdout**, **stdin**, and **stderr** (or **cout**, **cin**, **cerr**, and **clog**). Even though the program is aware of the console, the C library isn't because it initialized these handles before your program called **AllocConsole**. Of course, you only need to initialize the handles you plan to use.

It's fairly straightforward to use **freopen** with **CONIN$** or **CONOUT$** to initialize the standard C streams. Obviously, you use **CONIN$** for **stdin** and **CONOUT$** for **stdout** or **stderr**.

The C++ streams are a bit trickier. One way to cope with them is to use **freopen** first to set a standard handle, and then construct a **stdiobuf** on the heap to reflect the handle. You can assign this **stdiobuf** object directly to the standard handles like **cout** and **cin**.

If you don't want to bother, it's easy to use **ReadFile** and **WriteFile** (or the related console-specific calls) to directly access the new console. You can also use other standard library calls to directly open **CONIN$** or **CONOUT$** and work with them.

You can find a simple program in Listing 12.5 that creates a console in response to an item on the View menu. Once the console exists, the View menu will also contain an item to generate a few palindromes in the console. For variety, the program uses both **printf** and **cout** to generate its output.

The important code is in the **OnViewconsole** function. Here, you'll see that the program closes any existing console (using **FreeConsole**). Then a simple call to **AllocConsole** does all the work. It's easy to retrieve handles to the new console by calling **GetStdHandle**. One line of code reopens **stdout**, and another line sets **cout** so that it's useful.

Listing 12.5 Creating a console with a GUI program.

```
// newconView.cpp : implementation of the CNewconView class
//

#include "stdafx.h"
#include "newcon.h"

#include "newconDoc.h"
```

```
#include "newconView.h"

#include <stdiostr.h>  // only required if you want to use iostreams

#ifdef _DEBUG
#define new DEBUG_NEW
#undef THIS_FILE
static char THIS_FILE[] = __FILE__;
#endif

/////////////////////////////////////////////////
// CNewconView

IMPLEMENT_DYNCREATE(CNewconView, CEditView)

BEGIN_MESSAGE_MAP(CNewconView, CEditView)
   //{{AFX_MSG_MAP(CNewconView)
   ON_COMMAND(ID_VIEWCONSOLE, OnViewconsole)
   ON_COMMAND(ID_PALINDROME, OnPalindrome)
   ON_UPDATE_COMMAND_UI(ID_PALINDROME, OnUpdatePalindrome)
   //}}AFX_MSG_MAP
   // Standard printing commands
   ON_COMMAND(ID_FILE_PRINT, CEditView::OnFilePrint)
   ON_COMMAND(ID_FILE_PRINT_DIRECT, CEditView::OnFilePrint)
   ON_COMMAND(ID_FILE_PRINT_PREVIEW, CEditView::OnFilePrintPreview)
END_MESSAGE_MAP()

/////////////////////////////////////////////////
// CNewconView construction/destruction

CNewconView::CNewconView()
{
   // TODO: add construction code here
   m_console=NULL;
   m_connum=0;
}

CNewconView::~CNewconView()
{
}

BOOL CNewconView::PreCreateWindow(CREATESTRUCT& cs)
{
   // TODO: Modify the Window class or styles here by modifying
   //  the CREATESTRUCT cs
```

```
    BOOL bPreCreated = CEditView::PreCreateWindow(cs);
    cs.style &= ~(ES_AUTOHSCROLL|WS_HSCROLL);   // Enable word-wrapping

    return bPreCreated;
}

/////////////////////////////////////////////////////////////////////////////
// CNewconView drawing

void CNewconView::OnDraw(CDC* pDC)
{
    CNewconDoc* pDoc = GetDocument();
    ASSERT_VALID(pDoc);
    // TODO: add draw code for native data here
}

///////////////////////////////////////
// CNewconView printing

BOOL CNewconView::OnPreparePrinting(CPrintInfo* pInfo)
{
    // default CEditView preparation
    return CEditView::OnPreparePrinting(pInfo);
}

void CNewconView::OnBeginPrinting(CDC* pDC, CPrintInfo* pInfo)
{
    // Default CEditView begin printing.
    CEditView::OnBeginPrinting(pDC, pInfo);
}

void CNewconView::OnEndPrinting(CDC* pDC, CPrintInfo* pInfo)
{
    // Default CEditView end printing
    CEditView::OnEndPrinting(pDC, pInfo);
}

/////////////////////////////////////////////
// CNewconView diagnostics

#ifdef _DEBUG
void CNewconView::AssertValid() const
{
    CEditView::AssertValid();
}
```

```
void CNewconView::Dump(CDumpContext& dc) const
{
   CEditView::Dump(dc);
}

CNewconDoc* CNewconView::GetDocument() // non-debug version is inline
{
   ASSERT(m_pDocument->IsKindOf(RUNTIME_CLASS(CNewconDoc)));
   return (CNewconDoc*)m_pDocument;
}
#endif //_DEBUG

/////////////////////////////////////////////////////////////////////////////
// CNewconView message handlers


void CNewconView::OnViewconsole()
{
   if (m_console)
   {
      FreeConsole();
      m_console=NULL;
   }
   if (!AllocConsole())
      MessageBox("Can't make console!");
   else
   {
      // save console handle in case someone wants it
      m_console=GetStdHandle(STD_OUTPUT_HANDLE);


// Set STDOUT so it will work correctly
      freopen("CONOUT$","wt",stdout);

// Set cout so it will work correctly
      cout=new stdiobuf(stdout);

      printf("Console %d active!\n", ++m_connum);

   }

}

void CNewconView::OnPalindrome()
```

```
{
   // The next two statements are one way to print
   //DWORD dummy;
   //if (m_console) WriteConsole(m_console,(void *)
      // "Flee to me remote elf!\r\n",24,&dummy,NULL);
// however, since stdout is set right...
   printf("Rise to vote sir!\n");
   cout<<"Flee to me remote elf!\n";

}

void CNewconView::OnUpdatePalindrome(CCmdUI* pCmdUI)
{
  pCmdUI->Enable(m_console!=NULL);
}
```


Services

Services are a vital, yet mysterious, part of Windows 2000. If you've had any experience using or administering Windows, you surely have run into services before. But what are they? The simple answer is that they're programs that run outside of a particular user context. In other words, they continue running after you log off, and keep running even after another log in (possibly by another user). Services are the only programs that can perform this feat.

Windows itself uses services for many important features. For example, there's a service that allows you to log on to the computer—not a big surprise that this program must run even when no one is logged in. Other services allow disk sharing and printer sharing, and help drive devices.

From a programmer's point of view, services are easy (you can find a list of service-related calls in Table 12.2). They're really just ordinary programs (usually console programs) that have special provisions for interacting with the Service Control Manager (SCM). The SCM is the part of Windows that controls services. The user could work with the SCM by using the Services Control Panel applet under Windows NT 4. With Windows 2000, this same function is in a built-in MMC snap-in (see Chapter 10).

Like any console program, a service has a **main** function. The program can support a single service or it may supply multiple services. The **main** function supplies an array that describes the available services by calling **StartServiceCtrlDispatcher**. The array contains a text identifier and an entry point for each service the executable file contains.

Table 12.2 Service functions.

Function	Purpose
ChangeServiceConfig	Changes the configuration
ChangeServiceConfig2	Changes the optional configuration (Win2000)
CloseServiceHandle	Closes a service or SCM handle
ControlService	Sends a control request to a service
CreateService	Creates a service
DeleteService	Deletes a service
EnumDependentServices	Finds services that this service requires
EnumServicesStatus	Lists services in the SCM database
GetServiceDisplayName	Gets the display name
GetServiceKeyName	Finds the Registry key for this service
LockServiceDatabase	Locks the SCM database
OpenSCManager	Opens the SCM
OpenService	Opens an existing service
QueryServiceConfig	Requests the service configuration
QueryServiceConfig2	Requests the optional configuration (Win2000)
QueryServiceLockStatus	Requests information about the SCM lock status
QueryServiceObjectSecurity	Requests the service's security
QueryServiceStatus	Requests the service's status
RegisterServiceCtrlHandler	Registers a control handler function
SetServiceBits	Sets options specifying that the service is a particular system service
SetServiceObjectSecurity	Sets security information about a service
SetServiceStatus	Sets the service status
StartService	Starts a service
StartServiceCtrlDispatcher	Registers services with the SCM
UnlockServiceDatabase	Releases the lock on the SCM database

The entry point looks like a **main** function. It's a **void** function that receives the typical **argc** and **argv** arguments. These arguments aren't from the command line, but rather from the SCM.

Once the SCM calls the service entry point, the **SERVICE_STATUS** structure becomes very important. Most services keep a static copy of this structure and update it as appropriate. The entry point routine calls **RegisterServiceCtrlHandler** to register a callback that the SCM will use to communicate with the service. Also, the service initialization will call **SetServiceStatus** to inform the SCM if it's performing lengthy initialization, running, or stopped. If the initialization will take more than a few seconds, it's best to start a new thread to do the work there.

You'll also start a new thread if you have a service that just wants to run all the time in the background. For example, suppose you want to make a clock chime for your PC. This program would sound a beep every hour (or half-hour, or whenever you want). You'd want a thread that monitored the time of day and sounded the tone at the appropriate times.

When the SCM wants to do something, it will call the service's callback (the one set by **RegisterServiceCtrlHandler**). Generally, the SCM will call the function to ask the service to stop, pause, or continue after a pause. The SCM also uses the callback to query the current status of the service. A service can also define custom requests that others can send to it by calling the SCM's **ControlService** function. Of course, you have to have the appropriate security access to send requests to a service.

Installing Services

Installing a service requires a series of Registry entries. However, you usually won't directly make these Registry entries yourself. Instead, you'll open the SCM (using **OpenSCManager**) and then call **CreateService**. This function requires arguments that determine the file name of the service and other important information. It makes the correct Registry entries for you.

At first glance, **CreateService** is a bit intimidating, with 13 arguments, as shown in Table 12.3. However, most of them will usually require only the default values. The **dwServiceType** parameter is simply **SERVICE_WIN32_OWN_PROCESS** if you're making an executable that contains a single service. You can also specify **SERVICE_WIN32_SHARE_PROCESS** if your executable provides multiple services. Other flags allow you to specify that a service is a kernel driver or a file system driver.

If you ever want to get rid of a service, you can open the SCM, open the service in question (using **OpenService**), and then call **DeleteService**. You also use **OpenService** when you want to manipulate or communicate with an existing service.

Table 12.3 Arguments to CreateService.

Argument	Type	Description
hSCManager	SC_HANDLE	Handle to SCM
lpServiceName	LPCTSTR	Short name of service
lpDisplayName	LPCTSTR	Display name of service
dwDesiredAccess	DWORD	Requested security access to service
dwServiceType	DWORD	Type (see text)
dwStartType	DWORD	When to start the service
dwErrorControl	DWORD	Action to take if the service fails to start
lpBinaryPathName	LPCTSTR	File name that contains the service
lpLoadOrderGroup	LPCTSTR	Name of the group of services that will load at the same time
lpdwTagId	DWORD	Order of loading within the load order group
lpDependencies	LPCTSTR	Pointer to array of service names that this service requires
lpServiceStartName	LPCTSTR	Name of account to use when starting service (NULL is LocalSystem account)
lpPassword	LPCTSTR	Password for account (if required)

In the example service in this chapter (see Listing 12.6), I added code to register and unregister the service into the **main** function. If you run the program with the argument **setup**, the service automatically registers itself. If you run the program with the argument **delete**, the program removes itself from the SCM's list in the Registry.

Although this example contains internal code to install (and uninstall) the service, you'll often write a separate program to install the service. You can also have a program that knows how to communicate with the service (either via **ControlService** or some form of IPC). Microsoft refers to this sort of program as a *Service Control Program.*

When you install a service, you can specify that the service depends on other services. If this is the case, the SCM will load any services you require before it loads your service.

Listing 12.6 A simple service.

```
#include <windows.h>
#include <iostream.h>
#include <string.h>
#include <time.h>
#include <process.h>
```

```
SERVICE_STATUS          Service1Status;
SERVICE_STATUS_HANDLE   Service1StatusHandle;
int modtime=3600;  // chime on the hour

HANDLE thread;
BOOL manual=FALSE;

void ding(void *)
{
   time_t timeval;
   while (Service1Status.dwCurrentState!=SERVICE_STOPPED)
   {
      if (Service1Status.dwCurrentState!=SERVICE_PAUSED)
      {
         time(&timeval);
         if ((timeval%modtime)==0|| manual)
            PlaySound("DING",GetModuleHandle(NULL),
                              SND_RESOURCE|SND_SYNC|SND_NOSTOP);
         manual=FALSE;
      }
      Sleep(500);
   }
}

VOID __stdcall CtrlHandler (DWORD Opcode)
{
   DWORD status;
    switch(Opcode)
   {
   case SERVICE_CONTROL_PAUSE:
        // Do whatever it takes to pause here.
            Service1Status.dwCurrentState = SERVICE_PAUSED;
         break;
         case SERVICE_CONTROL_CONTINUE:
        // Do whatever it takes to continue here.
            Service1Status.dwCurrentState = SERVICE_RUNNING;
         // fake beep
         manual=TRUE;
            break;
       case SERVICE_CONTROL_STOP:
        // Do whatever it takes to stop here.
            Service1Status.dwWin32ExitCode = 0;
            Service1Status.dwCurrentState  = SERVICE_STOPPED;
            Service1Status.dwCheckPoint    = 0;
            Service1Status.dwWaitHint      = 0;
            if (!SetServiceStatus (Service1StatusHandle,
```

```
                &Service1Status))
        {
                status = GetLastError();
            // error!
            }
            return;
        case SERVICE_CONTROL_INTERROGATE:
        // Fall through to send current status.
          break;
        default:
            // unknown opcode?
          ;  // do nothing yet

   }
   // Send current status.
    if (!SetServiceStatus (Service1StatusHandle,  &Service1Status))
   {
        status = GetLastError();
      // error

   }
   return;
}

void __stdcall Service1Start (DWORD argc, LPTSTR *argv)
{
   DWORD status;
    DWORD specificError;
    if (argc>1) modtime=atoi(argv[1]);
   if (modtime==0) modtime=1

    Service1Status.dwServiceType        = SERVICE_WIN32;
    Service1Status.dwCurrentState       = SERVICE_START_PENDING;
    Service1Status.dwControlsAccepted   = SERVICE_ACCEPT_STOP |
        SERVICE_ACCEPT_PAUSE_CONTINUE;
    Service1Status.dwWin32ExitCode      = 0;
    Service1Status.dwServiceSpecificExitCode = 0;
    Service1Status.dwCheckPoint         = 0;
    Service1Status.dwWaitHint           = 0;
    Service1StatusHandle = RegisterServiceCtrlHandler(
        TEXT("Service1"),          CtrlHandler);
    if (Service1StatusHandle == (SERVICE_STATUS_HANDLE)0)
   {
        // error!
      return;
   }
```

```
     // Initialization code goes here.
    status=NO_ERROR;
     // Handle error condition
    if (status != NO_ERROR)
    {
         Service1Status.dwCurrentState       = SERVICE_STOPPED;
         Service1Status.dwCheckPoint         = 0;
         Service1Status.dwWaitHint           = 0;
         Service1Status.dwWin32ExitCode      = status;
         Service1Status.dwServiceSpecificExitCode = specificError;
         SetServiceStatus (Service1StatusHandle, &Service1Status);
         return;
    }      // Initialization complete - report running status.
     Service1Status.dwCurrentState       = SERVICE_RUNNING;
     Service1Status.dwCheckPoint         = 0;
     Service1Status.dwWaitHint           = 0;
     if (!SetServiceStatus (Service1StatusHandle, &Service1Status))
    {
         status = GetLastError();
     // error!
    }
     // This is where the service does its work.
    thread=(HANDLE)_beginthread(ding,0,NULL);
    return;
}

void main(int argc, char *argv[])
{
    SERVICE_TABLE_ENTRY   DispatchTable[] =
    {
         { TEXT("Service1"), Service1Start      },
         { NULL,             NULL               }
    };
    if (argc>1 && !stricmp(argv[1],"delete"))
    {
       SC_HANDLE scm=OpenSCManager(NULL,NULL,
         SC_MANAGER_CREATE_SERVICE);
       if (!scm)
       {
          cout<<"Can't open SCM\n";
          exit(1);
       }
       SC_HANDLE svc=OpenService(scm,"service1",DELETE);
       if (!svc)
       {
          cout<<"Can't open service\n";
          exit(2);
```

```
      }
      if (!DeleteService(svc))
      {
         cout<<"Can't delete service\n";
         exit(3);
      }
      cout<<"Service deleted\n";
      CloseServiceHandle(svc);
      CloseServiceHandle(scm);

      exit(0);

   }
   if (argc>1 && !stricmp(argv[1],"setup"))
   {
      char pname[1024];
      pname[0]='"';
      GetModuleFileName(NULL,pname+1,1023);
      strcat(pname,"\"");
      SC_HANDLE scm=OpenSCManager(NULL,NULL,
                 SC_MANAGER_CREATE_SERVICE),svc;
      if (!scm)
      {
         cout<<"Can't open SCM\n";
         exit(1);
      }
      if (!(svc=CreateService(scm,
                     "Service1","Service1",SERVICE_ALL_ACCESS,
         SERVICE_WIN32_OWN_PROCESS,SERVICE_DEMAND_START,
         SERVICE_ERROR_NORMAL,pname,NULL,NULL,NULL,
           NULL,NULL)))
      {
         cout<<"Registration error!\n";
         exit(2);
      }
      cout<<"Successfully registered "<<pname<<"\n";
      CloseServiceHandle(svc);
      CloseServiceHandle(scm);
      exit(0);
   }

   if (!StartServiceCtrlDispatcher( DispatchTable))
   {
      // error

   }
}
```

Inside The Example

Listing 12.6 shows a simple service that causes a beep to sound at the beginning of each hour (although you can adjust the time with a command line argument). This code contains four main functions:

- ***main***—The primary entry point
- ***Service1Start***—The service entry point
- ***CtrlHandler***—The service callback
- ***Ding***—A separate thread that monitors the time and causes a beep with **PlaySound** when the time is right

Notice that the global **Service1Status** is always up to date with the service's current status. This information allows the service to easily reply to requests for its status. At the end of **Service1Start**, the service starts the **Ding** function as a separate thread. This function mostly sleeps. When it wakes up, it examines the system time to see if the time is evenly divisible by 3,600 (the number of seconds in an hour). If it is, **Ding** sounds a bell.

You can change the number the service uses to test the time by setting it as the argument to the service. Notice that the argument appears in the **Service1Start** function, not in **main** as you might expect. Rememeber, **main** may apply to more than one service, so **Service1Start** is the logical place for the argument.

The loop in the **Ding** routine examines a few extra things other than just the time. The **manual** flag is normally **FALSE**, but if it's **TRUE**, the routine beeps regardless of the time. When the SCM pauses the service and resumes it, the code that handles the resume sets the manual flag; as a result, you can tell the service is actually doing something. The **Ding** routine also refuses to play audio if the service is in the pause mode.

Debugging Services

You can debug services several ways. One way is to open Visual Studio and select the Attach To Process option from the Debug menu. From there, you can select any running process that you want to debug (including a service). Of course, this option doesn't help you debug initialization code.

Another strategy is to change how Windows starts the service. You can create entries in the Systems Registry to accomplish this change. The entries will appear under HKEY_LOCAL_MACHINE\SOFTWARE\Microsoft\Windows NT\CurrentVersion to accomplish this change. Make a subkey named Image File Execution Options and under that key, create a key with the name of your service (for example, SERVICE2.EXE). For this key, create a string value named Debugger and make the value the name of your debugger. For this technique to work, the service can't start on boot and must be set to interact with the desktop.

Finally, you can call **DebugBreak** from within your service to start a debugging session. Doing so will cause an unhandled exception, which you can direct to the system debugger.

Other Service Considerations

When you register a service (using **CreateService**), you can tell the SCM that you want to allow the service to interact with the user. The user can also set this parameter. If this special flag isn't set, you'll be unable to see any user interface items the service might produce (a message box, for example).

You can use the special flag **MB_SERVICE_NOTIFICATION** to force the message box to display even if the service isn't set for user interaction. However, be careful not to do so when the SCM expects you to return immediately (for example, in the service entry point or the handler). Usually, you'll only want to create message boxes from a separate thread.

It's possible to change the configuration of a service on the fly. For example, from within a service control program, you can change the file name, the user interaction flag, or any other parameters you like by calling **ChangeServiceConfig**. However, before you do, you should lock the SCM database by calling **LockServiceDatabase**. If you don't do this, there could be conflicts if more than one program is changing the SCM database at one time. When you're done, call **UnlockServiceDatabase**. If you can't acquire a lock, you can always call **QueryServiceLockStatus** to find out who has the lock and how long they've had it.

There are other ways to create services. For example, the ActiveX Template Library includes a Wizard that will allow you to make an ActiveX object that can behave as a service. Of course, you can do the same thing with straight C++.

An Object-Oriented Service

If you look back at the code in Listing 12.6, you'll notice that most of it probably stays the same regardless of the actual function of the service. It makes sense to encapsulate these common portions in some sort of library, so why not use a C++ class?

That's exactly what the code in Listings 12.7 and 12.8 does. The base class **ServiceBase** is suitable for service executables that support a single service. To create a service, you need only derive a class from **ServiceBase** and, at a minimum, override **GetName** to return the service name.

Listing 12.7 The ServiceBase header.

```
// header for the service base abstract class
// This is useful only for executable services with one service
class ServiceBase
{
protected:
   static SERVICE_STATUS          ServiceStatus;
   static SERVICE_STATUS_HANDLE   ServiceStatusHandle;
   static HANDLE thread;
   DWORD lasterror;
   ServiceBase() { _this=this; };
   static void ServiceThread_(void *);
   static void __stdcall CtrlHandler(DWORD);
   static void __stdcall ServiceStart_ (DWORD argc, LPTSTR *argv);

   // These are the functions you may override if you wish
   virtual void ServiceThread(void) {};       // processing thread
   virtual void ServicePause(BOOL pause) {};  // pause
   virtual void ServiceStop() {};            // stop
   virtual void ServiceInterrogate() {};      // interrogate
       // user-defined opcode
   virtual void ServiceControl(DWORD opcode) {};
// init
   virtual DWORD ServiceInit(int argc, LPTSTR *argv)
    { return NO_ERROR; }; // You must supply a name
   virtual LPTSTR GetName()=0;

   // The main must be public
public:
   static void main(int argc, char *argv[]);
// This is really a pointer to the one and only derived class
   static ServiceBase *_this;

};
```

Listing 12.8 The ServiceBase class implementation.

```
#include <windows.h>
#include <iostream.h>
#include <string.h>
#include <process.h>
#include "servicebase.h"

SERVICE_STATUS  ServiceBase::ServiceStatus;
SERVICE_STATUS_HANDLE   ServiceBase::ServiceStatusHandle;
```

```
HANDLE ServiceBase::thread;
ServiceBase *ServiceBase::_this;

void ServiceBase::ServiceThread_(void *)
{
   _this->ServiceThread();
}

void __stdcall ServiceBase::CtrlHandler (DWORD Opcode)
{
    switch(Opcode)
   {
      case SERVICE_CONTROL_PAUSE:
        // Do whatever it takes to pause here.
            ServiceStatus.dwCurrentState = SERVICE_PAUSED;
         _this->ServicePause(TRUE);
         break;

      case SERVICE_CONTROL_CONTINUE:
        // Do whatever it takes to continue here.
            ServiceStatus.dwCurrentState = SERVICE_RUNNING;
         _this->ServicePause(FALSE);
            break;

       case SERVICE_CONTROL_STOP:
        // Do whatever it takes to stop here.
            ServiceStatus.dwWin32ExitCode = 0;
            ServiceStatus.dwCurrentState  = SERVICE_STOPPED;
            ServiceStatus.dwCheckPoint    = 0;
            ServiceStatus.dwWaitHint      = 0;
         _this->ServiceStop();
            if (!SetServiceStatus (ServiceStatusHandle,
                &ServiceStatus))
         {
                _this->lasterror = GetLastError();
            }
            return;
       case SERVICE_CONTROL_INTERROGATE:
        // Fall through to send current status.
          _this->ServiceInterrogate();
          break;
        default:
            _this->ServiceControl(Opcode);

   }
```

```
    // Send current status.
     if (!SetServiceStatus (ServiceStatusHandle,  &ServiceStatus))
         _this->lasterror = GetLastError();
    return;
}

void __stdcall ServiceBase::ServiceStart_ (DWORD argc, LPTSTR *argv)
{
     ServiceStatus.dwServiceType        = SERVICE_WIN32;
     ServiceStatus.dwCurrentState       = SERVICE_START_PENDING;
     ServiceStatus.dwControlsAccepted   = SERVICE_ACCEPT_STOP |
         SERVICE_ACCEPT_PAUSE_CONTINUE;
     ServiceStatus.dwWin32ExitCode      = 0;
     ServiceStatus.dwServiceSpecificExitCode = 0;
     ServiceStatus.dwCheckPoint         = 0;
     ServiceStatus.dwWaitHint           = 0;
     ServiceStatusHandle = RegisterServiceCtrlHandler(
         _this->GetName(),CtrlHandler);
     if (ServiceStatusHandle == (SERVICE_STATUS_HANDLE)0)
    {
         _this->lasterror=GetLastError();
       return;
    }
     // Initialization code goes here.
    _this->lasterror=_this->ServiceInit(argc,argv);
     // Handle error condition
    if (_this->lasterror != NO_ERROR)
    {
         ServiceStatus.dwCurrentState       = SERVICE_STOPPED;
         ServiceStatus.dwCheckPoint         = 0;
         ServiceStatus.dwWaitHint           = 0;
         ServiceStatus.dwWin32ExitCode      = _this->lasterror;
         ServiceStatus.dwServiceSpecificExitCode = _this->lasterror;
         SetServiceStatus (ServiceStatusHandle, &ServiceStatus);
         return;
    }      // Initialization complete - report running status.
     ServiceStatus.dwCurrentState       = SERVICE_RUNNING;
     ServiceStatus.dwCheckPoint         = 0;
     ServiceStatus.dwWaitHint           = 0;
     if (!SetServiceStatus (ServiceStatusHandle, &ServiceStatus))
    {
         _this->lasterror = GetLastError();
     // error!
    }
     // This is where the service does its work.
```

```
   thread=(HANDLE)_beginthread(ServiceThread_,0,NULL);
   return;
}

void ServiceBase::main(int argc, char *argv[])
{
   SERVICE_TABLE_ENTRY   DispatchTable[] =
   {
        { TEXT(""), ServiceStart_      },
        { NULL,               NULL                }
   };
   DispatchTable[0].lpServiceName=_this->GetName();
   if (argc>1 && !stricmp(argv[1],"delete"))
   {
      SC_HANDLE scm=OpenSCManager(NULL,NULL,SC_MANAGER_CREATE_SERVICE);
      if (!scm)
      {
         cout<<"Can't open SCM\n";
         exit(1);
      }
      SC_HANDLE svc=OpenService(scm,_this->GetName(),DELETE);
      if (!svc)
      {
         cout<<"Can't open service\n";
         exit(2);
      }
      if (!DeleteService(svc))
      {
         cout<<"Can't delete service\n";
         exit(3);
      }
      cout<<"Service deleted\n";
      CloseServiceHandle(svc);
      CloseServiceHandle(scm);

      exit(0);

   }
   if (argc>1 && !stricmp(argv[1],"setup"))
   {
      char pname[1024];
      pname[0]='"';
      GetModuleFileName(NULL,pname+1,1023);
      strcat(pname,"\"");
      SC_HANDLE scm=OpenSCManager(NULL,NULL,
```

12. Console Applications And Services

```
                SC_MANAGER_CREATE_SERVICE),svc;
        if (!scm)
        {
           cout<<"Can't open SCM\n";
           exit(1);
        }
        if (!(svc=CreateService(scm,_this->GetName(),
                _this->GetName(),SERVICE_ALL_ACCESS,
           SERVICE_WIN32_OWN_PROCESS,SERVICE_DEMAND_START,
           SERVICE_ERROR_NORMAL,pname,NULL,NULL,NULL,NULL,NULL)))
        {
           cout<<"Registration error!\n";
           exit(2);
        }
        cout<<"Successfully registered "<<pname<<"\n";
        CloseServiceHandle(svc);
        CloseServiceHandle(scm);
        exit(0);
     }

     if (!StartServiceCtrlDispatcher( DispatchTable))
     {
        // error but what?

     }
  }


  void main(int argc, char *argv[])
  {
     ServiceBase::_this->main(argc,argv);
  }
```

Of course, just overriding **GetName** won't make a very interesting server. However, you can also override **ServiceInit**, **ServicePause**, **ServiceStop**, and **ServiceInterrogate**, if you want to handle those events. You can also provide a **ServiceControl** function to handle user-defined SCM callbacks. If you need to do processing in a thread (like the last example), you can override **ServiceThread**.

Listings 12.9 and 12.10 show a service that's almost identical to the first service; but it uses the **ServiceBase** class. Because there can be only one object instantiated from the **ServiceBase**-derived class, it's easy for the code to find a pointer to the object and use it in various static and global functions (including a standard **main** function).

Listing 12.9 The Chime server header.

```
#include "servicebase.h"

class Chime : public ServiceBase
{
   LPTSTR GetName() { return "Chime"; }
   void ServiceThread(void);
   DWORD ServiceInit(int argc, LPTSTR *argv);
   int modtime;
public:
   Chime() { modtime=3600; }
};
```


Listing 12.10 The Chime server.

```
#include <windows.h>
#include <time.h>
#include "chime.h"

void Chime::ServiceThread(void)
{
    time_t timeval;
    while (ServiceStatus.dwCurrentState!=SERVICE_STOPPED)
        {
        if (ServiceStatus.dwCurrentState!=SERVICE_PAUSED)
            {
            time(&timeval);
            if ((timeval%modtime)==0)
            PlaySound("DING",GetModuleHandle(NULL),
              SND_RESOURCE|SND_SYNC|SND_NOSTOP);
            }
        Sleep(500);
        }
}

DWORD Chime::ServiceInit(int argc, LPTSTR *argv)
{
   if (argc>1) modtime=atoi(argv[1]);
   if (modtime==0) modtime=1;
   return NO_ERROR;
}

// Create the object (only 1)
Chime chime;
```

The core code in **ServiceBase** is very similar to the code in the original service. The code handles the self-installation and removal. However, at key points in the code, the base class calls virtual functions. If you override these functions, you can control the behavior of the service.

Notice that the only function you must override is **GetName**, which returns the name of your service. Other than that, the core code does all the required work. You need to override other functions only when you're interested in supplying behavior for the service.

Summary

Console programming isn't as glamorous as GUI programming, but it's a very useful technique. Although this book uses many console programs to illustrate basic ideas, this chapter shows that console programs can actually do quite a bit—including responding to mouse events, setting colors, reading characters off the console, and providing large virtual output spaces.

Another important use of console programs is in the creation of services. You can easily write a console program from scratch that's a service, but you can also use ATL or the C++ base class provided in this chapter.

Services are similar to DOS terminate-and-stay-resident (TSR) programs or Unix daemons. Anytime you need a simple program that's always present, you should think about using a service.

Immediate Solutions

Starting A Console Program

It's quite simple to create a console program. You can create a Win32 console program by using the New Project dialog box from Visual Studio to create an empty project set for console operations. You'll need to manually add at least one C or C++ source file and supply an ordinary **main** function.

Inside the program, you can use ordinary standard I/O (or I/O stream calls). If you want to print, use **printf** or the **<<** operator with **cout**. Of course, you'll want to include stdio.h (or iostream.h).

It's also perfectly permissible to include windows.h and make Windows calls. **MessageBox** is very useful, as well as any of the memory management and IPC calls. In general, you won't want to use any calls that require a message loop (although you can add consoles to programs with Windows; see below). Don't forget that modal dialog boxes don't require an external message loop, so they're easy to use from a console.

Using MFC From Console Programs

You can use some parts of MFC from console programs, although you incur a great deal of overhead if you do. If you want to use simple MFC classes like **CString** and **CFile**, you need only go to the project's settings dialog box and indicate that you're using MFC. You'll also want to include afx.h.

You incur so much overhead when doing this because you must include the MFC library (either statically or via a DLL) when you use any of these classes. A console program can't readily use much of this library, so the rest of it goes to waste.

Methods For Accessing Consoles

In addition to using calls like **printf** and **scanf**, you can use several calls in the Windows API to access a console. You can find a complete list in Table 12.1.

Although not specific for the console, you can always use the standard **ReadFile** and **WriteFile** calls to access the console. You can obtain a handle to the console by calling **GetStdHandle**.

The elementary calls that you can use include **ReadConsole** and **WriteConsole**. These calls work in a similar way to **ReadFile** and **WriteFile**, but they use the appropriate character set (ANSI or Unicode) regardless of what the program ordinarily uses.

For more control, you can also use **ReadConsoleInput** and **WriteConsole-Output**. **ReadConsoleInput** allows you to respond to mouse events, window-resizing events, and regular keyboard input. If you want mouse events, you must set the console mode (using **SetConsoleMode**) to include **ENABLE_MOUSE_INPUT** (the default). If you want window-resize events, you must set the **ENABLE_WINDOW_INPUT** flag (which isn't set by default). **ReadConsoleInput** returns an **INPUT_RECORD** structure that allows you to differentiate between the types of input (including keyboard input).

WriteConsoleOutput allows you to write characters and set their attributes at the same time. These attributes let you set the foreground and background colors to any combination of red, green, and blue. You can also set either color to be bright or dim. If you want to just write characters or just change attributes, you can use **WriteConsoleOutputCharacter** or **WriteConsoleOutputAttribute**. It's possible to read what the console is displaying by using **ReadConsoleOutput**, **ReadConsoleOutputCharacter**, or **ReadConsoleOutputAttribute**.

Just to make everything equal, you can also write characters into the console's input buffer so that the program will believe the user typed them in directly. You simply need to call **WriteConsoleInput**. You supply an **INPUT_RECORD** to this call, so you can fake mouse input as well as keyboard input.

Creating A Main Console For A GUI Program

Creating a standard console for a GUI program is quite simple: Just call **AllocConsole**. This simple call takes no arguments. Although the console is set as the program's standard input and standard output, the C library doesn't know that because it initialized itself at a time when the console didn't exist.

Luckily, this situation is simple to remedy. You can use **freopen** with the special filenames CONOUT$ and CONIN$ to reopen the **stdout**, **stdin**, and **stderr** handles. You can also reset **cout**, **cin**, **cerr**, and **clog** by assigning them a new **stdiobuf** object based on the appropriate standard handle (you can find an example in Listing 12.5).

Creating And Using Auxiliary Consoles

It's possible to have more than one console per program, although only a single console can be active at one time. To create a new console, you can call **CreateConsoleScreenBuffer**. This new console won't be active (nor will it appear) until you call **SetConsoleActiveScreenBuffer**. The new console won't be attached to any standard I/O handles, so you'll want to read and write the console using functions that take a console handle.

Handling Console Events

Your console program can receive notifications when the program is about to shut down. To do this, you must write a callback function that accepts a **DWORD** argument and returns a **BOOL**. You register your callback by calling **SetConsoleCtrlHandler**. This function takes a pointer to your callback function and a **BOOL** flag. If the flag is **TRUE**, the system adds your callback to the list of event handlers for this console. If the flag is **FALSE**, the system removes your callback.

When any shutdown is requested (via the close box, a Ctrl+C, a Ctrl+Break, a log off, or a system shutdown), Windows calls the console's callbacks in the reverse order that you registered them (in other words, the most recently registered callback receives a notification first). The **DWORD** argument to your callback indicates what type of event occurred.

If the handler wishes to allow the shutdown to proceed, it should return **FALSE**. If any handler returns **TRUE**, then the system quits calling handlers and aborts the shutdown. The first handler installed is the system default handler (so it's called last). Its behavior is to call **ExitProcess** to kill the program. So if no user-installed handlers return **TRUE**, this default handler will kill the process.

Depending on the console's mode, you may not get Ctrl+C notifications (but you'll always get Ctrl+Break notices). In particular, if you've cleared the **ENABLED_PROCESSED_INPUT** flag (using **SetConsoleMode**), the Ctrl+C character is just ordinary input and has no special meaning. You can also specify a **NULL** event handler and a **TRUE** flag to force the program to ignore Ctrl+C. Using the **FALSE** flag restores the default processing.

If you want to, you can generate fake events in your program. Do this by calling **GenerateConsoleCtrlEvent**.

You can find an example console event handler in Listing 12.4. This simple handler prompts the user with a message box and takes the appropriate action.

Finding A Console's Window Handle

Often, you'll want to know the console's window handle so that you can pass it to Windows API calls. Unfortunately, there's no easy way to learn the handle for a console program.

There's a trick you can use (documented in Microsoft's Knowledge Base article Q124103). The idea is to use the **FindWindow** call to locate the window based on some sort of unique title. Here are the basic steps:

1. Read the console's title (using **GetConsoleTitle**).
2. Change the title to something unique (using **SetConsoleTitle**).
3. Wait for at least 40 milliseconds (using **Sleep**) to ensure the title actually had time to change.
4. Call **FindWindow** to locate a window with the given title.
5. Set the console title back to its original value.
6. Wait another 40 milliseconds.
7. Call **GetWindowText** to verify that the window's title is the same as the original console title.

You can see these steps at work in the program in Listing 12.4.

Inside Services

Services are programs (usually console programs) that run regardless of the user logged on to the system. In fact, services run even when there are no users. They're similar to MSDOS TSR programs or Unix daemons. Windows manages services via the Service Control Manager (SCM). Services use the SCM to inform Windows about its status. Service control programs can use the SCM to start, stop, and otherwise control the service.

Services reside in a normal EXE file, and one EXE file can support more than one service (although usually you'll have only one service per file). The **main** function of a service simply calls **StartServiceCtrlDispatcher** to inform the SCM of the number of services provided by this EXE and their entry points.

The SCM then calls each service's entry point, passing any command-line arguments to this function (not the normal **main** function). This entry point will do any brief initialization required, update the service's status (using **SetServiceStatus**), and return to the SCM. If your service requires a lot of time to initialize, you should set the status to **SERVICE_START_PENDING** and do the initialization in a separate thread. Doing so allows you to return to the SCM immediately.

You'll also want to use a separate thread if you want to leave the service running all the time. For instance, the example service in this chapter (see Listing 12.6) chimes on the hour. It does so by sleeping in a separate thread.

The service entry point must also register a control handler. The SCM will use this handler to send notifications to the service. Some notifications inform the service that it is to stop or pause. You can also define a number of notifications that are specific to your service, if you like.

Accessing A Service

Any program that wants to control a service must open the SCM (using **OpenSCManager**) and then retrieve a handle to the particular service you want to manipulate (using **OpenService**). Then a simple call to **ControlService** will send notifications to the service handler. You can find a list of common service-related calls in Table 12.2.

Once you have an open service, you can learn its status or change its configuration as well. Of course, the handle you have for the service must have the correct security to allow you to do this. Like all objects, you request a particular access when you open the handle. If you don't have the proper security privileges, the system won't allow you to open the handle.

The C++ Service Base Class

For many simple services, you can utilize the C++ base class in this chapter (see Listings 12.7 and 12.8). This class contains most of the core functionality of a basic service. To use this class, you derive a new class from it and provide at least a **GetName** override. This function simply returns the name of your service.

You can override several other functions to provide your service's functionality:

- ***ServiceInit***—Performs initialization

- ***ServicePause***—Handles pause notifications from the SCM
- ***ServiceStop***—Responds to stop notifications from the SCM
- ***ServiceInterrogate***—Handles status queries from the SCM
- ***ServiceControl***—Processes user-defined service notifications (from **ControlService**)
- ***ServiceThread***—Performs long-term processing in a separate thread

Debugging Services

Services have a bad reputation when it comes to debugging. Since the service isn't an ordinary program, you can't run it with the debugger the way you usually do. The easiest way to debug a service is to open Visual Studio and select the Attach To Process option from the Debug menu. From there, you can select the service from the list of running processes the debugger provides. This method won't help you with service initialization code, however, since the debugger only recognizes the service after it starts.

You can also call **DebugBreak** from within your service to start a debugging session. Doing so will cause an unhandled exception that you can direct to the system debugger (presuming the service isn't set for starting on boot).

Another strategy is to change how Windows starts the service. You can create entries in the Systems Registry to accomplish this change. The entries will appear under HKEY_LOCAL_MACHINE\SOFTWARE\Microsoft\Windows NT\CurrentVersion to accomplish this. Make a subkey named Image File Execution Options and under that key, create a key with the name of your service (for example, SERVICE2.EXE). For this key, create a string value named "Debugger" and set the value the full path of your debugging program. For this technique to work, the service can't start on boot and must be set to interact with the desktop.

Appendix A

Beyond The Frontier

I grew up in a very small town on the Mississippi Gulf Coast (Bay St. Louis, to be exact). When I was in high school, there was big excitement because a Burger King opened on the highway. Before that, if you wanted fast food, you had to drive 20 or 30 miles into another town.

I left Bay St. Louis to live in many other parts of the country (now I'm a naturalized Texan). However, I still have family there and I return from time to time for a visit.

As I drive the streets of my boyhood hometown, everything seems the same—almost. Coast Electric, from which my Dad retired, is still there, and so is the Burger King. A lot of the old landmarks are still around, but somehow they're different. The corner grocery is now on the highway and the old building houses an electronics company that gave me my first real job. Bobbie Ann's bakery is no more, and the post office across the street is closed, too. Did I mention they have casino gambling now?

So, things seem familiar and yet different. Windows can be a lot like this. You burrow down into a project for six months or a year and you don't pay much attention to what's happening. Then when you resurface, Windows seems familiar, but different. The industry in general, and Windows in particular, changes at a dizzying rate. How do you keep up?

Know It All?

There's an old joke about a college philosophy class exam that had only one question: "Write down everything you don't know." This is often the same situation programmers face. Learning about new technology isn't always as hard as locating the one or two new technologies you find interesting.

In this book, you've read about many technologies that you can employ in Windows programs. It shouldn't surprise you to learn that there are many other areas of Windows that might be useful to you. One book can't cover everything, but in this chapter, you'll read a little about other parts of Windows that you may want to explore on your own.

With the rise of the Internet, it's never been easier to find information on new technology (Windows or otherwise). Still, it helps to know what you're looking for to start with. In this appendix I'll point out a few resources that can help you both online and offline.

Database Technologies

If you work with databases—and most programmers have some involvement with some sort of database—you know that Microsoft offers a bewildering array of database options. At the heart of most of them is the Open Database Connectivity standard (ODBC). ODBC provides a standardized wrapper around databases so that programs don't need to concern themselves with the details of the specific database.

However, few programmers actually program directly to ODBC. Instead, they use some form of ActiveX object to communicate with the database. In some cases, the object may use a direct method to talk to the underlying database (usually for improved speed). However, these objects often simply provide a layer over ODBC, hiding its complexities from you.

The problem is that Microsoft has made several attempts to provide these ActiveX objects, and each release is subtly different from the one before. The OLE DB objects appear to be the most recent incarnation at this time. This specification allows you to use databases by accessing the OLE DB objects. If you've ever worked with databases using Visual Basic, the model is similar.

OLE DB lets you create *consumers*—that is, programs that access data via OLE DB. It also allows for *providers*—"databases" that other programs access via OLE DB. Of course, the data you provide need not come from an actual database. You might write an OLE DB provider that looks up records from an Internet site, for example.

Using MAPI

Just as ODBC provides a standard interface to a multitude of databases, the Messaging API (MAPI) provides a standard interface around a variety of electronic mail and messaging programs. If your program needs to manipulate email, you'll be interested in MAPI.

Your initial thoughts might be that you don't care about email. However, many modern programs have a Send To item on the File menu; this item emails the current document. If you want your program to include this feature, you might be interested in MAPI.

If you're an MFC programmer using the document view architecture, implementing this feature couldn't be simpler. The **CDocument** class has two special functions that help you. The **OnFileSendMail** method can directly handle the menu and the **OnUpdateFileSendMail** function is the update command handler for the menu. If your document can save itself using **Serialize**, you'll have no problems. Simply use Class Wizard to connect these two functions to your menu item and you're done.

For more advanced techniques, you'll have to delve into the MAPI calls directly. In reality, you can use MAPI several ways. Which one you'll want to use depends on what features you need and how comfortable you are with ActiveX programming.

There are three types of MAPI client applications: messaging aware, messaging enabled, and messaging based. Messaging-aware and messaging-enabled applications typically incorporate messaging as a secondary function. For example, word processing or spreadsheet applications may offer limited email capabilities, but that isn't their primary focus. Messaging-based applications employ messaging as a central part of their processing and offer extensive messaging features. Electronic mail, or integrated mail and schedule applications (like Outlook 2000) are examples of messaging-based applications.

MAPI offers its services via ActiveX objects. However, these objects are relatively complex and useful primarily for messaging-based applications. To accommodate less complicated clients, MAPI also offers services via the Simple MAPI API. This is a function call-based API that offers limited functionality.

For clients that need more specialized functions, MAPI offers the Common Messaging Calls (CMC) or Collaboration Data Objects (CDO). These APIs offer more power than Simple MAPI but are less complex than using MAPI directly.

Color Management

Computers have come a long way from the days of black and white text-only terminals. Today's computers display color images and can often print them as well. Besides that, many computers have color input devices including video capture devices, digital cameras, and scanners.

This wealth of devices leads to a problem. If you take a picture with a digital camera, you'd like the color you see in real life to match the color you see on the screen and on your printed output. Practical devices, however, don't all match exactly. The colors displayed by your camera's imaging device probably do not exactly match what you see on your screen. Your screen's colors don't precisely match those on your laptop's LCD panel, and neither device matches your color inkjet printer's output.

For ordinary use, you probably aren't overly concerned with exact color matching. However, if you're preparing artwork for printing for a serious photographer or graphic artist, color matching is of paramount importance. To meet these needs, Windows supports color matching via Image Color Management (ICM). ICM allows you to prepare and use color profiles that describe the subtle differences between various color input and output devices. If programs use ICM properly, the tangerine on your screen will look exactly like the tangerine that you print on your color printer.

DirectX

Windows provides access to a wide range of hardware, including video adapters, sound cards, and input devices. Prior to Windows, your program had to know how to deal with all the various types of devices you might encounter. Windows makes this process much easier, because if you can interact with Windows, you can let Windows worry about the specific device type.

The problem is, when you make a call to draw a line on screen, for example, there's a large amount of overhead as Windows processes the call and decides how to handle your request. For many applications this overhead isn't a big deal, but some high-performance applications (mostly games) need higher performance.

To address this problem, Microsoft developed a set of technologies known as DirectX. DirectX is really several different libraries, including DirectDraw for screen operations, DirectInput for reading input devices, and DirectSound for audio operations.

In general, working with DirectX is more like directly controlling a device than working in Windows. For example, with DirectDraw, it's possible to get a drawing surface (much like a standard device context) that directly points to video memory. Therefore, when you request an operation on the surface, the drawing takes place directly on screen.

OpenGL

OpenGL is a library of drawing operations that originated at Silicon Graphics and has since become a *de facto* standard for drawing high-end graphics. OpenGL offers both 2D and 3D capabilities. Under Windows you rarely see OpenGL's 2D calls used, because Windows has good support for 2D drawing.

For 3D work, however, OpenGL is widely used. Even Microsoft's 3D screen savers (the pipe, maze, and flower box screen savers, for example) use OpenGL. With OpenGL, you specify objects as a series of vertices, set lighting, and then project the resulting image into a viewing area.

OpenGL is quite powerful and has become a *de facto* standard, but using it effectively does require some practice. A good understanding of geometry is helpful, as well, particularly when you're wading through the documentation's discussion of tessellating polygons (subdividing complex polygons into several convex polygons) and frustums (a shape like a pyramid with the top cut off).

Still Image

With the growing proliferation of scanners and digital cameras, there's a need to isolate programs from the specifics required to interface with these devices. This is where Still Image comes into play. Still Image is a means for programs to operate digital cameras, flatbed scanners, sheet scanners, or even handheld scanners.

Still Image is still in its infancy, but it promises big rewards for imaging software. Programs that use Still Image can ask devices for data or have the image device push data into the application as necessary.

Finding More Information

Even with all of these technologies available, there's still more to learn. Just for Internet programming, dozens of different techniques exist. So when you're looking for more information about one of these technologies or a whole new one, your first stop should probably be the Microsoft Developer Network (MSDN) Web site (**msdn.microsoft.com**). You have to register for most of the site's content, but doing so is well worth the effort (and doesn't cost anything as of this writing).

On MSDN, you'll find a great deal of documentation and news about what Microsoft has planned. If you're willing to spring a few dollars, you can also subscribe to MSDN on CD. You get some additional content on the CDs (depending on which level of subscription you purchase) and you can browse them without an Internet connection.

Speaking of subscriptions, don't forget to read programming magazines to find out the latest news. You can find my *Windows Commando* column in Visual Developer magazine (**www.visual-developer.com**).

Here are a few other Web sites you might find interesting and useful:

- ***www.al-williams.com***—My Web site.
- ***www.codeguru.com***—A great site with plenty of code examples.
- ***www.program.com***—A nice portal site for programmers (lots of links).
- ***devcentral.iftech.com***—DevCentral has a lot of content and a free MFC extension library.
- ***www.programmersheaven.com***—A lot of information about many languages.
- ***www.wotsit.org***—A collection of file format specifications that can be very useful.

Appendix B

Windows 2000: A Programming Odyssey

In 1969, I weathered hurricane Camille in a house about two blocks from the beach. Camille was a powerful storm and it came at night, which made it especially frightening. We spent the night in our bathroom, because it was the only room in the house that didn't have windows or an outside wall.

I can remember sitting in the candle-lit room (of course, the power was out) waiting for the storm to be over—it made for a long night.

What I didn't realize at the time was that the end of the storm wasn't the end of the ordeal; it was the beginning. The next morning a carpet of debris was on the ground. Our roof was damaged (our neighbor had no roof at all), our windows were blown out, and it would be weeks before we had electricity, running water, or telephones.

I sincerely hope this book has been less of an ordeal than a hurricane. However, as in the aftermath of a hurricane, you're just getting started. In this appendix, you'll find some thoughts about tomorrow's technology.

The Future?

The truth is, everyone wants to predict the future. I'd rather take my chances prognosticating about the lottery than make a bet on the future of computers. However, a few things seem fairly certain for the immediate future.

For Windows programming, it's certain that Windows 2000 will be the standard platform, especially for business users. How you'll program this platform is another matter. For the present, many large-scale projects use MFC. However, other languages are making inroads on MFC's (and C++'s) traditional dominance.

Visual Basic, long known for rapid application development, has grown enough that many developers find it useful. Another major contender is Java. Java's big advantage is that it produces code that runs on a variety of computers. What is the drawback to Java? Today it isn't typically speedy at runtime. A well-crafted C++ program will outperform a Java program in nearly all cases.

Microsoft did add features to make Java speedier (and to make it easier to implement Windows-like features). However, these features can lock your program into Windows, which violates the spirit of Java. Besides, Sun (the owner of Java) has Microsoft in court over some of these features—a situation that makes some developers nervous about using Microsoft's Visual J++.

But don't count Java out yet. In the days to come, you'll see more and more non-PC computers in specialized roles. These computers will be smart printers, network gateways, and storage devices, among other things.

To make all of these devices work together (and with the PC), you'll need Java. In particular, a Java technology known as Jini will allow devices to discover each other and load device drivers (written in Java so they're platform independent).

Using Jini, you can connect a database device to your network. Because of Jini, the PCs on the network will discover the database server and automatically load the correct drivers from the database server itself.

Consider another scenario: You're carrying a handheld computer with a wireless connection. When you walk into a room, the computer scans for devices using Jini. It might find a printer, an Internet gateway, and a digital video camera. The handheld would load whatever drivers it needed.

The Big Threat

Perhaps the biggest threat to traditional Windows development is—in a way—the Internet. Even today, you can use Web pages for managing contacts, tasks, and your calendar (check out **calendar.yahoo.com**, for example). You can even use the Web for email (like **www.hotmail.com**) or newsgroups (**www.talkway.com** or **www.deja.com**).

This is just the tip of the iceberg. As the Internet becomes more pervasive, you'll see more applications move to the Web. In the not-too-distant future, I wouldn't be surprised to see all programs, in a way, run as Web applications. Combined with protocols like Jini, your "browser"—which might be on a PC or on a handheld device—will control the application.

This new reality could lead to a dichotomy between programs and user interfaces. In the future you might carry a handheld device that acts as your telephone, your Web browser, your TV remote, and more. Your user interface would know your native language, your color preferences, and so forth. Wireless connectivity would hook the device to storage and services.

What Does It Mean To Me?

What does this scenario mean to today's programmers? Assuming it comes to pass, it means programmers will be more concerned with content and less concerned with appearance.

It also means you'll rely more on device-independent languages like Java (or its eventual successor) for programming. Don't get me wrong: C++ will continue to be viable for a long time. Perhaps C++ will evolve to be more device-independent. But just as DOS gave way to Windows and C gave way to C++, the tools we enjoy today will one day pass the torch to something new. My best guess is, that something will accommodate heterogeneous networks.

Be Prepared

There is, however, a big difference between keeping an eye on things and blindly jumping on every bandwagon that goes by. History is full of sure things that didn't quite make it. OS/2 and SmallTalk are great examples of programs that were supposedly sure things, but that never captured the market.

So be sure to watch the newer products and technologies, but don't be too eager to adopt something that will be a flash in the pan. Hard to tell the difference? That's the problem with predicting the future!

Advice For Today

Interoperable handheld computers running network applications may be the wave of the future. Of course, your immediate problem is keeping up with the rapid rate of change that characterizes Windows. However, some of the strategies are the same as trying to guess the future. Microsoft has been known to introduce things that didn't fare well and were eventually replaced. Look at DDE, for example. Many Microsoft database technologies have yielded to newer strategies. Are the new ways better? Yes, but that's small comfort if you've invested in the older product.

Making predictions about the future is a fool's errand. Only one thing is certain: Wherever your odyssey takes you, change will be your constant companion.

Index

A

A2W, 485
AAWSound.CPP, 88-91
AAWSOUND.H, 86-88
AAWSound server, 65
AbortBox code, 156
Abort dialog box, 156-159
Abort DLL, 152-154
Abort thread, 154-155
Absolute security descriptors (SDs), 377
accept(), 270, 271, 288
ACCESS_ALLOWED_ACE_TYPE, 359
AccessCheck, 367-368
Access Control Element (ACE), 359, 363
Access Control List (ACL), 359, 363-367
ACCESS_DENIED_ACE_TYPE, 359
ACCESS_MASK, 359
AccountLog function, 25
ACE (Access Control Element), 359, 363
ACF (Application Configuration File) files, 312, 329
ACL (Access Control List), 359, 363-367
ACL_REVISION, 363
Active Directory Services (ADS), 529-531
ActiveX, 23, 323
  aggregation, 27-28, 35-37
  C++ connection, 40-41
  class factory, 66
  clients, 60-64, 66-68
  code reuse, 27-28, 35, 115
  containment, 27-28, 35-37
  definitions, 24
  DLL servers, 65, 78-81, 82
  EXE server, 65, 68-78, 82, 83-92, 93
  HRESULT, 30-31
  IDispatch interface, 83-85, 97-113
  IDL, 75-77
  impersonating objects, 53-54
  IPC and, 239
  IUnknown, 32-33
  macros, 57, 60, 92-93
  marshalling, 38-40, 75, 77
  multiple interfaces, 82-83
  reference counts, 34-35
  Registry, 41-53, 78, 82, 117-118
  server design, 64-66
  Structured Storage System (SSS), 539, 557
  threads, 11, 12, 18, 40, 114, 132-135
  type libraries, 37, 42, 54-59
  UUID, 31-32
  vs. Java, 23-24
ActiveX Template Library (ATL). *See* ATL.
AddAccessAllowedAce, 363, 378
AddAccessDeniedAce, 363, 378
AddExtension, 449
AddRef, 33, 34, 36, 64, 116, 429
AddReg, 401
Addresses, sockets, 269
ADS (Active Directory Services), 529-531
ADSI, 529-531
ADsPath, 529
AfxBeginThread, 133, 135, 147, 148, 151
AfxCreateThread, 151
AfxEndThread, 151
AFXMT.H file, 193
AfxParseURL, 527
Aggregation, 27-28, 35-37, 95-97
Alertable timer, 174
Alertable waits, 174
AllocConsole, 564, 586
Anonymous pipes, 238, 252-255, 322, 325
ANSI, 13-14, 485
ANSI strings, 8
Apartment threading model, 114
APC (Asynchronous Procedure Call), 141-143, 174
API (Applications Programming Interface), 5, 8, 9, 18-20
AppWizard, 84-86, 94, 423, 477
AsciiChar, 563
.ASHARE segment, 324
AssignProcessToJobObject, 131

Asynchronous I/O, 201, 209, 227-231
ATL (ActiveX Template Library), 119, 422, 423-425, 436
  ATL Wizard, 448-449
  MMC snap-ins, 446, 448, 451-469, 473-474
  shell extensions, 422, 423-428, 436, 470
  smart pointers, 440-441
Auto binding handle, 318
Automation DLL, 94
Automation object, 428
Automation server, 83
AutoTreatAs, 54
AVC program, 539-552, 557-558

B

Battlefield game, as **CSockets** example, 293-309
beepthread routine, 135
BEGIN_INTERFACE_MAP macro, 92, 430
BEGIN_INTERFACE_PART macro, 86, 93, 429
bind(), 270
Binding handle, 311-312
Binding time, 112-113
BIN file, 405, 416
bInheritHandle, 357
Blocking calls, 293
BSTR, 98, 99
Buffers, 340

C

C++, 16, 17
  calling API from, 18-19
  derivation in, 27
  early binding, 112
  exception handlers, 347
  IUnknown, 33
  new operator, 34
  service base class, 589-590
  threads and, 146
  VTBLs, 40
C++ objects, 27
CAbortThread, 156
CallNamedPipe, 256
CancelIo, 208, 230
CancelWaitableTimer, 174
CAsyncSocket, 292-293, 309
CawcData object, 451
CawcNumData object, 452
CCmdTarget, 83, 84, 86, 104, 118, 429
CComPtr, 440
CComQIPtr, 441, 449
CEditView, 477-486
CEvent, 192
CFile, 536, 585
CFileDialog, 505
CFormView, 505
CGopherFile, 518, 536
Change notifications, 185
ChangeServiceConfig, 577
CHAR_INFO, 563
Checker program, as sockets example, 267, 273-290
CHECKIN command, 558
CHECKOUT command, 558
CHTMLDialog, 502, 535
CHtmlView, 486, 494-498, 532, 534, 536
CHttpConnection, 518, 536
CHttpFile, 518, 519, 528, 536
CInet control, 513
CInternetFile, 518, 536
CInternetSession, 517-518, 532, 536
CInternetSession::GetHttpConnection, 518
CLASSFAC.CPP, 78
Class factory, 66, 85
Class Identifier (CLSID), 31, 42, 46-47, 117
Class Wizard, 104-106, 309
Client (ActiveX), 24, 60-64, 66-68
  CSocket, 291
  debugging, 74
  RPC, 313-315, 317-318
  sockets, 270-271, 328
Clipboard, 238, 330
CList, 485
CListpostView::OnPublish, 506
close(), 271
CloseHandle, 167, 190, 204
closesocket(), 271
CLSID (Class Identifier), 31, 42, 46-47, 117
CLSIDFromCLSID(), 48
CLSID_InternetShortcut, 532
CLSID_ShellLink, 471
CMD_CLICK, 293
CMD_REPLY, 293
CMD_RESIGN, 293
CMultiLock, 192
CMutex, 192
CObject, 528
coclass keyword, 57

CoCreateAsClass(), 54
CoCreateGuid, 31
CoCreateInstance, 34, 37, 49, 64, 68, 442, 443, 471, 484
CoCreateInstanceEx, 113
Code reuse, ActiveX, 27-28, 35, 115
CoGetMalloc, 62
CoInitialize, 61, 442
COleVariant, 514
COM object, MFC to create, 431
COM+, 113-114
Completion ports, 210-211, 215-219, 232
Component (ActiveX), 24, 33, 37
CONIN$, 564
connect(), 271
ConnectNamedPipe, 256
ConnectTemplate, 86
CONOUT$, 564
Console applications, 538-568, 585-588
  auxiliary consoles, 587
  AVC program, 539-552, 557-558
  console calls, 560-563
  console window, 558-560
  dialog box callback program, 552-557
  events, 563
  GUI, 564-568, 586
  services, 568-584, 588-590
Console calls, 560-563
Console events, 563, 587
Console handles, 185-186, 560
Console program, starting, 585
Console window, 558-560
Container (ActiveX), 24
Containment, 27-28, 35-37, 116
Control (ActiveX), 24, 512
ControlService, 570
ConvertThreadToFiber, 139, 159
Cooperative multitasking, 12-13
COPYDATASTRUCT, 240, 323
CopyFile, 445
CoRegisterClassObject, 65, 77
CoWaitForMultipleHandles, 114
CREATE_ALWAYS, 225
CreateConsoleScreenBuffer, 560, 537
CreateEvent, 189
CreateFiber, 159
CreateFile, 185, 202-204, 225, 326, 327
CreateFileHandle, 202
CreateFileMapping, 219-220, 232, 251, 325
CreateIoCompletionPort, 210
CreateJobObject, 131
CreateMailSlot, 257, 258, 327
CreateMutex, 188, 190
CreateNamedPipe, 256, 326, 361, 362
CREATE_NEW, 225
CreatePipe, 253, 325
CreatePrivateObjectSecurity, 368
CreatePrivateSecurityObject, 379
CreateProcess, 11-12, 123, 124, 126-131, 144-145
CreateSemaphore, 191
CreateService, 577
CreateStdDispatch, 104
CREATE_SUSPENDED, 151
CreateThread, 132, 146
CreateWaitableTimer, 174
CRITICAL_SECTION, 175, 187, 190
Critical section calls, 176
Critical sections, 174-175, 187, 190-191
CSemaphore, 192
CSingleLock, 192
CSocket, 290-308
  archives with, 292
  battlefield game as example, 293-309
  as client, 291
  as server, 291
CStdioFile, 518, 528
CString, 485, 513, 585
CSynchObject, 192
CWinApp, 146
CWinThread, 146, 147, 148, 150-151
CWnd, 310

D

DACL (discretionary access control list), 357, 358, 359, 376
Datagrams, 257
Data types
  BSTR, 98, 99
  Registry, 387
  SAFEARRAY, 98
  VARIANTs, 98, 100-102
DCOM (Distributed COM), 113
DDE (Dynamic Data Exchange), 239, 322, 330
Deadlock, 189
DebugBreak, 590
Debugging
  client, 74
  heaps, 350

server, 74-75
services, 576-577, 590
DECLARE_INTERFACE_MAP macro, 92, 430
DECLARE_OLE_CREATE macro, 85, 93, 106, 430, 431
DefaultInstall, 401
DEF file, 324
DeleteCriticalSection, 191
DeleteFiber, 159
DeleteService, 570
Delphi (Borland), 16, 17
DelReg, 401
DeregisterEventSource, 408, 417
DestroyPrivateObjectSecurity, 368
Development tools, 15-16, 17
DHTML (dynamic HTML), 486
Dialog box
callback routine, 552-557
HTML dialog boxes, 499-502, 535
Ding function, 576
DisconnectNamedPipe, 257
Discretionary access control list (DACL), 357, 358, 359, 376
Dispatch map, 84
DispGetParam function, 103
DISPID, 97, 98
DISPPARAMS structure, 102, 112
Distinguished name, 529
Distributed COM (DCOM), 113
DllCanUnloadNow, 74, 81
DllGetClassObject, 74, 81
DLLMAIN.CPP, 78-81
DllMain function, 81
DllRegisterServer(), 53
DLLs (Dynamic Link Libraries), 15, 18, 77, 238, 247
as IPC mechanism, 248, 322
message DLL, 416-417
self-registering, 53
for shared memory, 247-251, 324
shell extensions, 422-431
DLL servers, 65, 78-81, 82, 94-95
DllUnregisterServer(), 53
Document Object (ActiveX), 24
DoScan, 484, 528
DoSomething, 34
DragAcceptFiles, 445
Dual interface, 112-113
Dual-mode snap-ins, 448
DuplicateHandle, 149, 183, 226, 253
DWORD, 76, 151, 347, 587
dwReserved, 511
Dynamic Data Exchange (DDE), 239, 322, 330
Dynamic HTML (DHTML), 486
Dynamic Link Libraries. *See* DLLs.

E

Early binding, 112
Embedding, 71
EnableAutomation, 95
ENABLE_MOUSE_INPUT, 562, 586
ENABLE_WINDOW_INPUT, 562
Encapsulation, 115
END_INTERFACE_MAP macro, 93, 430
END_INTERFACE_PART macro, 86, 93, 429
EnterCriticalSection, 175, 187, 190
Enumerator interface, 63
Enumerators, 63
EOF detection, 209, 226, 231
Error codes, 272
ERROR_HANDLE_EOF, 209
ERROR_INVALID_USER_BUFFER, 208
ERROR_IO_INCOMPLETE, 208, 231
ERROR_IO_PENDING, 207, 230, 231
Error message, logging, 407-408, 418
ERROR_NOT_ENOUGH_MEMORY, 208
ERROR_OPERATION_ABORTED, 208
ERROR_PIPE_LISTENING, 214
EventMessageFile, 406
Events, 163, 168-170, 187, 189-190
console applications, 563, 587
with overlapped I/O, 208-209
Event sources, 404-405
Exception code, 347-348
exec, 11
Executive, 9
EXE debugging, 74
EXE server, 65, 68-78, 82, 92-93
EXEs, self-registering, 52-53
ExitInstance, 146
ExitProcess, 135, 145
ExitThread, 149
ExitWindows, 132
Expand, 449
ExpandEnvironmentStrings, 45, 387
ExpandURL, 527
ExternalAddRef, 86, 95
ExternalQueryInterface, 86, 95
ExternalRelease, 86, 95

F

Facility, 406
FAT, 14
fdwFlags, 511
Fibers, 139-141, 159
Fibonacci numbers, code to create, 254-255
FILE_FLAG_OVERLAPPED, 207
File handles
  completion port, 210
  duplicating, 226-227
File mapping object, 219-223, 232
  shared memory, 251-252, 325
FILE_READ_SHARE, 327
Files
  closing, 227
  opening, 225
File system, 14
File types, Registry, 399-400, 402-404
File upload control, 512
FindCloseChangeNotification, 185
FindFirstChangeNotification, 185
FindFirstFile, 484
FindNextChangeNotification, 185
FindNextFile, 484
FindWindow, 558, 588
FLG_ADDREG_NOCLOBBER, 415
FlushFileBuffers, 257
fopen, 405
Foreground thread, 148
fork call, 123
Forking, 11-12
FormatMessage, 407, 418
FORMAT_MESSAGE_FROM_SYSTEM, 418
free, 313
Free threading model, 40
FTP, 518, 519
Function calls, 8

G

GenerateConsoleCtrlEvent, 587
GENERIC_ALL, 359, 367
GENERIC_EXECUTE, 359
GENERIC_MAPPING structure, 368
GENERIC_READ, 225, 359, 367
GENERIC_WRITE, 225, 359
getbuffer, 340
GetConsoleScreenBufferInfo, 563
GetConsoleTitle, 558, 588
GetCurrentFiber, 159
GetCurrentProcess, 127
GetCurrentProcessId, 129
GetCurrentThread, 149, 183
get_Document, 490, 534
GetExitCodeProcess, 145
GetExitCodeThread, 149
GetFiberData, 159
GetFileSecurity, 374, 375
gethostbyname(), 272
get_HWND, 486
GetIconLocation, 432, 471
GetIDsOfNames, 105
GetLastError, 45, 207, 230, 387
GetMailslotInfo, 258
GetModuleFileName, 432
GetModuleHandle, 552
GetMOTD, 312, 313, 318
GetNamedPipeHandleStatus, 256
GetNamePipeInfo, 257
GetOverlappedResult, 208, 209, 215
GetPath, 471
GetProcAddress, 499, 535
GetProcessHeap, 343
GetProcessWorkingSetSize, 131
GetQueuedCompletion Status, 210
GetResultPaneColInfo, 448, 450, 452
GetScopePaneInfo, 449
GetSecurityDescriptorOwner, 375
getservbyname(), 288, 289
GetStdHandle, 185, 253, 327
GetStockData function, 25
GetUserName, 359
GetWindowText, 588
GIL_NOTFILENAME, 426
Global atom table, 330
Global catalog, 529
Gopher, 519
GUI, console applications, 564-568, 586
GUID (Globally Unique Identifier), 31, 117

H

HAL (Hardware Abstraction Layer), 9, 18
(HANDLE)0xFFFFFFFF, 251, 252
Handles, 253
  auto binding handle, 318
  binding handle, 311-312

closing, 167, 190, 204
implicit handle, 312
key handle, 43
process handle, 149, 184
replacing with pipe, 327
for status bar, 309
thread handle, 149, 183, 184
waitable handles, 184
HeapAlloc, 343, 349
HeapCompact, 350
HeapCreate, 343, 348
HeapDestroy, 349
HeapFree, 343, 349
HEAP_GENERATE_EXCEPTIONS, 348, 349
HEAP_NO_SERIALIZE, 343, 348, 349, 350
Heaps, 343-344, 348-350
HeapSize, 349
HeapValidate, 350
HeapWalk, 350
HEAP_ZERO_MEMORY, 349
H file, 416
HICON, 432
HKEY, 42-44, 385, 412
HKEY_CLASSES_ROOT, 402, 421
HKEY_CLASSES_ROOT\CLSID, 75
HKEY_CLASSES_ROOT\INTERFACES, 75
HPFS file system, 14, 15
HRESULT, 30-31
HTML, 486
HTML dialog boxes, 499-502, 535
htons(), 269
HTTP, 518-519
Hyperlinks, link checker, 519-529

I

IAAWSound interface, 64-65, 75
IADs, 530
IADsComputer, 530
IADsContainer, 530
IADsPropertyList, 530
IADsUser, 530
IClassFactory interface, 37, 66
IClassFactory2 interface, 66
IComponent, 447
IComponentData, 447
Icon handler, 421, 422, 431-436
IConsole, 447
IConsoleNameSpace interface, 449, 450
Icon tray programs, 436-444, 469, 472-473
IDirectoryObject, 530
IDispatch interface, 83-85, 97-113, 118, 490, 534
MFC, 104, 118-119
IDL (interface description language), 75-77
Idle processing, 159-160
IDL files, 312, 316-317, 329
IEnumIDList, 63, 64
IEnum interface, 118
IExtractIcon::Extract, 426, 432
IExtractIcon::GetIconLocation, 426, 432
IExtractIcon interface, 422, 424, 425
IGetStockInfo, 26
IHTMLDocument2 interface, 534
IID (Interface Identifier), 31, 75
IID_IAAWSound interface, 75
IID_IShellLink interface, 471
ILog interface, 25
IMalloc interface, 61-63, 64, 118, 485
ImpersonateLoggedOnUser, 362
ImpersonateSelf, 362, 367
Impersonation, 362
IMPLEMENT_OLE_CREATE macro, 85, 93, 106, 430, 431
Implicit handle, 312
importlib keyword, 57
InetXTest, 515
INF files, 401-402
INI files, 41, 383-384, 400, 413-414, 415-416, 477
InitDialog function, 72
InitializeAcl, 363, 378
InitializeCriticalSection, 175, 190, 191
InitializeCriticalSectionAndSpinCount, 175
InitializeSecurity Descriptor, 358, 376
InitInstance, 71-72, 86, 146
InprocHandler32 key, 32
INPUT_RECORD, 562, 586
Insertable key, 48
InsertColumn, 452
InsertItem, 449, 452
INTERFACE_AGGREGATE macro, 93, 95
Interface description language (IDL), 75-77
Interface Identifier (IID), 31, 75
interface keyword, 58
Interface map, 85
INTERFACE_PART macro, 85, 93, 430
Interfaces, 25, 27, 116, 118
defined, 311
dual interface, 112-113
finding, 33

IUnknown, 32-33
MFC, 119
multiple interfaces, 82-83
predefined, 37
Interface table, 25
Interlocked calls, 167-168, 191-192
InterlockedCompareExchange, 167
InterlockedIncrement, 176, 184
Internet communication
Active Directory Services (ADS), 529-531
HTML dialog boxes, 499-502, 535
Internet Explorer, 486-502, 532, 534
MFC support, 517-529, 535-536
resource URLs, 498-499
shortcuts, 477-486
WebPost API, 502-517, 532
Internet Explorer, 486-502, 532, 534
Internet resources, 20
InternetShortcut::GetURL, 485
InternetShortcut object, 484
Interprocess communications (IPC), 124, 235-237
mailslots, 239, 257-264, 322, 327
Microsoft Message Queue (MSMQ), 114, 239, 319-320, 323
remote procedure calls (RPCs), 239, 310-319, 322, 329-330
serial number checking, 264-266
shared memory, 238, 247-252, 322
sockets, 239, 267-310, 322, 328
threads and, 237-238
Win2000 mechanisms, 238-240
INVALID_HANDLE_VALUE, 252
INVALID_SOCKET, 271
Invoke function, 97, 102
I/O
asynchronous I/O, 201, 227-231
completion ports, 210-211, 215-219, 232
file I/O review, 201-206
overlapped I/O, 207-209, 211-215, 224, 230
synchronous, 226
ioctl(), 271
ioctlsocket(), 271
IParam, 437
IPersistFile::Load, 426, 431, 484
IPersistFile::Save, 471
IPersistFile interface, 422, 426, 440-441, 442, 443, 471, 484, 532
IPersist::Load, 443
IPersistStorage, 447
IPersistStream, 447, 451
IPersistStreamInit interface, 447, 451
IResultData interface, 450-451
IShellExtInit interface, 422
IShellFolder interface, 60, 61, 62, 63
IShellLink interface, 442, 443, 471
IShellLink::Resolve, 444
IsKindOf, 428
ISnapInAbout interface, 451
IUniformResourceLocator interface, 532
IUnknown, 32-33, 36, 75, 86, 116, 424
IWebBrowser2 interface, 486-490, 534
IWPSite, 511

J

Java, ActiveX vs., 23-24
J/Direct (Microsoft), 19

K

Kerberos security system, 372
Key Distribution Center (KDC), 372
KEY_EXECUTE, 19
Key handle, 43
KEY_READ, 19
Korn, David, 12

L

Language, 406
Language, type library, 56-57
LanguageNames, 406
Late binding, 112
Latency, 293
LCIDs, 56
LDAP (Light-Weight Directory Access Protocol), 529
LeaveCriticalSection, 175, 187, 190
Library version number, 56
Light-weight Directory Access Protocol (LDAP), 529
Link checker, 519-529
LIST command, 558
Load, 484
Load balancing, COM+, 113-114
LoadLibrary, 499
LoadLibraryEx, 406
LoadModule, 124

Locale, 56
Localserver variable, 73
LocalServer32 keyword, 47
Local storage, threads, 136-139, 158-159
LockServer, 77
LockServiceDatabase, 577
Logging, 404-411, 417
 error message, 407-408, 418
 event sources, 404-405
 message files, 405-407
 using, 408-411
LogIn function, 25
LogonUser, 362
LookupAccountName, 358, 363
LookupAccountSid, 358, 359, 375
LookupQueue, 320
lpProcessAtrributes, 126
lpProcessInformation, 126
lpSecurityDescriptor, 357
lpStartupInfo, 126
lpThreadAtrributes, 126
ls command, 236

M

Macros, 60
 MFC, 92-93
 type library language, 57
 VARIANT macros, 102
Mailslots, 239, 257-264, 322
 creating, 258
 listening to, 259-261
 sending to, 261-264
 serial number checking, 264-266
 using, 327
MAILSLOT_WAIT_FOREVER, 257
MakeAbsoluteSD, 358
MakeSelfRelativeSD, 358
malloc, 313, 343
Manual event, 168
Manual event handle, 208
MapGenericMask, 368
MAPI (messaging API), 529
Mapped files, 219-223, 232, 251
MapViewOfFile, 252, 325
MapViewOfFileEx, 252
Marshalling, 38-40, 75, 77
m_bAutoDelete, 150, 151
MB_SERVICE_NOTIFICATION, 577
MB_SETFOREGROUND, 148
MC file, 405, 406, 416
MEM_COMMIT, 335, 346, 347
MEM_DECOMMIT, 346
Memory, 8
MEMORY_BASIC_INFORMATION, 347
Memory management, 332-351
 file mapping object, 219-223, 232, 325
 heaps, 343-344, 348-351
 shared memory, 238
 sparse memory techniques, 339-342
 VirtualAlloc, 334-339
Memory management unit (MMU), 333
Memory-mapped files, 219-223, 232
Memory paging, 333-334
MEM_RELEASE, 346
MEM_RESERVE, 335, 346
MessageBox, 8-9, 14, 18
Message box, appearing on top, 148-149
Message compiler, 405, 406
Message DLL, 416-417
Message files, 405-407
MessageId, 406
Message mode pipes, 256
Messaging API (MAPI), 529
Metadata, 530
METHOD_PROLOGUE macro, 86, 93, 429, 430
MFC, 59, 83
 aggregation, 95-97
 class factory, 85
 DLL server, 94-95
 example, 152-158
 EXE server, 92-93
 from console programs, 585
 icon handler, 432-433
 IDispatch, 104, 118-119
 Internet support, 517-529, 535-536
 REG file, 93
 Registry, 388-389
 return value with, 151-152
 shell extensions, 428-431, 436
 synchronization and, 192-197
 threads and, 135-136, 146-147, 150-151
MFC mutex, 193-197
Microsoft Management Console (MMC), 421
 ATL snap-ins, 446, 448, 451-469, 473-474
Microsoft Message Queue (MSMQ), 114, 239, 319-320, 323
Microsoft Transaction Server (MTS), 113
MIDL (Microsoft Interface Description Language), 40, 75
midl_user_allocate, 313, 318

midl_user_free, 313, 318
MKTYPLIB, 37, 57
MMC (Microsoft Management Console), 421
  ATL snap-ins, 446, 448, 451-469, 473-474
MMC_CALLBACK, 450
MMCN_DBLCLICK, 452
MMCN_EXPAND, 448, 449, 474
MMCN_SHOW, 448, 450, 474
MMU (memory management unit), 333
module keyword, 58
more program, 236
move(), 288
MsgWaitForMultipleObjects, 192
MsgWaitForMultipleObjectsEx, 173, 174
MSMQ (Microsoft Message Queue), 114, 239, 319-320, 323
MSMQMessage, 320
MSMQQueue, 320
MSMQQueueInfos, 319-320
MTS (Microsoft Transaction Server), 113
MultiByteToWideChar, 471, 485
Multiple interfaces, 82-83
Multiple objects, 191
Multiple threads, 40, 114
Multitasking, 11
  cooperative, 12-13
  preemptive, 13, 124
  Windows versions, 123
Multithreading, 310
Mutex calls, 170
Mutexes, 167, 170-171, 174-175, 183, 187, 188

N

nacn_nb_tcp, 317
nacn_np, 317
NamedPipeClient, 362
Named pipes, 238, 256-257, 322, 326, 361
Nested classes, 85-86
NetBios, 239, 322, 330
Neutral language, 57
new, 343
NIM_ADD, 436, 472
NIM_DELETE, 436, 472
NIM_MODIFY, 436, 472
Notify, 452
NOTIFYICONDATA, 437, 472
NTFS file system, 14, 15
ntohs(), 269
NULL, security descriptor and, 357, 377
NumMethods, 75

O

Object (ActiveX), 116
  automation object, 428
  creating, 33-34, 115
  impersonating, 53-54
  ownership, 374-375
  polymorphism, 29-30
  registering, 46-49
  shell extensions, 470
  shortcuts, 441-446, 470-472
  structure, 25-27
Object containment, 28
Object Wizard (ATL), 423
ODL script, 57
OFN_NODEREFERENCELINKS, 442, 470
OLE32.DLL, 47
OnConnect, 307
OnCopyData, 247
OnHost, 307
OnIdle member, 160
OnInitDialog, 396
OnInitialUpdate, 484, 510
OnReceive, 293, 308
OnScan, 527
OnUpdateAbout, 309
OnUpdateStatus, 309
OnViewConsole, 564
OpenEvent, 189
OpenEventLog, 408
OPEN_EXISTING, 225, 327
OpenFile, 519, 536
OpenFileMapping, 252, 325
OpenJobObject, 131
OpenMutex, 188, 190
OpenProcess, 127, 129, 149
OpenRequest, 519, 536
OpenSemaphore, 191
OpenService, 570
OpenURL, 518, 528, 536
OpenWaitableTimer, 174
OutputBase, 406
Overlapped I/O, 207-209, 224
  EOF detection, 209
  example, 211-215
  starting, 230
OVERLAPPED structure, 204, 207, 208, 216, 226

P

Page attributes, altering, 337-339
Page protection, 334-335, 346-347
ParseURL, 527
PeekMessage, 159-160
PeekNamedPipe, 257
Pentium processor, 6, 8
Persistence, 447
Pipes
  anonymous, 238, 252-255, 322, 325
  message mode pipes, 256
  named, 238, 256-257, 322, 326, 361
  used at DOS prompt, 236
PLAYREC structure, 289
Polymorphism, 29-30, 115-116, 117
Ports, sockets, 269, 272
POSIX subsystem, 9, 12
PostFiles, 511
PostMessage, 240, 484
PostQuitMessage, 148, 151
Preemptive multitasking, 13, 124
Private security, 368-371, 379
Privileges, 355-356, 372
PROCESS_ALL_ACCESS, 129
Process calls, 128
PROCESSED_INPUT, 587
Processes, 18, 124-132
Process handle, 149, 184
PROCESS_HEAP_ENTRY, 350
PROCESS_QUERY_INFORMATION, 129, 145
PROCESS_TERMINATE, 129
ProgID, 47, 117
ProgIDFromCLSID(), 48
Protection constants, 334
Proxies, 38-40
Proxy, 77
ProxyStubCLSID32, 75
pThis variable, 86
PulseEvent, 168, 187, 190
putbuffer, 340

Q

QueryInformationJobObject, 132
QueryInfoStatusCode, 528
QueryInterface, 33-34, 36, 74, 116, 442, 443, 449, 490
QueryServiceLockStatus, 577
Queue, 210, 319
QueueUsersPC, 142, 174

R

RC file, 405, 416
ReadConsole, 562
ReadConsoleInput, 215, 586
ReadConsoleOutput, 563
ReadConsoleOutputAttribute, 563
ReadConsoleOutputCharacter, 563
ReadFile, 204, 207, 209, 226, 253, 325, 326, 562
ReadFileEx, 209, 231-232
recv(), 271
REG_BINARY type, 387, 399
RegCloseKey, 44, 385
REGCLS_MULTIPLEUSE, 65, 77
REGCLS_SINGLEUSE, 65, 77
RegCreateKeyEx, 43, 385, 412
RegDeleteKey, 44, 385, 387
RegDeleteValue, 45, 399
REGDEMO, 388-389
REG_DWORD_BIG_ENDIAN type, 387
REG_DWORD_LITTLE_ENDIAN type, 387
REG_DWORD type, 387, 399
REGEDIT, 42, 50-51, 77, 118, 384, 400-401
REGEDIT4, 400, 414
REGEDT32, 42, 118, 384
RegEnumKeyEx, 44, 385, 412
RegEnumValue, 44, 385, 386, 412-413
REG_EXPAND_SZ type, 45, 387
REG files, 93, 118, 400-401, 414
RegisterEventSource, 405, 408, 417
RegisterServiceCtrlHandler, 570
Registry, 117-118, 383-387, 412-414
  class installation, 50-51
  contents, 399-400
  data types, 387
  file types, 399-400, 402-404
  INI files, 41, 383-384, 400, 413-414, 415-416
  MFC, 388-389
  REG files, 93, 118, 400-401, 414
  registering objects, 46-49
  self-registration, 50, 51-53, 78, 82
  type library, 55-60
  using, 413-414
Registry calls, 385-386
Registry key, 412
REG_LINK type, 388

REG_MULTI_SZ type, 45, 388
REG_NONE type, 388
RegOpenKey, 406
RegOpenKeyEx, 43, 385, 406
RegQueryValue, 44, 385, 386
RegQueryValueEx, 44, 45, 385, 399, 406, 412-413
REG_RESOURCE_LIST type, 388
RegSetValueEx, 44, 45, 385, 399
REGSVR32.EXE, 82
REG_SZ type, 388, 399
Release, 33, 34-35, 36, 116
ReleaseMutex, 167, 187, 188, 190
ReleaseSemaphore, 167, 191
Remote Procedure Call (RPC), 239, 310-319, 322, 329-330
REMOVE command, 558
ReportEvent, 408, 417
ResetEvent, 168
RES file, 405
Resource URLs, 498-499
ResumeThread, 147, 151
Reuse, ActiveX, 27-28, 35, 115
RevertToSelf, 362
rgvarg array, 103
Rights, 356, 367-368
RPC (Remote Procedure Call), 239, 310-319, 322, 329-330
RpcBindingFromStringBinding, 329
RpcMgmtStopServerListening, 318
RPCPROXY.H, 75
RPCRT4.LIB, 75
RpcServerListen, 318, 330
RpcServerRegisterIf, 330
RpcServerUnregisterIf, 318
RpcServerUseProtseqEp, 318, 329
RpcStringBindingCompose, 317, 329

S

SACL (system access control list), 357, 358, 376
SAFEARRAY, 98
SaveStdHandle, 327
Schema, 530
SCM (Service Control Manager), 568
SCODE, 30
SCOPEDATAITEM structure, 449
Scripting object model, 490-494, 534
ScrollConsoleScreenBuffer, 563
SDs. *See* Security descriptors.
Security, 354-379
  AccessCheck, 367-368
  impersonation, 362
  Kerberos, 372
  objectives of, 354-355
  private security, 368-371, 379
  privileges, 355-356, 372
  synchronization and, 172-173
  tokens, 362-363
SECURITY_ATTRIBUTE, 188
SECURITY_ATTRIBUTES structure, 357-358
SECURITY_DESCRIPTOR, 357
Security descriptors (SDs), 360-362, 376
  absolute, 377
  default, 357, 377
  specific security descriptor, 378
  universal descriptor, 378
Security ID (SID), 357, 358-359, 375, 376
Security objects, 360
SELFREG_E_CLASS, 53
SELFREG_E_TYPELIB, 53
Self-registration, 50, 51-53, 78, 82
Semaphores, 171-172, 183, 187, 188
SEM_FAILCRITICALERRORS, 204
send(), 271
SendMessage, 240
SendRequest, 519, 536
Serial number checking, 264-266
Server (ActiveX), 24
  automation server, 83
  CSocket, 291
  debugging, 74-75
  DLL servers, 65, 78-81
  EXE server, 65, 68-78
  RPC, 315-316, 318
  sockets, 269-270, 328
SERVER.CPP, 78
Service1Start, 576
Service1Status, 576
ServiceBase, 577-582, 584
ServiceControl, 582
Service Control Manager (SCM), 568, 588
Service Control Program, 571
ServiceInit, 582
ServiceInterrogate, 582
ServicePause, 582
Services, 568-584, 588-590
  accessing, 589-590
  debugging, 576-577, 590
  installing, 570-576

SERVICE_START_PENDING, 589
ServiceStop, 582
SERVICE_WIN32_OWN_PROCESS, 570
SERVICE_WIN32_SHARE_PROCESS, 570
SE_TCB_NAME, 129
setcell(), 288, 289
SetConsoleActiveScreenBuffer, 587
SetConsoleCtrlHandler, 563, 587
SetConsoleCursorInfo, 563
SetConsoleCursorPosition, 563
SetConsoleMode, 562, 587
SetConsoleTitle, 558, 588
SetCriticalSectionSpinCount, 176
SetErrorMode, 204
SetEvent, 168, 190
SetForegroundWindow, 148
SetIconLocation, 471
SetInformationJobObject, 132
SetMailslotInfo, 258
SetNamedPipeHandleStatus, 256
SetPath, 471
SetProcessShutdownParameters, 563
SetProcessWorkingSetSize, 131
SetSecurityDescriptorDacl, 376, 378
SetSecurityDescriptorGroup, 376
SetServiceStatus, 570, 589
SetStdHandle, 253
Severity, 406
SHAddToRecentDocs, 445, 473
Shared DLLs, 247-251
Shared flag, 163
Shared memory, 238, 322
  DLLs for, 247-251, 324
  file mapping object, 251-252, 325
SHChangeNotify, 473
Shell calls, 446, 473
ShellExec(), 50
ShellExecute, 125, 144, 145, 445
ShellExecuteEx, 125
Shell extensions, 421-436, 470
  ATL, 422, 423-428, 436, 470
  DLLs, 422-431
  MFC, 428-431, 436
  smart pointers, 440-441, 442
Shell_NotifyIcon, 436, 437, 472
Shells, 420-474
  icon tray programs, 436-444, 469, 472-473
  shell extensions, 421-436, 470
  shortcuts, 441-446, 470-472
  smart pointers, 440-441, 442
SHEmptyRecycleBin, 473
SHGetDesktopFolder, 60-61, 62
SHGetMalloc, 485
Shortcuts, 441-446, 470-472, 477-486
ShowHTMLDialog, 499, 535
ShowWindow, 124, 144, 558
SHQueryRecycleBin, 473
SID (Security ID), 357, 358-359, 375, 376
SID_NAME_USE, 358
Signal EOF, 209
Single event, 168
SleepEx, 174, 209
Smart pointers, 440-441, 442
Snap-ins, 446-448
  function of, 447
  MMC snap-ins, 446, 448, 451-469, 473-474
  types, 448
SOCKADDR_IN, 270
socket(), 270
SOCKET_ERROR, 271
Sockets, 239, 267-310, 322
  addresses, 269
  checker game using, 267, 273-290
  client, 270-271, 328
  CSocket, 290-308
  custom sockets, 308-309
  MFC sockets, 290
  number formats, 269
  ports, 269, 272
  server, 269-270, 328
  TCP sockets, 317
  Unix, 267, 269, 271, 272
  using, 328
  Windows, 271-272
Soft link, 441
sort program, 236
Sparse memory techniques, 339-342
SSS (Structured Storage System), ActiveX, 539, 557
Standalone snap-in, 448
STARTF_USESTDHANDLES, 253
StartServiceCtrlDispatcher, 568, 588
STARTUPINFO structure, 253, 327
Status bar, 309
STDAFX.H file, 193
STDMETHODIMP macro, 60, 430
STDMETHODIMP_ macro, 60, 430
STDMETHOD macro, 60, 430
STDMETHOD_ macro, 60, 430
STILL_ACTIVE, 145

Strings, 8
Structured exception handling (SEH), 347
Structured Storage System (SSS), ActiveX, 539, 557
Stub function, 38, 77
Subkeys, 412
Subsystem, 9
SuspendThread, 183
SwitchToFiber, 159
SW_MAXIMIZED, 144
SW_MINIMIZED, 144
SW_SHOW, 144
Symbolic link, 441
SymbolicName, 406
Synchronization, 124, 145, 163-167
  critical sections, 174-175, 187, 190-191
  events, 163, 168-170
  example, 176-184
  interlocked calls, 167-168, 191-192
  MFC and, 192-197
  mutexes, 167, 170-171, 174-175, 183, 187, 188, 190
  security and, 172-173
  selecting method, 187-188
  semaphores, 171-172, 183, 187, 188, 191
Synchronous I/O, 226
System access control list (SACL), 357, 358, 376
SYSTEM_AUDIT_ACE_TYPE, 359
System Registry. *See* Registry.
System tray, 420, 436

T

TCP sockets, 317
TerminateJobObject, 132
TerminateProcess, 145
TerminateThread, 149
Thread handle, 149, 183, 184
Thread local storage (TLS), 136-139, 158-159
THREAD_QUERY_INFORMATION, 149
Threads, 11, 12, 18, 132-135
  alternatives to, 159-160
  apartment threading model, 114
  APCs, 141-143
  asynchronous I/O with, 228-229
  C++ library and, 146
  converting into fiber, 139
  creating, 132, 146, 147
  deadlock, 189
  exit code, 149
  foreground thread, 148
  free threading model, 40
  interprocess communication and, 237-238
  I/O threads, 206-207
  local storage, 136-139, 158-159
  MFC and, 135-136, 146-147, 150-151
  multiple threads, 40, 114
  safety, 136
  synchronization, 163-167
  worker thread, 147
TLB file, 37
  distribution, 55-60
  generating, 57
TlsAlloc, 137, 158
TlsFree, 137
TlsGetValue, 137, 158
TlsSetValue, 158
Tokens, 362-363
transact(), 288
TransactNamedPipe, 256
Translator function, 348
TreatAs, 54
TryEnterCriticalSection, 175, 187, 191
typedef keyword, 57
Type libraries, 37, 42, 54-59
  creating, 57-59
  defined, 54
  elements, 54
  language, 56-57
  shell extension, 424

U

uFlags, 472
UNICODE, 8, 13-14, 485
UnicodeChar, 563
Universally Unique Identifier (UUID), 31-32, 85, 117, 311
Unix
  forking, 11-12
  ls command, 236
  multitasking, 11
  sockets, 267, 269, 271, 272
  Windows, differences between, 123
UNKWN.IDL, 75
UnlockServiceDatabase, 577
UnmapViewOfFile, 220, 252, 325

UpdateWindow, 310
URLs
converting, 477-486
resource URLs, 498-499
UserHandleGrantAccess, 132
User objects, security, 361
User principal name, 529
USES_CONVERSION, 485
UUID (Universally Unique Identifier), 31-32, 85, 117, 311
UUIDGEN, 31-32

V

Values, 412-413
VARIANT, 98, 100-102
VARIANT macros, 102
VFAT file system, 14, 15
VirtualAlloc, 334-339, 344, 345
Virtual container, 529
VirtualFree, 345-346
Virtual memory manager, 219
VirtualProtect, 335, 339, 346
VirtualProtectEx, 335
Virtual Tables (VTBLs), 40, 428
Visual Basic (VB), 16, 17, 18
Visual J++, calling API from, 19-20
VTBLs (Virtual Tables), 40, 428
VT_EMPTY, 103
VT_ERROR, 103

W

Waitable handles, 184
Waitable timers, 174
Wait calls, 174, 184, 191
WaitForMultipleObjects, 114, 166, 173, 188, 209
WaitForMultipleObjectsEx, 174
WaitForSingleObject, 129, 135, 145, 166, 183, 184, 188, 190
WaitForSingleObjectEx, 174, 209
WaitNamedPipe, 256
WebPost API, 502-517, 532
WebPost Wizard, 510
WebPublishing Wizard (Microsoft), 502, 511
Win16, DLLs, 249
Win32, DLLs, 249
Win32 multitasking, 123
Win32S library, 6, 10
WIN32_FIND_DATA structure, 484
Win2000 COM. *See* COM+.
Window, appearing on top, 148-149
Windows (Microsoft)
Advanced Server version, 7
architecture, 7-10, 17-18
Datacenter Server version, 7
error codes, 272
history, 4, 23
Professional edition, 7
Server edition, 7
sockets, 271-272
Unix, differences between, 123
versions, differences between, 4-15
Windows 3.1 (Microsoft)
DLLs, 15
features, 12
history, 4, 6, 9, 10
multitasking, 123-124
sockets, 271
Windows 3.11 (Microsoft), history, 4
Windows 3.5 (Microsoft), history, 6
Windows 3.51 (Microsoft), history, 6
Windows 95 (Microsoft)
API, 5
DLLs, 249
history, 5-6, 9, 10
sockets, 271
Windows 98 (Microsoft)
history, 9, 10
sockets, 271
Windows 2000 (Microsoft)
Active Directory Services (ADS), 529-531
console applications, 538-568, 585-588
DLLs, 249
Internet Explorer, 486-502, 532, 534
Internet shortcuts, 477-486
interprocess communications, 238-240
Kerberos, 372
logging, 404-411, 417
memory management, 332-351
MFC support, 517-529
Registry, 41-53, 78, 82, 117-118, 383-387, 412-414
security, 354-379
services, 568-584, 588-590
shells, 420-474
shortcuts, 441-446, 470-472
sockets, 271
WebPost API, 502-517, 532
Windows NT (Microsoft)